Psychology:
A New Introduction
STUDY GUIDE

2nd edition

Nick Shackleton-Jones
Richard Gross
Rob McIlveen

Hodder & Stoughton

A MEMBER OF THE HODDER HEADLINE GROUP

British Library Cataloguing in Publication Data
A catalogue record for this title is available from the British Library

ISBN 0 340 80415 7

First published 2001

Impression number 10 9 8 7 6 5 4 3 2 1
Year   2005 2004 2003 2002 2001

Typeset by GreenGate Publishing Services, Tonbridge, Kent.

Printed and bound in Great Britain for Hodder and Stoughton Educational,
a division of Hodder Headline plc, 338 Euston Road, London NW1 3BH,
by The Bath Press Ltd.

CONTENTS

UNIT 5 INDIVIDUAL DIFFERENCES AND PERSPECTIVES

PREFACE

Several years ago I told a group of students that all the facts they needed to know to pass an A level in psychology would fit on two sides of a single A4 page. They didn't believe me. To prove them wrong I sat down to produce the document, only to find that by the time I had finished I had about eighty pages of notes in tiny type.

How could I have been so wrong? I was wrong because casual introspection had revealed that I actually needed to know very little in order to teach the entire syllabus – what I had failed to see is that the few things that I knew about psychology were actually cues for other things – which in turn acted as cues for more information. In this way four pieces of information quickly become 1024 pieces of information ($4 \times 4 \times 4 \times 4 \times 4$). The secret to remembering all the information was, as Bower put it, 'organisation'.

The first notes that I produced were in tabular form. It is a common mistake to assume that others learn in the same ways that we do, but putting as much information as possible on a single page and splitting it into sections seemed to help most students, although it might have contributed to the mistaken belief that an A level is all about learning 'key facts'. Without understanding something about the structure of the material it is not only very difficult to remember it all, it's also very difficult to make sense of it or draw comparisons.

The idea of using schemas (mental maps) is not new, but the approach was novel: rather than simply linking labels in a more or less idiosyncratic fashion, chunks of information were organised in a hierarchical fashion, with cues placed clearly within this structure. The intention was not merely to provide a map of the relationships between concepts, but rather to provide the information itself, together with a good way to remember and structure it. Without organising information in this way memory cues can very quickly become overburdened and fail: if I have to remember more than four items at the supermarket, I will usually forget at least one.

Early maps were well received by students who liked the idea that thirty maps could summarise three hundred pages of text or replace a folder full of illegible notes. They blew them up to A3 size, scribbled on them and even stuck them on bedroom walls! I encouraged them to 'immerse' themselves in the material. In this way the information was able to take on a real dimension: students could picture maps in exams, take 'routes' through them to form essay structures and navigate around the syllabus like they might around a building.

Soon I began using OHPs of the maps for teaching so that as I taught, students could see what we were doing, where we had come from and where we were going. It also helped me a great deal, as I found that I now only needed one folder, rather than ten, in order to teach.

From an evolutionary perspective, our memory systems are not really 'designed' to acquire large amounts of information presented in symbolic form. In fact, we are better at remembering the plot of a good movie, how to get to our favourite places, how our teachers talked and acted or unusual things that happened to us. However, the 'information age' means that we are increasingly required to assimilate information rapidly, and I strongly believe that adapting information to suit our specialised processing capabilities will prove to be the way forwards.

This Study Guide represents a step in that direction, and is a companion to the second edition of the textbook *Psychology: A New Introduction*, following its structure closely with a study chapter for each chapter in the textbook. By ensuring a high degree of consistency with this text, the Study Guide is able to consolidate and deepen students' understanding of the main text whilst attempting to answer the questions 'What do I need to know?', 'How can I remember it?' and 'How can I do well in an exam?' as directly as possible. The Guide also contains additional materials to assist students in their preparation for exams, essay-writing and completion of coursework, although there is no separate references section (since these can all be found in the main textbook).

For each chapter of the main text there is a corresponding *schema* and a set of *self-test questions and answers* in the Study Guide. There are also several additional 'super-schemas', which provide an overview of entire syllabus areas (e.g. developmental psychology) at a single glance.

The *schemas* summarise central information contained in the corresponding textbook chapter and organise information into an overall structure by the use of links and headings. They possess the following properties:

- Central information contained in corresponding text-book chapters is condensed, summarised and broken into discrete 'chunks', which are presented in a visual arrangement. Where helpful, diagrams are also included.
- Items of information are contained in boxes whose borders and style indicate the type of information contained in them.

  - Black boxes indicate the main topic area.

  Attribution Theories & Bias

  - The main areas into which the topic can be divided are indicated by shaded, rounded boxes, connected to the main topic by heavy lines.

  Attribution Biases

  - Sub-headings are contained in non-shaded rounded boxes.

  Pursuit of common goals

  - Theory, applications and evaluation are mostly contained in boxes with a normal border.

  Conflict approaches
  Hostility arises from competition.
  Solutions:
  - remove competition and replace it with goals requiring co-operation

  - Important research studies are contained in boxes with a heavy dotted border.

  Conflicting Research:
  - Gilligan (1982): Kohlberg's stages are based on male morality and female morality is oriented more towards compassion.

  - A light dotted border above and below a piece of text indicates the introduction of a key term or definition.

  Attribution: an explanation of why an individual behaved in a certain way

The boxes are connected in such a way as to suggest the structure of the material. Where boxes are connected to the main topic box by a narrow line, this suggests material which might be used by way of introduction of a topic. In many cases, the schemas can provide the basis for an essay structure.

The *self-test questions* are aimed at developing students' critical abilities, as well as providing a way for students to monitor and vary their own learning. Each section contains questions which range in type and difficulty, so that most students should find it difficult to answer all questions correctly. Moreover, the questions tend to focus on information which is central to a topic and would therefore be useful in answering an exam question.

N.B. The Appendices on Exam Preparation, Essay Writing and Coursework apply *specifically* to the AQA syllabus. However, these also contain a great deal of advice and guidance that are relevant to other A level syllabuses.

ACKNOWLEDGEMENTS

Nick would like to thank his wife Rose and daughter Nadia for their love and support. Rob would like to thank Gill for her usual patience. Richard sends his love as usual to Jan, Tanya and Jo. Many thanks to Tim at Hodder & Stoughton, Dave, Anna and the team at GreenGate Publishing. Our best wishes go to all the unforgettable students who shared the adventure.

The publisher would like to thank Routledge for permission to reproduce the figure on page 161, previously Figure 37.3 in *The Nature of Adolescence* (1990, 2nd edition) by J.C. Coleman and L. Hendry.

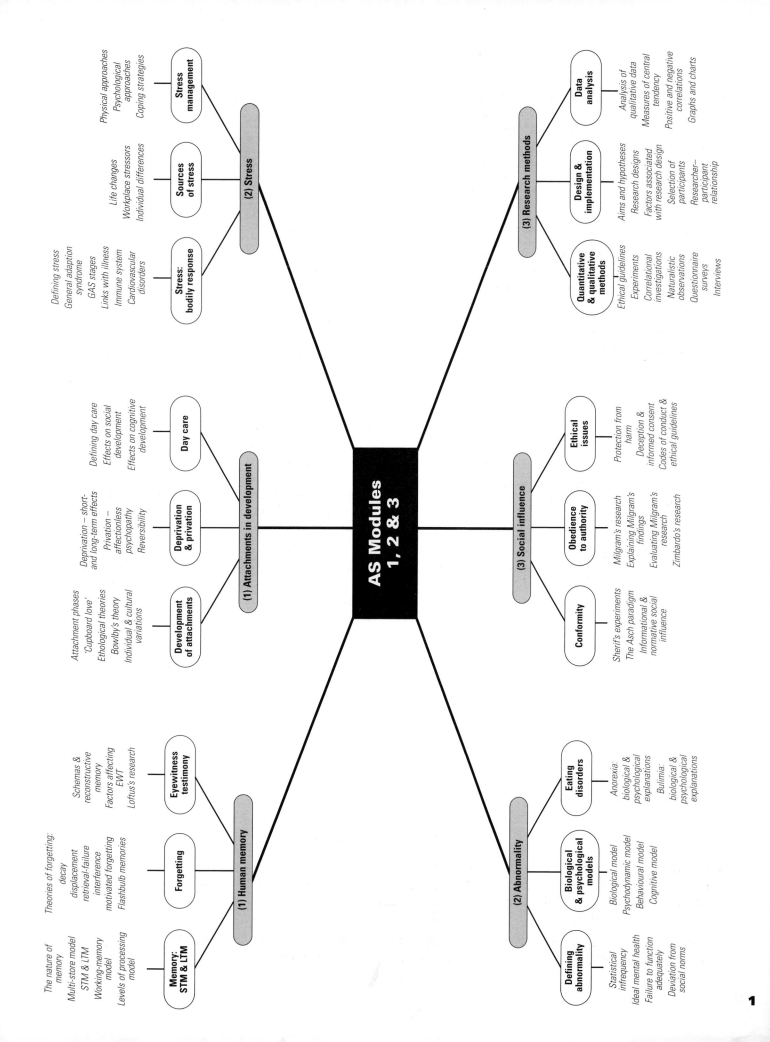

AS Modules 1, 2 & 3

(1) Attachments in development

Development of attachments
- Attachment phases
- 'Cupboard love'
- Ethological theories
- Bowlby's theory
- Individual & cultural variations

Deprivation & privation
- Deprivation – short- and long-term effects
- Privation – affectionless psychopathy
- Reversibility

Day care
- Defining day care
- Effects on social development
- Effects on cognitive development

(1) Human memory

Memory: STM & LTM
- The nature of memory
- Multi-store model
- STM & LTM
- Working-memory model
- Levels of processing model

Forgetting
- Theories of forgetting: decay, displacement, retrieval-failure, interference, motivated forgetting
- Flashbulb memories

Eyewitness testimony
- Schemas & reconstructive memory
- Factors affecting EWT
- Loftus's research

(2) Stress

Stress: bodily response
- Defining stress
- General adaption syndrome
- GAS stages
- Links with illness
- Immune system
- Cardiovascular disorders

Sources of stress
- Life changes
- Workplace stressors
- Individual differences

Stress management
- Physical approaches
- Psychological approaches
- Coping strategies

(2) Abnormality

Defining abnormality
- Statistical infrequency
- Ideal mental health
- Failure to function adequately
- Deviation from social norms

Biological & psychological models
- Biological model
- Psychodynamic model
- Behavioural model
- Cognitive model

Eating disorders
- Anorexia: biological & psychological explanations
- Bulimia: biological & psychological explanations

(3) Social influence

Conformity
- Sherif's experiments
- The Asch paradigm
- Informational & normative social influence

Obedience to authority
- Milgram's research
- Explaining Milgram's findings
- Evaluating Milgram's research
- Zimbardo's research

Ethical issues
- Protection from harm
- Deception & informed consent
- Codes of conduct & ethical guidelines

(3) Research methods

Quantitative & qualitative methods
- Ethical guidelines
- Experiments
- Correlational investigations
- Naturalistic observations
- Questionnaire surveys
- Interviews

Design & implementation
- Aims and hypotheses
- Research designs
- Factors associated with research design
- Selection of participants
- Researcher–participant relationship

Data analysis
- Analysis of qualitative data
- Measures of central tendency
- Positive and negative correlations
- Graphs and charts

AN INTRODUCTION TO PSYCHOLOGY AND ITS APPROACHES

KEY QUESTIONS
- What is psychology?
- What do psychologists do?
- What are the major theoretical approaches in psychology?

Q

Section 1: What is psychology?
1. What do the two Greek words *psyche* and *logos* mean?
2. What does *introspection* mean?
3. What name was given to Wundt's (1879) approach, in which he attempted to analyse the structure of conscious thought?
4. What criticism did Watson (1913) make of introspectionism?
5. Complete the sentence: 'Watson proposed that psychologists should confine themselves to studying _____, since this is measurable and observable'.
6. What is the difference between Freud's *psychodynamic approach* and *psychoanalysis*?
7. What were Gestalt psychologists mainly interested in?
8. What are *cognitive processes*?
9. What is the *computer analogy*?

Section 2: Classifying psychologists' work
10. What is the difference between pure research and applied research?
11. How does the *process approach* to psychology differ from the *person approach*?
12. Identify two areas of study in which a biopsychologist might be interested.
13. What is the *nature–nurture issue* concerned with?
14. Identify four cognitive processes which are of interest to cognitive psychologists.
15. What do developmental psychologists study?
16. Why might some psychologists claim that all psychology is social psychology?
17. What is the study of interpersonal perception concerned with?
18. What types of investigatory methods are most likely to be employed by the process and person approaches to psychology, respectively?
19. According to Hartley & Branthwaite (1997), in what way can the psychologist be seen as a 'toolmaker'?
20. What might be the role of a clinical psychologist in working with the elderly?

21. What do criminological (or forensic) psychologists attempt to do?
22. Which type of psychologist is most likely to be involved in planning educational programmes for people with learning difficulties?
23. What are the main responsibilities of occupational psychologists?

Section 3: Major theoretical approaches
24. What does a *methodological behaviourist* believe?
25. How does this view differ from that of a *radical behaviourist*?
26. What are the two types of conditioning (or learning) which are central to the behaviourist approach?
27. What do the letters 'S' and 'R' stand for, in the term *S–R psychology*?
28. Identify one practical contribution of behaviourist principles to the field of abnormal psychology.
29. How can the behaviourist approach be criticised for the way in which it defines the *response*?
30. Identify one further criticism of the behaviourist approach.
31. Identify one technique which Freud believed could be used to access the unconscious mind.
32. What is *repression*?
33. What claim is made by the *theory of infantile sexuality*?
34. What was the principal difference between Adler's psychodynamic approach and Freud's?
35. What is the link between rational emotive therapy (RET) and psychoanalysis?
36. What does it mean to say that Freudian theories are *unfalsifiable*?
37. Complete the sentence: 'Humanistic psychologists believe in ____ ____ and people's ability to choose how they act'.
38. What is an *actualising tendency*?
39. What is a *phenomenal field*?
40. What is 'lay therapy', to which Rogers contributed?
41. Why is the humanistic approach subject to the *nominal fallacy*?

Section 1: What is psychology?

1 Psyche means mind, soul or spirit, whilst logos means discourse or study.

2 Introspection describes the attempt of an individual to observe and analyse his/her own mental processes.

3 Wundt's (1879) approach was called *structuralism*.

4 Watson (1913) pointed out that the results of introspection could never be proved or disproved, and were therefore subjective and unscientific.

5 'Watson proposed that psychologists should confine themselves to studying *behaviour*, since this is measurable and observable.'

6 Freud's psychodynamic approach is based on his psychoanalytic theory, whilst psychoanalysis describes the therapeutic techniques which he developed.

7 Gestalt psychologists were mainly interested in perception.

8 Cognitive processes are mental processes, such as perception, attention, memory and thinking in general.

9 The computer analogy is the notion that human cognitive processes can be compared with the operation of computer programs.

Section 2: Classifying psychologists' work

10 Pure research is research done for its own sake, and intended to increase our knowledge, whilst applied research is aimed at solving a particular problem.

11 The process approach investigates the mechanisms underlying behaviour, whilst the person approach focuses more directly on the individual.

12 A biopsychologist might be interested in the functions of the nervous system, the endocrine (hormonal) system, brain activity, and genetics.

13 The nature–nurture issue is concerned with the degree to which characteristics are inherited (nature) or a product of learning and the environment (nurture).

14 Attention, memory, perception, language, thinking, problem-solving, reasoning and concept-formation are all of interest to cognitive psychologists.

15 Developmental psychologists study the biological, cognitive, social and emotional changes that occur in people over time.

16 Because all behaviour takes place within a social context and our behaviour may be influenced by others even when we are alone.

17 The study of interpersonal perception is concerned with how we form impressions of others and judge the causes of their behaviour.

18 The process approach is typically confined to the laboratory, where experiments are undertaken, whilst the person approach makes greater use of field studies and non-experimental methods.

19 Hartley & Branthwaite (1997) see psychologists as 'toolmakers' in their use and development of measures and techniques to help in the analysis and assessment of problems.

20 The clinical psychologist may be involved in assessing the elderly for their fitness to live independently.

21 Criminological psychologists attempt to apply psychological principles to the criminal justice system.

22 An educational psychologist.

23 Occupational psychologists are involved in the selection and training of individuals for jobs, and in vocational guidance, including the administration of aptitude tests and tests of interest.

Section 3: Major theoretical approaches

24 A methodological behaviourist believes that the subject matter of psychology should be behaviour.

25 The radical behaviourist believes not only that we should not study mental activities, but that these can be explained by (reduced to) an analysis of behaviour.

26 Respondent conditioning and operant conditioning.

27 Stimulus and response.

28 The behaviourist approach has led to the development of behaviour therapy and behaviour modification, used in the treatment of psychological disorders.

29 The behaviourist approach tends only to consider the frequency of a behaviour (the response) and not its intensity, duration or quality.

30 The behaviourist approach fails to account for the influence of people's *thoughts* on their behaviour.

31 Free association, dream interpretation and transference are all psychoanalytic techniques used to access the unconscious mind.

32 Repression refers to the process whereby threatening or unpleasant experiences are 'forgotten' by being removed to the unconscious.

33 The theory of infantile sexuality claims that the sexual instinct is active from birth and develops through a series of psychosexual stages.

34 Adler rejected Freud's emphasis on sexuality, stressing instead the will to power (striving for superiority and the rejection of inferiority).

35 The founder of rational emotive therapy, Ellis, was originally trained in Freudian techniques.

36 Unfalsifiable means 'incapable of being disproved'. For example, the claim that some unacceptable impulses are concealed in the unconscious mind is impossible to falsify.

37 'Humanistic psychologists believe in *free will* and people's ability to choose how they act.'

38 An actualising tendency is an intrinsic desire to grow, develop and enhance our capacities.

39 A phenomenal field refers to the way in which we each create our own world, shaped by our perceptions.

40 'Lay therapy' is therapy which is provided by non-medically qualified therapists.

41 The humanistic approach describes but does not explain personality. This is the nominal fallacy.

A

What is psychology?

- The word *psychology* derives from the Greek *psyche* (mind, soul or spirit) and *logos* (discourse or study).
- Wilhelm Wundt (1879) opened the first psychological laboratory at the University of Leipzig, attempting to record and measure conscious mental processes, using *introspection* under controlled conditions (*structuralism*).
- Watson (1913) proposed that psychologists should confine themselves to studying behaviour, since this can be measured and studied objectively (*behaviourism*).
- Freud (1900) published his *psychoanalytic theory* of personality, in which the *unconscious mind* plays a central role.
- Cognitive psychology emerged in the late 1950s, as psychologists became able to model cognitive processes on *computers*.

Process approach — **Classifying psychologists' work** — **Person approach**

Biopsychology
(Ch 17–25)
- Interested in the biological basis of behaviour (e.g. nervous system, endocrine system)
- Genetics and the role of the environment (nature vs nurture) are central issues.

Cognitive psychology
(Ch 26–34)
- Studies processes such as attention, memory, perception, language and thought
- Links to social psychology (social cognition) and developmental (Piaget's theory of cognitive development).

Developmental psychology
(Ch 35–43)
- Studies the biological, social, cognitive and emotional changes which take place over time.

Social psychology
(Ch 8–16)
- Studies the way in which our behaviour is influenced by others (e.g. interpersonal perception, attraction, prejudice).

Abnormal psychology
(Ch 53–61)
- Studies the underlying causes of deviant behaviour and psychological abnormality.

Introducing Psychology

Clinical psychologists – major functions
- Assessing people with learning difficulties/brain damage/the elderly
- Planning/carrying out programmes of therapy
- Carrying out research into abnormal psychology (e.g. therapeutic effectiveness)
- Involvement in community care
- Teaching other groups of professionals (e.g. nurses, social workers).

Applied psychology

Seven major skills/roles
- **Counsellor:** helping people to overcome problems
- **Colleague:** focusing on human issues, as part of a team
- **Expert:** drawing on specialised knowledge in advising on issues
- **Toolmaker:** using and developing psychometric measures
- **Detached investigator:** assessing the evidence for a point of view
- **Theoretician:** attempting to explain observed phenomena
- **Agent for change:** helping people and institutions to change for the better.

Criminological psychologists – research areas
- Jury selection and presentation of evidence
- Eyewitness testimony
- Improving the recall of child witnesses
- False memory syndrome
- Offender profiling and crime prevention
- Treatment programmes (e.g. anger management).

Educational psychologists – responsibilities
- Administering psychometric tests
- Planning and supervising remedial teaching
- Research into teaching, interview and counselling methods
- Planning educational programmes for people with impairments/special educational needs
- Advising parents and teachers on how to deal with children with impairments/behaviour problems
- Teacher training.

Occupational psychologists – responsibilities
- The selection and training of people for jobs
- Helping people who need to re-train for a new career (industrial rehabilitation)
- Designing training schemes as part of 'fitting the person to the job'
- Helping design equipment as part of 'fitting the job to the person'
- Maximising productivity
- Helping with communication and industrial relations (organisational psychology)
- Helping to sell products (advertising).

Major theoretical approaches

The behaviourist approach — **The psychodynamic approach** — **The humanistic approach**

Assumptions

The behaviourist approach
- Advocates the study of observable behaviour (*methodological behaviourism*) and rejects introspectionism.
- Emphasises the role of learning (either *respondent* or *operant* conditioning) and environmental factors in influencing behaviour.
- Stresses the use of *operational definitions* (where concepts are defined in measurable terms).
- Holds that a science of behaviour should aim to *predict* and *control* behaviour.

The psychodynamic approach
- Sees much of our behaviour as determined by *unconscious* thoughts, desires and memories.
- Experiences or thoughts which are threatening or unpleasant may be *repressed* (a major form of ego defence).
- The mind is composed of three interacting (often conflicting) forces: the *id*, *ego* and *superego*.
- Infants are sexually active from birth and pass through a series of *psychosexual stages* which influence adult personality.

The humanistic approach
- Believes that people are *free* to choose how they act.
- Argues that behaviour must be understood in terms of the individual's subjective interpretation of it (*phenomenological approach*).
- Individuals aim to grow, develop and enhance their capacities (*'self-actualisation'*), unless blocked by external factors.
- Stresses the importance of understanding the whole person (not 'bits' of behaviour).

Contributions

The behaviourist approach
- Used to explain learning, language development, moral development, gender development, memory (e.g. interference theory of forgetting) and abnormal behaviour.
- Used in *behaviour therapy* and *behaviour modification*. Also used in biofeedback and programmed learning (e.g. computer assisted learning).

The psychodynamic approach
- Used to explain motivation, dreams, forgetting, attachment, moral and gender development and abnormality. Influenced Erikson ('psychosocial stages'), Jung ('analytical psychology') and Adler ('individual psychology').
- Psychoanalysis is used in the treatment of disorders such as depression and anxiety.

The humanistic approach
- Rogers' *client-centred therapy* is used widely, and Rogers helped develop lay therapy (administered by psychoanalysts and others who are not medically qualified).
- Rogers helped develop ways of measuring self-concept and ideal self, in order to explore the importance of therapist qualities.

Evaluation

The behaviourist approach
- Behaviourists have tended to measure frequency of responses (e.g. of a rat in a Skinner box) and ignore intensity, duration and quality of responses.
- What people think is often very important in determining their behaviour (Garrett, 1996) and this is not recognised by the behaviourist.

The psychodynamic approach
- Freudian theories are *unfalsifiable* (incapable of being disproved).
- Freudian ideas about repression, early sexuality and the unconscious have become a part of Western culture.
- 'Hermeneutic strength': the theory allows us to interpret meaning in a way appropriate to our complex human experience.

The humanistic approach
- The theory has wide appeal as an alternative to more mechanistic theories, but its concepts are difficult to test empirically and it only succeeds in describing, not explaining personality.
- The approach counterbalanced behaviourist and psychodynamic approaches, recognising the importance of the self.

SHORT-TERM AND LONG-TERM MEMORY

KEY QUESTIONS
- What basic processes are involved in memory?
- What are the capacity, duration and coding of the various types of memory?
- How do the three main theories of memory explain memory function?

Section 1: Introducing memory

1 How did Ebbinghaus (1885) investigate the nature of memory?
2 What did he conclude about the nature of forgetting over time?
3 What is the difference between *recall* and *recognition tests* of learning?
4 What three basic information-processing operations are involved in memory?
5 Which of the following refers to the inability to retrieve stored information: *unavailability* or *inaccessibility*?

Section 2: The nature of memory

6 What is the principal function of sensory memory?
7 How long does it take for *iconic memory* to fade?
8 Which takes longer to fade, *echoic memory* (auditory sensory memory) or *visual sensory memory*?
9 What, according to Miller (1956), is the capacity of short-term memory?
10 What is *chunking*?
11 When Conrad (1964) presented participants with lists of six consonants for a brief period of time, what sort of errors did they make in recalling these consonants?
12 How is it possible to maintain information in short-term memory for long periods of time?
13 How did Peterson & Peterson (1959) discover the duration for which information is held in STM?
14 What is the capacity of long-term memory?
15 When Baddeley (1976) investigated the nature of long-term memory, what type of information did his participants have most difficulty recalling?

Section 3: Models of memory

16 What is another name for Atkinson & Shiffrin's (1969, 1971) *multi-store model of memory*?
17 What are the two permanent structural components referred to by this model?

18 What is the key process which accounts for the transfer of information from STM to LTM?
19 When Murdock (1962) tested participants by asking them to free-recall from a list of forty words presented to them, what did he discover?
20 How can the multi-store model account for the *primacy effect*?
21 How can the multi-store model account for the *recency effect*?
22 What would you expect to find if participants were asked to count backwards for thirty seconds after the presentation of the words to be recalled?
23 Which ability is commonly impaired in people suffering from Korsakoff's syndrome?
24 Which type of memory was impaired in the case of K.F. (Shallice & Warrington, 1970)?
25 What feature of the multi-store model did Baddeley & Hitch's (1974) *working-memory model* elaborate?
26 What is meant by the claim that the central executive in this model is *modality-free*?
27 What are the three slave-systems which make up working memory?
28 Why is the distinction between *maintenance rehearsal* and *elaborative rehearsal* a key element in Craik & Lockhart's (1972) alternative to the multi-store model?
29 What features of a stimulus are analysed at a shallow level?
30 At which level is a word's meaning analysed?
31 How did Craik & Tulving's (1975) experiment make participants process tachistoscopically presented words at different levels?
32 What is *elaboration*?
33 Apart from elaboration and level of processing, which other factor is most likely to determine whether or not a word is remembered?
34 What is meant by the criticism that the model is descriptive rather than explanatory (Eysenck & Keane, 1995)?

Q

Section 1: Introducing memory

1 Ebbinghaus (1885) investigated the nature of memory by inventing nonsense syllables, learning these lists, then testing himself on his ability to recall them at different times.

2 He concluded that memory declines sharply at first, but then levels off after a couple of days.

3 Recall tests require participants to remember items without any cues being present, whilst recognition tests involve deciding whether or not a piece of information has been presented previously.

4 Registration, storage and retrieval are the three basic information-processing operations involved in memory.

5 Inaccessibility refers to the inability to retrieve stored information.

Section 2: The nature of memory

6 The principal function of sensory memory is to retain information long enough for us to decide if it is worthy of further processing.

7 Iconic memory fades in less than a second.

8 Echoic memory (auditory sensory memory) fades more slowly than visual sensory memory.

9 Miller (1956) claimed that, for most people, the capacity of short-term memory is seven items (plus or minus two items).

10 Chunking refers to the process of combining independent pieces of information into larger 'chunks' of information.

11 Conrad (1964) found that acoustic confusion errors occurred when participants attempted to recall consonants from their short-term memory.

12 Information can be maintained indefinitely in short-term memory by rehearsing (repeating over and over) the information.

13 Peterson & Peterson (1959) discovered the duration of STM by presenting participants with a list of trigrams (such as XPJ) and asking them to count backwards for varying time periods after presentation (which prevents rehearsal). They were then asked to recall the information.

14 The capacity of long-term memory is not known, but no limit has ever been discovered. However, we do not remember all that we experience or every aspect of a stimulus, so some 'cognitive economising' seems likely.

15 Baddeley (1976) found that his participants had most difficulty recalling semantically similar words from LTM suggesting that information is coded semantically in LTM (i.e. converted into its meaning).

Section 3: Models of memory

16 Atkinson & Shiffrin's (1969, 1971) multi-store model of memory is also called *the dual-memory model.*

17 The two permanent structural components are short-term memory and long-term memory.

18 The key process which accounts for the transfer of information from STM to LTM is rehearsal.

19 Murdock (1962) discovered that participants were most likely to recall the words presented early on or towards the end of the list, but recalled few of those presented in the middle.

20 The multi-store model claims that the primacy effect results from the transfer of the first few words into LTM through rehearsal.

21 The multi-store model claims that the recency effect results from the last few words remaining in STM at the time of recall.

22 Counting backwards for thirty seconds at the end of presentation of a list of words would tend to eliminate the recency effect.

23 People suffering from Korsakoff's syndrome are commonly unable to transfer information from STM to LTM.

24 K.F. (Shallice & Warrington, 1970) had impaired STM but normal LTM.

25 Baddeley & Hitch's (1974) working-memory model constitutes an elaboration of short-term memory (STM).

26 The central executive is modality-free in the sense that it can process information in any sensory form (e.g. visual or acoustic information).

27 The three slave systems which make up working memory are the articulatory loop, the primary acoustic store, and the visuo-spatial scratchpad.

28 According to Craik & Lockhart (1972), maintenance (or rote) rehearsal serves only to maintain information in STM, whilst elaborative rehearsal (forming meaningful links) is more likely to transfer information to LTM. This suggests that simple rehearsal is not sufficient for information to be transferred to LTM.

29 The surface features of a stimulus (such as whether a word is in upper or lower case) are analysed at a shallow level.

30 The deepest level of analysis, semantic analysis, involves analysis of a word's meaning.

31 In Craik & Tulving's (1975) experiment, participants were presented with words tachistoscopically, then asked one of four questions (e.g. Is the word in capital letters? Does the word rhyme with 'wait'? Would the word fit the sentence …?). Different question types required different types of processing.

32 Elaboration refers to the amount of processing of a particular type at a particular level.

33 Distinctiveness has been shown to have a strong influence on whether or not a word is remembered.

34 The model is descriptive in that it accurately describes the findings that different types of processing lead to differential memories, but it does not explain how this works or why it should be so.

Memory as information-processing

- **Registration:** transformation of sensory input into a form which can be stored.
- **Storage:** holding or retaining information in memory.
- **Retrieval:** extracting stored info from memory.
- **Forgetting:** may occur because information is stored but irretrievable (*inaccessible*) or it may never have been stored (*unavailable*).

Measuring memory

Relearning: recording the number of repetitions needed to learn material vs the number required to relearn it (e.g. revision speed).
Recognition: deciding whether or not a piece of information has been encountered before (e.g. multiple choice questions).
Recall: recalling items either in the order of presentation (*serial recall*) or any order (*free recall*) (e.g. essay questions).
Paired-associates: participants learn a list of paired items, are later presented with the one and must remember the other.

Types of memory

Sensory memory

capacity
Sperling (1960) investigated visual sensory memory (*iconic store*) by flashing up a grid of letters and then testing recall immediately afterwards.
Results: almost all information could be retrieved but memory faded very quickly with a delay.

duration
- Sperling found that iconic store faded within 1 second.
- Auditory sensory memory (*echoic store*) lasts longer – about 4 seconds.
- Echoic store needs to be longer so that all sounds in a word can be processed.

coding
Sensory memory holds info long enough for it to be processed by attentional systems – as such, coding is **modality-specific** i.e. information is held in a relatively raw state close to the relevant sensory system (e.g. the retina), rather than centrally.

Short-term memory

capacity
- Miller (1956): 7 (±2) independent items or 'chunks'.
- Bower & Springston (1970): the letters FBIPHDTWAIBM could be remembered if 'chunked' so as to relate to items in long-term memory (FBI, etc.).

duration
- Info can be held indefinitely by *rehearsal*.
- Peterson & Peterson (1959) prevented rehearsal by getting participants to count backwards before recalling nonsense 'trigrams' (e.g. XPJ).
Results: recall fell to 5% after 18 seconds.

coding
Conrad (1964) presented participants with 5 consonants (e.g. BKSJLR) for less than 1 second.
Results: mistakes were often similar in sound to the target, suggesting that coding is principally acoustic.

Long-term memory

capacity
There is no evidence of a limit to LTM's capacity. Nevertheless, we do not remember images or stories precisely, which suggests that some 'cognitive economising' occurs.

duration
Ebbinghaus (1885) memorised lists of nonsense syllables, then tested himself at intervals.
Results: memory declined sharply at first, then levelled off after a couple of days.

coding
Baddeley (1966): participants required to recall acoustically similar ('mad', 'mat') or semantically similar ('big', 'long') words.
Results: semantically similar words were harder to recall in the long-term, suggesting LTM is largely coded semantically.

Models of memory

Multi-store model

Atkinson & Shiffrin (1968, 1971) attempted to explain flow of information from short-term to long-term memory:
- STM and LTM are permanent **structural components**.
- **Control processes** are transient and control flow of info.
- **Rehearsal** is a process which functions as a buffer between sensory memory and LTM and enables transfer of information to LTM.

Levels-of-processing processing

Craik & Lockhart (1972):
- It is not the *amount* but the *type* of rehearsal which is important.
- Memory is seen as a *by-product* of perceptual analysis.
- Incoming information is subjected to a series of analyses of increasing depth – the greater the depth the more likely it is to be retained.
- The level used depends on the stimulus and the time available.

Working-memory model

Baddeley & Hitch (1974):
- STM is more complex and versatile than the multi-store model proposed, and it is not unitary.
- Emphasised that it is an active store, combining a *central executive* (which allocates resources and can process any kind of information) and *slave/sub-systems*:
  1. **Phonological loop:** a verbal rehearsal loop, also used to hold words we are preparing to speak.
  2. **Visuo-spatial scratch-pad:** a visual rehearsal system, used to recall spatial layouts and images.

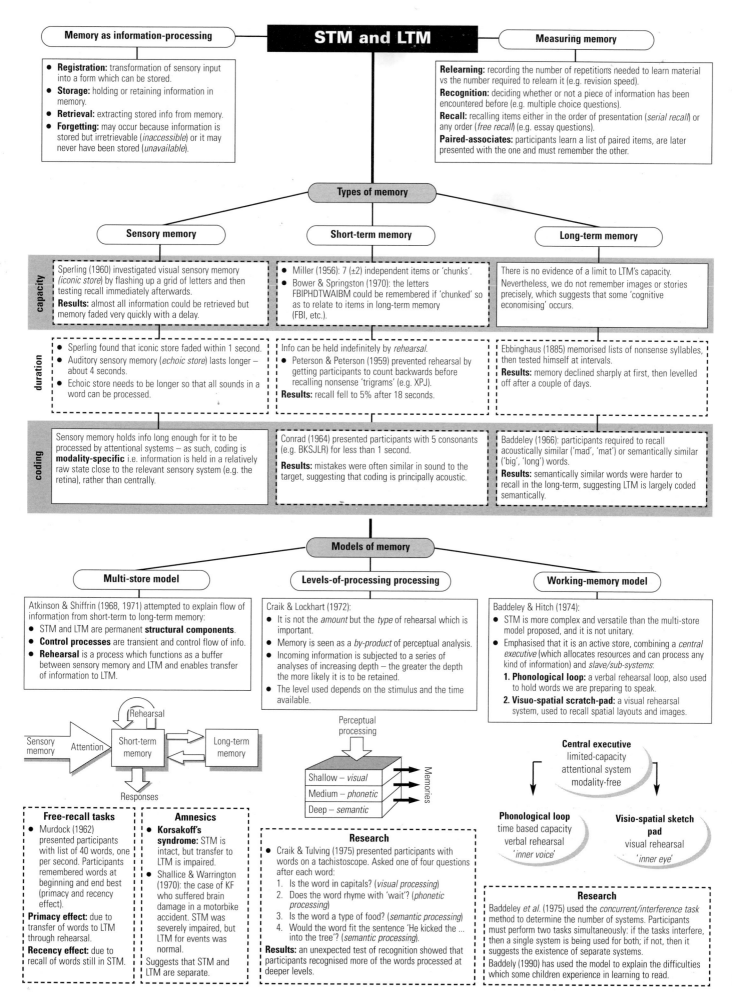

Free-recall tasks
- Murdock (1962) presented participants with list of 40 words, one per second. Participants remembered words at beginning and end best (primacy and recency effect).
Primacy effect: due to transfer of words to LTM through rehearsal.
Recency effect: due to recall of words still in STM.

Amnesics
- **Korsakoff's syndrome:** STM is intact, but transfer to LTM is impaired.
- Shallice & Warrington (1970): the case of KF who suffered brain damage in a motorbike accident. STM was severely impaired, but LTM for events was normal. Suggests that STM and LTM are separate.

Research
- Craik & Tulving (1975) presented participants with words on a tachistoscope. Asked one of four questions after each word:
  1. Is the word in capitals? (*visual processing*)
  2. Does the word rhyme with 'wait'? (*phonetic processing*)
  3. Is the word a type of food? (*semantic processing*)
  4. Would the word fit the sentence 'He kicked the ... into the tree'? (*semantic processing*).
Results: an unexpected test of recognition showed that participants recognised more of the words processed at deeper levels.

Research
Baddeley et al. (1975) used the *concurrent/interference task* method to determine the number of systems. Participants must perform two tasks simultaneously: if the tasks interfere, then a single system is being used for both; if not, then it suggests the existence of separate systems.
Baddely (1990) has used the model to explain the difficulties which some children experience in learning to read.

FORGETTING

KEY QUESTIONS
- What are availability and accessibility?
- How do decay and displacement theories explain forgetting?
- How do interference and retrieval-failure theories explain forgetting?
- How might emotional factors influence forgetting?

Q

Section 1: Introducing forgetting

1 What is the distinction between the *availability* and *accessibility* of information?
2 Which of these two is most likely to account for failures of short-term memory?

Section 2: Decay theories

3 What is an *engram*?
4 According to decay theories, under what circumstances will the engram tend to decay?
5 What, according to Hebb (1949), are the two stages in the formation of an engram?
6 What types of memory are not lost through decay?
7 What did Jenkins & Dallenbach's (1924) study of recall in sleeping participants conclude about the role of decay in forgetting?

Section 3: Displacement theory

8 In what sort of memory system would you expect displacement of material to occur?
9 What was involved in Waugh & Norman's (1965) *serial probe task*?
10 What were their findings?

Section 4: Retrieval-failure theory

11 According to retrieval-failure theory, why are we sometimes unable to recall memories?
12 What is the *tip-of-the-tongue phenomenon*?
13 What did Brown & McNeill (1966) discover when investigating the tip-of-the-tongue phenomenon?
14 When Tulving & Pearlstone (1966) asked participants to recall words which they had tried to memorise, why was the experimental group able to recall many more than the control group?
15 What is Tulving & Thomson's (1973) *encoding specificity principle*?
16 Tulving (1974) used the term *cue-dependent forgetting* to apply to which two types of forgetting?

17 Would you prefer to take your A level psychology exam in the same room or a different room to the one in which your lessons were held? Why?
18 Why might people sometimes claim to forget what they did whilst under the influence of alcohol?
19 What did Godden & Baddeley (1975) discover when testing the recall of divers who had learned word-lists underwater?

Section 5: Interference theory

20 What are the two types of interference which may occur between information which is learned?
21 How is *paired-associate learning* used to investigate these two types of interference?
22 What term describes the interference of later learning with material learned earlier?
23 What, based on Wickens' (1972) research, is the most likely cause of *proactive interference*?
24 Why have the results of interference experiments been criticised for possessing *low ecological validity*?

Section 6: Motivated forgetting

25 According to Freud, what is *repression*?
26 What sort of information does Freud suggest we are likely to repress?
27 What is *psychogenic amnesia*?
28 Which aspect of psychogenic amnesia does the *motivated forgetting theory* have most difficulty accounting for?
29 According to Parkin (1993), in what circumstances may motivated forgetting have a beneficial role?
30 How, according to Loftus (1997), are *false memories* constructed?
31 According to Brown & Kulik (1977), what kind of event most commonly produces flashbulb memories?
32 What further discovery did they make when investigating flashbulb memories for the death of Martin Luther King?
33 Why, according to evolutionary explanations, do flashbulb memories occur?

Section 1: Introducing forgetting

1 Availability refers to whether or not material has been stored, whereas accessibility refers to whether or not the information can be retrieved.

2 Failures of short-term memory are most likely to be due to the information being unavailable.

Section 2: Decay theories

3 An engram is a structural change in the brain which accompanies learning.

4 Decay theories claim that metabolic processes will degrade the engram over time, unless it is maintained by repetition or rehearsal.

5 According to Hebb (1949), an engram is initially delicate and liable to disruption (the active trace). With learning, it grows stronger and becomes permanent (the structural trace).

6 Procedural memories (involving motor skills, such as riding a bike) appear not to be lost through decay.

7 Jenkins & Dallenbach's (1924) study of recall in sleeping participants found that recall-score declined far less than in participants who were awake, suggesting that interference, not decay, plays the major role in forgetting.

Section 3: Displacement theory

8 Displacement is most likely to occur in limited-capacity memory systems, such as STM.

9 The serial probe task involved presenting participants with a series of digits, then a 'probe' digit from the list to discover whether participants could recall the digit immediately following the probe.

10 Waugh & Norman (1965) found that when the number of digits following the probe was small, recall was good, but when the number of digits was large, recall was poor. This supports displacement theory.

Section 4: Retrieval-failure theory

11 Retrieval-failure theories argue that poor recall occurs because the correct retrieval cues are not being used.

12 The tip-of-the-tongue phenomenon is when we know that we know something, but cannot recall it.

13 Brown & McNeill (1966) discovered that participants in the 'tip-of-the-tongue' state could recall some of the features of the word (such as its first letter), despite being unable to recall the whole word.

14 Tulving & Pearlstone (1966) found that presenting participants with the category headings of the words which they had learned boosted recall.

15 Tulving & Thomson's (1973) encoding specificity principle states that recall improves if the same cues are present during recall as were present during learning.

16 Tulving (1974) uses the term cue-dependent forgetting to refer to state- and context-dependent forgetting.

17 Abernathy's (1940) participants recalled material best when in the same room as they had learned it. Ideally you should take exams in your teaching room.

18 Physiological states represent internal cues (e.g. alcohol acts as a cue) and memories may become inaccessible when they are absent, having been present during learning. In addition, alcohol may also impair the transfer of information from short-term to long-term memory.

19 Godden & Baddeley (1975) found that divers' recall was best under the same conditions as they had learned.

Section 5: Interference theory

20 Proactive interference (or inhibition) and retroactive interference (or inhibition) may occur when similar material is learned within a short time-span.

21 Paired-associate learning involves participants learning two lists of word-pairs one after the other. The first word of each word pair is the same on both lists, but is paired with a different word in each case. Participants are then asked to recall which words were paired on either the first or second list.

22 Retroactive inhibition refers to interference of later learning with material learned earlier.

23 Wickens' (1972) research suggests that the major cause of proactive interference is interference with the retrieval of information from STM.

24 Interference experiments typically involve participants recalling similar lists of nonsense syllables within a short time-span. When meaningful material is used, interference effects are difficult to demonstrate. Some psychologists have argued that this shows that such explanations bear little relation to real life.

Section 6: Motivated forgetting

25 Freud claims that repression is an unconscious process in which certain memories are made inaccessible.

26 Freud claims that memories which elicit guilt, shame or anxiety are most likely to be repressed.

27 Psychogenic amnesia is amnesia which does not have a physical cause.

28 The motivated forgetting theory cannot account for the sudden return of memories in people suffering from psychogenic amnesia after a period of hours or years.

29 Parkin (1993) claims that motivated forgetting may have a beneficial role in cases of post-traumatic stress disorder, where it may help sufferers to adjust.

30 Loftus (1997) claims that false memories are often constructed by combining actual memories with the content of suggestions from others.

31 Brown & Kulik (1977) found that shocking personal events were most likely to precipitate flashbulb memories (commonly, the sudden death of a relative).

32 Brown and Kulik also discovered that whilst 75 per cent of black participants had flashbulb memories for the assassination of Martin Luther King, only 33 per cent of whites did, suggesting that personal relevance is an important factor.

33 Evolutionary explanations suggest that flashbulb memories occur in response to events which threaten survival, so that the organism can remember and avoid recurrences of the event.

A

Decay theory

- Explain why forgetting increases over time.
- Memories are stored in the brain as structural changes (*engrams*).
- Metabolic processes will tend to degrade the engram unless maintained by rehearsal (*'use it or lose it'*).

Hebb (1949) identified two stages in engram formation:
1. During learning, engram is delicate and liable to disruption (the *active trace*). Equivalent to STM.
2. After learning, a stronger, permanent engram is formed (the *structural trace*), corresponding to LTM.

Jenkins & Dallenbach (1924): participants learned lists of nonsense syllables, then went to sleep and were tested for recall after either 1, 2, 4 or 8 hours.
Results: far more forgetting occurred in participants who did not go to sleep after learning words. This suggests that interference from new material, *not* decay, is most responsible for forgetting.

Retrieval failure

- Memories cannot be recalled because the correct retrieval cues are not being used.
- Demonstrated by the *tip-of-the-tongue phenomenon*, where we know that we know something but cannot retrieve it then and there.
- Tulving (1974) uses the term *cue-dependent forgetting* to refer to two types of forgetting.

cue-dependent forgetting

state-dependent forgetting

Clark *et al.* (1987): victims' inabilities to recall details of a violent crime may be due in part to their change in emotional state.

context-dependent forgetting

Abernathy (1940): participants recalled material best when in the same room in which they learned it.

Tulving & Pearlstone (1966): participants attempted to recall words from list of words in different categories.
Results: participants were able to recall more words if supplied with category headings. (e.g. 'animals', 'tools').

Availability refers to whether or not material has been stored in the first place. Mostly concerns forgetting occurring in STM.

Forgetting in STM & LTM

Accessibility refers to whether or not what has been stored can be retrieved. Mostly concerns forgetting occurring in LTM.

Interference

- Forgetting is influenced more by what we do *before* or *after* learning than by the passage of time.
- Studied using *paired-associate lists* where two lists of word pairs are learned, the same words paired differently on each list (list A and list B).
- **Retroactive interference** involves later learning interfering with material learned earlier. (A ← B)
- **Proactive interference** involves earlier learning interfering with material learned later on. (A → B)

- Wickens (1972): participants became poorer at retaining information in STM on successive trials. However, if category of information was changed performance improved (release from proactive inhibition).
- This suggests that the major cause of proactive interference is interference with the retrieval of information from STM, rather than its storage.
However, Baddeley (1990) argues that such studies are not clearly related to real life and so lack ecological validity.

Displacement

- Forgetting occurs due to the limited capacity of STM.
- When the system is full, oldest material is pushed out by incoming new material ('bookshelf' model).

Waugh & Norman (1965) used a *serial probe task*, presenting participants with 16 digits, then asking them to say which digit followed a digit from the list (the 'probe').
Results: the greater the number of digits following the probe, the poorer participants' recall, suggesting that later material had, indeed, displaced earlier material.

The Influence of Emotional Factors

Motivated forgetting

- **Repression:** according to Freud, forgetting is a motivated process.
- **Defence mechanisms:** act to repress memories likely to cause guilt, shame or anxiety.
- **Unconscious mind:** where repressed memories reside, so they are not 'erased'.
- Freud (1901) reports on the case of a man who continually forgot the line following 'with a white sheet' in a poem. Freud claims that he was repressing a fear of death associated with seeing his dead father covered by a white sheet.

- Cases of *psychogenic amnesia* (amnesia without any physiological cause), which is linked to stressful events, may support this theory – but the theory cannot explain why these memories return when they do.
- Parkin (1993): repression may be beneficial in helping people to cope with traumatic events.
- Loftus (1997): it is difficult to investigate repressed memories, and some of the 'repressed memories' unearthed by psychiatrists may well be *false memories*.

Flashbulb memories

- According to Brown & Kulik (1977) a 'flashbulb memory' is an especially vivid and detailed kind of episodic memory, typically associated with a major public event.
- They argue that the brain possesses a special memory mechanism, triggered by important or emotionally arousing events, which causes an entire scene to become 'printed' on the memory.
- FMs are likely to be durable as they are frequently rehearsed.

Brown & Kulik (1977): asked participants about their memories of actual or attempted assasinations or personal shocks in the past 15 years.
Results: 73 out of 80 participants reported FMs associated with personal shock. They also discovered that more black participants reported a FM for the assassination of Martin Luther King than did white participants, suggesting that personal relevance matters.

CRITICAL ISSUE – EYEWITNESS TESTIMONY

KEY QUESTIONS
- What did Bartlett discover regarding memory?
- How accurate is eyewitness testimony?
- What factors may influence eyewitness testimony?
- How accurate is facial recognition?

Section 1: Reconstructive memory

1. Identify one of the criticisms Bartlett (1932) made of Ebbinghaus's research.
2. Name one method used by Bartlett to investigate human memory for meaningful material.
3. Identify *two* of the ways in which the *War of the Ghosts* story changed, following re-telling.
4. In what way did Wynn & Logie's (1988) findings differ from Bartlett's?
5. What is a *schema*?
6. Name two features of schemas.
7. How did Allport & Postman (1947) investigate the distorting effect of schemas?

Section 2: Eyewitness testimony research

8. Which aspect of memory has cast doubts on the reliability of eyewitness testimony?
9. Which significant recommendation regarding eyewitness testimony was made by the Devlin Committee?
10. What is the difference between *episodic memory* and *semantic memory*?
11. What did Memon & Wright (1999) discover regarding the relationship between identity parades and the mugshots shown to witnesses before the parade?
12. What sort of questions did Loftus investigate in her research into eyewitness testimony?
13. What did Loftus (1974) discover about the importance of testimony submitted by discredited witnesses?
14. Why, according to Brigham & Malpass (1985), are errors in identifying a suspect most likely to occur when the suspect is of a different race to the witness?
15. How did the study reported by Memon & Wright (1999) investigate the importance of social influence?

16. What is a *leading question*?
17. Participants in Loftus & Palmer's (1974) experiment gave widely differing estimates of how fast two cars were going, after watching a video clip of an accident. Why?
18. In a follow-up experiment, Loftus asked participants if they had seen broken glass. What did she find?
19. According to Loftus & Zanni's (1975) research, which of the two questions 'Did you see *the* broken headlight?' and 'Did you see *a* broken headlight?' is most likely to elicit a positive response?

Section 3: Evaluating EWT research

20. How does *source misattribution* explain the tendency of participants to recall seeing items which they have never actually seen when these have been (falsely) suggested to them?
21. What name is given to the phenomenon in which memories of details from various sources are combined with memories of another event?
22. Do leading questions merely affect individuals' responses at the time of questioning, or do they actually distort memories for events?
23. Identify two conditions under which it is easiest to mislead eyewitnesses, according to Cohen (1993)?
24. Describe two of the ways in which the quality of CCTV images may vary, according to Bruce (1998).
25. What explanation can you give for Harrower's (1998) conclusion that people recall details and faces not from memory but in terms of what they believe criminals should look like?
26. Complete the sentence: 'Bekerian & Bowers (1983) have argued that Loftus questions her witnesses in a rather ___ way'.

Q

Section 1: Reconstructive memory

1 Bartlett (1932) criticised Ebbinghaus's use of nonsense syllables (which excluded 'all that is central to human memory'), the study of 'repetition habits' (as having little to do with everyday life memory) and his focus on passive responses to stimuli, rather than people's active search for meaning.

2 Bartlett used both the serial reproduction (in which one person re-tells a story to another and so on) and repeated reproduction (in which one person recalls a story repeatedly, over time) methods to study memory.

3 The story became shorter, more coherent, more conventional and more clichéd.

4 Contrary to Bartlett's findings, Wynn and Logie (1988) found that the accuracy of descriptions of an event was maintained across intervals and regardless of the number of recalls.

5 A schema is a mental map or representation of a given area of knowledge.

6 Schemas provide us with preconceived expectations, help us to interpret information, and affect the way that memories are encoded.

7 Allport & Postman (1947) investigated the distorting effect of schemas by showing participants a picture of a white man threatening a black man with a razor. After several re-tellings of the story, the razor changed from the white man's hand to the black man's hand in participants' accounts.

Section 2: Eyewitness testimony research

8 The reconstructive nature of memory, in particular the tendency of people to 'fill in the gaps' or modify memories so as to match existing schemas, has cast doubts on the reliability of eyewitness testimony.

9 The Devlin Committee recommended that the trial judge instruct the jury that it is not safe to convict on a single eyewitness's testimony alone, except in exceptional circumstances.

10 Episodic memory refers to our memory for the events, people, objects which we have personally encountered, whilst semantic memory is our store of general factual information.

11 Memon & Wright (1999) discovered that people presented to witnesses in mug-shots were more likely to be identified in a line-up regardless of whether or not they actually committed the crime.

12 Loftus was interested in questions such as 'Can the wording of questions cause witnesses to remember events differently?', and 'Can witnesses be misled into remembering things which did not actually occur?'.

13 Loftus (1974) discovered that even discredited witnesses were highly influential on participants' perceptions of guilt or innocence.

14 According to Brigham & Malpass (1985), people of a given race tend to have difficulty recognising the faces of people from other races.

15 Memon & Wright (1999) reported a study in which participants were asked in pairs whether they had seen several cars in a previous phase of a study. People's responses were influenced by the first person's answers (compare this with Sherif's (1935) or Asch's (1951) studies).

16 A leading question is one that suggests to a person the answer that should be given.

17 Participants in Loftus & Palmer's (1974) experiment gave widely differing speed estimates depending on whether the term used in the question 'How fast were the cars going when they ...?' was 'hit', 'smashed', 'collided', 'bumped', or 'contacted'.

18 Loftus found that participants who had been asked questions using the term 'smashed' were far more likely to remember broken glass than those for whom the term was 'hit'.

19 According to Loftus & Zanni's (1975) research, the question 'Did you see the broken headlight?' is most likely to elicit a positive response.

Section 3: Evaluating EWT research

20 Source misattribution proposes that witnesses are confusing information obtained outside of the witnessed event with the witnessed event itself, i.e. they correctly recall the information, but forget where they got it from.

21 This phenomenon is termed *memory blending*.

22 The above experiment suggests that it is participants' memories, not merely their answers at the time, which have been affected, since in the follow-up experiment both groups of participants were asked the same question, concerning information which had not been questioned previously.

23 Eyewitnesses are most easily misled if the information concerned is peripheral to the main event, if the information is given after a delay, or if they have no reason to mistrust it.

24 Bruce (1998) identified the following three variables: camera and lighting angles, the difficulty in judging different images as being of the same individual and the degree of familiarity of the witness with the individual captured on tape.

25 Harrower's (1998) conclusion is consistent with the view that memory works in a reconstructive fashion, using schemas to fill in the gaps in memory.

26 'Bekerian & Bowers (1983) have argued that Loftus questions her witnesses in a rather *unstructured* way.'

Reconstructive Memory

The Bartlett 'approach'

Bartlett (1932) argued that Ebbinghaus's studies of memory had little to do with memory in everyday life. Instead, he studied participants who repeated a story to each other (*serial reproduction*).

The *War of the Ghosts*, a North American folk tale, was reproduced by English participants. During reproduction:

- the story became shorter
- the story became more coherent
- the story became more conventional & clichéd.

Bartlett concluded that interpretation plays a major role in remembering, and that remembering is an *active* process (compare this with Gregory's model of perception).

Schemas

- A schema is a '*mental map*' of events, objects or people, containing relevant information.
- Schemas provide us with preconceived *expectations*.
- Schemas help us to *interpret* the world, and to make it more predictable.
- Schemas affect the way memories are encoded and can have a *distorting* effect (see below).

Allport & Postman (1947): showed participants a drawing of two men in an argument (one white, one black). The white man held a cut-throat razor.

Results: When participants described the scene to another, who in turn described it to another, the razor typically 'changed hands' in line with prevailing prejudice.

Eyewitness Testimony

The importance of eyewitness testimony

Loftus (1974): asked students to judge a man accused of robbing a grocer's and murdering the owner and his 5-year-old-daughter.

- 9 out of 50 judged him guilty on the evidence alone.
- 36 out of 50 judged him guilty when told an assistant had witnessed the man commit the crime.
- 34 out of 50 judged him guilty even when told the assistant was short-sighted, without his glasses and could not have seen the accused's face.

Conclusion: Even a discredited/mistaken witness can be very influential.

The influence of leading questions

Loftus & Palmer (1974):

- Participants were shown a 30-second video of two cars colliding.
- Speed estimates differed depended on wording of question: 'How fast were the cars going when they …

smashed ?'	hit ?'
40.8 mph	*31.8 mph*

Follow-up experiment:

- Participants were asked if they remembered seeing broken glass (there was none).
- Answers varied depending on the wording of the question in the first experiment:

smashed ?'	hit ?'
32% 'yes'	*14% 'yes'*

Suggests that memories had been permanently altered by the earlier leading questions.

Loftus & Zanni (1975) showed participants a short film of a car travelling through the countryside.

- Participants were asked either 'How fast was the white sports car going when it passed the 'Stop' sign?' (there *was* a stop sign) or 'How fast was the white sports car going when it passed the barn?' (there *was no* barn!)

Results: 17.3% of the participants in the second group recalled seeing the (non-existent) barn, vs only 2.7% in the first group, when questioned a week later.

Conflicting research

- Loftus (1979): 98% of participants could not be misled about the colour of a purse they had seen stolen.

Suggests that participants are less likely to be misled about *central* information, or when misinformation is blatantly wrong.

Cohen (1993) argues that people are less likely to be misled if:

- the false information concerns insignificant details,
- the false information is given after a delay,
- they have no reason to distrust it.

Other influences on EWT

Race

- '**Own race bias**' (Brigham & Malpass, 1985): members of different races were found to be good at recognising faces of members of their own race, but poor at telling apart faces of other races.

Clothing

- Sanders (1984): clothing was more influential than height and facial features when participants identified criminals from identity parades.

Social influence

- Memon & Wright (1999): describe a study in which participants' responses to questions regarding whether or not they had seen cars previously, were influenced by the responses given by another participant earlier.

Misleading questions & suggestibility

Both children and adults seem prone to reconstructive errors when recalling events, particularly if presented by misleading information. Such information includes leading questions and after-the-fact information, as illustrated by Loftus's research.

Closed-circuit television

Bruce (1998): argues that although CCTV is increasingly able to provide footage of criminals, the belief that this will eliminate the problems associated with human recall is incorrect. Bruce has identified a number of reasons why a CCTV image alone might not be sufficient to establish a suspect's identity.

Bruce (1998): discovered that human vision has difficulty dealing with subtle differences between two images – a problem exaggerated by the following aspects of CCTV images:

- camera & lighting angles may provide only a poorly lit, messy image of the top or back of someone's head.
- even with relatively high quality images, judging different images to be of the same individual may be prone to error.
- people find it much easier to identify familiar faces than unfamiliar faces, using CCTV images.

THE DEVELOPMENT AND VARIETY OF ATTACHMENTS

SYLLABUS

10.2 Attachments in development – the development and variety of attachments
- the development of attachments (e.g. Schaffer). Research into individual differences, including secure and insecure attachments (e.g. Ainsworth) and cross-cultural variations. Explanations of attachment (e.g. learning theory, Bowlby's theory)

KEY QUESTIONS
- What are sociability and attachments?
- Which theories exist to explain the processes of attachment-formation?
- How do attachments vary between individuals and across cultures?

Q

Section 1: The nature of sociability and attachment

1 Which three dimensions of temperament are taken to be present at birth and inherited?
2 How can *sociability* be defined?
3 How do Kagan *et al.* (1978) define *attachments*?
4 Why is our first attachment widely recognised to be crucial for healthy development?
5 How does the *discriminate attachment phase* differ from the *indiscriminate attachment phase*?
6 At what age do infants begin to become more independent from the caregiver?

Section 2: Theories of the attachment process

7 Complete the following sentence: 'According to psychoanalytic accounts, infants become attached to their caregivers because of the caregiver's ability to satisfy _____ _____'.
8 What, according to Freud, are the causes of unhealthy attachments?
9 According to the behaviourist account, what is the first step in the formation of an attachment?
10 Why does Harlow's (1959) finding that infant rhesus monkeys spend more time clinging to cloth surrogates than to wire and bottle ones cast doubt on '*cupboard love*' theories of attachment?
11 What was the consequence for the rhesus monkeys in Harlow & Suomi's (1970) experiment of being raised exclusively with cloth mothers?
12 What did Schaffer & Emerson (1964) discover (in their longitudinal study) about the target of infant attachments?
13 Define *imprinting*.
14 Why are *precocial species* most likely to employ imprinting as an attachment mechanism?
15 What is a *critical period*?
16 Does imprinting occur in humans in the same way as it does in ducklings?

17 Complete the following sentence: 'Bowlby argued that because new-born infants are entirely helpless, they are _____ _____ to behave towards their mothers in ways that ensure their survival'.
18 How do infants use looking behaviour to promote the formation of a parent–child bond?
19 Why might we think that smiling is an innate behaviour?
20 Bowlby (1951) believed that there was a critical period beyond which mothering is useless – what was that period?
21 What term did Bowlby use to describe (what he believed was) the child's innate tendency to become attached to one particular individual?
22 What did Klaus and Kennell's *extended contact hypothesis* propose?
23 What did Rutter (1981) conclude about the kinds of attachment behaviour that infants display towards different attachment figures?
24 According to Bowlby, what is the value of a father to the infant?
25 What did Yogman *et al.* (1977) discover when looking at differences in the quality and quantity of mothers' and fathers' caregiving?

Section 3: Individual and cultural variations

26 What *two* behaviours were significantly correlated with infant attachment styles, according to Ainsworth's (1967) Ganda project?
27 What is the *Strange Situation* and what is it used for?
28 According to Ainsworth *et al.* (1978), what is the difference between *anxious–avoidant* and *anxious–resistant attachments*?
29 Are attachment styles permanent characteristics?
30 Identify *two* of the main conclusions reached by Ijzendoorn & Kroonenberg's (1988) review of cross-cultural studies employing the Strange Situation.

Section 1: The nature of sociability and attachment

1   Sociability, emotionality and activity are dimensions of temperament which are taken to be present at birth and inherited.

2   Sociability can be defined as seeking and being gratified by rewards from social interaction, preferring to be with others, sharing activities and being responsive to and seeking responsiveness from others.

3   Kagan *et al.* (1978) define attachments as an intense emotional relationship that is specific to two people, that endures over time, and in which prolonged separation from the partner is accompanied by stress and sorrow.

4   Our first attachment may well act as a *prototype* for all later attachments.

5   During the discriminate attachment phase, children develop specific attachments and become distressed when separated (separation anxiety). They may also develop a fear of strangers.

6   Infants begin to become more independent of the caregiver from about nine months onwards (though this varies from child to child).

Section 2: Theories of the attachment process

7   'According to psychoanalytic accounts, infants become attached to their caregivers because of the caregiver's ability to satisfy *instinctual needs*.'

8   Freud claims that either overgratification or undergratification of instinctual needs are likely to be the cause of unhealthy attachments.

9   The behaviourist account holds that the first step in attachment formation is to associate the primary caregiver with the satisfaction of physiological needs.

10 Harlow's (1959) finding suggests that contact comfort may be a more important factor in determining attachments than food alone.

11 The rhesus monkeys in Harlow & Suomi's (1970) experiment, having been raised exclusively with cloth mothers, were extremely aggressive as adults, rarely interacted with other monkeys and made inappropriate sexual responses.

12 Schaffer & Emerson (1964) discovered that infants often become attached most strongly to people who do not perform caregiving activities.

13 Imprinting refers to the tendency of some species to form an automatic bond with whatever moving object is present during a certain critical period soon after hatching.

14 Precocial species are mobile from birth and therefore need a mechanism which allows them to identify caregivers and stay close to them.

15 A critical period is a restricted time period during which certain events must take place if development is to progress normally.

16 No. Humans are unlikely to attach to moving objects simply because they are present soon after birth. Human attachments are flexible and complex.

17 'Bowlby argued that because new-born infants are entirely helpless, they are *genetically programmed* to behave towards their mothers in ways that ensure their survival.'

18 Infants look to return a parent's gaze, inviting them to respond. Infants are distressed by lack of eye contact.

19 Smiling is probably innate since it occurs soon after birth, before the child has had an opportunity to learn, and before it has mastered control of its facial muscles.

20 Bowlby's (1951) critical period, beyond which mothering is useless, was two-and-a-half to three years (12 months for most children).

21 Bowlby used the term *monotropy* to describe an innate tendency to attach to a particular individual.

22 Klaus and Kennell's extended contact hypothesis proposed that mothers who had a lot of contact with their new-borns were more likely to cuddle, soothe and enjoy their babies later on.

23 Rutter (1981) discovered that infants display a range of attachment behaviours towards a variety of individuals (not just the mother).

24 Bowlby claimed that the father is of no direct emotional significance to the child, but is only indirectly important as support for the mother.

25 Yogman *et al.* (1977) found no differences in the quality and quantity of mothers' and fathers' caregiving.

Section 3: Individual and cultural variations

26 Ainsworth found that ratings of the mother's sensitivity and holding behaviour were significantly correlated with attachment styles.

27 The Strange Situation is a series of interactions between a mother, infant and a stranger, and was designed by Ainsworth *et al.* (1978) as a way of measuring the attachment styles of different infants.

28 An anxious–avoidant attachment is characterised by indifference towards the mother and similar behaviours towards the stranger, whilst an anxious–resistant attachment is characterised by an ambivalent attitude towards the mother, with distress on her departure and anger on her return.

29 Ainsworth *et al.* believed that attachment styles were permanent characteristics; however, Vaughn *et al.* (1980) demonstrated that attachment styles can change, depending on the circumstances.

30 Ijzendoorn & Kroonenberg (1988) found that there are marked differences within cultures in the distribution of attachment types, that the overall worldwide pattern was similar to Ainsworth *et al.*'s 'standard', and that type A is more common in Western Europe and type C in Israel and Japan.

A

Early Social Development

Sociability: seeking and being gratified by rewards from social interaction, preferring to be with others, sharing activities, being responsive and seeking responsiveness from others.

Attachment: an intense emotional relationship that is specific to two people, that endures over time, and in which prolonged separation from the partner is accompanied by stress and sorrow (Kagan *et al.*, 1978).

Attachment phases

Age	Stage and characteristics
6 weeks– 3 months	**Pre-attachment phase:** infants attracted to humans in preference to inanimate objects. Nestling, gurgling and smiling are directed towards anyone.
3 months– 7 months	**Indiscriminate attachment phase:** infants distinguish familiar and unfamiliar faces. Infants will allow careful strangers to handle them without distress.
7 months– 9 months	**Discriminate attachment phase:** infants begin to develop specific attachments and display separation anxiety. Linked to emergence of object permanence. Many display a fear of strangers response.
9 months +	**Multiple attachments phase:** infants become increasingly independent. Strong additional bonds formed with other caregivers and peers.

Variations in attachment

Ainsworth's (1967) Ganda project

Studied 28 unweaned babies over a 9-mth period. Found that quality of attachment was correlated with mother's *sensitivity* – how well she interprets and responds to her baby's needs – and the amount of *holding* by the mother. The study was subsequently replicated in Baltimore, using the *Strange Situation* (see below).

The 'Strange Situation' technique for studying attachment
(Ainsworth & Wittig, 1969)

A series of interactions between a mother, child and stranger in which the child's behaviour is studied. Using the Strange Situation, Ainsworth *et al.* (1978) were able to classify children's behaviour as belonging to one of three types:

Type A (15%) **Anxious–avoidant**
Baby ignores/indifferent to mother. Both adults treated similarly.

Type B (70%) **Securely attached**
Distressed when mother leaves. Seeks contact and is calmed when mother returns.

Type C (15%) **Anxious–resistant**
Cries more and explores less than types A or B. Very distressed when mother leaves. Anger towards her on return.

Cross-cultural studies using the Strange Situation

3 main conclusions (van Ijzendoorn & Kroonenberg, 1988):
- Marked differences between cultures of distribution of types A, B, C – e.g. Japan has a high proportion of type C, very little type A.
- The overall worldwide pattern was similar to Ainsworth's standard.
- Though type B is most common, type A is more common in Western Europe and type C in Israel and Japan.

Theories of attachment

'Cupboard love' theories

Psychoanalytic account
(Freud, 1926)

- Infants become attached to their caregivers (usually the mother) because they satisfy instinctual needs.
- Healthy attachments result from feeding practices which satisfy needs for food, security and libidinal impulses.
- Unhealthy attachments result from over- or under-gratification of these needs.

Behaviourist account

Infants become attached to those who satisfy physiological needs:
1. Caregivers become **associated** with gratification.
2. Caregivers become **conditioned reinforcers**.
3. Gratification **generalises** to a feeling of security when caregiver is present.

Conflicting research

Harlow (1959) placed infant rhesus monkeys in cages with a choice of two mothers:
- **wire mother** – made from wire with a feeding bottle attached
- **cloth mother** – covered in terry cloth but with no feeding bottle.

Results: The infants spent most of their time clinging to the cloth mother and would run to it when distressed, indicating that contact comfort was more important than feeding alone.

Schaffer & Emerson (1964): a longitudinal study of infants. Roughly a third were most strongly attached to someone who *did not* perform caretaking duties (feeding, bathing, etc.)

Ethological theories

Imprinting (Lorenz, 1935)

- Some non-humans (especially precocial species) form a strong bond with the first moving object they encounter.
- The bond occurs without feeding taking place and allows the young to recognise the caregiver and stay close to it.
- A **critical period** is a restricted time-period in which certain events necessary for normal development must take place.
- Lorenz saw imprinting as being switched on and off genetically.
- Led some researchers to propose the existence of a **sensitive period** in humans.

- Lorenz found that imprinting reached a peak (in ducklings) at between 12 and 17 hours after hatching
- Imprinting was measured by following behaviour towards a model of a moving male duck.
- Lorenz saw imprinting as irreversible – supported by the finding that it affects sexual preferences later on.

Bowlby's theory

'[M]other love in infancy is as important for mental health as are vitamins and proteins for physical health' (Bowlby, 1951).

Maternal-sensitive period

- New-born infants are genetically programmed to behave in ways which ensure their survival (e.g. cuddling, eye-contact, smiling and crying).
- Also, the mother inherits a genetic blueprint for responding to the baby, producing an attachment at a critical period.
- Mothering is therefore useless if delayed for $2\frac{1}{2}$–3 years (12 months for most infants) (Bowlby, 1951).

Extended contact hypothesis

Klaus & Kennel (1976) proposed that mothers who spent more time with their new-borns would form stronger bonds with them. This led to changes in maternity ward practices.

Monotropy

Bowlby believed that children display a strong innate tendency to become attached to one particular figure (monotropy).

This attachment is qualitatively different from all others.

Conflicting research

- Rutter (1981): infants show each type of attachment behaviour towards figures other than the mother.
- Schaffer & Emerson (1964): infants form multiple attachments, in which the mother is not always the main attachment.

DEPRIVATION AND PRIVATION

Section 1: The maternal-deprivation hypothesis

1 Bowlby based his hypothesis on two claims, one of which was that there is a 'critical period' for attachment formation. What was the other claim?

2 What, according to Bowlby, would be the consequence of breaking the mother–child bond in the first few years of life?

3 What did Goldfarb (1943) discover when investigating the development of institutionalised and fostered children?

4 Spitz (1945, 1946) and Spitz & Wolf (1946) investigated poor South American orphanages. What clinical condition resulted from the minimal attention which the children received?

5 Complete the following sentence: 'Unfortunately, Bowlby, Goldfarb, Spitz and Wolf all failed to recognise that the _____ nature of the institutional environment could be responsible for the effects they observed'.

6 What is meant by Rutter's (1981) point that Bowlby failed to distinguish *deprivation* from *privation*?

Section 2: Deprivation

7 What is the first stage in the *distress response* which a young child shows in response to short-term separation?

8 What are the important features of the final stage of distress (i.e. detachment)?

9 At what age are children likely to find separation most distressing?

10 Why?

11 Describe one way in which the distress experienced by the child following separation could be reduced.

12 What two events are most likely to result in long-term deprivation for the child?

13 Name any four characteristics associated with *separation anxiety*.

14 What, according to Bowlby, is *school phobia*?

15 Based on Richards' (1995) research, identify any four common consequences of divorce for the child.

16 Richards' (1995) findings concerning the effects of divorce are *correlational*. How does this affect the way in which we interpret them?

17 What, according to Schaffer (1996a), is the single most damaging factor before, during and after the separation of parents?

18 What did Harlow discover about the behaviour of rhesus monkeys reared only by 'surrogate' (artificial) mothers?

Section 3: Privation

19 What would you expect an *affectionless psychopath* to be like?

20 What did Bowlby discover, when investigating the histories of 14 juvenile thieves, all of whom showed characteristics of affectionless psychopathy?

21 How might you criticise the methodology of this particular study?

22 What was the conclusion of Bowlby *et al.*'s (1956) study of children who had been separated from parents whilst in a tuberculosis sanitorium?

23 In Tizard & Hodges' (1978) study of children who were adopted or returned to their natural families, which group was most likely to form close attachments?

24 What were Tizard and Hodges able to conclude?

25 What did Quinton & Rutter (1988) attempt to determine by observing women, brought up in care, interacting with their own children?

26 Complete the sentence: 'The considerable variability of parenting skills within the group brought up in care could be explained in terms of ____ ____'.

Section 1: The maternal-deprivation hypothesis

1 The two claims on which Bowlby based his hypothesis were that infants undergo a 'critical period' for attachment formation, and that infants have a strong innate drive to form a unique attachment with a single individual (monotropy theory).

2 Bowlby claimed that the consequence of breaking the mother–child bond in the first few years of life would be serious and permanent damage to emotional, social and intellectual development.

3 Goldfarb (1943) discovered that the institutionalised children fell behind the fostered group on a variety of measures, ranging from IQ to tests of social maturity, from the age of three onwards.

4 Spitz (1945, 1946) and Spitz & Wolf (1946) observed high levels of anaclitic depression, involving symptoms such as poor appetite and morbidity.

5 'Unfortunately, Bowlby, Goldfarb, Spitz and Wolf all failed to recognise that the *unstimulating* nature of the institutional environment could be responsible for the effects they observed.'

6 Rutter (1981) pointed out that, whilst Bowlby's conclusions concerned the effects of deprivation (separation from the primary attachment figure), the studies on which he based his claims were actually studies of privation (the absence of *any* attachment).

Section 2: Deprivation

7 Protest is the first stage in the distress response, involving crying, kicking, screaming and struggling.

8 Detachment is often characterised by a superficial and uniform treatment of others, and following reunion with the mother 'rejection' of her often ensues.

9 Maccoby (1980) suggests that the period between 12 months and 18 months is associated with maximum distress.

10 Children at this age may not be able to maintain an image of the absent parent in memory, and may not be able to understand that the separation is temporary.

11 Distress may be reduced if the child has had previous positive experiences of separation (such as staying with grandparents), or if he/she has been able to form multiple attachments. Finally, the quality of substitute care is important in keeping distress to a minimum.

12 Death and divorce are the events most likely to result in long-term deprivation for a child.

13 Increased aggressive behaviour, increased demands on the mother, clinging behaviour, detachment, psychosomatic reactions and fluctuations between clinging and detachment, are all characteristics associated with separation anxiety.

14 According to Bowlby, school phobia is an expression of separation anxiety, the child fearing that something dreadful will happen to its mother while it is at school.

15 Richards' (1995) research identifies lower levels of academic achievement and self-esteem, higher incidence of conduct disorders, earlier social maturity and transitions to adulthood, a tendency towards more changes of job and lower socio-economic status, a higher frequency of depression and more distant relationships with relations, as common consequences of divorce for the child.

16 Richards' (1995) findings are correlational: as such, they do not tell us whether the above factors are caused by divorce, or are just 'side effects' of other factors which may lead to divorce (e.g. parental discord).

17 Schaffer (1996a) claims that inter-parental conflict is the single most damaging factor before, during and after the separation of parents.

18 Harlow discovered that rhesus monkeys reared only by 'surrogate' mothers were disturbed in later sexual behaviour and, if female, became inadequate mothers.

Section 3: Privation

19 An affectionless psychopath is commonly incapable of deep feelings and consequently unable to form meaningful interpersonal relationships.

20 Bowlby discovered that seven of the 14 juvenile thieves had suffered complete or prolonged separation from their mothers, and a further two had spent nine months in hospital as two-year-olds.

21 Bowlby's study was methodologically flawed. It was a retrospective study and, as such, relied on fallible human memories for events.

22 Bowlby *et al.*'s (1956) study of children staying in a tuberculosis sanitorium concluded that 'part of the emotional disturbance can be attributed to factors other than separation'.

23 Tizard & Hodges (1978) found that the adopted children were more likely to form close attachments than the children who were returned to their natural families.

24 Tizard and Hodges concluded that children who are initially deprived of attachments can form attachments later on, providing that adults nurture such attachments.

25 Quinton & Rutter (1988) aimed to determine whether children deprived of parental care in turn became depriving parents.

26 'The considerable variability of parenting skills within the group brought up in care could be explained in terms of *developmental pathways*.'

Deprivation and Privation

Bowlby's maternal-deprivation hypothesis

Based on his ideas regarding a **critical period** for attachment-formation, and his **monotropy theory**, Bowlby argued that the mother–infant attachment could not be broken in the first few years of life without serious and permanent damage to social, emotional and intellectual development. Based his claims on studies such as:

Goldfarb (1943):
- Fifteen children raised in institutions compared with 15 fostered children.
- Institutionalised group raised in 'social isolation' during first year.
- Institutionalised group did poorly on tests of abstract thinking, social maturity, rule-following, and at age 14 IQs averaged 72 (vs. 95 for the fostered group).

Spitz (1945, 1946):
- Studied very poor South American orphanages where children only received minimal attention.
- The children were apathetic and displayed *anaclitic depression*. After 3 months of such deprivation, complete recovery was rare.

Bowlby believed the studies showed the effects of maternal deprivation; however:
- Bowlby, Goldfarb, Spitz failed to recognise that such institutional environments were extremely *unstimulating* (not just lacking in maternal care).
- Rutter pointed out that Bowlby had failed to distinguish *deprivation* from *privation*. In fact, the results relate to privation.

Deprivation

Short-term effects (associated with e.g. hospitalisation)

The stages of distress
Protest: initial reaction takes the form of crying, screaming, clinging to mother/struggling.
Despair: child calms, may appear apathetic. Keeps anger 'locked up' and wants nothing to do with people.
Detachment: with prolonged separation, child begins to respond to others but superficially. If reunited, may 'reject' mother.

Factors influencing distress
Age: separation is most distressing between 7/8 months and 3 years (when attachments are being formed).
Gender: boys are generally more distressed than girls. Any behavioural problems are likely to be accentuated.
Separation experience: positive previous experiences of separation reduce distress.
Multiple attachments: children with multiple attachments are less likely to be distressed.

Long-term effects (associated with e.g. death or divorce)

Separation anxiety
Aggressive behaviour: increased together with demands on the mother.
Clinging behaviour: may not let mother out of sight – this may generalise to other relationships.
Detachment: child may appear to become self-sufficient.
Fluctuation: between clinging and detachment.
Psychosomatic reactions: e.g. bed-wetting.

Effects of divorce
(Richards, 1995)
Academic achievement: lower.
Self-esteem: lower.
Conduct: higher incidence of problems.
Social maturity: develops earlier, with transitions to adulthood (e.g leaving home, having children) occurring earlier.
Depression: higher incidence.
Relationships: more distant towards parents and kin.

Research – divorce
- Richards' research is correlational – Elliot & Richards (1991) found some of the above effects to be present before divorce.
- Schaffer (1996a): it is inter-parental conflict which is the most damaging factor.
- Amato (1993): conflict between parents who live together is associated with low self-esteem in children.

Privation

Effects

Affectionless psychopathy
Bowlby claimed that separation experiences in early childhood cause affectionless psychopathy – an inability to have deep feelings for others resulting in a lack of meaningful relationships.

Bowlby (1946) studied 44 juvenile thieves:
- Fourteen showed features of affectionless psychopathy (AP).
- Seven of these had experienced prolonged separation as children.
- None of a control group of juveniles showed AP.

Bowlby took this to show that AP resulted from maternal deprivation, though *privation* is a more likely cause.

Developmental retardation
- Dennis (1960): there is a critical period for intellectual development before age 2.
- Based claims on a study of Iranian orphanages where children adopted after age 2 seemed unable to catch up.

Skeels & Dye (1939):
- Studied 25 children raised in an unstimulating orphanage.
- At age 2 those with lower IQs were transferred to a school for the mentally retarded where older girls provided one-to-one care.

Results: the average IQ of this group rose by 36 points, whilst the IQ of those remaining behind dropped by 21 points.

Reversibility

Studies of late adoption
Tizard & Hodges (1978): looked at children who were either adopted or returned to own families on leaving care.
- Children had little opportunity to form relationships whilst in institutions.
- By age 8 majority of adopted children had formed close attachments, whereas only some of those returned to their natural families had done so (biological parents often had mixed feelings about having the children back).
- By age 16 adopted group had better family relationships than children returned to their own families.
- However, *outside* family *both* groups more likely to seek adult affection, experience difficulties with peers, less likely to have special friends, more likely to befriend *any* peer.

Overall, suggests the importance of *nurturing adults* in reversing effects.

Extreme early privation
Koluchova (1972): describes the case of two Czechoslovakian boys brought up in a cellar.
- Boys were discovered aged 7, and by age 14 showed no psychopathological symptoms.

Developmental pathways
Quinton & Rutter (1988): investigated whether deprived children would become depriving parents:
- Women brought up in care were, as a whole, less sensitive, supportive and warm.

However, this may be due to a chain of events *following* care (e.g. teenage pregnancy, marital breakdown etc.) and such *developmental pathways* may explain why some possessed better parenting skills than others.

CRITICAL ISSUE – THE EFFECTS OF DAY CARE ON CHILDREN'S DEVELOPMENT

Section 1: Understanding day care

1 How does Scarr (1998) use the expression 'day care'?

2 What does it mean to say that shared childcare is actually a normative experience for contemporary American and British children?

3 Complete the sentence: 'According to Scarr (1998), non-maternal shared care is normative both _____ and _____'.

4 Roughly what percentage of mothers of school-age children are in the labour force?

5 What is the '*motherhood mystique*'?

6 According to Scarr (1998), what is the main difference between research into the effects of day care in the 1970s, and research in the 1990s?

7 Identify four of the criteria which are most commonly agreed on as measures of the quality of care.

8 Why is it difficult to interpret the findings of reports which link poor quality care with lower cognitive scores and social adjustment ratings?

Section 2: Effects on social development

9 What does Bowlby predict will be the consequence of maternal separation for the child, following the formation of a maternal bond?

10 What two conditions need to be met in order for children not to suffer any ill effects resulting from day care, according to Schaffer (1996a)?

11 What did Belsky & Rovine (1988) discover when they studied children who had been receiving day care for at least four months and for more than 20 hours per day?

12 What is the principal criticism of Belsky and Rovine's research?

13 How does the distribution of insecure infants of working mothers in the USA compare with the distribution of insecure infants of (mainly non-working) mothers?

14 Why is it not fair to assume that children who are emotionally insecure with their mothers are insecure in general?

Section 3: Effects on cognitive development

15 Compete the sentence: 'According to Scarr (1998), children from low-income families definitely _____ from high quality care'.

16 For which groups are the effects of day care on cognitive development least clear?

17 Baydar & Brooks-Gunn (1991) studied 1181 children, comparing those whose mothers went out to work before their children were a year old with those whose mothers started work later. What did they find?

18 What did Scarr & Thompson (1994) discover when studying 1100 Bermudan children, some of whom had received day care?

19 What general criticism do Horwood & Fergusson (1999) make of the majority of research into the effects of day care?

20 What overall conclusion do Mooney and Munton (cited in Judd, 1997) draw from their review of 40 years' research into day care?

21 Complete the sentence: 'In more than __ per cent of British two-parent families with dependent children, both parents work'.

Section 1: Understanding day care

1 Scarr (1998) uses the expression to refer to all varieties of non-maternal care of children who reside with their parents or close relatives.

2 Shared childcare is normative for British and American children, because at the moment most children have mothers who are employed.

3 'According to Scarr (1998), non-maternal shared care is normative both *historically* and *culturally*.'

4 Roughly 75 per cent of the mothers of school-age children are in the labour force.

5 The 'motherhood mystique' refers to the widespread belief that women are born and bred to be mothers, primarily.

6 According to Scarr (1998), research in the 1970s did not look into the quality of non-maternal care, but simply compared it with maternal care, whilst in the 1990s research has focused on variations in the type and quality of care.

7 Quality of care involves: health and safety requirements, responsive and warm staff–child interaction, developmentally appropriate curricula, limited group sizes, age-appropriate caregiver–child ratios, adequate indoor and outdoor space, adequate staff training and low staff turnover.

8 The quality of care selected by parents is correlated with personal characteristics or circumstances. These – not the quality of day care – may explain the observed results.

Section 2: Effects on social development

9 Bowlby predicts that such separation may lead to distress, and even separation anxiety.

10 Schaffer (1996a) claims that the quality and stability of care are essential in averting ill effects.

11 Belsky and Rovine found that these children were more likely to develop insecure attachments than children who stayed at home.

12 Belsky and Rovine's study used only one method of assessing attachment – the 'Strange Situation'. This may not have been an appropriate technique.

13 The distribution is almost identical (USA: 22% Type A, 14% Type C; Non-USA 21% Type A, 14% Type C).

14 Since an attachment is a relationship, not a global personality trait, insecurity towards the mother-figure may not generalise to all situations.

Section 3: Effects on cognitive development

15 'According to Scarr (1998), children from low-income families definitely *benefit* from high quality care'.

16 For middle-class and upper-income families, the cognitive effects of day care are not clear.

17 Baydar & Brooks-Gunn (1991) found that those children whose mothers went out to work before they were a year old were worse off, both cognitively and in behavioural terms, as compared to the group whose mothers went out to work later.

18 Scarr and Thompson found *no* differences in either cognitive or socioemotional development between children who had been placed in day care before or after 12 months, or for more or less than 20 hours per week.

19 Horwood and Fergusson point out that much of the research into the effects of day care has been carried out in the USA and may not apply to other societies and cultures.

20 Mooney and Munton conclude that there is no evidence that working mothers stunt their children's emotional or social development.

21 'In more than *70* per cent of British two-parent families with dependent children, both parents work.'

A

Day Care

Day Care: all varieties of non-maternal care of children who reside with their parent(s) or close relatives (Scarr, 1998).

Investigating day care (Scarr, 1998)

- In the 1970s, maternal and non-maternal care were compared without regard for the quality of either, on the implicit assumption that non-maternal care was necessarily damaging.
- During the 1980s studies began to look at the quality and variety of care settings to see if children's reactions to day care differed.
- Non-maternal shared care is normative culturally and historically (Scarr, 1998).
- During the late 1980s/1990s, researchers investigated variation of day-care quality and type in relation to both family characteristics and individual differences.

Taken together, these changes represent a shift away from the *motherhood mystique* – the idea that women are born and reared to be, first and foremost, mothers.

Measuring the quality of day care (Scarr, 1998)

There is extraordinary international agreement regarding the nature of quality care:

- health and safety requirements;
- responsive and warm interaction between staff and children;
- developmentally appropriate curricula;
- limited group size;
- age-appropriate caregiver-child ratios;
- adequate indoor and outdoor space
- adequate staff training (in either early childhood education or child development);
- low staff turnover (as a measure of the stability of care)

Although poor quality care has been correlated with poorer cognitive and social skills, this may be because of the personal characteristics of parents who choose poor care, rather than the care itself.

Day care – facts

- Examples include day nurseries, childminders, non-resident grandparents.
- Childcare is normative for American & British children – 75% of mothers of school-age children are in the labour force, and more than 50% of mothers of children under 12 mths.
- Non-maternal shared care is normative culturally and historically (Scarr, 1998).
- By 2000 the number of women in paid employment will outnumber men (though with a far higher percentage in part-time jobs).

The effects of day care

Effects on social development: attachments

Bowlby's prediction

- Bowlby predicts that deprivation of an attachment figure during the child's first year may result in *no* attachment being formed, and that deprivation *after* an attachment has been formed may result in separation anxiety.
- Schaffer (1996a) found that children do not suffer such ill-effects, provided there is sufficient *stability* and *quality* of care.

So, are there *any* studies showing harmful social effects?

- Belsky & Rovine (1988): infants who had been receiving day care for at least four months before their first birthday and for more than 20hrs per week were more likely to develop insecure attachments than those who stayed at home.
- However, these results were obtained using the 'Strange Situation' which may not be appropriate in assessing day-care children: their familiarity with separation may lead them to be classified as 'avoidant'.

Additional research

- Ijzendoorn & Kroonenberg (1988): found that the distribution of insecure children amongst working mothers in the USA (22% Type A; 14% Type C) virtually identical to that for mainly non-working mothers around the world (21% Type A, 14% Type C).
- Clarke-Stewart (1989): studies of children of working mothers across a range of situations, with a variety of attachment figures shows that they perform as well as children raised solely by their mothers. Even if day-care children are more likely to demonstrate insecurity with their mothers, there is no reason why this should generalise to other situations or individuals.

Effects on cognitive development

Overall picture

Scarr (1998): children from low-income families definitely benefit from high quality care, showing better school achievement and more socialised behaviour. High quality day care provides learning opportunities and emotional supports not provided at home.

However, for middle-class and upper-income families the picture is less clear:

Harmful cognitive effects?

- Baydar & Brooks-Gunn (1991): studied 1181 children and found that they were worse off, both cognitively and in behavioural terms if mothers went out to work before they were a year old (compared with those whose mothers worked later). This supports the claim that day care of more than 20hrs per wk, before one year old, can be harmful.
- Scarr & Thompson (1994): tested this claim in a study of 1100 children in Bermuda. Teacher ratings of children at ages 5, 6, 7 found no differences between those placed in care before or after 12 mths of age, or for more or less than 40hrs per wk.

Beneficial cognitive effects?

- Horwood & Fergusson (1999): conducted a longitudinal study of 1200 New Zealand children between the ages of 8 and 18. Children whose mothers worked tended to have slightly higher average test scores (e.g. on word recognition, mathematical reasoning and examination success) than those whose mothers did not work. However these differences largely disappeared when related factors (e.g. mother's education, socioeconomic status, ethnic background, etc) were taken into account.

Overall conclusions

- Horwood & Fergusson (1999): much of the research carried out into the effects of day-care has been conducted in the USA and may not generalise to other cultures.
- Mooney & Munton (cited in Judd, 1997): there is no evidence that working mothers stunt their children's emotional or social development.
- As the proportion of children requiring day-care rises, a national strategy to ensure proper training and payment of carers is essential.

STRESS AS A BODILY RESPONSE

SYLLABUS
11.1 Stress – stress as a bodily response
- the body's response to stressors, including the general adaptation syndrome (Seyle). Research into the relationship between stress and physical illness, including cardiovascular disorders and the effects of stress on the immune system

KEY QUESTIONS
- What is stress?
- How does stress affect the body?
- What is the relation between stress and illness?
- How does stress affect cardiovascular disorders and the immune system?

Section 1: Introducing stress
1 What did Seyle (1936) discover when he exposed rats to conditions like extreme cold, fatigue, electric shock or the injection of toxic fluids?
2 What term is used to describe any stimulus which produces stress?
3 What is *eustress* (Selye, 1980)?
4 Complete Lazarus & Folkman's (1984) definition of stress: 'Stress is a pattern of ___ physiological states and ___ responses occurring in situations where people perceive ___ to their well-being which they may be unable to meet'.
5 What name is given to the *non-specific response* discovered by Selye?

Section 2: The role of the nervous system
6 Name the three main components identified by MacLean's (1982) *triune model* of the brain.
7 Which CNS structure is responsible for regulating the *pituitary gland*?
8 What are the two essential functions of the *peripheral nervous system* (PNS)?
9 To what do the nerves of the autonomic nervous system (ANS) connect the central nervous system (CNS)?
10 What are the major functions of the *parasympathetic branch* of the ANS?
11 What is the primary function of the ANS?
12 According to Cannon (1927), what is the major function of the sympathetic branch of the ANS?
13 Apart from direct neural stimulation, how does the ANS exert its effects on the body?

Section 3: The stages of the GAS
14 What name is given to the first of the three stages of this response?
15 What is the role of *corticosteroids*, released during the first stage?
16 Identify three physiological factors that are increased by the action of *adrenaline* and *noradrenaline*.
17 What general name is given to the response in which we prepare for physical action?

18 How is the *immune system* affected during the second stage (the *resistance stage*)?
19 During which stage are *stress-related illnesses* most likely to occur?
20 Why is Selye's emphasis on the physiological response to stressors problematic?
21 What is involved in the *primary appraisal* of a stressor?
22 Identify two negative emotional states associated with stress.

Section 4: Stress and illness
23 Why, from an evolutionary perspective, might stress be bad for us?
24 Identify two illnesses with which stress is apparently linked.
25 What is the relationship between *antibodies* and *antigens*?
26 How does the persistent secretion of *steroids* affect the immune system?
27 Identify three events which have been found to cause immunological deficiencies in non-humans.
28 What was the stressor that caused wounds to heal more slowly in Sweeney's (1995) study?
29 What are the effects of *acute* and *chronic stressors* on the levels of defensive agents?
30 What are endorphins?
31 What explanation did Friedman and Rosenman propose for the finding that men are more susceptible to heart disease than women?
32 What are the major characteristics of *Type A personalities* (Friedman & Rosenman, 1974)?
33 Complete the sentence: 'The relationship between stress and CHD is not straightforward. One proposal is that chronic stress produces _____ formation in the cardiovascular system. Additionally, stress may increase blood _____ levels through the action of adrenaline and noradrenaline on the release of free fatty acids'.
34 What did Harburg *et al.* (1973) discover when they measured the blood pressure of Americans from 'high' and 'low' stress areas of Detroit?

Section 1: Introducing stress

1 Seyle (1936) discovered that the same (non-specific) pattern of physiological responses occurred.

2 A stressor.

3 Eustress is stress which is healthy and necessary to keep us alert.

4 'Stress is a pattern of *negative* physiological states and *psychological* responses occurring in situations where people perceive *threats* to their well-being which they may be unable to meet.'

5 Selye (1936) called the non-specific response the *general adaptation syndrome* (GAS).

Section 2: The role of the nervous system

6 MacLean's (1982) triune model of the brain identifies the central core, the limbic system and the cerebral cortex.

7 The hypothalamus is responsible for regulating the pituitary gland.

8 The peripheral nervous system sends information to the CNS from the outside world, and transmits information from the CNS to the muscles.

9 The nerves of the autonomic nervous system (ANS) connect the central nervous system (CNS) to the skeletal muscles.

10 The parasympathetic branch of the ANS stimulates processes that serve to restore or conserve energy, and those which carry out the body's 'maintenance needs'.

11 The primary function of the ANS is to regulate internal bodily processes.

12 Cannon (1927) claims that the major function of the sympathetic branch of the ANS is to mobilise the body for an emergency ('fight-or-flight').

13 The ANS stimulates the release of hormones (from the endocrine glands).

Section 3: The stages of the GAS

14 The first of the three stages is the alarm reaction.

15 Corticosteroids help to fight inflammation and allergic reactions.

16 Adrenaline and noradrenaline increase: heart rate and blood pressure, the release of glucose from the liver, respiration rate, blood coaguability, and sweating.

17 The 'fight-or-flight' response is the general name given to the response in which we prepare for physical action.

18 During the second stage (the resistance stage), the immune system's ability to deal with infection or physical damage is reduced.

19 Stress-related illnesses are most likely to occur during the exhaustion stage (the third stage) of the GAS.

20 Selye's emphasis on physiological factors fails to take into account psychological factors in the production of stress.

21 The primary appraisal of a stressor involves deciding whether it has positive, negative or neutral implications.

22 Anger, hostility, embarrassment, depression, helplessness and anxiety are all associated with stress.

Section 4: Stress and illness

23 In essence, the evolutionary perspective suggests that stress is an outdated response, designed to help us cope with 'fight-or-flight' situations, but maladaptive in dealing with everyday stressors.

24 A link apparently exists between stress and headaches, asthma, cancer, cardiovascular disorders, hypertension and the malfunctioning of the immune system.

25 Antibodies are produced by the immune system and bind to antigens, identifying them as targets for destruction.

26 The persistent secretion of steroids depresses the immune system by interfering with antibody production.

27 Separation from the mother, electric shocks, and exposure to loud noise all cause immunological deficiencies in non-humans (Esterling & Rabin, 1987).

28 Caring for an elderly relative with dementia caused participants' wounds to heal more slowly in Sweeney's (1995) study.

29 Acute stressors are associated with an increase in the levels of defensive agents, whilst chronic stressors are associated with a decrease in these levels.

30 Endorphins are morphine-like substances which are produced by the endocrine system as the body's own natural painkillers.

31 Friedman and Rosenman proposed that the finding that men are more susceptible to heart disease than women may be due to job-related stress.

32 Type A personalities are ambitious, competitive, easily angered, time-conscious, hard-driving and demanding of perfection (Friedman & Rosenman, 1974).

33 'The relationship between stress and CHD is not straightforward. One proposal is that chronic stress produces *plaque* formation in the cardiovascular system. Additionally, stress may increase blood *cholesterol* levels through the action of adrenaline and noradrenaline on the release of free fatty acids.'

34 Harburg *et al.* (1973) discovered that the highest blood pressures were found in those living in the highest stress areas.

The central nervous system

- The central nervous system (CNS) consists of the brain and the spinal cord.
- MacLean's (1982) *triune model*: distinguishes the *central core* (oldest part) from the *limbic system* and the *cerebral cortex* (newest part).
- The *hypothalamus* helps to regulate the sympathetic branch of the *autonomic nervous system* and controls the *endocrine glands* via the *pituitary gland*.

The peripheral nervous system

The peripheral nervous system consists of nerves that connect the CNS with the sense organs, muscles and glands.
- The PNS has two main functions: to send information to the CNS from the outside world, and to transmit information from the CNS to produce a particular behaviour.
- The PNS has two parts: the *somatic nervous system* and the *autonomic nervous system*.

The endocrine system

- Endocrine glands are glands without ducts which release their products directly into the bloodstream.
- Such glands secrete *hormones* (powerful chemical messengers) which act on certain receptors at locations around the body.
- Information is fed back to these glands (via a negative feedback loop), enabling the hormones to maintain a steady state.
- The system is regulated by the *hypothalamus*, which exerts its influence via the *pituitary gland*.

The somatic nervous system (external world)

- The somatic nervous system receives sensory information from the external world and sends signals to the striped (striated) skeletal muscles which are involved in voluntary movements.

The autonomic nervous system (internal world)

- The autonomic nervous system (ANS) connects the CNS to the internal organs (viscera), glands and smooth muscles (e.g. those involved in digestion).
- The ANS functions to regulate internal bodily processes, by sending information to and from the CNS.
- The ANS appears to operate autonomously (independently), controlling functions such as urination and defecation in the absence of conscious control. The ANS is divided into two branches:

The sympathetic branch

- Comprises bundles of neurons which form a long vertical chain on either side of the spinal cord.
- The interconnections between the neurons allow the sympathetic branch to act as a unit.
- The sympathetic branch prepares the body to expend energy.
- Cannon (1927) suggested that the major function of the sympathetic branch was to prepare the body for *fight-or-flight*.

The parasympathetic branch

- The parasympathetic branch stimulates processes that restore or conserve energy.
- Also carries out the body's maintenance needs (e.g. digestion, waste elimination, tissue repair) and is most active when we are inactive.

Lazarus & Folkman (1984): stress is a pattern of negative physiological states and psychological responses occurring in situations where people perceive threats to their well-being which they may be unable to meet.

Stress

Selye (1936): discovered a common, non-specific pattern of physiological responses after injecting rats with toxins, exposing them to cold, electric shocks or fatigue. He called this response the **general adaptation syndrome**.

The general adaptation syndrome (GAS)

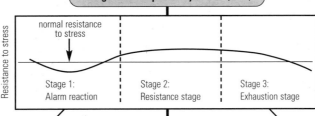

normal resistance to stress

Resistance to stress

Stage 1: Alarm reaction
Stage 2: Resistance stage
Stage 3: Exhaustion stage

Alarm reaction

Triggered by the perception and evaluation of a stimulus as a stressor. Blood pressure and muscle tension drop (shock phase) followed by the countershock phase, in which the hypothalamus exerts two parallel effects:

Hypothalamic–pituitary–adrenal axis

The *hypothalamus* stimulates the *pituitary* to release ACTH. This stimulates the *adrenal gland* to produce corticosteroids, which stimulate the liver to produce glucose and help fight inflammation and allergic reactions.

The sympatho-adrenomedullary axis

Sympathetic branch of ANS: releases *adrenaline* and *noradrenaline* causing accelerated heart rate and respiration, raised blood pressure and coagulability, tensing of muscles. Blood is diverted from the internal organs and digestion stopped.

Resistance stage

If the stressor continues the body recovers from the initial alarm and begins to cope:
- corticosteroids depress immune system
- repair of cells is inhibited
- resources are depleted.

Exhaustion stage

If a stressor is not removed or cannot be dealt with higher brain centres prevent the body returning to normal and maintain the *pituitary–adrenal excitation*. The adrenal glands enlarge and lose their store of adrenal hormones. Continual depletion of the body's resources causes the following effects:
- tissues show signs of wear
- muscles become fatigued
- blood sugar levels drop.
- the endocrine glands, kidneys and other organs are damaged.
It is during this stage that stress-related illnesses occur.

Stress and illness

Stress & the immune system

Whilst acute stressors (e.g deadlines) can *increase* defensive agents, consistent production of corticosteroids (as with chronic stressors) interferes with antibody production which decreases inflammation and suppresses leucocyte production. Stress may also lead to heightened *endorphin* levels – which in turn may suppress immune system function.

- Sweeney (1995): found that biopsy wounds healed more slowly on patients caring for elderly relatives with dementia.
- Kiecolt-Glasner *et al*. (1995): found that wounds took nine days longer to heal in women caring for relatives with Alzheimer's disease (as compared to a similar group who were not).

Stress & evolution

From an evolutionary perspective the arousal caused by the ANS in response to stress was *adaptive*. But in response to everyday stressors – few of which present physical danger – it is probably *maladaptive*.

Stress & cardiovascular disorders

In the late 1950s Friedman & Rosenman found that American men were more susceptible to heart disease than women, despite sharing the same diet. They speculated that job-related stress might be a factor.

Type 'A' & Type 'B' personalities

Friedman & Rosenman (1974): conducted a 9-yr study of 3000 middle aged men, classifying them as *Type A* (ambitious, competitive, easily angered, perfectionist) and *Type B* (relaxed, easy-going, not easily angered, forgiving). In the course of the 9-yr study, 70% of the 257 men who died were type A personalities – however Type A personalities may be a *response* to, rather than a *cause* of physiological risk factors (such as high blood pressure).

STRESSORS: SOURCES OF STRESS

SYLLABUS

11.1 Stress – sources of stress
- research into sources of stress, including life changes (e.g. Holmes and Rahe), and workplace stressors (e.g. work overload, role ambiguity). Individual differences in modifying the effects of stressors, including the role played by personality (e.g. Friedman and Rosenman), culture and gender

KEY QUESTIONS
- What is a stressor?
- What is the relationship between life changes and stress?
- What is the relationship between stress and the workplace?
- How might individual variation affect stress?

Section 1: Life changes

1 When Holmes & Rahe (1967) examined the hospital records of 5000 patients, what did they find?
2 Complete the sentence: 'Holmes and Rahe worked on the assumption that stress is caused by undesirable *or* ____ events which require ____'.
3 How was the social readjustment rating scale (SRRS) constructed?
4 What did Holmes and Rahe discover was positively correlated with high SRRS scores?
5 Name two of the problems identified by Cohen *et al.* (1998) as being associated with high SRRS scores.
6 Give one possible explanation for the inability of the SRRS to predict with any certainty future illness and disease.
7 Why is the retrospective nature of research using the SRRS a difficulty?
8 Why can the *correlational* nature of SRRS research be used as a criticism?
9 Which basic assumption, made by Holmes and Rahe, concerning the nature of life changes might be challenged?
10 What did Kanner *et al.* (1981) believe to be a better predictor of both physical and psychological health than life changes?

Section 2: Workplace stressors

11 Name two occupations which have been found to be amongst the most stressful.
12 What did Marmot *et al.* (1997) discover when investigating the incidence of cardiovascular disorders within organisations?
13 Which of the contributory factors explored by Marmot *et al.* was considered to be the most significant?
14 Complete the following sentence: 'Women are confronted with ____ and ____ employment-related stressors than men (Long & Khan, 1993)'.
15 What are *quantitative underload* and *qualitative overload* in relation to employment?
16 What is *role ambiguity*?

17 Identify three conditions associated with low decision latitude/control.
18 What interpersonal factors can promote health for an individual and an organisation?
19 Identify one behaviour which Chen & Spector (1992) found to be most strongly linked with workplace stressors.
20 What did Kahn & Cuthbertson (1998) discover when comparing the stress experienced by working mothers with that experienced by full-time homemakers?

Section 3: Individual differences

21 What did Greer *et al.* (1979) discover regarding '*fighting spirit*'?
22 Besides the stressor itself, what key factor determines the physiological response to stress?
23 What particular characteristic have Booth-Kewley & Friedman (1987) shown to be a better predictor of coronary heart disease than 'Type A' personality as a whole?
24 What characteristics does a 'Type C' personality possess, according to Temoshok (1987)?
25 With what risk has a 'Type ER' personality been associated?
26 What term is used by Anderson (1991) to refer to the emotional challenges faced by an African-American minority in a white American majority?
27 Anderson identifies three types of stressor. Which of these types is most likely to account for race-related stress in black Americans?
28 How much more likely are black Americans to die of hypertension than are white Americans?
29 Complete the sentence: 'Whilst women have a lower mortality rate than men, the ____ rate for women is higher'.
30 What biological explanation for the lower mortality rate of women was suggested by Frankenhauser (1983)?
31 What explanation did Friedman and Rosenman propose for the finding that men are more susceptible to heart disease than women?
32 Identify one way in which women's personalities may have a bearing on the stress they experience.

Section 1: Life changes

1. Holmes & Rahe (1967) were able to identify (43) life events that appeared to cluster in the months preceding the onset of illness.
2. 'Holmes and Rahe worked on the assumption that stress is caused by undesirable or *desirable* events which require *change*.'
3. Holmes and Rahe assigned an arbitrary value of 50 'life change units' to 'marriage' and asked people to assign a value to each of the other 42 events, relative to this value.
4. Holmes and Rahe found a relationship between high SRRS scores and the likelihood of experiencing some sort of physical illness within the following year.
5. Cohen *et al.* (1998) identified heart disease, cancer and relapses amongst those diagnosed with mental disorders as being associated with high SRRS scores.
6. There are many causes of illness and disease besides stress, the SRRS takes a simplistic approach to measurement and does not take into account the differences between individuals' ability to withstand stress.
7. Retrospective research relies on people recalling both their illness and life events. This recollection may be inaccurate or biased – for example, a person might focus on minor physiological sensations and report them as being 'symptoms of illness'.
8. SRRS research is correlational, meaning that it tells us that some relationship exists between two variable but not that one causes the other (e.g. people with larger shoe sizes have a lower life expectancy – can you guess why?).
9. The basic assumption that stress is caused by any event which requires change may be incorrect. Positive change may be less stressful than negative change.
10. Kanner *et al.* (1981) found hassles to be a better predictor of both physical and psychological health than life changes.

Section 2: Workplace stressors

11. Nursing, social work, teaching and working in the police force have been found to be amongst the most stressful.
12. Marmot *et al.* (1997) found that people on the 'bottom rung' (in clerical or office support positions) were much more likely to develop cardiovascular disorders than those in administrative positions.
13. Marmot *et al.* found that a low degree of control was the biggest contributory factor.
14. 'Women are confronted with *more* and *different* employment-related stressors than men.' (Long & Khan, 1993)
15. Quantitative underload refers to having too little work to do, whilst qualitative overload refers to having work which is too difficult or which requires too much attention.
16. Role ambiguity occurs when an employee is unclear about his/her work role in an organisation.

17. Low decision latitude/control is associated with low self-esteem, anxiety, depression, apathy, exhaustion and symptoms of coronary heart disease.
18. Supportive interpersonal relationships from superiors and colleagues can promote individual and organisational health.
19. Chen & Spector (1992) found sabotage, hostility and intention to quit to be most strongly linked with workplace stressors.
20. Kahn & Cuthbertson (1998) discovered that full-time homemakers experienced more depression than working mothers and experienced more stress when spouses did not contribute to childcare or chores.

Section 3: Individual differences

21. Greer *et al.* (1979) discovered that women showing 'fighting spirit' were significantly more likely to be free of cancer five years after being diagnosed with breast cancer, as compared with similar women who accepted the diagnosis stoically.
22. The physiological response to stress is determined partly by the psychological impact – the way a stressor is perceived or evaluated.
23. Booth-Kewley & Friedman (1987) showed that hostility is a better predictor of coronary heart disease than 'Type A' personality as a whole.
24. Temoshok (1987) suggests that 'Type C' personalities have difficulty in expressing emotion, and tend to suppress or inhibit emotions.
25. 'Type ER' personality has been associated with an increased risk of another heart attack in heart attack victims.
26. Anderson (1991) uses the term *acculturative stress* to refer to the emotional challenges faced by an African-American minority in a white American majority.
27. Race-related stress is most likely to be experienced in terms of daily events/hassles.
28. Black Americans are twice as likely to die of hypertension than are white Americans.
29. 'Whilst women have a lower mortality rate than men, the *morbidity* rate for women is higher.'
30. Frankenhauser (1983) found that females failed to show significant increases in adrenaline output when faced with a stressful situation, and suggested that as a consequence they might experience less stress-related damage.
31. Friedman and Rosenman proposed that the finding that men are more susceptible to heart disease than women may be due to job-related stress.
32. Women are less likely to be 'Type A' personalities and less likely to be hostile than are men.

A

Stressors

The social readjustment rating scale (SRRS)
Holmes & Rahe (1967): examined the hospital records of 5000 patients and identified 43 life events which clustered in the months preceding their illness. They then asked people to assign a value to each, given an arbitrary value of 50 for marriage, and developed the social readjustment rating scale (SRRS).

- Holmes & Rahe found a relationship between high SRRS scores in one year and the chances of experiencing physical illness in the next: a person scoring 200–300 life change units has a 50% chance of developing a physical illness.
- Cohen *et al.* (1998) found that high SRRS scores are associated with physical & psychological problems including heart disease & mental disorder relapse.

Examples of items from the SRRS scale

Rank	Life event	Mean value
1	Death of a spouse	100
2	Divorce	65
4	Jail term	63
6	Personal illness or injury	53
7	Marriage	50
25	Outstanding personal achievement	28
33	Change in schools	20
38	Change in sleeping habits	16
42	Christmas	12

Evaluation
- The overall relationship between life changes and illness is small and of little predictive power. Individuals may experience life events differently depending on how they perceive them.
- SRRS research is usually *retrospective*, and people under stress might be prone to recall minor physiological sensations as symptoms of illness.
- SRRS research is correlational – do the life changes cause illness, or are (mentally) ill people more likely to undergo change?
- Holmes and Rahe assumed that any event requiring change causes stress – but positive events requiring change may cause less stress than negative ones requiring a similar amount of change.
- Kanner *et al.* (1981) developed a 'hassles scale' and claim that there is a stronger relationship between everyday annoyances/pressures and illness than there is between major life changes and illness.

The relationship between stress & the workplace was first systematically investigated in the 1970s. Although the precise relationship is not clear, it seems that all employees experience some degree of stress as a result of their work.

- Studies have indicated that four of the most stressful occupations are nursing, social work, teaching and working in the police force.
- Whilst some studies suggest that senior executives experience most stress, others indicate that people on the 'bottom rung' may experience more: Marmot *et al.* (1997) found that clerical staff were more likely to develop cardiovascular complaints than administrators.
- Marmot *et al.* identified a *low degree of control* as being the biggest contributory factor.
- Women are confronted with *more* and *different* stressors to men (Long & Khan, 1993).

Factors affecting employment-related stress
- **Work overload/underload:** both conditions may be *quantitative* (too much/too little) or *qualitative* (too difficult/too easy) and lead to boredom & frustration.
- **Role ambiguity/conflict:** role ambiguity occurs when an employee is unclear of his/her role, conflict occurs when roles are incompatible or conflict with other beliefs.
- **Job insecurity/redundancy:** both are associated with anxiety, which may be heightened by feelings of unfairness.
- **Degree of latitude/control:** both responsible positions and those in which the employee is relatively helpless can be stressful.
- **Interpersonal relationships/support:** poor relationships or support networks are associated with stress and poor mental health.

Research
- Chen & Spector (1992): used questionnaires to investigate the link between job stressors & harmful behaviours in 400 employees. They found a relationship between high levels of stress and directly aggressive actions (e.g. sabotage & hostility).
- Kahn & Cuthbertson (1998): found that full-time homemakers experienced more depression than working mothers and reported greater stress when spouses did not contribute to childcare or chores.

Stressors & individual differences

Personality, culture and gender may all affect an individual's *perception* of a stressor, and as a result its psychological *impact*.

'Type A' personality
Although early studies linked Type A personality to cardiovascular disorders, Booth-Kewley & Friedman (1987) showed that hostility is a better predictor of these disorders than Type A personality alone (although how the two are linked is unclear).

'Type C' personality
Temoshok (1987): proposed the existence of a 'Type C' personality who tends to suppress or inhibit emotions. Such types have been linked to cancer and decreased sperm production, though it is not clear that there is a causal relationship.

'Types D & ER' personality
Type D personalities are anxious, gloomy, socially inept worriers, whilst Type ER ('emotional responder') personalities are highly volatile and prone to mood swings. Both may increase the risk of further attacks in people who have experienced heart attacks.

One key criticism of the SRRS is that it fails to take into account cultural and ethnic variation in the kinds of stressors to which people are exposed. For example, the physical and mental health of African-Americans is generally poorer than that of white Americans, even when the effects of poverty are taken into account:

- 35% of black Americans suffer from hypertension and it accounts for 20% of deaths (twice the amount for whites). Racism may well be a contributory factor.

Acculturative stress (Anderson, 1991)
Refers to the emotional challenges faced by African-Americans living in a majority white community. Anderson distinguishes 3 types:

- *Level 1* (chronic stressors): including racism & overcrowding.
- *Level 2* (major life events): including those in the SRSS
- *Level 3* (daily hassles): This is the level at which most pressure is faced by African-Americans (compare 'stop & search' harassment of British blacks).

Although men have a higher *mortality* rate than women, women have a higher *morbidity* rate (are more likely to suffer ill-health).

- This difference might be due to the protective effect of female hormones, such as *oestrogen*.
- It may also be that women are less likely to be 'Type A' personalities or be hostile.
- Lifestyle differences (such as drinking & smoking) may also account for the differences – and for the fact that these have decreased in the last 30 yrs.

Research
- Frankenhauser (1983): found that female students failed to show a significant increase in adrenaline levels when faced with a stressful situation. They may therefore experience less stress-related damage during their lifetime.
- Frankenhauser *et al.* (1991): showed that female engineering students & bus drivers showed male patterns of adrenaline response, suggesting the importance of gender roles and socialisation.

CRITICAL ISSUE – STRESS MANAGEMENT

SYLLABUS

11.1 Critical issue – stress management
• methods of managing the negative effects of stress, including physical (e.g. drugs, biofeedback) and psychological approaches (e.g. Meichenbaum – stress-inoculation, and Kobasa – hardiness). The role of 'control' in the perception of stress. The strengths and weaknesses of methods of stress management

KEY QUESTIONS
• What are the negative effects of stress?
• Can psychological approaches reduce the effects of stress?
• What is the role of 'control' in perceptions of stress?
• What are the strengths and weaknesses of different methods of stress management?

Section 1: Physical approaches

1 According to Lefcourt *et al.* (1997), how can *humour* help in reducing stress?
2 Upon which part of the nervous system do anxiolytic drugs act?
3 What is the function of these drugs?
4 Identify two reasons for preferring alternatives to anxiolytic drugs in treating stress.
5 What does a *biofeedback machine* do?
6 What condition were students able to reduce through the use of an *electromyogram* in Bradley's (1995) experiment?
7 Identify one disadvantage of using this technique to reduce stress.
8 What did Morris (1953) discover in his study of London bus drivers and conductors?
9 When Daley & Parfitt (1996) measured mood states, physical well-being and job satisfaction in a British food retail company, which employees did they find scored most highly on these measures?
10 How is Jacobson's (1938) *progressive relaxation technique* carried out?
11 According to Green (1994), under what conditions is the progressive relaxation method most likely to have long-term benefits?
12 Name one further relaxation technique.

Section 2: Psychological approaches

13 To what does the general term *cognitive restructuring* refer?
14 Complete the sentence: 'Meichenbaum's approach assumes that people sometimes find situations stressful because they think about them in ____ ways'.
15 The second stage of Meichenbaum's stress inoculation training is called 'skill acquisition and rehearsal'. What does this involve?

16 Which type of *preparation statement* is the following: 'It worked; you did it'?
17 What name is given to the final stage of self-instructional training?
18 Identify two of the three main ways in which *hardy* and *non-hardy individuals* differ according to Kobasa (1979, 1986).
19 What does Kobasa mean by the term *focusing*?
20 What is involved in Kobasa's *compensation through self-improvement* approach to dealing with stressors?
21 What did Weiss (1972) discover when subjecting rats to electric shocks?
22 What is *learned helplessness* (Seligman, 1975)?
23 In what way did Glass & Singer (1972) demonstrate that the mere knowledge that one can exert control over a stressful situation seems to reduce stress?
24 What two terms refer to the extremes of Rotter's (1966) *locus of control* scale?
25 Which locus of control is generally shared by 'hardy' individuals?
26 What is the difference between *primary control* and *secondary control* (Wade & Tavris, 1993)?
27 Cohen & Lazarus (1979) identify five classes of coping strategy. To what strategy does the term *intrapsychic* refer?
28 What is meant by *inhibition of action* as a class of coping strategy?
29 What two terms do Lazarus & Folkman (1984) use to distinguish different *coping strategies*?
30 Complete the sentence: 'By their nature defence mechanisms involve some degree of ____ of reality and self-____'.

Q

Section 1: Physical approaches

1 Lefcourt *et al.* (1997) have suggested that humour can help by stimulating endorphin production.

2 Anxiolytic drugs act on the autonomic nervous system (the sympathetic branch).

3 Anxiolytic drugs reduce anxiety.

4 These drugs are associated with side-effects (such as drowsiness, lethargy), physical dependence (and addiction), withdrawal symptoms, and tolerance.

5 A biofeedback machine produces precise information (or feedback) about bodily processes such as heart rate and/or blood pressure.

6 Students were able to reduce the occurrence of tension headaches through the use of an electromyogram which monitors muscle tension.

7 The biofeedback method requires a specialised physiological measuring device and regular practice in order to be effective.

8 Morris (1953) discovered that the conductors were far less likely to suffer from cardiovascular disorders than the sedentary drivers.

9 Daley & Parfitt (1996) found that employees who were members of the corporate health and fitness club scored most highly.

10 Jacobson's (1938) progressive relaxation technique involves tightening, then relaxing, groups of muscles until the whole body is relaxed.

11 Green (1994) claims that progressive relaxation needs to be incorporated into a person's lifestyle/routine in order to cause the cognitive change necessary for long-term benefits.

12 Meditation is another relaxation technique.

Section 2: Psychological approaches

13 Cognitive restructuring refers to various methods of changing the way people think about their life situation and selves.

14 'Meichenbaum's approach assumes that people sometimes find situations stressful because they think about them in *catastrophising* ways.'

15 Skill acquisition and rehearsal involves replacing negative self-statements with incompatible positive coping statements.

16 'It worked; you did it' is an example of a reinforcing self-statement.

17 The final stage of self-instructional training is termed *application and follow-through*.

18 Hardy people are highly committed to/involved in whatever they do, view change as a challenge, and have a stronger sense of control over events in their lives, as compared with non-hardy individuals (Kobasa, 1979).

19 Kobasa uses the term *focusing* to refer to learning to identify the physical signs of stress.

20 Kobasa's compensation through self-improvement is the suggestion that when a stressor cannot be avoided or dealt with, we should take on a challenge which *can* be dealt with.

21 Weiss (1972) discovered that rats that were unable to control the electric shocks were more susceptible to peptic ulcers and had a lower immunity to disease than rats who could control the shocks.

22 Learned helplessness refers to the generalised expectation that events are independent of our control.

23 Glass & Singer (1972) exposed participants to a loud noise. Participants who believed they could stop the noise by pressing a button showed less evidence of stress than those who lacked the option of control (even though both were exposed to the same noise).

24 Rotter's (1966) 'locus of control' scale extends from high internal control to high external control.

25 Hardy individuals generally possess a high internal locus of control (i.e. they feel able to control events around them).

26 Primary control involves influencing reality by changing other people, events or circumstances whilst secondary control involves trying to accommodate to reality by changing one's own perceptions, goals or desires.

27 Intrapsychic refers to strategies which involve reappraising the situation (e.g. Freudian defence mechanisms) or changing the internal environment (e.g. through drug use, meditation).

28 These strategies involve doing nothing.

29 Lazarus & Folkman (1984) use the terms *problem-focused* and *emotion-focused strategies* to distinguish different coping strategies.

30 'By their nature defence mechanisms involve some degree of *distortion* of reality and self-*deception*.'

Psychological approaches

Stress inoculation

The *cognitive model of abnormality* (Ch. 5) focuses on irrational thoughts – *cognitive restructuring* is used to refer to changing the way people think in order to change their responses.

Stress inoculation training
(Meichenbaum, 1976, 1997)

People sometimes find situations stressful because they think about them in catastrophising ways. Therapy involves 3 stages:

1. *Cognitive preparation:* therapist and client explore the ways situations are thought about and identify 'self-defeating internal dialogues'.
2. *Skill acquisition and rehearsal:* the client learns to replace negative thoughts by learning 'preparation statements' (see below).
3. *Application & follow-through:* client is guided through successively more stressful situations by the therapist.

Examples of coping statements
Preparing for a stressful situation:
　You can develop a plan to deal with it.
　Don't worry; worry won't help anything.
Handling a stressful situation:
　One step at a time; you can handle the situation.
　Relax; you're in control. Take a slow deep breath.
Coping with fear of being overwhelmed:
　You should expect your fear to rise.
　It will be over shortly.
Reinforcing self-statements:
　It worked; you did it.
　It wasn't as bad as you expected.

Relaxation

- Jacobson (1938): noticed that people experiencing stress tend to add to their discomfort by tensing their muscles, and developed the 'progressive relaxation' to reduce the level of arousal.

Problems: only effective if incorporated into a regular routine since it requires a cognitive change.

Meditation

During meditation a person assumes a comfortable position, closes their eyes and attempts to clear all disturbing thoughts from their mind. They may also repeat a single syllable (or *mantra*).

- Wallace & Fisher (1987) found that meditation reduces oxygen consumption and induces brain activity indicative of a calm mental state.

Coping strategies

5 categories of strategy
(Cohen & Lazarus, 1979)

1. *Direct action response:* change or manipulate stressful situation.
2. *Information seeking:* understand and predict stressor(s).
3. *Inhibition of action:* doing nothing.
4. *Intrapsychic:* reappraising the situation (e.g. stress inoculation).
5. *Turning to others:* using others for help and support.

Problem-focused vs emotion-focused
(Lazarus & Folkman, 1984)

- *Problem-focused (optimistic) strategies:* a plan for dealing with a stressor is made and implemented.
- *Emotion-focused (pessimistic) strategies:* reducing the negative emotions associated with the stressor by using short-term cognitive or behavioural strategies.

Both intrapsychic coping strategies and Freudian 'ego defence mechanisms' are examples of emotion-focused coping. The latter invariably involve some form of self-deception or distortion of reality and, as such, are likely to lead to anxiety over the long term.

Developing hardiness

The nature of hardiness

Kobasa (1979, 1986): claimed that 'hardy' and 'non-hardy' individuals differ in three main ways. Hardy people:

1. Are highly committed to whatever they do & see their activities as meaningful.
2. View change as a challenge rather than as a threat.
3. See themselves as having control over their lives (high internal locus of control).

Developing hardiness

Kobasa suggests three ways of increasing hardiness:

1. *Focusing:* teaching people to identify the physical signs of stress.
2. *Reconstructing stressful situations:* analysing how stressful experiences might have been better dealt with.
3. *Compensation through self-improvement:* turning our attention from stressors we cannot deal with to those that we can.

The role of control

- Rotter (1966): developed the concept of locus of control, and a scale running from high internal to high external control.
- Wade & Tavris (1993): distinguish primary control (in which we change the environment to suit ourselves) from secondary control (in which we change ourselves to suit the environment).

Research into control

- Seligman (1975): used the term 'learned helplessness' to refer to the apathy exhibited by dogs after having been exposed to unavoidable electric shocks.
- Glass & Singer (1972): found that participants who could control their exposure to loud noise suffered less stress than those who could not.

Stress Management

Physical approaches

Psychotherapeutic drugs

Anxiolytic drugs

These drugs act directly on the autonomic nervous system in order to reduce the physiological effects of stress.

- The benzodiazepine group includes *chlordiazepoxide* (*Librium*) and *diazepam* (*Valium*).
- Side effects include drowsiness and lethargy.
- They may also cause physical dependence and, when stopped, lead to withdrawal symptoms including insomnia, tremors and convulsions.
- Critics argue that such drugs merely treat the symptoms without addressing the disorder or causes of the disorder.

Biofeedback

A biofeedback machine enables us to become aware of subtle changes in internal physiological states so that we can bring autonomic functions (such as heart rate, muscle tension and blood pressure) under voluntary control.

- Bradley (1995) cites a study in which college students were able to significantly reduce muscle tension and headaches through use of an electromyogram (EMG) which provided feedback about muscle tension).

Problems

- Biofeedback requires specialised equipment.
- Regular practice seems to be needed for beneficial effects to be achieved.
- It is not known exactly how biofeedback works.

Physical activity & exercise

- Morris (1953) found that conductors (who move around the bus) were less likely to suffer from cardiovascular disorders than the seated drivers.
- Daley & Parfitt (1996) found that employees of a UK food retail company scored highest on measures of mood states, physical well-being & job-satisfaction if members of the corporate health & fitness club.

The reduction of stress-related illnesses in fit individuals may be due to improved circulation, strengthened heart muscles and heightened self-esteem.

DEFINING PSYCHOLOGICAL ABNORMALITY

SYLLABUS

11.2 Abnormality – defining psychological abnormality
- attempts to define abnormality in terms of statistical infrequency, deviation from social norms, a 'failure to function adequately', and deviation from ideal mental health. Limitations associated with these attempts to define psychological abnormality (including cultural relativism)

KEY QUESTIONS

Can we define abnormality as:
- a deviation from statistical norms?
- a deviation from ideal mental health?
- a failure to function adequately?
- a deviation from social norms?

Section 1: Statistical infrequency

1 What is the literal definition of *abnormality*?
2 What is the *'statistical infrequency'* definition of abnormality?
3 In what way does this definition fail to take into account the *desirability* of a behaviour or characteristic?
4 How does this definition fail to take into account the *undesirability* of a behaviour or characteristic?
5 Identify one further difficulty with the *deviation from statistical norms* definition of abnormality.

Section 2: Deviation from ideal mental health

6 How does the *deviation from ideal mental health* approach define abnormality?
7 Identify three of the 'characteristics of ideal mental health' proposed by Jahoda (1958).
8 What is the difficulty with using such characteristics to define abnormality?
9 What is an important difference between judgements of *physical health* and judgements of *mental health*?
10 What argument does Chance (1984) advance regarding the cultural variability of standards for mental health?
11 Complete the following sentence: 'Not only does the mental health definition change across cultures, it changes over ___ within a culture (it is ___-dependent)'.

Section 3: Failure to function adequately

12 What two things should every human being achieve, according to the *failure to function adequately model* of abnormality?
13 Why do Sue *et al.* (1994) use the terms *practical* and *clinical* criteria to describe the ways in which people fail to function adequately?
14 What do Miller & Morley (1986) have to say in support of the *personal distress model of abnormality*?

15 Give two reasons why this model may not be an adequate definition of abnormality.
16 Identify one other form of distress which may be used in defining abnormality.
17 Identify one difficulty with using 'others' distress' as a criterion for abnormality.
18 What does *maladaptiveness* mean in relation to defining abnormality?
19 What constitutes *unexpected behaviour*, according to Davison & Neale (1994)?
20 Identify one further criterion according to which an individual could be seen as failing to function adequately.
21 What is the principal difficulty in using 'bizarreness' as a criterion for abnormality?

Section 4: Deviation from social norms

22 What is a *norm*?
23 Identify the five classes of behaviour which exist on the continuum of normative behaviour (Gross, 1995).
24 Complete the sentence: 'If abnormality is defined in terms of ____, criminal behaviour is normal because it is statistically ____'.
25 What did Malinowski (1929) discover when studying the Trobriand Islanders?
26 Social norms clearly change across cultures. In what other way do they change?
27 How many of the characteristics which have been suggested as definitions of abnormality would you expect to be reflected in behaviours actually *classified* as being mental disorders?
28 What solution do Sue *et al.* (1994) propose to the lack of consensus on the 'best definition' of abnormality?

Section 1: Statistical infrequency

1 Literally, abnormality means deviating from the norm or average.
2 The deviation from statistical norms definition says that behaviours or characteristics which are statistically infrequent are abnormal.
3 Behaviours may be statistically infrequent but nevertheless desirable (such as creativity) and we would not want to classify such behaviours as abnormal.
4 Behaviours which are undesirable, and which we might wish to classify as abnormal (such as child abuse, eating disorders and depression), may in fact be statistically quite common.
5 This definition implies a 'cut-off' point for what is normal, which must be necessarily arbitrary (e.g. what is a 'normal' height?), and will clearly vary between cultures.

Section 2: Deviation from ideal mental health

6 By identifying the characteristics which people should possess in order to be considered 'normal', we can define abnormality as a deviation from these characteristics.
7 Amongst others, Jahoda (1958) identifies individual choice, resistance to stress, an accurate perception of reality, and self-actualisation as characteristics of ideal mental health.
8 Most of us would fall foul of at least one of these criteria, with the consequence that most of us would be considered abnormal.
9 Judgements of physical health make reference to the objective physical state of the individual and can be stated in anatomical and physical terms. Judgements of mental health are essentially value judgements.
10 Chance (1984) proposes that there must be universal standards to which we should all aspire, regardless of culture and regardless of the popularity of certain behaviours (e.g. murder can never be considered mentally healthy).
11 'Not only does the mental health definition change across cultures, it changes over *time* within a culture (it is *era*-dependent).'

Section 3: Failure to function adequately

12 According to this model, we should all achieve some sense of personal well-being and make some contribution to the larger social group.
13 Sue *et al.* (1994) use these two terms since they are often the basis on which people come to the attention of psychologists or other professionals.

14 Miller & Morley (1986) point out that people present themselves to clinics principally because their feelings or behaviours cause them distress.
15 Personal distress may sometimes be the appropriate response to certain circumstances, and in some cases we may wish to classify behaviours as abnormal where the individual is not experiencing any personal distress (such as with dissocial personality disorder).
16 The distress to others, caused by an individual's behaviour, may sometimes be used to determine whether or not a behaviour is abnormal.
17 Using others' distress can lead to an individual being unfairly classified as abnormal, by involving others' subjective judgements and values.
18 Maladaptiveness is where individuals are prevented from efficiently satisfying their occupational and social roles.
19 Davison & Neale (1994) claim that unexpected behaviour involves reacting to a situation or event in ways which could not be predicted or reasonably expected from what is known about human behaviour (e.g. acting in a way which is 'out of all proportion to the situation').
20 If an individual's behaviour is bizarre it may constitute a failure to function adequately.
21 What is 'bizarre' will vary depending on the context and the justification for the behaviour.

Section 4: Deviation from social norms

22 A norm is an expectation about how people should behave and think.
23 The continuum of normative behaviour includes unacceptable, tolerable, acceptable/permissible, desirable, and required/obligatory behaviours.
24 'If abnormality is defined in terms of *infrequency*, criminal behaviour is normal because it is statistically *frequent*.'
25 Malinowski (1929) discovered that Trobriand Islanders were expected to clean the bones of their dead relatives and wear them as ornaments.
26 Social norms change across time and are, therefore, era-dependent.
27 Any of the behaviours classified as mental disorders may reflect one, a combination, or none of the characteristics used to define abnormality.
28 Sue *et al.* (1994) have proposed a multiple-perspectives (or multiple-definitions) approach, according to which all points of view are considered as part of the evaluation of an individual.

Statistical infrequency

- The most obvious and intuitive way of defining abnormality: individuals possessing *statistically infrequent characteristics or behaviours* are abnormal.
- Someone who behaves in a way unlike the vast majority of people may be labelled 'abnormal'.

Problems

- Some behaviours are statistically abnormal but *desirable*: e.g. genius (Zuleika Yusoff sat A level maths at the age of 5, Mozart performed his own concerto aged 3).
- Some behaviours are statistically normal but *undesirable*: Hasset & White (1989) point out that one in two Americans is either depressed and/or involved in child abuse.
- How far must one deviate from the average? At what point does someone's height become abnormal, for example? Any chosen cut-off point will be arbitrary.

Deviation from social norms

- Norms are expectations about how people should behave and think. All societies have norms, but these will differ from one society to another and over time.
- Abnormality can be considered in terms of breaking society's standards or norms.

Problems

- Most people deviate from some norms: Gibson (1967) found high 'confession rates' amongst people for prosecutable offences from which they had escaped conviction.
- Norms change with time: some behaviours come to be viewed as differences in lifestyle, rather than abnormal, over time (e.g. homosexuality, which was classed as a mental disorder until 1973).
- Norms are culture-bound: social norms vary between cultures and any such definition of abnormality will be culture-relative.

Norms across cultures

- Malinowski (1929) studied the Trobriand Islanders, where the bones of dead relatives are normally cleaned and worn as ornaments.

Defining Abnormality

Deviation from ideal mental health

- Abnormality can be defined as deviating from the characteristics and abilities which one *should* possess in order to be considered mentally healthy.
- This may mean possessing characteristics which should *not* be possessed (e.g. hearing voices) or *not* possessing characteristics which *should* be possessed (e.g. being able to cope with stress).
- Jahoda (1958) has suggested a number of ideals, including individual choice, resistance to stress, accurate perception of reality, self-actualisation (being who you want to be) as possible characteristics of mental health.

Problems

- **Most of us fail to demonstrate all these characteristics, all the time:** Maslow (1968) points out that few people achieve self-actualisation, and some of us may not always feel that we are coping with stress. As a result, most of us would be considered abnormal at some time.
- **Such ideals are value judgements, not objective judgements:** unlike physical health, which can be defined in clear physical terms (Szasz, 1960), judgements about mental health may involve cultural and personal values about what is healthy. This leaves the decision open to bias.
- **Ideals of mental health vary between cultures:** in the Sambia of New Guinea, male youths are taught that females are poison and the males engage in prescribed unlimited fellatio. On the island of Java, soccer is played with a ball that is soaked in petrol then set alight.
- **Ideals of mental health vary with time and context:** Chance (1984) claims that there are certain universal standards and that, for example, murder cannot be considered healthy even if it is popular. However, during war-time, pacifists may be considered negatively, and schizophrenic symptoms (such as hallucinations) would be seen as healthy 'visions' in a 13th-century monk (Wade & Tavris, 1993).

Failure to function adequately

- Every human being should achieve a sense of personal well-being and make some contribution to a larger social group. Abnormality is defined as a failure to function adequately in this respect.
- Such failures include the '*practical*' and '*clinical*' criteria below (Sue *et al.*, 1994):

Personal distress

Most people come to clinics because their feelings/behaviours cause them distress (Miller & Morley, 1986). These feelings may take forms such as *anxiety*, *depression*, and *loss of appetite*, and may not be obvious to other people.

Problems

- We cannot use this as a definition on its own since such feelings may be appropriate responses under some circumstances (e.g. the death of a loved one).
- Some mental disorders are not accompanied by personal distress (e.g. repeated acts of crime with dissocial personality disorder).

Others' distress

Some psychological states may not be distressing for the individual him/herself, but lead to distress in *others*. Being the cause of others' distress can thus constitute a failure to function adequately.

Maladaptiveness

If behaviour is maladaptive (i.e. prevents the person from efficiently satisfying social and occupational roles), then it may be classed as abnormal even if not causing distress (e.g. substance-use disorders).

Unexpected behaviour

If a person reacts in ways which could not reasonably be predicted, then we may see them as functioning inadequately, for example, behaviour which is out of all proportion to the situation (such as extreme over-reactions: Davison & Neale, 1994).

Problems

- Unexpected behaviours may also involve under-reactions, which may be more difficult to identify.

Bizarreness

A person is failing to function adequately if behaviour would be considered bizarre in the circumstances (e.g. walking around a university naked).

Problems

- Under some circumstances, bizarre behaviours are not abnormal (e.g. transvestitism is common in pantomimes).

BIOLOGICAL AND PSYCHOLOGICAL MODELS OF ABNORMALITY

SYLLABUS

11.2 Abnormality – biological and psychological models of abnormality
- assumptions made by biological (medical) and psychological (including psychodynamic, behavioural and cognitive) models of abnormality in terms of their views of the causes of abnormality and implications for treatment

KEY QUESTIONS
How do the following models explain and approach the treatment of mental disorders:
- the medical model?
- the psychodynamic model?
- the behavioural model?
- the cognitive model?

Section 1: The medical model

1 Which model of abnormality was replaced by the emergence of the *medical model* in the eighteenth century?
2 What central claim regarding the nature of mental disorders is made by the medical model?
3 Upon what evidence were the early successes of the medical model based?
4 From what observation do *genetic theories* of mental disorders originate?
5 How do *biochemical theories* explain mental disorders?
6 What other term is used to describe *medical therapies*?
7 Identify two problems associated with the use of *drug therapies*.
8 Name the two other principal forms of therapy associated with the medical model.
9 Identify one criticism common to both these forms of therapy.

Section 2: The psychodynamic model

10 How did Freud explain *hysteria*, in which physical symptoms are experienced but there are no underlying physical causes?
11 Name the three interacting structures which Freud believed comprise the personality.
12 What is 'normality' according to the *psychodynamic model*?
13 According to Freud, which *psychosexual stage* of development is experienced between the ages of three and five or six?
14 What are *defence mechanisms*?
15 What did Freud call the defence mechanism in which we redirect our emotional responses from a dangerous object to a safe one?
16 What is the first aim of *psychoanalysis*?
17 Name two further psychodynamic therapies, apart from psychoanalysis.
18 Identify two criticisms of the methodology used by Freud in developing his psychodynamic model.

19 What is meant by the criticism that Freud's model is both *reductionist* and *deterministic*?

Section 3: The behavioural model

20 Complete the sentence: 'Whilst the medical and psychodynamic models explain disorders in terms of internal factors, the behavioural model sees disorders as _____ _____ which are learned and maintained'.
21 According to the behavioural model, where should we look if we wish to explain mental disorders?
22 What were Watson & Rayner (1920) able to demonstrate with Little Albert?
23 According to Thorndike, what types of behaviours were animals likely to repeat?
24 What two forms of conditioning are held to explain the origins of mental disorders?
25 Identify two things that therapies based on the behavioural model have in common.
26 Name one example of a behaviour therapy, and one example of a behaviour modification technique.

Section 4: The cognitive model

27 How do *social learning theorists* believe we learn new behaviours?
28 What is the main difference between the *cognitive model* and the *behavioural model*?
29 How does the *information-processing approach* view mental disorders?
30 Complete the sentence: 'Beck (1974) argues that disorders like depression are often 'rooted' in the ____ ways people think about themselves and the world'.
31 Identify the five types of illogical thinking which Beck (1974) identified as contributing to depression.
32 What is *cognitive restructuring*?

Q

Section 1: The medical model

1 The demonological model, which saw mental disorders as resulting from supernatural forces.

2 The medical model claims that mental disorders are forms of illness which can be treated with medical techniques.

3 Early successes were largely based on showing that mental disorders could be linked to gross destruction of brain tissue.

4 Genetic theories of mental disorders originate from the observation that some mental disorders have a tendency to run in families.

5 Biochemical theories explain mental disorders as a result of imbalances of neurotransmitters.

6 Medical therapies are also known as somatic therapies.

7 Drug therapies are rarely cures, and usually only treat the symptoms of a disorder. They frequently have unpleasant side-effects, and have been accused of being used as a form of 'social control'.

8 Electroconvulsive therapy (ECT) and psychosurgery.

9 Both these forms of therapy lack a convincing scientific rationale to explain their effects.

Section 2: The psychodynamic model

10 Freud explained hysteria as a result of unresolved and unconscious sexual conflicts originating in childhood.

11 The id, the ego, and the superego.

12 Normality is a balance between the conflicting demands of the id, ego, and superego.

13 The phallic stage.

14 Defence mechanisms are ways in which the ego prevents anxiety-arousing impulses and thoughts from reaching consciousness.

15 Freud termed this redirection of impulses *displacement*.

16 The first aim of psychoanalysis is to make the unconscious conscious, thereby providing people with insight into their problems.

17 Additional psychodynamic therapies include psychoanalytically oriented therapies, psychodynamic approaches to group therapy (including psychodrama and transactional analysis).

18 Freud's methods lacked scientific rigour (depending largely on inference rather than objective evidence) and his samples were biased (consisting largely of upper middle-class Viennese women aged 20–44).

19 Freud's model reduces the complexity of human behaviour to the interplay of three forces (reductionist), and sees people as helpless to change themselves since 'the die is cast early in life' (deterministic).

Section 3: The behavioural model

20 'Whilst the medical and psychodynamic models explain disorders in terms of internal factors, the behavioural model sees disorders as *maladaptive behaviours* which are learned and maintained.'

21 According to this model, we should look at the environmental conditions in which the behaviour is displayed.

22 Watson & Rayner (1920) were able to demonstrate that a phobia (in Albert's case, a phobia of white rats) could be acquired through classical conditioning.

23 According to Thorndike, animals are likely to repeat behaviours which lead to pleasurable consequences.

24 Operant conditioning and classical conditioning.

25 Therapies based on the behavioural model focus on maladaptive behaviours rather than speculating as to their cause, base the success or failure of the treatment on specific observable changes, and believe that the value claimed for a treatment should be related to evidence from experimental studies.

26 Behaviour therapies include implosion, flooding, systematic desensitisation, aversion therapy and covert sensitisation, whilst behaviour modification techniques include behaviour shaping and token economies.

Section 4: The cognitive model

27 Social learning theorists point out that certain behaviours can be acquired simply by watching them being performed.

28 Unlike the behavioural model, the cognitive model believes that cognitions such as thoughts, expectations and attitudes play an important role in causing mental disorders.

29 The information-processing approach views mental disorders as resulting from a disturbed 'input–output sequence' in the storage, manipulation and retrieval of information.

30 'Beck (1974) argues that, disorders like depression are often 'rooted' in the *maladaptive* ways people think about themselves and the world.'

31 Beck (1974) identified magnification, minimisation, selective abstraction, arbitrary inference and overgeneralisation as examples of illogical thinking.

32 Cognitive restructuring involves identifying maladaptive thoughts or ways of thinking, and challenging and attempting to change them.

The medical model

- Emerged in the 18th century, replacing the '*demonological*' model, which saw supernatural forces as responsible for mental disorders.
- Proposed that all mental disorders are actually forms of physical *illness* (*pathology*) which could be treated with appropriate medical techniques.
- Proposed that the brain plays a central role in 'psychic functioning'. Early successes were largely based on showing that mental disorders could be linked to gross destruction of brain tissue.
- More recently, the model has looked at the role played by neurotransmitters and genetics in mental disorders.

Somatic (physical) therapies

- *Chemotherapy* (drugs) alleviate symptoms, do not offer a cure, have unpleasant side effects.
- *Electroconvulsive* therapy (electricity): effective for depression, but lacks a convincing rationale and causes some amnesia.
- *Psychosurgery* (surgery): irreversible, dangerous, and poorly understood.

Biochemical and genetic theories

- *Biochemical* theories explain mental disorders in terms of an imbalance of neurotransmitters.
- *Genetic* theories derive from the discovery that some disorders run in families, and proposes that DNA may transmit disorders.

The cognitive model

- Accepts the behavioural account of learning but focuses on the thoughts, expectations, and attitudes (*cognitions*) which accompany behaviour and which may cause mental disorders.
- Social learning theorists point out that behaviours can be acquired through *observational learning* (Bandura, 1969).
- Proposes that 'mediating processes', such as thoughts, interpretations and perceptions of ourselves, are important in causing disorders (not just conditioning).
- Some approaches see individuals as *information-processors* whose input–output sequences may become disordered (e.g. by faulty storage or manipulation of information).
- Other approaches see mental disorders as resulting from faulty patterns of thinking (see below).

Cognitive therapies
(Beck & Weishaar, 1989)
Aim to teach people to:
- *monitor* their negative, automatic thoughts
- *recognise* the connection between cognition, affect and behaviour
- *examine* the evidence for and against distorted thoughts
- *replace* these with more reality-oriented interpretations
- *identify and alter* beliefs which pre-dispose them to distort their experiences.

Cognitive restructuring
(Beck, 1974)
Disorders such as depression often involve maladaptive ways of thinking, e.g.:
- *Magnification and minimisation*: magnifying failures and minimising successes.
- *Arbitrary inference*: arriving at a conclusion about oneself without any supporting evidence.
Therapy aims to identify and challenge such beliefs.

Models of Abnormality

The psychodynamic model

- Freud argued that mental disorders were caused by *psychological conflicts* which originated in *childhood* and are *unconscious*.
- The personality is composed of three interacting structures (see below). When these are in balance, normality is attained, but when unconscious conflicts cannot be managed, disorders arise. *Neurotic symptoms* may represent compromises between these structures and reflect the stage of development at which the conflict occurred. '*Defence mechanisms*' serve to protect us from these conflicts.

Structures of the personality

ID (operates on the *pleasure principle*): present at birth, impulsive and pleasure-seeking.

EGO (operates on the *reality principle*): negotiates compromises between id and superego and helps us cope with reality.

SUPEREGO (*conscience + ego-ideal*): governs moral judgements and feelings.

Psychosexual stages

Oral stage (0–1 yr) pleasure achieved through the mouth.
Anal stage (1–3 yrs) pleasure achieved through anal membranes.
Phallic stage (3–5/6 yrs) pleasure through self-manipulation of genitals.
Latency stage (5/6–12 yrs) sexual motivations recede in importance.
Genital stage (after puberty) pleasure through heterosexual relationships.

Some defence mechanisms

Repression: unacceptable thoughts/impulses are pushed into the unconscious.
Reaction formation: the opposite of an unacceptable impulse is expressed.
Rationalisation: socially acceptable reasons are given for unacceptable motives.
Displacement: an emotional response is redirected towards a 'safe' object.
Projection: unacceptable motives/impulses are transferred to others.

Psychodynamic therapy – psychoanalysis

The aim of therapy is to make the *unconscious conscious* and to provide people with *insight* into their problems. Often involves therapeutic *regression* and *interpretation* (e.g. of dreams) in order to unearth *repressed* material.

The behavioural model

- Rejects references to internal factors and claims that mental disorders are *maladaptive behaviours*.
- Sees maladaptive behaviours as *learned* and *maintained* in the same way as adaptive behaviours (*conditioning*).
- Maintains that the best way of explaining disorders is to consider the environmental conditions in which a behaviour is displayed.
- Theorists use the case of 'Little Albert' (below) as a model for the acquisition of all abnormal fears.

Pavlov & classical conditioning
Ivan Pavlov found that a dog would learn to *associate* one stimulus (such as a bell) with another stimulus (such as meat) if the two were repeatedly paired. The dog would then salivate at the sound of the new stimulus (the bell).

Thorndike & operant conditioning
Thorndike noticed that animals will repeat behaviours which have led to pleasurable consequences and not repeat behaviours with unpleasurable consequences.

Little Albert
(Watson & Rayner, 1920)
- Albert, an 11-month-old boy, was conditioned to fear a white rat by presenting the rat at the same time as striking a steel bar behind his head.
- After seven combinations, Albert not only feared the rat, but this fear had *generalised* to a white rabbit, cotton wool, a fur coat and the experimenter's white hair.

Skinner & operant conditioning
Skinner coined the term 'operant conditioning' to describe the way in which our voluntary behaviours are shaped and maintained by their consequences. A behaviour (such as avoiding something we fear) can be 'reinforced' because it leads to a pleasurable consequence (such as a reduction in fear)

Behavioural therapies
- Therapies attempt to change behaviour by systematically applying learning principles.
- The success or failure of a treatment is based on *specific* and *observable* changes in behaviour and therapists believe that the value of a therapy must be supported by evidence from experimental studies.
- Therapies based on *classical conditioning* are termed '*behaviour therapy*' (which includes implosion therapy, flooding, systematic desensitisation & aversion therapy)
- Therapies based on *operant conditioning* are termed '*behaviour modification*' (which includes behaviour shaping and token economies).

CRITICAL ISSUE – EATING DISORDERS:
ANOREXIA NERVOSA AND BULIMIA NERVOSA

SYLLABUS

11.2 Abnormality – critical issue: eating disorders – anorexia nervosa and bulimia nervosa
- the clinical characteristics of anorexia nervosa and bulimia nervosa. Explanations of these disorders in terms of biological and psychological models of abnormality, including research studies on which these explanations are based

KEY QUESTIONS
- What are the characteristics of anorexia nervosa and bulimia nervosa?
- How do genetic/neurological and social/psychological factors contribute to these eating disorders?

Q

Section 1: Characteristics of anorexia nervosa

1 How long have the characteristics of what is now called *anorexia nervosa* been known?
2 By what ratio do female anorectics outnumber male anorectics?
3 At what age is onset of the disorder most common?
4 What is the principal characteristic of anorexia nervosa?
5 Complete the sentence: 'For a diagnosis of anorexia nervosa to be considered, the individual must weigh less than __ per cent of normal or expected weight for height, age and sex'.
6 Identify two physical problems which frequently accompany anorexia nervosa.
7 In what percentage of cases is anorexia nervosa fatal?
8 What is the literal meaning of anorexia nervosa?
9 What is the difference between the *restricting sub-type* and *binge eating/purging sub-type* of the disorder, as identified by DSM-IV?
10 Why do anorectics fail to recognise their bodies' thinness?

Section 2: Explaining anorexia nervosa

11 Which area of the brain plays an important role in the regulation of eating?
12 How does the action of *noradrenaline* on this area affect the behaviour of non-humans?
13 What is the relationship between the neurotransmitter *serotonin* and appetite?
14 What is the principal problem in drawing conclusions from studies of changes in neurotransmitter levels?
15 What is the *concordance rate* for anorexia nervosa in MZ twins brought up in the same environment?
16 According to the *psychodynamic model*, why might an overdependence on parents lead to anorexia?
17 A further psychodynamic explanation proposes that anorexia represents an attempt to avoid a particular issue. What is that issue?

18 According to Bemis (1978), why is there a link between being a 'good girl', doing well in school, and anorexia nervosa?
19 What types of family systems produce anorexia nervosa, according to Minuchin *et al.* (1978)?
20 Identify two criticisms of psychodynamic accounts of anorexia nervosa.
21 Crisp (1967) believes that anorexia nervosa can be seen as a specific *phobia*. What is it a fear of?
22 What general research finding suggests that Western societal norms may be influential in causing anorexia nervosa?

Section 3: Characteristics of bulimia nervosa

23 What behaviours are characteristic of *bulimia nervosa*?
24 How many times more likely are women to be bulimics than men?
25 What percentage of the population may be affected by bulimia?
26 Identify two reasons why many cases of bulimia go unnoticed by friends and family.
27 Name any three physiological effects associated with *purging*.

Section 4: Explaining bulimia nervosa

28 What is the relation between *plasma endorphins* and bulimia nervosa?
29 Explain how Ruderman's (1986) *disinhibition hypothesis* accounts for bulimia nervosa.
30 Identify the reasons given by Garner (1992) for believing that it is misleading to see anorexia nervosa and bulimia nervosa as psychologically dissimilar.
31 According to Cooper (1995), in what two ways may *depression* relate to eating disorders?
32 What general conclusions can be drawn regarding the causes of eating disorders?

Section 1: Characteristics of anorexia nervosa

1 The characteristics of what is now known as anorexia nervosa have been known for several hundred years (Hartley, 1997).

2 Female anorectics outnumber male anorectics by 15:1.

3 Onset is most common in adolescence, peaking at between 14 and 16 years of age.

4 The principal characteristic of anorexia nervosa is a prolonged refusal to eat adequate amounts of food, resulting in deliberate weight loss.

5 'For a diagnosis of anorexia nervosa to be considered, the individual must weigh less than *85* per cent of normal or expected weight for height, age and sex.'

6 These include a decline in general health, low blood pressure, low body temperature, constipation and dehydration.

7 Between 5–15 per cent of anorexia cases are fatal (Hsu, 1990).

8 'Anorexia nervosa' literally means nervous loss of appetite.

9 The restricting sub-type of anorectics loses weight through constant fasting and physical activity, whilst the binge eating/purging sub-type alternates between fasting and bingeing.

10 Due to a distorted body image, the individual does not recognise the body's thinness.

Section 2: Explaining anorexia nervosa

11 The hypothalamus plays an important role in the regulation of eating.

12 Noradrenaline acts on the hypothalamus to cause non-humans to begin eating, with a preference for carbohydrates.

13 Serotonin induces satiation and suppresses appetite.

14 Conclusions from studies of changes in neurotransmitter levels do not tell us whether these changes are causes of the disorder, effects of it, or merely correlates.

15 Askevold & Heiberg (1979) report a concordance rate for MZs of 50 per cent, whilst Holland *et al.* (1984) found a concordance rate of 55 per cent for MZ twins.

16 The psychodynamic model suggests that girls who are over-dependent on parents may fear becoming sexually mature and independent, becoming anorectic in an effort to remain pre-pubescent and avoid adult responsibilities.

17 A further psychodynamic explanation proposes that it is adult sexuality, particularly pregnancy, which is feared.

18 Bemis (1978) argues that females who are habitually co-operative and well-behaved may feel controlled by others, and attempt to assert their individuality by assuming control over their bodies.

19 Minuchin *et al.* claim that dysfunctional family systems produce anorexia nervosa.

20 Some psychodynamic accounts seem to apply only to females, and they have difficulty explaining the occurrence of the disorder in adulthood.

21 Crisp (1967) believes that anorexia nervosa is a phobia of gaining weight.

22 Research which shows that in at least some non-Western societies the incidence of anorexia nervosa is much lower, suggests that cultural and social norms may influence its prevalence.

Section 3: Characteristics of bulimia nervosa

23 Bulimia nervosa is characterised by periodic episodes of 'binge' eating, followed by 'purging' of the digestive tract using laxatives, self-induced vomiting or diuretics.

24 Women are fifty times more likely to be bulimics than are men.

25 Bulimia may affect as much as five per cent of the population.

26 Bulimics are often secretive in their behaviours, and appear to eat normally in public. Also, there is not a constant weight loss as there is in anorexia nervosa.

27 Purging may lead to 'puffy' facial appearance, a deterioration in tooth enamel, calluses on the back of the hand, digestive tract damage, dehydration and nutritional imbalances.

Section 4: Explaining bulimia nervosa

28 Plasma endorphins are elevated in people with bulimia nervosa (and in those who self-mutilate: Parkin & Eagles, 1993), although it is not clear if this is a cause, effect, or correlate of the disorder.

29 Ruderman's (1986) disinhibition hypothesis proposes that 'restricted' eaters who have 'all-or-nothing' rules regarding dieting may feel that they have over-eaten, and, having broken their diet, feel disinhibited about consuming more food. Alcohol may also lead to disinhibition.

30 Garner (1992) points out that anorectics and bulimics share many psychological traits (such as perfectionism) and the goal of maintaining a sub-optimal weight, and that individuals may move between the two disorders.

31 Cooper (1995) suggests that depression may contribute to the initiation or the maintenance of an eating disorder.

32 No single theory emerges as a definitive account of the origins of eating disorders. It seems likely that disorders do not have single discrete causes, but result from a combination of factors.

A

Anorexia nervosa

Facts
- *Anorexia nervosa* literally means 'nervous loss of appetite', but anorectics are often both hungry and pre-occupied with thoughts of food.
- The characteristics of the disorder have been known about for several hundred years (Hartley, 1997).
- Female anorectics outnumber males by 15:1.
- Onset is usually in adolescence, with the 14–16 period being most common (Hsu, 1990).
- Estimates of the disorder's incidence range from 1 in 100 to 4 in 100 (Sahakian, 1987).

Characteristics
- Characterised by a prolonged refusal to eat adequate amounts of food, resulting in deliberate weight loss (85% of normal weight for anorexia diagnosis).
- Physical consequences include cessation of menstruation, low blood pressure and body temperature, constipation and dehydration.
- Restricting types lose weight through fasting and physical activity.
  Binge eating/purging types use laxatives and vomiting, alternating between fasting and binge eating.
- Distorted body image causes the individual not to recognise her/his body's thinness.

Explanations

Biological explanations
- A dysfunction of the *hypothalamus* (which plays an important role in regulating eating).
- Changes in neurotransmitter levels (*noradrenaline* can trigger eating in non-humans, whilst *serotonin* suppresses appetite).
- Lask (cited in Kennedy, 1997) believes a deficient blood flow to the anterior temporal lobes, which interpret vision, may explain why anorectics see themselves as fat.

Genetic explanations
- First and second degree relatives of anorectics are significantly more likely to develop the disorder (Strober & Katz, 1987).
- Holland *et al.* (1984): found concordance rates of 55% for MZ (*identical*) twins and 7% for DZ (*non-identical*) twins. However, twins were raised together and the genetic component is likely to be small.

Psychodynamic explanations
- The disorder represents an unconscious effort to remain *pre-pubescent* (anorexia may cause menstruation to cease and retard puberty). Sexual maturity is feared because the girl is over-dependent on parents.
- Alternatively, the disorder prevents the girl from having to address the issue of her sexuality (especially pregnancy), allowing her to take on a 'boy-like' appearance.
- Finally, the disorder may reflect an attempt by anorectics to assert their own independence and individuality by assuming *control* over their bodies. Many anorectics are 'good girls' who are co-operative and well-behaved, and this may lead them to feel that they are being controlled by others.
- However, some of the above can only be applied to females, and cannot explain anorexia in adults.

Behavioural explanations
- Anorexia is a 'weight phobia' (Crisp, 1967) resulting from social norms, values and roles.
- Hill (cited in Uhlig, 1996a): classmates, mothers and toys (such as Sindy dolls) are more influential than fashion magazines, shaping young girls' perceptions of desirability.
- The cultural idealisation of the slender female in the West may be one cause of a fear of being fat (Petkova, 1997).
- Wooley & Wooley (1983): cultural standards of thinness are related to the increase in the incidence of eating disorders.
- Lee *et al.*, (1992): much lower incidences of anorexia in other cultures support this explanation.

Conflicting research
- Touyz *et al.* (1988): describe the case of an anorectic who was blind from birth. This is difficult for the behavioural model to explain.

Anorexia & Bulimia

Bulimia nervosa

Facts
- The word '*bulimia*' comes from the Greek *bous* meaning 'ox' and *limos* meaning hunger.
- Fewer than 5% of cases are men (Cooper, 1995).
- *Bulimia nervosa* is more common than anorexia nervosa and may affect up to 5% of the population.
- The disorder usually begins in adolescence/early adulthood.
- The frequency with which *binges* occur ranges from 2–3 times a week to 30 times a week.
- Associations between self-mutilative behaviour and bulimia have been found (Parry-Jones & Parry-Jones, 1993).

Characteristics
- Characterised by periodic episodes of compulsive 'binge' eating which are terminated either by abdominal pain or (in the purging type) the expulsion of food using diuretics, laxatives or self-induced vomiting.
- Like anorectics, bulimics are unduly concerned with their body shape and weight and they fluctuate between weight gain and loss.
- Guilty feelings resulting from the behaviour mean that it is often carried out in secret and the disorder may go unnoticed.
- Physiological effects of purging include puffy facial appearance, deterioration in tooth enamel, calluses on the back of the hand, digestive tract damage, dehydration and nutritional imbalances.

Explanations

Biological explanations
- Abnormal neurotransmitter levels may be involved (e.g. *serotonin* levels are increased by carbohydrate bingeing).
- Hormones and endorphins may be involved – elevated levels of *plasma endorphins* have been found in bulimics and those who self-mutilate (Parkin & Eagles, 1993).
- However, it is not clear whether these changes are a cause, consequence or correlate of the disorder.

Genetic explanations
- The genetic evidence is much weaker than with anorexia.
- Kendler *et al.* (1991): concordance rate of only 23% for MZs and 9% for DZs.

Other explanations
- Garner (1986): it is misleading to regard bulimia and anorexia as being psychologically dissimilar. Anorectics and bulimics share the same goal of maintaining a sub-optimal body weight and may move between the two disorders.

Parental domination and BN
- Bruch (1991): argues that *parental domination* produces perceptual and cognitive disturbances and the affected child is unable to correctly identify its own internal needs (e.g. hunger) and its own emotions or fatigue levels.
- Halmi (1995): found that bulimics have difficulty distinguishing hunger from other bodily needs and emotions – so anxiety may be misinterpreted as hunger, leading to overeating.

The disinhibition hypothesis
- Ruderman (1986): distinguishes between *restrained* eaters (who constantly diet) and *unrestrained* eaters.
- Restrained eaters may believe they have over-eaten and since they have broken their diet feel disinhibited and consume more food. Alcohol is also a 'disinhibiting factor'.
- This is later followed by purging in an attempt to reduce this weight gain.
- This 'all-or-nothing' rigidity makes people susceptible to binge eating.

CONFORMITY AND MINORITY INFLUENCE

SYLLABUS

12.1 Social influence – conformity and minority influence
- research studies into conformity (e.g. Sherif, Asch, Zimbardo) and minority influence (e.g. Moscovici, Clark). Explanations of why people yield to majority (conformity) and minority influence

KEY QUESTIONS
- What is conformity?
- What have investigators discovered about conformity?
- Why do people conform?
- Is conformity good or bad?

Section 1: Introducing conformity

1. How do Zimbardo & Leippe (1991) define *conformity*?
2. What is the difference between a *membership group* and a *reference group*?
3. What is the *autokinetic effect*?
4. Complete the sentence: 'By observing the convergence of participants' individual estimates when placed in a group, Sherif was able to study the development of a ____ ____ in the laboratory'.
5. Why, according to Asch (1951), did Sherif's experiments fail to demonstrate conformity?

Section 2: The Asch paradigm

6. What task did Asch devise in order to study conformity?
7. In what important way did this task differ from Sherif's task?
8. How many errors were made on Asch's task when participants were not influenced by group pressure?
9. How did Asch create *group pressure* in order to study its effects on a single participant?
10. What was the *mean conformity rate* in Asch's first studies of group pressure effects?
11. Identify five explanations given by Asch's participants in explaining their conforming behaviour.
12. When a single confederate was instructed to give the wrong answer when in a group of 16 naïve participants, what was their reaction?
13. What did Bogdonoff *et al.* (1961) discover when investigating *stress* in naïve participants in Asch-type experiments?
14. Does an increase in group size always result in an increase in conformity?
15. What is the relationship between *unanimity* and conformity?
16. How did Sistrunk & McDavid (1971) use groups of men and women to demonstrate that *task familiarity* influences conformity?

17. Do men or women conform more?
18. Identify four other factors which have been found to influence the likelihood of participants conforming to group pressure.
19. Give two criticisms of the original experimental procedure used by Asch to investigate conformity.
20. How did Crutchfield (1954) attempt to overcome criticisms of Asch's procedure?
21. According to Moscovici & Faucheux (1972), why should we see the naïve participants in Asch's studies as the *majority*?
22. What can Asch-type studies tell us about minorities, according to Moscovici and Faucheux?
23. Name three of the reasons why, according to Hogg & Vaughan (1995), *consistency* is an important factor in minority influence?

Section 3: Why do people conform?

24. What is the difference between *informational social influence* and *normative social influence*?
25. When Schachter (1951) instructed a confederate to disagree with the majority over the issue of sentencing a delinquent, how was the confederate treated?
26. What is the difference between *internalisation* and *compliance*?
27. Complete the sentence: 'The dual-process dependency model of social influence underestimates the role of ____ ____ in determining the degree of conformity'.
28. According to Abrams *et al.* (1990), when does social influence occur?

Section 4: Conformity: good or bad?

29. What valuable social purpose served by conformity is identified by Zimbardo & Leippe (1991)?
30. What assumption, implicit in much research into conformity, was made explicit by Asch (1952)?
31. Why might a conforming response sometimes be a rational response?

Q

Section 1: Introducing conformity

1 Zimbardo & Leippe (1991) define conformity as 'a change in belief or behaviour in response to real or imagined group pressure when there is no direct request to comply with the group, nor any reason to justify the behaviour change'.

2 A membership group is a group to which one belongs, whilst a reference group is a group which, although one is not a member, one admires and respects.

3 The autokinetic effect refers to the apparent movement of a stationary point of light in an otherwise dark room.

4 'By observing the convergence of participants' individual estimates when placed in a group, Sherif was able to study the development of a *group norm* in the laboratory.'

5 Asch (1951) argued that since Sherif's task was ambiguous, with no right or wrong answer, one could not draw conclusions about conformity.

Section 2: The Asch paradigm

6 Asch devised a simple perceptual task involving the estimation of line lengths in order to study conformity.

7 Unlike Sherif's task, Asch's task was unambiguous, with responses which were clearly correct or incorrect.

8 When participants were not influenced by group pressure, very few errors were made (0.42 per cent).

9 Asch instructed several confederates to give unanimously wrong answers on certain critical trials. Since 'naïve participants' heard these incorrect responses before giving their own responses, they experienced pressure to conform.

10 Thirty-two per cent of the incorrect responses were agreed with in Asch's first studies (the mean conformity rate).

11 Asch's participants explained their conforming behaviour by saying that they didn't wish to upset the experiment, that they doubted they could see the task material properly or were suffering from eye-strain, that they didn't wish to appear foolish/different, or that they had been unaware of giving incorrect answers.

12 When a single confederate gave the wrong answer, the 16 naïve participants reacted with laughter and sarcasm.

13 Bogdonoff *et al.* (1961) discovered that naïve participants showed increases in measures of arousal associated with stress when hearing incorrect responses, and could reduce this arousal by conforming.

14 No. The relationship is not linear; a single confederate has little effect, two confederates typically produce 14 per cent conformity in Asch-type experiments, three confederates produce near-maximum conformity of 32 per cent, and subsequent increases make little difference.

15 If the unanimity of a group is punctured, it seems to exert far less group pressure, and conformity levels decrease.

16 Sistrunk & McDavid (1971) asked men and women to identify kitchen utensils and tools. The women were more likely to conform when identifying tools, and the men when identifying kitchen utensils.

17 Women tend to conform more than men when responses are public, but when responses are made privately this difference seems to disappear (Eagly & Steffen, 1984).

18 Self-esteem, concern about social relationships, a need for social approval and attraction towards other group members have all been found to influence the degree to which participants conform to group pressure.

19 Asch's original experimental procedure was time consuming to set up, and uneconomical in that only one naïve participant at a time could be tested.

20 Crutchfield (1954) automated Asch's procedure, placing participants in a booth with a set of lights which supposedly indicated other participants' responses. However, they were in fact controlled by the experimenter, and so no confederates were needed.

21 Moscivici & Faucheux (1972) argue that since the naïve participants are actually expressing the conventional or self-evident view, we should see them as the majority.

22 Asch-type studies can tell us how the active minority manages to influence the views of the majority.

23 Hogg & Vaughan (1995) see consistency as disrupting the majority norm, drawing attention to the minority, identifying an alternative view, demonstrating certainty, and revealing the minority viewpoint as the only possible solution to a conflict.

Section 3: Why do people conform?

24 Informational social influence involves making reference to others in order to determine social reality, whereas normative social influence is used to determine what is acceptable.

25 Schachter (1951) found that the group tried to convince the confederate to agree, and when he did not, largely ignored him.

26 Internalisation involves changing one's private beliefs so as to be consistent with a public belief, whilst compliance involves a change in behaviour which does not correspond to the individual's private beliefs.

27 'The dual-process dependency model of social influence underestimates the role of *group membership* in determining the degree of conformity.'

28 Abrams *et al.* (1990) claim that social influence occurs when we see ourselves as belonging to a group and possessing the same characteristics as others.

Section 4: Conformity: good or bad?

29 Zimbardo & Leippe (1991) believe that conformity enables us to structure our social behaviour and predict the reactions of others.

30 The assumption that independence is 'good' and conformity 'bad'.

31 If the information which we have about a situation is biased or limited, then conforming to the views or behaviour of others may be the most rational option.

Conformity

Conformity: a change in belief or behaviour in response to real or imagined group pressure (Zimbardo & Leippe, 1991).
Groups: may be those to which the individual belongs (*membership groups*) or those whom the person admires or respects (*reference groups*) but does not belong.

Group norms
Sherif (1935): had participants make estimates of the amount by which a spot of light in a dark room appeared to move (*autokinetic effect*).
Results: the private estimates made by participants converged towards an average when they were members of a group (emergence of a group norm).

Asch's research

Factors affecting conformity

Using the Asch paradigm, researchers have manipulated variables in order to discover their influence:

Group size
With one confederate only, conformity is low (3%). This rises to 14% with two confederates, and 32% with three. Further increases in group size have no effect.

Unanimity
When unanimity is 'punctured' (e.g. by a single non-conforming stooge), conformity decreases greatly.

Task difficulty, ambiguity and familiarity
With difficult or ambiguous tasks, conformity *increases*. Where the task is familiar (e.g. identifying familiar objects), conformity decreases.

Gender/individual differences
Men conform less than women when their conformity/independence will be made public. Conformity increases when naïve participants are low in *self-esteem*, have a strong need for *social approval*, or are *attracted* to other group members.

The Asch paradigm

Unlike Sherif's study, Asch (1951) presented participants with an *unambiguous* situation to see if they would conform to an obviously wrong answer.
- Asch devised a simple perceptual task involving judging which of three lines matched a comparison line in length.
- Pilot studies found an error rate of less than 0.5% when participants performed alone.
- Some participants were then selected as *confederates* and instructed to give *incorrect* answers when given a secret signal.
- A single naïve participant was placed in this group, and was last or next to last to respond.

Results: when confederates gave incorrect answers, naïve participants would give incorrect responses about one-third of the time. About three-quarters of participants conformed at least once.

Participants' explanations
- Didn't want to 'upset the experiment'.
- Didn't want to appear different/foolish.
- Weren't aware they had given incorrect responses.
- Wondered if they were suffering from eye-strain.

Bogdonoff *et al.* (1961): naïve participants experienced stress when hearing incorrect responses, but this decreased if they conformed.

Automating Asch's procedure
(Crutchfield, 1954)
Asch's experiment was time-consuming to set up and uneconomical, requiring many confederates for each naïve participant.
- Crutchfield seated participants in a cubicle with a panel of lights supposedly representing the responses of participants in other cubicles.
- In fact, the lights were controlled by the experimenter and the need for confederates was removed altogether.

Minority vs majority influence

- Moscovici & Faucheux (1972): although naïve participants are numerically a minority, it is more profitable to think of them as the *majority*, since they embody the conventional view.
- We need, therefore, to understand how active minorities (in this case the *confederates*) were able to influence the majority.
- Moscovici (1976): the *consistency* of the minority appeared to be the most important factor.

Why is consistency important?
(Hogg & Vaughan, 1995)
- It *disrupts* the majority norm and produces uncertainty.
- It draws attention to the minority as an entity.
- It identifies an alternative, coherent point of view.
- It demonstrates commitment to that view.
- It shows that the solution to the conflict is the minority view.

Informational social influence (ISI)

Festinger's (1954) *social comparison theory* states that people have a basic need to confirm that their beliefs are correct. In ambiguous/novel situations, we look to others for 'guidance' about our social reality. The less we are able to rely on our own perceptions, the more we will be susceptible to informational influence from others.

Normative social influence (NSI)

People need to be *accepted* by others and create a favourable *impression*, so they accept the view of the majority rather than risking rejection.

Non-conformity and rejection
Schachter (1951): when a confederate was instructed to disagree with the majority over the sentencing of a fictitious delinquent ('Johnny Rocco'), the group initially tried to get him to conform to their views, then largely ignored and rejected him when he failed to do so.

Why do people conform?
(Deutsch & Gerard, 1955)

Internalisation and compliance

Internalisation occurs when a private belief becomes consistent with a public belief or opinion. The individual conforms 'truly', accepting the majority view.
Compliance occurs when people give answers which they do not really believe. Conformity may sometimes be more accurately described as 'internalisation' (as in Sherif's experiments) or 'compliance' (as is more likely in Asch's experiments).

Group belongingness

The distinction between NSI and ISI has been called the dual process dependency model of social influence and has been criticised for underestimating the role of group 'belongingness' in conformity.

Referential social influence
Abrams *et al.* (1990): social influence only occurs when we disagree with those with whom we expect to agree (e.g. when others are similar to us or belong to the same group). On this model, the degree of similarity or common group membership will influence conformity.

OBEDIENCE TO AUTHORITY

KEY QUESTIONS
- What is obedience?
- How did Milgram investigate obedience?
- How valid are the findings of research into obedience?
- How can we explain these findings?
- How can obedience be resisted?

Section 1: Milgram's research

1 What three differences did Milgram (1992) identify between *conformity* and *obedience*?

2 What was the original purpose of Milgram's research into obedience?

3 How did Milgram obtain participants for his investigation?

4 What was the role of *Mr Wallace*?

5 What were the '*teachers*' in Milgram's experiment instructed to do?

6 In the '*voice feedback*' variation of Milgram's experiments, what did the learner do as the experiment progressed?

7 In what way did the experimenter (*Mr Williams*) deal with participants' reluctance to continue?

8 What percentage of the participants in Milgram's 'voice feedback' variation administered the highest voltage to the 'learners'?

9 Milgram describes a number of behaviours common to the participants in the role of 'teacher'. Describe three of them.

10 How did Milgram subsequently vary the *institutional context* of his experiments?

11 What result did Milgram obtain when the teacher was in the same room as the learner or had to force the learner's hand onto a shock plate?

12 In what way did Milgram vary the *remoteness* of the authority figure in his experiments?

13 Which of Milgram's variations on his basic design produced the highest levels of obedience?

14 Complete the following sentence: 'The effects of ___ _____ are most impressive in undercutting the experimenter's authority'.

15 Which of Milgram's variations produced the lowest levels of obedience?

Section 2: Explaining and evaluating Milgram's findings

16 What effect does Milgram refer to in explaining the atrocities committed by the Nazis, and Eichmann's defence that he was 'just carrying out orders'?

17 What is the difference between an *agentic state* and an *autonomous state*?

18 How was the impact of visible symbols of authority demonstrated by Bickman (1974)?

19 What experiment involving caged puppies casts doubt on the 'credibility' explanation?

20 What experiment did Hofling *et al.* (1966) carry out, suggesting that high levels of obedience are not limited to laboratory settings?

21 According to Gilbert (1981), how might the '*foot-in-the-door*' phenomenon have influenced Milgram's participants?

22 What did Milgram find when he replicated his experiment using *female* participants?

23 What have researchers discovered when looking at the cross-cultural replicability of Milgram's findings?

24 Give one criticism of studies which have attempted to replicate Milgram's finding cross-culturally.

Section 3: Resisting obedience

25 Identify two of the three social processes identified by Hirsch (1995) as being related to the occurence of genocide?

26 Identify two of the three ways in which Milgram felt that obedience might be reduced.

27 When are we most likely to *rebel* against authority?

28 What two roles were allocated to students in Zimbardo *et al.*'s (1973) prison study simulation?

29 Why did Zimbardo *et al.* (1973) have to terminate their study after only six days, when it was planned to run for two weeks?

30 Complete the sentence: 'According to Banuazizi & Mohavedi (1975), the behaviour of both guards and prisoners may have arisen from the ____ ____ of their respective roles'.

Section 1: Milgram's research

1 According to Milgram (1992), obedience involves an explicit instruction to act in a certain way, the presence of a higher authority who is of a different status, and a social hierarchy which sanctions the power of the authority figure (rather than a need for acceptance by one's peers).

2 Milgram wished to test the '"Germans are different" hypothesis', used as an explanation for Nazi atrocities.

3 Participants were obtained by placing an advertisement in a local newspaper.

4 Mr Wallace was a confederate who always took the role of learner.

5 The 'teachers' were instructed to teach a list of word-pairs to the learners, punishing incorrect responses with increasing levels of electric shock.

6 As the experiment progressed, the learner was heard to utter grunts, screams, protests, then fall ominously silent after refusing to answer any more questions. The learner was a confederate, suffered no shock, and all protests were played on a tape recorder.

7 The experimenter was permitted to use four verbal 'prods' ('please continue', 'the experiment requires that you continue', 'it is absolutely essential that you continue', 'you have no other choice, you must go on') to encourage participants to continue.

8 Sixty-two-and-a-half per cent in the initial study (remote victim) administered the highest voltage.

9 Participants displayed great anguish, verbally attacked the experimenter, twitched nervously, or broke into nervous laughter.

10 Milgram varied the institutional context of his experiments by moving to a rundown office in downtown Bridgeport.

11 When the teacher was in the same room as the learner, or had to force the learner's hand onto a shock plate, the 450 volt-obedience rate dropped to 40 and 30 per cent, respectively.

12 Milgram varied the remoteness of the authority figure by having the experimenter leave the room, after giving the essential instructions, and give the remaining instructions by telephone.

13 Having the teacher paired with another (confederate) teacher who administered the shocks whilst the participant simply read out the word pairs, produced the highest levels of obedience.

14 'The effects of *peer rebellion* are most impressive in undercutting the experimenter's authority.'

15 When the learner demanded to be shocked, or when there were two authorities giving contradictory commands, the levels of obedience were lowest.

Section 2: Explaining and evaluating Milgram's findings

16 Milgram uses the expression 'diffusion of responsibility' to refer to the tendency of participants to allocate responsibility to the authority figure.

17 Individuals in an agentic state see themselves as an agent of an external authority, whereas individuals in an autonomous state act of their own accord and assume responsibility for their actions.

18 Bickman (1974) found that people were twice as likely to pick up a paper bag or give a coin to a stranger when instructed to do so by a uniformed guard rather than by a civilian.

19 Sheridan & King (1972) had participants administer real electric shocks to a caged puppy as part of a study of 'learning'. Seventy-five per cent of the participants administered the maximum voltage.

20 Hofling *et al.* (1966) instructed nurses by telephone to administer twice the maximum dose of a drug. Twenty-one out of 22 complied unhesitatingly.

21 Gilbert (1981) says that participants may have found it difficult to extricate themselves from the experiment, having agreed to a series of gradually escalating demands (the 'foot-in-the-door' phenomenon).

22 Milgram obtained very similar levels of obedience with female participants compared with male participants.

23 Attempts to replicate Milgram's findings cross-culturally have produced a wide range of levels of obedience, ranging from 16 per cent for Australian female students (Kilham & Mann, 1974) to 92 per cent for Dutch citizens (Meeus & Raaijmakers, 1986).

24 Such studies have varied in the degree to which they accurately reproduced Milgram's experimental set-up.

Section 3: Resisting obedience

25 Hirsch (1995) identified authorisation (obeying orders originating in authority), routinisation (massacre becoming a routine/mechanical operation) and dehumanisation (where the victims are seen as less than human) as being related to the occurence of genocide.

26 Milgram felt obedience might be reduced by educating people about the dangers of blind obedience, encouraging people to question authority, and exposing them to the actions of disobedient models.

27 We are most likely to rebel against authority when we feel that our freedom is in danger of being lost.

28 Students in Zimbardo *et al.*'s (1973) prison simulation study were allocated either prisoner or guard roles.

29 Zimbardo *et al.* (1973) had to terminate their study prematurely because of the pathological reactions of the students in the role of 'prisoners'.

30 'According to Banuazizi & Mohavedi (1975), the behaviour of both guards and prisoners may have arisen from the *stereotyped expectations* of their respective roles.'

Obedience: involves an explicit instruction to behave in a certain way, a higher authority who influences behaviour, and a hierarchical structure which legitimises this authority

Stanley Milgram's studies of obedience to authority
Milgram (1963, 1964, 1974)

Milgram wished to test the idea that Nazism was the product of a German character defect (a readiness to obey authority).

- Participants (aged 20–50 years), from all walks of life, answered a newspaper advertisement for a 'study of memory' (paid $4.50).
- Participants introduced to Mr Williams (experimenter) and Mr Wallace (confederate), whom they believed was a harmless accountant in his 50s. Told that experiment concerned effects of punishment on learning. Drew lots – rigged so that the confederate was the learner.
- 'Teacher' looked on as learner was strapped into chair, given mild sample shock, and told both of a slight heart condition (*voice feedback variation*).
- Teacher introduced to shock generator (15–450 volts), marked *'slight, moderate, strong, very strong, intense, intense to extreme, danger: severe shock, XXX'*. Teacher is given a sample shock.
- Teacher instructed to teach word pairs to learner and told to move one switch higher on the shock generator for every incorrect response.
- Teacher heard tape-recorded grunts, screams, objections and, ominous silence after 330 volts (*voice feedback variation*).
- 4 verbal prods used by experimenter: *'Please continue'*, *'The experiment requires that you continue'*, *'It's absolutely essential that you continue'*, *'You have no other choice – you must go on'*.
- After the experiment (when participants refused to continue or administered the maximum shock four times) full debriefing was given.

Results: Approximately 65% of participants went up to 450 volts, all to 300 (*voice feedback variation*). Psychiatrists had predicted that less than 1% of participants would administer the highest voltage. Participants trembled, sweated, broke into nervous laughter, or verbally attacked the experimenter. Three participants suffered seizures.

Variations on Milgram's basic procedure (% going to 450 V)

A peer administers shocks (92.5%)
- The teacher is paired with another (bogus) teacher and had only to read out the word-pairs, whilst the other teacher administered the shock.
- Participants shifted responsibility onto the other teacher and obedience rose to 92.5%

Institutional context (47.5%)
- Many participants claimed that they continued administering shock because the experiment was being conducted at prestigious Yale University.
- When Milgram transferred the experiment to a rundown office in downtown Bridgeport, the 450-volt obedience rate was still 47.5%.

Proximity (40%) and touch proximity (30%)
- When learner and teacher were in the same room, the 450-volt obedience rate dropped to 40%.
- When the teacher had to force the learner's hand onto a shock plate the 450-volt obedience rate was still 30%.

Two peers rebel (10%)
- The teacher is paired with two confederate (bogus) teachers.
- The first teacher refused to continue at 150 V, the second at 210 V.
- Only 10% of participants continued on to 450 V, most stopping when one or the other teachers refused to continue.

Resisting obedience

- Milgram felt that obedience could be reduced by *educating* people about the dangers of blind obedience, encouraging them to *question* authority, exposing them to *disobedient* models.
- Brehm (1966): when people believe they are *entitled* to freedom they experience *reactance* (an unpleasant emotional state which they are motivated to reduce) when attempts are made to restrict their freedom of choice, and will disobey.

The Stanford prison simulation (Zimbardo *et al.*, 1973)
- Zimbardo *et al.* created a mock prison in the university basement, randomly assigning students to prisoner or guard roles.
- Prisoners wore 'smocks' and were referred to by numbers. Guards wore uniforms and sunglasses, and were referred to as 'Sir'.
- Experiment had to be stopped after six days as guards became increasingly sadistic, and prisoners suffered pathological reactions.

Evaluating & explaining Milgram's results

Experimental realism
Participants may not have believed the experimental set-up, and guessed that the learner was not receiving shocks.

Puppies and electric shocks (Sheridan & King, 1972)
- Participants were required to deliver real and increasing electric shocks to a caged puppy as part of a learning task.
- After a time, an odourless anaesthetic was released into the cage, causing the puppy to appear to 'die'.
- 75% of participants continued, and delivered the maximum shock.

Demand characteristics
Participants may simply have responded to cues in Milgram's experimental setting, making this an unusual result.

Obedience in nurses (Hofling *et al.*, 1966)
- Nurses were instructed by telephone to deliver twice the maximum dosage of a drug (in fact a harmless tablet) to a patient.
- 21 out of 22 obeyed unhesitatingly.

Personal responsibility
Participants show signs of relief when the experimenter said 'I'm responsible for what goes on here'. Milgram saw this '*diffusion of responsibility*' as crucial to understanding Nazi atrocities.

Legitimate authority
In an organised society, individuals must give up responsibility to those of higher status (indicated by visible symbols) in order to ensure smooth functioning. Participants may have entered this '*agentic*' state, rather than acting independently ('*autonomous*' state).

The 'foot in the door'
Gilbert (1981): the demands escalated gradually beginning with harmless co-operation, so that participants may not have known at what point to stop, having begun.

Methodological and generalisation issues

- **Representative sample?** Milgram studied 636 participants from the New Haven area. Although participants who went to 450 V tended to be more authoritarian, people who volunteer for experiments tend to be less authoritarian on average.
- **Gender bias?** Although Milgram used mainly male participants, the 40 females in one of his experiments produced the same results as men.
- **Cross-cultural validity?** Reproducing the study in different countries produced obedience rates ranging from 16% (Australian female students) to 92% (members of the Dutch population). However, such studies often only replicated Milgram's procedure partially.
- **Ecological validity?** Clearly there are differences between Nazi Germany and Milgram's laboratory. Some psychologists argue that his findings do not generalise well to real-life situations. However, Hofling *et al.* (1966) (see above) showed that high levels of obedience could be obtained outside the laboratory.

CRITICAL ISSUE – THE DEVELOPMENT OF ETHICAL GUIDELINES FOR RESEARCH

SYLLABUS

12.1 Critical issue: ethical issues in psychological research
- ethical issues surrounding the use of deception, informed consent and the protection of participants from psychological harm, including the relevance of these issues in the context of social influence research. Ways in which psychologists deal with these issues (e.g. through the use of ethical guidelines)

KEY QUESTIONS
- Which ethical concerns are raised by research into social influence?
- How have ethical guidelines been applied to psychological research?
- What problems are there in applying these guidelines?

Section 1: Studying social influence

1 What accusation did Baumrind (1964) level against Milgram?
2 How did Milgram respond to this criticism?
3 How could Milgram claim that the experimenter *did not make* the participant shock the learner?
4 Complete the sentence: 'A broader ethical issue concerns protecting the ____ versus benefitting ____'.
5 What was Zimbardo *et al.*'s (1973) view of the ethical concerns in his 'prison simulation experiment', as compared to Milgram's?
6 How long was Zimbardo *et al.*'s prison simulation supposed to last, and how long did it actually last?
7 Roughly what proportion of conformity and obedience experiments deceive participants, according to Vitelli (1988)?
8 Identify one of the two main reasons why deception is considered unethical.
9 What term is used to describe the procedure used by Milgram (and others) to minimise the adverse effects of deception.
10 Why, according to Milgram, were his 'technical illusions' ultimately justified?
11 What did Christensen (1988) discover about the acceptability of deception (so long as it was not extreme)?
12 What was Aronson's (1988) defence of Milgram's use of research?
13 What was the only area of Zimbardo *et al.*'s experiment to involve deception?
14 Although Zimbardo *et al.* acknowledged that their procedure had caused suffering, what comment did Zimbardo make regarding the nature of that suffering?

Section 2: Ethical guidelines

15 What are the two major *professional bodies* responsible for publishing ethical guidelines?
16 Identify three of the four guiding principles considered to be amongst the most important.
17 Identify one reason why ethical guidelines must be continually updated.
18 Why, according to Gale (1995), do modern psychologists use the term *participants* rather than *subjects*?
19 Which type of psychologists have been responsible for this change in terminology?
20 Why, according to the *Ethical Principles*, are ethical guidelines necessary?
21 Complete the sentence: 'The essential principle is that the investigation should be considered from the ____ of all ____'.
22 Explain what is required for *informed consent* to be given.
23 Identify one common condition under which special care might need to be taken in obtaining informed consent.
24 Why is it difficult to argue that prior knowledge of a procedure can ever be guaranteed?
25 What ethical requirement might be affected by factors such as the status of the experimenter, or the desire to please others/not look foolish?
26 Complete the sentence: 'Participants should never be misled without extremely strong ____ or ____ justification'.
27 Identify one of the two ways in which participants can be protected from stress related to the disclosure of confidential information.
28 According to Brown (1997), what difficulty is caused by the way in which formal ethical codes focus on the *individual* participant?

Section 1: Studying social influence

1. Baumrind (1964) accused Milgram of failing to protect his participants from stress and emotional conflict.

2. Milgram responded that the stress caused was not an intended or expected outcome of the procedure.

3. Milgram believed that every person who came into the laboratory was free to accept or reject the demands of authority.

4. 'A broader ethical issue concerns protecting the *individual* versus benefitting *society*.'

5. Zimbardo (1973) felt that the ethical concerns were even greater in his experiments than in Milgram's.

6. Zimbardo's prison simulation was supposed to last for two weeks but was stopped after only six days.

7. Vitelli claims that almost all conformity and obedience experiments involve the deception of participants.

8. Deception is considered unethical because it prevents the participant from giving informed consent and because participants may learn harmful things about themselves.

9. Milgram debriefed his participants, explaining the procedure thoroughly, in order to minimise the adverse effects of deception.

10. Milgram's claims that his 'technical illusions' were ultimately justified because they were in the end accepted and approved of by those exposed to them.

11. Christensen (1988) discovered that so long as deception was not extreme, participants did not seem to mind.

12. Aronson (1988) argued that without deception Milgram could not obtained results which reflect how people behave in real situations.

13. The only deception in Zimbardo *et al.*'s experiment was to do with the arrest of the 'prisoners' at the start of the experiment.

14. Zimbardo claimed that the suffering was 'stimulus bound' and did not extend beyond the boundaries of the prison simulation itself.

Section 2: Ethical guidelines

15. The British Psychological Society (BPS) and the American Psychological Association (APA).

16. The guiding principles considered to be amongst the most important include consent/informed consent, deception, debriefing and protection of participants.

17. They must be updated to take into account the changing political and social contexts.

18. Gale (1995) believes that the change of wording represents a genuine shift in the perception of the individual – from object to person.

19. Feminist psychologists have been largely responsible for the change in terminology.

20. According to the *Ethical Principles*, ethical guidelines are necessary to clarify the conditions under which psychological research is acceptable.

21. 'The essential principle is that the investigation should be considered from the *standpoint* of all *participants*.'

22. Participants need to be informed of the objective of the study and any other aspects which might reasonably be expected to influence their willingness to participate.

23. Special care needs to be taken where participants' condition or circumstances may affect their ability to give informed consent – such as with detained persons (e.g. those in prison, psychiatric hospital) or with children or persons suffering from mental disorder.

24. It is difficult for either the researcher or the participant to fully grasp the procedure without actually experiencing it.

25. The *Ethical Principles* require that participants consent freely to the procedure and this might be affected by factors such as the status of the experimenter, or the desire to please others/not look foolish.

26. 'Participants should never be misled without extremely strong *scientific* or *medical* justification.'

27. Participants can be protected from stress related to their experimental results by making this information anonymous as soon as possible, and by according them the right to witness the destruction of records which they do not wish to be kept.

28. Brown (1997) argues that formal ethical codes focus on the individual participant and ignore broader questions regarding the risks to a group to which the participant belongs (e.g. research into race-related differences in IQ).

Ethical Issues

The *Ethical Principles for Conducting Research with Human Participants* (British Psychological Society, 1990, 1993) identifies the responsibilities and obligations common to both the scientist and practitioner roles.

Gale (1995) points out that guidelines need to be continually updated and reviewed in the light of changing social and political contexts and do not depend on absolute or universal ethical truths.

The introduction to the *Ethical Principles* states:
'Psychological investigators are potentially interested in all aspects of human behaviour and conscious experience. However, for ethical reasons, some areas of human experience and behaviour may be beyond the reach of experiment ...'
'The essential principle is that the investigation should be considered from the standpoint of all participants ...'.

Consent/Informed consent

Principle
- The *Ethical Principles* states that participants should be informed of the objectives of the research, all other aspects of the research which might reasonably be expected to influence their willingness to participate ...
- In addition, [investigators] ... should not be allowed to pressurise the participants to take part in or remain in the investigation.

Evaluation
- How easy is it to inform participants? Participants will not have full knowledge until they have experienced the procedure, and the investigators may not have experienced it themselves.

Example – Milgram
- Milgram deceived his participants as to the real nature of the experiment and did not, therefore, obtain full informed consent from participants (see Aronson's comments to the right).
- Other criticisms of Milgram have focused on the extent to which he pressurised participants to remain in the investigation – both the initial payment and the verbal prods used by the experimenter can be seen as forms of pressure.

Example – Zimbardo
- Zimbardo's participants were told of everything that would happen to them and gave their permission for invasion of privacy, loss of civil rights, and harassment.
- Although they gave consent, it is unlikely that either the participants or the researchers fully understood what the *experience* of the procedure was like.

Deception

Principle
- The *Ethical Principles* states that intentional deception of participants should be avoided where possible.
- Where there are no alternatives to deception, participants should be debriefed at the earliest possible opportunity.

Evaluation
- According to Vitelli (1988), almost all conformity & obedience experiments deceive participants over the purpose of the research, the accuracy of the information they are given and/or the true identity of other participants/the experimenter.
- Deception is unethical because it prevents the participant from giving informed consent, and may be potentially harmful where participants risk learning things about themselves as *people*.

Example – Milgram
- Milgram's study has been criticised for its use of deception. However, Aronson (1988) defended its use, pointing out that realistic results could not have been obtained otherwise.
- In defence of his experiments, Milgram pointed out (1974) that all participants were thoroughly debriefed and that the procedures were justified because participants ultimately accepted and approved of them.
- Psychologists must consider whether or not a means can be sufficiently justified by an end.
- Christensen (1988) found that participants do not seem to mind deception, so long as it is not extreme.

Example – Zimbardo
- The only deception in Zimbardo's prison simulation involved the arrest – which came as a surprise to participants.

Debriefing

Principle
- The *Ethical Principles* states that the investigator should provide the participant with any necessary information to complete their understanding of the nature of the research ... [and] ... monitor any unforeseen negative effects.
- Some effects which may be produced by an experiment will not be negated by a verbal description following the research.

Evaluation
- According to Aronson (1988), the experimenter must take steps to ensure that the subjects leave the experimental situation in a frame of mind that is at least as sound as it was when they entered.
- Although debriefing is commonly used to protect participants from any harmful effects – such as those resulting from deception – in some circumstances longer-term measures (such as psychiatric assessment) are required.

Example – Milgram
- Milgram thoroughly debriefed his participants immediately following the procedure, and one year later participants were assessed by an independent psychiatrist for signs of psychological harm. Most participants said that they were happy to have participated.

Example – Zimbardo
- Zimbardo *et al.* held debriefing sessions and participants returned post-experimental questionnaires at intervals of weeks, months and years.

Protection of participants

Principle
- The *Ethical Principles* states that investigators have a responsibility to protect participants from physical and mental harm.
- Debriefing, confidentiality and the right to withdraw are all means of ensuring that this happens.

Evaluation
- Brown (1987) argues that codes focus too narrowly on risks to individual participants whilst neglecting risks to the wider group to which the participant may belong (e.g. research into racial differences in IQ).

Example – Milgram
- Baumrind (1964): criticised Milgram for exposing participants to stress and emotional conflict.
- Milgram (1974): stress was neither an *anticipated* nor *intended* outcome and *'momentary excitement'* is not harm.
- Despite this, surely Milgram should have stopped when it became clear that distress was being caused?
- Milgram:
  1. Participants were reunited with Mr Wallace & informed that no shock had been delivered and assured that their behaviour was entirely normal.
  2. The experimenter did not *make* the participant deliver the shocks – they were free to obey/disobey the authority figure.
- There is also a broader ethical issue concerning protecting the individual vs benefitting society, which in turn relates to the question 'Does the end justify the means?'.

Example – Zimbardo
- Zimbardo (1973): '... prisoners suffered physical and psychological abuse hour after hour for days, while volunteer guards were exposed to the new self-knowledge that they enjoyed being powerful and had abused this power ...'.
- Savin (1973): the benefits resulting from Zimbardo *et al.*'s experiment did not justify the distress, mistreatment & degradation.
- However, Zimbardo *did* halt the expt. after six days when the intensity & seriousness of the distress were clear.

RESEARCH METHODS –
QUANTITATIVE AND QUALITATIVE RESEARCH

KEY QUESTIONS
- What are the essential features of an experiment?
- What types of experimental and non-experimental research are there?
- What are the advantages and disadvantages of each type of study?

Section 1: Experimental designs

1 What does the word *empirical* mean, in the phrase 'empirical research'?
2 Complete the following sentence: 'Biases can enter into the data-gathering process and challenge the ____ of the findings obtained'.
3 What is the difference between *descriptive statistics* and *interpretative statistics*?
4 What is the name of the organisation which publishes the Code of Conduct for Psychologists?
5 What is a *research question*?
6 What is the difference between *quantitative* data and *qualitative* data?
7 Which is the most exclusively *quantitative* approach of gathering data?
8 In the phrase 'one variable has an effect on another', what is the term *effect* really shorthand for?
9 Complete the sentence: 'In experimental research we observe the effect of an ____ variable on a ____ variable whilst holding all other variables constant'.
10 What name is given to variables other than the ones we are studying which might affect the outcome of the experiment?
11 Why is it so important to control or account for variables other than those we are studying?
12 What is the name given to a group used for comparison purposes with other experimental groups?
13 Complete the sentence: 'In an experiment a ____ ____ is often used, in which all participants are tested in the same place under the same conditions'.
14 What are *participant variables*?
15 What procedure is normally used to minimise the effect of participant variables?

16 What is the difference between an experiment and a *quasi-experiment*?
17 In what way does a *non-equivalent groups design* constitute a quasi-experiment?
18 What name is given to the type of experiment in which the experimental conditions are not controlled by the experimenter?
19 What name is given to the effect on participants' behaviour, caused by their knowing that they are objects of research?

Section 2: Non-experimental designs

20 What type of study is being carried out when a researcher investigates sex differences (for example)?
21 What is the essential difference between the conclusions which may be drawn from experimental and non-experimental designs?
22 What does the term *correlation* refer to, strictly speaking?
23 What term is used to describe the type of observational study in which behaviour is observed in an everyday, normal setting?
24 What is an *undisclosed observation*?
25 Identify one ethical problem with undisclosed observations.
26 Identify one problem with *disclosed* observations?
27 What is meant by the expression *observer bias*?
28 What is the difference between *open-ended* and *closed questions*?
29 Complete the sentence: 'Fixed-choice items have the advantage of being ____'.
30 To what does the *validity* of a scale or measure refer?
31 What is a *leading question*?
32 Identify two ways in which the *interview* differs from the *questionnaire*.

Section 1: Experimental designs

1 The word empirical means based on real-world observations.

2 'Biases can enter into the data-gathering process and challenge the *validity* of the findings obtained.'

3 Descriptive statistics summarise data, whilst interpretative statistics are used to analyse the data.

4 The Code of Conduct for Psychologists is published by the British Psychological Society.

5 A research question is the question that a researcher poses when considering how to support a theory or extend its scope.

6 Quantitative data are measures in numerical form, whilst qualitative data are unquantified data (such as conversations or pictures).

7 The most exclusively quantitative approach of gathering data is the experiment.

8 The term *effect* is really shorthand for 'a presumed cause and effect relationship between two variables'.

9 'In experimental research we observe the effect of an *independent* variable on a *dependent* variable whilst holding all other variables constant.'

10 Such variables are known as extraneous variables.

11 It is important to control or account for these extraneous variables, otherwise they may affect the outcome of the experiment and we may not be able to draw a conclusion about cause and effect.

12 A control group is used for the purpose of comparison with other experimental groups.

13 'In an experiment a *standardised procedure* is often used, in which all participants are tested in the same place under the same conditions.'

14 Participant variables are pre-existing differences between people which might explain differences between groups in an experiment.

15 Random allocation of participants to the various experimental conditions is usually used to minimise participant variables.

16 In a quasi-experiment the experimenter lacks complete control over all relevant variables.

17 In a non-equivalent groups design participants are not randomly allocated to the experimental conditions.

18 When the experimental conditions are not controlled by the experimenter, the experiment is termed a *natural experiment*.

19 The effect on participants' behaviour, caused by their knowing that they are objects of research, is termed *participant reactivity*.

Section 2: Non-experimental designs

20 An investigation of sex differences is termed a *group difference study*.

21 Experimental designs allow us to draw conclusions about cause and effect, whilst non-experimental designs rarely allow us to do so.

22 Strictly speaking, the term *correlation* refers to the degree of statistical relationship between one variable and another.

23 The term *naturalistic observation* is used to describe the type of observational study in which behaviour is observed in an everyday, normal setting.

24 An undisclosed observation is one in which the participants under study do not know that they are being observed.

25 One ethical problem with undisclosed observations is that it is difficult to gain consent. Another is that researchers could gain access to confidential information which participants might not have shared if they knew that they were under study.

26 In a disclosed observation a participant's awareness of being observed might affect their behaviour.

27 Observer bias refers to the problem that different observers differ in how they perceive, evaluate and label behaviours.

28 Open-ended questions allow a respondent to answer using whatever words they wish whilst closed questions restrict responses to a number of fixed responses.

29 'Fixed-choice items have the advantage of being *quantifiable*.'

30 The validity of a scale or measure refers to the extent to which a scale actually measures what it is intended to measure.

31 A leading question is one in which the desired answer is implied in the question.

32 In an interview researchers usually have more time with each respondent, do not impose an exact structure on the information to be obtained and have the opportunity to obtain people's unique and personal views.

A

Quantitative data: measures in numerical form (e.g. reaction times). Produces data suitable for statistical analysis.

Qualitative data: measures in non-numerical form (e.g. a recorded conversation). Can be analysed at a descriptive level. Most often used to generate theories which may then be tested quantitatively.

Quantitative & Qualitative Research

Hypothesis testing
To support a theory a researcher may pose a *research question*. This has to be phrased as a *hypothesis* – a prediction that can be tested empirically.

The results of this research can be summarised (*descriptive* statistics, e.g. as a bar chart) and analysed (*interpretive* statistics, e.g. a *t*-test for differences).

How does research work?
The research process varies, but in general terms:
- researchers gather data ('*empirical*' research)
- and come up with a *theory* which explains their data.

To test the theory they use it to generate *hypotheses*
- which are then tested in a systematic way,
- leading to support/rejection of the hypothesis.

Experimental designs

Variables (things that change)
- *Independent variable (IV)*: the factor which is under the experimenter's control.
- *Dependent variable (DV)*: the factor which is measured, and may be dependent on the IV.
- *Extraneous variable*: a factor which *might* affect the DV, but which we are not investigating
- *Confounding variable*: an uncontrolled extraneous variable which could explain the change in the DV.

What is an experiment?
An experiment involves manipulating a single variable, whilst controlling others, allowing psychologists to draw inferences about cause and effect.
- Researchers may use a '*control group*' (where the variable being investigated is absent) to compare results with an '*experimental group*' (e.g. to test the effects of caffeine on memory one group might learn material after a large cup of coffee, the other after no coffee).
- Since it is important that groups to be compared are as similar as possible, researchers may use '*random allocation*' (of participants to groups) and *large group sizes* in order to average out differences between the groups.

Standardised procedure
A standardised procedure helps to reduce extraneous variables, by ensuring that all conditions are the same (except the IV) across experimental groups (e.g. by ensuring that the experimenter behaves in the same way towards all participants). It also helps other researchers to test the hypothesis by replicating the procedure.

Quasi-experimental designs

Non-equivalent groups: participants not randomly allocated to conditions
It's not always possible to randomly allocate people to experimental conditions:
- Example: a teacher might wish to test the effectiveness of a new textbook by measuring exam scores .She might not be able to assign students randomly to different groups (old/new textbook) and so have to use existing groups.
- The problem with this design is that the groups may differ significantly in the first place (e.g. one group may comprise better students than the other).

Natural experiments: treatment not controlled by the experimenter
It is not always possible to manipulate the experimental conditions:
- Example: a teacher wishing to test the effectiveness of a new textbook may find that different groups are already using different textbooks, and only be able to step in to record the results.
- In some cases behaviour is studied 'in the field'. In such field studies *participant reactivity* (the way in which the research context affects the participant's behaviour) may be avoided – at the cost of reducing control over extraneous variables.

Non-experimental designs

Group difference studies
In such studies no treatment occurs, so there are no variables that are manipulated or controlled. Instead, two groups (such as men and women) are balanced and compared. Since it is impossible to know how many of the differences have been balanced (e.g. education) we cannot know to what extent the results are due to the main difference between the groups (e.g. gender).

Correlational studies
A 'correlation' refers to the statistical relationship between two variables.
- Correlations can be **positive** (where an increase in one variable is associated with an increase in another) or **negative** (where an increase in one variable is associated with a decrease in another).
- In a correlational study, researchers simply measure two variables and correlate the results (for example researchers might measure time spent watching television and violent behaviours).

Problems
Just because a relationship exists between two variables, we cannot assume that there is any *causal* connection. For example, shoe size and life expectancy are negatively correlated – but only because men tend to have shorter life expectancies and larger feet than women.

Observational studies
The direct observation of relatively unconstrained behaviour as it occurs.

Types of observational studies
- **Naturalistic vs laboratory:** naturalistic observations study behaviour as it occurs in an everyday, normal setting (as opposed to a laboratory setting).
- **Disclosed vs undisclosed:** in disclosed observations participants know that they are being observed.
- **Participant:** researchers themselves may participate in the group being observed (e.g. a cult).
- **Systematic vs qualitative:** systematic observations used a clearly organised and agreed classification system whilst qualitative observations are more likely to be in the form of a tape recording, diary or video.

Problems
- **Observer bias:** each observer may differ in how they perceive, value and label behaviours.
- **Ethical problems:** in undisclosed observations consent is not usually obtained – however where consent is obtained (disclosed observations) behaviour may be affected by **demand characteristics**.
- **Control:** in a naturalistic setting variables which may influence behaviour are uncontrolled so cause & effect cannot be studied.
- **Reliability & replicability:** results may vary greatly over time & are difficult to reproduce. Structuring the observation may cause important behaviour to be missed.

Questionnaires
These are used as part of a *survey* (information-gathering exercise) to determine attitudes.
- **Closed vs open questions:** open-ended questions (e.g. 'how do you feel about hunting?') provide responses which may be difficult to summarise or quantify. Closed questions typically comprise a number of fixed choices (e.g. the *Likert scale*) but may not allow the participant to give the response they wish to give.
- **Reliability vs validity:** reliability refers to how consistently a scale measures a variable and is often checked by re-testing. Validity refers to how accurately a scale measures what it is intended to measure.
- **Common problems:** questions may be leading, too complex, or unclear.

Interviews
In interviews researchers typically have more time with each respondent and impose less structure on the information to be obtained.
- **Semi-structured interviews:** set out to obtain personal views by using open-ended sets of questions. Respondents are encouraged to respond normally and openly. The interviewer is able to order the questions in a way which feels natural and conversational and to follow up points in detail.
- **Problems:** interviews are more likely to be subject to interpersonal variables, such as the relationship between interviewer and interviewee and the potentially leading nature of questions.

RESEARCH METHODS –

RESEARCH DESIGN AND IMPLEMENTATION

KEY QUESTIONS
- What are hypotheses, samples, validity and operational definitions?
- What types of experimental design are there?
- What sources of bias may affect experiments?

Section 1: Research aims and hypotheses

1 Define an *operational definition*.
2 What is the difference between a *directional hypothesis* and a *non-directional hypothesis*?
3 Why do researchers use samples?
4 Complete the sentence: 'In order to consider a sample to be ____ of a population we must assume that it has been drawn at ____ from that population'.
5 What is a *sampling error*?
6 What term applies to a statistical difference so large that it is unlikely to have occurred by chance alone?
7 What does a *null hypothesis* claim?
8 What is the name of the hypothesis that is provisionally supported if the null hypothesis is rejected?
9 What level of probability is normally used in psychological research?
10 What does the term *experimental validity* refer to?
11 What does the term *external validity* refer to?
12 What is the difference between *population validity* and *ecological validity*?

Section 2: Experimental designs

13 What is the defining feature of an *independent groups design*?
14 Identify two disadvantages of the independent groups design.
15 How does the *repeated measures design* differ from the independent groups design?
16 Identify two advantages of the repeated measures design.
17 What is *counterbalancing* intended to reduce?
18 What is a *matched pairs design*?

19 Identify two advantages associated with the matched pairs design.

Q

Section 3: Sources of bias

20 What name is given to variables other than the ones under study which could have caused the experimental effects?
21 What is the purpose of a *pilot study*?
22 In general, how do researchers rule out variables other than those under study which might interfere with the results?
23 In what way did Rosenthal & Lawson (1964) demonstrate *experimenter bias*?
24 What is a *double-blind experiment*?
25 How does Orne (1962) define *demand characteristics*?
26 What cues did Orne & Scheibe (1964) provide in order to demonstrate the effect of demand characteristics in their experiment?
27 Identify one way in which *social desirability* may affect the behaviour of participants in psychological experiments.
28 What is the criterion which must be met in order for a sample to be considered *random*?
29 What term is used to apply to the type of sample in which people volunteer?
30 Why is a *stratified sample* sometimes used in research?
31 What type of sample is one in which every tenth person on a list is selected?
32 Complete the following sentence: 'A captive group, such as a psychology class at school or college can be termed an ____ or ____ sample'.

Section 1: Research aims and hypotheses

1 An operational definition is one which defines a variable in terms of the steps taken to measure it.

2 A directional hypothesis predicts a difference and the direction of the difference whilst a non-directional hypothesis predicts only that there will be a difference and not the direction.

3 Researchers use samples because it is often impractical to test an entire population.

4 'In order to consider a sample to be *representative* of a population we must assume that it has been drawn at *random* from that population.'

5 A sampling error refers to the differences between samples drawn at random from a population.

6 A statistical difference so large that it is unlikely to have occurred by chance alone is termed a *significant difference*.

7 A null hypothesis claims that there is no significant difference between experimental groups – i.e. that the experimental samples are drawn from the same population.

8 If the null hypothesis is rejected the alternate hypothesis is provisionally accepted.

9 The 5 per cent level of probability (a 5 per cent chance) is normally used in psychological research.

10 The term experimental validity refers to the extent to which a researcher can be sure that the effect apparently demonstrated is real.

11 External validity refers to the degree to which a demonstrated effect can be generalised.

12 Population validity concerns the extent to which a result can be generalised to other groups whilst ecological validity concerns the extent to which a result applies in other environments.

Section 2: Experimental designs

13 An independent groups design tests different participants in each condition of an experiment.

14 Disadvantages: participant variables may confound any effects, and more participants are needed to fill the conditions.

15 The repeated measures design uses the same participants in each of the experimental conditions.

16 Advantages: no participant variables; fewer participants are needed to fill the conditions.

17 Counterbalancing is a technique used to reduce order effects.

18 A matched pairs design is one in which participants across different experimental groups are matched as closely as possible on relevant variables.

19 Advantages: participant variable differences are minimised and there are no order effects.

Section 3: Sources of bias

20 Such variables are termed *confounding variables*.

21 A pilot study can expose and highlight any difficulties in an experimental procedure and allow for adjustments to be made before data-gathering begins.

22 In general, researchers try to control all variables except those under study.

23 Rosenthal & Lawson (1964) demonstrated experimenter bias by allocating rats randomly to groups of students and telling students that the groups of rats were 'bright' or 'dull'. Researchers who believed their rats to be bright did indeed record that their rats learned more quickly.

24 A double-blind experiment is one in which neither the researcher nor the participants know which conditions they (the participants) have been allocated to.

25 Orne (1962) defines demand characteristics as: 'The totality of cues that convey an experimental hypothesis to the subject …'.

26 Orne & Scheibe (1964) provided participants in one experimental condition with a consent form and a 'panic button'.

27 Social desirability may cause participants in psychological experiments to try to produce the 'right results' or to be a 'good participant'.

28 In order for a sample to be considered random every item in the population must have an equal probability of selection.

29 A sample in which people volunteer is called a *self-selecting sample*.

30 A stratified sample is sometimes used to ensure that important sections of a population are proportionately represented in a sample.

31 Such a sample would be called a *systematic sample*.

32 'A captive group, such as a psychology class at school or college, can be termed an *opportunity* or *convenience* sample.'

Research Design and Implementation

Experimental validity

Internal

Refers to the certainty with which we can claim that it was a change in the independent variable that caused a change in the dependent variable:

- **Experimental validity:** is a specific form of internal validity and refers to the extent to which a researcher can be sure that the effect apparently demonstrated is real.
- **Threats to the validity:** of the findings occur due to variables which are not controlled and might, therefore, lead to a mistaken assumption of an effect.

External

Refers to the how general an effect is; the extent to which it might apply to different cultures or in different environments, for example.

- **Populational validity:** concerns the extent to which the researchers can be confident that they would obtain the same effect among different groups of people.
- **Ecological validity:** concerns the generalisation of the effect from the environment (e.g. laboratory) in which it was demonstrated to a different environment.

Experimental designs

Independent groups

Different participants in each condition

Advantages
- No order effects (e.g. participants improving on the second test).
- Loss of one participant from one condition does not entail a loss of the result across all conditions.

Disadvantages
- Participant variables may confound effects.
- More participants are needed to fill conditions.

Repeated measures

Same participants in each condition

Advantages
- No participant variables (since participants are the same in each condition).
- Fewer participants required to obtain results.

Disadvantages
- Order effects (often dealt with by *counterbalancing*: splitting participants into groups who take the conditions in a different order).
- Loss of one participant entails loss of results from all conditions.

Matched pairs

Participants matched between groups

Advantages
- Participant variable effects minimised.
- No order effects.

Disadvantages
- More participants needed to fill conditions.
- Matching is never perfect.

Sources of bias

Confounding

These are variables other than those under study (i.e. the independent and dependent variables) which can affect the outcome of the experiment (e.g. participant variables, order effects). If these are not controlled for other researchers may criticise the design and claim that the effects were not really demonstrated.

Key study: 'bright' rats and 'dull' rats
Rosenthal & Lawson (1964): randomly allocated rats to students, telling one group that its rats were 'bright' and the other that its rats were 'dull'.
Results: the 'bright' rats did learn more quickly, presumably because of the students' expectancies.

Solutions
- **Piloting:** a pilot study can help to identify any flaws in the procedure before the actual data-gathering begins.
- **Single/double blind:** participants may be affected if they know the expected outcome. In single-blind experiments the participants do not know which condition they have been assigned to and in double-blind experiments neither the data-gatherer nor the participants know which conditions have been assigned.

Demand characteristics

Orne (1962): 'The totality of cues that convey an experimental hypothesis to the subject …'.

Key study: panic!
Orne & Scheibe (1964): compared the reactions of two groups of participants left alone in a room. One group had to sign a consent form and had a 'panic button' pointed out. The other group did not.
Results: the group given the cues reacted in a more extreme fashion that those who were not — perhaps attempting to produce the reactions expected by the researchers.

Social desirability
People like to be seen to think and do the 'right thing'. In the research context this may extend to trying to produce the 'right' results or attempting to be a 'good' participant.

Sampling issues

In order to draw conclusions about a population from a study involving a sample of that population, that sample must be representative, and therefore free from bias. The following are commonly used sampling methods:

- **Simple random sampling:** in order to be random every individual in the population must have an equal probability of being selected. This is difficult to achieve and in practice many participants in psychological experiments are *self-selected* (volunteers).
- **Stratified sampling:** in order to represent different sections of the population, it may be divided up into groups and random samples taken from those groups (e.g. ensuring that 5% of the sample are left-handed, but selecting these at random).
- **Systematic sampling:** selecting participants according to a system (e.g. every tenth person in a list).
- **Non-random samples – haphazard, opportunity and convenience:** selecting participants in a shopping mall would not yield a representative sample and would be selected haphazardly. A captive group (e.g. a first-year psychology class) would be termed an opportunity or convenience sample.

RESEARCH METHODS –
DATA ANALYSIS

KEY QUESTIONS
- What are the different levels of measurement?
- What types of descriptive statistics are there?
- How can data be represented graphically?
- How can qualitative data be analysed?

Q Section 1: Descriptive statistics

1 Define *data*.
2 What are *nominal* level data?
3 What are *ordinal* level data?
4 What are *interval* level data?
5 What is a *sampling error*?
6 Which of the above levels of data does not tell us whether a difference is a qualitative or quantitative difference?
7 What is a general problem with reducing data to lower levels?
8 What are *descriptive statistics*?
9 What does a measure of *central tendency* tell us?
10 What does a *measure of dispersion* tell us?
11 What is the difference between the *mode* and the *median* as measures of central tendency?
12 How is the mean value calculated for a data set containing a number of items of information?
13 Identify one disadvantage associated with the mean as a measure of central tendency.
14 Identify two advantages associated with the mode as a measure of central tendency.
15 What is the *range* of a set of values?
16 Complete the sentence: 'A problem with the range is that it tells us nothing about how scores are ____ ____ within the range'.
17 What is the *deviation* of a score?
18 What does a small standard deviation imply about the 'shape' of the data set?

Section 2: Graphical representations

19 What does a *histogram* show?
20 What name is given to a line drawn so as to join the mid points of each of the columns of a histogram?
21 Describe one feature of the columns used in a histogram.
22 In what way does a *bar chart* represent data differently to a histogram?
23 Why are the columns on a bar chart usually separated?
24 Complete the sentence: 'A chart must be a useful, fair and clear ____ of data'.
25 Complete the sentence: 'A chart should have clear ____ and ____'.
26 What name is given to the type of distribution which is commonly assumed by many psychological measures (such as personality and intelligence tests)?
27 What numerical values can a *correlation* take?
28 What does it mean if there is a *negative* correlation between two variables?
29 What is the most common means of representing a correlation graphically?
30 What is the basic problem with interpreting correlational evidence?
31 Historically, what have been the two general reactions to the question of what to do with qualitative data?
32 What general approach is adopted by *content analysis*?
33 Why might researchers undertaking a content analysis be kept unaware of the hypothesis under test?
34 Identify two common possible aims of purely qualitative analysis.
35 What approach to qualitative data is suggested by *grounded theory*?

Section 1: Descriptive statistics

1 Data are items of information.

2 Nominal level data have been classified into categories (e.g. yes/no, anxious/secure).

3 Ordinal level data are data organised into rank order (e.g. a class arranged in height order).

4 Interval level data are data relating to a scale with equal intervals between measurement units (e.g. the height in centimetres of each individual).

5 A sampling error refers to the differences between samples drawn at random from a population.

6 Nominal level data does not tell us whether a difference is a qualitative or quantitative.

7 When we reduce data to lower levels we lose information.

8 Descriptive statistics are tools/methods of summarising sets of data in order to provide a clearer picture of trends within the data set.

9 A measure of central tendency tells us which is the typical or central value in a data set.

10 A measure of dispersion tells us the extent to which data are spread around the centre.

11 The mode is the most common value in a data set, whilst the median is the middle value in a data set which has been arranged in rank order.

12 The mean is calculated by adding up (summing) the scores and dividing the total by the number of scores.

13 The mean can be greatly affected by extreme values in one direction and by *skew*. In addition it is usually not an actual value appearing in the data set.

14 The mode is a simple measure, is equal to at least one of the scores in the data set, and is unaffected by a few extreme scores.

15 The range of a set of values is the distance in units from the top to the bottom value.

16 'A problem with the range is that it tells us nothing about how scores are *spread out* within the range.'

17 The deviation of a score is the distance of that score from its group's mean value.

18 A small standard deviation implies that the scores are grouped more tightly around the mean.

Section 2: Graphical representations

19 A histogram shows the frequency of values in a data set (i.e. the number of times each value occurred).

20 Such a line is termed a *frequency histogram*.

21 The columns in a histogram must be the same width for the same size interval and they should not be separated.

22 Whilst a histogram can only represent frequencies, a bar chart can represent any values (e.g. totals, means, percentages).

23 The columns on a bar chart are usually separated because the categories on the *x*-axis are discrete (i.e. not a continuous scale).

24 'A chart must be a useful, fair and clear *summary* of data.'

25 'A chart should have clear *headings* and *labels*.'

26 Many psychological measures assume a *normal distribution* of aptitudes or characteristics.

27 A correlation can vary between +1 and −1, taking any value in between.

28 If there is a negative correlation between two variables then an increase in one is associated with a decrease in the other and vice versa.

29 A correlation is commonly represented using a *scattergram* (or *scattergraph*).

30 The basic problem with interpreting correlational evidence is that although we may know that two variables are related in some way, we do not know if there is any *causal* connection between the two, or what *direction* any causal connection might take.

31 The two general reactions have been either to find some way to turn the qualitative data into quantitative data, or to deal with the data in purely qualitative terms.

32 Content analysis involves the use of some sort of coding system to categorise qualitative data, in order to convert it to quantitative frequencies.

33 Researchers undertaking a content analysis might be kept unaware of the hypothesis under test in order to ensure that their own biases or expectancies do not somehow guide their data analysis.

34 Purely qualitative analysis may be aimed at exploring and describing the data, testing hypotheses using the data, and generating theories from the data.

35 In grounded theory data are thoroughly searched and cross-referenced with the aim of detecting 'emerging themes' and categories.

A

Data Analysis

Levels of measurement

Nominal level data *(categories)*
Data is classified according to categories, to which labels are attached, e.g. a teacher might classify students according to the subjects they study. There may be *qualitative* differences and *quantitative* differences between the categories.

Ordinal level data *(ranked)*
Data is sorted into rank order, e.g. the overall position of students in the class (such as 'top', 'third'). The intervals between ranks are not known (e.g. we do not know if the difference in marks between 'top' and 'second' is the same as between 'second' and 'third').

Interval level data *(measured units)*
Data represents values on a scale made up of equal intervals (measurement units), e.g. the no. of days absence each student has had. Because these measurements have been standardised it is meaningful to compare the data quantitatively.

Descriptive data

Central tendency
the typical or central value

Mode
The value which occurs most frequently in a data set.
- Unreliable in small data sets but is unaffected by extreme scores ('*outliers*').

Median
The middle value when the values have been placed in order.
- Better than the mode for small data sets but affected badly by skewed data.

Mean
The 'average': calculated by adding up scores & dividing them by the no. of scores.
- Sensitive to all values, but affected by outliers and skewed data.

Dispersion
the extent to which the data are spread around the centre

Range
The distance in units between the top and bottom values of a data set, e.g. 5, 8. Range = 4 (difference + 1).
- Problem: range tells us nothing about how scores are spread out within the range (e.g. 1, 7, 7, 7, 9 vs. 1, 3, 5, 7, 8, 9).

Standard deviation
The deviation of a score refers to how much it differs from the mean value. The standard deviation (SD) is something like the average deviation.
- A large SD tells us the scores are spread out whilst a small SD tells us the scores are clustered around the mean.

Graphical representations

Histograms and frequency polygons
- Each column in a histogram represents the frequency of a value (shown below).
- A frequency polygon is formed by drawing a line joining the midpoints of the columns (shown below, overlaid on histogram).

Bar charts
- Each column represents a *value* (such as group means, percentages, etc.).
- Where values are discrete categories (as below) columns are *separated*.

Correlations and scattergraphs
- A scattergraph illustrates the correlation between two values, with a cross representing each pair.
- In a positive correlation an increase in one score is correlated with an increase in the other. In a negative correlation (shown below) an increase in one variable is correlated with a *decrease* in the other.

Important points to remember
- **A chart must be a useful, clear summary of the data** (not just a representation of it): e.g. a graph with a bar for each person's score doesn't summarise the data meaningfully.
- **Headings should be clear and axes clearly labelled:** a legend may be required, and axes should show the exact units being used.
- **Don't rely on a computer to get it right:** a computer can produce graphs, but only you can take the decisions about what to present and how to present it.

Analysing qualitative data

Qualitative data is data in non-numerical form – such as *descriptions* of participants' behaviours or the *reasons* which they give for their behaviours. These may be combined with quantitative measures and suggest areas for further research. There are two general approaches to qualitative data: one is to reduce the data into quantitative form (typically by categorising) the other resists this reduction and reports the data in qualitative terms (e.g. a written document in which the results are considered).

Content analysis
This involves changing qualitative data into quantitative data by rating or coding it in order to categorise it.
- e.g.: researchers investigating the portrayal of children in advertising might identify a number of possible roles (e.g. consumer, problem, playmate, etc.). The researchers would agree these definitions and then be trained in applying them. Results may then be presented as frequencies or percentages.

Purely qualitative analysis
Typically a complete record of behaviour or talk is obtained, and analysed not statistically but in terms of significant themes or ideas. As far as possible the data are kept in their original form.
- In '*grounded theory*' data (such as transcripts of interviews) are thoroughly searched and cross-referenced with the aim of detecting 'emerging themes' and categories.

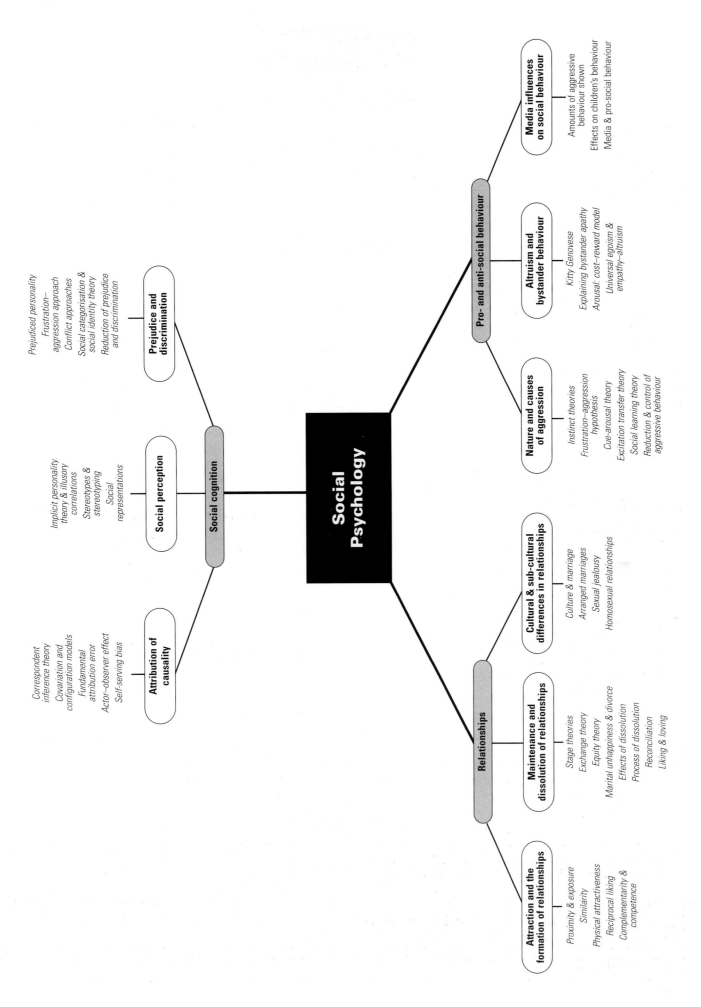

Social Psychology

Social cognition

Attribution of causality
Correspondent inference theory
Covariation and configuration models
Fundamental attribution error
Actor–observer effect
Self-serving bias

Social perception
Implicit personality theory & illusory correlations
Stereotypes & stereotyping
Social representations

Prejudice and discrimination
Prejudiced personality
Frustration–aggression approach
Conflict approaches
Social categorisation & social identity theory
Reduction of prejudice and discrimination

Relationships

Attraction and the formation of relationships
Proximity & exposure
Similarity
Physical attractiveness
Reciprocal liking
Complementarity & competence

Maintenance and dissolution of relationships
Stage theories
Exchange theory
Equity theory
Marital unhappiness & divorce
Effects of dissolution
Process of dissolution
Reconciliation
Liking & loving

Cultural & sub-cultural differences in relationships
Culture & marriage
Arranged marriages
Sexual jealousy
Homosexual relationships

Pro- and anti-social behaviour

Nature and causes of aggression
Instinct theories
Frustration–aggression hypothesis
Cue–arousal theory
Excitation transfer theory
Social learning theory
Reduction & control of aggressive behaviour

Altruism and bystander behaviour
Kitty Genovese
Explaining bystander apathy
Arousal: cost–reward model
Universal egoism & empathy–altruism

Media influences on social behaviour
Amounts of aggressive behaviour shown
Effects on children's behaviour
Media & pro-social behaviour

ATTRIBUTION OF CAUSALITY

KEY QUESTIONS
* What are attribution theories?
* How does the correspondent inference theory explain the attribution process?
* How does the covariation model explain the attribution process?
* What biases affect how attributions are made?

Q

Section 1: Introducing attribution

1 What are *attribution theories* concerned with?
2 Why did Heider believe that the ordinary person was like a *naïve scientist*?
3 Why is it important that members of a culture share a *common psychology*?
4 What is a *dispositional* (or *internal) attribution*?
5 What is a *situational* (or *external) attribution*?

Section 2: Correspondent inference theory

6 What do Jones & Davis (1965) mean by the term *correspondent inference*?
7 Complete the sentence: 'Jones and Davis argue that a precondition for a correspondent inference is the attribution of _____'.
8 Once this precondition has been met, we can look for a disposition which may explain it. According to Jones and Davis, we employ an *analysis of non-common effects* for this purpose. What does this involve?
9 What influence does information regarding the *expectedness* and *social desirability* of a behaviour have on a correspondent inference?
10 Name two other factors which may influence the inference which we draw.

Section 3: Co-variation and configuration models

11 According to Kelley (1967), what is the *principle of covariation*?
12 What is the difference between *distinctiveness information* and *consensus information*?
13 If a behaviour is accompanied by *high consensus* information, is a dispositional or situational attribution more likely?
14 How do we use *consistency, distinctiveness* and *consensus* information, according to the *abnormal conditions focus model*?
15 What is the problem with Kelley's claim that we require three types of information in order to make an attribution?

16 What are *causal schemata*?
17 What is the difference between a behaviour which falls into the *multiple necessary causes* schema and one which falls into the *multiple sufficient causes* schema?
18 How is the *discounting principle* used?
19 Why is Kelley's model a *normative* model of the attributional process?
20 Complete the sentence: 'Our tendency to act as "cognitive _____" means that we do not analyse the interactions between personal and situational factors even if a lot of information is available'.

Section 4: Attributional biases

21 What is the *fundamental attribution error*?
22 Napolitan & Goethals (1979) had students talk with a young woman who behaved in either a cold or a warm manner. Half of the students were told that she was instructed to behave in this manner. What was the effect of this information on the students' attributions?
23 What two explanations for the fundamental attribution error were proposed by Jones & Nisbett (1971)?
24 What did Miller (1984) discover about the attributional process in India?
25 How do the *consequences* of a person's behaviour affect the attributions made for that behaviour?
26 What is the *actor–observer effect*?
27 How does a dislike of being 'pigeon-holed' help us to explain this effect?
28 Complete the sentence: '... another possible explanation suggests that actors do not perceive _____ as they act and are therefore more likely to attribute their behaviour to the situation'.
29 What experiment did Storms (1973) carry out in order to investigate the actor–observer effect?
30 What is the *self-serving bias*?
31 According to this bias, what kind of attribution are you most likely to make to explain a good exam result?
32 In which *clinical condition* is the self-serving bias reversed?

Section 1: Introducing attribution

1 Attribution theories are concerned with the ways in which we explain behaviour, in particular the general principles governing our selection and use of information to arrive at causal explanations for behaviour.

2 Heider believed that we are naïve scientists in that we try to link observable behaviours to unobservable causes.

3 Without a common psychology, members of a culture would find it difficult to understand and be understood by others. Social life would be impossible.

4 A dispositional (or internal) attribution is an explanation of a behaviour in terms of the enduring characteristics of the actor, such as his/her personality, motivation or abilities.

5 A situational (or external) attribution is an explanation of behaviour by reference to external events not under the direct control of the actor, such as illness, accidents, and environmental pressures.

Section 2: Correspondent inference theory

6 A correspondent inference (Jones & Davis, 1965) is made when we infer whether or not a person's dispositions correspond to their behaviour.

7 'Jones and Davis argue that a precondition for a correspondent inference is the attribution of *intentionality*.'

8 An analysis of non-common effects involves looking at the number of differences between the chosen course of action and those that are not. These can be used to explain why the individual chose a particular behaviour.

9 Behaviour which is expected or socially desirable tells us very little about a person. For example, teachers can tell very little about the characters of their students so long as they behave as students are expected to. When behaviour is unexpected or undesirable, we find it more informative.

10 Free choice and prior expectations also influence the inference we draw.

Section 3: Co-variation and configuration models

11 The principle of covariation states that 'an effect is attributed to one of its possible causes with which, over time, it co-varies'.

12 Distinctiveness information tells us whether or not the person reacts in the same way towards other similar stimuli or entities, whilst consensus information tells us whether or not others behave in the same way towards the same stimulus.

13 If a behaviour is accompanied by high consensus information a situational attribution is more likely.

14 We use this information to determine whether it is the actor or some aspect of the situation which is abnormal, attributing the cause to whatever is abnormal.

15 We frequently make attributions without having access to all three types of information.

16 Causal schemata are ready-made beliefs or preconceptions about how certain kinds of causes interact to produce certain effects.

17 Behaviour falling into the multiple sufficient causes schema could be caused by any number of things, whilst one which falls into the multiple necessary causes schema must have involved many causes.

18 The discounting principle is used to discount the least plausible of the explanations for a behaviour falling into the multiple sufficient causes schema.

19 Kelley's model is normative because it tells us how people should make attributions rather than how they actually do.

20 'Our tendency to act as "cognitive *misers*" means that we do not analyse the interactions between personal and situational factors even if a lot of information is available.'

Section 4: Attributional biases

21 The fundamental attribution error is the tendency to overestimate the importance of dispositional or personal or situational factors, and underestimate external or situational factors for other people's behaviours.

22 Nothing whatsoever. The students completely disregarded the 'situational' information in making their attributions.

23 Nisbett (1971) proposed that there is a different focus of attention when we see ourselves from when we judge others and that different types of information (such as how consistent the behaviour is) are available when judging our own behaviour.

24 Miller (1984) found that in India people were far more likely to give situational attributions for others' behaviour.

25 The more negative and serious the consequence of a person's behaviour, the more likely we are to blame them for it (e.g. reporters after the death of Princess Diana).

26 The actor–observer effect is the tendency to make different attributions for behaviour depending on whether we are performing or observing it.

27 We dislike being 'pigeon-holed', and so are less likely to explain our own behaviour in terms of trait labels (dispositional attribution).

28 '… another possible explanation suggests that actors do not perceive *themselves* as they act and are therefore more likely to attribute their behaviour to the situation.'

29 Storms (1973) showed participants a video of their behaviour from another person's perspective, and found that the direction of attributions was reversed.

30 The self-serving bias is the tendency to 'take credit' for positive events and 'deny responsibility' for negative events.

31 A good exam result must surely be the result of your hard work and high ability (internal attribution).

32 Those suffering from clinical depression seem to blame themselves for negative events and attribute positive events to external factors.

A

Attribution: an explanation of why an individual behaved in a certain way.
Attribution theory: the general principles governing our selection and use of information to arrive at causal explanations for behaviour.

Heider (1958)
The ordinary person is like a *naïve scientist*, linking behaviours to causes.
Explanations are either:
- *dispositional/internal* (e.g. ability or effort)
- *situational/external* (e.g. illness or luck).

Correspondent inference theory

Jones & Davis (1965)
- An attribution involves deciding whether or not a person's *dispositions* (e.g. kindness) correspond to their intentions (e.g. buying flowers).
- If behaviour and dispositions do not correspond, we may decide that the *situation* has caused the behaviour.
- In order to make an inference, we must first decide if the behaviour was intentional.
- If behaviour is intentional, an analysis of *non-common effects* is carried out in order to see why the person chose this option (e.g. this was the *only* available option which would have impressed a particular member of the opposite sex).
- Other important factors may then be considered:
  - **Free choice:** if the person was pressurised, their behaviour may not reflect their dispositions.
  - **Expectedness/social desirability:** expected/desirable behaviours tell us little about dispositions.
  - **Prior expectations:** help us to judge whether or not a particular behaviour is in character.

Covariation and configuration models

Covariation model
Kelley (1967)
An attribution about the cause of a behaviour depends on the extent to which it covaries with three types of information:

e.g. Why is Pete always late for psychology?

Consensus	**Distinctiveness**	**Consistency**
Extent to which others behave in the same way.	Extent to which the person behaves in the same way to similar stimuli.	The stability of the behaviour across time.
Is everyone late for psychology?	*Is Pete also late for sociology?*	*Is Pete always late for psychology?*
no = low consensus	no = high distinctiveness	no = low consistency
yes = high consensus	yes = low distinctiveness	yes = high consistency

Research
- McArthur (1972): people do make attributions in the direction suggested by the model when given the three types of information.
- **Abnormal conditions focus model** (Hilton & Slugoski, 1986): the three types of information help tell if it is the *situation* or the actor which is *abnormal* (*e.g. if everyone else is on time, Pete is abnormal*).

Configuration model
Kelley (1972)
- In many situations we do not have all three kinds of information.
- In these '*single-event attributions*', we make attributions by slotting behaviour into '*causal schemata*' ('stereotyped' explanations).
- Causal schemata are a shorthand way of explaining events; two principal types:

Multiple sufficient causes
Any number of causes could explain the behaviour.
e.g. a pop-star advertising cola.
A *discounting principle* is used to eliminate unlikely causes.

Multiple necessary causes
Many causes are needed to produce the behaviour.
e.g. winning a marathon.

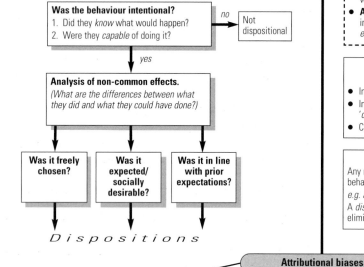

Was the behaviour intentional?
1. Did they *know* what would happen?
2. Were they *capable* of doing it?

no → Not dispositional

yes

Analysis of non-common effects.
(What are the differences between what they did and what they could have done?)

Was it freely chosen? | **Was it expected/ socially desirable?** | **Was it in line with prior expectations?**

D i s p o s i t i o n s

Attributional biases

The fundamental attribution error

The tendency for observers to underestimate situational influences and overestimate dispositional influences upon others' behaviour (Ross, 1977).

Napolitan & Goethals (1979)
- Students talked with a young woman who was either warm and friendly or cold and critical.
- Half were told behaviour was spontaneous, half that she was instructed to behave that way.

Results: both groups inferred that she was warm when she was friendly, and cold when unfriendly, regardless of whether they knew that she was acting as instructed.

Explanations (Jones & Nisbett, 1971)
1. *Focus of attention*: when we act, we focus on the situation; when another acts, we focus on them and not the situation.
2. *Types of information*: we have more consistency information available when judging ourselves, and know what it is we are attending to.

The actor–observer effect

The tendency to make different attributions about a behaviour depending on whether we are *performing* (acting) or *observing* it. If acting, we tend to make external attributions, if observing we tend to make dispositional attributions.

Storms (1973):
- Pairs of participants talked across a table and were videoed.
- When shown the video of their behaviour, they tended to make *internal* attributions, not external attributions as is typical.

Explanations
1. We do not like to be pigeon-holed, so do not explain our behaviours with trait-labels.
2. Observers assume actors always behave in the way they have seen; actors know they have behaved differently.
3. People do not *perceive* themselves, they focus on their situation. When observing, they focus on the actor, not the actor's situation.

The self-serving bias

The tendency for us to 'take the credit' (*internal attribution*) when things go right, and 'deny responsibility' (*external attribution*) when things go wrong.

- Lau & Russell (1980): American football players attributed wins to internal causes (e.g. determination) and defeats to external causes (e.g. injuries).
- Arkin *et al.* (1980): students regard exams in which they do well as good indicators of their abilities, and those in which they do badly as poor indicators.
- Abramson *et al.* (1978): depressed people reverse this pattern, attributing success to luck and failure to a lack of ability.

Explanations
Greenberg *et al.* (1982): the bias serves our *needs*, such as the need to maintain self-esteem. 'Taking the credit' is a *self-enhancing bias*, denying responsibility is a *self-protecting bias*.

SOCIAL PERCEPTION

SYLLABUS

13.1 Social cognition – social perception
- social and cultural influences on the perception of the social world, including the nature of social representations and of social and cultural stereotyping

KEY QUESTIONS
- What is implicit personality theory?
- What are stereotypes and how can we explain them?
- What are social representations and how are they formed?

Section 1: Implicit personality theory

1. What did the participants in Asch's (1946) study do when presented with a list of characteristics describing a fictitious individual?
2. What is the difference between a *central trait* and a *peripheral trait*?
3. What is the *halo effect*? Can you give an example of a term likely to induce a positive halo?
4. Bruner & Tagiuri (1954) coined the term *implicit personality theory*. What does it describe?
5. What sort of people are likely to share similar implicit personality theories?
6. What is an *illusory correlation*?

Section 2: Stereotypes

7. What is a *social stereotype*?
8. What did Katz & Braly (1933) find in their investigation of stereotyping in Princeton University students?
9. When Gagahan (1991) criticises studies of stereotyping for *social desirability responding*, what does she mean?
10. How did Razran (1950) overcome the problem of social desirability responding?
11. According to Campbell (1967), why must stereotypes contain a *'grain of truth'*?
12. Why do illusory correlations cast doubt on the 'grain of truth' hypothesis?
13. When Hamilton & Gifford (1976) read equal proportions of positive and negative statements about members of either small or large groups, what effect did they observe?
14. According to Wegner & Vallacher (1976), how do we explain 'odd' behaviour?
15. What is the *confirmation bias*?
16. Complete the following sentence: 'Tajfel sees stereotyping as a special case of categorisation which involves an exaggeration of _____ within groups and of _____ between groups'.

17. According to Brislin (1993), why should we not view stereotyping as an *abnormal cognitive process*?
18. We often assume that a stereotype is intended to apply to *all* members of a stereotyped group. What did McCauley & Stitt (1978) find when investigating stereotypes of Germans?
19. Why do we rely on stereotypes to form impressions of strangers?
20. Complete the sentence: 'Perhaps stereotypes are resistant to change because they represent ways of _____ our complex social world'.

Section 3: Social representations

21. How does Moscovici define *social representations*?
22. What is an *anchor* in social representations research?
23. What two processes are used to *objectify* an abstract concept, in order to make it concrete?
24. How has *figuration* been applied to Freud's psychodynamic model?
25. What social representation has resulted from *split-brain* studies?
26. According to Durkin (1995), why do children make use of social representations?
27. What is the role of social representations in child-rearing practices?
28. How might social representations concerning 'intelligence' influence the way in which children are taught?
29. Why did a student protest staged by Belgian student-leaders fail, according to Di Giacomo's (1980) research?
30. According to Moscovici (1984), what features of social representations allow them to be both *durable* and *open to change*?
31. What is perhaps the major weakness with social representations theory?

Q

Section 1: Implicit personality theory

1 The participants in Asch's (1946) study inferred further character traits from a list of characteristics describing a fictitious individual.

2 Central traits, such as 'warm' or 'cold', exert a major influence on our perceptions of others, whilst peripheral traits, such as 'polite' or 'blunt', exert only a minor influence on our overall impressions.

3 The halo effect involves attributing to someone a range of characteristics we associate with a particularly favourable or unfavourable characteristic. Such characteristics are usually evaluative, such as 'generous' (positive halo) or 'cruel' (negative halo).

4 Implicit personality theory describes the unconscious inference processes that enable us to form impressions of others based on very little evidence.

5 People from the same culture or group are the most likely to share similar implicit personality theories.

6 An illusory correlation is the belief that two variables (such as race and aggressiveness) are correlated, when in fact they are not.

Section 2: Stereotypes

7 A social stereotype is a grossly oversimplified and generalised abstraction that people share about their own or another group.

8 Katz & Braly (1933) found that Princeton University students held strong traditional stereotypes about ethnic minorities, especially derogatory stereotypes, despite having (in most cases) no personal contact with members of the stereotyped groups.

9 Gagahan (1991) is pointing out that participants in research into stereotypes may simply give the response which they believe is most socially acceptable or desirable and, as a consequence, not reveal their true attitudes.

10 Razran (1950) deceived his participants into believing that they would be rating pictures of girls according to their psychological characteristics. In fact, the same picture was given a different ethnic group name, and differences in the traits reported attributed to ethnic stereotyping.

11 Campbell (1967) claims that stereotypes originate in at least one person's experience before being communicated to others, so must contain a 'grain of truth'.

12 In order for stereotypes to contain a grain of truth, traits must have been correctly inferred from behaviour. However, illusory correlations demonstrate that we may associate certain traits with certain behaviour without there being any such relationship.

13 Hamilton & Gifford (1976) found that participants rated members of the smaller group as being less desirable, despite there being no relationship between the group and this characteristic.

14 Wegner & Vallacher (1976) claim that we explain 'odd' behaviour as being due to the actor's membership in an unusual group.

15 The confirmation bias is the tendency for us to seek out information which confirms our existing beliefs.

16 'Tajfel sees stereotyping as a special case of categorisation which involves an exaggeration of *similarities* within groups and of *differences* between groups.'

17 Brislin (1993) argues that stereotypes are 'categories about people', and simply reflect a general need to organise, remember and retrieve potentially useful information.

18 McCauley & Stitt (1978) found that traits stereotypically assigned to Germans were not believed by their participants to apply to all Germans.

19 It might be ethically correct to form impressions based only on unique characteristics of individuals, but this attribute-driven processing involves more cognitive effort than category-driven processing, where judgements are based on group membership.

20 'Perhaps stereotypes are resistant to change because they represent ways of *simplifying* our complex social world.'

Section 3: Social representations

21 Social representations are ' ... a set of concepts, statements and explanations originating in daily life in the course of inter-individual communications'.

22 An anchor is a concept established within a pre-existing system of beliefs to which new experiences can be related.

23 Personification and figuration are used to objectify an abstract concept in order to make it concrete.

24 Figuration has led people to portray the impulsive id as a demon perched on one shoulder, with the moral superego balanced on the other.

25 Moscovici & Hewstone (1983) argue that Sperry's (1964) split-brain studies have become transformed into a social representation of a logical left-brained type person and an intuitive right-brained type person.

26 Durkin (1995) claims that children make use of social representations in order to understand the adult world, making 'the unfamiliar familiar' by incorporating the puzzling features of the adult world into their own collective practices.

27 Social representations help adults to know what to expect of children and what should be done with them.

28 Teachers who believe that 'intelligence' is inherited will be less inclined to stimulate under-achievers than those who believe that 'intelligence' is a product of experience.

29 Di Giacomo (1980) found that the social representation of students differed between the student-leaders and the students themselves. Leaders were more likely to associate students with solidarity.

30 Moscovici (1984) sees social representations as having a solid 'central figurative nucleus', surrounded by 'peripheral elements' which may change.

31 Social representations theory is vague and 'fuzzy', and as a consequence largely unfalsifiable since it does not suggest many hypotheses which can be tested experimentally.

Social Perception

Implicit personality theory

Bruner & Taguiri (1954)
Implicit personality theory (IPT): beliefs about which personality traits belong together. We use IPTs to 'fill in the gaps' when we have little information about people. IPTs are consistent within a culture.

Illusory correlations: may result from IPTs where we see certain variables as being related when in fact they are not.

Stereotypes

The nature of stereotypes

Stereotyping: a form of IPT where a single item about a person (appearance or verbal label) is used to generate inferences about their character.

Individual stereotype: judgements about what a person from a given group is like.

Group stereotype: belief that all people from a given group share the same characteristics.

Social stereotypes: grossly oversimplified and generalised abstractions that people share about their own or other groups (Oakes *et al.*, 1994).

Explaining stereotyping

The 'grain of truth' hypothesis
Campbell (1967) believes that stereotypes arise from two sources:
- a person's experience of another person.
- communicating that experience to others.

Stereotypes therefore originate in at least one person's experience.

However, this assumes that people make logical inferences, whereas in fact *illusory correlations* may cause people to infer traits wrongly from their experiences.

Explaining illusory correlations

- Wegner & Vallacher (1976): illusory correlations (ICs) arise from a tendency to attribute 'odd' behaviours to membership of an unusual group.
- **The confirmation bias:** ensures that once we have made an IC we seek out information which supports it.

Stereotyping as a cognitive process

- Tajfel (1971): stereotyping is a special case of *categorisation* involving an exaggeration of differences *between* groups and similarities *within* groups.
- Brown (1986): stereotypes are 'an intrinsic, essential and primitive aspect of cognition'.
- Other psychologists see generalisations as false and illogical. However, people may not believe a stereotype applies to every member of a group (see below).

Social representations

The nature of social representations

Anchoring and objectifying
Anchors: established concepts within a pre-existing system to which new experiences can be related.

Objectifying: making abstract things concrete in a way that most people can understand. Achieved by:
1. *personification* (linking ideas with a person's name, e.g. Freud)
2. *figuration* (converting complex ideas into images and metaphors, e.g. 'black holes').

Social representations (SRs): the shared beliefs and expectations held by the society or group to which we belong (Moscovici, 1981).
- SRs provide the *framework* within which we can make sense of and communicate about the world.
- SRs are 'the essence of social cognition' (Moscovici, 1981).

SRs in childhood
Durkin (1995) argues that SRs apply in two ways to childhood:
1. They are used by children to make sense of the world (e.g. the rules which adults impose on them).
2. They are used by members of a society to know what expectations and beliefs to have towards children, and how to treat them as a result (e.g. whether or not intelligence is inherited).

Other research
- Di Giacomo (1980): studied a protest staged by Belgian students. Leaders' SRs saw students as 'workers' needing 'solidarity'. The students did not. The protest failed.
- Moscovici (1984): SRs are stable because they combine a stable 'nucleus' with changeable peripheral elements.

65

PREJUDICE AND DISCRIMINATION

Section 1: Introducing prejudice

1   What are the three components common to all attitudes?
2   What is the difference between prejudice and discrimination?

Section 2: The frustration–aggression approach

3   What was the aim of Adorno *et al.*'s (1950) research?
4   What did Adorno *et al.* believe about the link between upbringing and prejudice?
5   Which of Adorno's inventories was found to be highly correlated with scores on all of the other inventories?
6   What name did Adorno *et al.* give to individuals who scored highly on this particular inventory?
7   What historical aspect of prejudice suggests that Adorno *et al.*'s theory is inadequate as an explanation of prejudice?
8   What did Minard (1952) discover when assessing the attitudes of white coal-miners towards their black fellow workers above ground and underground?
9   What does Dollard *et al.*'s (1939) *frustration–aggression hypothesis* state?
10 How was Weatherley (1961) able to demonstrate *scapegoating* of Jews under laboratory conditions?

Section 3: Conflict approaches

11 Complete the sentence: 'According to relative deprivation theory, the discrepancy between our _____ and _____ _____ produces frustration'.
12 What is the principal source of inter-group conflict, according to *realistic conflict theory*?
13 What experiment did Sherif *et al.* (1961) carry out which supports realistic conflict theory?
14 How did Sherif *et al.* (1961) succeed in reducing the prejudice which they had created?
15 What was involved in Aronson *et al.*'s (1978) *jigsaw classroom technique*?
16 How successful was Aronson *et al.*'s approach at reducing prejudicial attitudes?

Section 4: Social categorisation and social identity

17 How were the boys in Tajfel *et al.*'s (1971) minimal group experiments assigned to their groups.
18 What did Tajfel *et al.* discover about the boys' allocation of points?
19 *Social categorisation theory* claims that people tend to divide up the world into two categories. What are these?
20 According to social categorisation theory, how is prejudice caused?
21 What, according to *social identity theory*, are the two components of a positive self-image?
22 How can social identity theory be criticised?
23 What term is used to describe the phenomenon in which both groups come to see themselves in the right and the opposition in the wrong?
24 Why might *increased contact* not be sufficient in itself for a reduction in prejudice to occur?
25 Which two additional suggestions for the reduction of prejudice are made in Allport's (1954) *contact hypothesis*?
26 What did Deutsch & Collins (1951) find when they studied the effects of integrated housing projects?

Section 5: Social learning theory

27 According to *social learning theory*, what is the source of negative racial attitudes?
28 What does it mean to say that 'parents should encourage self-examination in their children'?
29 How did Elliot (1977) enable her students to experience the effects of prejudice and discrimination directly?
30 Identify two ethical concerns which might apply to Elliot's study.
31 According to Milner, what is the *primary motivation* behind the development of prejudicial attitudes in children?
32 How does this motivation relate to the phenomenon of *misidentification*?

Section 1: Introducing prejudice

1 All attitudes have cognitive, affective and behavioural components.

2 An unjustified negative attitude towards a group and its members is called *prejudice*. Discrimination is the behavioural component of this attitude.

Section 2: The frustration–aggression approach

3 Adorno *et al.* (1950) aimed to discover whether or not a link between personality and prejudice existed, in an attempt to understand the emergence of anti-Semitism and ethnocentrism in Nazi Germany.

4 Adorno *et al.* believed that an excessively harsh disciplinary attitude might create aggression which could not be directed at parents, and so might be displaced onto an alternative target.

5 The potentiality for fascism scale (F scale) was found to be highly correlated with scores on the other scales.

6 Adorno *et al.* called such individuals *authoritarian personalities*.

7 Historically, prejudice has been widespread in certain cultures at certain times. It is hard to see how this could result from personality differences alone.

8 Minard (1952) discovered that 80 per cent of the white miners were friendly to their black fellow workers underground as opposed to only 20 per cent when they were above ground. This suggests that conformity to social norms plays a significant role in prejudicial attitudes.

9 Dollard *et al.*'s (1939) frustration–aggression hypothesis states that frustration always leads to aggression, and aggression is always a result of frustration.

10 Weatherley (1961) insulted students who scored either high or low on an anti-Semitism scale, then had all participants write short stories about pictures of men, some of whom had Jewish-sounding names.

Section 3: Conflict approaches

11 'According to relative deprivation theory, the discrepancy between our *expectations* and *actual achievements* produces frustration.'

12 Realistic conflict theory maintains that the principal source of inter-group conflict is competition for scarce resources.

13 Sherif *et al.* (1961) generated competition between two groups of white American boys at summer camp (the 'Rattlers' and the 'Eagles'). The boys competed for rewards, and negative attitudes quickly arose.

14 Sherif *et al.* (1961) engineered a problem with their shared water supply, requiring the boys to work together to restore the supply. Working to achieve this superordinate goal reduced prejudice.

15 Aronson *et al.*'s (1978) jigsaw classroom technique involved children working in small inter-racial groups. Each child was given part of a task, but all were tested on the whole, so they had to work together to succeed.

16 The approach reduced prejudice between the students concerned, but changes in attitudes may not be long-term or generalised to whole groups.

Section 4: Social categorisation and social identity

17 The boys in Tajfel *et al.*'s (1971) minimal group experiments were assigned arbitrarily (e.g. by the toss of a coin).

18 Tajfel *et al.* discovered that the boys would always allocate more points to their own groups, even when a co-operative strategy would have been to both groups' advantage.

19 People tend to divide up the world into ingroups ('us') and outgroups ('them').

20 Prejudice is caused by categorising individuals into groups, since people favour their own groups (categorisation is a sufficient condition for prejudice).

21 A positive self-image is comprised of a personal identity and a social identity.

22 Support for social identity theory is principally from minimal group experiments, which may lack ecological validity. Additionally, research only shows a positive bias towards the ingroup, not derogatory attitudes towards the outgroup.

23 The mirror-image phenomenon.

24 Increased contact may fail if groups are of unequal status. In particular the 'superior' group may rationalise the inequality.

25 Allport's (1954) contact hypothesis suggests that equal status contact and the pursuit of common goals may reduce prejudice.

26 Deutsch & Collins (1951) found that residents of integrated housing schemes were less prejudiced than those who did not live in integrated housing.

Section 5: Social learning theory

27 Negative racial attitudes arise from 'significant others' (such as parents, peers or teachers) or from the media (especially television and films).

28 Children should be encouraged to look more closely at the things they do or say to determine whether or not they reflect prejudice or discrimination (e.g. statements like 'You're alright – you're just like a white person').

29 Elliot artificially created prejudice and discrimination amongst some students by encouraging discrimination towards other students based on their eye-colour.

30 The children were only nine years old and not in a position to give informed consent for the experiment. In addition, some may have suffered stress and discomfort as a consequence of the study.

31 Children are motivated by a need to locate themselves and their groups within the social world in a way which promotes positive personal and social identities.

32 Children from minority groups may choose to identify with the majority group (misidentification) if they are prevented from forming a positive image of their own group.

Prejudice & Discrimination

The prejudiced personality — Emotional sources — Frustration–aggression hypothesis

The authoritarian personality (Adorno *et al.*, 1950)

Prejudice is the result of personality development. Children who are harshly disciplined might displace their aggression onto alternative targets (such as minority groups), especially those who are weaker or who cannot fight back.

- Adorno *et al.* (1950) devised several personality inventories to measure: anti-semitism (*AS scale*) (negative opinions of Jews), Ethnocentrism (*E scale*) (belief in own group's superiority), political–economic conservatism (*PEC scale*) (resistance to change), potentiality for fascism (*F scale*) (authoritarian trends).

Results: those who scored highly on the F-scale scored highly on the other scales, and were likely to have had the childhood described above.

Problems with Adorno *et al.*'s research

- Their scales consisted of statements which would always indicate authoritarianism if agreed with. This can produce biases due to *response set*.
- The original sample was biased (white, middle-class, non-Jewish Americans).
- The theory cannot explain widespread prejudice at times in history.

Dollard *et al.* (1939)

- Frustration always gives rise to aggression, and aggression is always caused by frustration.
- Frustration (caused by being blocked from achieving a desirable goal) cannot always be dealt with by direct aggression and we may displace the aggression onto a 'scapegoat'.

Laboratory studies (Weatherley, 1961)

Weatherley had experimenters insult students who scored either low or high on measures of anti-semitism.

- Both groups had to write short stories about pictures of men, two of whom had Jewish-sounding names.
- Groups did not differ in aggression shown towards non-Jews, but high-scorers showed more aggression when writing about those with Jewish names.

Relative deprivation theory — Conflict approaches — Realistic conflict theory

- Frustration is produced by the discrepancy between our *expectations* and our actual *attainments*.
- Relative deprivation occurs when attainments fall short of rising expectations.
- *Fraternalistic deprivation* occurs when individuals compare their attainments with a dissimilar group (e.g. the Los Angeles riots, based on the poor treatment of Rodney King in comparison with treatment of whites).
- *Egoistic relative deprivation* occurs when individuals make comparisons with other similar individuals.
- Vivian & Brown (1995): the most militant blacks were those with high educational status, presumably because their expectations are high and their treatment still poor.

Robber's Cave field experiment (Sherif *et al.*, 1961)

- Sherif (1966) proposes that prejudice arises as a consequence of *competition* for scarce resources. Competition is a sufficient condition for the occurrence of hostility or conflict.
- He divided twenty-two 11- and 12-year-old white middle-class boys attending summer camp into two groups who were housed separately out of sight of each other.
- Groups created strong group identities (the 'Rattlers' and the 'Eagles').
- Competitive events were organised and the two groups came to view each other in negative ways, fighting with each other.
- Attempts to resolve this by having them eat together failed (*desegregation*).
- However, when the shared water supply was 'cut off', and groups had to work together to restore it, prejudices and negative stereotypes were greatly reduced (*superordinate goals*).

Jigsaw classroom technique (Aronson *et al.*, 1978)

- Students are allocated to small inter-racial groups & each child is given a part of the lesson to be learned, and the group is tested on the whole lesson.
- In order to succeed, students must co-operate.

Social categorisation & social identity

- People divide themselves into *ingroups* ('us') and *outgroups* ('them').
- This is necessary for discrimination, and sufficient by itself to produce discrimination.
- Ingroups see themselves positively and tend to see differences among themselves (the ingroup differentiation hypothesis).
- Outgroups are evaluated less favourably and seen to be all alike (*the illusion of outgroup homogeneity*).

Minimal group experiments (Tajfel *et al.*, 1971)

- 14–15-year-old Bristol schoolboys were randomly assigned to one of two groups.
- Boys were told which group they belonged to but did not meet any of the others.
- Boys worked on tasks involving allocating points to members of both groups.
- Boys allocated more points to their own groups, even when a co-operative strategy would have earned more points overall.

Tajfel concluded that just knowing that another group exists is sufficient for discrimination to occur.

Social Identity (Tajfel & Turner, 1986)

- People strive to maintain a *positive self-image*.
- There are two components to this: personal identity (our personal traits) & social identity (derived from group membership)

In order to enhance self-esteem, individuals make social comparisons with other groups, each trying to evaluate itself more highly. This leads to social competition.

The 'contact hypothesis' of prejudice reduction

Contact hypothesis (Allport, 1954): 'Prejudice … may be reduced by equal status contact between minority and majority groups in the pursuit of common goals'.

Coalminers

Minard (1952) studied white coalminers in the USA, and found that underground 80% were friendly towards blacks, with only 20% being friendly above ground.

This suggests that equal status below ground and social norms above ground decreased, and increased prejudice.

Social learning & childhood identity

Social learning theory suggests that children acquire negative attitudes as a result of parents, peers, teachers and the media (e.g. seeing groups in comic or demeaning roles on TV or film).

Experience of prejudice and discrimination

Jane Elliot (1977): divided her 9-year-old pupils into blue-eyed and brown-eyed groups.

- Treated groups differently depending on eye-colour.

Results: children who were treated more poorly did more poorly in homework, and became depressed and angry. Children 'on top' treated outgroup very badly. When treatment was reversed, patterns reversed.

Racism & childhood identity

Milner (1996, 1997): disagrees with the social learning view that the development of children's racial attitudes is a passive process in which children simply 'absorb' implicit or explicit racism from their culture.

- Children are actively engaged in constructing a sense of identity.
- This identity must locate themselves and their groups in a way which establishes and sustains a positive self-and social-regard.
- Negative racial attitudes may help the child to align itself with the majority group.
- However, the minority group cannot gain in self-esteem through negative racial attitudes and misidentification may occur, resulting in self-denigration.

Clark & Clark (1947): asked black and white children aged 3–7 to choose between a black or white doll to play with.

Regardless of their own colour, children chose to play with the white dolls, describing them as prettier and nicer.

11

ATTRACTION AND THE FORMATION OF RELATIONSHIPS

SYLLABUS

13.1 Relationships – attraction and the formation of relationships
- explanations and research studies relating to interpersonal attraction (e.g. matching hypothesis). Theories and research studies relating to the formation of relationships (e.g. reward/need satisfaction, sociobiological theory)

KEY QUESTIONS
- How is the formation of relationships affected by proximity and exposure?
- How significant is similarity in relationship formation?
- How does attractiveness influence relationship formation?
- How do reciprocity, complementarity and competence influence liking?

Section 1: Affiliation

1 How do psychologists define *affiliation*?
2 Under what circumstances would you expect the need for affiliation to be greatest?
3 What did Schachter (1959) find when he led groups of female students to believe they were about to receive either painful or painless electric shocks?
4 Complete the sentence: 'According to Clore & Byrne (1974), we are attracted to people whose presence is _____ for us'.

Section 2: Proximity and exposure

5 What did Festinger *et al.* (1950) discover when investigating the patterns of relationships formed between students living in campus accommodation?
6 According to Hall (1959), what are *proxemic rules*?
7 What is meant by saying that successful relationships may require an initial establishment of *boundary understandings*?
8 What is Zajonc's (1968) *mere exposure effect*?

Section 3: Similarity

9 What did Newcomb (1961) discover when comparing the effects of *similarity* and *familiarity*?
10 What is the relationship between sharing of attitudes and liking?
11 Identify Rubin's (1973) five reasons why similarity is *rewarding*.
12 What explanation for the effect of similarity on liking is offered by *balance theory* (Heider, 1946; Newcomb, 1953)?
13 How does balance theory differ from Rosenbaum's (1986) *repulsion hypothesis*?

Section 4: Physical attractiveness

14 Give five differences between the ways in which attractive and unattractive people are perceived.

15 Are there any exceptions to the rule 'what is beautiful, is good', according to psychological research?
16 What did Dion (1972) find when investigating *attributions* made for the bad behaviour of *attractive* or *unattractive children*?
17 Give four examples of the different criteria that different *cultures* have for physical attractiveness.
18 What did Brehm (1992) conclude was the primary '*resource*' offered by females in her study of commercial dating services?
19 What did Langlois & Roggman (1994) discover about '*average*' faces?
20 Which features did Perrett *et al.* (1994) find were consistently rated as being attractive in their cross-cultural study?
21 What did Wells *et al.* (1995) discover were correlates of high levels of hair loss?
22 If, according to *social exchange theory*, we look to maximise our rewards in our choice of partner, why do we settle for partners who are anything less than perfectly rewarding?
23 What is a *value-match*?
24 Are we most satisfied when *matched* with the partner we most desire?
25 What did Lykken & Tellegren (1993) discover when investigating *mate selection* in 738 sets of identical twins?

Section 5: Reciprocity and competence

26 What is *reciprocal liking*?
27 Who does Aronson & Linder's (1956) *gain–loss theory* predict we should like the most?
28 How much evidence is there to support the view that '*opposites attract*'?
29 What is the general rule concerning the relationship between *competence* and *attraction*?
30 How has Duck (1995) criticised research into the formation of relationships?

Q

Section 1: Affiliation

1 Psychologists define affiliation as the basic need for the company of others.

2 The need for affiliation has been found to be greatest when moving to a new neighbourhood, on termination of a close relationship, and during times of anxiety.

3 Schachter (1959) found that those expecting to receive painful electric shocks (the high anxiety condition) were twice as likely to want to wait for the experiment in a room with another participant, rather than alone.

4 'According to Clore & Byrne (1974), we are attracted to people whose presence is *rewarding* for us.'

Section 2: Proximity and exposure

5 Festinger *et al.* (1950) discovered that students were most friendly with their next-door neighbours and least friendly with those living at the end of the corridor. Those living near stairways also had more friends than those living at the end of a corridor.

6 Hall (1959) sees proxemic rules as rules which prescribe the physical distance that is appropriate between people in daily situations, and the kinds of situation in which closeness or distance is proper.

7 Successful relationships may require that in the initial stages partners are invited into each other's personal space, rather than invading it.

8 The mere exposure effect (Zajonc, 1968) refers to a general tendency of people to prefer stimuli with which they are more familiar.

Section 3: Similarity

9 Newcomb (1961) discovered that whilst *similarity* was important in determining liking, the key factor was *familiarity*, which frequently led dissimilar room-mates to like each other.

10 Individuals are strongly attracted to people who share their attitudes, and the degree of liking is proportional to the proportion of attitudes shared.

11 Rubin (1973) believes that similarity may provide the basis for shared activities, increase our confidence and self-esteem, encourage us to believe that the person is sensitive and praiseworthy, and make it easier to communicate.

12 Balance theory (Heider, 1946; Newcomb, 1953) proposes that similarity is a consequence of our need for a 'balanced' world; to have different views to those of a friend would produce an imbalance, which can be resolved by changing our views or rejecting our friend.

13 Rosenbaum's (1986) repulsion hypothesis suggests that disagreement is more strongly motivating than agreement, and that it is this discomfort which motivates us to seek out those with similar views.

Section 4: Physical attractiveness

14 Attractive people are perceived as sexually warm and responsive, kind, strong, outgoing, nurturant, interesting, intelligent, more likely to be sought after and popular, more likely to be employed and as happier, more socially skilled and successful.

15 Dermer & Thiel (1975) found that extremely attractive females were judged to be egoistic, vain, materialistic and less likely to be successfully married.

16 Dion (1972) found that bad behaviour was explained in situational terms for attractive children and dispositional terms for unattractive children.

17 Chipped teeth, body scars, artificially elongated heads and bound feet have all been regarded as attractive in certain cultures.

18 Brehm (1992) concluded that the primary 'resource' offered by females was physical attractiveness.

19 Langlois & Roggman (1994) found that producing an 'average' face from digitised pictures of students resulted in a face which was more attractive than 96 per cent of the individual faces.

20 High cheek bones, a thinner jaw and large eyes (relative to facial size) were consistently regarded as attractive.

21 Wells *et al.* (1995) discovered that low self-esteem, depression, neuroticism and psychoticism were all correlates of hair loss.

22 If everybody is looking to maximise their rewards, then we must strike a compromise and settle for somebody who is roughly as rewarding as we are.

23 A value-match is the most rewarding person we could realistically hope to find (in our judgement).

24 No. We are most satisfied with the partner who we feel will not reject us.

25 The mates selected by the identical twins were no more similar than those selected by random pairs of adults. In addition, less than half reported finding their co-twin's mate attractive.

Section 5: Reciprocity and competence

26 Reciprocal liking refers to our tendency to like those who like us.

27 According to Aronson & Linder's (1956) theory, we should like most those people who come to like us after initially disliking us.

28 Very little. Winch (1958) found some degree of complementarity of needs between marriage partners.

29 In general we are more attracted to competent than incompetent people.

30 Duck (1995) argues that much of the research in this area is based on analyses of interactions where the partners are students, and tends to focus on immediate judgements of attractiveness or expressions of desire to see another person again. Additionally, follow-up studies or longitudinal research are rarely carried out.

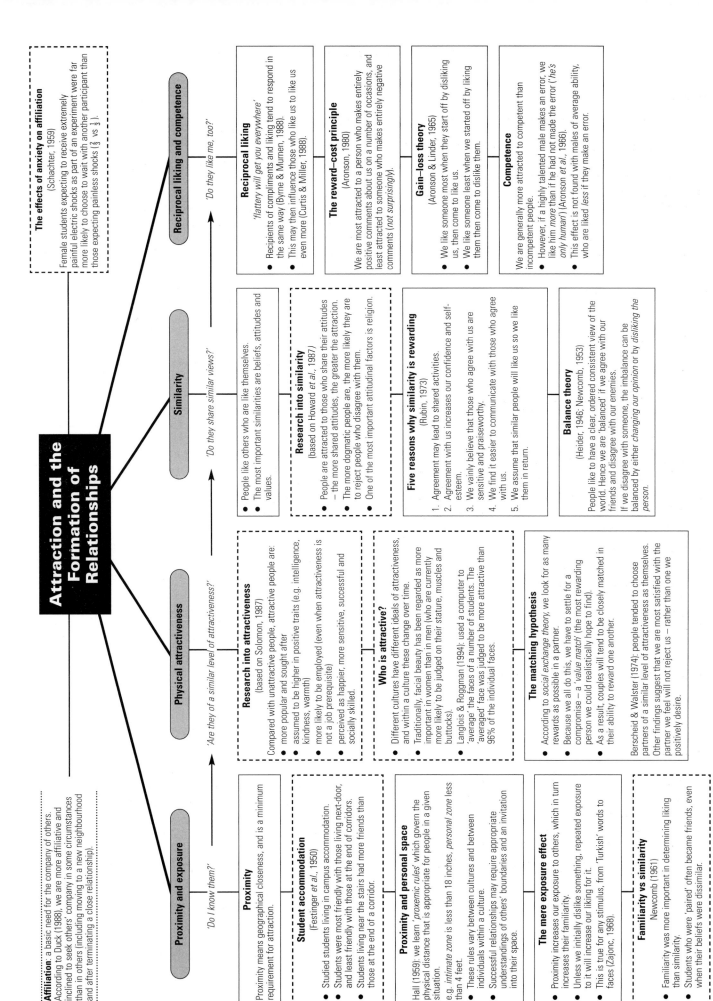

Attraction and the Formation of Relationships

Affiliation: a basic need for the company of others. According to Duck (1988), we are more affiliative and inclined to seek others' company in some circumstances than in others (including moving to a new neighbourhood and after terminating a close relationship).

The effects of anxiety on affiliation
(Schachter, 1959)
Female students expecting to receive extremely painful electric shocks as part of an experiment were far more likely to choose to wait with another participant than those expecting painless shocks (⅔ vs ⅓).

Reciprocal liking and competence

'Do they like me, too?'

Reciprocal liking
'flattery will get you everywhere'
- Recipients of compliments and liking tend to respond in the same way (Byrne & Murnen, 1988).
- This may then influence those who like us to like us even more (Curtis & Miller, 1988).

The reward–cost principle
(Aronson, 1980)
We are most attracted to a person who makes entirely positive comments about us on a number of occasions, and least attracted to someone who makes entirely negative comments (*not surprisingly*).

Gain–loss theory
(Aronson & Linder, 1965)
- We like someone most when they start off by disliking us, then come to like us.
- We like someone least when we started off by liking them then come to dislike them.

Competence
We are generally more attracted to competent than to incompetent people.
- However, if a highly talented male makes an error, we like him *more* than if he had not made the error ('*he's only human!*') (Aronson et al., 1966).
- This effect is not found with males of average ability, who are liked *less* if they make an error.

Similarity

'Do they share similar views?'

- People like others who are like themselves.
- The most important similarities are beliefs, attitudes and values.

Research into similarity
(based on Howard et al., 1987)
- People are attracted to those who share their attitudes – the more shared attitudes, the greater the attraction.
- The more dogmatic people are, the more likely they are to reject people who disagree with them.
- One of the most important attitudinal factors is religion.

Five reasons why similarity is rewarding
(Rubin, 1973)
1. Agreement may lead to shared activities.
2. Agreement with us increases our confidence and self-esteem.
3. We vainly believe that those who agree with us are sensitive and praiseworthy.
4. We find it easier to communicate with those who agree with us.
5. We assume that similar people will like us so we like them in return.

Balance theory
(Heider, 1946; Newcomb, 1953)
People like to have a clear, ordered consistent view of the world. Hence we are 'balanced' if we agree with our friends and disagree with our enemies.
If we disagree with someone, the imbalance can be balanced by either *changing our opinion* or by *disliking the person*.

Physical attractiveness

'Are they of a similar level of attractiveness?'

Research into attractiveness
(based on Solomon, 1987)
Compared with unattractive people, attractive people are:
- more popular and sought after
- assumed to be higher in positive traits (e.g. intelligence, kindness, warmth)
- more likely to be employed (even when attractiveness is not a job prerequisite)
- perceived as happier, more sensitive, successful and socially skilled.

Who is attractive?
- Different cultures have different ideals of attractiveness, and within a culture these change over time.
- Traditionally, facial beauty has been regarded as more important in women than in men (who are currently more likely to be judged on their stature, muscles and buttocks).
- Langlois & Roggman (1994): used a computer to 'average' the faces of a number of students. The 'averaged' face was judged to be more attractive than 96% of the individual faces.

The matching hypothesis
- According to *social exchange theory*, we look for as many rewards as possible in a partner.
- Because we all do this, we have to settle for a compromise – a '*value match*' (the most rewarding person we could realistically hope to find).
- As a result, couples will tend to be closely matched in their ability to reward one another.

Berscheid & Walster (1974): people tended to choose partners of a similar level of attractiveness as themselves. Other findings suggest that we are most satisfied with the partner we feel will not reject us – rather than one we positively desire.

Proximity and exposure

'Do I know them?'

Proximity
Proximity means geographical closeness, and is a minimum requirement for attraction.

Student accommodation
(Festinger et al., 1950)
- Studied students living in campus accommodation.
- Students were most friendly with those living next-door, and least friendly with those at the end of corridors.
- Students living near the stairs had more friends than those at the end of a corridor.

Proximity and personal space
Hall (1959): we learn '*proxemic rules*' which govern the physical distance that is appropriate for people in a given situation.
e.g. *intimate zone* is less than 18 inches, *personal zone* less than 4 feet.
- These rules vary between cultures and between individuals within a culture.
- Successful relationships may require appropriate understandings of others' boundaries and an invitation into their space.

The mere exposure effect
- Proximity increases our exposure to others, which in turn increases their familiarity.
- Unless we initially dislike something, repeated exposure to it will increase our liking for it.
- This is true for any stimulus, from 'Turkish' words to faces (Zajonc, 1968).

Familiarity vs similarity
Newcomb (1961)
- Familiarity was more important in determining liking than similarity.
- Students who were 'paired' often became friends, even when their beliefs were dissimilar.

12

MAINTENANCE AND DISSOLUTION OF RELATIONSHIPS

SYLLABUS

13.1 Relationships – maintenance and dissolution of relationships
- theories and research studies relating to the maintenance (e.g. social exchange theory, equity theory) and dissolution of relationships. Psychological explanations of love (e.g. romantic and companionate love)

KEY QUESTIONS
- Are there stages in the development of relationships?
- Why do people stay together?
- What are the effects and process of dissolution?
- What is love?

Section 1: Stage theories and staying together

1 Which is the first of the three filters in Kerckhoff & Davis's (1962) *filter theory*, and determines the likelihood of couples meeting?

2 What do the letters SVR stand for, in Murstein's (1976, 1987) *stage theory*?

3 According to Levinger's (1980) *five-stage theory of relationships*, what is the third stage, which follows acquaintance/initial attraction, and building up the relationship?

4 Complete the sentence: 'According to Homans (1974), we view our feelings for others in terms of ____'.

5 What is the extra component added to *reward*, *cost* and *profit* in *equity theory*?

6 According to equity theory, what is most likely to make us feel differently about a relationship?

7 Explain what is meant by the statement: 'When CL alt. exceeds the current ratio, then the relationship will be unlikely to continue'.

8 According to Argyle (1988), when are people in close relationships likely to begin thinking about rewards and costs?

9 What factors do Hill *et al.* (1976) see as important predictors of whether or not relationships would break up?

10 According to Duck (1992), what are the characteristics of happy couples?

Section 2: Unhappiness and dissolution

11 Name the factors identified by Duck (1988, 1992) as contributing to *marital unhappiness* and *divorce*.

12 According to McGhee (1996), what kind of communication strategy is a good predictor of dissatisfaction experienced by wives?

13 How do women differ from men with regard to the number and type of problems reported within relationships?

14 What two factors determine changes in marital satisfaction on Pineo's (1961) *linear model*?

15 According to Burr's (1970) *curvilinear model*, when is marital satisfaction likely to be high?

16 What type of attribution is an individual employing a *relationship-enhancing approach* to conflict resolution likely to make for their partner's negative behaviour?

17 Identify three rules which are common to most relationships, according to Argyle & Henderson (1984).

18 Identify the ill effects that Duck (1992) found that people in disrupted relationships are susceptible to.

19 According to Cochrane (1983, 1996), how much more likely are the *divorced* to be admitted to mental hospital in any one year than married people?

20 What important difference exists between the way men and women suffer the detrimental effects of divorce?

21 How does Fincham (1997) attempt to account for the differences between the way in which divorce affects men and women?

22 Name three of the five stages of pre-marital romantic break-ups in Lee's (1984) model.

23 Which of Lee's stages are experienced as the most dramatic and exhausting stages of the break-up?

24 Which phase follows the *intrapsychic phase* in Duck's (1982, 1988) model of relationship dissolution?

25 What is the purpose of the '*grave-dressing*' *phase*, the final phase in Duck's model?

26 What is the *constructive–passive response* to relationship dissatisfaction, according to Rusbult's (1987) model?

Section 3: Liking and loving

27 According to Rubin (1973), what are the three components of *love*?

28 What are the differences between *liking* and *loving*?

29 How does the nature of women's and men's loving differ?

30 According to Berscheid & Walster (1978), what is the difference between *romantic* and *companionate love*?

31 What are the three basic components of Sternberg's (1986b, 1988) *love triangle*?

32 How do *individualistic cultures* differ from *collectivist cultures*?

33 What did Gupta & Singh (1992) discover when they compared Indian couples who had *married for love* with couples who had entered into *arranged marriages*?

Section 1: Stage theories and staying together

1 The first of the three filters in Kerckhoff & Davis's (1962) filter theory is the sociological/demographic filter (for example, determining the likelihood of individuals from a certain class, race, religion, meeting).

2 The letters SVR stand for stimulus, value, role (Murstein, 1976, 1987).

3 The third of Levinger's (1980) five stages of relationships is the consolidation or continuation stage.

4 'According to Homans (1974), we view our feelings for others in terms of *profits*.'

5 Equity theory proposes the extra component of investment.

6 Equity theory predicts that a change in the ratio of rewards to costs within a relationship is most likely to make us feel differently about that relationship.

7 Comparison-level theory proposes that we make comparisons between the ratio of rewards and costs we are currently receiving with the level we could receive elsewhere (comparison level for alternatives). If we could do better elsewhere, we will feel dissatisfied.

8 Argyle (1988) maintains that people begin thinking about rewards and costs in a relationship when they start to feel dissatisfied.

9 Hill *et al.* (1976) found that similarities of age, intelligence, attractiveness, education and career plans were important predictors of a lasting relationship, as well as equal involvement in the relationship and the partners describing themselves as being 'in love'.

10 Duck (1992) found that happy couples give more positive and consistent non-verbal cues than unhappy couples, express more agreement with and approval of their partners, talk more about their relationships, and are more willing to compromise.

Section 2: Unhappiness and dissolution

11 Duck (1988, 1992) identifies marriages in which the partners are younger than usual, from lower socioeconomic groups and educational levels, from different demographic backgrounds, and who have experienced parental divorce as children, as prone to marital unhappiness and divorce.

12 McGhee (1996) found that partners' manipulative and coercive communication strategies were good predictors of dissatisfaction experienced by wives.

13 Women report more problems, and stress basic unhappiness and incompatibility, than do men.

14 Pineo's (1961) linear model suggest that the fading of the romantic 'high' and a reduction over time of compatibility cause changes in marital satisfaction.

15 According to Burr's (1970) curvilinear model, marital satisfaction is likely to be high in the earliest and later years of marriage.

16 An individual employing a relationship-enhancing approach to conflict resolution is likely to make an external attribution for their partner's negative behaviour.

17 Argyle & Henderson (1984) identified 'respecting other people's privacy', 'not discussing what has been said in private' and 'being emotionally supportive' as rules which apply to most relationships.

18 Duck (1992) found that people in disrupted relationships are susceptible to coronary heart disease, alcoholism, drug dependency and sleep disturbances.

19 Cochrane (1983, 1996) found that the divorced are five-and-a-half times more likely to be admitted to mental hospital in any one year than married people.

20 Men tend to suffer detrimental effects after divorce, whereas women tend to suffer detrimental effects before divorce.

21 Fincham (1997) argues that women value relationships more than men, and feel greater responsibility for making the relationship work. When it does not, this can cause depression.

22 The five stages of pre-marital romantic breakups are dissatisfaction, dissatisfaction exposed, negotiation, attempts to resolve the problem, and relationship terminated (Lee, 1984).

23 Lee found that exposure and negotiation are experienced as the most dramatic and exhausting stages.

24 The dyadic phase follows on from the intrapsychic phase.

25 The 'grave-dressing' phase involves providing a credible and socially acceptable account of the relationship's life and death, helping to save face and 'justify' the original commitment.

26 The constructive–passive response is 'loyalty'.

Section 3: Liking and loving

27 According to Rubin (1973), love comprises attachment, caring and intimacy.

28 Rubin maintains that loving is more than an intense liking, and differs qualitatively in the ways described above.

29 Women are more likely to report loving same-sex friends and appear able to experience loving in a wider variety of contexts than are men, who channel loving into a single sexual relationship.

30 Romantic love is characterised by intense feelings of tenderness, elation, anxiety, and sexual desire, whilst companionate love is the affection remaining after this has subsided and is less intense, involving thoughtful appreciation of one's partner.

31 Sternberg's (1986b, 1988) love triangle proposed that love is comprised of passion, intimacy and commitment (or decision).

32 Individualistic cultures place the greatest emphasis on personal achievement and self-reliance, whilst collectivist cultures prioritise the welfare and unity of the group.

33 Gupta & Singh (1992) discovered that couples who had married for love reported diminished feelings of love after five years, whereas couples in arranged marriages (who were not newly-weds) reported more love.

A

Maintenance and Dissolution of Relationships

Stage theories

'Filter' theory (Kerckhoff & Davis, 1962)
Relationships pass through a series of filters which predict likelihood of forming a relationship, stability and long-term commitment:
similarity of sociological/demographic factors (e.g. social class) ➡ similarity of psychological/basic values ➡ complementarity of emotional needs

Levinger's theory (Levinger, 1980)
Relationships proceed through five stages:
Acquaintance/Initial attraction ➡ Building up the relationship ➡ Consolidation/continuation ➡ Deterioration and decline ➡ Ending

Stimulus–value–role (SVR) theory (Murstein, 1987)
Relationships proceed through three stages:
Stimulus stage (attraction based on external attributes) ➡ **Value stage** (similarity of values is more important) ➡ **Role stage** (commitment based on successful performance of roles e.g. husband/wife)

Staying together

Social exchange theory (Homans, 1974; Blau, 1964)
Relationships are seen in economic terms:
● Our feelings for others depend on profits (a relationship's rewards minus its costs).
● Relationships are 'expensive' (e.g. in time and energy) and we want to get out more than we put in.

Conflicting research
Mills & Clark (1980): identify two types of couple, only one of which is selfish:
● *exchange couple*: keep a mental record of who is 'ahead' in the relationship.
● *communal couple*: each partner gives out of concern for the other.

Similarity
As a general rule the more similar two people see themselves as being, the more likely the relationship will be maintained
● Hill *et al.* (1976) studied 231 steadily dating couples and found that many of the 45% that broke up cited differences in interests, background, sexual attitudes and ideas about marriage as reasons.

Equity theory
Relationships are seen in economic terms:
● Equity means a constant ratio of rewards to costs (so we may be happy contributing more than we receive).
● Changes in the ratio will lead to dissatisfaction.
● Investments are made to ensure longer term profits.

Comparison levels approach
We 'shop around' for the best deal we can get by comparing:
● comparison level (CL): the level of rewards and costs we are used to.
● comparison level for alternatives (CL alt): the level of rewards and costs we could receive elsewhere.

Unhappiness and divorce

Factors in marital unhappiness
(Duck, 1988, 1992)
● Partners are younger than usual.
● Partners are from lower socio-economic groups.
● Partners are from different demographic backgrounds.
● Partners have experienced parental divorce as children.
● Partners have had more than average number of pre-marital sexual relationships.

Gender differences
(Brehm, 1992)
● Women report more problems in relationships than do men.
● Women's reports are a better predictor of breakdown.
● Men's expectations of marriage may be better met than women's.
● Women are more likely to stress basic unhappiness and incompatibility.

Satisfaction changes over time
Pineo's linear model
Satisfaction decreases as:
● romantic love fades
● dissimilarities increase.

Burr's curvilinear model
● Marital happiness declines with arrival of children and increases with their departure.

Conflict resolution
(Bradbury & Fincham, 1990)
Relationship-enhancing couples:
● put partner's negative behaviour down to *external*, unstable causes. (e.g. stress at work)
● put their positive behaviour down to *internal*, stable causes. (e.g. personality traits)
Distress-maintaining couples:
● do the opposite.

Rule-breaking and deception
(Argyle & Henderson, 1984)
Rules: shared beliefs about what should and should not be done.
Rules for most relationships:
● Do not be deceptive.
● Respect other's privacy.
● Be emotionally supportive.
● Do not discuss confidential information.
Other rules apply to similar clusters of relationships.

Dissolution vs reconciliation

Dissolution

Lee's model (1984)
Five stages in the breakup of pre-marital romance.
1. *Dissatisfaction* (D): is discovered.
2. *Exposure* (E): dissatisfaction exposed.
3. *Negotiation* (N): about the dissatisfaction.
4. *Resolution* (R): attempts at resolution made.
5. *Termination* (T): relationship terminated.

Duck's model (1982, 1988)
Four phases in relationships breakup.
Intrapsychic phase: dissatisfaction is internal, focus on partner's inadequacy, assess alternatives.
Dyadic phase: decide to confront/avoid partner, negotiate repair/withdrawal.
Social phase: problems made public, blame-placing, 'intervention teams' (family/friends) may try to help.
Grave-dressing phase: each partner constructs an acceptable account of what went wrong to preserve their reputation.

Reconciliation

Exit–voice–loyalty–neglect model
Rusbult (1987)
4 basic responses to relationship dissatisfaction: *exit* (leaving), *neglect* (ignoring), *voice* (articulating concerns), *loyalty* (staying and accepting things.)

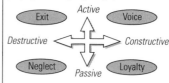

Marital reconciliation
Wineberg (1994)
Wineberg studied 506 white women who had attempted reconciliations. Overall, 30% were successful. The key factors linked with reconciliation were:
● Both partners were of the same religion.
● Cohabitation with a partner before marriage.
● Marriage with a partner of the same age.

Culture

Importance of cross-cultural research
(Goodwin, 1995)
● Allows us to see whether competing theories are true universally.
● Helps us to ease relationships in an age where inter-cultural contact is increasing.
● Understanding the rules of commerce cross-culturally is important for business.

Individualism vs collectivism
(Goodwin, 1995; Bellur, 1995)
● Individualistic cultures place more emphasis on personal achievement whilst collectivist cultures prioritise the welfare and unity of the group.
● In individualistic cultures, marriage is seen as the culmination of a loving relationship, whereas in collectivist cultures love often follows marriage.

Loving

Romantic and companionate love
(Berscheid & Walster, 1978)
● *Romantic love*: intense feelings of tenderness, elation, anxiety and sexual desire.
● *Companionate love*: the affection that remains after romantic love subsides.
The transition from romantic to companionate love is important if a relationship is to be maintained.

The triangular theory of love
(Sternberg, 1988)
Love has three basic components:
● *Intimacy* (sharing and closeness)
● *Passion* (romance and sexual desire)
● *Commitment* (deciding to maintain a relationship).
Different combinations of these produce different types of love.

CULTURAL AND SUB-CULTURAL DIFFERENCES IN RELATIONSHIPS

SYLLABUS

13.1 Relationships – cultural and sub-cultural differences in relationships
- explanations and research studies relating to differences in relationships between Western and non-Western cultures (e.g. individualist/collectivist, voluntary/involuntary, permanent/impermanent types of relationships). 'Understudied' relationships such as gay and lesbian, 'electronic' friendships (e.g. relationships formed on the Internet)

KEY QUESTIONS
- How do relationships differ between Western and non-Western cultures?
- How do gay and lesbian relationships differ from heterosexual relationships?
- What are 'electronic' friendships?

Section 1: Cultural differences

1 Complete the sentence: 'Research into relationships has tended to concentrate on ____ cultures and ____ individuals'.

2 Identify two general differences between interpersonal relationships in Western and non-Western cultures.

3 What term is used to describe marriage to a single individual at any one time?

4 What is *polygyny*?

5 Give one likely explanation for *fraternal polyandry* amongst some of the peoples of Tibet.

6 What did Levine (1988) discover regarding the central core of polyandrous families among the Nyinba?

7 What did Schuler (1987) discover regarding the status of unmarried women amongst the Chumik of Tibet?

8 Why do Chumik families prefer to keep daughters in the household as long as possible?

9 What is the popular 'Hollywood' view of relationships?

10 What did Kephart (1967) find when asking Americans 'If someone had all the other qualities you desired in a marriage partner, would you marry this person if you were not in love?'

11 What reason can you give for the finding that, twenty years later, more than 80 per cent of *both* men *and* women replied 'no' to the question above (Simpson *et al.*, 1986)?

12 What did Jankowiak & Fischer's (1992) study of songs and folklore in 166 societies discover regarding 'Western' romantic love?

13 Which country showed the highest percentage of 'yes' responses to the question 'Are you in love right now?' in Specher *et al.*'s (1994) study?

14 Complete the sentence: 'First generation Indian immigrants tend to endorse the idea that ___ precedes ___ more than second generation Indian immigrants'.

15 What did Gupta & Singh (1992) discover when comparing arranged marriages with 'love' matches?

16 When Hupka (1981) studied sexual jealousy in 92 societies, what was the observed relationship between marriage and jealousy?

17 What is the relationship between the expression of jealousy and social power within a society, according to Reiss (1986)?

18 When Buunk & Hupka (1987) studied sexual jealousy in different countries, what did they discover to be the two most common triggers?

Section 2: Understudied relationships

19 What do the terms *heterosexual*, *homosexual* and *bisexual* mean, respectively?

20 What percentage of American boys report some kind of homosexual experience before the age of 15, according to Hass (1979)?

21 How was homosexuality classified up until 1973, by DSM-II?

22 To what does the term *ego-dystonic homosexuality* refer?

23 What model has psychological research into homosexuality moved away from since the 1970s, according to Kitzinger & Coyle (1995)?

24 Identify the three factors which Kitzinger and Coyle found to differ significantly between heterosexual and homosexual couples.

25 How do homosexual couples tend to differ from heterosexual couples in the roles which they take within the relationship?

26 Roughly how much time per day does the typical student spend on the Internet for 'fun', according to Harlow (1999)?

27 Name three ways in which computer-users may communicate online.

28 What is *intersection frequency*?

29 What proportion of people responding to Scherer & Bost's (1997) survey had formed a personal relationship with someone in a newsgroup?

30 What percentage of online relationships are romantic?

Q

Section 1: Cultural differences

1 'Research into relationships has tended to concentrate on *Western* cultures and *heterosexual* individuals.'

2 Interpersonal relationships in Western cultures tend to be individualistic, voluntary and temporary whereas in non-Western cultures they tend to be more collectivist, involuntary and permanent.

3 Marriage to a single individual at any one time is termed *monogamy*.

4 Polygyny describes the situation in which one man has two or more wives.

5 Polyandry may minimise population growth in an area of scarce resources. It may also keep brothers together and slow the growth of families whilst preserving it as a single economic unit.

6 Levine (1988) discovered that the central core of polyandrous families was comprised of a group of men.

7 Schuler (1987) discovered that amongst the Chumik of Tibet unmarried women have low social status and are treated little better than slaves.

8 Chumik families prefer to keep daughters in the household as long as possible because their daughters' labour is economically important.

9 The popular 'Hollywood' view of relationships is that people fall in love and then commit themselves to each other through marriage.

10 Kephart found that well over twice as many men answered 'no' to the question than did women.

11 It may be that increasing financial independence on the part of women has allowed them to choose partners for reasons other than material necessity.

12 Jankowaik and Fischer's study of songs and folklore found that Western 'romantic love' was recognised in more than 85 per cent of the cultures they studied.

13 Russia showed the highest percentage of 'yes' responses to the question 'Are you in love right now?'.

14 'First generation Indian immigrants tend to endorse the idea that *marriage* precedes *love* more than second generation Indian immigrants.'

15 Gupta and Singh discovered that love was more likely to develop and grow during the course of arranged marriages as compared with 'love' matches.

16 Hupka found that the more important marriage was thought to be, the more jealousy people showed.

17 Reiss believes that the expression of jealousy by men and women is related to their social power – the greater the power, the greater the expression of jealousy.

18 When Buunk and Hupka found that the two most common triggers were flirting and sexual relations.

Section 2: Understudied relationships

19 Heterosexual refers to individuals with a sexual preference for the opposite sex, homosexual to individuals with a sexual preference for the same sex and bisexual to individuals who are attracted to people of both sexes.

20 According to Hass, 14 per cent of American boys report some kind of homosexual experience before the age of 15.

21 Until 1973 DSM-II classed homosexuality as a sexual deviation.

22 The term ego-dystonic homosexuality refers to someone who is homosexually aroused but who finds this a persistent source of distress and wishes to become heterosexual.

23 Kitzinger and Coyle claim that psychological research has moved away from a 'pathology model' since the 1970s.

24 Kitzinger and Coyle found that homosexual relationships differ in terms of cohabitation, sexual exclusivity and sex role.

25 Homosexual couples are more likely to prefer equality of status and power, and reject husband–wife or masculine–feminine roles.

26 According to Harlow, the typical student spends about one hour per day on the Internet for 'fun'.

27 Computer-users may communicate online using email, discussion forums, newsgroups, chatrooms or multiplayer games.

28 Intersection frequency refers to how often a person who participates in a chat-room is encountered.

29 Two-thirds of people responding to Scherer and Bost's survey had formed a personal relationship with someone in a newsgroup.

30 Less than 10 per cent of online relationships are romantic.

Cultural & Sub-cultural Differences in Relationships

Basic differences
Western cultures: emphasise romantic love in dyads (two-person groupings). Interpersonal relationships tend to be individualistic, voluntary and temporary.
Non-Western cultures: emphasise family ties and responsibilities. Interpersonal relationships tend to be collectivist, involuntary and permanent.

Polyandry – Key studies
- **Levine (1988):** studied polyandry among the Nyinba (ethnic Tibetans) and found that this led to families with a core of men (usually brothers) in which the relationship between fathers and children is emphasised. Such a system helps to minimise population growth in order to cope with scarce resources.
- **Schuler (1987):** studied polyandry in the Chumik (a Tibetan society) in which roughly a quarter of women over 35 have never been married. Families adopt strategies aimed at keeping their daughters unmarried in order to keep them working in the family. Unmarried women are of low social status.

Romantic love – a Western phenomenon?

Key study – the importance of love
- **Kephart (1967)** asked Americans 'If someone had all the other qualities you desired in a marriage partner, would you marry this person if you were not in love?'
Results: well over twice as many men replied 'no' as did women. However, by 1986 Simpson *et al.* found that 80% of both men and women said 'no' – perhaps reflecting the increasing financial independence of women.

Cultural similarities
The popular ('Hollywood') view of passionate romantic love as a Western phenomenon may be mistaken:
- **Moghaddam (1998)** argues that 'falling in love' is found in most human societies and that it is only the idea that everyone should marry only when in love that is limited to Western societies.

Cultural differences
Smith & Bond (1998) argue that although there are universal ways of describing attachments, the precise nature of love or romance varies:
- **Levine *et al.* (1995):** compared collectivist and individualistic cultures using Kephart's question (above). Collectivist cultures (such as India) were more likely to say 'yes'.
- **Sprecher *et al.* (1994):** found the highest number of 'yes' responses to the question 'are you in love right now?' in Russia. However the meaning of 'being in love' varies between cultures.

Arranged marriages: good or bad?

Prevalence
Arranged marriages are far more common in collectivist families, with one extended family 'marrying' another (as opposed to individualistic cultures where one individual marries another):
- **Gupta & Singh (1992):** found that love is more likely to develop and grow during an arranged marriage than a 'love' marriage (see Ch 12).

Divorce rates
- In general, divorce rates for arranged marriages are much lower than among those who marry for love.
- However, divorce rates among couples in arranged marriages are rising. This may be indicative of a shift away from traditional family values towards personal freedom.

Sexual jealousy

Research
According to Reiss (1986), all societies are aware of sexual jealousy, although the cultural rules for dealing with it differ:
- **Ford & Beach (1951):** only 53% of societies studied by anthropologists forbid extramarital sex by both husbands and wives.
- **Rivers (1906):** the Toda of the southern Deccan Plateau of India consider it inappropriate for a man to refuse his wife's request to have an affair.
- **Hupka (1981):** studied jealousy in 92 societies and found that the more importance was attached to marriage, the more jealousy was shown.

Key study – triggering sexual jealousy
- **Buunk & Hupka (1987):** studied over 2000 students from Hungary, Ireland, Mexico, the Netherlands, (former) Soviet Union, the USA and (former) Yugoslavia. Students were asked to rate 'sexual' behaviours (e.g. partner dancing, flirting with another) in terms of how uneasy it made them feel.
Results: overall similarities between countries were greater than differences; flirting & sexual relationships were the most likely causes of jealousy.

Homosexual relationships   Understudied relationships   'Electronic' friendships

Is homosexuality 'normal'?
Whilst *heterosexuals* display a sexual preference for people of the *opposite* sex, *homosexuals* prefer people of the *same* sex:
- **Frequency:** around 3–4% of men are exclusively homosexual, 1% of women, with 14% of boys reporting some kind of homosexual experience before age 15.
- **History:** Until 1960 homosexuality was illegal and until 1973 homosexuality was identified as a sexual deviation by DSM-II. By 1987 DSM-III-R only identified distress about one's sexual orientation as a disorder (in line with changing attitudes).

Changes in psychological research (Kitzinger & Coyle, 1995)
Since the 1970s research has moved away from a 'pathology' model & incorporated:
- A belief in a basic similarity between homosexuals and heterosexuals.
- A recognition of the diversity and variety of homosexuals as individuals.
- An assertion that homosexuality is natural, normal and healthy.
- A denial that homosexuals pose a threat to children, family or society.

Homosexual relationships – differences
- **Cohabitation:** is much less common for homosexuals. Reasons may range from concerns about 'visibility' to a desire for autonomy.
- **Exclusivity:** is much less common in gay relationships, although homosexual relationships may have norms which differ from the heterosexual couple.
- **Sex roles:** most gays & lesbians reject traditional husband–wife, masculine–feminine roles, preferring equality of status & power.

Basic facts
- **History:** started out as a research network some 30 yrs ago and now incorporates over 30,000,000 web sites. The typical student now uses the Net for an hour a day for 'fun'.
- **Means of communication:** Communicating with others may take the form of email, discussion forums, newsgroups, chatrooms and multiplayer games.

Factors influencing the formation of relationships
- **Proximity/exposure/familiarity:** in physical form are translated into 'intersection frequency' online (how often another individual is encountered online – facilitated by 'buddy' lists).
- **Similarity:** similarities of beliefs, attitudes and values are traditionally most significant and is likely to affect the frequency of correspondence as individuals disclose information about themselves.
- **Physical attractiveness:** individuals' physical attractiveness is usually concealed, which may remove the effects of the physical attractiveness stereotype and matching hypothesis (see Ch 11).
- **Complementarity:** little research has been conducted, although people with technical expertise tend to like those who seek their help.

Key study
Parks & Floyd (1996) and Scherer & Bost (1997) found that:
- Two-thirds of people in their survey had formed a personal relationship online, these people were more likely to be women, self-disclosure is an important part of online relationships and less than 10% of online relationships are 'romantic'.

77

14

THE NATURE AND CAUSES OF AGGRESSION

SYLLABUS

13.1 Pro- and anti-social behaviour – nature and causes of aggression

- social psychological theories of aggression (e.g. social learning theory, deindividuation, relative deprivation) including research studies relating to these theories. Research into the effects of environmental stressors on aggressive behaviour

KEY QUESTIONS

- What is aggression?
- What theories have been advanced to explain aggressive behaviour?
- What effects do environmental stressors have on aggression?

Section 1: Introducing aggression

1 How do Baron & Richardson (1994) define *anti-social behaviours*?

2 How can *aggression* be defined?

Section 2: Theories of aggression

3 Dollard *et al.* (1939) proposed the *frustration–aggression hypothesis* in an effort to explain aggressive behaviour. What does this hypothesis state?

4 According to this account, what causes frustration?

5 What experiment, involving young children, did Barker *et al.* (1941) carry out in order to investigate the effects of frustration?

6 According to Berkowitz's (1966, 1978, 1989) cue-arousal theory, what two conditions act together to produce aggression when frustration occurs?

7 In Geen & Berkowitz's (1966) experiment, in which participants were insulted by a stooge and then required to administer electric shocks to the same stooge, did they administer more shock when the stooge was called 'Kirk Anderson' or 'Bob Anderson'?

8 In a similar experiment conducted by Berkowitz & LePage (1967), a stooge was subjected to higher levels of shock in the presence of certain cues. What were these cues?

9 What is the main principle behind Zillman's (1982) *excitation-transfer theory*?

10 Why did Zillman & Bryant (1974) require their participants to ride bicycles?

11 Which type of pornography is most likely to lead to a *decrease* in aggressive behaviour?

12 According to *social learning theory*, which two processes are responsible for the learning of aggressive behaviours?

13 How did Bandura (1965) use a 'Bobo doll' to demonstrate *vicarious reinforcement*?

14 Why, according to Le Bon, does *anonymity* cause individuals to indulge in behaviour which would normally be controlled?

15 What is Festinger *et al.*'s (1952) explanation for why deindividuation may lead to uncharacteristic behaviours?

16 How did Zimbardo (1969) demonstrate anonymity in big cities?

17 What was the effect on Zimbardo's (1969) female participants administering electric shocks when they were dressed in lab coats and hoods which hid their faces?

18 What is Diener's (1980) explanation for deindividuation?

19 What are the two types of *self-awareness*, according to Prentice-Dunn & Rogers (1982, 1983)?

20 Give any one example of a factor which may reduce each type of self-awareness, respectively.

21 What expression do Prentice-Dunn and Rogers use to describe the state that we enter as a result of *decreased self-awareness*?

22 According to Prentice-Dunn and Rogers, a deindividuated state does not, in itself, cause anti-social or aggressive behaviour. How does it relate to these behaviours?

23 Give one criticism of Zimbardo's (1969) study, in which women wearing hoods were more likely to administer high levels of electric shock.

Section 3: The effects of stressors

24 What three major causes of aggression relating to the physical environment does Baron (1977) identify?

25 Under what conditions did Donnerstein & Wilson (1976) discover that 'angered' participants would deliver more and longer shocks to a confederate?

26 In what environment has a high correlation between crowding and violence been found?

27 What did Baron (1972) find when exposing angered and non-angered participants to very high temperatures (91–95° Fahrenheit)?

28 Complete the sentence: 'Taylor & Sears (1994) found that participants who had consumed alcohol were more susceptible to ____ pressure'.

29 What did Taylor *et al.* (1994) discover when investigating the link between marijuana and aggression?

Section 1: Introducing aggression

1 Baron & Richardson (1994) define anti-social behaviours as those which show a lack of feeling and concern for the welfare of others.

2 Aggression can be defined as behaviour intended to harm or destroy another person who is motivated to avoid such treatment.

Section 2: Theories of aggression

3 The frustration–aggression hypothesis states that aggression always results from frustration and that frustration always leads to aggression.

4 Frustration is caused by unfulfilled desires (when an expected reinforcer is prevented from occurring).

5 Barker *et al.* (1941) showed young children attractive toys, then prevented them from playing with them. When they were eventually allowed to play with them, they threw, stomped on, and smashed the toys.

6 The two conditions are a readiness to act aggressively and the presence of environmental cues.

7 Participants administered more shock when the stooge was called 'Kirk Anderson', having seen a film in which the actor Kirk Douglas was brutally beaten.

8 The cues were a shotgun and a revolver. The weapons effect refers to the tendency of weapons to stimulate violence (Berkowitz & LePage, 1967).

9 Zillman's (1982) excitation-transfer theory states that arousal from one source can be transferred to, and energise, some other response.

10 Zillman & Bryant (1974) had participants ride bicycles in order to raise their levels of arousal. They then investigated whether heightened arousal would affect the level of shock delivered to a stooge who had previously insulted them.

11 Donnerstein *et al.* (1987) found that 'soft' pornography either decreases or has no effect on aggression, whereas 'hard core' pornography can lead to an increase in aggression.

12 Reinforcement and the imitation of aggressive models (observational learning) may lead to aggressive behaviour.

13 Bandura (1965) showed children videos of adults attacking a 'Bobo doll' and then being rewarded/punished/ neither, and subsequently observed the children's behaviour in a similar situation.

14 Anonymity removes the sense of individuality from group members. Because moral responsibility is then shifted away from the individual onto the group, the individual feels free to indulge in behaviours which would normally be controlled.

15 Festinger *et al.* (1952) believe that group membership allows us to merge with that group, foregoing our individual identities, leading to a reduction of inner restraints and inhibitions.

16 Zimbardo (1969) abandoned a car in a big city location and a small town location and secretly filmed people's behaviour, recording the number of incidents of 'destructive contact'.

17 Zimbardo (1969) discovered that they delivered twice as much shock as females who could be easily identified.

18 Diener (1980) argues that we are prevented by situational factors from becoming self-aware. This results in a weakening of normal restraints, a lack of concern about what others will think of our behaviour, and a reduced capacity to think rationally.

19 Public self-awareness and private self-awareness.

20 Public self-awareness may be reduced by difficulty in recognising the individual in a crowd, by a diffusion of responsibility and by the presence of models who supply norms for behaviours. Private self-awareness may be reduced by drugs, arousal, physical involvement, hypnosis and chanting.

21 Prentice-Dunn and Rogers describe this state as an *irrational state of altered consciousness*.

22 The deindividuated state makes us susceptible to behavioural cues, such as others' behaviour or the presence of weapons.

23 The hoods worn by women in Zimbardo's (1969) study resembled the hoods worn by the Ku Klux Klan, and may have led participants to believe that extreme behaviours were expected of them.

Section 3: The effects of stressors

24 Baron (1977) identifies noise, crowding and temperature as being the three major causes of aggression relating to the physical environment.

25 Donnerstein & Wilson (1976) discovered that 'angered' participants who were exposed to bursts of high-intensity noise would deliver more and longer shocks to a confederate.

26 Cave (1998) found a high correlation between crowding and violence in prisons.

27 Baron (1972) found that very high temperatures actually reduced aggression in both angered and non-angered participants.

28 'Taylor & Sears (1994) found that participants who had consumed alcohol were more susceptible to *social* pressure.'

29 Taylor *et al.* discovered that marijuana tends to reduce aggression.

Anonymity

- Le Bon (1879): the more anonymous a crowd, the greater its potential for extreme action, because anonymity removes the sense of individuality from group members.
- Moral responsibility is shifted from the individual to the group, and the normal restraints are removed.
- Festinger *et al.* (1952) proposed the concept of *deindividuation* where individuals do not single out others as individuals and do not feel that they themselves are singled out by others.
- Individuals merge with the group and, becoming anonymous, experience a reduction of inhibitions.

Prentice-Dunn & Rogers' theory (1982, 1983)

Argue that there are two types of self-awareness:
- *Public self-awareness:* concern about the impression we are giving others. (This can be reduced by difficulty in identifying us, diffusion of responsibility, and by other members setting norms which can be imitated.)
- *Private self-awareness:* the attention we pay to our thoughts and feelings. (This can be reduced by drugs, chanting, physical involvement, excitement.)

These two can lead to an irrational state of altered consciousness, in which we are susceptible to behavioural cues (such as weapons, others' behaviour) and can behave in aggressive and antisocial ways.

Research

- Zimbardo (1969): left cars with number plates removed and bonnets up in the Bronx area of New York and Palo Alto, California. In the more anonymous 'big city', the car was mostly stripped by clean-cut whites within one day, whereas the car in Palo Alto was left alone for seven days.
- Zimbardo (1969): female undergraduates who wore hoods which hid their faces, or conspicuous name tags administered electric shock to another student who pretended to be in pain. Anonymous females administered twice as much shock, irrespective of whether the student was described as 'conceited and critical' or 'honest and warm'.

Deindividuation theory

Frustration–aggression hypothesis

- Dollard *et al.* (1939) translated Freud's work into social learning theory terms.
- Hypothesis proposes that aggression is always a consequence of frustration and frustration always leads to aggression.
- Frustration occurs when our goals are thwarted (i.e. when an expected reinforcer is prevented from occurring).
- Aggression will therefore emerge in specific situations and may be delayed, disguised, or directed towards a 'scapegoat'.

- Barker *et al.* (1941): children who were shown toys, then prevented from playing with them, were more likely to throw/smash them when allowed to play with them.
- Miller (1941): frustration is not sufficient for aggression, it can be expressed in ways other than aggression, and expression will depend partly on other situational factors (e.g. fear of retaliation).

Cue-arousal theory

- Berkowitz (1966, 1978, 1989): frustration does not always produce aggression. Frustration produces anger.
- Frustration is psychologically painful and psychological or physical pain can produce aggression.
- Two conditions act to produce aggression when frustration occurs:
  – a readiness to act aggressively
  – environmental cues associated with aggression/the frustrating object.

- The weapons effect (Berkowitz, 1968): stooges administered electric shocks to participants. Angry participants were then asked to administer shocks to the stooge. When a shotgun and revolver were placed on a nearby table, participants administered a higher level of shock than when they were absent.

Aggression

Aggression: some behaviour intended to harm or destroy another person who is motivated to avoid such treatment.

Antisocial behaviours: behaviours which show a lack of feeling and concern for the welfare of others (Baron & Richardson, 1994).

Excitation-transfer theory

- Zillman (1982): arousal from one source can be transferred to and energise some other response.
- There is a sequence in which arousal is generated then labelled, which produces a specific emotion such as anger.
- Arousal from any source (e.g. exercise, sex) can therefore produce heightened aggression (if mis-attributed).

- Zillman & Bryant (1974) aroused participants by requiring them to ride bicycles. Participants were then insulted by a stooge. Aroused participants delivered higher levels of harsh noise to stooges.

Social learning theory

- Aggressive behaviours are learned through *reinforcement* and *imitation* of aggressive models (Bandura, 1965, 1973, 1994).
- Reinforcement can take the form of praise for 'being tough,' or rewards for aggression.
- Observational learning involves observing others who serve as models for behaviour.

- 'Bobo Doll' study (Bandura, 1965): children watched a video of an adult being aggressive towards an inflatable 'Bobo doll'. Children who observed the adult being rewarded for behaviour were significantly more aggressive than those who had seen the adult punished (or not rewarded) when placed in the same situation.

The effects of environmental stressors

The effects of noise
- Donnerstein & Wilson (1976): participants were angered by a confederate's negative evaluation of an essay they had written. Participants were then given the opportunity to administer electric shocks to the confederate.
- Participants were more likely to administer more and longer shocks if subjected to high-intensity noise through headphones.

Evaluation: the heightened arousal produced by loud noise is only converted into aggression if this is already the dominant response (Bandura, 1973).

The effects of crowding
- Studies have produced mixed results with no correlation between urban density and crime, but a high correlation between crowding and violence in prisons. Laboratory studies (e.g. Freedman *et al.*, 1972) found increases of aggression in all-male groups but the opposite effect in all-female groups.
- Freedman (1975) claims that crowding only serves to intensify the individual's typical reactions to a situation.

The effects of temperature
- A large proportion of the serious violence in the late 1960s in major American cities occurred during heat-wave conditions (Goranson & King, 1970).
- Baron & Bell (1975) exposed participants to provocation and aggressive models expecting to find that temperature heightened this aggression. However, aggression was only increased in non-provoked participants and actually *reduced* in provoked participants (trying to minimise the discomfort became the dominant response).

Alcohol and other drugs
- Whilst intoxicated offenders commit 60% of murders in the USA, Taylor *et al.* (1960) found that marijuana tends to *reduce* aggression.
- Taylor & Sears (1994) assigned male students to an alcohol or placebo condition and then placed them in a competitive situation in which they delivered electric shocks to an opponent. Participants who had consumed alcohol were more susceptible to social pressure to increase the level of shock.

15

ALTRUISM AND BYSTANDER BEHAVIOUR

SYLLABUS

13.1 Pro- and anti-social behaviour – altruism and bystander behaviour
- explanations (e.g. empathy–altruism, negative-state relief) and research studies relating to human altruism and bystander behaviour. Cultural differences in pro-social behaviour

KEY QUESTIONS
- How can we explain bystander apathy?
- What explanations of bystander behaviour does the arousal model offer?
- Can egoism or altruism best account for bystander behaviour?

Section 1: Introducing bystander behaviour

1 How did Kitty Genovese respond when she was stabbed by her attacker?

2 How many of her neighbours in her apartment block were aware of the disturbance?

3 How many times did her attacker assault her?

4 What central question is raised by reports such as that of Kitty Genovese?

Section 2: The decision model

5 Latané & Darley (1968) proposed a 'five-step' decision model of bystander intervention. The first and last steps are *noticing the event* and *implementing the selected decision*, respectively. What are steps two, three and four?

6 What is *pluralistic ignorance*?

7 What experiment, involving the study of students completing questionnaires, did Latané & Darley (1968) carry out in order to demonstrate pluralistic ignorance?

8 Why is *social influence* one reason why groups of participants failed to respond to cries coming from an adjoining room (Latané & Rodin, 1969)?

9 What interesting result did Latané & Rodin (1969) obtain when, instead of placing *strangers* together, they placed two *friends* together, and measured their responses to a potential emergency?

10 What do Latané & Darley (1968) suggest underlies the *diffusion of responsibility* phenomenon?

11 How did Darley & Latané (1968) demonstrate diffusion of responsibility in a laboratory setting?

12 How did Darley and Latané account for the high levels of emotional arousal in participants who did not respond to a victim's plight?

13 What is the relationship between the *competence* of a bystander and his/her likelihood of intervening to help?

14 In what situations may competencies *reduce* the likelihood of bystanders intervening?

15 How did Bickman (1971) demonstrate the effect of a victim's proximity on the likelihood of a bystander intervening?

16 How can Latané and Darley's model be criticised?

17 Piliavin *et al.* carried out a number of experiments involving the collapse of a 'stooge' in a subway carriage (Piliavin *et al.*, 1969; Piliavin & Piliavin, 1972). Identify the factors which affected the likelihood of bystanders intervening.

18 What is the *reverse bystander effect* (Williams & Williams, 1983)?

Section 3: The cost–reward model

19 Piliavin *et al.*'s (1981) *cost–reward model* emphasises the interaction between two sets of factors. Give examples of factors from both sets.

20 What do Piliavin *et al.* mean by '*we-ness*'?

21 What is the role of *arousal* in the cost–reward model?

22 What name do Piliavin *et al.* give to the '*calculations*' in which bystanders weigh the benefits and costs of helping?

23 Give two examples of the *costs of helping* and two examples of *costs of not helping*.

24 In terms of the costs of helping and not helping, explain why bystanders are typically unlikely to help a 'stooge' who, clutching a bottle, collapses in a subway.

25 Give an example of both *personal costs* and *empathy costs*.

26 When is *indirect helping* most likely to occur?

27 Identify any two ways in which *cognitive reinterpretation* can be accomplished.

28 What is Piliavin *et al.*'s explanation for why *impulsive helping* occurs?

Section 4: Egoism and altruism

29 What is the difference between an *egoistic act* and an *altruistic act*?

30 What is the *paradox of altruism*?

31 What argument is advanced in the '*empathy–altruism*' *hypothesis*?

Section 1: Introducing bystander behaviour

1 Kitty Genovese responded by screaming 'Oh my God, he stabbed me!' and 'Please help me!'.

2 Thirty-eight of her neighbours were woken by her screams.

3 Her attacker assaulted her twice, stabbing her and returning to assault her and stab her a second time.

4 Such reports raise the question 'Why do bystanders intervene/fail to intervene?'

Section 2: The decision model

5 The second, third and fourth steps are: interpreting the event as one requiring help, assuming personal responsibility, and selecting a way to help.

6 Pluralistic ignorance refers to the lower likelihood of individuals defining a situation as dangerous if others are present.

7 Latané & Darley (1968) had smoke (actually steam) fill a room in which students were completing questionnaires. When others were present, they were far less likely to raise the alarm.

8 Social influence refers to the tendency of individuals to follow the reactions of others. For example, by appearing to remain calm, individuals may influence others into thinking that a situation is 'safe'.

9 Latané & Rodin (1969) found that when two friends were placed in an ambiguous situation, their response to a potential emergency was just as quick as when either was alone, and much quicker than when two strangers were together.

10 Latané & Darley (1968) suggest that a diffusion of responsibility occurs when individuals reason that somebody else should, and probably will, offer assistance.

11 Darley & Latané (1968) persuaded students that they were taking part in a discussion over an intercom with a number of other participants (either two or one). One of the other 'participants' (actually a tape-recording) was heard to have a seizure and response times were measured.

12 Darley and Latané believed that such participants were experiencing conflict between the fear of making fools of themselves/disrupting the experiment, and their own guilt and shame at doing nothing.

13 When bystanders have relevant competencies (e.g. first aid qualifications), helping is more likely.

14 If bystanders perceive others as being more competent they are less likely to help.

15 Bickman (1971) replicated Darley and Latané's 'seizure study', but led participants to believe that the other person in the discussion was either close to or distant from the victim. Participants were more likely to help when the other participant was far from the victim.

16 Latané and Darley's model does not tell us why 'no' decisions are taken at any of the five stages, and pays more attention to why people don't help, rather than why they do. Additionally, the model does not account for other factors which have been shown to affect helping (such as those identified by Piliavin *et al.*).

17 Whether or not the stooge was carrying a cane or a bottle (and smelled of alcohol), the appearance of fake blood from the victim's mouth as they collapsed, and the presence of an ugly facial birthmark all affected the likelihood of bystander intervention.

18 The reverse bystander effect refers to the increasing reluctance of victims to seek help as the number of potential helpers increases.

Section 3: The cost–reward model

19 The first set of factors includes situational, bystander and victim characteristics, whilst the second includes cognitive and affective reactions.

20 'We-ness' is used by Piliavin *et al.* (1981) to refer to the categorisation of another person as a member of one's own group.

21 The two sets of factors interact to produce arousal. This arousal is then attributed to some factor (such as the victim's plight), and attempts made to reduce this arousal.

22 They call it hedonistic calculus.

23 Costs of helping include time, effort, danger, embarrassment, disruption of activities and psychological aversion. Costs of not helping include guilt, others' disapproval, and the cognitive/emotional discomfort of knowing that another is suffering.

24 Such an individual may be perceived as dangerous or violent, and as not worthy of help. Hence the costs of not helping are low.

25 Personal costs include self-blame and public disapproval, whilst empathy costs refer to the knowledge that a victim continues to suffer.

26 Indirect helping is most likely to occur when both the costs of helping and the costs of not helping are high.

27 Cognitive reinterpretation can be accomplished by redefining the situation as one not requiring help, by denigrating the victim, or by diffusion of responsibility.

28 Piliavin *et al.* believe that impulsive helping occurs as a consequence of the individual being 'flooded' with arousal which focuses them toward the victim's plight, blocking out cost considerations. They suggest that the mechanism may have an evolutionary basis.

Section 4: Egoism and altruism

29 An egoistic act is performed solely with a view to benefit the individual acting, whilst an altruistic act is performed solely to benefit others.

30 The paradox of altruism refers to the Darwinian view that, in the long term, organisms who are altruistic are the least likely to survive.

31 The empathy–altruism hypothesis suggests that we feel empathic concern when others are in distress and act to reduce their distress.

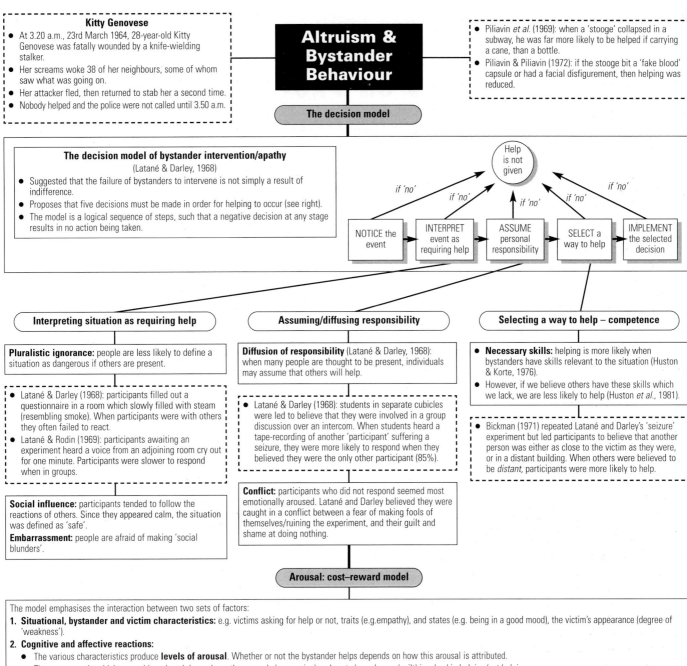

Altruism & Bystander Behaviour

The decision model

Kitty Genovese

- At 3.20 a.m., 23rd March 1964, 28-year-old Kitty Genovese was fatally wounded by a knife-wielding stalker.
- Her screams woke 38 of her neighbours, some of whom saw what was going on.
- Her attacker fled, then returned to stab her a second time.
- Nobody helped and the police were not called until 3.50 a.m.

- Piliavin *et al.* (1969): when a 'stooge' collapsed in a subway, he was far more likely to be helped if carrying a cane, than a bottle.
- Piliavin & Piliavin (1972): if the stooge bit a 'fake blood' capsule or had a facial disfigurement, then helping was reduced.

The decision model of bystander intervention/apathy
(Latané & Darley, 1968)

- Suggested that the failure of bystanders to intervene is not simply a result of indifference.
- Proposes that five decisions must be made in order for helping to occur (see right).
- The model is a logical sequence of steps, such that a negative decision at any stage results in no action being taken.

Help is not given

NOTICE the event → INTERPRET event as requiring help → ASSUME personal responsibility → SELECT a way to help → IMPLEMENT the selected decision

if 'no'

Interpreting situation as requiring help

Pluralistic ignorance: people are less likely to define a situation as dangerous if others are present.

- Latané & Darley (1968): participants filled out a questionnaire in a room which slowly filled with steam (resembling smoke). When participants were with others they often failed to react.
- Latané & Rodin (1969): participants awaiting an experiment heard a voice from an adjoining room cry out for one minute. Participants were slower to respond when in groups.

Social influence: participants tended to follow the reactions of others. Since they appeared calm, the situation was defined as 'safe'.

Embarrassment: people are afraid of making 'social blunders'.

Assuming/diffusing responsibility

Diffusion of responsibility (Latané & Darley, 1968): when many people are thought to be present, individuals may assume that others will help.

- Latané & Darley (1968): students in separate cubicles were led to believe that they were involved in a group discussion over an intercom. When students heard a tape-recording of another 'participant' suffering a seizure, they were more likely to respond when they believed they were the only other participant (85%).

Conflict: participants who did not respond seemed most emotionally aroused. Latané and Darley believed they were caught in a conflict between a fear of making fools of themselves/ruining the experiment, and their guilt and shame at doing nothing.

Selecting a way to help – competence

- **Necessary skills:** helping is more likely when bystanders have skills relevant to the situation (Huston & Korte, 1976).
- However, if we believe others have these skills which we lack, we are less likely to help (Huston *et al.*, 1981).

- Bickman (1971) repeated Latané and Darley's 'seizure' experiment but led participants to believe that another person was either as close to the victim as they were, or in a distant building. When others were believed to be *distant*, participants were more likely to help.

Arousal: cost–reward model

The model emphasises the interaction between two sets of factors:
1. **Situational, bystander and victim characteristics:** e.g. victims asking for help or not, traits (e.g.empathy), and states (e.g. being in a good mood), the victim's appearance (degree of 'weakness').
2. **Cognitive and affective reactions:**
   - The various characteristics produce **levels of arousal**. Whether or not the bystander helps depends on how this arousal is attributed.
   - The exact way in which arousal is reduced depends on the rewards (e.g. praise) and costs (e.g. danger/guilt) involved in helping/not helping.
   - **Hedonistic calculus** (weighing the costs and benefits) determines whether the bystander helps (see below).

Applications to research

- When person carrying a cane collapses, costs of helping (e.g. danger) are low and costs of not helping (e.g. criticism) are high.
- When person carrying a bottle collapses, costs of helping (e.g. danger) are high and costs of not helping (e.g. criticism) are low ('Who would blame me?').

'Personal costs' vs 'empathy costs'

- Personal costs (e.g. self-blame and disapproval) and empathy costs (e.g. knowing the victim continues to suffer) are associated with not helping.
- Where costs of helping and not helping are *both* high, individuals may help indirectly (getting someone else) or reinterpret the situation (e.g. by blaming the victim/deciding help is not required).

Impulsive helping

- Piliavin *et al.'s* model suggests that help is least likely to be offered in life-threatening situations.
- Impulsive helping, where people act in almost reflexive ways, irrespective of personal cost, does sometimes occur.
- Piliavin *et al.* argue that emergency situations flood the bystander with arousal which narrows their attention towards the victim's plight.

Universal egoism

- The view that people are fundamentally selfish, and altruism is impossible (Dovidio, 1995).
- Simple Darwinian theory suggests that altruistic species should die out. However, altruism among animals *is* observed.
- The '*paradox of altruism*' can be explained if we assume that altruism is really a subtle form of *egoism* (e.g. 'investing') and this is roughly the approach taken by Piliavin *et al.'s* model.

Egoism vs altruism

Is a bystander's response a selfish, *egoistic* act, or one performed to benefit others, with no expectation of benefit/gain (*altruistic*)?

Empathy–altruism

- The empathy–altruism hypothesis argues that sometimes we experience empathic concern for others and act to relieve their distress.
- The feelings produced by empathic concern are qualitatively different from those produced by personal distress.

16

MEDIA INFLUENCES ON PRO- AND ANTI-SOCIAL BEHAVIOUR

SYLLABUS
13.1 Pro- and anti-social behaviour – media influences on pro- and anti-social behaviour
- explanations and research studies relating to media influences on pro- and anti-social behaviour

KEY QUESTIONS
- How much aggressive behaviour is shown on television?
- What are the effects of media aggression on children's behaviour?
- Can the media also have pro-social effects?
- How is media influence studied?

Q

Section 1: Showing and watching aggression
1. What is the basic method used to quantify the amount of violence shown on television?
2. What was the principal finding of Gerbner's studies of violence on American television?
3. According to Cumberbatch's (1987) study of British television, what percentage of viewing time did violence occupy?
4. What was Cumberbatch's view regarding the increase in television violence in the decade up to 1987?
5. When Gunter & Harrison (1995) compared terrestrial and satellite channels for the percentage of programmes containing violent acts, what did they find?
6. According to Gunter and Harrison, in what type of programme were most of the violent acts contained?
7. What was the overall conclusion of Gunter and Harrison's study regarding the distribution of violence in television programmes?

Section 2: The effects of television on behaviour
8. What general conclusion, relevant to the study of the effects of television on children's behaviour, can be drawn from Bandura's (1965) 'Bobo doll' study?
9. How were Anderson et al. (1986) able to study the viewing habits of families?
10. Complete the following sentence: 'Anderson discovered that no-one watches the television for more than ___ per cent of the time it is on'.
11. Approximately how much time do adults spend watching television, per week?
12. At what age does the average number of hours of television watched per week peak?
13. Cumberbatch (1987) found that whilst violence in children's programmes was rare, there was one notable exception. What was it?
14. How do children differ from adults in their perception of violent acts on television?
15. How do *correlational studies* of television violence investigate the relationship between television violence and aggression?

16. What is the principal criticism of correlational studies of the effects of television violence on behaviour?
17. How did Liebert & Baron (1972) investigate the link between watching violent television and behaving aggressively?
18. Identify three problems associated with *laboratory studies* of media influences.
19. In general, what are the results of field experiments into the relationship between watching television violence and aggressive behaviour?
20. How did Williams (1986) conduct a *natural experiment* in her study of the 'Notel' community?
21. In 1994, a study began to look at the effects of the introduction of television to the island of St Helena. So far, what effects on pro-social behaviour have been found?
22. What relationship between television and arousal is proposed by Berkowitz (1993)?
23. How do the effects of television *disinhibition* and *desensitisation* differ?
24. What is probably the most direct link between watching television and the viewer's own behaviour?
25. Which type of individual is most likely to benefit from a *cathartic* effect of watching television violence?

Section 3: Pro-social effects of the media
26. Name six pro-social effects of the media which researchers have found from laboratory studies which used specially prepared television materials.
27. What conclusion do Gunter & McAleer (1990) draw regarding the effects of televised examples of good behaviour?
28. What is involved in *television literacy*?
29. According to Mitchell (1983), what relation may computer games have with social interaction amongst children?
30. Identify five benefits associated with the use of computer games.

Section 1: Showing and watching aggression

1 A simple counting technique is used, with researchers defining violence objectively, then coding samples of television for incidents which match those definitions.
2 Gerbner found that although the number of programmes containing violence had not increased significantly since 1967, the number of violent episodes per show had increased.
3 Violence occupied about one per cent of viewing time.
4 Cumberbatch argued that whilst violence in society and concerns about violence on television had risen, this was not reflected by similar increases in violence on television.
5 Gunter & Harrison (1995) found that roughly 28 per cent of terrestrial programmes contain violent acts, compared with 52 per cent of programmes on satellite channels.
6 Films and dramas contained 70 per cent of the violent acts.
7 The study concluded that television violence is concentrated principally in a small number of programmes.

Section 2: The effects of television on behaviour

8 Bandura's (1965) 'Bobo doll' study suggests that children can acquire new aggressive responses through exposure to a filmed model.
9 Anderson *et al.* (1986) installed automatic time-lapse video recording equipment in the homes of 99 families, with one camera recording people's behaviour in the room and the other focused on the television itself.
10 'Anderson discovered that no-one watches the television for more than *75 per cent* of the time it is on.'
11 Roughly ten hours per week (11.5 hours switched on, 7.56 hours looking at it).
12 The average number of hours of television watched per week peaks at the age of ten.
13 Cumberbatch (1987) found that children's cartoons contained relatively high amounts of violent behaviour.
14 Children differ from adults in their ratings of violence, and may not see violent acts which lack realism (such as cartoon violence) as being violent.
15 Correlational studies of television violence typically ask people which programmes they like most or watch most often, and then correlate this with measures of aggression, such as teacher's reports or self-reports.
16 Correlational studies can tell us whether there is a relationship between television violence and aggressive behaviour, but do not allow us to infer causation. It may be, for example, that naturally aggressive individuals choose to watch more violent television.
17 Liebert & Baron (1972) randomly assigned children to two groups. One group watched *The Untouchables,* which was violent, whilst the others watched a non-violent sports competition. They were then observed playing afterwards, and their aggressive acts measured.
18 Most laboratory studies use small and unrepresentative samples, under unnatural viewing conditions. Additionally, the measures of viewing and aggressive behaviour are often far removed from everyday behaviour. Overall, such studies lack ecological validity.
19 In general, the results show that children who watch violent television are more aggressive than those who do not (Parke *et al.*, 1977).
20 Williams (1986) studied a community where television had only recently been introduced (the 'Notel' community), comparing verbal and physical aggression with communities where there was either a single or several television channels.
21 The study of St Helena has shown that pro-social behaviours have not decreased since the introduction of television, and have actually increased slightly.
22 Berkowitz (1993) proposes that watching violence on television increases the viewer's overall level of emotional arousal and excitement.
23 Disinhibition is the reduction of inhibitions about behaving aggressively oneself (or coming to believe that aggression is a legitimate way of solving problems). Desensitisation is the reduction in emotional response to television violence (and an increased acceptance of it in real life) as a result of repeatedly viewing it.
24 Imitation is probably the most direct link between watching television and the viewer's own behaviour.
25 Individuals who score highly on cognitive measures of fantasy, daydreaming and imagination are most likely to benefit (Singer, 1989).

Section 3: Pro-social effects of the media

26 Courage, the delay of gratification, adherence to rules, charitable behaviour, friendliness and affectionate behaviour may all be influenced by the use of specially prepared TV material.
27 Gunter & McAleer (1990) conclude that televised examples of good behaviour can encourage children to behave in friendlier and more thoughtful ways to others.
28 Television literacy involves teaching children to be 'informed consumers' of television (e.g. distinguishing reality and make-believe, understanding the purpose of advertisements, and assessing stereotyping).
29 Mitchell (1983) points out that computer games may promote interaction in a beneficial way through co-operation and competition.
30 Computer games can act as motivating devices in the learning process, give children a sense of confidence in the use of IT, equip them with computer-related skills, can promote social interaction, allow the release of aggression and stress, enhance cognitive skills, provide a sense of mastery and accomplishment, and reduce youth problems (as a consequence of an addictive interest in computer games).

A

Media Influences on Behaviour

How much aggression is shown?

American TV – Gerbner's studies
(Gerbner, 1972; Gerbner & Gross, 1976; Gerbner et al., 1980, 1986)
- The percentage of TV shows containing violent incidents has remained the same since 1967.
- The number of violent episodes per show has gradually increased to around five violent acts per hour (prime time).
- On children's weekend shows, there were roughly 20 violent acts per hour.

UK TV – Cumberbatch's (1987) study
- 30% of programmes contained some violence (1.68 acts per hour, on average).
- Violence occupied just over 1% of viewing time.
- Death resulted from violence 26% of the time, but considerable blood and gore occurred in only 0.2% of cases.
- Perpetrators were more likely to be portrayed as 'baddies' than 'goodies'.

UK TV – Gunter & Harrison (1995)
- BBC 1 and 2, ITV, and Channel 4. 28% contained violent acts (52% for satellite channels).
- 70% of violence occurred in dramas and films, 19% in children's programmes.
- Most violent acts occurred in inner-city locations and the majority of perpetrators were young white males.
- 1% of programmes contained 19% of all violent acts.
Concluded that *violence is concentrated in a small number of programmes*.

How much do people watch?

Anderson *et al.* (1986):
- No one watches TV for more than 75% of the time it is on.
- Children average 12.8 hours (9.14 hours watching), adults 11.5 hours (7.56 hours watching) per week.
- Adult males look at the TV more than do adult females.
- Number of hours looking at TV increases up to age of 10 then decreases, levelling off at 17 years.

How is violence perceived?

- Cumberbatch (1987): children's cartoons contain relatively high amounts of violence.
- However, realism appears to be an important factor, since real life violence is judged as more violent than fictional violence (Gunter & McAleer, 1990).
- Although cartoons may *objectively* contain a large number of violent acts, children may *subjectively* perceive them as containing hardly any.

How does TV exert an influence?

Arousal
- Berkowitz (1993): watching violence increases a viewers' emotional arousal and excitement.
- More realistic violence is perceived by viewers as more arousing.

Disinhibition
- Refers to a reduction in the viewer's inhibitions about behaving aggressively.
- Relates to Berkowitz's 'cue-arousal' theory (see Ch 14).

Imitation
- Bandura (1965) showed that children may imitate aggressive adults (see Ch 38).
- However, cognitive factors (i.e. how violence is perceived and interpreted) will affect whether or not it is imitated.

Desensitisation
- A reduction in emotional response to TV violence and an acceptance of violence in real life.
- Increasingly violent programmes may be required to produce an emotional response (Gadow & Sprafkin, 1989).

Does viewing TV violence at an early age predict later aggression?

Comstock & Paik (1991): viewing TV violence at an early age *is* a predictor of later aggression (based on Huesmann & Eron's (1986) cross-cultural survey). However, Cumberbatch (1997) made the following criticisms:
- The Australian research showed *no* significant correlation between early TV viewing and later aggression.
- The Dutch researchers found no relationship and refused to allow their findings to be included.
- The American researchers found that when initial aggression was controlled for there was only a significant correlation in girls.
- The Polish researchers only found small effects which needed to be 'treated cautiously'.
- The Finnish researchers misunderstood their own data which in fact showed a *negative* correlation.

Media and pro-social behaviour

TV violence and catharsis
- Instinct theories suggest that watching TV violence might allow aggressive feelings to be released.
- Evidence suggests that if this effect does occur, it is restricted to individuals who score high on measures of fantasy and imagination (Singer, 1989)

Four areas of evidence for pro-social effects of TV
(Gunter & McAleer, 1990)
Laboratory studies with prepared materials: these have been shown to influence courage, delay of gratification, and promote adherence to rules, friendliness and affection.
Laboratory studies using broadcast materials specially designed for teaching (e.g. *Sesame Street*): children are able to identify and remember co-operative and helping behaviours emphasised.
Laboratory studies with materials from popular series: when pro-social behaviour is similar to that required of the child, programmes may influence behaviour in some circumstances.
Field studies relating pro-social viewing to pro-social behaviours: children who watch a high proportion of pro-social programmes are more likely to behave pro-socially; however, the correlations are weaker than with anti-social behaviour.

Computer games
- The long-term effects are unclear (Griffiths, 1997).
- They may promote interaction (through co-operation and competition) among children (Mitchell, 1983), have a cathartic effect (Kestenbaum & Weinstein, 1984) or provide a sense of achievement.

Methods of studying TV violence

Correlational studies
- Typically involve asking people what they watch and correlating these with reports of social behaviour by teachers, peers etc.
- Such studies are unable to infer cause and effect, and it may be that those who watch violent TV are different in some way.

Laboratory studies
- Designed to test for a causal link, and typically involve showing experimental groups of children violent programmes and observing their behaviour.
- Most use small and unrepresentative samples and unnatural viewing conditions, so it is unclear how they relate to the real world.

Field experiments
- Have greater ecological validity than laboratory experiments and typically involve assigning children to violent/non-violent viewing and measuring their behaviour.
- Poor control over extraneous variables mean that we cannot be certain what has caused differences between groups.

Natural experiments
- Researchers take advantage of naturally occurring divisions.
- Williams (1986) studied the 'Notel' community where TV was only recently introduced. Verbal and physical aggression *did* increase in the two year period following the introduction of TV.

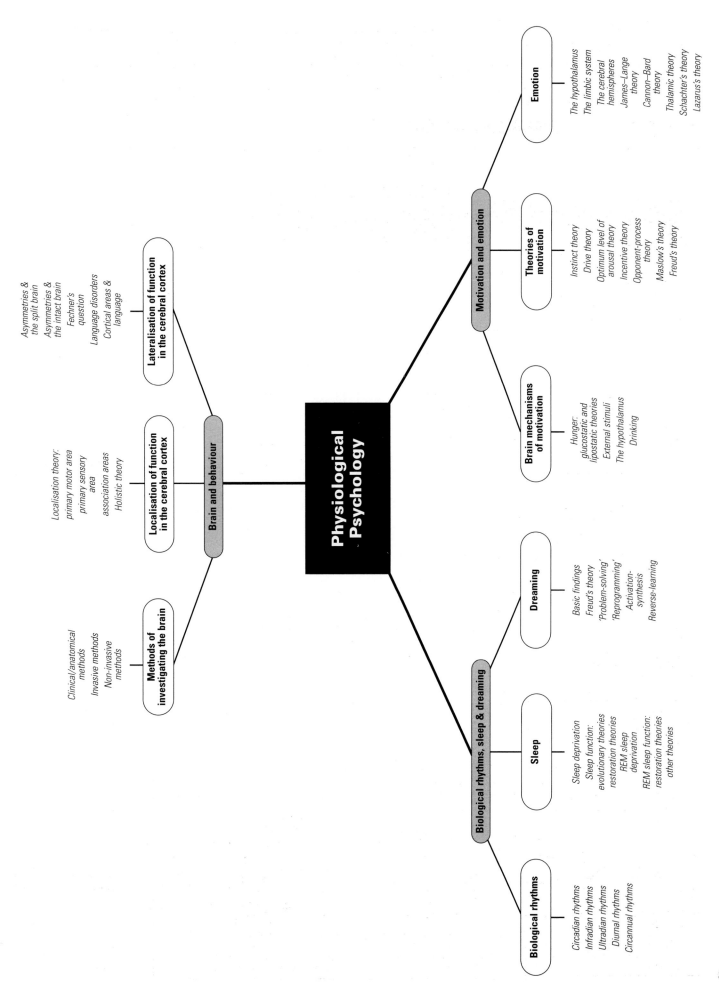

Physiological Psychology

Brain and behaviour

Methods of investigating the brain
- Clinical/anatomical methods
- Invasive methods
- Non-invasive methods

Localisation of function in the cerebral cortex
- Localisation theory: primary motor area
- primary sensory area
- association areas
- Holistic theory

Lateralisation of function in the cerebral cortex
- Asymmetries & the split brain
- Asymmetries & the intact brain
- Fechner's question
- Language disorders
- Cortical areas & language

Motivation and emotion

Brain mechanisms of motivation
- Hunger: glucostatic and lipostatic theories
- External stimuli
- The hypothalamus
- Drinking

Theories of motivation
- Instinct theory
- Drive theory
- Optimum level of arousal theory
- Incentive theory
- Opponent-process theory
- Maslow's theory
- Freud's theory

Emotion
- The hypothalamus
- The limbic system
- The cerebral hemispheres
- James–Lange theory
- Cannon–Bard theory
- Thalamic theory
- Schachter's theory
- Lazarus's theory

Biological rhythms, sleep & dreaming

Biological rhythms
- Circadian rhythms
- Infradian rhythms
- Ultradian rhythms
- Diurnal rhythms
- Circannual rhythms

Sleep
- Sleep deprivation
- Sleep function: evolutionary theories
- restoration theories
- REM sleep deprivation
- REM sleep function: restoration theories
- other theories

Dreaming
- Basic findings
- Freud's theory
- 'Problem-solving'
- 'Reprogramming'
- Activation-synthesis
- Reverse-learning

87

METHODS OF INVESTIGATING THE BRAIN

Section 1: Clinical/anatomical methods

1 In what way do *clinical/anatomical methods* study the brain?
2 What type of patients were studied in Broca and Wernicke's investigations into language?
3 Identify three difficulties with such studies.

Section 2: Invasive methods of investigation

4 What is involved in *ablation*?
5 What discovery was made by Flourens, using this technique with rabbits, birds and dogs?
6 Apart from the difficulty of generalising the results of ablation studies to humans, what is another problem with these studies?
7 What is involved in *lesion production*?
8 Complete the sentence: 'Lesions in one area of the hypothalamus cause extreme ___ in rats'.
9 Identify one therapeutic use of lesions in humans.
10 What do the letters ESB stand for?
11 How were Olds & Milner (1954) able to discover a '*pleasure centre*' in the brains of rats?
12 What classic research was carried out by Penfield during the 1940s and 1950s?
13 How has ESB been used therapeutically?
14 Identify three criticisms of ESB made by Valenstein (1977).
15 What does *micro-electrode recording* aim to measure?
16 Which sensory system has been investigated by Hubel and Wiesel using micro-electrode recording?
17 Identify two drawbacks associated with this method.

Section 3: Non-invasive methods of investigation

18 In what way can radioactive forms of sugar be used to study anatomic pathways?
19 What does an *EEG (electroencephalogram)* measure?
20 In what form are the results of an EEG machine produced?
21 When are *alpha waves* most likely to be be recorded by an EEG?

22 Identify three conditions in which the EEG can assist diagnosis.
23 Identify one further area in which the EEG has proved an indispensible tool for researchers.
24 What is the principal criticism of the EEG as a method of investigating cortical functioning?
25 In what way is *computerised electroencephalography* able to partially overcome limitations of the EEG?
26 In what way does a *magnetoencephalograph* (MEG) differ from an EEG?
27 How does EEG imaging allow brain functioning to be measured 'on a millisecond by millisecond basis' (Fischman, 1985)?
28 How does *computerised axial tomography* (CAT) allow researchers to investigate cortical functioning?
29 What type of information is yielded by a CAT scan?
30 What do the letters MRI stand for, when referring to scanning devices?
31 What is the role of radio waves in MRI scanning?
32 What limitation do CAT and MRI scans share, when providing us with information about the brain?
33 What is the first step in investigating the brain functioning of an individual when using *positron emission tomography* (PET)?
34 What is the biggest advantage of PET over MRI and CAT?
35 In what way is PET useful in the study of mental disorders?
36 What conclusion was reached by Gur *et al.* (1994) in studying the brain metabolism of men and women using this method?
37 What is the advantage of newer techniques (such as *SPET* and *SQUID*) over other scanning techniques?
38 How does SPET measure brain activity?
39 Complete the sentence: 'SPET is also useful in detecting the brain areas affected in people with ___ difficulties (Matthews, 1996a)'.

Section 1: Clinical/anatomical methods

1 Clinical/anatomical methods look at the behavioural consequences of accidental brain damage.
2 Broca and Wernicke studied patients who had suffered a stroke, and had difficulty producing or understanding speech.
3 Such studies are not very helpful in studying subtle changes, since accurate records of behaviour prior to the damage often do not exist. It is also difficult to determine the location and amount of damage, and researchers have to wait for the 'right kind' of injury to occur in order to study a given area.

Section 2: Invasive methods of investigation

4 Ablation involves surgically removing or destroying brain tissue and observing the behavioural consequences.
5 Flourens discovered that the cerebellum plays a vital role in co-ordination and balance.
6 Ablation methods cannot tell us if a removed part of the brain controlled a particular behaviour or was simply involved in it.
7 Lesion production involves deliberately injuring part of the brain, then observing the behavioural consequences.
8 'Lesions in one area of the hypothalamus cause extreme *overeating (or undereating)* in rats.'
9 Lesions are used to reduce the severity of epileptic seizures.
10 Electrical stimulation of the brain.
11 Olds & Milner (1954) fitted implanted electrodes to a control mechanism which the rat could operate. Since the rat would self-stimulate this region at over 100 times per minute, and in preference to food or water, it was assumed that this was a pleasure centre.
12 Penfield stimulated the cortex of conscious patients being treated for epilepsy, to map cortical functions.
13 ESB has been used to treat pain by 'blocking' pain messages in the spine before they reach the brain.
14 Valenstein (1977) points out that no single brain area is likely to be the sole source of a given behaviour, that ESB-provoked behaviour is not normal but compulsive and stereotypical, and that identical stimulation produces different effects at different times on the same individual.
15 Micro-electrode recording aims to measure the electrical activity in a single neuron.
16 Hubel and Wiesel used this technique to investigate the visual system in monkeys.
17 The method is slow (since only one neuron can be studied at a time), and is confined to non-humans since the electrodes can destroy brain tissue.

Section 3: Non-invasive methods of investigation

18 Radioactive forms of sugar can be injected into non-humans, the animal made to perform a task, and slices of the sacrificed animal's brain pressed against a radioactivity-sensitive film in order to determine which areas were most active.
19 An EEG measures changes in the electrical activity of the brain.
20 An EEG machine produces results by tracing the impulses in pen on paper attached to a revolving drum.
21 Alpha waves are most likely to be be recorded in adults who are awake, relaxed, with their eyes closed.
22 Tumours, damaged brain tissue, and epilepsy.
23 The EEG has also proved helpful in investigating sleep and dreaming.
24 The EEG only reflects the gross activity of neurons and tells us only that something is happening, not what is happening.
25 In computerised electroencephalography, a stimulus is repeatedly presented and a computer screens out activity unrelated to the stimulus.
26 A magnetoencephalograph (MEG) detects weak magnetic fields, whereas an EEG detects electrical activity.
27 During EEG imaging, the activity recorded by 32 electrodes is sent to a computer, which translates this information into coloured, moving images.
28 The CAT scan examines the brain by taking a large number of X-rays of the brain, using a rotating X-ray tube and detector.
29 A CAT scan yields structural information about the brain.
30 Magnetic resonance imaging.
31 Radio waves are used to excite hydrogen atoms in the brain which in turn disturb a magnetic field. This disturbance is measured.
32 Both CAT and MRI scans can only provide a still image of a cross-section of the brain.
33 The first step in PET is to inject the person with a small amount of radioactive material, bonded to a substance which is metabolised.
34 PET is able to examine the relationship between brain activity and mental processes.
35 PET can reveal differences in the pattern of neural activity between those with and without mental disorders.
36 Gur *et al.* (1994) concluded that men have a more active metabolism in the primitive brain centres controlling sex and violence.
37 Newer techniques (such as SPET and SQUID) are able to focus on very small areas of the brain.
38 SPET measures brain activity by monitoring blood flow to different brain areas.
39 'SPET is also useful in detecting the brain areas affected in people with *learning* difficulties (Matthews, 1996a).'

A

Investigating the Brain

Clinical/anatomical methods

- Involve looking at the behavioural consequences of accidental brain damage.
- Unfortunately it may be difficult to determine the precise *location* and *amount* of damage, and just how *much* behaviour change has resulted from the damage.

Invasive methods

Ablation and lesion production

Ablation involves surgically removing or destroying brain tissue and observing the behavioural consequences.

- Flourens pioneered the technique in the 1820s, showing that the removal of thin slices from the cerebellum of rabbits, birds and dogs resulted in poor co-ordination and balance.
- However, where behaviour does change, we cannot be sure if the brain region *controls* or is merely *involved* in a behaviour.

Lesion production involves deliberately injuring part of the brain and observing the behavioural consequences.

- Animals are placed under anaesthetic, an electrode inserted into a specific brain site, and used to 'burn' out a small area.
- Lesions to the hypothalamus of rats produce over- or under-eating.
- However, we cannot be sure that such findings can be generalised to humans.

Electrical stimulation of the brain (ESB)

ESB involves inserting one or more electrodes into a living animal's brain and applying an electric current which does not cause any damage.

- Olds & Milner (1954): electrical stimulation of the *hypothalamus* in rats caused them to increase the frequency of whatever they were engaged in.

Also used in studying the *cortex* of humans (Penfield, 1940s and 1950s) and can be used to 'map' brain regions, as well as *therapeutically* (e.g. by 'blocking' pain messages in the spine before they reach the brain).

Problems

Valenstein (1977): points out that (i) no single brain area is likely to be the sole source of a behaviour, (ii) ESB produces compulsive, not natural behaviours, and (iii) the effects of ESB on the *same* area vary over time.

Micro-electrode recording

The insertion of tiny electrodes to record a single neuron's activity in a living animal's brain. The electrode is attached to an electrical connector cemented to the brain, which leads to an apparatus which measures electrical activity.

- Hubel & Wiesel (1965): used this technique to investigate the ways in which a monkey's brain processes visual information.

Problems

- Since the brain contains billions of neurons, building up a picture of how the brain works using this method is very slow.
- Micro-electrodes can destroy brain tissue, so their use has been confined to non-humans, making it difficult to generalise findings to humans.

Chemical stimulation

Involves introducing a chemical into the brains of non-humans to determine its behavioural and physiological effects.

- The chemical is delivered using a small tube (*micro-pipette*).
- The most commonly used chemicals are those believed to affect synaptic transmission.

- Has been used to trace anatomic pathways in the brain, using a radioactive form of sugar. Cells involved in a task use more sugar, so radioactivity builds up in them.
- The animal is then 'sacrificed' and slices of brain tissue exposed to a photographic film sensitive to radioactivity.

Problems

- The data are often difficult to interpret, with different non-humans responding differently to the same chemical.
- As with all invasive methods, there are practical and ethical issues.

Non-invasive methods

Recording the brain's electrical activity

- Adrian & Matthews (1934): developed the *electroencephalogram* (or EEG) which measures changes in brain activity in different brain parts.
- The EEG allows researchers to measure brain activity in response to specific experiences, using an amplifier which passes information to pens which trace impulses onto paper.
- The EEG is used in *clinical diagnosis* since EEG patterns from tumours and damaged tissue are distinctive.
- The EEG is also used to investigate *sleep and dreaming*.
- Recordings can only represent the gross and simultaneous activity, revealing that *something* is happening but not *what*.

4 main types of 'brain waves'

- **Delta** (1–3 Hz): mainly found in infants, adults in 'deep' sleep, or adults with brain tumours.
- **Theta** (4–7 Hz): common in infants aged 2–5 years, observed in adults with antisocial personality disorder.
- **Alpha** (8–13 Hz): seen in adults who are awake, relaxed and whose eyes are closed.
- **Beta** (13Hz +): seen in adults who are awake, alert, have their eyes open, and are concentrating on a task.

Modern techniques

- *Computerised electro-encephalography*: involves repeatedly presenting a stimulus and having a computer filter out activity unrelated to it.
- *Magnetoencephalograms (MEGs)*: detect the weak magnetic fields caused by the brain's electrical activity.
- *EEG imaging*: allows researchers to measure brain functioning on a millisecond basis, by feeding information from 32 electrodes placed on the scalp into a computer which produces moving images.

Scanning and imaging devices

Computerised axial tomography (CAT)

- The brain is examined by taking a large number of X-ray photographs of it.
- A person's head is placed in a tube with an X-ray source and X-ray detector opposite each other. These two then rotate, and the amount of penetration of X-rays is recorded.
- Information is then fed into a computer which displays a 3-D representation of the brain's structures.

Magnetic resonance imaging (MRI)

- MRI uses a strong magnetic field, rather than X-rays, to form an image of the brain.
- A person is placed in a powerful magnetic field, then harmless radio waves, which excite hydrogen atoms in the brain, are emitted.
- The changes in the magnetic field are recorded by computer, producing a more sensitive and clearer picture than the CAT scan.

Positron emission tomography (PET)

- PET measures metabolic activity in the brain.
- A person is injected with a harmless radioactive substance 'bonded' to glucose.
- As the brain metabolises this glucose, the most active areas can be detected.
- PET can provide information about brain functioning *during* behaviour and *differences* of functioning in abnormality.

SPET and SQUID

- *Superconducting quantum imaging devices* (SQUIDs) and *single positron emission devices* (SPETs) are able to focus on the activity of very small areas of the brain.
- SPET measures blood flows into different brain areas, having first injected a person with a small amount of radioactive iodine.
- Useful in detecting areas of brain involved in learning difficulties.

18

LOCALISATION OF FUNCTION IN THE CEREBRAL CORTEX

SYLLABUS

13.2 Brain and behaviour – localisation of function in the cerebral cortex
- the function organisation of the cerebral cortex, including the primary motor, sensory and association areas (e.g. Broca's and Wernicke's areas). 'Distributed functions' as an alternative to localisation of function

KEY QUESTIONS
- What is localisation theory?
- What are the primary motor areas?
- What are the sensory motor areas?
- What are the primary association areas?
- What is holistic theory?

Section 1: Introducing localisation theory

1 What name is given to the *fissure* which runs down the middle of the brain, dividing it into two halves?
2 What is the central claim of *localisation theory*?
3 How did *phrenologists* claim to be able to detect the unusual development of the 'organs' which make up the brain?
4 Which *invasive method* is commonly used to assist in understanding localised brain function?

Section 2: The primary motor area

5 What did Delgado (1969) discover when he stimulated part of the *primary motor area* in a patient's left hemisphere?
6 What is a *contralateral connection*?
7 What did Penfield discover when he stimulated the top of the primary motor area?
8 What did Penfield discover regarding those body areas (such as fingers) which require more precise control?
9 What aspect of movement is the primary motor area *not* responsible for?

Section 3: The primary sensory areas

10 What is the principal role of the *primary somatosensory area*?
11 In what two ways is this area similar to the primary motor area?
12 According to Robertson (1995), what difference exists between the somatosensory areas of Braille readers and non-Braille readers?
13 What is a likely consequence of damage to the primary somatosensory area?
14 In which lobe is the *primary auditory area* located?
15 What did Penfield discover when stimulating this area in his patients?
16 What is meant by saying that hearing involves *ipsilateral connections* as well as *contralateral connections*?
17 What is a likely consequence of slight damage to the auditory area?
18 In which lobe is the *primary visual area* located?

19 What is a likely consequence of damage to part of the visual area?
20 What is the *optic chiasma*?
21 Why doesn't damage to one eye result in one hemisphere 'missing out' on visual input?

Section 4: Association areas

22 Complete the sentence: 'The motor association areas are involved in the ___ and ___ of movements'.
23 What do the *motor association areas* in the left parietal lobe keep track of?
24 What is *cross-modal matching*?
25 What is a likely consequence of damage to the *auditory association area* in the left hemisphere?
26 What is *visual agnosia*, and from what type of damage does it result?
27 What example of this phenomenon is given by Sacks (1985)?
28 Identify three other cognitive functions which are performed by association areas involved in neither motor nor sensory functions.
29 Complete the sentence: 'Frontal lobe damage does not cause significant impairments in ___ functioning'.
30 What example does Luria (1980) give of *perseveration*?
31 Identify three ways in which frontal lobe damage may affect intentions.
32 What is *behavioural inertia*, caused by excessive frontal lobe damage?
33 What name is given to the procedures in which brain damage is deliberately inflicted with the intention of treating mental disorders?
34 Identify three roles played by association areas in the *temporal lobes*.

Section 5: Holistic theory

35 What is the central claim made by *holistic theory*?
36 What did Lashley (1926) discover when studying the effects of destroying parts of rats' brains on their ability to remember their way through a maze?
37 What is the *law of mass action*?

Section 1: Introducing localisation theory

1 The longitudinal fissure.
2 According to localisation theory, different areas of the brain are specialised for different psychological functions.
3 Phrenologists claimed to be able to detect unusual developments of people's brains by the pattern of bumps on their skulls.
4 Electrical stimulation of the brain (ESB).

Section 2: The primary motor area

5 Delgado (1969) discovered that this caused the patient to form a clenched fist with his right hand.
6 A contralateral connection is one in which nerve fibres cross over, connecting one side of the body to the opposite hemisphere.
7 Penfield discovered that stimulating the top of the primary motor area resulted in twitching in the lower part of the body.
8 Those body areas which require more precise control have more cortical area devoted to them than areas requiring less precise control.
9 The primary motor area is not responsible for 'commanding' or planning movements.

Section 3: The primary sensory areas

10 The primary somatosensory area is responsible for receiving information from the skin senses (and the sense of taste).
11 This area also represents the body in an approximately 'upside-down' fashion, and more sensitive body parts have more cortex devoted to them.
12 Robertson (1995) found that Braille readers have more cortical area devoted to the tip of the right forefinger than do non-Braille readers.
13 Damage to the primary somatosensory area is likely to cause deficits or disturbances in the sense of touch.
14 The primary auditory area is located in the temporal lobe.
15 Penfield discovered that stimulation of this area caused patients to report hearing sounds.
16 Whilst much of the information from each ear crosses to the opposite hemisphere (contralateral connection), some information is processed by the hemisphere on the same side as the ear (ipsilateral connection).
17 Slight damage to this area is likely to produce partial hearing loss.
18 The primary visual area is located in the occipital lobe.
19 Damage to part of this area is likely to cause blindness in part of the visual field.

20 The optic chiasma is the location in the brain where nerve fibres from each eye meet and then divide.
21 Damage to one eye doesn't result in one hemisphere 'missing out' on visual input, since both hemispheres receive half of the visual input from each eye.

Section 4: Association areas

22 'The motor association areas are involved in the *planning* and *execution* of movements.'
23 The motor association areas in the left parietal lobe keep track of the location of the body's moving parts.
24 Cross-modal matching is a complex sensory function in which information from one sense modality (such as touch) may be translated into another (such as sight). This allows us to identify by sight something which we have previously only touched.
25 Damage to the auditory association area in the left hemisphere is likely to result in difficulties in producing or comprehending language.
26 Visual agnosia is an inability to recognise objects by sight, and results from damage to the visual association area.
27 Sacks (1985) gives an example of a man who, suffering from visual agnosia, mistook his wife for his hat.
28 Other association areas are involved in learning, thinking and memory.
29 'Frontal lobe damage does not cause significant impairments in *intellectual* functioning.'
30 Luria (1980) gives the example of a man who continued to try to light a match after it had been lit.
31 Frontal lobe damage may affect the ability to set goals, plan actions, and make decisions.
32 Behavioural inertia is a condition in which a person lacks spontaneity, remains motionless, and stares vacantly into space.
33 Psychosurgery.
34 Association areas in the temporal lobes play a role in memory, social behaviour, and certain emotional responses.

Section 5: Holistic theory

35 Holistic theory claims that psychological functions are controlled by neurons throughout the brain.
36 Lashley (1926) found that destruction of one particular area did not lead to greater difficulties than destruction of any other area.
37 The law of mass action says that the greater the amount of cortex destroyed, the greater are the behavioural effects.

The Cerebral Cortex – Localisation

- Delgado (1969) stimulated the primary motor area of a patient's *left* hemisphere, causing him to form a fist with his *right* hand.
- Nerve fibres cross the body as they pass through the medulla oblongata (*contralateral connection*).
- Penfield discovered that stimulating the top of the primary motor area (or *motor strip*) caused a twitching in the lower part of the body. He also found that body areas requiring precise control (e.g. fingers) have more cortical area devoted to them.

Localisation theory
different areas of the brain are specialised for different functions

The primary motor area

Association areas in the cortex

Other association areas
- A large number of other areas are believed to be involved in *learning, thinking, memory*, etc.
- Damage to frontal lobes does not (as one might expect) impair intellectual functioning, but the ability to set goals, plan and make decisions.
- Luria (1980) describes the case of a man with frontal lobe damage who continued trying to light a match that was already lit (*perseveration*).
- *Frontal lobe damage* is also associated with changes in personality, such as a lack of emotion, insight, or an inability to perceive sarcasm (McDonald & Pearce, 1996).
- Penfield (1947) found that association areas in the *temporal lobes* play an important role in memory.
- These association areas also play a role in *social behaviour* and *emotional responses*. In some cases, damage may cause a person to become a compulsive talker.

Sensory association areas
- Each of the primary sensory areas sends information to an adjacent sensory association area.
- Association areas in the parietal lobe play an important role in integrating complex sensory functions (e.g. *cross-modal transfer*).
- Damage to the left hemisphere's auditory association area causes severe disturbances of language. Right hemisphere damage affects the ability to perceive the location of sounds.
- Damage to the visual association areas does not produce blindness, but an inability to recognise objects by sight (e.g. '*The man who mistook his wife for a hat*', Sacks, 1985).
- Damage to the right parietal lobe results in a difficulty in integrating an object's parts into a coherent whole.

Motor association areas
- Involved in the planning and execution of movements.
- These areas receive information from several areas and integrate it into plans and actions.
- Left parietal lobe damage makes hand movements difficult.
- Motor association areas in the left parietal lobe also play an important role in keeping track of the body's moving parts (Carlson, 1988).
- Damage to this lobe may result in difficulty in pointing to parts of the body, suggesting that 'false data' are being sent to the primary motor area, resulting in poor execution of movement.

The primary sensory areas

Primary visual area
- Penfield found that stimulating areas of the *occipital lobe* caused patients to report seeing visual displays, convincing him that this was the primary visual area.
- Damage to this area causes blindness in part of the visual field.
- Information is converted to electrical impulses by the *retina*. These travel down the *optic nerve*, meeting and dividing up at the *optic chiasma*.
- Since only half of the information from each eyes crosses over to the opposing hemisphere, each hemisphere receives information from both eyes.
- Information from the left visual field is processed by the right hemisphere and vice versa.

Primary auditory area
- Located in the *temporal lobe* of each hemisphere, along the *lateral fissure*.
- Auditory information is transmitted from the ear, via the *thalamus*, causing neurons to fire in the primary auditory area.
- The neurons in this area are highly specialised, with some responding only to high or low pitched sounds.
- Penfield found that stimulation of this area caused patients to report hearing sounds.
- Although most information received by an ear travels to the primary auditory hemisphere on the opposite side, some information is processed on the same side (*ipsilateral connection*).

Primary somatosensory area
- A thin 'strip', located in the *parietal lobe*, just across the *central fissure*.
- Receives information from the skin senses, and sense of taste.
- Like the primary motor area, the body is represented in an 'upside-down' fashion, with more sensitive body parts (e.g. face) having more cortex devoted to them.
- The somatosensory area in the left hemisphere registers information from the right side of the body.
- Sensory deficits depend on the amount of damage (e.g. with mild damage, subtle temperature distinctions may be difficult but distinguishing 'hot' and 'cold' is still possible).
- Robertson (1995) found that in Braille readers, the cortical area devoted to the tip of the right forefinger is considerably enlarged as compared with the left.

Holistic theory
psychological functions are controlled by neurons throughout the brain

- **Holistic theory** argues that psychological functions are controlled by neurons throughout the brain.
- Although it seems clear that at least some mental processes and behaviours are localised in certain parts of the brain, this does not necessarily mean that we can reject holism.

- Lashley (1926) studied the effects of destroying parts of rats' brains on their ability to remember their way through a complex maze.
- Destruction of one particular area did *not* lead to greater difficulties than destruction of any other area, although in later experiments Lashley found that the *amount* of cortex destroyed influenced learning (*the law of mass action*).

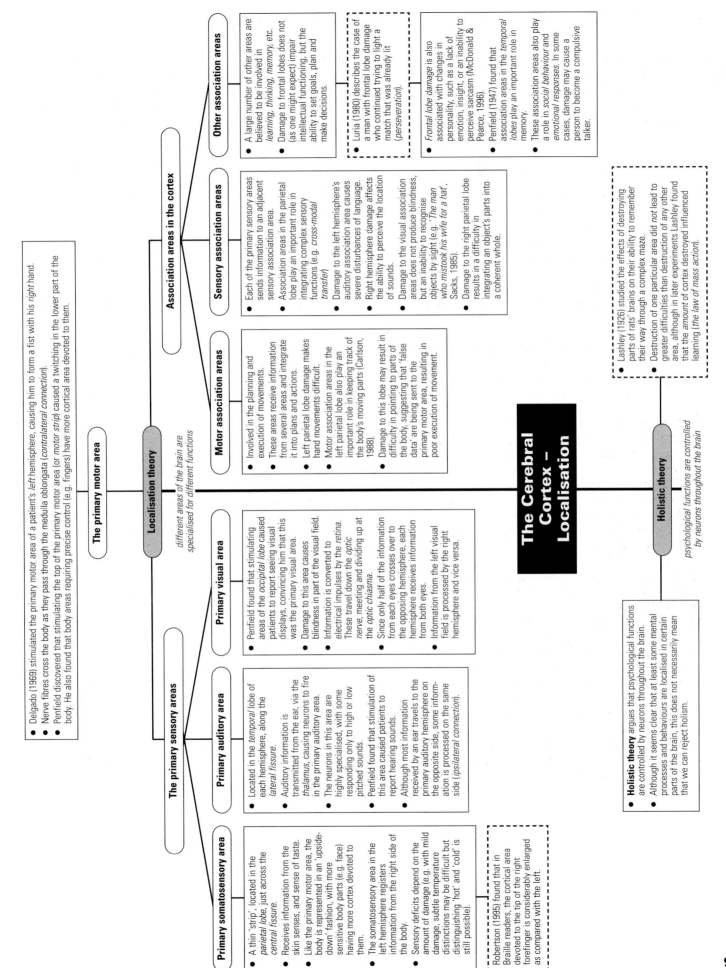

19

LATERALISATION OF FUNCTION IN THE CEREBRAL CORTEX

SYLLABUS
13.2 Brain and behaviour – lateralisation of function in the cerebral cortex
- lateralisation of function in the cerebral cortex, including the organisation of language in the brain and other hemisphere asymmetries of function (e.g. Sperry's research on the 'split-brain')

KEY QUESTIONS
- What is the relationship between cortical areas and language?
- What research has been done into cerebral asymmetries, using 'split-brain' patients?
- Does each half of the brain have a different conscious experience?

Q **Section 1: Language disorders, localisation and lateralisation**

1 What did Broca discover when he carried out a post-mortem on his patient 'Tan'?
2 What is an *aphasia*?
3 Complete the sentence: 'Usually a person with Broca's aphasia can ___ spoken or written language either normally or near normally, but has great difficulty in ___ speech'.
4 What is meant by saying that the speech of *Broca's aphasics* often has a '*telegraphic*' quality to it?
5 What are *phonemic paraphrasias*?
6 What does *Broca's area* store?
7 What is the major characteristic of *Wernicke's aphasia*?
8 What are *semantic paraphrasias*?
9 What is the probable function of *Wernicke's area*?
10 What is the major characteristic of *anomic aphasia*?
11 What is the likely role of the *angular gyrus*?
12 What is the typical symptom of *conduction aphasia*?
13 What are the symptoms of *transcortical aphasia*?
14 What is the essential difference between transcortical aphasia and Wernicke's or Broca's aphasia?
15 What is the difference between *localisation* and *lateralisation*?
16 In what percentage of right-handers is language lateralised in the left hemisphere?
17 What is *bilateral representation*?
18 What difference did Kimura (1993) discover between the ways in which speech production is organised in men and women?
19 According to Lashley (1926), what is the *law of equipotentiality*?
20 Connor (1997) cites the case of a ten-year-old boy who had his left hemisphere surgically removed in an effort to treat *Sturge–Weber syndrome*. What was the consequence of this operation?

Section 2: 'Split-brain' studies

21 What is a *commissurotomy*?
22 What was the *medical* aim of the commisurotomy?
23 What did Sperry *et al.* (1964) discover after conducting commissurotomies followed by surgery on the optic nerves of cats?
24 In what way does the *visual information* reaching each hemisphere differ in normal humans?
25 What was Sperry's method for delivering visual information to only one cerebral hemisphere?
26 How does the *divided field technique* differ from Sperry's technique?
27 What did Zaidel (1983) conclude about the *right* hemisphere's linguistic abilities?
28 What are *chimerics*?
29 In what sense is the left hemisphere an '*analyser*'?
30 What happens when different decision tasks are presented to both hemispheres of split-brain patients simultaneously?
31 Identify one reason why the results of split-brain studies should be treated with caution.
32 What is involved in the *Wada test*?
33 Identify additional ways in which it is possible to study cerebral asymmetries in the intact brain.
34 What is involved in a *dichotic listening task*?
35 Identify four activities in which the right hemisphere demonstrates superior synthetic ability.
36 What is Pucetti's (1977) argument concerning the nature of mind?
37 How does '*bundle theory*' explain the unity of consciousness?

Section 1: Language disorders, localisation and lateralisation

1 Broca discovered that 'Tan' had suffered stokes which had caused multiple lesions in a cortical area of the frontal lobe of the left hemisphere.

2 An aphasia is a language disorder arising from brain damage.

3 'Usually a person with Broca's aphasia can *understand* spoken or written language either normally or near normally, but has great difficulty in *producing* speech.'

4 The speech of Broca's aphasics contains few 'function words' and consists almost entirely of 'content words' (i.e. is 'telegraphic').

5 Phonemic paraphrasias are mispronunciations of certain words (e.g. saying 'likstip' instead of 'lipstick').

6 Broca's area stores the 'motor plans' for the formulation of words.

7 The major characteristic of Wernicke's aphasia is a difficulty in understanding spoken or written language.

8 In semantic paraphrasias, the word that is produced does not have the intended meaning, though it may be related to the intended word.

9 Wernicke's area probably stores memories of the sequence of sounds contained in words.

10 Anomic aphasics have few problems in producing or understanding language, but are unable to find correct nouns to name objects.

11 The angular gyrus is probably involved in retrieving the appropriate word for a given meaning from a memory store.

12 The typical symptom of conduction aphasia is difficulty in repeating a sentence that has just been heard.

13 Transcortical aphasics have few comprehension skills and/or cannot produce normal speech. They are, however, able to repeat back what somebody has just said.

14 In transcortical aphasia the damage has occurred beyond Wernicke's and Broca's areas.

15 Localisation is the view that specific functions and processes have relatively precise and circumscribed locations, whereas lateralisation is the view that certain functions occur only in one or other of the cerebral hemispheres.

16 Language is lateralised in the left hemisphere in 95 per cent of right-handers.

17 Bilateral representation is when the language structures are more or less equally represented in both hemispheres.

18 Kimura (1993) discovered that speech is more bilaterally organised in women than in men.

19 The law of equipotentiality (Lashley, 1926) refers to the ability of other areas of the brain to reorganise themselves and take over a damaged part's functions.

20 The operation resulted in the boy learning to speak at the age of ten, having previously been mute.

Section 2: 'Split-brain' studies

21 A commisurotomy is a surgical operation which involves severing the corpus callosum, which connects the two cerebral hemispheres.

22 The aim of the commisurotomy was originally to reduce the severity of epileptic seizures by preventing the corresponding brain activity from 'bouncing' back and forth between the two hemispheres.

23 Sperry *et al.* (1964) discovered that when each of the cat's hemispheres received information from one of its eyes, a cat which had learned a task with a patch over one eye behaved as if it had never learned the task when the patch was placed over the other eye.

24 Normally, the right hemisphere receives information about the left visual field, and the left hemisphere information about the right visual field.

25 Sperry's method involved presenting a visual stimulus for a tenth of a second in either the right or left visual field, causing it to be perceived in only the left or right hemisphere of split-brain patients.

26 In the divided field technique, a stimulus is presented to the left and right visual fields of patients simultaneously, whereas in Sperry's technique a stimulus is presented to either the right or left visual field.

27 Zaidel (1983) concluded that the comprehension abilities of the right hemisphere are roughly equivalent to those of a ten-year-old child.

28 Chimerics are composite pictures of two faces.

29 The left hemisphere is skilled at handling discrete information which can be stated verbally in the form of mathematical propositions. Hence it is an 'analyser'.

30 Split-brain patients are able to perform two tasks simultaneously better than are people with an intact corpus callosum (Ellenberg & Sperry, 1980).

31 Split-brain patients have all had a history of epileptic seizures and so may not be representative of people in general.

32 The Wada test involves injecting an anaesthetic (sodium amytal) into the left or right carotid artery, then observing what happens.

33 Cerebral asymmetries can be studied in the intact brain using an EEG, measurements of blood flow and glucose consumption, and through studying people who have suffered strokes.

34 A dichotic listening task involves presenting different auditory information to a person's right and left ears simultaneously.

35 The right hemisphere demonstrates superior synthetic ability in spatial tasks, artistic activities, body image and facial recognition.

36 Pucetti (1977) argues that even in normal people, in whom the two hemispheres are connected, the individual is two minds.

37 Bundle theory explains the unity of consciousness by claiming that a sense of self is no more than a collection ('bundle') of experiences (e.g. the sensations accompanying respiration, of the tongue and eyes, and so on).

A

Cortical areas and language disorders

Wernicke's aphasia

Damage to Wernicke's area causes Wernicke's aphasia:
- The major characteristic is difficulty in understanding written or spoken language.
- Wernicke's aphasics produce language which is virtually unintelligible and lacking in coherence. Sufferers may produce *jargon* (nonsense words) or *neologisms* (invented words).
- Wernicke's area may store memories of the sequences of sounds contained in words.

Cortical areas and language disorders

- Broca studied patients (such as 'Tan') who had difficulty in producing speech whilst Wernicke described patients who could produce speech but had difficulty understanding it.
- Post-mortems suggested that such language deficits arose from brain damage to the left frontal lobe.
- Such deficits are called *aphasias*. Milner (1971) argues that unless speech loss is complete, deficits should be called *dysphasias*.

Broca's aphasia

Damage to Broca's area causes 'Broca's aphasia':
- The major characteristic is great difficulty in producing speech. Usually, a Broca's aphasic can comprehend written or spoken language. However, speech is typically slow, non-fluent and difficult to understand, with grammatical words omitted.
- Broca's area stores the 'motor plans' for the formulation of words. Damage to this area causes faulty data to be sent to the primary motor area.

Conduction aphasia

Conduction aphasics can understand and produce speech relatively well.
- The major characteristic is difficulty in repeating a sentence that has just been heard.
- Probably occurs as a result of lesions interrupting the nerve fibres (*arcuate fasciculus*) which connects Broca's area with Wernicke's area.

Anomic aphasia

Anomic aphasics have few problems in understanding and producing language.
- The major characteristic is an inability to find the correct nouns to name objects.
- This happens to most of us at times, but the anomic aphasic has difficulty in naming common objects (e.g. a pen), causing them to *circumlocute* (speak in a roundabout way).
- Anomic aphasia seems to result from damage to the angular gyrus, which retrieves the word corresponding to a particular meaning.

Transcortical aphasia

Transcortical aphasics can repeat back what somebody has just said to them.
- The major characteristic of transcortical aphasia is poor comprehension skills and/or an inability to produce normal speech.
- Resembles Broca's aphasia and Wernicke's aphasia, although the damage has occurred beyond these areas.

Language: localisation, lateralisation and holism

Not only are certain language functions localised, but in most people they are found in one or other of the cerebral hemispheres (*lateralised*). For most of us, language is lateralised in the left hemisphere.
- **Handedness:** Satz (1979): in 95% of right-handed individuals, language is localised in the left hemisphere. 75% of left-handers have language localised in the left hemisphere, with language processed in both hemispheres in the remaining 25%.
- **Gender:** Kimura (1993): speech is more bilaterally organised in women. In addition, women are less likely to incur aphasia than men since women are more likely to suffer aphasia when the front of the brain is damaged, and damage to the back of the brain (which affects men more) is more common.
- **Holism:** The brain appears to have remarkable plasticity, so that when an area is damaged other areas are able to reorganise themselves and take over that area's functions. Connor (1997) reports on the case of a 10-year-old boy with 'Sturge–Weber syndrome', which caused the left side of the brain to become shrunken. Removal of the left side of his brain resulted in him learning to speak, having previously been mute.

Fechner's question

Fechner's question. In 1860 Fechner asked what would happen if a living person's brain were split in half along the two hemispheres. He believed that each half would have a separate conscious experience.

Language and the Brain

Answering Fechner's question
Ornstein (1986) suggests that a commissurotomy does not produce a 'splitting' of the mind, but helps to manifest a duality that is there all the time.

The split-brain procedure

The commissurotomy
- In the early 1960s, Vogel & Bogen suggested that epileptic seizures were caused by an amplification of brain activity which 'bounced' back and forth between the two hemispheres and suggested severing the *corpus callosum* as a therapy of last resort (a *commissurotomy*).

- Research with cats and monkeys revealed that the commissurotomy did not seem to cause any ill-effects, although cats who learned tasks with an eye patch over one eye behaved as if no learning had occurred when the patch was placed over the other eye!
Such findings suggested that the corpus callosum is a means of transferring information between the two hemispheres, and that if this is severed, each hemisphere is unaware of the sensations and processes occurring in the other.

Procedures for studying split-brain patients

Sperry's technique
Because of the way our eyes are connected to our brain, both hemispheres receive information from both eyes. However, the left hemisphere processes information from the right side of the visual field and the right hemisphere from the left side of our visual field. Normally, as our eyes move, both hemispheres are able to receive the same visual information.
- Sperry's method involved presenting a stimulus for one-tenth of a second on the right or left side of a projector screen, with the participant looking straight ahead so that the information is only received by one or other hemisphere.

The divided field technique
A word or picture is presented to the left visual field (right hemisphere) and a different word or picture presented simultaneously to the right visual field (left hemisphere).
Words and pictures are flashed up briefly onto a projector screen as in Sperry's technique.

Basic findings of split-brain studies

- When a picture is shown to the *right* visual field and a patient asked to report verbally what was shown, the task is done easily.
- When a picture is shown to the *left* visual field the patient cannot do the task (since the right hemisphere usually lacks language structures).
- However, in the above situation a patient is able to use the left hand (which is out of sight, beneath the screen) to select correctly the object seen by the right hemisphere (since the left hand is controlled by the right hemisphere).

- In one study the word 'case' was presented to the right visual field and the word 'key' to the left visual field. The patient reported that the word 'case' had been seen, but the left hand wrote the word 'key'.
- Other studies showed that when asked to find an object that corresponded to a word seen, right and left hands ignored objects that had been seen by the hemisphere controlling the other hand.

Hemispheres – differences

- The right hemisphere is superior to the left at copying drawings. The left hemisphere seems incapable of duplicating 3-D forms.
- Levy *et al.* (1972) showed patients chimerics (composite pictures of two different faces). When asked to describe the picture, the left hemisphere dominated, but the right hemisphere was better able to select a picture that had been seen.

Analytic and synthetic hemispheres
Analyser: the left hemisphere is better at using discrete information that can be handled verbally in the form of mathematical propositions.
Synthesiser: the right hemisphere is superior when information cannot be described adequately in words or symbols, but is able to synthesise it and recognise it as a whole.

Other findings
- Ellenberg & Sperry (1980) found that split-brain patients were able to perform two simple decision tasks simultaneously, and better than people with an intact corpus callosum.

BIOLOGICAL RHYTHMS

Section 1: Circadian rhythms

1 What is a *bodily rhythm*?
2 Over what period of time do *circadian rhythms* vary?
3 Which physiological variables vary in a circadian way.
4 What are *Zeitgebers*?
5 What is an *oscillator*?
6 The SN are the location of one of the oscillators. What do the letters SN stand for?
7 What research, conducted by Morgan (1995), supports the view that the cycle length of such rhythms is dependent on genetic factors?
8 According to Loros *et al.* (cited in Highfield, 1996b), what are the evolutionary origins of the *internal clock*?
9 What does it mean to say that circadian rhythms are primarily an *endogenous property*?
10 What did Luce & Segal (1966) discover when investigating the sleep patterns of people living in the Arctic Circle?

Section 2: Infradian rhythms

11 How long do *infradian rhythms* last?
12 Complete the sentence: 'The menstrual period is the ___ of a four-week cycle of activity'.
13 What is the role of the menstrual cycle?
14 Identify two psychological symptoms associated with pre-menstrual syndrome (PMS).
15 Identify the behavioural changes which Dalton (1964) claimed are clustered around the pre-menstrual interval.
16 Identify two reasons for thinking that PMS is not simply a 'denial of femininity'.
17 Which *gland* is responsible for governing the phases of the menstrual cycle?
18 What was shown in Reinberg's (1967) study of a young woman who spent three months in a cave?

Section 3: Ultradian rhythms

19 What are *ultradian rhythms*?
20 Which two discoveries were made in Loomis *et al.*'s (1937) pioneering studies of sleep using the EEG?
21 What do the letters '*REM*' stand for in the term *REM sleep*?
22 What did Dement & Kleitman (1957) discover about REM sleep?
23 When are *beta waves* replaced by *alpha waves*?
24 What type of waves mark the onset of *Stage 1 sleep*?
25 What is a *hypnagogic state* and when does it occur?
26 What are *sleep spindles* and during which stage of sleep are they most likely to occur?
27 What do *Stage 3 sleep* and *Stage 4 sleep* have in common?
28 After falling asleep, when do we enter REM sleep for the first time?
29 Why has REM sleep also been termed *paradoxical sleep*?
30 During which cycles of sleep do *Stages 3 and 4* of sleep occur?
31 How do sleep patterns change with age?

Section 4: Disrupting biological rhythms

32 What period do Monk & Folkard (1992) define as being the 'day working window'?
33 Identify two performance deficits which have been identified as resulting from shift work.
34 What is the shortest period which you might expect a reversal of bodily rhythms to take?
35 What change in shift pattern did Czeisler *et al.* (1982) recommend to a group of shift workers?
36 What general phenomenon does the term *jet lag* refer to?
37 In which compass direction does the body find it easiest to travel by jet?
38 Why is this?
39 What name is given to the '*hormone of darkness*'?

Section 1: Circadian rhythms

1. A bodily rhythm is a cyclical variation over some period of time in a physiological or psychological process.
2. Circadian rhythms vary over periods of about 24 hours.
3. Heart rate, metabolic rate, breathing rate, body temperature and hormones all vary in a circadian way.
4. Zeitgebers are external cues about the time of day.
5. An oscillator is an internal (or body) clock.
6. The letters SN stand for suprachiasmatic nuclei.
7. Morgan (1995) gave hamsters brain transplants of SN cells from a mutant strain whose cycles were shorter than those of the recipients. The recipients adopted the same cycles as the mutant strain.
8. Loros *et al.* argue that internal clocks were developed by primitive bacteria so that they could adjust their metabolism in anticipation of the sun's rays.
9. Circadian rhythms are primarily an internal (endogenous) property and do not depend on external cues.
10. Luce & Segal (1966) discovered that people living in the Arctic Circle slept for normal periods, despite the fact that the sun does not set during the summer months.

Section 2: Infradian rhythms

11. Infradian rhythms last for longer than one day.
12. 'The menstrual period is the *end* of a four-week cycle of activity.'
13. The menstrual cycle prepares the womb to house and nourish a fertilised egg (a zygote).
14. Irritability, depression, headaches, a decline in alertness and visual acuity, and changes in appetite are all associated with pre-menstrual syndrome.
15. Dalton (1964) claimed that crimes, suicides, accidents and a decline in the quality of schoolwork and intelligence test scores are all clustered around the pre-menstrual interval.
16. PMS occurs in all cultures, and similar effects occur in primates.
17. The pituitary gland is responsible for governing the phases of the menstrual cycle.
18. Reinberg's (1967) study found that the woman's day lengthened and her menstrual cycle shortened.

Section 3: Ultradian rhythms

19. Ultradian rhythms are rhythms which are shorter than one day.
20. Loomis *et al.*'s (1937) studies found that the brain is active during sleep and that certain types of activity seem to be related to changes in the type of sleep.

21. Rapid eye movement.
22. Dement & Kleitman (1957) found that people woken during REM sleep usually reported that they were dreaming.
23. Beta waves are replaced by alpha waves when people change from being awake and alert to relaxed with eyes closed.
24. Theta waves mark the onset of Stage 1 sleep.
25. A hypnogogic state is one in which we experience hallucinatory and dream-like images, and occurs at the transition from relaxation to Stage 1 sleep.
26. Sleep spindles are brief bursts of mental activity which usually occur during Stage 2 sleep.
27. Stage 3 sleep and Stage 4 sleep are both characterised by delta waves, unresponsiveness to the environment, a lack of eye movement and complete relaxation of the muscles.
28. We enter REM sleep for the first time having first 'descended' to Stage 4 sleep, then 'climbed' to Stage 2 sleep.
29. REM sleep is paradoxical sleep in that the eyes and brain are very active, whilst the body is virtually paralysed.
30. Stages 3 and 4 of sleep occur only during the first two cycles of sleep.
31. As we get older, we sleep for less time, and spend less time in REM sleep.

Section 4: Disrupting biological rhythms

32. Monk & Folkard (1992) define the hours between 07:00 and 18:00 as being the 'day working window'.
33. Decreased attention, a slowing down of reasoning skills, impaired reaction time and disturbed perceptual–motor skills are all performance deficits which have been identified as resulting from shift work.
34. Some people can apparently achieve reversal in five to seven days.
35. Czeisler *et al.* (1982) recommend a change in the shift rotation period for a group of shift-workers from seven to twenty-one days.
36. Jet lag refers to a cluster of symptoms suffered by most people when several time zones are crossed in a short space of time.
37. The body finds it easiest to travel west by jet.
38. The body's natural circadian rhythm is about 25 hours. Travelling west lengthens the day in the direction of this figure, whilst travelling east shortens the day beneath 24 hours.
39. The 'hormone of darkness' is *melatonin*.

Biological Rhythms

Circadian rhythms

These are consistent cyclical variations *over a period of about 24 hours*. Heart rate, metabolic rate, breathing rate, temperature and hormones all vary during the day, and such variations persist for a time if we reverse our activity patterns.

Internal clocks

- *External cues* (*Zeitgebers*) are used by the body to synchronise internal (or body) clocks called *oscillators*, in a process called *entrainment*.
- *Folkhard et al.* had students spend a month isolated from external cues. Recordings of mood, activity and temperature levels confirmed the existence of several internal clocks.
- **Location:** One of these clocks lies in the suprachiasmatic nuclei (SN), which receives information directly from the retina.
- **Evolution:** Loros *et al.* (cited in Highfield, 1996b): internal clocks were developed by primitive bacteria in order to adjust their metabolism in anticipation of the sun.

Research

- Hamsters given brain transplants of SN cells from a mutant strain adopt the same activity cycles as the mutants (suggesting a genetic basis).
- Luce & Segal (1966) found that people living near the Arctic Circle sleep normally even during the light summer months, suggesting that the sleep–waking cycle is an endogenous (internal) property.
- Some people take longer than others to adjust to changes e.g. 'jet lag' (see below).

Infradian rhythms

These are rhythms which last for *longer than one day*. The most commonly studied infradian rhythm is *menstruation* (an endocrine cycle).

Menstruation

The end of a 4-week cycle of activity in which the womb has prepared for the job of housing and nourishing a fertilised egg.

- Onset is irregular at first, but becomes well-established in a few months.
- Sabbagh & Barnard (1984): the menstrual periods of women who spend a lot of time together often become synchronised (possibly due to some chemical scent).

Pre-menstrual syndrome

- A variety of effects typically occurring 4/5 days before the onset of menstruation. Includes mild irritation, depression, headaches, a decline in alertness and sometimes changes in appetite.
- Dalton (1964) reported that crimes, suicides, accidents and a decline in the quality of schoolwork are all clustered around the pre-menstrual interval.
- Traditionally, PMS was attributed to a denial of femininity, although the finding that the effects of PMS occur in all cultures (and also in primates) challenges this.

Research

The *pituitary gland* governs menstruation by influencing changes in the walls of the uterus (the endometrium):

- Timonen *et al.* (1964): found that conceptions increased during the lighter (summer) months.
- Reinberg (1967): found that the menstrual cycle of a woman who spent 3 months in a cave shortened. Reinberg speculated that this was due to low light levels.

Ultradian rhythms

These are rhythms which are *shorter than a day* (e.g. heart rate and renal excretion). The most well-researched are those occurring during *sleep*.

- Loomis *et al.* (1937): used the EEG to discover that the brain is active during sleep and that types of activity seemed to relate to types of sleep.
- Dement & Kleitman (1957): found that people woken during REM (rapid eye movement) sleep usually reported dreaming.
- During REM sleep, the body's muscles are in a state of *virtual paralysis* although heart rate and blood pressure fluctuate.
- Rechtschaffen & Kales (1968): divided NREM (non-REM) sleep into four stages:

Stage and EEG	Characteristics
Stage 1 *theta waves*	Onset sometimes accompanied by a *hypnagogic* (hallucinatory) state. We are easily awoken.
Stage 2 *sleep spindles*	Characterised by brief bursts of activity. Brain responds to some external stimuli (*K-complexes*).
Stage 3 *delta waves*	In Stages 3 and 4, we are unresponsive and difficult to wake. Muscles are relaxed.
Stage 4 *delta waves*	Delta waves make up more than 50% of the EEG. Heart rate, temperature and blood pressure low.

- After we have 'descended' to Stage 4 sleep we 'climb' the *sleep staircase*, entering REM sleep instead of Stage 1.
- Typically, we have 5 or so such cycles of sleep, each lasting on average 90 mins.
- Stages 3 and 4 occur only in the first two cycles of sleep, whilst episodes of REM sleep increase in length.
- As we age we spend less time asleep, and the percentage of REM sleep decreases.

Disrupting biological rhythms

Shift work

Shift work

Monk & Folkard (1992) define shift work as 'any regularly taken employment outside the day working window, defined arbitrarily as the hours between 07:00 and 18:00'. Humans can adjust their bodily rhythms to some extent.

Problems associated with shift work

- Night workers sleep less than day workers, but some problems are additional to those caused by lack of sleep: decreased attention, slowing down of reasoning skills, impaired reaction time, disturbed perceptual–motor skills.
- People differ in how quickly they can reverse their biological rhythms; some achieving reversal in 5–7 days, others taking 14 days. In addition physiological functions reverse at different times: heart rate 'entrains' quickly whilst adrenocorticotrophic hormone production may take more than a week.
- The shift changeover period leaves the body in a state of internal desynchronisation which is stressful and exhausting.

Shifting shifts – research

- Czeisler *et al.* (1982): found that a group of shift-workers generally took around 16 days to adjust to a new shift pattern. They recommended that the shift rotation period changed from 7 to 21 days.

Results: workers reported liking the new schedules more & enjoying better health. Employers saw an increase in productivity and a decrease in the number of errors.

Jet lag

Jet lag

The term is used to describe the cluster of symptoms suffered by most people when they cross several time zones in a short space of time. When we fly to the west we 'gain' time, and 'lose' time when we fly to the east.

Problems associated with jet lag

- Tiredness during the new daytime and an inability to sleep at night.
- Decreased mental performance, especially on vigilance tasks.
- Decreased physical performance, especially when tasks require precision.
- Loss of appetite, indigestion & even nausea.
- Increased irritability, headaches & mental confusion.

Reducing jet lag – research

- Our natural circadian rhythm is around 25 hours. Travelling east shortens a day even more than 24 hours, whilst travelling west lengthens a day in the direction which the body 'prefers'.
- Melatonin, which is a hormone normally produced at night, takes several days to adjust its production cycle. When jet-lagged volunteers are given a synthetic form of melatonin on the afternoon before departure, far fewer report feeling jet-lagged than those given a placebo (Blakemore, 1988).

SLEEP

KEY QUESTIONS
- What have studies of total sleep deprivation shown?
- What theories of sleep function have been proposed?
- What have studies of REM sleep deprivation shown?
- What theories of REM sleep function have been proposed?

Q

Section 1: Studies of total sleep deprivation

1 What was the nature of Patrick & Gilbert's (1898) pioneering study of *sleep deprivation*?
2 Why was it impossible for researchers to assess the psychological functioning of Peter Tripp towards the end of his 'wakeathon'?
3 What pattern of sleeping is common in participants following sleep deprivation?
4 What are periods of *micro-sleep*?
5 According to Hüber-Weidman (1976), after how many nights without sleep may *delusions* be experienced?
6 What is the principal symptom of *sleep deprivation psychosis*?
7 How did Rechtschaffen *et al.* (1983) investigate the effects of sleep deprivation in rats?
8 What was the likely cause of death in Rechtschaffen *et al.*'s rats?

Section 2: Evolutionary and restoration theories

9 According to Meddis (1975), what two factors may affect the amount of time which an animal spends sleeping?
10 Complete the sentence: 'Webb (1982) argues that sleep is an ___ response which does not satisfy a ___ need in the way that food does'.
11 What is the principal claim made by the *hibernation theory* of sleep function?
12 Why are explanations which relate sleep function to risk of predation *non-falsifiable*?
13 According to Oswald's (1966) *restoration theory* of sleep function, what are the functions of sleep?
14 How does Shapiro *et al.*'s (1981) study of people who had completed an 'ultra-marathon' support Oswald's theory?
15 How does Ryback & Lewis's (1971) study of healthy individuals who spent six weeks in bed contradict Oswald's theory?

16 What did Kales *et al.* (1974) discover when studying insomniacs?

Section 3: Studies of REM sleep deprivation

17 How was Dement (1960) able to investigate the effects of *REM sleep deprivation* in volunteers?
18 What finding of Dement's suggests that his volunteers began to experience *REM starvation*?
19 What is the *REM rebound effect*?
20 What did Greenberg *et al.* (1972) discover after showing REM-deprived volunteers a film of a circumcision rite performed without anaesthetic?
21 Complete the sentence: 'Alcohol suppresses ___ sleep without affecting ___ sleep'.

Section 4: Restoration and other theories

22 What is synthesised more rapidly during REM sleep than during NREM sleep?
23 What percentage of a newborn baby's sleep is REM sleep?
24 What caused an increase in REM sleep in non-humans in Bloch's (1976) study?
25 Which aspect of REM sleep is difficult for restoration theorists to explain?
26 How did Empson & Clarke (1970) support the *memory consolidation theory* of sleep function?
27 Identify one other finding relating to humans which supports memory consolidation theory.
28 What does the *sentinel theory* propose is the function of REM sleep?
29 What is the main weakness of this theory?
30 What is the role of REM sleep according to the *oculomotor system maintenance theory*?

Section 1: Studies of total sleep deprivation

1 Patrick & Gilbert's (1898) study deprived three 'healthy young men' of sleep for a period of ninety hours.

2 Towards the end of Peter Tripp's 'wakeathon', he experienced intense delusions, which made tests of psychological functioning impossible.

3 Following sleep deprivation, participants typically sleep for longer than normal, then return to their usual pattern of sleeping on subsequent nights.

4 Micro-sleep occurs when we stop what we are doing and stare into space for a few seconds.

5 Hüber-Weidman (1976) claims that delusions may be experienced after five nights without sleep.

6 The principal symptom of sleep deprivation psychosis is depersonalisation (the loss of a clear sense of identity).

7 Rechtschaffen *et al.* (1983) placed a rat on a disc above a bucket of water, with an EEG monitoring its brain activity. When the rat attempted to sleep, the disc rotated, forcing the rat to walk to avoid falling into the water.

8 The rats were probably unable to regulate their own body heat.

Section 2: Evolutionary and restoration theories

9 Meddis (1975) suggests that the animal's method of obtaining food and its exposure to predators affect the amount of time it spends sleeping.

10 'Webb (1982) argues that sleep is an *innate* response which does not satisfy a *physiological* need in the way that food does.'

11 The hibernation theory of sleep function claims that sleep is an adaptive instinctual behaviour which keeps us quiet and out of harm's way.

12 Such explanations can explain both sleeping very little and sleeping a lot by reference to a decreased risk of predation. Hence they are impossible to falsify.

13 Oswald's (1966) restoration theory claims that the functions of sleep are to restore depleted energy reserves, eliminate waste products from the muscles, repair cells, and recover physical abilities lost during the day.

14 Shapiro *et al.*'s (1981) study found that people who had completed an 'ultra-marathon' slept for longer than normal for two nights following the race.

15 Ryback & Lewis (1971) found that healthy individuals who spent six weeks in bed did not sleep for less time than normal.

16 Kales *et al.* (1974) found that insomniacs suffer from far more psychological problems than healthy people.

Section 3: Studies of REM sleep deprivation

17 Dement (1960) deprived volunteers of REM sleep by waking them up every time they entered REM sleep, and compared them with volunteers who were woken during NREM sleep.

18 REM starvation was shown by volunteers because they made more and more attempts to enter REM sleep as the amount of REM deprivation increased.

19 The REM rebound effect refers to the increase in REM sleep following a period of deprivation.

20 Greenberg *et al.* (1972) discovered that the anxiety experienced when repeatedly viewing the film did not diminish in volunteers deprived of REM sleep, as would normally be the case in healthy individuals.

21 'Alcohol suppresses *REM* sleep without affecting *NREM* sleep.'

Section 4: Restoration and other theories

22 Proteins are synthesised more rapidly during REM sleep than during NREM sleep.

23 Around 50 per cent of a newborn baby's sleep is REM sleep.

24 Bloch's (1976) study found that REM sleep increases when non-humans are given training on a new task.

25 The fact that REM sleep uses a substantial amount of energy, which would prevent protein synthesis.

26 Empson & Clarke (1970) found that participants were less able to recall unusual phrases which they heard before bedtime if they were deprived of REM sleep.

27 The proportion of time spent in REM sleep decreases with age.

28 The sentinel theory proposes that awakening after REM sleep allows animals to check their surroundings for signs of danger.

29 The sentinel theory sees only the end of REM sleep as serving any function, not the time during REM sleep.

30 The oculomotor system maintenance theory proposes that the function of REM sleep is to keep the eye muscles 'toned up'.

A

Total sleep deprivation in humans

- Patrick & Gilbert (1998): deprived three 'healthy young men' of sleep for 90 hours. Desire to sleep increased gradually. Two of them experienced perceptual disorders after the second night. When allowed to sleep, all three slept for longer than usual, then returned to normal.
- In 1959, Peter Tripp staged a charity 'wakeathon', staying awake for eight days. Towards the end he experienced hallucinations and delusions.

The effects of sleep deprivation
(after Hüber-Weidman, 1976)

Night 1: experience is uncomfortable, but tolerable.
Night 2: urge to sleep is greatest between 3 and 5 a.m.
Night 3: complex information-processing is impaired.
Night 4: confusion, irritability, and micro-sleep occur.
Night 5: delusions may be experienced.
Night 6: *depersonalisation* and symptoms of *sleep deprivation psychosis*.

Total sleep deprivation in rats

- Rechtschaffen *et al.* (1983): placed a rat on a rotating disc above a bucket of water. An EEG monitored its brain activity, causing the disc to rotate whenever it showed signs of sleep. This forced the rat to walk to avoid falling into the water.
- **Result:** all sleep-deprived rats had died after 33 days. The rats had suffered progressive physical deterioration until they were unable to regulate their own body temperature.

Restoration theories of sleep

- Oswald (1966): the purpose of sleep is to restore depleted reserves of energy, eliminate waste products, repair cells and recover physical abilities.
- The pituitary gland releases a hormone during Stage 4 sleep which is important for tissue growth, formation of red blood cells and protein and RNA synthesis.

- Shapiro *et al.* (1981): people completing an ultramarathon slept for 1½ hours longer than normal following the race.
- Ryback & Lewis (1971): healthy individuals who spent 6 weeks in bed did not sleep for less time (*contradicting* the theory).
- Kales *et al.* (1974): insomniacs suffer from more *psychological* problems, suggesting a psychologically restorative function.

Evolutionary theories of sleep

Predators and prey

- Meddis (1975): points out that animals that cannot find a safe place to sleep have high metabolic rates (which require a lot of food-gathering) or are at risk from predators (e.g. sheep) sleep very little, whilst predators sleep more.

The hibernation theory of sleep function

The enforced inactivity of sleeping aids survival by:
1. reducing the risk of predation or accidents by night
2. preventing us from wasting energy foraging or hunting

However, Evans (1984) points out that we are potentially *vulnerable* during sleep, and that such accounts are 'non-falsifiable' since they can explain either more or less sleep by reference to reduced vulnerability.

Sleep

Dement (1960): volunteers were allowed to sleep normally but woken every time they entered REM sleep. A control group was woken the same number of times during NREM sleep.
- Compared with the control group, the REM-deprived group were more irritable, aggressive and less able to concentrate on tasks.
- After several nights they began to show *REM-starvation*: they attempted to go into REM sleep as soon as they slept and were increasingly hard to wake. The number of attempts to enter REM sleep also increased greatly.

REM sleep deprivation

REM rebound
When people are allowed to sleep normally after REM-deprivation, they show a REM rebound effect (they spend longer in REM sleep than is normal), suggesting that they are trying to make up for 'lost' REM sleep time.

REM, anxiety and alcohol

- Greenberg *et al.* (1972): participants watched an anxiety-provoking film of a circumcision rite (performed without anaesthetic). Repeated viewing usually causes the anxiety to subside, but this did not occur in REM-deprived participants.
- Alcohol suppresses REM sleep without affecting NREM sleep. With severe alcohol abuse, a REM rebound effect may manifest itself as the disturbing hallucinations experienced during alcohol withdrawal (Greenberg & Pearlman, 1967).

Restoration theories

- Oswald (1966): REM sleep is related to brain restoration and growth.
- Studies have shown a greater rate of *protein synthesis* during REM sleep than in NREM sleep, and this may be an organic basis for changes in the personality (Rossi, 1973).
- Infants spend 50% of their sleep time in REM sleep (compared with 20% for adults) and REM sleep may promote the cell manufacture and growth necessary for the developing nervous system.

Bloch (1976): REM sleep increases when non-humans are given training on a new task, suggesting that protein synthesis during REM sleep may be involved in the formation of new memories.
Problem: REM sleep uses a substantial amount of energy which would actually *prevent* high levels of protein synthesis.

Other theories

Memory consolidation theory
REM sleep may stimulate neural tissue and consolidate memories:
- Empson & Clarke (1970): found that REM-deprived participants who heard unusual phrases before bedtime were less likely to remember them the next morning than those deprived of NREM sleep.

The sentinel theory
- Short periods of wakefulness sometimes occur at the end of REM sleep. Snyder (cited in Borbely, 1986) believes this allows animals to check for danger.
- However, this does not suggest a function for REM sleep itself.

The oculomotor system maintenance theory
- The function of REM sleep is to keep the eye muscles toned up.

DREAMING

KEY QUESTIONS
What is the function of dreaming, according to:
- Freud's theory
- 'problem-solving' theory
- 'reprogramming' theories
- 'activation–synthesis' theory
- 'reverse-learning' theory?

Section 1: Dreams: some basic findings

1 Approximately how many episodes of REM sleep do we experience per night?

2 What percentage of the time do we report vivid dreams when woken from REM sleep?

3 Identify the major differences between dreams occurring in REM sleep and those occurring in NREM sleep.

4 How did Dement & Wolpert (1958) demonstrate that external events can be incorporated into a dream?

5 Identify two differences between men's dreams and women's dreams.

6 Why can't sleepwalking occur during REM sleep?

Section 2: Freudian and problem-solving theories

7 Complete the sentence: 'Freud argued that a dream was a sort of 'psychic ___ ___'.

8 According to Freud, why is a dream's content disguised in symbolic form?

9 What term describes the *real (deeper) meaning* of a dream?

10 Which of the following would Freud *not* consider to be symbols for the male genital organs: hoses, bottles, feet, trees, ships, umbrellas?

11 In what way have Foulkes & Cohen (1973) challenged Freud's claim that part of the function of dreaming is to 'protect sleep'?

12 What is probably the major problem for Freud's theory of dream function?

13 How does Webb & Cartwright's (1978) *problem-solving theory* view the function of dreams?

14 Complete the sentence: 'Like Freud, Cartwright makes much use of the role of ___ in dreaming'.

15 How does Hartmann's (1973) research support Webb & Cartwright's (1978) theory of dream function?

Section 3: Reprogramming and activation-synthesis theories

16 According to Evans' (1984) *reprogramming theory*, what are the two functions of REM sleep?

17 What did Herman & Roffwarg (1983) discover caused participants to spend longer than usual in REM sleep?

18 According to Foulkes (1985), how does 'spontaneous activity' in the nervous system relate to the content of dreams?

19 Identify the four functions which Foulkes attributes to dreams.

20 According to Koukkou & Lehmann's (1980) theory, with what do we combine recently acquired information during dreams?

21 What was Hobson (1989) able to demonstrate regarding the activity of neurons in sleeping cats?

22 What do Hobson & McCarley (1977) mean by saying. that the dream is the brain's effort 'to make the best out of a bad job'?

23 According to Hobson (1988), what is the effect of *acetylcholine* on *giant cells*?

24 Why, according to Hobson & McCarley's (1977) *activation–synthesis theory*, are we unable to remember dreams?

25 How does Foulkes criticise Hobson and McCarley's theory?

Section 4: Reverse-learning theory

26 According to Crick & Mitchison's (1983) *reverse-learning theory*, what is the function of dreams?

27 How does the finding that neither the dolphin nor the spiny anteater dream provide some support for this theory?

28 What does Crick and Mitchison's theory suggest regarding the significance of a dream's content?

29 Complete the sentence: 'All theories of dreaming have difficulty in accounting for the observation that something very like REM sleep occurs in the ___ ___'.

30 What is Jouvet's (1983) explanation for the above observation?

31 What did Maquet *et al.* (cited in Highfield, 1996d) find when using PET scans to investigate brain activity during dreaming?

Section 1: Dreams: some basic findings

1 We experience four or five episodes of REM sleep per night.

2 People woken from REM sleep report dreaming about 80 per cent of the time.

3 Dreams occurring during REM sleep are clearer, more detailed, more vivid, and more likely to have a plot than those occurring during NREM sleep.

4 Dement & Wolpert (1958) lightly sprayed cold water onto dreamers' faces and found that they were more likely to dream about water.

5 Men's dreams are more likely to take place in outdoor settings and be more aggressive and sexual in content than women's dreams.

6 Sleepwalking can't occur during REM sleep since the body is in a state of virtual paralysis.

Section 2: Freudian and problem-solving theories

7 'Freud argued that a dream was a sort of "psychic *safety valve*".'

8 A dream's content is disguised in symbolic form since it consists of drives and wishes that would be threatening if expressed directly.

9 The real (deeper) meaning of a dream is its latent content.

10 Bottles and ships symbolise the female genital organs, according to Freud.

11 Foulkes & Cohen (1973) point out that disturbing events during the day tend to be followed by disturbing dreams, rather than 'protective imagery'.

12 The major problem is that the interpretation of a dream is not something which can be objectively achieved.

13 Webb & Cartwright's (1978) theory sees dreams as a way of dealing with problems (such as those relating to work, sex, health and relationships).

14 'Like Freud, Cartwright makes much use of the role of *metaphor* in dreaming.'

15 Hartmann (1973) found that people experiencing inter-personal or occupational problems spend longer in REM sleep than people without such problems.

Section 3: Reprogramming and activation-synthesis theories

16 Evans (1984) claims that during REM sleep the brain assimilates/processes new information, and updates information already stored.

17 Herman & Roffwarg (1983) discovered that spending a day wearing distorting lenses (that turned the world upside-down) caused participants to spend longer than usual in REM sleep.

18 Foulkes (1985) argues that spontaneous activity in the nervous system is interpreted by cognitive processes, presenting them as more structured dreams.

19 Foulkes believes that dreams may relate newly acquired knowledge to our own self-consciousness, help integrate newly acquired specific knowledge with past general knowledge, prepare us to deal with new, unexpected events and reveal the nature of our cognitive processes.

20 Koukkou & Lehman (1980) believe that during dreams we combine recently acquired information with ideas and strategies of thinking that originated in childhood.

21 Hobson (1989) demonstrated that neurons deep within the brain fire in a seemingly random way during sleep.

22 Hobson & McCarley (1977) argue that during dreams the brain receives signals which suggest that it is moving, and attempts to synthesise this random activity by imposing order on it.

23 Hobson (1988) argues that giant cells fire in an unrestrained way in the presence of acetylcholine.

24 We are unable to remember dreams since the neurons in the cortex that control the storage of new memories are turned 'off'.

25 Foulkes (1985) points out that the content of dreams is influenced by our waking experiences, so that they cannot be as random and meaningless as Hobson and McCarley suggest.

Section 4: Reverse-learning theory

26 According to Crick and Mitchison (1983), the function of dreams is to enable the brain to get rid of information it does not need.

27 Both the dolphin and the spiny anteater have an unusually large cortex for their size (possibly to accommodate all the useless information which cannot be disposed of).

28 A dream's content is an accidental result that does not lend itself to meaningful interpretation.

29 'All theories of dreaming have difficulty in accounting for the observation that something very like REM sleep occurs in the *developing foetus*.'

30 Jouvet's (1983) explanation is that REM sleep serves to program the brain for genetically determined functions (such as instincts).

31 Maquet *et al.* (cited in Highfield, 1996d) found that both the left and right amygdalas are active during sleep.

Dreaming

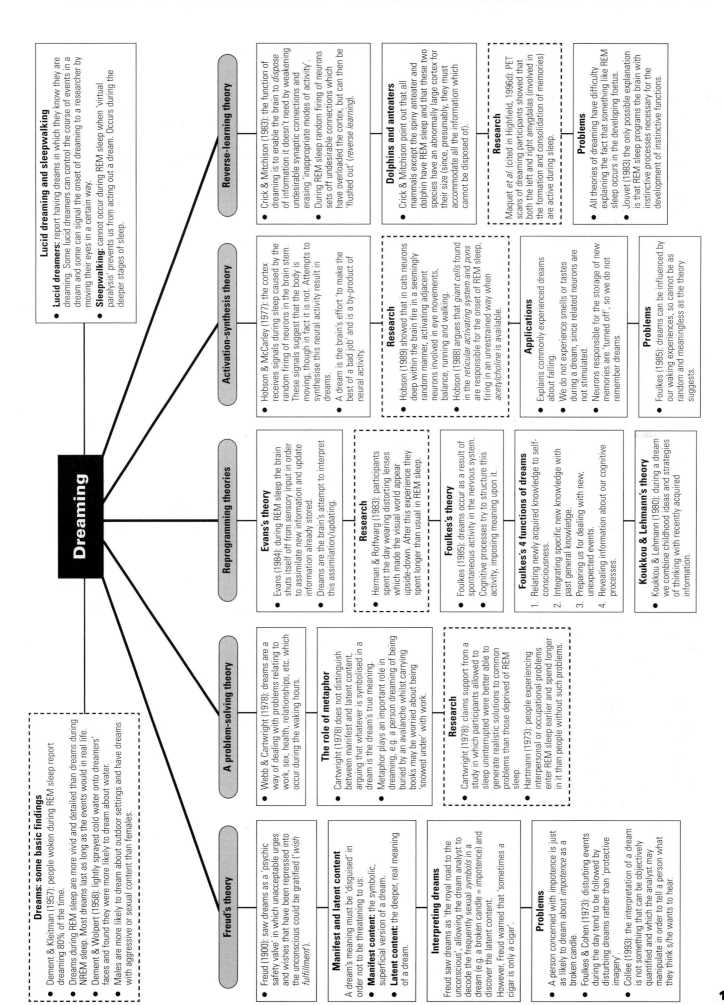

Dreams: some basic findings

- Dement & Kleitman (1957): people woken during REM sleep report dreaming 80% of the time.
- Dreams during REM sleep are more vivid and detailed than dreams during NREM sleep. Most dreams last as long as the events would in real life.
- Dement & Wolpert (1958): lightly sprayed cold water onto dreamers' faces and found they were more likely to dream about water.
- Males are more likely to dream about outdoor settings and have dreams with aggressive or sexual content than females.

Lucid dreaming and sleepwalking

- **Lucid dreamers:** report having dreams in which they know they are dreaming. Some lucid dreamers can control the course of events in a dream and some can signal the onset of dreaming by moving their eyes in a certain way.
- **Sleepwalking:** cannot occur during REM sleep when 'virtual paralysis' prevents us from acting out a dream. Occurs during the deeper stages of sleep.

Reverse-learning theory

- Crick & Mitchison (1983): the function of dreaming is to enable the brain to *dispose* of information it doesn't need by weakening undesirable synaptic connections and erasing 'inappropriate modes of activity'.
- During REM sleep random firing of neurons sets off undesirable connections which have overloaded the cortex, but can then be 'flushed out' (*reverse learning*).

Dolphins and anteaters

- Crick & Mitchison point out that all mammals except the spiny anteater and dolphin have REM sleep and that these two species have an abnormally large cortex for their size (since, presumably, they must accommodate all the information which cannot be disposed of).

Research

Maquet *et al.* (cited in Highfield, 1996d): PET scans of dreaming participants showed that both the left and right amygdalas (involved in the formation and consolidation of memories) are active during sleep.

Problems

- All theories of dreaming have difficulty explaining the fact that something like REM sleep occurs in the developing foetus.
- Jouvet (1983) the only possible explanation is that REM sleep programs the brain with instinctive processes necessary for the development of instinctive functions.

Activation–synthesis theory

- Hobson & McCarley (1977): the cortex receives signals during sleep caused by the random firing of neurons in the brain stem. These signals suggest that the body is moving, though in fact it is not. Attempts to synthesise this neural activity result in dreams.
- A dream is the brain's effort 'to make the best of a bad job' and is a by-product of neural activity.

Research

- Hobson (1989) showed that in cats neurons deep within the brain fire in a seemingly random manner, activating adjacent neurons involved in eye movements, balance, running and walking.
- Hobson (1988) argues that *giant cells* found in the *reticular activating system and pons* are responsible for the onset of REM sleep, firing in an unrestrained way when *acetylcholine* is available.

Applications

- Explains commonly experienced dreams about falling.
- We do not experience smells or tastes during a dream, since related neurons are not stimulated.
- Neurons responsible for the storage of new memories are 'turned off', so we do not remember dreams.

Problems

- Foulkes (1985): dreams can be influenced by our waking experiences, so cannot be as random and meaningless as the theory suggests.

Reprogramming theories

Evans's theory

- Evans (1984): during REM sleep the brain shuts itself off from sensory input in order to assimilate new information and update information already stored.
- Dreams are the brain's attempt to interpret this assimilation/updating.

Research

Herman & Roffwarg (1983): participants spent the day wearing distorting lenses which made the visual world appear upside-down. After this experience they spent longer than usual in REM sleep.

Foulkes's theory

- Foulkes (1985): dreams occur as a result of spontaneous activity in the nervous system.
- Cognitive processes try to structure this activity, imposing meaning upon it.

Foulkes's 4 functions of dreams

1. Relating newly acquired knowledge to self-consciousness.
2. Integrating specific new knowledge with past general knowledge.
3. Preparing us for dealing with new, unexpected events.
4. Revealing information about our cognitive processes.

Koukkou & Lehmann's theory

- Koukkou & Lehmann (1980): during a dream we combine childhood ideas and strategies of thinking with recently acquired information.

A problem-solving theory

- Webb & Cartwright (1978): dreams are a way of dealing with problems relating to work, sex, health, relationships, etc. which occur during the waking hours.

The role of metaphor

- Cartwright (1978) does not distinguish between manifest and latent content, arguing that whatever is symbolised in a dream is the dream's true meaning.
- Metaphor plays an important role in dreaming, e.g. a person dreaming of being buried by an avalanche whilst carrying books may be worried about being 'snowed under' with work.

Research

Cartwright (1978): claims support from a study in which participants allowed to sleep uninterrupted were better able to generate realistic solutions to common problems than those deprived of REM sleep.

Hartmann (1973): people experiencing interpersonal or occupational problems enter REM sleep earlier and spend longer in it than people without such problems.

Freud's theory

- Freud (1900): saw dreams as a 'psychic safety valve' in which unacceptable urges and wishes that have been repressed into the unconscious could be gratified (*wish fulfillment*).

Manifest and latent content

A dream's meaning must be 'disguised' in order not to be threatening to us:

- **Manifest content:** the symbolic, superficial version of a dream.
- **Latent content:** the deeper, real meaning of a dream.

Interpreting dreams

Freud saw dreams as 'the royal road to the unconscious', allowing the dream analyst to decode the frequently sexual *symbols* in a dream (e.g. a broken candle = impotence) and discover the latent content.

However, Freud warned that 'sometimes a cigar is only a cigar'.

Problems

- A person concerned with impotence is just as likely to dream about *impotence* as a broken candle.
- Foulkes & Cohen (1973): disturbing events during the day tend to be followed by disturbing dreams rather than 'protective imagery'.
- Collee (1993): the interpretation of a dream is not something that can be objectively quantified and which the analyst may manipulate in order to tell a person what they think s/he wants to hear.

105

BRAIN MECHANISMS OF MOTIVATION

KEY QUESTIONS
- What causes hunger?
- What is the role of the hypothalamus in eating?
- What causes drinking?

Section 1: The causes of hunger

1 Define the term *motive*.
2 What is *homeostasis*?
3 Complete the sentence: 'An early theory proposed that the ___ sent information about hunger to the brain via the ___ ___.'
4 How did Cannon & Washburn (1912) study the relation between hunger pangs and stomach contractions?
5 Identify two reasons why hunger mechanisms are more complex than early theories suggest.
6 What finding suggests that the liver also plays a role in controlling hunger?
7 According to *glucostatic theory*, what is the primary stimulus for hunger?
8 In what way do *insulin injections* support glucostatic theory?
9 Where did Meyer & Marshall (1956) believe glucoreceptors to be, following their experiments with mice?
10 What does the finding that animals who eat diets high in fats, but maintain a relatively constant calorie intake, suggest?
11 What are *adipose tissues*?
12 According to Nisbett's (1972) version of *lipostatic theory*, what determines the *body-weight set-point*?
13 Identify one finding relating to humans which supports lipostatic theory.
14 What condition usually results in rats in whom the *lateral hypothalamus* (LH) has been damaged?
15 What is the likely role of the lateral hypothalamus?
16 Identify four *external factors* which may influence eating.
17 What is encouraged by *sensory-specific satiety*?

Section 2: The hypothalamus and eating

18 What did Hetherington & Ranson (1942) discover was the effect of producing lesions in the *ventromedial hypothalami* (VMH) of rats?
19 What is the difference between the *dynamic* and *static phases* of VMH *hyperphagia*?
20 What role does the *dual hypothalamic control theory* of eating give to the LH and the VMH?
21 Under which conditions do VMH-damaged rats *not* eat more food than normal?
22 Under which conditions can LH damaged rats be persuaded to eat normally?
23 Identify three other effects of LH damage in rats.
24 What overall conclusion concerning the importance of the LH and VMH can be reached, based on the research findings?
25 Which *neurotransmitter level* is increased by *carbohydrates*?
26 O'Rahilly *et al.* (cited in Radford, 1997) found low levels of *leptin* in the bodies of two obese cousins. What is the likely role of leptin?

Section 3: Drinking

27 What explanation for drinking does the *dry-mouth theory* of thirst propose?
28 Identify one problem with the dry-mouth theory.
29 To what are certain cells in the *lateral preoptic area* of the hypothalamus sensitive?
30 What is *osmosis*?
31 What is the role of *antidiuretic hormone*, which is produced by osmoreceptors in response to fluid depletion?
32 What causes *volumetric thirst*?
33 What is the role of the hormone *angiotensin*?
34 Which aspect of drinking behaviour is particularly difficult for researchers to explain?
35 What is the difference between *primary* and *secondary* drinking?

Section 1: The causes of hunger

1   A motive is an inner directing force which arouses an organism and directs its behaviour towards some goal.

2   Homeostasis refers to the body's tendency to maintain a steady state.

3   'An early theory proposed that the *stomach* sent information about hunger to the brain via the *vagus nerve*.'

4   Washburn swallowed a balloon attached to a tube so that his stomach contractions could be measured, whilst at the same time recording his hunger pangs.

5   People whose stomachs have been removed still report feeling hungry, and cutting the connections between the gastrointestinal tract and the brain has little effect on food intake (Pinel, 1993).

6   Injections of glucose into the liver cause a decrease in eating.

7   According to glucostatic theory, the primary stimulus for hunger is a decrease in the level of blood-glucose below a certain set-point.

8   Insulin injections lower blood glucose levels and stimulate eating.

9   Meyer & Marshall (1956) believed that glucoreceptors were located in the ventromedial hypothalamus.

10   The finding suggests that it cannot be glucose levels alone which regulate eating behaviour, since the animals' blood glucose levels are lowered slightly despite the constant calorie intake.

11   Adipose tissues are the fatty tissues of the body.

12   Nisbett's (1972) theory claims that fat levels in the adiposites (fat cells) determine the body-weight set-point.

13   Short-term dieting programmes do not produce long-term weight loss in humans.

14   Hypophagia (the cessation of eating to the point of starvation) usually results in rats in whom the lateral hypothalamus has been damaged.

15   The lateral hypothalamus affects feeding by altering the body-weight set-point.

16   Habit, environment, culture, and palatability of foods may all influence eating.

17   Sensory-specific satiety (we become tired of one food after a time) encourages the consumption of a varied diet.

Section 2: The hypothalamus and eating

18   Hetherington & Ranson (1942) discovered that lesions in the ventromedial hypothalamus of rats caused them to overeat, doubling or trebling their body weight.

19   In the *dynamic phase* of VMH *hyperphagia*, the animal eats rapidly for several weeks and gains weight. During the *static phase*, the animal attempts to defend a stable level of obesity.

20   The dual hypothalamic control theory of eating proposes that the LH 'turns' hunger on and the VMH 'turns' it off.

21   VMH-damaged rats do not eat more food than normal if they have to work for their food.

22   LH damaged rats can be persuaded to eat normally if they are fed for several weeks through a tube.

23   LH damage in rats also causes them to cease grooming themselves, have difficulty with balance, and show little interest in any stimuli.

24   The LH and VMH are likely to affect the body-weight set-point, but are not absolutely essential in regulating eating in the long-term.

25   Carbohydrates increase serotonin levels.

26   Leptin's role is apparently to keep the brain informed and regulate appetite and the rate at which calories are consumed.

Section 3: Drinking

27   The dry-mouth theory of thirst proposes that receptors in the mouth and throat play a major role in determining thirst.

28   When water is prevented from passing into the stomachs of animals who have swallowed it, they quickly resume drinking ('sham drinking' studies).

29   Certain cells in the lateral preoptic area of the hypothalamus are sensitive to cellular dehydration (an increase in salt levels in the blood).

30   Osmosis is the process whereby fluid levels in the cells are affected by salt levels in the blood.

31   Antidiuretic hormone causes the kidneys to reabsorb water which would otherwise be excreted as urine.

32   Volumetric thirst is caused by a lowering of the volume of blood in the body, which in turn lowers blood pressure.

33   Angiotensin is released by the kidneys and circulates to the hypothalamus, resulting in the initiation of drinking behaviour.

34   It is difficult to explain why we normally stop drinking well before the new supply of fluid reaches the blood.

35   Primary drinking occurs when there is a physiological need, whilst secondary drinking is drinking not caused by such a need.

A

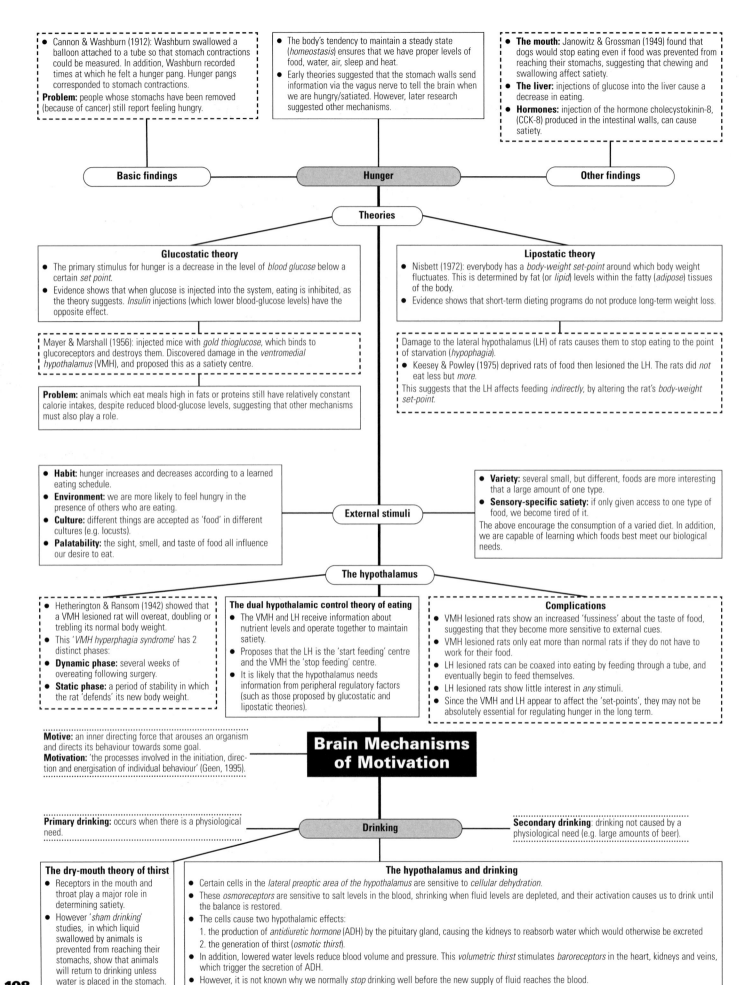

- Cannon & Washburn (1912): Washburn swallowed a balloon attached to a tube so that stomach contractions could be measured. In addition, Washburn recorded times at which he felt a hunger pang. Hunger pangs corresponded to stomach contractions.
  Problem: people whose stomachs have been removed (because of cancer) still report feeling hungry.

- The body's tendency to maintain a steady state (*homeostasis*) ensures that we have proper levels of food, water, air, sleep and heat.
- Early theories suggested that the stomach walls send information via the vagus nerve to tell the brain when we are hungry/satiated. However, later research suggested other mechanisms.

- **The mouth:** Janowitz & Grossman (1949) found that dogs would stop eating even if food was prevented from reaching their stomachs, suggesting that chewing and swallowing affect satiety.
- **The liver:** injections of glucose into the liver cause a decrease in eating.
- **Hormones:** injection of the hormone cholecystokinin-8, (CCK-8) produced in the intestinal walls, can cause satiety.

Basic findings   **Hunger**   **Other findings**

Theories

Glucostatic theory
- The primary stimulus for hunger is a decrease in the level of *blood glucose* below a certain *set point*.
- Evidence shows that when glucose is injected into the system, eating is inhibited, as the theory suggests. *Insulin* injections (which lower blood-glucose levels) have the opposite effect.

Mayer & Marshall (1956): injected mice with *gold thioglucose*, which binds to glucoreceptors and destroys them. Discovered damage in the *ventromedial hypothalamus* (VMH), and proposed this as a satiety centre.

Problem: animals which eat meals high in fats or proteins still have relatively constant calorie intakes, despite reduced blood-glucose levels, suggesting that other mechanisms must also play a role.

Lipostatic theory
- Nisbett (1972): everybody has a *body-weight set-point* around which body weight fluctuates. This is determined by fat (or *lipid*) levels within the fatty (*adipose*) tissues of the body.
- Evidence shows that short-term dieting programs do not produce long-term weight loss.

- Damage to the lateral hypothalamus (LH) of rats causes them to stop eating to the point of starvation (*hypophagia*).
- Keesey & Powley (1975) deprived rats of food then lesioned the LH. The rats did *not* eat less but *more*.
- This suggests that the LH affects feeding *indirectly*, by altering the rat's *body-weight set-point*.

- **Habit:** hunger increases and decreases according to a learned eating schedule.
- **Environment:** we are more likely to feel hungry in the presence of others who are eating.
- **Culture:** different things are accepted as 'food' in different cultures (e.g. locusts).
- **Palatability:** the sight, smell, and taste of food all influence our desire to eat.

External stimuli

- **Variety:** several small, but different, foods are more interesting that a large amount of one type.
- **Sensory-specific satiety:** if only given access to one type of food, we become tired of it.
- The above encourage the consumption of a varied diet. In addition, we are capable of learning which foods best meet our biological needs.

The hypothalamus

- Hetherington & Ransom (1942) showed that a VMH lesioned rat will overeat, doubling or trebling its normal body weight.
- This '*VMH hyperphagia syndrome*' has 2 distinct phases:
- **Dynamic phase:** several weeks of overeating following surgery.
- **Static phase:** a period of stability in which the rat 'defends' its new body weight.

The dual hypothalamic control theory of eating
- The VMH and LH receive information about nutrient levels and operate together to maintain satiety.
- Proposes that the LH is the 'start feeding' centre and the VMH the 'stop feeding' centre.
- It is likely that the hypothalamus needs information from peripheral regulatory factors (such as those proposed by glucostatic and lipostatic theories).

Complications
- VMH lesioned rats show an increased 'fussiness' about the taste of food, suggesting that they become more sensitive to external cues.
- VMH lesioned rats only eat more than normal rats if they do not have to work for their food.
- LH lesioned rats can be coaxed into eating by feeding through a tube, and eventually begin to feed themselves.
- LH lesioned rats show little interest in *any* stimuli.
- Since the VMH and LH appear to affect the 'set-points', they may not be absolutely essential for regulating hunger in the long term.

Motive: an inner directing force that arouses an organism and directs its behaviour towards some goal.
Motivation: 'the processes involved in the initiation, direction and energisation of individual behaviour' (Geen, 1995).

Brain Mechanisms of Motivation

Primary drinking: occurs when there is a physiological need.

Drinking

Secondary drinking: drinking not caused by a physiological need (e.g. large amounts of beer).

The dry-mouth theory of thirst
- Receptors in the mouth and throat play a major role in determining satiety.
- However '*sham drinking*' studies, in which liquid swallowed by animals is prevented from reaching their stomachs, show that animals will return to drinking unless water is placed in the stomach.

The hypothalamus and drinking
- Certain cells in the *lateral preoptic area* of the hypothalamus are sensitive to *cellular dehydration*.
- These *osmoreceptors* are sensitive to salt levels in the blood, shrinking when fluid levels are depleted, and their activation causes us to drink until the balance is restored.
- The cells cause two hypothalamic effects:
  1. the production of *antidiuretic hormone* (ADH) by the pituitary gland, causing the kidneys to reabsorb water which would otherwise be excreted
  2. the generation of thirst (*osmotic thirst*).
- In addition, lowered water levels reduce blood volume and pressure. This *volumetric thirst* stimulates *baroreceptors* in the heart, kidneys and veins, which trigger the secretion of ADH.
- However, it is not known why we normally *stop* drinking well before the new supply of fluid reaches the blood.

THEORIES OF MOTIVATION

KEY QUESTIONS
- What different types of motive are there?
- How do instinct theories explain motivation?
- How do drive theories explain motivation?
- How do optimum level of arousal and incentive theories explain motivation?
- How do Maslow and opponent-process theorists explain motivation?

Section 1: Types of motive

1. What name is given to *motives* which are rooted primarily in body tissue needs?
2. What are *sensation-seeking motives*?
3. Identify two effects of sensory deprivation.
4. Identify two types of sensation-seeking motive which are often activated by the new or unknown.
5. What is the sensation-seeking motive known as *manipulation*?
6. What does Brehm (1966) mean by *psychological reactance*?
7. What do psychologists generally believe is the purpose of the motivation to *seek stimulation*?
8. In what important way do complex *psychosocial motives* differ from other classes of motive?
9. What psychosocial need does McClelland (1958) suggest can be measured using the *thematic apperception test*?
10. What is the *need for affiliation*?
11. Identify two other complex psychosocial needs.

Section 2: Instinct theories

12. What is the principal claim made by *instinct theories* of motivation?
13. Why were such theories particularly popular in the early twentieth century?
14. In what way was the reasoning of early instinct theorists 'circular'?
15. What does the term *fixed action pattern*, used by ethologists, mean?
16. What is the role of the self-vocalisations produced by ducklings whilst still within the egg?

Section 3: Drive theories

17. What do *sociobiologists* see as the primary motivation for all our behaviours?
18. To what did Woodworth (1918) liken human behaviour?
19. What is the major difference between *homeostatic drive theory* and *drive reduction theory*?
20. How did Cannon (1929) define *homeostasis*?

21. Complete the sentence: 'When we are thirsty a ___ need leads to an internal ___ which causes a ___ drive'.
22. According to drive reduction theory, what is a *drive state*?
23. In what way do such states activate behaviour?
24. In what way are *primary drives* different from *secondary drives*?
25. Why is it difficult for drive theories to explain behaviours such as 'stamp collecting'?
26. Why do people who refuse to eat snacks (despite being hungry) in order to enjoy their lunch more, apparently contradict drive reduction theory?

Section 4: Arousal and incentive theories

27. What did Olds & Milner (1954) discover when they allowed a rat to stimulate its own '*pleasure centre*' by means of an electrode placed in its hypothalamus?
28. What does *optimum level of arousal* (OLA) theory suggest is an important motivation?
29. According to Zuckerman (1979), what are *sensation-seekers*?
30. What is the major problem with OLA theory?
31. How does *incentive theory* differ from other theories of motivation mentioned above?
32. How do experiments with rats and saccharin (Sheffield & Roby, 1955) support incentive theory?
33. What is *work motivation*?
34. Under which three conditions is work motivation high?
35. How do *intrinsic* and *extrinsic rewards* differ?

Section 5: Opponent-process and Maslow's theories

36. According to *opponent-process theory*, what does every emotional experience elicit?
37. What has opponent-process theory been particularly useful in explaining?
38. According to Maslow (1954), how can our needs be organised?
39. How do *D-motives* and *B-motives* differ?
40. What is the principal difficulty with concepts such as *self-actualisation*?

Q

Section 1: Types of motive

1 Biologically based motives.

2 Sensation-seeking motives are apparently largely unlearned needs for certain levels of stimulation.

3 Sensory deprivation commonly produces hallucinations, difficulty in thinking clearly, boredom, anger and frustration.

4 Curiosity and exploration are often activated by the new or unknown.

5 Manipulation refers to our desire to touch, handle or play with a specific object before we are satisfied.

6 Psychological reactance is the term that describes our tendency to re-assert our freedom when it is threatened.

7 The motivation to seek stimulation probably evolved to increase an organism's chances of survival by motivating it to gather information about its surroundings.

8 Complex psychosocial motives, unlike other classes of motive, are acquired by learning, and aroused by psychological events.

9 McClelland (1958) suggests that need for achievement can be measured using the thematic apperception test.

10 The need for affiliation is the desire to maintain close, friendly relations with others.

11 The need for power and the need for approval are both psychosocial needs.

Section 2: Instinct theories

12 Instinct theories of motivation see us as possessing innate predispositions to act in a particular way in response to a certain stimulus.

13 Such theories were popular largely due to Darwin's emphasis on the similarity between humans and other animals.

14 Early instinct theorists argued for the existence of instincts on the basis of observed behaviours, and also explained behaviours by reference to these instincts.

15 A fixed action pattern is an unlearned behaviour (universal to all members of a species) which occurs in the presence of a naturally occurring stimulus.

16 The self-vocalisations enable the duckling to discriminate maternal calls.

Section 3: Drive theories

17 Sociobiologists see the desire to ensure the future survival of our genes as the primary motivation for all our behaviours.

18 Woodworth (1918) likened human behaviour to the operation of a machine.

19 Homeostatic drive theory is a physiological theory whilst drive reduction theory is primarily a learning theory.

20 Cannon (1929) defined homeostasis as an optimum level of physiological functioning that maintains an organism in a constant internal state.

21 'When we are thirsty a *tissue* need leads to an internal *imbalance* which causes a *homeostatic* drive.'

22 A drive state is an unpleasant state of bodily arousal.

23 Drive states activate behaviour by motivating us to reduce the tension associated with them.

24 Primary drives are biological needs, whilst secondary drives help reduce primary drives and are learned by association.

25 Stamp collecting is not a behaviour which can sensibly be explained by proposing a 'stamp collecting drive'.

26 Such behaviours seem to increase rather than reduce certain drives.

Section 4: Arousal and incentive theories

27 Olds & Milner (1954) discovered that rats would stimulate this area in preference to doing anything else, and that this behaviour never satiated.

28 Optimum level of arousal theory suggests that the desire for a certain level of stimulation is an important motivation.

29 Zuckerman (1979) identifies sensation-seekers as those people with high optimum levels of arousal.

30 OLA theory cannot be tested since we cannot measure an organism's level of arousal.

31 Incentive theory proposes that we are motivated by external stimuli (incentives) rather that internal states.

32 Sheffield & Roby (1955) found that rats will work hard for a sip of saccharin even though saccharin cannot reduce a tissue need (it has no nutritional value).

33 Work motivation is our tendency to expend effort and energy on a job.

34 Work motivation is high when hard work will improve performance, performance will yield rewards and these rewards are valued.

35 Intrinsic rewards are the pleasure and satisfaction which a task brings, whilst extrinsic rewards are those which are given beyond a task's intrinsic pleasures.

Section 5: Opponent-process and Maslow's theories

36 According to opponent-process theory, every emotional experience elicits a more intense opposite emotional experience.

37 Opponent-process theory been particularly useful in explaining drug addiction.

38 Maslow (1954) argues that our needs can be organised in a hierarchy, with basic physiological needs at the bottom, and more complex and psychological needs higher up.

39 D-motives are those relating to deficiencies which are associated with our survival, whilst B-motives give rise to behaviours which relate to 'self-actualisation' or 'being'.

40 Concepts such as self-actualisation are difficult to define operationally, and consequently difficult to study experimentally.

Theories of Motivation

Types of motive

Sensation-seeking motives
Needs for certain levels of stimulation, largely learned:
- **Activity:** all animals need to be active; sensory deprivation studies show that inactivity is intolerable.
- **Curiosity and exploration:** humans and non-humans are motivated by the unknown and the desire to 'find out'.
- **Manipulation:** primates seem to have the need for tactile experiences which they direct towards a specific object.

In addition, many species demonstrate a need for *play* (which is often 'practice play'), *contact* (touching others), and *control* (the need to determine our own actions).

Biologically based motives
- Rooted primarily in body tissue needs (e.g. need for food, air, water, sleep).
- Although these needs are in-built, their expression is often learned.

Complex psychosocial motives
Needs aroused by psychological events and acquired by learning:
- **Need for achievement** (*nAch*): the need to meet or exceed some standard.
- **Need for affiliation** (*nAff*): the desire to maintain close, friendly relations with others.
- **Need for power** (*nPower*): a concern with being in charge, having status and prestige.
- **Need for approval** (*nApp*): the desire for some sign that others like us or think we are good.

Instinct theories
Propose that we possess *innate* or *genetically pre-determined dispositions* to act in a certain way. Largely due to the Darwinian emphasis on the similarity of humans to animals.
- Early theories fell into disrepute due to disagreement over the number of instincts (up to 15,000 were identified), and a tendency of theorists to propose a new instinct to explain any observed behaviour (e.g. a 'cleanliness instinct').
- *Ethologists* revived and revised instinct theory, coining the term '*fixed action pattern*' to describe unlearned behaviours which are 'released' automatically in the presence of certain stimuli (e.g. aggressive behaviour in sticklebacks in response to a red patch (Tinbergen, 1951)).

Sociobiology
- Sociobiologists argue that innate tendencies play an important role in complex human behaviour, with the primary motive to ensure the survival of one's genes.
- However, such 'selfish gene' explanations of human behaviour may underestimate the role of situational and personal variables.

Drive theories

Homeostatic drive theory
- Cannon (1929) saw organisms as trying to achieve an optimum level of physiological functioning by maintaining a constant internal state (*homeostasis*).
- Tissue needs (e.g. dehydration) lead to imbalances which lead to homeostatic drives, causing the organism to behave in a way which restores the balance (e.g. eating when hungry).

Drive-reduction theory
- States of need lead to unpleasant states of bodily arousal (*drive states*) which activate behaviours required to reduce them.
- *Primary drives* (such as hunger) are supplemented by *secondary drives* (e.g. the drive for money), which we acquire through association.
- However, not all behaviours are obviously motivated by drives – and some seem to *increase* rather than reduce certain drives (e.g. carefully preparing a meal). Finally, Olds & Milner (1954) discovered that a rat that could stimulate an electrode placed in the 'pleasure centre' of its hypothalamus, would do so *endlessly*.

Optimum level of arousal theory
- We have a preference for an optimum level of arousal (OLA) and that when arousal falls *below* this level, we are motivated to raise it by increasing stimulation; when arousal rises *above* this level, we decrease stimulation.
- People with a *low* OLA may prefer sedentary lifestyles, whereas those with a *high* OLA ('sensation-seekers') may prefer to engage in activities such as driving fast cars.
- Unfortunately, there is no way of measuring an organism's OLA independently of its behaviour.

Incentive (expectancy) theory
- *External* stimuli (instead of internal drives) motivate us in certain directions in the absence of physiological states.
- The expectation of achieving a desirable goal (incentive) motivates us to perform behaviours. Undesirable goals inhibit behaviours.
- *Work motivation* describes our tendency to expend effort and energy on a job and will be increased if a) hard work improves performance, b) good performance yields rewards, c) such rewards are valued (Mitchell & Larson, 1987).
- Rotter (1966) proposes that expectations and values affect whether a behaviour is performed or not.

Opponent-process theory
Solomon & Corbit (1974) point to the fact that some motives are clearly acquired.
- They argue that every emotional experience elicits a more intense *opposite* emotional experience which persists long after the primary emotion it developed from, and diminishes the intensity of the primary emotion.
- Repeated pleasurable experiences eventually lose their pleasantness (shifting the driving force from pleasure to pain).
- Repeated unpleasurable experiences eventually lose their unpleasantness (shifting the driving force from pain to pleasure).

Drug addiction
- The initial pleasure produced by the drug is followed by a gradual decline and then a minor craving for it.
- When addiction occurs the drug is taken to avoid the pain of withdrawal rather than the experiences of pleasure.

Maslow's theory
Maslow (1954): behaviour is motivated by the desire for personal growth (*self-actualisation*).
- Human needs can be organised into a hierarchy. Lower needs need to be satisfied before higher, more complex needs.
- Behaviours related to survival have '*deficiency*' (D-motive) causes. Behaviours related to self-actualisation have '*being*' (B-motive) causes.
- Critics point out the 'self-actualisation' is difficult to define, and that the order in which needs are satisfied often differs from the order in the hierarchy.

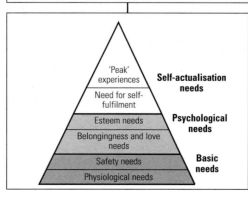

Freud's theory
Behaviour is controlled by unconscious motives closely related to instincts.
- Originally Freud saw all human behaviour as rooted in '*Eros*' (the drive for 'bodily pleasure').
- Later he argued that '*Thanatos*' (a drive for self-destruction) also influences behaviour.
- Unfortunately, it is difficult to test such a theory since unconscious motives cannot be observed directly.

EMOTION

KEY QUESTIONS
• What is the role of the hypothalamus in emotion?
• What is the role of the limbic system in emotion?
• What is the role of the cortex in emotion?
• How do different theories explain emotion?

Q

Section 1: The hypothalamus

1 What did Bard (1928) discover was the effect of destroying parts of the cerebral cortex in cats and dogs?
2 What was the consequence of removing the *hypothalamus* following decortication?
3 What did Sem-Jacobsen (1968) discover when investigating *hypothalamic stimulation* in humans?

Section 2: The limbic system

4 What is *Klüver–Bucy syndrome*?
5 What is *hyperorality* (one of the symptoms of Klüver–Bucy syndrome)?
6 According to Klüver & Bucy (1937), how does damage to the *limbic system* affect fearfulness and aggression in monkeys?
7 What is the effect of destroying the *amygdala* of wild monkeys?
8 In the case study conducted by Mark & Ervin (1970), what procedure was carried out to reduce Julia's aggressive behaviour?
9 What did Brady & Nauta (1953) discover was the effect of lesions in the *septum* of rats?
10 What evidence did Delgado (1969) produce for the existence of an *aggression centre*?
11 What was Valenstein's (1973) criticism of Delgado's claims?

Section 3: The cerebral hemispheres

12 What is the role of the *corpus callosum*?
13 Which side of the body is likely to be paralysed in a patient displaying an *indifference reaction* following brain damage?
14 What stimuli were used by Ley & Bryden (1979) in studying the processing of emotional states in people with normally functioning hemispheres?
15 Complete the sentence: 'PET scans have shown that the left hemisphere is more active during ___ emotional experiences'.
16 According to Day & Wong (1996), how does the hemispheric functioning of *dissocial individuals* differ from that of normal people?

Section 4: Theories of emotion

17 Complete the sentence: 'For the James–Lange theory, emotions are a ___-___ of automatic behavioural or physiological responses'.
18 Which brain structure is responsible for interpreting bodily changes as emotions?
19 What does the James–Lange theory imply about the pattern of physiological responses fed back to the brain with respect to different emotions?
20 What findings were reported by Wolf & Wolff (1947)?
21 What was demonstrated in Marañon's (1924) study, in which participants were injected with adrenaline?
22 What claim is made by *facial feedback theory*?
23 What is the name of the physiological response which Cannon saw as underlying all emotional states?
24 According to the *thalamic theory*, to which two areas does the thalamus simultaneously send impulses?
25 Identify the two brain structures which are likely to play a more central role in emotion than the thalamus.
26 According to *Schachter's theory*, what are the two factors upon which an emotion depends?
27 According to Schachter's theory, what determines the *intensity* of an emotion and the *particular emotion* that is experienced?
28 What was the purpose of Schachter & Singer (1962) injecting participants with *epinephrine*?
29 Why should participants in the 'epinephrine-informed' condition *not* experience changes in their emotional states?
30 What are people taught in *misattribution therapy*?
31 What does Lazarus (1982) regard as an *essential pre-requisite* for the experience of emotion?
32 Complete the sentence: 'According to Lazarus, emotion reflects a constantly changing ___-___ relationship'.
33 What argument has Zajonc (1984) raised against Lazarus's theory?
34 What does Lazarus use the term *primitive evaluative perception* to describe?

Section 1: The hypothalamus

1 Bard (1928) discovered that destroying parts of the cerebral cortex in cats and dogs caused a lower threshold of emotional excitation.
2 The rage produced by decortication disappeared if the hypothalamus was also removed.
3 Sem-Jacobsen (1968) discovered that hypothalamic stimulation in humans had little effect on emotional experiences.

Section 2: The limbic system

4 Klüver–Bucy syndrome is the name given to the five main consequences of damage to the temporal lobes of monkeys.
5 Hyperorality is the tendency of monkeys to eat any food given to them, and to put moveable objects into their mouths.
6 Klüver and Bucy (1937) found that damage to the limbic system decreases fearfulness and increases aggression in monkeys.
7 Destroying the amygdala causes the monkeys to become tame and placid.
8 Julia's aggressive behaviour was reduced by psychosurgery in the form of a small lesion to her amygdala.
9 Brady & Nauta (1953) discovered that lesions in the septum of rats resulted in the lowering of the rat's 'rage threshold'.
10 Delgado (1969) showed that stimulating a charging bull's limbic system resulted in the bull stopping in its tracks.
11 Valenstein's (1973) argued that the bull was simply 'confused' and 'frustrated' and gave up (rather than ceasing to be aggressive).

Section 3: The cerebral hemispheres

12 The corpus callosum connects the two cerebral hemispheres and allows them to exchange information.
13 An indifference reaction is most likely to be produced in people with left-sided paralysis.
14 Ley & Bryden (1979) showed participants drawings of faces displaying different emotional expressions.
15 'PET scans have shown that the left hemisphere is more active during *positive* emotional experiences.'
16 Day & Wong (1996) found that dissocial individuals do not show a right ('emotional') hemisphere advantage as do normal people when responding to negative emotional words.

Section 4: Theories of emotion

17 'For the James–Lange theory, emotions are a *by-product* of automatic behavioural or physiological responses.'
18 The cortex is responsible for interpreting bodily changes as emotions.
19 The theory implies that the pattern of physiological responses would have to be different for each emotion, if the cortex were to be able to determine which emotion should be experienced.
20 Wolf & Wolff (1947) found that different people display different patterns of physiological activity whilst experiencing the same emotion.
21 Marañon (1924) found that participants did not report emotional overtones to the physiological changes caused by adrenaline.
22 Facial feedback theory claims that facial expressions can produce changes in emotional state as well as mirror them.
23 Cannon saw the 'fight-or-flight' response as underlying all emotional states.
24 The thalamus simultaneously sends impulses to the cortex and the hypothalamus.
25 The limbic system and the hypothalamus are likely to play a more central role in emotion than the thalamus.
26 According to Schachter's theory, an emotion depends on physiological arousal in the ANS and the cognitive appraisal (interpretation) of this arousal.
27 The intensity of an emotion is determined by the degree of arousal, whilst the particular emotion that is experienced is determined by the interpretation of the arousal.
28 Epinephrine was injected in order to produce increased heart rate, respiration rate, blood pressure and muscle tremors.
29 Participants in the 'epinephrine-informed' condition should experience arousal, but since they are expecting these effects they will attribute them to the drug and not to a change in emotional state.
30 During misattribution therapy, people are taught to attribute maladaptive arousal (e.g. a phobia) to some other source (e.g a pill they have just taken).
31 Lazarus (1982) regards some cognitive processing as an essential pre-requisite for the experience of emotion.
32 'According to Lazarus, emotion reflects a constantly changing *person–environment* relationship.'
33 Zajonc (1984) argues that cognition and emotion operate as independent systems.
34 Lazarus uses the term primitive evaluative perception to describe the sorts of unconscious cognitive appraisal involved in primitive emotional responses (such as fear).

A

Emotion

The limbic system

Klüver & Bucy's (1937) research

Klüver–Bucy syndrome
The five main consequences of damage to the temporal lobes of monkeys:
1. *Hyperorality*: the monkeys tried to eat anything given to them.
2. *Visual agnosia*: they were unable to recognise objects by sight.
3. *Hypersexuality*: increased and often inappropriate sexuality.
4. Tamer and safer to handle.
5. Displayed a complete lack of fear.

Further research
- Showed that damage to the limbic system affected the emotional behaviour of monkeys (e.g. increased aggression and decreased fearfulness).
- Noted that the destruction of the *amygdala* made wild and ferocious monkeys tame and placid. Similar results were found in other species.

Applications – psychosurgery
Klüver, Bucy and others' findings were instrumental in developing psychosurgery:
- Mark & Ervin (1970): cite the case of Julia, a young woman who committed unprovoked attacks on 12 people. Tests suggested that the amygdala was damaged, and a small lesion produced by surgeons in the amygdala greatly reduced her aggressive behaviour.

The cerebral hemispheres

The corpus callosum and hemispheric specialisation
The two cerebral hemispheres are connected by the *corpus callosum*. Split-brain studies suggests that this acts as a 'channel of communication' between the two hemispheres which are specialised for different tasks (see Ch 19).

Studies of brain-damaged patients
- People with right hemisphere damage suffer paralysis of the left side but seem unmoved by this (*indifference reaction*), whereas those with left hemisphere damage suffer anxiety and depression in response to their paralysis (*catastrophic reaction*).
- This suggests that the right hemisphere is specialised for recognising and responding to emotion-provoking stimuli (such as brain damage), whilst the left hemisphere is not.

Studies of people with normal hemispheric function
- Ley & Bryden (1979): showed participants drawings of faces depicting emotional expressions, in such a way that they were only perceived by one or other of the hemispheres.
- The right hemisphere made fewer recognition errors when the drawings depicted clear emotional states, suggesting that the right hemisphere has an advantage in recognising clear facial expressions of emotion.

James–Lange theory

- According to this theory, an emotional experience is the result (not the cause of) bodily and/or behavioural changes (e.g. crying) to some emotion-provoking stimulus. James argued that 'we feel sorry because we cry'.

Perception of emotion-arousing stimulus *(e.g. a bear)*	→	**Bodily changes** both visceral and skeletal *(e.g. running away)*	→	**Interpretation by cortex** of changes as an emotion *(e.g. fear)*

feedback of bodily changes (thalamus)

3 criticisms of the theory (Cannon, 1927)

Each emotion would need a distinct pattern of physiological activity or the cortex would be unable to determine which is to be felt:
- Wolf & Wolff (1947): different people have different patterns of physiological activity when experiencing the same emotion.

Physiological changes do not themselves produce changes in emotional state:
- Marañon (1924) injected participants with adrenaline which caused a physiological change but participants did not report an emotional change.

Total separation of the viscera from the CNS does not eliminate emotions:
- Cannon found that when visceral feedback was abolished in cats and dogs, emotional experience was unaffected.

Cannon–Bard theory

- Cannon saw all emotions as producing the same pattern of responses (the fight-or-flight response).
- External stimuli activate the *thalamus* which sends information to the cortex for interpretation and messages to the viscera and skeletal muscles (via the PNS), so that the emotion and physiological responses are independent of one another.

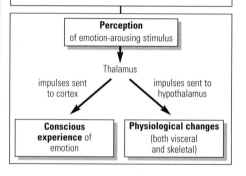

Perception of emotion-arousing stimulus

Thalamus

impulses sent to cortex — **Conscious experience** of emotion

impulses sent to hypothalamus — **Physiological changes** (both visceral and skeletal)

Schachter's theory

- Schachter's (1964) '*two-factor theory of emotion*' proposes that emotional experience depends on two factors: physiological arousal in the ANS, and cognitive appraisal (interpretation of this arousal).
- Unlike the James–Lange theory, Schachter argues that the same physiological changes underlie all emotional states, and that it is the meaning attributed to them that determines different emotions. The interpretation may be influenced by situational cues.

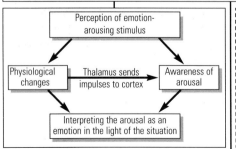

Perception of emotion-arousing stimulus

Physiological changes — Thalamus sends impulses to cortex — Awareness of arousal

Interpreting the arousal as an emotion in the light of the situation

Schachter & Singer (1962):
- Participants were given an injection of *epinephrine* (which causes physiological arousal) and either informed or misinformed as to its effects.
- Participants were exposed to 'stooges' who behaved in either an angry or euphoric way.
- Participants who were not informed of the drug's effects reported similar feelings to those of the stooge to whom they were exposed (apparently interpreting their arousal similarly).

Other research
- Dutton & Aron (1974) found that male participants approached by a female researcher whilst crossing an unstable suspension bridge were more likely to invent stories with a high amount of sexual imagery than those approached on a solid wooden bridge (the former interpreting their arousal as sexual attraction).

Lazarus's theory

- Lazarus (1982): argues that some cognitive processing is an essential pre-requisite for the experience of emotion.
- Emotion occurs when '*central life agendas*' (e.g. survival, personal values) become an issue in the changing person–environment relationship.

Problems
- Zajonc (1984): argues that cognition does not have primacy over emotion, and that they operate as independent systems.
- Zajonc argues that we have evolved the ability to detect affective qualities without *cognitive mediation* (e.g. when we meet a person for the first time and form a positive or negative impression despite having processed very little information about the person).

- Lazarus disagrees and argues that even primitive emotional responses (e.g. fear) require some unconscious appraisal (*'primitive evaluative perception'*).
- Ekman *et al.* (1985) point out that there is no known stimulus which reliably produces the same response in all people, supporting Lazarus's theory.

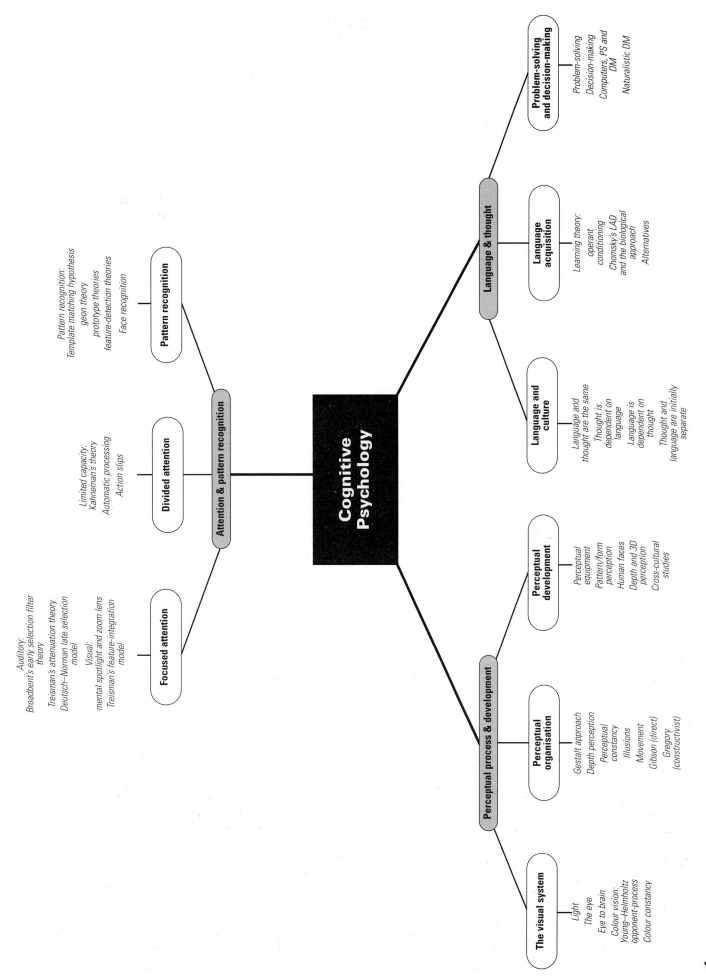

Cognitive Psychology

Attention & pattern recognition

Focused attention

Auditory:
Broadbent's early selection filter theory
Treisman's attenuation theory
Deutsch–Norman late selection model
Visual:
mental spotlight and zoom lens
Treisman's feature-integration model

Divided attention

Limited capacity:
Kahneman's theory
Automatic processing
Action slips

Pattern recognition

Pattern recognition:
Template matching hypothesis
geon theory
prototype theories
feature-detection theories
Face recognition

Language & thought

Language and culture

Language and thought are the same
Thought is dependent on language
Language is dependent on thought
Thought and language are initially separate

Language acquisition

Learning theory:
operant conditioning
Chomsky's LAD and the biological approach
Alternatives

Problem-solving and decision-making

Problem-solving
Decision-making
Computers, PS and DM
Naturalistic DM

Perceptual process & development

The visual system

Light
The eye
Eye to brain
Colour vision:
Young–Helmholtz
opponent-process
Colour constancy

Perceptual organisation

Gestalt approach
Depth perception
Perceptual constancy
Illusions
Movement
Gibson (direct)
Gregory (constructivist)

Perceptual development

Perceptual equipment
Pattern/form perception
Human faces
Depth and 3D perception
Cross-cultural studies

FOCUSED ATTENTION

SYLLABUS

13.3 Attention and pattern recognition – focused attention

- studies of focused (selective) attention (e.g. Cherry). Explanations of focused attention, including early-selection (e.g. Broadbent, Treisman) and late-selection models (e.g. Deutsch and Deutsch)

KEY QUESTIONS
- Why do psychologists study attention?
- What theories are there to explain focused auditory attention?
- What theories are there to explain focused visual attention?
- What are the strengths and weaknesses of these theories?

Section 1: Early studies of attention

1. Why did behaviourists argue that attention was not worthy of experimental study?
2. What important claim did Broadbent make in his 1958 book *Perception and Communication*?
3. What is the *cocktail-party phenomenon* (Cherry, 1953)?
4. What is a *binaural listening task*?
5. What is a *dichotic listening task*?
6. What is involved in *shadowing*?
7. How much of a shadowed message is remembered?
8. Broadbent (1954) used a *split-span procedure* to investigate attention. What did this involve?

Section 2: Focused auditory attention

9. What is the common feature of all *single-channel theories of attention*?
10. According to Broadbent's (1958) theory, at what stage does filtering occur in the processing of information?
11. What is the purpose of the *short-term store* in this model?
12. What features of the stimulus does the selective filter operate upon?
13. What does the *limited-capacity channel* correspond to?
14. How does this model suggest that we deal with two simultaneous stimuli?
15. Why is Moray's (1959) finding that we will sometimes switch our attention to a 'non-attended ear' if our name is presented in that ear a problem for Broadbent's model?
16. What did Treisman (1960) discover when she switched information, mid-sentence, to a non-attended ear?
17. What were Underwood's (1974) participants, trained in shadowing, able to do?
18. According to Treisman's *attenuation theory*, what types of analyses are carried out on incoming information?
19. What does it mean to say a message is attenuated?
20. What types of information is attention likely to be switched to, according to this theory?
21. According to the Deutsch–Norman theory, when does filtering or selection occur?

22. Why is this theory sometimes called *pertinence theory*?
23. Why is the finding (Treisman & Riley, 1969) that target words are best identified in a shadowed message (vs the non-shadowed message) a problem for this theory?
24. What is meant by saying that the major problem with these single-channel theories is that they are inflexible?

Section 3: Focused visual attention

25. Which area of the retina allows maximum visual processing?
26. What is *covert attention* (Posner, 1980)?
27. What did Posner liken covert attention to?
28. What conclusion can be drawn from LaBerge's (1983) experiment, in which participants identified numbers at varying distances from the centre of their attention?
29. What did LaBerge discover when he investigated the 'width' of the 'mental spotlight'?
30. What did Eriksen (1990) mean by the *zoom-lens model* of visual attention?
31. When Neisser & Becklen (1975) superimposed two films, what implications did their results have for the the *spotlight model*?
32. What is a *visual search procedure*?
33. According to Treisman's (1988) *feature–integration theory* of visual processing, what are the two stages of visual processing?
34. In Treisman & Gelade's (1980) experiments, which of the two letters 'Y' or 'Z' increased the time taken by participants to spot a letter 'T', and why?
35. When McLeod *et al.* (1991) asked participants to identify a moving 'X' from among moving 'O's and stationary 'X's, what did they find?
36. Does this support Treisman's feature integration theory – why/why not?
37. Overall, what do the above studies suggest regarding the fate of unattended information?

Section 1: Early studies of attention

1 Behaviourists argued that since attention was not directly observable, it was not worthy of study.

2 Broadbent's book *Perception and Communication* argues that humans cannot cope with all the information available to their senses, and must therefore selectively attend to some of it.

3 The cocktail-party phenomenon (Cherry, 1953) describes our ability to focus attention on one conversation, whilst ignoring other conversations.

4 A binaural listening task involves listening to pairs of messages spoken simultaneously, using both ears.

5 A dichotic listening task involves presenting different messages to participants' right and left ears, respectively.

6 Shadowing is a procedure which requires participants to repeat out loud one or other of the messages presented in a dichotic listening task.

7 Moray (1959) found that very little of the shadowed message is remembered.

8 Broadbent's (1954) split-span procedure involved presenting six numbers to participants, three in one ear and three in the other, and recording how many were recalled.

Section 2: Focused auditory attention

9 All single-channel theories of attention propose that at some stage in the processing of information there is a 'bottleneck' or filter, which limits the amount of information to be passed on for further processing.

10 Broadbent's (1958) early selection filter theory claims that filtering occurs early on in processing.

11 The short-term store is a temporary buffer which holds information until it can be processed further.

12 The selective filter operates upon purely physical characteristics of the stimulus (such as tone and volume).

13 The limited-capacity channel corresponds to our 'stream of consciousness', i.e. all that we are aware of, now.

14 According to this model, it is possible for us to process two simultaneous stimuli by returning to the stimuli still held in the short-term store (one at a time).

15 Moray's (1959) finding is a problem since, according to Broadbent's model, selective filtering does not involve analysis of meaning, so we should not notice that our name is presented in a non-attended ear.

16 Treisman (1960) found that participants would occasionally shift their attention to the non-attended ear.

17 Underwood's (1974) participants, trained in shadowing, were able to recall most of the material presented to the non-shadowed ear.

18 Treisman's attenuation theory claims that incoming information is analysed in terms of its grammar, meaning and sound patterns.

19 An attenuated message is not rejected completely but 'turned down', so that it is still processed to some extent.

20 According to this theory, attention is likely to be switched to biologically relevant or important information.

21 The Deutsch–Norman theory claims that filtering and selection of information occur late in processing, only after all inputs have been analysed at a high level.

22 This theory is sometimes called pertinence theory, since the pertinence (or relevance) of information plays a key role in determining whether or not it is selected for attention.

23 The finding (Treisman & Riley, 1969) that target words are best identified in a shadowed message (vs. the non-shadowed message) is a problem for this theory, since both sensory inputs should have been analysed in terms of their meaning before being attended to: target words should be equally easy to identify.

24 Single-channel theories are inflexible in that they claim that certain amounts of processing occur at certain stages, whereas this may vary depending on the task and the nature of the information.

Section 3: Focused visual attention

25 The fovea (an area of the retina with the densest concentration of receptor cells) allows maximum visual processing.

26 Covert attention (Posner, 1980) refers to our ability to shift our attention without shifting our gaze (i.e. making eye movements).

27 Posner likened covert attention to an internal mental spotlight.

28 LaBerge (1983) asked participants to identify numbers at varying distances from the centre of their attention, concluding that visual attention is most concentrated at the centre of the internal spotlight.

29 LaBerge discovered that the 'width' of the mental spotlight's 'beam' varied, depending on the task.

30 Eriksen's (1990) zoom-lens model of visual attention proposed that the beam of the internal mental spotlight may be very narrow or broad.

31 Neisser & Becklen (1975) found that when they superimposed two films, participants could attend to one or the other, but not both. This contradicts the spotlight model, since both films were at the centre of attention.

32 A visual search procedure involves presenting participants with an array of stimuli, from which they must identify a 'target' item.

33 Treisman's (1988) two stages of visual processing are processing the features of a stimulus, and combining those features to form objects.

34 Treisman & Gelade's (1980) experiments found that the letter 'Z' increased the time taken by participants to spot a letter 'T' (since it shares the horizontal bar).

35 McLeod *et al.* (1991) found that participants could quickly identify a moving 'X' from among stationary 'X's and moving 'O's.

36 No, since the surrounding stimuli shared features with the moving 'X'.

37 Overall, these studies support the idea that unattended information is processed to some extent, but to what extent and how this is done is still unclear.

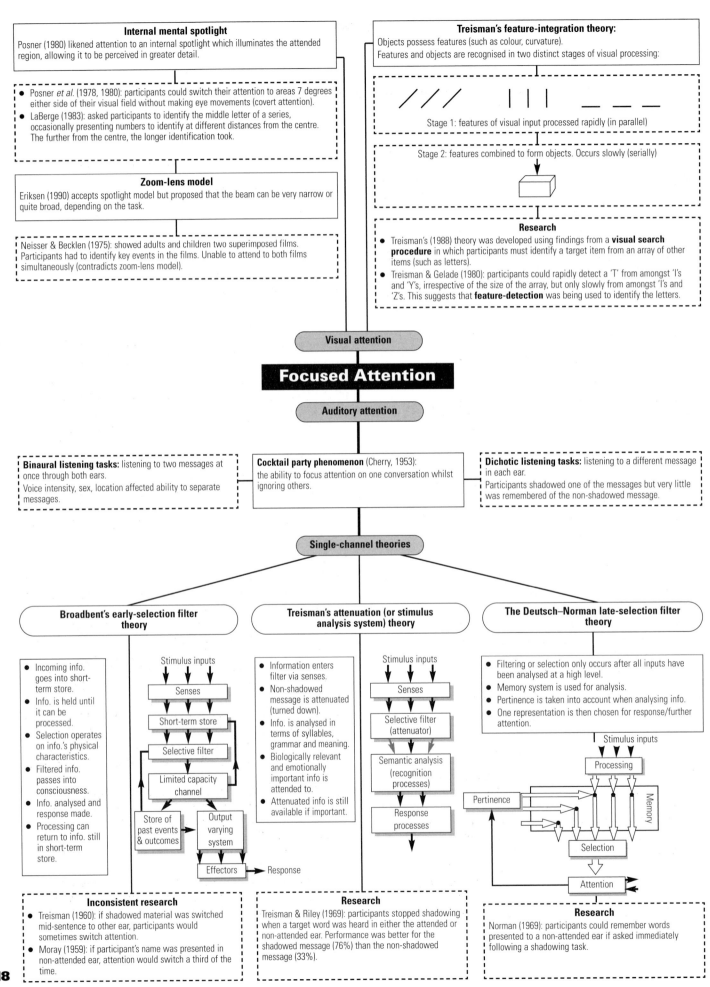

Internal mental spotlight
Posner (1980) likened attention to an internal spotlight which illuminates the attended region, allowing it to be perceived in greater detail.

- Posner *et al.* (1978, 1980): participants could switch their attention to areas 7 degrees either side of their visual field without making eye movements (covert attention).
- LaBerge (1983): asked participants to identify the middle letter of a series, occasionally presenting numbers to identify at different distances from the centre. The further from the centre, the longer identification took.

Zoom-lens model
Eriksen (1990) accepts spotlight model but proposed that the beam can be very narrow or quite broad, depending on the task.

Neisser & Becklen (1975): showed adults and children two superimposed films. Participants had to identify key events in the films. Unable to attend to both films simultaneously (contradicts zoom-lens model).

Treisman's feature-integration theory:
Objects possess features (such as colour, curvature).
Features and objects are recognised in two distinct stages of visual processing:

Stage 1: features of visual input processed rapidly (in parallel)

Stage 2: features combined to form objects. Occurs slowly (serially)

Research
- Treisman's (1988) theory was developed using findings from a **visual search procedure** in which participants must identify a target item from an array of other items (such as letters).
- Treisman & Gelade (1980): participants could rapidly detect a 'T' from amongst 'I's and 'Y's, irrespective of the size of the array, but only slowly from amongst 'I's and 'Z's. This suggests that **feature-detection** was being used to identify the letters.

Visual attention

Focused Attention

Auditory attention

Binaural listening tasks: listening to two messages at once through both ears.
Voice intensity, sex, location affected ability to separate messages.

Cocktail party phenomenon (Cherry, 1953):
the ability to focus attention on one conversation whilst ignoring others.

Dichotic listening tasks: listening to a different message in each ear.
Participants shadowed one of the messages but very little was remembered of the non-shadowed message.

Single-channel theories

Broadbent's early-selection filter theory

- Incoming info. goes into short-term store.
- Info. is held until it can be processed.
- Selection operates on info.'s physical characteristics.
- Filtered info. passes into consciousness.
- Info. analysed and response made.
- Processing can return to info. still in short-term store.

Stimulus inputs → Senses → Short-term store → Selective filter → Limited capacity channel → Store of past events & outcomes / Output varying system → Effectors → Response

Inconsistent research
- Treisman (1960): if shadowed material was switched mid-sentence to other ear, participants would sometimes switch attention.
- Moray (1959): if participant's name was presented in non-attended ear, attention would switch a third of the time.

Treisman's attenuation (or stimulus analysis system) theory

- Information enters filter via senses.
- Non-shadowed message is attenuated (turned down).
- Info. is analysed in terms of syllables, grammar and meaning.
- Biologically relevant and emotionally important info is attended to.
- Attenuated info is still available if important.

Stimulus inputs → Senses → Selective filter (attenuator) → Semantic analysis (recognition processes) → Response processes

Research
Treisman & Riley (1969): participants stopped shadowing when a target word was heard in either the attended or non-attended ear. Performance was better for the shadowed message (76%) than the non-shadowed message (33%).

The Deutsch–Norman late-selection filter theory

- Filtering or selection only occurs after all inputs have been analysed at a high level.
- Memory system is used for analysis.
- Pertinence is taken into account when analysing info.
- One representation is then chosen for response/further attention.

Stimulus inputs → Processing / Pertinence / Memory → Selection → Attention

Research
Norman (1969): participants could remember words presented to a non-attended ear if asked immediately following a shadowing task.

DIVIDED ATTENTION

KEY QUESTIONS
- What is dual-task performance and which factors affect it?
- How do limited-capacity and multi-channel theories explain divided attention?
- How does automatic processing occur?
- What are 'action slips'?

Section 1: Dual-task performance

1 What is the difference between studies of focused attention and studies of divided attention?
2 What did Spelke *et al.* (1976) discover about students' abilities to perform two tasks simultaneously?
3 According to Hampton (1989), why do factors which make one task easier tend to make the other easier too?
4 What three factors do Eysenck & Keane (1995) identify as affecting our ability to perform two tasks simultaneously?

Section 2: Theories of divided attention

5 Name two factors which (according to Kahneman's, 1973, model of attention) may affect how capacity is allocated.
6 What is the role of arousal in Kahneman's model?
7 What is meant by the *allocation policy* in Kahneman's (1973) model?
8 According to Norman & Bobrow's (1975) *central capacity interference theory*, in what two ways may performance be limited?
9 What does it mean to say that this theory is *unfalsifiable*?
10 What is meant by the term *module* in Allport's *multi-channel approach*?
11 Why, according to this model, can dissimilar tasks be performed simultaneously?
12 Give one criticism of this approach.
13 How do *synthesis models* attempt to combine capacity and module accounts of attentional processing?

Section 3: Automatic processing

14 What does it mean to say that a task is processed automatically?
15 According to Schneider & Shiffrin (1977), what is the distinction between *controlled* and *automatic processing*?
16 Give an everyday example of a task which is initially controlled, but through practice becomes automatic.

17 What two suggestions have been made as to how we change from controlled to automatic processing?
18 What is the *Stroop Effect* (Stroop, 1935)?
19 According to Manstead & Semin (1980), what is the distinction between *open-loop control* and *closed-loop control*?
20 According to Abrams & Manstead (1981), why does our performance on simple tasks improve when we are being watched?
21 Why does our performance on complex tasks worsen when we are being watched?
22 What are the two separate control systems which Norman & Shallice (1986) proposed in their attentional model?
23 According to this model, when does partially automatic processing occur?

Section 4: Action slips

24 What is an *action slip*?
25 Name three of the five categories of action slip identified by Reason (1979, 1992).
26 What relationship does Reason (1992) suggest exists between action-slips and open-loop control?
27 Name two reasons why action slips occur, according to Sellen & Norman's (1992) *schema theory* of action slips.
28 What, according to this theory, is the difference between a parent schema and a child schema?
29 What, according to Eysenck (1994), would be one way of avoiding all action-slips?
30 What is one criticism of the *diary method* employed by Reason to record his participants' data concerning action-slips?
31 What overall conclusion can we draw regarding whether or not it is possible to divide attention between two tasks?

Section 1: Dual-task performance

1 Studies of focused attention require participants to process information from one of two inputs, whereas studies of divided attention require participants to process both stimulus inputs.

2 Spelke *et al.* (1976) discovered that students could learn to take notes and read short stories simultaneously, but only after six weeks of training.

3 Hampton (1989) claimed that factors which make one task easier will make the other easier, since such factors reduce the interference occurring between the two tasks.

4 Eysenck & Keane (1995) identify difficulty of task, amount of practice at task, and similarity of tasks as affecting dual-task performance.

Section 2: Theories of divided attention

5 Kahneman's (1973) model of attention claimed that enduring dispositions, momentary intentions and an evaluation of attentional demands all affect the way that processing capacity is allocated.

6 Arousal plays a key role in Kahneman's (1973) model, with more attentional resources being available when we are aroused.

7 The allocation policy was Kahneman's (1973) attempt to explain the system of rules used by an attentional system for deciding which possible activities should be allocated attention.

8 Norman & Bobrow's (1975) central capacity interference theory claims that performance may be data-limited (e.g. reading at a distance) or resource-limited (e.g. holding a conversation whilst negotiating a roundabout).

9 An unfalsifiable theory is one which cannot be disproved, i.e. which is consistent with any set of findings.

10 A 'module', according to Allport's multi-channel approach, is a specialised processing mechanism.

11 Dissimilar tasks can be performed simultaneously, because they use separate processing modules and so do not interfere with each other.

12 The approach is unfalsifiable, since we can propose any number of modules to explain observations. In addition, the number and function of the modules has yet to be specified, as has the manner in which they co-operate to produce behaviour.

13 Synthesis models propose the existence of a modality-free central processor which co-ordinates and controls the operation of more specific processing systems. Baddeley's (1986) working memory model is an example.

Section 3: Automatic processing

14 A task which has become automatic is one which makes no attentional demands.

15 Schneider & Shiffrin (1977) claim that controlled processing makes heavy demands on attentional resources, is slow, and involves conscious attention to a task. Automatic processing makes no demands on attentional resources, is fast, unavoidable, unaffected by capacity limitations and difficult to modify.

16 Such tasks include learning to drive a car, tying one's shoelaces, and reading.

17 Psychologists are unsure as to how, precisely, controlled processing may become automatic, although it may involve a speeding up of the processing or a change in the nature of the processing.

18 The Stroop Effect (Stroop, 1935) refers to the difficulty of naming the colour of words which themselves refer to a different colour.

19 According to Manstead & Semin (1980), open-loop control is equivalent to automatic processing and closed-loop control to controlled processing.

20 Abrams & Manstead (1981) claim that our performance on simple tasks improves when we are being watched, because we normally leave them under open-loop control and pay little attention to what is going on. We focus our attention when we are being watched.

21 Manstead & Semin (1980) explain that when performing complex tasks which require all our attentional capacity, an audience acts as a distraction.

22 Norman & Shallice's (1986) attentional model proposes the existence of contention scheduling and the supervisory attentional system.

23 Partially automatic processing results from the monitoring of fully automatic processes by the contention scheduling system.

Section 4: Action slips

24 An action slip is the performance of an action which is unintended.

25 Reason (1979, 1992) identified storage failures, test failures, sub-routine failures, discrimination failures and programme assembly failures as the five categories of action slip.

26 Reason (1992) suggests that action-slips occur because we become over-reliant on open-loop control (automatic actions) when we should be paying more attention (closed-loop control).

27 Sellen & Norman's (1992) schema theory claims that action slips occur because of errors in the formation of intentions, activating incorrect schema, activation of the correct schema is lost, or faulty triggering of an active schema.

28 A parent schema corresponds to overall intentions, whilst a child schema corresponds to sets of actions involved in achieving the intention.

29 Eysenck (1994) claims that we could avoid all action slips by relying solely on closed-loop control.

30 Reason's diary method is flawed in that participants may not have detected all of their action slips.

31 It does sometimes seem possible to divide attention between two tasks, although how this is achieved has not yet been satisfactorily explained.

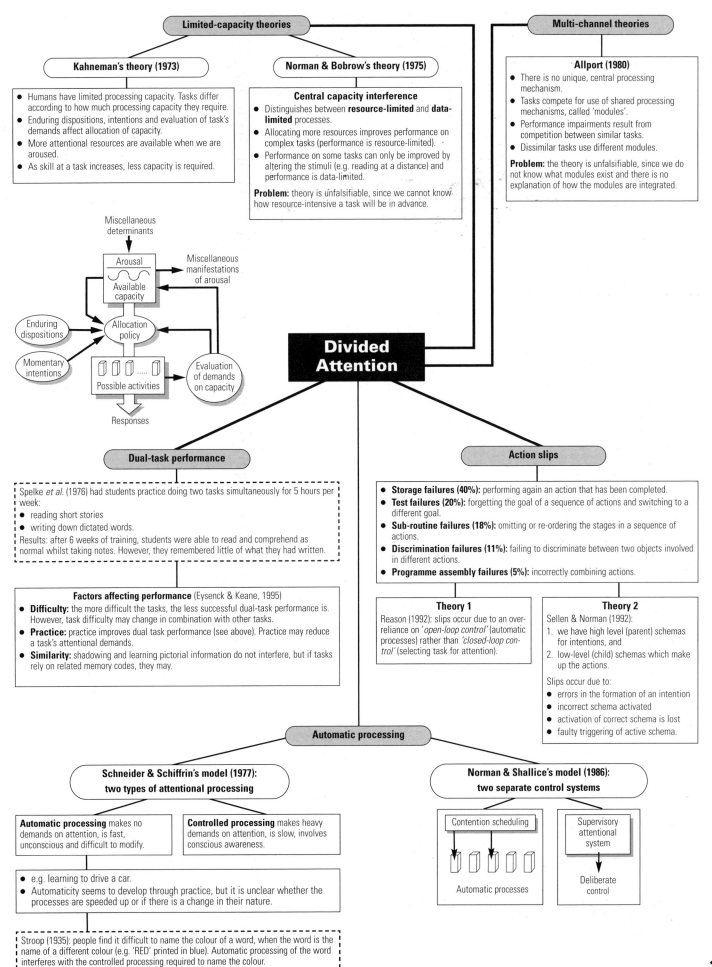

Kahneman's theory (1973)

- Humans have limited processing capacity. Tasks differ according to how much processing capacity they require.
- Enduring dispositions, intentions and evaluation of task's demands affect allocation of capacity.
- More attentional resources are available when we are aroused.
- As skill at a task increases, less capacity is required.

Norman & Bobrow's theory (1975)

Central capacity interference

- Distinguishes between **resource-limited** and **data-limited** processes.
- Allocating more resources improves performance on complex tasks (performance is resource-limited).
- Performance on some tasks can only be improved by altering the stimuli (e.g. reading at a distance) and performance is data-limited.

Problem: theory is unfalsifiable, since we cannot know how resource-intensive a task will be in advance.

Multi-channel theories

Allport (1980)

- There is no unique, central processing mechanism.
- Tasks compete for use of shared processing mechanisms, called 'modules'.
- Performance impairments result from competition between similar tasks.
- Dissimilar tasks use different modules.

Problem: the theory is unfalsifiable, since we do not know what modules exist and there is no explanation of how the modules are integrated.

Miscellaneous determinants

Arousal

Available capacity

Miscellaneous manifestations of arousal

Enduring dispositions

Momentary intentions

Allocation policy

Possible activities

Evaluation of demands on capacity

Responses

Divided Attention

Dual-task performance

Spelke *et al.* (1976) had students practice doing two tasks simultaneously for 5 hours per week:
- reading short stories
- writing down dictated words.
Results: after 6 weeks of training, students were able to read and comprehend as normal whilst taking notes. However, they remembered little of what they had written.

Factors affecting performance (Eysenck & Keane, 1995)
- **Difficulty:** the more difficult the tasks, the less successful dual-task performance is. However, task difficulty may change in combination with other tasks.
- **Practice:** practice improves dual task performance (see above). Practice may reduce a task's attentional demands.
- **Similarity:** shadowing and learning pictorial information do not interfere, but if tasks rely on related memory codes, they may.

Action slips

- **Storage failures (40%):** performing again an action that has been completed.
- **Test failures (20%):** forgetting the goal of a sequence of actions and switching to a different goal.
- **Sub-routine failures (18%):** omitting or re-ordering the stages in a sequence of actions.
- **Discrimination failures (11%):** failing to discriminate between two objects involved in different actions.
- **Programme assembly failures (5%):** incorrectly combining actions.

Theory 1
Reason (1992): slips occur due to an over-reliance on 'open-loop control' (automatic processes) rather than 'closed-loop control' (selecting task for attention).

Theory 2
Sellen & Norman (1992):
1. we have high level (parent) schemas for intentions, and
2. low-level (child) schemas which make up the actions.

Slips occur due to:
- errors in the formation of an intention
- incorrect schema activated
- activation of correct schema is lost
- faulty triggering of active schema.

Automatic processing

Schneider & Schiffrin's model (1977):
two types of attentional processing

Automatic processing makes no demands on attention, is fast, unconscious and difficult to modify.

Controlled processing makes heavy demands on attention, is slow, involves conscious awareness.

- e.g. learning to drive a car.
- Automaticity seems to develop through practice, but it is unclear whether the processes are speeded up or if there is a change in their nature.

Stroop (1935): people find it difficult to name the colour of a word, when the word is the name of a different colour (e.g. 'RED' printed in blue). Automatic processing of the word interferes with the controlled processing required to name the colour.

Norman & Shallice's model (1986):
two separate control systems

Contention scheduling

Supervisory attentional system

Automatic processes

Deliberate control

28

PATTERN RECOGNITION

SYLLABUS

13.3 Attention and pattern recognition – pattern recognition

- explanations of pattern recognition (e.g. template and feature-detection theories), including the role of biological mechanisms (e.g. Hubel and Wiesel) and of context (e.g. top-down vs bottom-up processing). Research studies and theories of face recognition (e.g. Bruce and Young)

KEY QUESTIONS

- How do the following approaches attempt to explain pattern recognition: template-matching, prototype and feature-detection?
- What criticisms may be made of each approach?
- How does face recognition occur?

Section 1: Theories of pattern recognition

Q

1 How does Eysenck (1993) define pattern recognition?
2 What is the central principle behind the template-matching hypothesis (TMH) of pattern recognition?
3 Identify one serious criticism of the template-matching hypothesis.
4 What does the term *geon* stand for in Biederman's (1987) geon theory of pattern recognition?
5 What basic strategy does Biederman claim we adopt when we are asked to describe a familiar or unfamiliar object?
6 What is significant about the 'regions of greatest concavity', according to this theory?
7 Briefly outline the way in which pattern recognition occurs, according to geon theory.
8 What would we need to store (besides geons) in order to be able to recognise familiar objects?
9 Complete the sentence: 'According to Roth (1995), Biederman's theory was designed to provide an ____ plausible account of how we recognise objects in terms of their recognisable components'.
10 How was Beiderman (1987) able to provide experimental support for his theory?
11 What was Beiderman's basis for identifying the basic set of 36 geons?
12 In what way do prototype theories differ from template theories of pattern recognition?
13 How does Eysenck (1993) define a *prototype*?
14 What is the main weakness of prototype theories in explaining pattern recognition?
15 How do feature-detection theories of pattern recognition view a visual stimulus?
16 What is required of participants in a *visual scanning task*?
17 Identify one further type of research which provides experimental support for feature-detection theories.
18 What types of entity can be *simple*, *complex* and *hypercomplex* according to Hubel & Weisel (1968)?
19 How did Selfridge's (1959) *Pandemonium model* of feature detection differ from typical feature-detection models?

20 What is the difference between *image demons* and *feature demons*, according to this model?
21 Complete the sentence: 'A general criticism of feature-detection theories is their failure to take sufficient account of the role played by ____ in pattern recognition'.

Section 2: Face recognition

22 In what way is face recognition unlike other cases of everyday object recognition?
23 Identify one of the meanings of the term *configural* which Bruce (1995) identifies?
24 What is the name of the system used by both the police and Bradshaw & Wallace (1971) to produce artificially constructed faces?
25 What did Bradshaw and Wallace discover when presenting pairs of faces and asking participants to decide whether or not they were different?
26 Which particular facial feature did Sergent (1984) discover led to faster 'difference' decisions when it was altered?
27 What is Thompson's (1980) *Thatcher illusion*?
28 How does Bartlett & Searcy's (1993) *configural processing hypothesis* explain the Thatcher illusion?
29 What are the symptoms of *prosopagnosia*?
30 What pattern recognition task was W.J. (McNeill & Warrington, 1993) able to learn, despite his prosopagnosia?
31 According to Young *et al.*'s (1985) model of facial recognition, what do recognition units contain?
32 What is a 'PIN', according to this model?
33 The revised model, produced by Bruce & Young (1986), identifies three independent routes for the processing of facial information. What are they?
34 Which phenomenon was used by Brennen *et al.* (1990) in supporting their revised model?
35 Which phenomenon, occasionally exhibited by prosopagnostic patients, does not support the revised model?
36 In facial recognition, what is the *orienting response*?
37 What is the main symptom of *Capgras delusion*?

122

Section 1: Theories of pattern recognition

1 Eysenck (1993) defines pattern recognition as 'the process by which we assign meaning to visual input by identifying the objects in the visual field'.

2 The template-matching hypothesis (TMH) maintains that incoming sensory information is matched against copies (or templates) of previously presented objects stored in long-term memory.

3 First, the TMH would require an unfeasibly large number of templates for object recognition to occur in all conditions, and secondly we would never be able to recognise unfamiliar patterns.

4 Geon stands for geometrical icon in Biederman's (1987) geon theory.

5 Biederman claims that we begin by dividing the objects into parts, comprising 3D shapes or objects.

6 The 'regions of greatest concavity' (such as corners), are the points at which we divide an object into its components geons.

7 Geon theory claims that we extract geon-based information from the visual object (breaking it into its component geons) and then match it with stored representations.

8 We would also need to store descriptions of the geons and their relationships for every single object for which we are familiar.

9 'According to Roth (1995), Biederman's theory was designed to provide an *intuitively* plausible account of how we recognise objects in terms of their recognisable components.'

10 Beiderman produced line drawings of everyday objects and tested participants to recognise 'partial' versions from which some geons were missing.

11 Beiderman's basis for the basic set of 36 geons is largely 'hunch' rather than empirical evidence.

12 Prototype theories propose that instead of storing templates we store a relatively small number of abstract forms, called prototypes, which define a category of visual stimuli.

13 Eysenck (1993) defines a prototype as an abstract form representing the basic elements of a set of stimuli.

14 Prototype theories fail to explain how pattern recognition is affected by context as well as by the visual stimulus itself.

15 Feature-detection theories of pattern recognition view a visual stimulus as a configuration of elementary features (such as vertical lines or closed curves).

16 In a visual scanning task participants search lists of letters as quickly as possible to find a randomly placed target letter.

17 Studies of eye movement and fixation also provide experimental support for feature-detection theories.

18 Simple, complex and hypercomplex are all types of cortical cells, according to Hubel and Weisel.

19 Selfridge's (1959) Pandemonium model of feature detection differed from typical feature-detection models in that it suggested that feature detection occurred in parallel rather than in series.

20 Image demons simply copy the pattern presented whilst feature demons analyse the information from the image demons in terms of combinations of features.

21 'A general criticism of feature-detection theories is their failure to take sufficient account of the role played by *context* in pattern recognition.'

Section 2: Face recognition

22 Face recognition is unlike other cases of everyday object recognition since we are recognising instances of a class (e.g. 'that's Bob') rather than classes of objects ('that's a table').

23 Bruce (1995) identifies three meanings: faces are processed holistically, facial features interact with one another and the spatial relationships between features are as important as the features themselves.

24 Both the police and Bradshaw & Wallace (1971) used Identikit.

25 Bradshaw and Wallace discovered that the more difference between two faces (the fewer features they had in common), the faster participants were able to decide if two faces were different.

26 Sergent (1984) discovered that 'difference' decisions were faster when the chin was altered.

27 Thompson's (1980) Thatcher illusion involves inverting the eyes and mouth of a photograph of the ex-Prime Minister. The end result looks grotesque when upright but near normal when inverted.

28 The configural processing hypothesis argues that the strangeness of the image only appears when the configuration of features can be seen, and that this does not occur when the image is inverted.

29 Prosopagnosia refers to the inability to recognise familiar faces.

30 W.J. was able to learn to tell the faces of his sheep apart.

31 Recognition units contain stored representations of familiar faces.

32 A 'PIN' is a 'person identity node' containing information about personal identity.

33 There are three independent routes for the processing of emotional expressions, lip-reading and identification.

34 The 'tip-of-the-tongue' phenomenon was used.

35 Covert recognition by prosopagnostic patients does not support the revised model.

36 The orienting response is a preparatory emotional response in anticipation of the interaction that is likely to follow.

37 The main symptom of the Capgras delusion is a belief that one or more close relatives have been replaced by near-identical impostors.

A

Pattern Recognition

Pattern recognition: the process by which we assign meaning to visual input by identifying the objects in the visual field (Eysenck, 1993)

Template-matching hypothesis (TMH)

Incoming sensory information is matched against copies of patterns stored in memory (*templates*).

Problems

- We would need to possess an impossibly large no. of templates to match every visual input we receive.
- We would never recognise unfamiliar patterns.

Prototype theories

Instead of storing templates we store a small number of 'prototypes' – 'an abstract form representing the basic elements of a set of stimuli' (Eysenck, 1993). Visual stimuli of the same category share properties with the prototype.

Problems

- The theory cannot explain how pattern recognition is affected by *context*.

Geon theory (Biederman, 1987)

We divide objects up into simple geometric shapes (geometric icons) such as 'block' or 'cylinder'. This overcomes the limitations of the TMH since a large number of objects can be described by combining a small number of simple geometric 'primitives'.

1. Information about an object's components is extracted from the visual object.
2. This information is then matched in parallel against 36 stored basic geons.
3. The object is identified according to which stored representation provides the best fit (this requires the relationships between geons to be stored for every object).

Evaluation

Biederman (1987): produced line drawings of 36 common objects (e.g. cup, scissors) then produced 'partial' versions in which one of more geons were missing. These were then presented briefly to participants who tried to identify the partial drawings.

Results

- Participants recognised partial objects drawings as quickly as the complete drawings, with 90% accuracy.
- Complex, complete objects were recognised slightly more quickly than simple complete objects.

Both results are consistent with geon theory, object recognition occurring even when not all geons are present/visible. In addition the more geons an object contains, the less time it is likely to take to match enough geons to make an identification.

Feature-detection theories

Every stimulus can be thought of as a configuration of elementary features (e.g. vertical lines, horizontal lines and closed curves).

Research

- Visual scanning tasks: challenge participants to search lists of letters as quickly as possible to find a target. If feature-detection theory is correct, tasks should be more difficult when letters have more features in common (e.g. E, F) which is exactly what researchers have found.
- Studies of eye movements: e.g Yarbus, 1967 showed that different features of a complex scene were focused on, depending on what information participants were required to extract from it.
- Hubel & Weisel (1968): identified three types of cell in the visual cortex of monkeys which respond only to certain types of stimuli ('simple', 'complex' and 'hypercomplex' cells).

Evaluation

- Most feature-detection theories assume a serial form of processing (feature detection, then feature combination, then pattern recognition).
- Selfridge's (1959) 'Pandemonium' model suggests that PR occurs in parallel with 'image demons', 'feature demons', 'cognitive demons', and 'decision demons'. Describing the sub-processes which occur in order to recognise letters.
- However, neither approach to feature-detection takes into account the way in which humans use *context* in identifying object (i.e. these theories are based on data-driven processing rather than concept-driven processing).

Face recognition

Are faces more than the sum of their parts?

Early theorists assumed that faces could be described as a set of parts (such as features) and their relationships. More recently Bruce (1995) argues that faces are viewed in a more 'configural' way.

- She identifies 3 meanings of 'configural': holistic processing of faces, the interaction of features with one another, and the significance of the spatial relationships between features.

Research

Sergent (1984): reviewed studies which showed that the more differences between two *Identikit* faces, the faster a 'difference' decision was made. However, Sergent found that certain features (e.g. chins) made more difference than others, suggesting that there is an *interactive* processing of features.

Face recognition and the brain

Studies of brain-injured participants suggest that the brain 'farms out' different aspects of face recognition to specialised areas.

- Ellis & Young (1990): when we recognise a familiar person, a separate neurological pathway sets up a preparatory emotional response ('orienting response').
- In the *Capgras' delusion* patients come to believe that close relatives have been replaced by near-identical impostors (since recognition occurs but the orienting response does not).

Processing upright and inverted faces

Sergent and others found that when faces are inverted, features are processed independently:

- Yin (1969) points out that whilst upright faces are recognised extremely accurately, inverted faces are not – inverted features cannot be integrated into a coherent impression.
- Thompson (1980) produced the *Thatcher Illusion* by inverting the eyes and mouth alone. When viewed upright the face appears grotesque, but when inverted it appears similar to the 'normal' version.

Disorders of face processing – prosopagnosia

- McNeil & Warrington (1993) report the case of W.J. who, following a series of strokes, could no longer distinguish famous & unfamiliar faces. He did, however, learn to tell a number of his sheep apart whilst still remaining prosopagnostic for human faces.

In addition, some case studies show that emotional expressions may still be interpreted from faces that cannot be recognised, or a failure to recognise emotions in familiar faces may occur – suggesting that the two processes are separate (see 'face recognition and the brain' above).

Models of face recognition

Bruce & Young (1986) revised Young *et al.*'s (1985) model in which face recognition occurs in a number of distinct stages. According to the revised model:

- The model comprises several different processing 'modules' linked in sequence or parallel.
- There are independent routes for the processing of emotional expressions, lip reading and identification.
- The route by which familiar faces are identified involves separate stages of representation of the face (*structural encodings*), access of stored structural descriptions of known faces (*face recognition units/FRUs*), access of information about personal identity (via *person identity nodes/PINs*) and finally retrieval of proper names.

Evaluation

- Brennet *et al.* (1990): found that participants in a tip-of-the-tongue state while trying to recall a name from a description were not helped by photographs of the person. This is consistent with the model, since face recognition units are activated before the PINs.
- However, evidence of 'covert recognition' of faces in prosopagnostic patients does not, since if FRUs are not activated, no deeper level information should be accessible.

124

29

THE VISUAL SYSTEM

SYLLABUS

13.3 Perceptual process and development – the visual system

- structure and functions of the visual system: the eye, retina and visual pathways. Research into the nature of visual information processing (e.g. sensory adaptation and the processing of contrast, colour and features)

KEY QUESTIONS
- What are light and colour?
- How do the eye and visual pathways function?
- How can colour vision and colour constancy be explained?

Section 1: Light and the eye

1 What name is given to the *energy particles* of which light consists?
2 Which two forms of electromagnetic radiation lie either side of the visible spectrum?
3 What determines the *intensity* of a light wave?
4 What is *hue*?
5 What determines our experience of *saturation*?
6 What did Sir Isaac Newton discover when light was passed through a prism?
7 What name is given to the tough outer coat which encloses the eyeball?
8 How is the amount of light which enters the eye controlled?
9 What is the next structure which light reaches when it has passed through the aqueous humour?
10 What is the role of the *ciliary muscles*?
11 What do *cones, rods, bipolar cells* and *ganglion cells* all have in common?
12 What type of cell are *rods* and *cones,* and what is their role?
13 Complete the sentence: 'Rods help us to see ___ colour, whilst cones respond to different wavelengths allowing us to see ___ colour'.
14 How does the distribution of rods and cones around the retina differ?
15 What is the *optic disc*?
16 Place the following in order according to which is most and least numerous in the retina: bipolar cells, rods and cones, ganglion cells.
17 According to Hubel & Wiesel (1962), what is a *receptive field*?

Section 2: From the eye to the brain

18 Describe what occurs at the *lateral geniculate nucleus* (LGN).
19 What is the *geniculostriate path*?
20 What is *blindsight*?

21 Name the three types of cortical cell Hubel & Wiesel (1965) propose decode light information.
22 What are *hypercolumns*?
23 What is *ocular dominance*?
24 What did Zeki (cited in Highfield, 1997b) discover when studying GY, a man blinded in an accident when he was seven?

Section 3: Understanding colour vision

25 What was the principle behind Newton's *colour circle*?
26 What term is used to describe the type of colour mixing which occurs when we mix different coloured paints? Why is this term used?
27 What type of colour mixing takes place in the visual system?
28 How does the *Young–Helmholtz theory* explain colour vision?
29 What did Ohtsuka (1985) discover about the way in which light of a certain wavelength stimulates receptor cells?
30 Identify two perceptual phenomena which cannot be explained by the Young–Helmholtz theory.
31 Name the three types of receptor proposed by the *opponent-process theory* of colour vision.
32 Why is the *opponent-process theory* of colour vision so called?
33 Which two types of individuals suffer from *dichromatic vision*?
34 How can the opponent-process theory explain why we see a green after-image having stared for some time at a red patch?
35 Complete the sentence: 'Opponent-process theory does not seem to operate at the level of the ___, but along the ___ ___ from the cones to the visual area'.
36 What is *colour constancy*?
37 What was Land (1977) able to demonstrate, using a *colour Mondrian*?
38 What theory did Land advance to explain his findings?

Q

Section 1: Light and the eye

1 Light consists of energy particles called photons.
2 Ultraviolet rays and infrared rays lie either side of the visible spectrum.
3 The number of photons in a stream of light determines the wave's intensity.
4 Hue refers to the colour we perceive something to be.
5 Our experience of saturation is determined by the proportion of coloured light to non-coloured light in a light stream.
6 Sir Isaac Newton discovered that white light is a mixture of wavelengths corresponding to all colours in the visible spectrum.
7 The tough outer coat which encloses the eyeball is called the *sclera*.
8 The amount of light which enters the eye is controlled by the iris, which contracts or expands, altering the size of the pupil.
9 Having passed through the aqueous humour, light reaches the lens.
10 The ciliary muscles expand or contract so as to change the shape of the lens, allowing light to be focused on the retina.
11 Cones, rods, bipolar cells and ganglion cells are all neurons (and are all present in the retina).
12 Rods and cones are photosensitive cells (or photoreceptors), which convert light energy into electrical nerve impulses.
13 'Rods help us to see *achromatic* colour whilst cones respond to different wavelengths allowing us to see *chromatic* colour.'
14 Rods are fairly evenly distributed around the retina whilst cones are much more numerous towards its centre (especially at the fovea).
15 The optic disc is the part of the retina where the optic nerve leaves the eye.
16 Rods and cones are the most numerous, followed by bipolar cells and ganglion cells.
17 Hubel and Wiesel define a receptive field as the area of the retina to which a single ganglion cell is sensitive.

Section 2: From the eye to the brain

18 At the lateral geniculate nucleus (LGN), the optic nerve fibres terminate at synapses with cells belonging to the thalamus, which combine the information from both eyes before sending it to the cortex.
19 The geniculostriate path is the neural pathway which carries visual information from the thalami to the cortex.
20 Blindsight is a term used to describe the ability to identify objects without being consciously aware of them.
21 Hubel & Wiesel (1965) suggested the existence of simple cells, complex cells and hypercomplex cells, each involved in decoding information.

22 Hypercolumns are 1 mm square blocks of tissue which extend from the surface of the cortex down to the white matter below.
23 Ocular dominance refers to the manner in which cells in the visual cortex always respond more strongly to a stimulus in one eye or the other.
24 Zeki discovered that GY could detect fast moving cars and the direction in which they were travelling, and that such detection did not involve the primary visual processing area.

Section 3: Understanding colour vision

25 Newton's colour circle was designed so that colours which produced either white or neutral grey were placed at opposite ends of the circle's diameter.
26 When we mix different coloured paints, subtractive colour mixing occurs. This term is used since each colour absorbs all those wavelengths which it does not reflect. Mixing the paints causes both sets of absorbed wavelengths to be 'subtracted' from the light reflected.
27 Additive colour mixing takes place in the visual system.
28 The Young–Helmholtz theory proposes that the eye contains three types of receptor, responding to red, green and blue light respectively, and that the perception of colour is created by combining information from them.
29 Ohtsuka (1985) discovered that light of a particular wavelength may stimulate more than one type of receptor.
30 Neither colour blindness nor negative after-images can be explained by the Young–Helmholtz theory.
31 The opponent-process theory of colour vision proposes the existence of red–green, yellow–blue and black–white receptors.
32 The theory is so called since each member of a pair is opposed to the other, so that when one is excited the other is inhibited.
33 People who are red–green, or yellow–blue colourblind suffer from dichromatic vision.
34 According to the opponent-process theory, staring at a red patch causes the red component to tire, so that only the green component is 'fresh' enough to fire when we stare at a neutral surface.
35 'Opponent-process theory does not seem to operate at the level of the *cones*, but along the *neural path* from the cones to the visual area.'
36 Colour constancy refers to the manner in which the colours we perceive are not determined solely by the wavelength of light reflected from an object, but by other factors such as knowledge and experience.
37 Land (1977) was able to demonstrate that participants would judge a colour to be the same, despite alterations in the wavelength of the light actually reflected from it.
38 Land's retinex theory attempts to explain his findings.

The Visual System

The eye

About 90% of the information about the external world reaches us through the eye, which has a complex structure:
- **The sclera:** a tough outer coat, which is opaque except for the front, where it bulges out to form a transparent membrane (cornea).
- **The lens:** a crystalline structure which focuses light waves, and whose shape is controlled by a ring of **ciliary muscles**.
- **The vitreous humour:** a jelly-like substance through which light passes, which helps the eye to maintain its shape.
- **The retina:** a delicate membrane lining the back of the eye, containing photosensitive cells.

The **iris** controls the amount of light entering the eye by expanding or contracting to vary the size of the **pupil**. Abnormalities in the shape of the eye make it impossible for the lens to focus light (*accommodation*) correctly, causing short- or long-sightedness.

The retina

Contains two types of *photoreceptor* cells, which convert light into electrical nerve impulses:
- **Rods:** (120 million, evenly distributed around the retina) help us to see *achromatic* colour (black, white and greys) and are specialised for vision in dim light (*scotopic vision*).
- **Cones:** (7 million, packed densely around the centre of the retina, especially the *fovea*) help us to see *chromatic* colour (red, green, blue, etc.) and are specialised for bright light vision (*photopic vision*).

These cells convert light to neural signals which are passed to smaller numbers of **bipolar cells** which in turn pass signals to **ganglion cells**. These travel across the retina's inner surface and converge to form the **optic nerve**. A single ganglion cell is connected to all/most of the rods in its *receptive* field.

Types of ganglion cells
- *On-centre and off-surround:* most active when light falls on the centre of its receptive field.
- *Off-centre and on-surround:* most active when light falls on the edge of the receptive field.
- *Transient cells:* respond to movements in the receptive field.

Eye to brain

Visual sensory information travels to the **thalamus** and on to the **primary visual area** of the cortex:
- Optic nerve fibres terminate at synapses at the **lateral geniculate nucleus** (LGN), a part of the thalamus.
- The LGN in each thalamus combines the information from both eyes before sending it to the cortex, via the **geniculostriate path**.

Types of cortical cells

Hubel & Wiesel (1965) suggested the existence of 3 types of cortical cells, which play a role in decoding light information:
- **Simple cells:** respond *only* to particular features of a stimulus in a particular orientation and location in the visual field.
- **Complex cells:** respond to particular features of a stimulus in a particular orientation *no matter where they occur* in the visual field.
- **Hypercomplex cells:** respond to corners, angles, bars of a particular length moving in a certain direction.

- Hubel & Wiesel (1977): showed that the visual area is divided into roughly 1 mm square blocks of tissue extending down through the cortex to the white matter below. These *hypercolumns* contain cells with the same 'orientation preference'. In addition, cells always respond more strongly to a stimulus in one eye rather than the other (*ocular dominance*).
- Maunsell & Newsome (1987): have identified as many as 19 areas, besides the primary visual area, which are involved in vision and which transmit and receive information from each other.

Light

Light is a form of electromagnetic radiation, consisting of energy particles called *photons*, which travel in waves.

2 important characteristics:
- The number of photons in a stream of light determines its *intensity*.
- The distance between peaks of a light wave determines its *wavelength*.

3 important properties:
- *Brightness:* determined by the intensity of a wave.
- *Hue:* the colour we perceive is partly determined by a light's wavelength.
- *Saturation:* how colourful light is (determined by the proportion of coloured light to non-coloured light).

Colour vision

Sir Isaac Newton discovered that white light is a mixture of all the colours of the spectrum. He also discovered that mixing two colours far apart in the spectrum produced white, and produced a 'colour circle' to record which these were.

Subtractive and additive colour mixing
- *Subtractive colour mixing:* blue and yellow paint appears blue and yellow because they absorb all other wavelengths. Mixing them causes all wavelengths except green to be absorbed.
- *Additive colour mixing:* when lights with different wavelengths strike the retina, these are combined by the visual system.

Colour constancy

Familiarity with, and knowledge of, an object, can both affect the perception of an object's colour (*colour constancy*)

- Land (1977): Asked participants to select two colours from a *colour Mondrian* (a patchwork of different colours). Land adjusted the red, green and blue light being reflected from the second colour, so that it matched the first – nevertheless, participants still saw the colour as remaining the same!

Land proposed the '*retinex theory of colour constancy*' to explain this phenomenon.

Theories of colour vision

The Young–Helmholtz theory
- Proposes that the eye contains *3 types of receptor cells* corresponding to red, green and blue.
- The perception of colour is created by *combining* the information from these receptors, the ratio of blue:green:red receptors activated determining the colour perceived.
- Over 100 years later, research confirmed the existence of three such receptors, each containing a *photopigment* sensitive to different wavelengths of light.
- The wavelengths to which the cone types are sensitive *overlap*, so that light of a particular wavelength may stimulate more than one type of cone (Ohtsuka, 1985).
- However, *colour blindness* and the perception of *negative after-images* cannot easily be explained by this theory.

The theory is also called *trichromatic theory* and derives from the work of Young (who in 1802 demonstrated that combinations of red, green and blue light could produce all the colours of the spectrum) and von Helmholtz (who, 50 years later, suggested that the eye contains 3 types of receptor corresponding to these wavelengths).

Opponent-process theory
- Hering (1870) also proposed the existence of *3 types of receptor cells*, with two responsive to pairs of colours (red–green receptors and yellow–blue receptors) and one sensitive to black–white (contributing to the perception of brightness and saturation).
- A response to one of the colours for which a receptor is sensitive means that the other colour of the pair is 'inhibited' (so that a colour can be reddish-yellow, but never 'reddish-green').
- Hering's theory *can* explain *colour blindness* (e.g. where red and green cannot be seen but blue and yellow can) and *negative after images* (where receptors become 'overstimulated' by a colour causing the opposite of the pair to fire more readily).

Opponent-process theory does *not* seem to operate at the level of the cones, but along the neural pathways connecting them to the visual area:
- Studies of the bipolar, ganglion and LGN cells suggest that messages from the cones may be relayed to the brain in an opponent-process fashion (DeValois & Jacobs, 1984), e.g. some neurons are excited by red light but inhibited by green.

PERCEPTUAL ORGANISATION

KEY QUESTIONS
- How does the Gestalt approach explain perception?
- In what ways do we organise our perceptions?
- How do constructivist and direct theories explain perception?

Q Section 1: Describing perception

1 How do psychologists define *perception*?
2 Ehrenfels (1890) claimed that many stimuli acquire a pattern quality which gave them 'emergent properties' (e.g. 'squareness') – what name did he give this characteristic?
3 According to Gestalt psychologists, where do the principles for organising sensory information originate?
4 What are *figure* and *ground*?
5 Gestalt psychologists believed that objects are perceived as *Gestalten*. What does this mean?
6 What is the *law of Prägnanz*?
7 Name three Gestalt laws of perception.
8 What experiment did Navon (1977) perform to test the idea that the whole is perceived before the parts?
9 What is depth perception?
10 What is the difference between *monocular* and *binocular depth cues*?
11 What is *retinal disparity*?
12 What is *accommodation*?
13 What is *perceptual constancy*?
14 Define the term *size constancy*.
15 Why is shape constancy needed when perceiving objects?
16 Define an *illusion*.
17 Name two of the four types of illusion identified by Gregory.
18 What perceptual tendency is demonstrated by the *horizontal–vertical illusion*?
19 What do Rubin's vase and the Necker cube have in common?
20 Why, according to Gregory (1973), does the *autokinetic effect* occur?
21 What is *induced movement*?

Section 2: Theories of perception

22 What do *top-down theorists* of perception believe?
23 What is another name for bottom-up processing?
24 According to Gregory (1966), what does our perceptual system 'search for' when it detects a stimulus?
25 How do perceptual constancies show that perception is an indirect process?
26 What is an illusion, according to Gregory?
27 Why do illusions support Gregory's top-down approach to perception?
28 How does Gregory's *misapplied size constancy theory* apply to the Müller–Lyer illusion?
29 What is meant by Gibson's claim that perception is 'direct'?
30 What term does Gibson (1966) use to describe the pattern of light extended over time and space?
31 What three main forms of information does this pattern contain?
32 What kinds of information are provided by the flow of the environment around a moving observer?
33 What are *affordances*?
34 What, according to Fodor & Pylyshyn (1981), is the difference between 'seeing' and 'seeing as'?
35 What do *transactionalists* argue?
36 How does the *Ames room* work?
37 Name two things which Gibson's and Gregory's approaches have in common.
38 How do Gregory and Gibson differ in their views of perceptual learning?
39 What is the name of Neisser's (1976) model which proposes that perception involves a perceptual cycle?

Section 1: Describing perception

1 Perception is the organisation and interpretation of incoming sensory information to form internal representations of the external world.

2 Ehrenfels (1890) called 'emergent properties', such as 'squareness', *Gestalt qualität*.

3 Gestalt psychologists claimed that the principles for organising sensory information are innate.

4 Figure and ground are the object and surroundings respectively in any scene.

5 Gestalten are 'organised wholes', 'configurations' or 'patterns'. Gestalt psychologists believe that we perceive these rather than combinations of sensations.

6 'Psychological organisation will always be as good as the prevailing conditions allow' (Koffka, 1935). Often this means that we prefer simple, stable patterns to more complex ones.

7 The Gestalt laws of perception are: proximity, similarity, good continuation, closure, the part–whole relationship, simplicity, common fate.

8 Navon (1977) constructed alphabetical letters made up of smaller letters. He found that participants perceived the larger letters more readily.

9 Depth perception is the ability to organise three-dimensional perceptions from the two-dimensional information which falls on our retinas.

10 Monocular depth cues can be perceived with one eye, whilst binocular depth cues require both eyes in order to be perceived.

11 Retinal disparity describes the difference between the images cast upon each retina.

12 Accommodation describes the thickening or flattening of the lenses of the eye in order to focus on an object.

13 Perceptual constancy is the ability to perceive objects as unchanging despite changes in the sensory information which reaches our eyes.

14 Size constancy refers to the perception of objects as remaining of fixed size, despite their casting smaller images on the retina as they get further away.

15 Shape constancy is needed in order to perceive an object as staying the same despite changes in the retinal image at different orientations.

16 An illusion is a perception of an object which does not match its true physical characteristics.

17 Gregory (1983) identifies distortions, ambiguous figures, paradoxical figures and fictions.

18 The horizontal–vertical illusion illustrates our tendency to overestimate the size of vertical objects.

19 They are both ambiguous figures; i.e. both can be perceived in more than one way.

20 Gregory (1973) claims that the autokinetic effect occurs due to small, uncontrollable eye movements which, in the absence of any surroundings, cannot be filtered out.

21 Induced movement is the apparent movement of an object which is stationary, when its surroundings are moving.

Section 2: Theories of perception

22 Top-down theorists of perception believe that our perception is the end result of a process which involves making inferences about what things are like.

23 Bottom-up processing can also be called *data-driven processing*.

24 Gregory (1966) claims that our perceptual system searches for the best interpretation of a stimulus.

25 Perceptual constancies show that perceptions must 'go beyond' the often sketchy information provided in the retinal image, drawing on expectations and past experience.

26 An illusion is a perceptual hypothesis which is not confirmed by the data.

27 Illusions support Gregory's approach because they show that perception is an active process of suggesting and testing hypotheses.

28 Gregory's misapplied size constancy theory suggests that we interpret the 'fins' of the Müller–Lyer illusion as perspective cues, and therefore overestimate the length of the apparently more distant line.

29 Gibson's claim that perception is 'direct' means that perception involves 'picking up' information provided by the optical array in a way which involves little or no information processing.

30 Gibson (1966) uses the term *optical array* to describe the pattern of light extended over time and space.

31 This pattern contains information such as optic flow patterns, texture gradients and affordances.

32 The flow of the environment provides information regarding direction, speed and altitude.

33 Affordances are directly perceivable, potential uses of objects.

34 Fodor & Pylyshyn (1981) claim that 'seeing' depends on what a thing is and 'seeing as' depends on knowing what a thing is (e.g. a Martian might well 'see' a table but not see it as a table).

35 Transactionalists argue that past experience is used to select interpretations of ambiguous sensory data.

36 The Ames room works by being constructed in such a way as to give the impression that the people standing at either corner are of unusual sizes.

37 Gibson's and Gregory's approaches both see visual perception as mediated by reflected light, as requiring physiological systems, and as an active process influenced by learning.

38 For Gregory, perceptual learning involves using experience and memory to make sensations coherent; for Gibson, we learn to identify features given in the optical array.

39 Neisser's (1976) model was called the *analysis-by-synthesis model*.

A

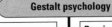

Gestalt psychology

Maintains that perceptions are organised, acquiring a *'Gestalt qualität'* (emergent property), so that a perception is greater than the sum of its parts. Comprises 2 key principles:
1. **Law of Prägnanz:** psychological organisation will always be as good as the prevailing conditions allow. In this definition, good is undefined (Koffka, 1935).
2. **Figure–ground:** to perceive we must separate objects (*figures*) from their surroundings (*ground*). Surroundedness, contour, size, orientation and symmetry are important.

Laws of Prägnanz

Proximity: close elements, spatially or temporally, tend to be grouped.
Similarity: similar figures tend to be grouped together.
Good continuation: we perceive continuous patterns in preference to discontinuous ones.
Closure: we tend to close incomplete figures, giving them familiar meaning.
Part–whole relationship: patterns are recognised despite changes in their parts.
Simplicity: a stimulus is organised into its simplest components.
Common fate: elements seen moving together belong together.

Illusions

When our perception of an object does not match its true physical characteristics.

Types of illusions

(Gregory, 1983)

- **Distortions:** perception distorts the stimulus. e.g. horizontal–vertical illusion.
- **Ambiguous figures:** two or more possible interpretations of a single stimulus. e.g. Rubin's vase and Necker cube.
- **Paradoxical figures:** parts of the stimulus are possible, but overall it is impossible. e.g. Penrose impossible triangle.
- **Fictions:** what we perceive is not physically present in the stimulus e.g. Kanizsa Triangles.

Depth perception

The ability to organise 3-D perceptions from the 2-D images that fall on our retinas.

Binocular cues

- **Retinal disparity:** the difference between the images perceived by each eye.
- **Stereopsis:** the process of combining two retinal images.
- **Convergence:** rotation of the eyes inwards as objects become close.
- **Accommodation:** changes in the shape of the lenses of the eyes when focusing.

Monocular cues

- Relative size
- Superimposition
- Relative height
- Texture gradient
- Shadowing
- Relative brightness
- Aerial haze
- Aerial perspective
- Motion parallax

Constancies

The ability to perceive an object as unchanging despite changes in the sensory information reaching our eyes.

- **Size constancy:** the smaller retinal images cast by receding objects are interpreted as an object of constant size changing location.
- **Shape constancy:** we perceive objects as being of constant shape despite changes in the shape of the image on the retina.
- **Location constancy:** our perceptual system 'filters out' head and eye movements in order to prevent the world from seeming to spin wildly.
- **Brightness constancy:** objects seem to keep their familiar brightness despite changes in the amount of light which they reflect.
- **Colour constancy:** familiar objects retain their hue under varying lighting conditions.

Top-down/ indirect/constructivist approach: perception is an active process involving knowledge and experience, and hypotheses or 'best guesses' about the world (conceptually driven processing).

Perceptual Organisation

Bottom-up/direct approach: the perceptual environment is information-rich, containing many cues which allow us to perceive without interpretation (data-driven processing).

Gregory

Gregory (1966): 'Perception is not determined simply by stimulus patterns. Rather, it is a dynamic searching for the best interpretation of the available data … [which] involves going beyond the immediately given evidence of the senses. We draw inferences from sensory information, forming hypotheses/best guesses as to what we see'.

Illusions

A perceptual hypothesis which is not confirmed by the data.

Key example: Müller–Lyer illusion where:
1. figure is interpreted in 3-D using fins as depth cues
2. size constancy is misapplied, the more 'distant' lines being scaled up to appear larger.

Constancies

Supplementing available sense data to give objects familiar meaning.

Perceptual set

A perceptual bias or readiness to perceive particular features of a stimulus (Allport, 1955).

Shows that perception can be influenced by perceiver and stimulus variables, e.g.
- motivation
- context/expectations
- beliefs and values.

Gibson

Optical array – The pattern of light striking the retina.
Perception involves 'picking up' the rich information provided by the optical array, in a way which requires little or no information processing. The optic array contains 'physical invariants':

Optic flow

The flow of the visual environment around a moving observer.

Texture gradients

The greater roughness of textures when close up.

Affordances

Directly perceivable potential uses of objects – linked to the concept of 'ecological optics'.

Research
- Lee & Lishman (1975): built a 'swaying room' which appeared to sway around a stationary participant standing in it. They found that adults adjust their balance and children fall over.
- Lee & Lishman (1975): also argue that *'time to contact'* estimations are an important function of perception and that optic flow plays a key role in this calculation.

Research: Ames' distorted room (cited in Ittelson, 1952) showed that whether the distortion resulted in a judgement that the person is very small or that the room is abnormal depended on familiarity/unfamiliarity with the person in the room.

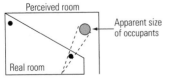

Comparing top-down and bottom-up processing

Transactionalists argue that whether top-down or bottom-up processing is used will depend on past experience.

Neisser (1976) developed the *analysis-by-synthesis model*, which assumed an ongoing perceptual cycle involving the search for features to match schemata in memory (*top-down*) and a process of feature analysis used to identify patterns in the stimulus environment (*bottom-up*).

Analysis-by-synthesis model

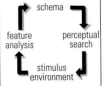

PERCEPTUAL DEVELOPMENT

KEY QUESTIONS
- How does the nature–nurture debate apply to the study of perception?
- What methods are used in the study of infant perception?
- What perceptual abilities do infants have?

Section 1: Infant perception

1 Why are psychologists interested in studying the perceptual abilities of human infants?
2 What is the nature–nurture debate as it applies to perception?
3 What is a *nativist*?
4 What is an *empirist*?
5 How does the *preferential looking technique* work?
6 What two things can this technique tell us?
7 What would you expect to happen to a baby's sucking rate when it detects a novel stimulus?
8 What is *habituation*?
9 What is a *visually evoked potential* and how is it measured?
10 How good is an infant's colour perception when it is a few months old?
11 Which technique did Bornstein (1976) use to discover that infants could distinguish between yellow and green?
12 What is the *pupillary reflex*?
13 When is the *blink reflex* first present?
14 What is the *optokinetic reflex*?
15 When do babies first show *convergence* and *accommodation*?
16 What is *visual acuity*?
17 How far can neonates see before things start to become blurred?
18 Which technique did Fantz (1961) use to investigate the perceptions of 1–15-week-old infants?
19 What was Fantz's first finding, using this technique?
20 In a later experiment, Fantz used six discs, each with a different appearance. Which was the most popular stimulus?
21 When scanning a triangle, which areas do babies spend longest looking at?
22 Give two explanations for the finding that infants prefer looking at human faces.
23 What was Fantz's aim in presenting children with normal and 'scrambled' faces?

24 What did Hershenson *et al.* (1965) discover when presenting infants with a real face, a distorted picture and Fantz's 'scrambled' face?
25 How do babies respond to facial expressions, minutes after birth?
26 What did Gibson & Walk (1960) call their apparatus, used to test depth perception in infants?
27 What was the reaction of 6–14-month-old infants placed on their apparatus?
28 What is the principal problem with their study?
29 How did Campos *et al.* (1970) overcome this problem?
30 What is an *integrated avoidance response*?
31 How did infants respond when unable to grasp the 'virtual object' created by Bower's (1979) apparatus?
32 What method did Bower (1966) use to investigate size constancy in his 'peek-a-boo' experiments?
33 What can we conclude from this?
34 How did Bower use triangles to investigate whether or not infants exhibited the Gestalt principle of *closure*?

Section 2: Cross-cultural studies

35 What did Rivers (1901) discover when comparing the responses to the Müller–Lyer Illusion of English participants with those of Murray Islanders?
36 What is the central claim made by Segall *et al.*'s *carpentered world hypothesis*?
37 Did the findings of Mundy-Castle & Nelson's (1962) study of Knysma forest-dwellers support this hypothesis?
38 Which perceptual ability was not displayed by the pygmy in Turnbull's (1961) study?
39 What was the aim of Hudson's (1960) study in which he showed African participants hunting scenes?
40 What does Serpell (1976) mean by saying that research may have mistaken 'stylistic preference' for perceptual differences?
41 What is the *transactional perspective*?

A Section 1: Infant perception

1 Psychologists are interested in studying the perceptual abilities of human infants, since it is a direct way of assessing which abilities are present at birth.

2 The nature–nurture debate, in the area of perception, concerns whether or not perceptual abilities are inborn or the product of experience and learning.

3 A nativist is someone who argues that we are born with capacities to perceive the world in certain ways.

4 An empirist argues that our perceptual abilities develop through experience.

5 The technique works by presenting the infant with two stimuli simultaneously, and observing which the infant spends most time looking at.

6 This technique tells us whether the infant can discriminate between two stimuli, and which it prefers.

7 A baby's sucking rate tends to increase or decrease when it detects a novel stimulus.

8 Habituation is the weakening of a response to a stimulus to which an organism has become accustomed.

9 A visually evoked potential is a measure of brain activity made by attaching electrodes to an infant's scalp.

10 An infant's colour perception is almost as good as an adult's by the time it is a few months old.

11 Bornstein (1976) used habituation to discover that infants could distinguish between yellow and green.

12 The pupillary reflex is the narrowing of the pupil as a result of the contraction of the muscles of the iris. It protects the retina from bright light.

13 The blink reflex is present at birth.

14 The optokinetic reflex is a reflex which allows the infant to follow moving objects with its eyes.

15 Babies do not show convergence and accommodation until a few months old.

16 Visual acuity refers to the ability to discriminate fine detail.

17 Neonates can only see about twenty centimetres before things start to become blurred.

18 Fantz (1961) used the preferential looking technique to investigate the perceptions of 1–15-week-old infants.

19 Fantz found that infants demonstrated a distinct preference for complexity.

20 The most popular of the six discs which Fantz (1961) presented to infants was the picture of a face.

21 When scanning a triangle babies spend longest looking at the corners of the triangle, the areas of highest contrast.

22 Infants may prefer looking at human faces because this preference is innate, or simply because a face combines complexity, pattern and movement, all of which babies prefer.

23 Fantz presented children with normal and 'scrambled' faces in an attempt to discover whether they preferred faces, or just complexity and contrast.

24 Hershenson *et al.* (1965) claimed that infants did not show any preference when presented with a real face, a distorted picture and Fantz's 'scrambled' face.

25 Shortly after birth babies will tend to imitate facial expressions.

26 Gibson & Walk's (1960) apparatus was called *the visual cliff.*

27 Six- to 14-month-old infants placed on the visual cliff would not crawl onto the deep side, even when beckoned by their mothers.

28 The infants in Gibson and Walk's study were not neonates and may have learned to perceive depth by the time they were able to crawl.

29 Campos *et al.* (1970) got round this problem by placing younger babies on the deep side and monitoring their heart rates.

30 An integrated avoidance response occurs when an infant shields its face, throws back its head and even cries in response to an object moving towards its face.

31 Infants unable to grasp Bower's (1979) 'virtual object' appeared surprised and occasionally distressed.

32 Bower's (1966) experiments used conditioned head rotation to discover whether an infant could recognise cubes of different sizes at different distances.

33 This experiment found that size constancy does appear to be innate.

34 Bower conditioned infants to respond to a triangle partially covered by a rectangle – and found they responded similarly to a complete triangle.

Section 2: Cross-cultural studies

35 Rivers (1901) discovered that Murray Islanders were less susceptible than the English participants.

36 Segall *et al.*'s carpentered world hypothesis holds that Westerners are more likely to interpret angles in 3D terms, since we live in a world where most angles are realistically interpretable as right-angled corners.

37 No. Mundy-Castle & Nelson's (1962) study of Knysma forest-dwellers found that they were not susceptible to the Müller–Lyer illusion, despite living in carpentered buildings.

38 The pygmy in Turnbull's (1961) study did not appear to possess size constancy.

39 Hudson's (1960) 'hunting scenes' study aimed to classify participants as having 2D or 3D vision, depending on their interpretation of the scene.

40 Serpell (1976) points out that non-Westerners may 'reject' Western pictorial representations on aesthetic grounds ('stylistic preference'), because they do not conform to their notions of artistic representation.

41 The transactional perspective holds that we are born with certain capacities whose development is strongly influenced by environmental influences.

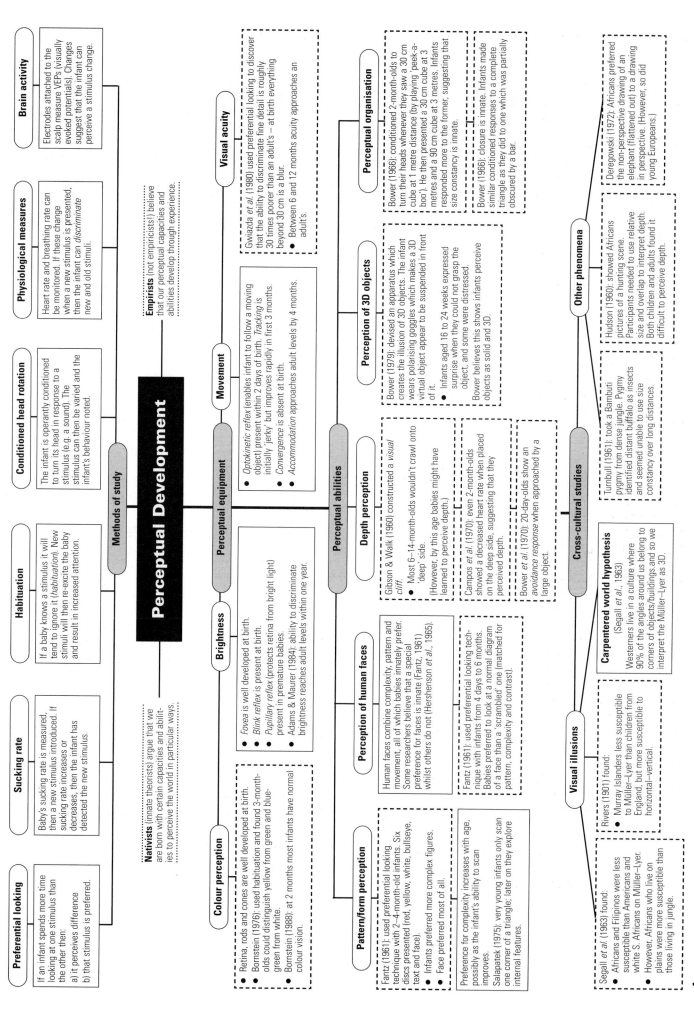

Perceptual Development

Methods of study

Brain activity
Electrodes attached to the scalp measure VEP's (visually evoked potentials). Changes suggest that the infant can perceive a stimulus change.

Physiological measures
Heart rate and breathing rate can be monitored. If these change when a new stimulus is presented, then the infant can *discriminate* new and old stimuli.

Conditioned head rotation
The infant is operantly conditioned to turn its head in response to a stimulus (e.g. a sound). The stimulus can then be varied and the infant's behaviour noted.

Habituation
If a baby knows a stimulus it will tend to ignore it (*habituation*). New stimuli will then re-excite the baby and result in increased attention.

Sucking rate
Baby's sucking rate is measured, then a new stimulus introduced. If sucking rate increases or decreases, then the infant has detected the new stimulus.

Preferential looking
If an infant spends more time looking at one stimulus than the other then:
a) it perceives difference
b) that stimulus is preferred.

Nativists (innate theorists) argue that we are born with certain capacities and abilities to perceive the world in particular ways.

Empirists (not empiricists) believe that our perceptual capacities and abilities develop through experience.

Perceptual equipment

Movement
- *Optokinetic reflex* (enables infant to follow a moving object) present within 2 days of birth. *Tracking* is initially 'jerky' but improves rapidly in first 3 months.
- *Convergence* is absent at birth.
- *Accommodation* approaches adult levels by 4 months.

Visual acuity
Gwiazda *et al.* (1980) used preferential looking to discover that the ability to discriminate fine detail is roughly 30 times poorer than an adult's – at birth everything beyond 30 cm is a blur.
- Between 6 and 12 months acuity approaches an adult's.

Brightness
- *Fovea* is well developed at birth.
- *Blink reflex* is present at birth.
- *Pupillary reflex* (protects retina from bright light) present in premature babies.
- Adams & Maurer (1984): ability to discriminate brightness reaches adult levels within one year.

Colour perception
- Retina, rods and cones are well developed at birth.
- Bornstein (1976): used habituation and found 3-month-olds could distinguish yellow from green and blue-green from white.
- Bornstein (1988): at 2 months most infants have normal colour vision.

Perceptual abilities

Perceptual organisation
Bower (1966): conditioned 2-month-olds to turn their heads whenever they saw a 30 cm cube at 1 metre distance (by playing 'peek-a-boo'). He then presented a 30 cm cube at 3 metres and a 90 cm cube at 3 metres. Infants responded more to the former, suggesting that size constancy is innate.

Bower (1966): closure is innate. Infants made similar conditioned responses to a complete triangle as they did to one which was partially obscured by a bar.

Perception of 3D objects
Bower (1979): devised an apparatus which creates the illusion of 3D objects. The infant wears polarising goggles which makes a 3D virtual object appear to be suspended in front of it.
- Infants aged 16 to 24 weeks expressed surprise when they could not grasp the object, and some were distressed. Bower believes this shows infants perceive objects as solid and 3D.

Depth perception
Gibson & Walk (1960) constructed a *visual cliff*.
- Most 6–14-month-olds wouldn't crawl onto 'deep' side.
(However, by this age babies might have learned to perceive depth.)

Campos *et al.* (1970): even 2-month-olds showed a decreased heart rate when placed on the deep side, suggesting that they perceived depth.

Bower *et al.* (1970): 20-day-olds show an *avoidance response* when approached by a large object.

Perception of human faces
Human faces combine complexity, pattern and movement, all of which babies innately prefer. Some researchers believe that a special preference for faces is innate (Fantz, 1961) whilst others do not (Hershenson *et al.*, 1965).

Fantz (1961): used preferential looking technique with infants from 4 days to 6 months. Babies preferred to look at a normal diagram of a face than a 'scrambled' one (matched for pattern, complexity and contrast).

Pattern/form perception
Fantz (1961): used preferential looking technique with 2–4-month-old infants. Six discs presented (red, yellow, white, bullseye, text and face).
- Infants preferred more complex figures.
- Face preferred most of all.

Preference for complexity increases with age, possibly as the infant's ability to scan improves.
Salapatek (1975): very young infants only scan one corner of a triangle; later on they explore internal features.

Cross-cultural studies

Other phenomena
Deregowski (1972): Africans preferred the non-perspective drawing of an elephant (flattened out) to a drawing in perspective. (However, so did young Europeans.)

Hudson (1960): showed Africans pictures of a hunting scene. Participants needed to use relative size and overlap to interpret depth. Both children and adults found it difficult to perceive depth.

Turnbull (1961): took a Bambuti pygmy from dense jungle. Pygmy identified distant buffalo as insects and seemed unable to use size constancy over long distances.

Carpentered world hypothesis
(Segall *et al.*, 1963)
Westerners live in a culture where 90% of the angles around us belong to corners of objects/buildings and so we interpret the Müller–Lyer as 3D.

Visual illusions
Rivers (1901) found:
- Murray Islanders less susceptible to Müller–Lyer than children from England, but more susceptible to horizontal–vertical.

Segall *et al.* (1963) found:
- Africans and Filipinos were less susceptible than Americans and white S. Africans on Müller–Lyer.
- However, Africans who live on plains were more susceptible than those living in jungle.

32

LANGUAGE AND CULTURE

SYLLABUS

13.3 Language and thought – language and culture
- research into the relationship between language and thought, including the linguistic relativity hypothesis. Investigations into the social and cultural aspects of language use (e.g. Bernstein, Labov)

KEY QUESTIONS
- Are language and thought the same?
- Is thought dependent on language?
- To what extent is language dependent on thought?
- Do language and thought develop independently?

Q

Section 1: Language and thought are the same

1 What, according to Watson's (1913) view, are *thought processes*?
2 Why was Watson's view called *peripheralism*?
3 What is curare and why did Smith (Smith *et al.*, 1947) inject himself with it?
4 If Watson's view were correct, what would be the consequence for people born unable to speak?

Section 2: Thought is dependent on language

5 According to *social constructionists*, what is the source of our ways of understanding the world?
6 What is meant by the expression *linguistic relativity hypothesis* (LRH)?
7 What does Whorf (1956) mean by the expression *linguistic determinism*?
8 Give three examples which support the Sapir–Whorf linguistic relativity hypothesis.
9 What is the difference between the strong and weaker versions of the LRH?
10 What did Carroll & Casagrande (1958) discover when they tested the strong version of the LRH, using Navaho-speaking and English-speaking children?
11 What did Brown & Lenneberg (1954) discover when testing the colour perceptions of Zuni Indians?
12 What did Berlin & Kay (1969) discover when investigating the use of colour terms in different cultures?
13 What are *focal colours*?
14 In Heider & Oliver's (1972) study, who were better at identifying colours which they had seen 30 seconds before – the Dani or English speakers?
15 Complete the sentence: 'Whorf's evidence was _____ rather than empirical, and he _____ the differences between Hopi and other languages' (Berry *et al.*, 1992).
16 What is a possible explanation for why Inuit Indians have many words for snow?
17 According to Hunt & Agnoli (1991), who would you expect to perform mental arithmetic more quickly – French speakers or English speakers?

Section 3: Linguistic relativity, class and race

18 When Bernstein (1961) looked at the difference between verbal intelligence scores and non-verbal intelligence scores for groups of middle-class children and groups of working-class children, what did he discover?
19 What was the name which Bernstein gave to the two types of 'codes' used by the two classes, respectively?
20 Identity four features of the 'code' which tends to be used by working-class children?
21 What is one criticism of the choice of terms 'restricted' and 'elaborated' as used to describe middle-class and working-class speech.
22 What is one major difference between Black English and White English?
23 How does Labov (1973) respond to the view that Black English is sub-standard and illogical?
24 Labov described the behaviour of a young black boy called Leon. What was Leon like?

Section 4: Language is dependent on thought

25 What was Piaget's view of the relationship between language and thought?
26 Complete the following sentence: 'As language develops it _____ onto previously acquired _____ structures, and so language is dependent on thought'.
27 What cognitive ability did children have to demonstrate in Corrigan's (1978) tests before they were capable of talking about absent objects?

Section 5: Language and thought are initially separate

28 What was the central claim made by Vygotsky (1962) with respect to the relation of language and thought?
29 What terms did Vygotsky use to describe *thinking which occurs without language* and *language which occurs without thought*?
30 According to Vygotsky, what is the difference between the *internal* and *external functions* of speech?
31 What is *egocentric speech*?

Section 1: Language and thought are the same

1 Watson (1913) believed 'thought processes' to be no more than the sensations produced by tiny movements of the speech organs too small to produce audible sounds.

2 Watson's view was called peripheralism, since it held that 'thinking' occurs peripherally, in the larynx, rather than in the brain.

3 Curare is a poison which produces paralysis in the skeletal muscles. Smith injected himself with it in order to discover if thought continued whilst his vocal apparatus was paralysed (Smith *et al.*, 1947).

4 If Watson were correct, people born unable to speak would also be unable to think.

Section 2: Thought is dependent on language

5 Social constructionists believe that we derive our ways of understanding the world from other people and our culture, rather than from objective reality.

6 The linguistic relativity hypothesis is the view that, since language determines how we think and what we think about, people with different languages think about the world differently.

7 Whorf's (1956) linguistic determinism claims that language determines our concepts. Since we can think only through the use of concepts, acquiring a language involves acquiring a world view.

8 Inuit Eskimo's have over 20 words for snow (according to Whorf), the Hanuxoo people use 92 terms for rice, the Shona people of Zimbabwe have only three words for colour and the Dani have only two.

9 The strong version of the LRH holds that language determines thought, whilst weaker versions hold that language affects perception or memory.

10 Carroll & Casagrande (1958) discovered that Navaho-only-speaking children had better shape-recognition abilities than English-speaking children (though this was not true for Navaho–English speaking children).

11 Brown & Lenneberg (1954) discovered that the Zuni Indians made more mistakes than English speakers when discriminating yellow and orange.

12 Berlin & Kay (1969) discovered that all cultures draw their basic colour terms from only 11 colours and that colour terms emerge in a sequence common to the history of all languages.

13 Focal colours are the basic 11 colours common to all languages.

14 Heider & Oliver (1972) found that the Dani were just as good at identifying colours which they had seen previously as English speakers.

15 'Whorf's evidence was *anecdotal* rather than empirical, and he *exaggerated* the differences between Hopi and other languages.' (Berry *et al.*, 1992)

16 Inuit Indians may have many words for snow, because snow is a very significant environmental feature for the Inuit and they therefore have more ways of describing it.

17 Hunt & Agnoli (1991) argue that the French should be better at mental arithmetic, since many of their number-words contain fewer syllables than the equivalent words in English.

Section 3: Linguistic relativity, class and race

18 Bernstein (1961) found that there was no difference between verbal intelligence and non-verbal intelligence scores in groups of middle-class children, whilst groups of working-class children would often show large differences between the two measures of intelligence.

19 Bernstein claimed that middle-class children tended to use an elaborated code, whilst their working-class counterparts were more likely to use a restricted code.

20 The restricted code is grammatically crude, tends to be context-bound (i.e. assumes the listener's familiarity with the topic of discourse), rarely uses the word 'I', frequently uses uninformative emotionally reinforcing phrases ('I mean', 'you know', 'like').

21 The terms 'restricted' and 'elaborated' imply value judgements, with the latter being superior.

22 Black English tends to omit the verb 'to be' (the present tense copula).

23 Labov (1973) points out that many languages omit the verb 'to be' (such as Russian), and yet we do not consider them inferior or illogical. He argues that such a view of Black English is rooted in prejudice.

24 Leon was very different, depending on the situation. In the more formal situation, when questioned by a white or black interviewer, he was uncommunicative and silent for much of the time. With friends, he was outgoing and conversational.

Section 4: Language is dependent on thought

25 Piaget believed that language is more or less dependent on thought, or a child's level of cognitive development.

26 'As language develops it *'maps'* onto previously acquired *cognitive* structures, and so language is dependent on thought.'

27 Children had to be capable of advanced object permanence (knowing that objects continue to exist when they cannot be seen) before they were capable of talking about absent objects.

Section 5: Language and thought are initially separate

28 Vygotsky (1962) believed that language and thought develop independently as separate activities which interact at a certain stage of development.

29 Vygotsky used the term *pre-linguistic thought* to describe thinking which occurs without language and *pre-intellectual language* to describe language which occurs without thought.

30 The internal function of speech is to monitor and direct thoughts, whilst the external function of speech is to communicate the results of thinking to others.

31 Egocentric speech is talking out loud about one's plans and actions and occurs in individuals who do not adequately distinguish the internal and external functions of speech.

Language & Culture

Language and thought are the same

Peripheralism (Watson, 1913)
- 'Thought processes' are no more than the sensations produced by tiny, inaudible movements of the speech organs (thought is silent speech).
- Thinking therefore occurs 'peripherally', in the larynx.

Smith *et al.* (1947):
- Tested Watson's theory by injecting himself with *curare* – a drug causing total paralysis of the skeletal muscles.
- Despite being unable to speak, Smith was subsequently able to report on his thoughts during the paralysis.

Language is dependent on thought

Piaget (1950)
- As language develops, it is 'mapped' onto pre-existing cognitive structures.
- Children can be taught words, but will only be 'parroting' them if they have not yet achieved adequate cognitive growth.
e.g. Corrigan (1978): children were unable to talk about absent objects until they demonstrated an advanced level on an *'object permanence'* test.

Conflicting research
Luria & Yudovich (1971):
- Studied five-year-old twin boys with only a primitive (synpraxic) level of speech, used only to accompany actions/objects.
- When they learned to use an objective language system, they were able to plan and engage in meaningful play.

Thought and language are initially separate

Vygotsky (1962)
- Language and thought begin as separate activities (thinking mainly in images, language used as a social tool).
- At age two, *pre-linguistic thought* and *pre-intellectual language* join to form **verbal thought** and **rational speech**.
- Between ages 2 and 7, language performs two functions:
  1. **Internal function** – monitoring and directing thought
  2. **External function** – communicating results of thinking.
- Because children cannot distinguish these functions clearly, their speech is often *egocentric* (unable to think privately).
e.g. Vygotsky (1962): when 6/7-year-olds encounter a mishap in solving a problem, they often speak out loud.

Pre-linguistic thought (images, etc.) / Verbal thought and rational speech / Pre-intellectual language (crying, etc.)

Thought is dependent on language

The Sapir–Whorf linguistic relativity hypothesis
Language determines how we think about the world and what we are able to think of.

The Whorfian hypothesis (1956)

- **Linguistic determinism** – language determines our concepts and we can only think through the use of concepts. Acquiring a language involves acquiring a 'world-view'. People who speak different languages have different world views.
- The grammar of a language may also determine an individual's thoughts and perceptions – e.g. Hopi indians do not distinguish past, present and future, and instead talk about time as it appears to the observer.

Examples
- The Hanuxoo people from the Philippines use 92 words for different types of rice.
- Eskimos have over 20 words for snow.
- The Shona people (Zimbabwe) have only three words for colour and the Dani (New Guinea) only two ('mola' for bright, warm hues, 'mili' for dark, cold hues).

Experimental tests of the linguistic relativity hypothesis

'Strong' version: language determines thought

Carroll & Casagrande (1958):
- Compared three groups on their form recognition abilities and the sequence in which they develop:
  1. Navaho-only speaking children
  2. Navaho-American children
  3. American children.
Results:
Navaho-only children did show superior form recognition and developed these abilities in a different sequence from Americans.
This may be because Navaho language stresses the importance of form.

'Weak' version: language affects perception/memory

Brown & Lenneberg (1954):
- Tested Zuni Indians (who have one word to describe yellow and orange) on their recognition of colours.
Results: compared with English speakers, they made more mistakes.

Conflicting research
Heider & Oliver (1972):
- Tested Dani (who have only two colour words) by showing them a colour, then later asking them to identify it from a range.
Results: Dani did not make more mistakes than English speakers in identifying the colour.

Links to social class and race

Bernstein (1961):
- Working-class and middle-class children speak two different kinds of language:
  1. **Restricted code**
  2. **Elaborated code.**
Lack of an elaborated code resulted in lower scores on tests of verbal intelligence in working-class children.

Restricted code	Elaborated code
Grammatically crude	Grammatically complex
Context-bound	Context-independent
'I' rarely used	'I' often used
Stresses present	Stresses past and future
Doesn't allow abstract expression	Allows abstract thought expression

Black English

- Black English differs from White English (e.g. by omitting the verb 'to be': 'he gone').
- Bernstein argues that this makes Black English a restricted code, and others regard it as illogical and sub-standard.
- Labov (1973): whilst the rules of Black English differ, it is not illogical or sub-standard (other languages omit the verb 'to be') – it is prejudice which motivates such judgements.

Labov (1970) illustrated **the influence of the social situation**:
- A boy called 'Leon' would say very little in a 'formal' situation when asked by white/black interviewers about a toy.
- However, when chatting with a friend and using local dialect he was a 'lively conversationalist'.

33

LANGUAGE ACQUISITION

SYLLABUS

13.3 Language and thought – language acquisition
- research into the process of language acquisition. Explanations of language development, including environmental (e.g learning) and nativist theories (e.g. Chomsky)

KEY QUESTIONS
- What are the major components of grammar?
- What are the major stages in language development?
- How do learning theory and biological approaches explain language development?
- What are the problems with these explanations?

Section 1: Language and language stages

1. What is *psycholinguistics*?
2. Define *grammar*.
3. What do psycholinguists mean when they talk about *phones* (phonetic segments)?
4. What are *phonological rules*?
5. Complete the following sentence: 'Semantics is the study of the ___ of a language'.
6. What is a *morpheme*?
7. To what does the term *syntax* refer?
8. What form of communication do babies tend to use most in the first month of life?
9. Why do babies 'coo'?
10. What is *phonemic contraction*?
11. At what age do children tend to produce their first word (the one-word stage)?
12. What is *jargon*?
13. What does it mean to say that the child's early word-use is very much 'context-bound'?
14. What is a *holophrase*?
15. Nelson (1973) undertook a careful analysis of children's early word use – what did she discover?
16. Name the two sub-stages which make up the two-word sentences stage.
17. What does Brown (1965) mean when he says that between 18 and 30 months the child's speech is largely *telegraphic*?
18. What is the purpose of *motherese*?
19. What is the difference between the *pivotal rules* and *categorical rules* used by children in combining words (Brown, 1970)?
20. What does it mean to say that the MLU of children increases rapidly from about 30 months?
21. If a child who has never heard of a 'wug' tells us that two of them are two 'wugs', what can we conclude?
22. What is the term used to describe the tendency among young children to talk about 'gooses' and 'sheeps'?

Section 2: Theories of language development

23. What is the technical term used by behaviourists to describe the *reinforcement of successive approximations* to the desired behaviour?
24. When children produce *echoic responses* to their parents, what are they engaging in?
25. According to Slobin (1975), how good are parents at teaching grammar to their children?
26. According to Bandura (1977), what aspect of adults' sentences do children imitate?
27. Why does the spontaneous application of grammatical rules by children pose a problem for learning theory?
28. What is the central claim made by Chomsky in order to explain how children acquire language?
29. What does LAD stand for?
30. What is the difference between the *deep structure* and the *surface structure* of a sentence?
31. What does this mean: 'Rule (1): S $\longrightarrow$ NP + VP'?
32. What is a *linguistic universal*?
33. According to Lenneberg (1967), how can we explain the existence of a critical period for language development?
34. According to the *language and social interaction approach*, what is the source of language?
35. What, according to Snow (1977), is the relationship between language and an infant's social world?
36. What is *proto-conversation* (Snow, 1977)?
37. What does LASS (Bruner, 1983) stand for?
38. According to this view, what do mothers do with language in order to assist the language acquisition process?
39. What does Gauker (1990) mean when he says that language is a *cause–effect analytic device*?

Q

Section 1: Language and language stages

1 Psycholinguistics is the study of the perception, understanding and production of language.

2 Grammar can be defined as the system of rules which are used to generate sentences in a given language.

3 Phones (or phonetic segments) refer to the basic and discrete speech sounds within a language.

4 Phonological rules are rules concerning which phonemes can be combined to form morphemes.

5 'Semantics is the study of the *meaning* of a language.'

6 Morphemes are the basic units of meaning within a language.

7 The term syntax refers to the rules used when combining words into phrases and sentences.

8 Babies' communication during the first month of life largely takes the form of crying.

9 Babies' 'cooing' is associated with pleasurable states.

10 'Phonemic contraction' refers to the restriction of the infant's phonemes to those used in its native language.

11 Children tend to produce their first word at about 12 months.

12 Jargon is the technical term for non-words produced by children during the beginning of the one-word stage.

13 The child's early word-use tends to be restricted to specific situations or contexts and it is in this sense that it is 'context-bound'.

14 A holophrase is a single word used to convey a complex message, such as 'Juice!' ('Please can I have some juice?').

15 Nelson (1973) discovered that the first 50 words produced by children tended to fall into six categories, with nominals and action words forming the largest groups.

16 Stage 1 grammar and Stage 2 grammar are the two substages within the two-word sentences stage.

17 Telegraphic is the term used by Brown (1965) to describe the near absence of purely grammatical terms (functors) in a child's early speech.

18 Motherese is a simplified form of language used by parents with children who have not yet mastered the full complexity of language.

19 Pivotal rules combine a single constant term with other terms, whilst categorical rules combine words in a constant category-to-category relation (Brown, 1970).

20 The mean length of utterance (MLU – the average number of words in a child's sentences) increases rapidly from about 30 months.

21 If a child uses the term 'wugs' without ever having come across the term before, it cannot be imitating language use, so must have internalised the rule for forming a plural.

22 Over-regularisation describes the tendency among young children to talk about 'gooses' and 'sheeps'.

Section 2: Theories of language development

23 Shaping describes the reinforcement of successive approximations to a desired behaviour.

24 Echoic responses are produced when children engage in imitation of their parents.

25 Very poor. Slobin (1975) points out that parents frequently reinforce incorrect grammar.

26 According to Bandura (1977), children imitate the general form of adults' sentences, not the exact form.

27 This is a problem because the rules have never been explicitly taught and are applied in new situations where no reinforcement can have occurred.

28 Chomsky's central claim is that children are born with an innate mechanism which enables them to understand and formulate sentences in any language.

29 LAD stands for 'language acquisition device'.

30 The deep structure of a sentence is roughly that sentence's meaning, whereas the surface structure of a sentence is the way it is expressed in words.

31 'Rule (1): S $\longrightarrow$ NP + VP' is a phrase-structure rule, meaning that a sentence is comprised of a noun phrase and a verb phrase.

32 A linguistic universal is a feature common to all languages (such as nouns).

33 Lenneberg (1967) maintains that up until the age of puberty, the brain is relatively unspecialised and hence can still develop language-processing abilities.

34 According to the language and social interaction approach, language arises from the child's pre-linguistic knowledge, especially its knowledge of social interactions.

35 Snow (1977) maintains that language is 'mapped' onto the infant's social world.

36 Proto-conversation (Snow, 1977) describes adults' attempts to 'involve' the infant in conversation by interpreting its grunts, gurgles, burps and giggles as primitive language.

37 LASS (Bruner, 1983) stands for 'language acquisition support system'.

38 According to this view, mothers simplify linguistic input and break it down into helpful, illustrative segments.

39 Gauker's (1990) cause–effect analytic device is the use of language to bring about and understand changes in the speaker's environment.

Components of grammar

Phonology (sound system)
- **Phones** are the basic speech sounds of a language (such as [p] or [d]).

Phonological rules: regulate how we can combine **phonemes** (e.g. 'plort' is possible, 'xydrfq' is not).

Language: 'an arbitrary set of symbols which, taken together, make it possible to transmit and understand an infinite variety of messages' (Brown, 1965).

Semantics (meaning system)
- **Morphemes** are a language's basic units of meaning.
- Morphemes are mostly words, but also include prefixes and suffixes.

Morphological rules: regulate how we can combine phonemes into **morphemes**.

Language Acquisition

Syntax (system for relating sound to meaning)
- Syntax refers to the rules used in combining words into phrases and sentences (e.g. subject, verb, object).

Syntactical rules: regulate how we can combine morphemes to form sentences.

Grammar: an overall description of a language, a formal device with a finite set of rules that generate the sentences in the language (Carroll, 1986).

Language development stages

Stage 1: Pre-linguistic (0–12 months)
- **Crying** dominates in the first month, with parents learning to discriminate different cries (Gustafson & Harris, 1990).
- **Cooing** begins at about 6 weeks and is associated with pleasurable states.
- **Babbling** begins between 6 and 9 months, with the baby producing combinations of consonants and vowels (e.g. 'mama', 'dada').
- **Phonemic expansion** begins shortly after babbling, with babies producing all possible phonemes.
- **Phonemic contraction** begins at 9 or 10 months, where the baby restricts its phonemes to those used in its native language.

Stage 2: One-word stage (12–18 months)
- **Context-bound:** early words are produced only in very limited or specific situations (Barrett, 1989) (e.g. using 'duck' only to refer to toy duck whilst in bath).
- **Expressive function:** some words communicate internal states (e.g. pleasure and surprise).
- **Directive function:** the behaviour of others is directed.
- Nelson (1973): identified six categories of words: *general nominals* (51% – names of types of objects), *specific nominals* (14% – names for unique objects), *action words* (13% – describe/accompany actions), modifiers (9% – refer to properties of things), *personal–social words* (8% – relate to feelings/relationships), *function words* (4% grammatical function words).
- Nelson (1973): it is a child's involvement with the environment which determines early word use.

Stage 3: Two-word sentences

Stage 1 grammar (18–30 months)
- *Telegraphic speech* (Brown, 1965): purely grammatical terms (*'functors'*) are omitted from speech.
- Semantic relationships: children combine pairs of words according to *pivotal* or *categorical* rules.

Stage 2 grammar (30+ months)
- *Mean length of utterance* (MLU): the average word length of a child's sentences increases rapidly.
- Over-regularisation occurs, where children apply rules too rigidly (e.g. 'gooses').

Berko (1958):
- Showed children a picture of a 'wug'.
- Then showed picture of two of them and asked to complete the sentence *'now there are two …'*.
3 & 4-year-olds were able to apply the rule for pluralising a new word (so rule must have been 'internalised').

Theories of language development

Chomsky's LAD and the biological approach
- Chomsky (1957): environmental factors alone (such as reinforcement) cannot explain language development.
- Children are born with an innate *'language acquisition device'* (LAD) which contains *transformational grammar* (TG) – TG is made up of *phrase structure rules*, which specify how to combine types of words to generate sentences.
- Phrase structure rules allow people to convert the *surface structure* of language (the actual words used to express something) into its *deep structure* (what it means).
- Children look for features common to all languages (*'linguistic universals'*) such as nouns, verbs, which fit into the rules.

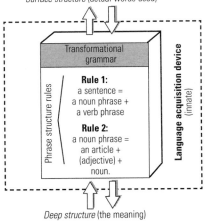

Surface structure (actual words used)

Transformational grammar

Phrase structure rules

Rule 1:
a sentence = a noun phrase + a verb phrase

Rule 2:
a noun phrase = an article + (adjective) + noun.

Language acquisition device (innate)

Deep structure (the meaning)

Research
- Different languages do appear to have features in common and some form of TG is acquired by all people (unless brain damaged). Even those with learning difficulties acquire language, suggesting the skill is separate from learning.

Alternative approaches

Social interaction approach
Language arises from pre-linguistic knowledge
- Smith & Cowie (1991): language is used to communicate needs and intentions and as a means of entering into a community.
- Snow (1977): babies initially master a social world onto which they 'map' language.
- *Proto-language* involves adults responding to and attributing meaning to a baby's grunts, cooing and eye-contact.

LASS (Bruner, 1983)
Language acquisition support system
Language acquisition requires more than just a model to input information into the LAD.
The parent provides the LASS:
- simplified linguistic input, breaking language down for the child, and
- 'formats' which are familiar games or routines in which the child can learn language.
Language is an extension of the interactions that the infant and caregiver have built up over the previous months.

Learning theory

Classical conditioning
- A neutral sound (such as 'mama') is repeatedly paired with an *unconditioned stimulus* (such as the mother).
- Words become *conditioned stimuli*, eliciting conditioned responses (e.g. salivating at the sound of the word 'cake').

Operant conditioning
Skinner (1957) argued that verbal behaviours are the result of *selective reinforcement*.
1. Children imitate adult language, producing echoic responses (*tacts*).
2. Adults shape the baby's sounds by reinforcing those closest to real words.
3. *Reinforcement* takes the form of touch, feeding, attention.
4. Later, correct sentences and grammar are reinforced through others' responses – incorrect grammar is ignored.

Conflicting research
- Slobin (1975): children learn grammatical rules despite their parents, whose use of grammar is often very poor and who frequently reinforce incorrect grammar.
- Nelson (1973): vocabulary develops more slowly in children whose mothers systematically correct poor pronunciation.

Other problems
- Slobin (1986): learning theory cannot explain universal stages in language development, since reinforcement will vary from one individual to the next.
- Chomsky (1968): learning theory cannot explain the *creativity* of language, since most of the sentences used by adults are original and therefore have never been reinforced before.
- Learning theory cannot explain how children begin using grammatical rules, which they have never been taught, to apply to new words.

PROBLEM-SOLVING AND DECISION-MAKING

KEY QUESTIONS

- What is the nature of a problem?
- How do we go about solving problems?
- What types of errors do we make in solving problems?
- How can we explain the decision-making process?

Section 1: The nature of problems

1 What is the definition of a *problem*?
2 If the first two stages in problem-solving are 'representing the problem' and 'generating possible solutions', what is the third stage?
3 What is the difference between *adversary* and *non-adversary problems* (Garnham, 1988)?

Section 2: Approaches to problem-solving

4 According to the behavioural perspective, how do we go about solving problems?
5 What, according to the Gestalt approach, is *productive thinking*?
6 What name did Köhler give to the process by which his chimp, Sultan, solved the bananas-hanging-from-the-ceiling problem?
7 What is an *algorithm*?
8 What is the principal problem with using algorithms to solve problems (e.g. solving anagrams)?
9 What are *heuristics*?
10 What are the advantages of heuristic approaches to problem-solving?
11 How is a search for a solution carried out when undertaking a *means–end analysis*?

Section 3: Errors in problem-solving

12 What is *mental set*?
13 What experiment did Duncker (1945) carry out in order to demonstrate *functional fixedness*?
14 What is *confirmation bias*?

Section 4: Decision-making models and biases

15 How is *decision-making* different from *problem-solving*?
16 According to the *additive compensatory model*, how do we decide which alternative to choose?
17 What is meant by the terms *utility* and *probability* in the *utility–probability model of decision-making*?

18 What is the difference between *compensatory* and *non-compensatory models* of the decision-making process?
19 How is a *minimax strategy* applied to decision-making?
20 According to the explanation offered by the *availability heuristic model* of decision-making, why do people overestimate the chances of being a victim of violent crime (Tyler & Cook, 1984)?
21 How, according to the *representativeness heuristic*, do we judge the likelihood of something (such as the likelihood of a shy person being a librarian)?
22 In what way can this heuristic distort our judgement concerning the likelihood of events?
23 What do psychologists mean by *belief perseverance*?
24 How can *entrapment* affect our decisions?
25 What is the term used to describe our tendency to overestimate the probability that something would have happened after it has happened (the 'I-knew-it-all-along phenomenon')?
26 Why are people likely to prefer hamburgers that are 75 per cent meat to those that are 25 per cent fat?

Section 5: Computer vs naturalistic studies

27 What name is given to the view that human cognition can be understood by comparing it with the functioning of computers?
28 What was Newell *et al.*'s (1958) *general problem solver* attempting to do?
29 When psychologists have compared experts and novices on adversarial tasks (such as chess-playing), what have they discovered about why experts make better decisions?
30 What is an *expert system*?
31 What is one criticism of such systems?
32 Why do some researchers argue that studies of decision-making should investigate *naturalistic decision-making* (NDM)?

Section 1: The nature of problems

1 A problem is a situation in which there is a discrepancy between a present state and some goal state, with no obvious way of reducing it.

2 The third stage in problem-solving, following on from 'representing the problem' and 'generating possible solutions', is 'evaluating possible solutions'.

3 Adversary problems are those in which two or more people compete for success, whereas non-adversary problems are those in which other people are involved only as 'problem-setters' (Garnham, 1988).

Section 2: Approaches to problem-solving

4 The behavioural perspective maintains that we go about solving problems by trial-and-error.

5 The Gestalt approach identifies productive thinking as the solution of a problem by reorganisation, or perceiving new relations among its elements.

6 According to Köhler, Sultan solved the problem by sudden insight.

7 An algorithm is a systematic exploration of every solution to a problem until the correct one is found.

8 Algorithms (e.g. as used by some chess computers) can be effective, but where the number of possible solutions is large they can be extremely time-consuming.

9 Heuristics are rules of thumb used in problem-solving.

10 Heuristic approaches, whilst not guaranteeing a solution, tend to reach solutions quickly.

11 A means–end analysis involves 'working backwards', searching for a solution by beginning with the goal and working backwards to the current state.

Section 3: Errors in problem-solving

12 Mental set is the tendency to continue using a previously successful strategy to solve problems, even when more efficient strategies exist.

13 Duncker (1945) investigated functional fixedness by providing participants with a box of drawing pins and a candle and instructing them to attach it to a wall in an upright position. They did not think to use the box as a stand which could be pinned to the wall.

14 Confirmation bias is a tendency to look for information which confirms our ideas and overlook contradictory information.

Section 4: Decision-making models and biases

15 Decision-making is a special case of problem-solving in which we already know the possible solutions (or choices) to a problem.

16 The additive compensatory model claims that we weigh up alternatives, listing features common to both and assigning weights which reflect their value. The alternative with the highest score is the most rational.

17 Utility refers to the value placed on potential positive or negative outcomes, whilst probability is the likelihood that the choice will produce the potential outcome.

18 Compensatory models assume that we are rational in weighing up the pros and cons of each option, whilst non-compensatory models assume that we do not consider all the features of alternatives, and that features do not compensate for one another.

19 A minimax strategy involves selecting the option with the strongest best feature, or the least weak feature.

20 According to the availability heuristic model of decision-making, information about violent crimes is likely to be vivid and memorable, and therefore readily available in LTM. As a consequence, we overestimate how likely it is to occur.

21 The representativeness heuristic allows us to judge the likelihood of something by intuitively comparing it with our preconceived ideas, which we believe represent a category.

22 The representativeness heuristic can distort our judgement by leading us to overlook important information concerning the actual frequency of objects/events in the world.

23 Belief perseverance refers to the tendency to cling to a belief even in the face of contrary evidence.

24 Entrapment refers to the reluctance to withdraw from a situation or retract a choice because of the costly investments which we have made in it.

25 The term *hindsight bias* refers to our tendency to overestimate the probability that something would have happened after it has happened.

26 People often make choices which depend to some extent on the way in which options are presented (or 'framed'), even if the choices are actually equivalent but framed differently.

Section 5: Computer vs naturalistic studies

27 The computer analogy is the view that human cognition can be understood by comparing it with the functioning of computers.

28 Newell *et al.*'s (1958) general problem solver was an attempt to simulate the entire range of human problem-solving.

29 Psychological studies suggest that experts make better decisions, not because they are faster thinkers or cleverer than non-experts, but because they make better use of working memory.

30 An expert system is a computer program which applies knowledge in a specific area, enabling the computer to mimic the function of a human expert.

31 Expert systems are less flexible than their human counterparts.

32 NDM researchers argue that only by studying experienced people can we understand how decision-makers utilise both their domain knowledge and contextual information.

A

Problem-solving

Problem: a situation in which there is a discrepancy between a present state and some goal state with no obvious way of reducing it.

Problems in PS

Mental set

The tendency to continue using a previously successful strategy when more efficient strategies exist.

Luchins & Luchins (1959):
- Participants imagined using containers to solve three tasks where the goal was to obtain precise amounts of water.
- **Results:** participants continued to use strategy which was successful for Task 1 on Tasks 2 and 3, though it was not efficient (Task 2) or successful (Task 3).

Functional fixedness

A type of mental set in which we fail to see that an object may have functions other than its normal ones.

Duncker (1945):
- Gave participants a box of drawing pins and a candle.
- Told to attach upright candle to wall.
- Failed to see that empty pin box could be pinned to the wall.

Generating solutions

Heuristics

- Heuristics are 'rules of thumb': they do not guarantee a solution but can be quick.
- They are based mainly on intuition and past experience.

Include

Analogies: recognising that a problem is similar to another.

Means–end analysis: search for a solution begins at the goal (or end) and works backwards. Often involves breaking main goal into sub-goals (e.g. Hobbits & Orcs problem).

Algorithms

- Algorithms are systematic explorations of every possible solution until correct one is found.
- Can be very time-consuming.

Stages of problem-solving (PS)

1. *Defining / representing* the problem.
2. *Generating* possible solutions.
3. *Evaluating* possible solutions.

Types of problem

- **Adversary** – two or more competitors.
- **Non-adversary** – others involved only as problem-setters.

Perspectives on PS

Gestalt

- We re-structure a problem by understanding the relations between its elements.
- Approach distinguishes *reproductive* and *productive* thinking.
- Kohler's chimp '*Sultan*' solved problems with sudden 'insight'.

Behaviourist

- Problem-solving is essentially trial-and-error involving accidental success.
- Successful behaviours are reinforced and PS improves.

Information-processing

- PS involves cognitive processes that are analysed in terms of separate stages, namely

---

Decision-making

A special case of problem-solving in which we already know the possible solutions.

Models

Compensatory models

Additive compensatory model
- We start the DM process by evaluating the features of alternatives and giving each a score.
- The alternative with the highest score is the rational choice.

Utility-probability model

DM process proceeds by weighting the *desirability* of each outcome according to:
Utility: value placed on outcome.
Probability: likelihood that choice will produce potential outcome.

Non-compensatory models

Elimination by aspects
We eliminate options if they do not meet certain criteria, starting with the most important criterion.

Minimax strategy
We select the option with the strongest best feature or the least weak feature.

Conjunctive strategy
We set minimum acceptable values for each criterion, then eliminate options which do not meet these.

Computer vs naturalistic DM

- **Computer analogy:** the assumption that human cognition can be understood by comparing it with a digital computer.
- **Expert systems:** computer programs which apply knowledge in a specific area (e.g. MYCIN which assists medical diagnoses). Whilst useful, they are much less flexible than humans.
- **Naturalistic decision-making:** researchers argue that more can be learned by studying the DM process in experienced humans who make decisions in changing environments.

Heuristics

Availability heuristic

- We base decisions on information readily available in LTM.
- We assume (often wrongly) that information is most readily available about events when they are frequent.
- Therefore, if we can easily think of information about an event, it is more likely to happen.

People tend to overestimate the probability of dying in a plane crash (Tyler & Cook, 1984) – since information about plane crashes is readily available (as compared with information about car crashes).

Representativeness heuristic

Making a decision by intuitively comparing alternatives with preconceived ideas about which characteristics belong to which categories (e.g. stereotypes).

Tversky & Kahneman (1973): gave participants a description of 'Steve' as shy, withdrawn, lover of detail.
Results: Participants were most likely to identify Steve as being a librarian when given a choice of occupations.

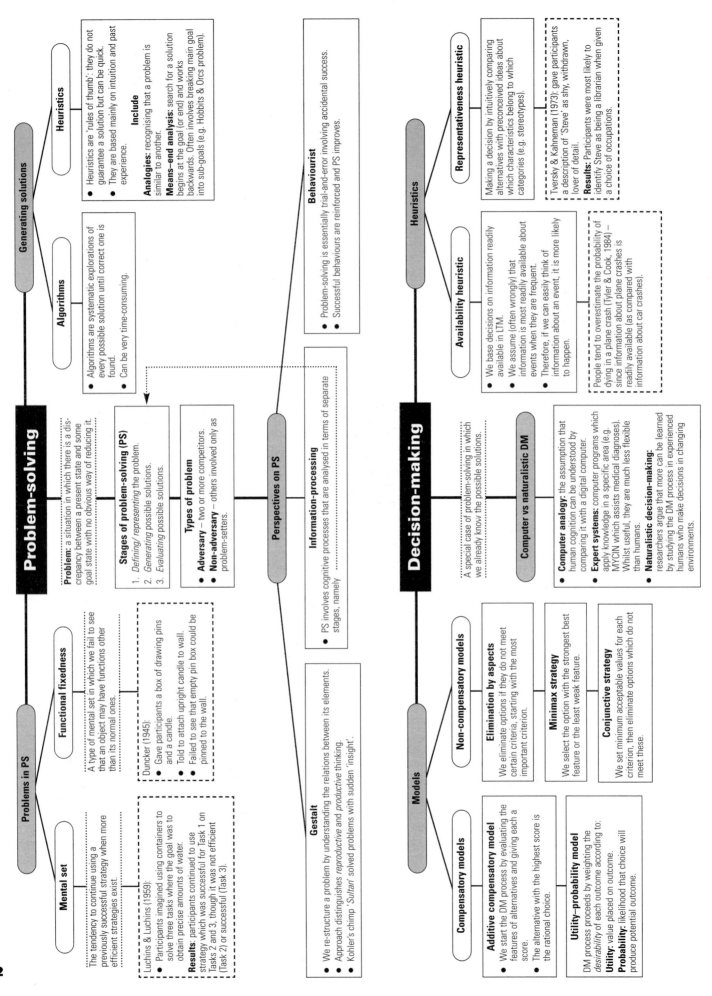

142

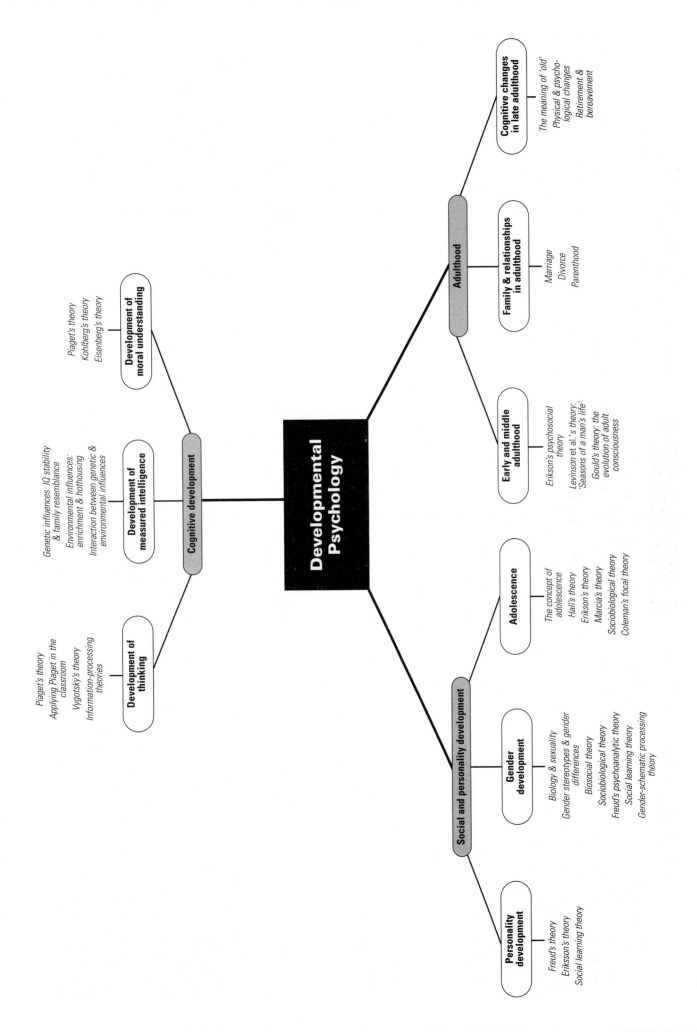

Developmental Psychology

Cognitive development

Development of thinking
- Piaget's theory
- Applying Piaget in the classroom
- Vygotsky's theory
- Information-processing theories

Development of measured intelligence
- Genetic influences: IQ stability & family resemblance
- Environmental influences: enrichment & hothousing
- Interaction between genetic & environmental influences

Development of moral understanding
- Piaget's theory
- Kohlberg's theory
- Eisenberg's theory

Adulthood

Early and middle adulthood
- Erikson's psychosocial theory
- Levinson et al.'s theory: 'Seasons of a man's life'
- Gould's theory: the evolution of adult consciousness

Family & relationships in adulthood
- Marriage
- Divorce
- Parenthood

Cognitive changes in late adulthood
- The meaning of 'old'
- Physical & psychological changes
- Retirement & bereavement

Social and personality development

Personality development
- Freud's theory
- Eriksson's theory
- Social learning theory

Gender development
- Biology & sexuality
- Gender stereotypes & gender differences
- Biosocial theory
- Sociobiological theory
- Freud's psychoanalytic theory
- Social learning theory
- Gender-schematic processing theory

Adolescence
- The concept of adolescence
- Hall's theory
- Erikson's theory
- Marcia's theory
- Sociobiological theory
- Coleman's focal theory

THE DEVELOPMENT OF THINKING

KEY QUESTIONS
- What theories are proposed by Piaget, Vygotsky and the information-processing approach?
- What implications does each approach have for education?

Q Section 1: Piaget's theory

1 Upon what research did Piaget originally base his conclusions regarding cognitive development?
2 Complete the following sentence: 'Piaget concluded that younger children's intelligence is _____ different as well as _____ different from older children's'.
3 What is a *functional invariant*?
4 What, according to Piaget, is a *schema*?
5 What term did Piaget use to apply to the process of modifying our existing schemas to match new objects?
6 According to Piaget, what are the stages of cognitive development?
7 What is *object permanence*?
8 Towards the end of the sensorimotor stage *symbolic thought* emerges. What is it?
9 What is *artificialism*?
10 Children are unable to *decentre* at this stage. What is it that they cannot do?
11 How did Piaget & Inhelder (1956) demonstrate *egocentrism* in the pre-operational child?
12 If a child is shown equal amounts of water in identical beakers, then one of these amounts is poured into a tall, thin beaker and the child states that there is now more water in this beaker, what conclusions can we draw?
13 What can a concrete-operational child do that a pre-operational child cannot?
14 What is a *transitivity task*?
15 What is the difference between *horizontal* and *vertical décalage*?
16 What is the central difference between the child's abilities at the concrete operational and *formal operational* stages?
17 What experiment did Inhelder & Piaget (1958) conduct in order to investigate the problem-solving abilities of children at different ages?

18 How might misunderstandings concerning the use of the word 'more' confuse children attempting to complete a conservation task?
19 What is one criticism of Piaget & Inhelder's (1956) '*three-mountains' task*?
20 What did McGarrigle & Donaldson (1974) discover by using 'Naughty Teddy'?
21 What is one methodological criticism of Piaget's work?
22 How can the concept of *readiness* be applied in the classroom?
23 What is meant by the expression *discovery learning*?
24 What is achieved by the teacher in creating *disequilibrium*?
25 What is the educational value of encouraging children to listen to others' points of view?

Section 2: Alternatives to Piaget

26 Piaget believes that cognitive development follows a course which is largely pre-determined, but for Vygotsky cognitive development arises from an entirely different source. What is this source?
27 What does the term *scaffolding* mean, in Vygotsky's theory?
28 Which strategy was most efficient in Wood *et al.*'s (1976) study of mothers helping four- and five-year-olds on a construction task?
29 What does Vygotsky mean by the *zone of proximal development*?
30 What is the value of *collaborative learning* (involving peer groups as well as teachers)?
31 What metaphor is central to the information-processing approach to cognitive development?
32 What is a *task analysis*?
33 What is *metacognition*?
34 Complete the sentence: 'One of the teacher's main roles is to help children find strategies for reducing their _____ load' (Sutherland, 1992).

Section 1: Piaget's theory

1 Piaget originally based his conclusions regarding cognitive development on observations of his own three children.

2 'Piaget concluded that younger children's intelligence is *qualitatively* different as well as *quantitatively* different from older children's.'

3 A functional invariant is a fundamental aspect of the developmental process which remains the same throughout cognitive development.

4 A schema, according to Piaget, is a basic building block of intelligent behaviour – a mental structure which allows us to organise past experiences and understand future experiences.

5 Piaget used the term *accommodation* to describe the process of modifying our existing schemas to match new objects.

6 There are four stages of cognitive development: sensori-motor, pre-operational, concrete operational and formal operational.

7 Object permanence is the ability to maintain a mental representation of an object which is out of sight for a period of time.

8 Symbolic thought is the capacity to construct a mental representation of an object and deal with this as though it were the object.

9 Artificialism is the belief that natural features (such as the sky) have been designed and constructed by people.

10 Pre-operational children are unable to decentre; they cannot classify things logically or systematically, since they can only focus on a single perceptual quality at a time.

11 Piaget & Inhelder (1956) demonstrated egocentrism by presenting children with a papier-mâché model of three mountains, placing a doll somewhere in this scene, then asking them to pick out the picture most closely resembling what the doll would see. Pre-operational children could not do this.

12 A child who cannot see that the amount of water remains the same is demonstrating an inability to conserve liquid quantity.

13 A concrete-operational child can decentre and take another's point of view (a decline in egocentrism).

14 A transitivity task involves a type of inferential reasoning such as: 'If Alan is taller than Bob and Charlie is taller than Alan, who is tallest?'.

15 Horizontal décalage refers to inconsistencies in a child's abilities within the same kind of operation (e.g. ability to conserve number but not weight); vertical décalage to inconsistencies between different abilities.

16 A concrete-operational child is still concerned with manipulating things, whereas a formal-operational child can manipulate ideas or propositions.

17 Inhelder & Piaget (1958) asked children of different ages to discover which combinations of four colourless liquids would produce a yellow liquid.

18 Children may use 'more' to refer to 'larger, longer, occupying more space', whereas adults use it to mean 'containing a greater number'.

19 Piaget & Inhelder's (1956) 'three-mountains' task may have been an especially difficult task.

20 McGarrigle & Donaldson (1974) used 'Naughty Teddy' to rearrange the counters in a number conservation experiment, and found that children were more likely to give the correct response than if an adult had rearranged the counters.

21 Piaget's principal technique was observation, which is not methodologically rigorous, is difficult to replicate and open to bias.

22 Readiness (the idea that children become 'ready' to learn certain concepts at certain stages) means that the teacher must assess the child's current level of development carefully and adjust tasks as appropriate.

23 Discovery learning is an expression used to convey the Piagetian view that children learn from actions, rather than from passive observation.

24 In creating disequilibrium, the teacher provides the opportunity and the motivation for children who are ready to advance to the next stage.

25 According to Piaget, listening to others' points of view may help to break down egocentrism, as well as enabling them to learn from each other.

Section 2: Alternatives to Piaget

26 Vygotsky maintains that cognitive development arises from a social process, involving interaction with others.

27 Scaffolding refers to the role played by parents, teachers and others, by which children acquire skills and knowledge. These people provide a 'framework' which helps to support the child during development.

28 Wood *et al.* (1976) found that mothers who provided specific and general interventions, according to the child's progress, were the most efficient instructors.

29 The zone of proximal development is the range of abilities and skills which a child is potentially capable of, but is not yet capable of alone.

30 Collaborative learning enables more advanced children to assist younger children, as well as allowing children to internalise the communicative process.

31 The computer metaphor is central to the information-processing approach to cognitive development, with human beings seen as information-processors.

32 A task analysis involves analysing a task's component steps in order to discover the processes necessary to solve a problem.

33 Metacognition is 'thinking about thinking': in this context, it is making children aware of their own learning processes.

34 'One of the teacher's main roles is to help children find strategies for reducing their *memory* load.' (Sutherland, 1992)

Functional invariants: fundamental aspects of the developmental process which stay the same and work in the same manner throughout the stages of development.

Genetic epistemology: the study of the development of knowledge. Piaget believed that cognitive development occurs through the interaction of innate capacities and environmental events.

Structure of the intellect

- **Schemas** are mental structures which organise experience.
- **Concepts** are rules which describe the properties of events and their relations to one another.
- We begin life with simple schemas (e.g. sucking and grasping).
- Through **accommodation** and **assimilation** (adaptation) the child matches its schemas and the world, achieving a state of **equilibrium** (mental balance).

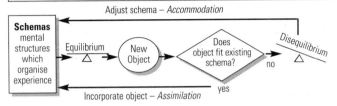

Alternatives

Vygotsky's theory

- Opposed to Piagetian theory – saw children as acquiring knowledge and skills through graded collaboration with those who already possess them.
- Ability to think and reason for ourselves is the result of a *social process*.

Scaffolding

- Refers to the role played by parents, teachers and others by which children acquire knowledge and skills (Wood *et al.*, 1976).
- As a task becomes more familiar to the child, those who provide support leave more for the child to do.

Research

- Wood *et al.* (1976): on a construction task with 4- and 5-year-olds, mothers used different strategies.
- The most effective were those who combined general and specific interventions according to the child's progress.

Zone of proximal development

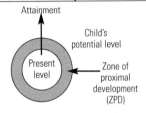

- The ZPD is those functions which have not yet matured but are in the process of maturing (Vygotsky, 1978).
- The ZPD varies from one child to another, but with support from others the child can attain more than it would have been able to alone.

Educational applications

- Teachers should scaffold children to competence, guiding pupils in paying attention, concentrating and learning effectively.
- Rejects approaches advocating rigid control over learning.
- Collaborative learning is important, where small peer groups enable more advanced children to help less advanced children.
- For Vygotsky, there is value in direct teaching but with the child as an active learner.

Information-processing approach

- Shares the Piagetian view that there are psychological structures in people's minds which explain their behaviour.
- Uses the central metaphor of computers (e.g. inputs and outputs).
- Problem-solving failures occur because of faults in basic processes (see below).

Task analysis

To understand problem-solving, we must break it down into its component steps, e.g: 1. perceive and encode the facts, 2. store them in working memory (WM), 3. combine components in WM to form an integrated representation, 4. encode the question, 5. scan the representation to formulate an answer.

Educational applications

- Teachers must help children to reduce the load on WM, e.g. by encouraging them to write down the facts involved in a problem.
- *Metacognition* – making children aware of their own learning plays a vital role.
- Children should be encouraged to a) test hypotheses and b) use visual imagery to apply their answers to real-life situations.

Stages of cognitive development

Stage	Age	Key features
Sensorimotor	*0–2 years*	Developing motor skills. Object permanence develops.
Pre-operational	*2–7 years*	Egocentrism. Inability to decentre/conserve. Representational thought.
Concrete operational	*7–11 years*	Logical thinking, but requires real objects.
Formal operational	*11+ years*	Abstract and hypothetico-deductive thought.

Sensorimotor stage

Object permanence increases – children begin to search for hidden objects
- *Sub-stage 1* (0–1 mth) No understanding of object ('out of sight, out of mind').
- *Sub-stage 2* (1–4 mths) Infants look briefly at where an object has disappeared.
- *Sub-stage 3* (4–10 mths) Partially hidden object found. Object permanence emerges.
- *Sub-stage 4* (10–12 mths) A completely hidden object can be found.
- *Sub-stage 5* (12–18 mths) An object hidden under several covers can be found.
- *Sub-stage 6* (18–24 mths) An object placed in a container, then hidden, can be found.

Pre-operational stage

- **Inability to conserve:** not understanding that quantities remain the same despite changes in appearance: (e.g. number – counters, volume – tall/short beakers.)
- **Centration:** Inability to focus on more than one perceptual quality at a time. (e.g. unable to sort pencils according to colour and size).

Egocentrism
Piaget & Inhelder (1956): 'three-mountain scene' – children were unable to pick out the picture corresponding to the view seen by a doll placed within the scene.

Concrete operational stage

- **Logical operations** can now be performed, but only when using actual objects (e.g. dividing a cake).
- **Decentring** is now possible, and egocentrism declines.
- **Transitivity tasks** are still difficult: e.g. 'Alan is taller than Bob, and Charlie is taller than Alan' – who is shortest?
- **Décalage** occurs, with some types of conservation mastered before others.

Formal operational stage

- Ideas/propositions can be manipulated verbally, without real objects.
- Hypothetical thought is also possible (e.g. what if people had tails?)

Systematic problem-solving (Inhelder & Piaget, 1958)
Gave participants beakers filled with a clear liquid which turned yellow when mixed in a certain combination.

Results
Pre-operational children simply mixed the liquids randomly, concrete operational children were more systematic but failed to test all possible combinations whilst formal operational children worked systematically, testing all alternatives.

Educational applications

Discovery learning: learning must be an active process of discovery where children construct knowledge for themselves.
- **Readiness:** The teacher should assess each child's stage of cognitive development, setting tasks which are appropriate and intrinsically motivating.
- **Curriculum:** Teachers guide children's discovery and should adapt the curriculum to each child's needs. Content might include maths (number), logic (transitive inferences) and science (conservation).
- **Teaching methods:** Teachers should try to create a state of *disequilibrium* to encourage children to advance to the next stage. Teachers should encourage children to learn from each other. Teaching materials should involve real objects.

36

THE DEVELOPMENT OF MEASURED INTELLIGENCE

SYLLABUS

6.2 Cognitive development
- factors associated with the development of intelligence test performance, including genetic and environmental influences

6.1 Early socialisation
- theories and research into the effects of enrichment and deprivation on the child

KEY QUESTIONS
- To what extent are IQ scores a product of genetic factors?
- To what extent do environment and upbringing influence IQ scores?
- Can an enriched environment significantly improve IQ scores?

Section 1: Genetic influences on IQ scores

1 Why is it important to distinguish *measured intelligence* and *intelligence*?
2 What did Tryon (1940) discover when he bred 'maze-bright' and 'maze-dull' rats separately?
3 Why is the *stability* of IQ scores over time an important issue?
4 What is the difference between *IQ* and *DQ*?
5 What did McCall *et al.* (1973) find when they looked at IQ scores in 140 middle-class children between the ages of two-and-a-half and 17?
6 What sorts of events are most likely to cause short-term fluctuations in measured IQ?
7 What can we conclude from the low stability coefficients which we find when looking at IQ scores in individuals over time?
8 If genetic factors *do* influence IQ, why would one expect to find greater concordance between the IQ scores of brothers than between those of cousins?
9 What is the difference between *monozygotic twins* and *dizygotic twins*?
10 What is the concordance rate between monozygotic twins raised together?
11 Give two possible explanations for this finding.
12 How 'separate' were the twins raised 'separately' in Shields' (1962) and Juel-Nielsen's (1965) studies of monozygotic twins?
13 When do monozygotic twins necessarily share an environment?
14 In what way is bias introduced by the agencies responsible for placing separated twins?
15 What net effect have the problems with twin studies had on the conclusions drawn from them?
16 Why are studies of *adopted children* of relevance to the debate concerning whether or not IQ scores are a result of genetic influences?
17 What did Munsinger (1975) find when he compared correlations between adopted children and their biological

parents with correlations between adopted children and their adoptive parents?
18 Identify one problem with such studies.
19 What was found by Scarr & Weinberg's (1976) 'transracial' study (black children adopted into high-income white families)?

Section 2: Environmental influences

20 What term is used to describe pre-natal factors including rubella, toxic chemicals and pollutants?
21 What syndrome may result from a mother's excessive alcohol use during pregnancy?
22 What did Rutter *et al.* (1998) discover when reviewing the progress at age four of Romanian children who had experienced extreme privation in their first two years?
23 According to Zajonc & Marcus's (1975) study, how can family size and birth order affect IQ scores?
24 Give one example of an *environmental insult* which may affect IQ.
25 What was discovered by Skeels & Dye's (1939) study comparing children in orphanages with those raised by foster mothers?
26 What was the aim of 'Operation Headstart', begun in 1965 in the United States?
27 How long-lasting were the IQ gains resulting from this programme?
28 Give two criticisms of the 'Headstart' programme.
29 What overall conclusion can you draw about the usefulness of enrichment programmes?
30 What caution regarding the effects of enriched environments was identified by White (1971), when he provided infants with enriched visual environments?
31 Describe ways in which parents can encourage learning in their children.
32 If a certain trait is highly heritable, can we conclude that environmental factors are unlikely to influence it significantly?

Section 1: Genetic influences on IQ scores

1 Measured intelligence and intelligence may well not be the same thing. There may be different types of intelligence, aspects of which are not measured by intelligence tests, and intelligence tests may not actually measure intelligence.

2 Tryon (1940) found that the offspring of 'maze-bright' rats were also good at learning mazes and 'maze-dull' rats had offspring which were slow to learn.

3 If IQ is largely inherited, then we would expect it to be stable over time, since genetic material is stable over time. If IQ scores are not stable, then this suggests that environment may influence scores.

4 IQ stands for Intelligence Quotient and DQ stands for Developmental Quotient and is usually used with children aged two or less. DQ assesses a child's developmental rate against the average.

5 McCall *et al.* (1973) found that IQ scores fluctuated by an average of 28 points between the ages of two-and-a-half and 17, and in one case by as much as 74 points!

6 Disturbing factors (such as parental divorce) are most likely to cause short-term fluctuations in measured IQ.

7 The low stability coefficients which we find when looking at IQ scores in individuals over time suggest that, although genetic factors may play a significant role in IQ scores, a simple genetic account cannot tell the whole story.

8 Brothers share roughly 50 per cent of their genetic material, whereas cousins share only 12 per cent: if the genetic account is correct, brothers are more likely to have similar IQs.

9 Monozygotic twins develop from a single egg (zygote) and are therefore identical (share 100 per cent of their genes), whereas dizygotic twins arise from two eggs and are not identical (share 50 per cent of genes on average).

10 The concordance rate for monozygotic twins raised together is roughly 0.85 (Bouchard & McGue, 1981).

11 This may be due to the fact that they share identical genes, or that they both have similar upbringing and environments.

12 Not very separate: some of the twins went to the same school and/or played together (Farber, 1981; Horgan, 1993) and some were raised in related branches of the parents' families.

13 Monozygotic twins necessarily share the mother's womb for the first nine months of life.

14 The agencies responsible for placing separated twins often try to match the families as closely as possible, thereby increasing the similarity of their environments.

15 The problems with twin studies probably led to an over-estimation of genetic influences.

16 By studying adopted children we can see whether or not their IQ scores correlate best with their natural or adoptive parents, which in turn suggests whether genetic or environmental factors are more influential.

17 Munsinger (1975) found a correlation of 0.48 between the IQ scores of adopted children and their biological parents as opposed to only 0.19 between adopted children and their adoptive parents.

18 Such studies do not take into account the similarity between the adoptive and biological parents' environments.

19 Scarr & Weinberg's (1976) 'transracial' study found that adopted children could make significant IQ gains (16 points) when adopted into families of above average intelligence, income and social class.

Section 2: Environmental influences

20 The term *teratogen* is used to refer to any of these deleterious pre-natal factors.

21 *Foetal alcohol syndrome* may result from a mother's excessive alcohol use during pregnancy.

22 Rutter *et al.* (1998) discovered that the children showed considerable physical and developmental 'catch-up' and 'spectacular' cognitive catch-up.

23 Zajonc & Marcus (1975) found that members of larger families had lower than average IQ scores, and that intelligence also declines with birth order, with the youngest children scoring lower on average.

24 Environmental insults include toxins, such as lead-based paint, which may be ingested by the child causing lower IQ scores (Needleman *et al.*, 1990).

25 Skeels & Dye (1939) found that most of the children raised by foster mothers showed significant improvements in their measured intelligence.

26 'Operation Headstart' was a compensatory programme designed to give culturally disadvantaged pre-school children enriched opportunities in early life.

27 Initial results suggested that the IQ gains were not long-lasting, disappearing within a couple of years.

28 Hunt (1969) argued that the programme was inappropriate to the children's needs. Additionally, it emphasised IQ changes as a measure of its effectiveness, rather than social competence or emotional health.

29 Enrichment programmes can be effective with children from deprived backgrounds, but are unlikely to have much of an impact on children raised in 'normal' environments (Scarr, 1984).

30 White (1971) found that the infants were advanced in some respects but delayed in others as a result of their enriched surroundings.

31 Parents can encourage learning by making learning informal; by not persisting in encouraging the child to learn when she/he is reluctant; by not being critical of the child's efforts; by giving the child their full attention sometimes; by including them in their everyday activities; talking *to* not *at* them; trying to see things from the child's perspective and directing their child towards learning opportunities.

32 No. A trait may be highly heritable but nevertheless dependent on environmental influences for its development.

Development of Measured Intelligence

Tryon (1940) divided rats into 'maze-bright' and 'maze-dull' groups. Groups bred separately in identical pens. Offspring were found to have inherited their parents' ability to learn mazes.

Genetic influences

IQ stability

An individual's genetic inheritance remains constant during his/her life, if IQ depends largely on genetics, IQ scores should be stable.
- Many studies have shown little fluctuation over time (e.g. Honzik *et al.*, 1973) with high stability coefficients.
- However, these tend to be of large groups which obscure individual differences. The stability coefficients are also lower than simple genetic theory suggests.
- Short-term fluctuations can be caused by disturbing life-events.

Conflicting research
McCall *et al.* (1973): in 140 middle class children, the average IQ change between 2½ and 17 years was 28 points. One child increased by 74 points!

Family resemblance studies

If genetic factors influence IQ, then the closer the genetic relationship between two people, the higher the correspondence between their IQ scores.
- **Monozygotic** (identical) twins (MZs) share 100% of their genes.
- **Dizygotic** (non-identical) twins (DZs) share on average 50% of genes.
- Bouchard & McGue (1981): the highest concordance rate for IQ scores is between MZ twins (supporting the genetic account).
- However, this result could be due to shared environment.

Separated twin studies
Allow us to see if concordance rates are just as high when MZs are raised apart.

Bouchard *et al.* (1990): concordance rates for MZs raised apart were lower than MZs raised together but still higher than for DZs raised together.
Suggests a strong genetic influence

Adoption studies
Allow us to see if concordance rates are closer to biological or adoptive parents.

Munsinger (1975): correlation between adoptees and biological parents was 0.48, and only 0.19 between adoptees and adoptive parents. Suggests a strong genetic influence.

Criticisms
- 'Separated' twins often turn out to have attended same schools, or been raised in branches of the same family.
- Twins will have had same experiences whilst in the womb.
- Agencies responsible for separating twins try to match families as closely as possible.
- Where twins have come forward to take part in the study, they may not be a representative sample.
- Different studies have used different IQ tests, making them difficult to compare.
- Burt's (1966) studies of MZ twins were partially fabricated.

Criticisms
- Assessing the degree of similarity between the environments of the biological and adoptive parents is difficult.

Scarr & Weinberg (1976): studied black children adopted into white families of above average intelligence and income.
Results: Average IQ changed from 90 (before adoption) to 106 (after adoption). Suggests a strong environmental component.

Environmental influences

Pre-natal influences

Teratogens
Include infections (e.g. rubella), toxic chemicals (e.g. heroin, alcohol), radiation & pollutants. Incompatibility between the mother/child rhesus factors may also produce toxins.

Foetal alcohol syndrome
Excessive alcohol use during pregnancy may lead to small children with *microcephaly* (small head and brain) and mild retardation and heart defects.

Post-natal influences

Extreme malnutrition
Stock & Smythe (1963): children suffering extreme malnutrition during infancy averaged 20 IQ points less than those with adequate diets.

Stressful circumstances
Samerof & Seifer (1989): children with no risk factors (e.g. father not living with the family) averaged 30 IQ points higher than those with 7 or 8 risk factors.

Family size
Zajonc & Markus (1975): intelligence declines with family size, and also with birth order (younger children average lower IQs).

Environmental insults
Needleman *et al.* (1990): children ingesting lead-based paint from peeling walls had lower IQs.

Enrichment studies

Milwaukee Project
- Heber & Garber (1975): worked with 40 poor, mostly black, families, (average IQ 75). Half were given job training and sent to school.
  Results
- Enriched group had an average IQ score of 126.
- However, IQ gains decreased over time.

Hothousing

White (1971): infants in enriched visual surroundings were advanced in some respects but delayed in others.

Howe (1995): children in hothousing regimes may miss out on experiences important for healthy development.

Operation Headstart
Begun in 1965, gave culturally disadvantaged pre-school children enriched opportunities, over 1 year period.
Results
- Initial IQ gains disappeared within a couple of years.
- However, reviews of the long-term effects have revealed a 'sleeper effect' with lasting IQ gains re-emerging.

Encouraging learning
Howe & Griffey (1994)
- Learning should be informal.
- Parents should not encourage learning if child is reluctant.
- Children's efforts should not be criticised.
- Parents should sometimes give children full attention.
- Children should participate in parents' everyday activities.
- Talk to children, not at them.
- See things from the child's perspective.
- Guide children towards learning opportunities.

Interaction

- Both genetic and environmental factors influence measured intelligence.
- Early heritability estimates for IQ of 80% are now more likely to be 50–60%.
- Even where a trait is highly heritable, it can still be heavily influenced by environmental variables (e.g. malnourishment can stunt growth).
- Ultimately, it is impossible to separate out environmental and genetic influences entirely.

37

DEVELOPMENT OF MORAL UNDERSTANDING

SYLLABUS

13.4 Cognitive development – development of moral understanding
- theories of moral understanding (e.g. Piaget, Kohlberg) and pro-social reasoning (e.g. Eisenberg), including the influence of gender (e.g. Gilligan) and cultural variation

KEY QUESTIONS
- How does Piaget explain moral development?
- How does Kohlberg explain moral development?
- How does Eisenberg explain moral development?
- What problems are associated with these approaches?

Q

Section 1: Piaget's theory

1 Complete the following sentence: 'According to Piaget (1932), morality develops gradually during childhood and adolescence with children passing through _____ different _____ of moral development'.
2 Why were the rules of marbles important to Piaget?
3 What is meant by saying that to younger children the rules of marbles were *external laws*?
4 What did children aged ten or more believe was the function of the rules of marbles?
5 Who were more likely to break the rules, older children or younger children?
6 What is the difference between *mutual respect* and *unilateral respect*?
7 When Piaget told children aged between five and ten stories about children who had broken something, what factor was most influential in determining how naughty they thought the children were?
8 What did older children feel was the most important element in determining the degree of naughtiness?
9 Why are younger children far more likely to accept collective punishment than older children?
10 What is *immanent justice*?
11 What is the difference between *heteronomous* and *autonomous morality*?
12 How much can Piaget's work tell us about practical morality?
13 What is the explanation offered by the *information-processing approach* as to why young children are more likely to concentrate on the damage done when assessing a child's naughtiness?

Section 2: Kohlberg's theory

14 Describe one similarity between Kohlberg's and Piaget's views of moral development.

15 How did Kohlberg investigate moral reasoning in children aged between seven and 17?
16 Name the three *levels of moral development* proposed by Kohlberg.
17 Upon what basis are decisions made about right and wrong during the first stage of moral development?
18 According to Kohlberg, what is the highest stage of moral development attainable?
19 Which stage of moral reasoning is characteristic of adults who engage in robbery (Thornton & Reid, 1982)?
20 What problems exist with the *story-book morality technique* used by Kohlberg to assess morality?
21 According to Gilligan (1982), in what way does Kohlberg's work suffer from a *gender bias*?
22 Which of Piaget's cognitive stages corresponds to Kohlberg's *post-conventional level of morality*?

Section 3: Eisenberg's theory

23 Complete the sentence: 'In contrast to Eisenberg's approach, which involves *prosocial moral reasoning*, Kohlberg's approach is _____-_____'.
24 What is meant by *prosocial moral reasoning*?
25 What name is given to Level 1 of Eisenberg's stages of moral reasoning?
26 Describe the type of moral reasoning typical of the 'approval and interpersonal orientation' stage.
27 How does level 4b (transitional level) differ from level 5 (strongly internalised stage)?
28 What is the significance of Eisenberg's finding that individuals who typically used higher-level reasoning occasionally reverted to lower-level reasoning?
29 Complete the sentence: 'According to Eckensberger (1999), _____ are increasingly being seen as the basis for moral development'.

Section 1: Piaget's theory

1 'According to Piaget (1932), morality develops gradually during childhood and adolescence with children passing through *qualitatively* different *stages* of moral development.'

2 Piaget believed that a study of children's understanding of the rules of marbles could reveal the way in which their moral reasoning develops.

3 The rules of marbles were external laws to younger children: they were perceived as created by others, and incapable of being changed in any way.

4 Children aged ten or more believed that the function of the rules of marbles was to prevent quarrelling and ensure fair play.

5 Older children were far less likely to break the rules than younger children, who often broke them to suit themselves.

6 Mutual respect involves a moral orientation towards peers, whereas unilateral respect is the moral attitude shown by children towards adult authority.

7 Children aged between five and ten believed that the severity of the outcome of the behaviour was the most important factor in assessing the naughtiness of the children who had broken something.

8 Older children understood that the child's intentions were the most important element in determining the degree of naughtiness.

9 Younger children are more likely to accept collective punishment than older children, because it is decreed by authority and accepted simply because of its source.

10 Immanent justice is the idea that misfortunes which befall wrong-doers are actually a form of punishment.

11 Heteronomous morality involves accepting and being subject to another's rules and laws, whereas autonomous morality involves a view of rules as the product of social agreements and co-operation.

12 Although Piaget's work was intended to increase our knowledge of practical morality, his method involved gaining answers to theoretical questions and situations, and so may not tell us very much about how people actually behave in practice.

13 The information-processing approach suggests that young children are unable to remember all of the details of the story, such as who did the damage.

Section 2: Kohlberg's theory

14 Both Kohlberg and Piaget believe that moral development passes through stages.

15 Kohlberg presented children with moral dilemmas (short stories in which they had to choose between two alternatives and justify their decision).

16 Pre-conventional, conventional and post-conventional morality.

17 During the first stage of moral development (punishment and obedience orientation), children believe that right and wrong are determined by what is punishable and what is not.

18 The highest level of moral development (universal ethical principles orientation) involves acting in accordance with the universal principles laid down by one's conscience.

19 Thornton & Reid (1982) found adults who engage in robbery to be characterised by stage 2 reasoning ('right and wrong are determined by what brings rewards').

20 The story-book morality technique used by Kohlberg presents people with hypothetical moral situations. In reality, their behaviours might be very different.

21 Kohlberg's work was based solely on interviews with males. Gilligan (1982) argues that since women tend to be oriented more towards compassion and care, the gender bias causes them to be rated as conventional, rather than post-conventional in their reasoning.

22 The formal operational stage.

Section 3: Eisenberg's theory

23 'In contrast to Eisenberg's approach, which involves *prosocial moral reasoning*, Kohlberg's approach is *prohibition-oriented*.'

24 Prosocial moral reasoning involves the way in which children consider the conflict between their needs and those of others, with minimal influence of laws and rules.

25 Level 1 of Eisenberg's stages of moral reasoning is called the 'hedonistic, self-focused orientation'.

26 At the 'approval and interpersonal orientation' stage the child uses stereotyped images of good and bad persons and behaviours in justifying their behaviour.

27 Level 4b (transitional level) differs from level 5 (strongly internalised stage) in that at the former the individual's internalised values are not clearly or strongly stated whilst in the latter stage they are.

28 Eisenberg's finding that individuals who typically used higher-level reasoning occasionally reverted to lower-level reasoning is significant since it is contrary to Kohlberg's theory.

29 'According to Eckensberger (1999), *emotions* are increasingly being seen as the basis for moral development.'

Eisenberg (1982, 1986; Eisenberg *et al.*, 1991): argues that 'prohibition-oriented' theories (such as Kohlberg's, below) do not apply to contexts in which the role of laws, rules & authority is minimal.
- Children are typically faced with a conflict between their own needs and those of others. In these situations, children apply prosocial moral reasoning.

Stages of prosocial moral reasoning		Characteristics	Predominant at age
Level 1	**hedonistic, self-focused**	Concerned with selfish, pragmatic consequences and what is 'right' is whatever is instrumental in achieving the individual's own desires/needs.	*preschool & primary*
Level 2	**needs of others**	Concern for physical & psychological needs of others even though they may conflict with the individual's own. Concern expressed in simplest terms.	*pre-school & primary*
Level 3	**approval & inter personal**	Stereotyped images of good and bad persons or behaviours used in justifying helping (e.g. 'It's the nice thing to do').	*primary & secondary*
Level 4a	**self-reflective empathic**	Evidence of self-reflection and role-taking (e.g. 'putting oneself in their shoes') in forming judgements.	*primary & secondary*
Level 4b	**transitional level**	Justifications involve internalised values or responsibilities and, though not clearly stated, the rights of others.	*minority of secondary*
Level 5	**strongly internalised**	As above, but much more strongly stated. Wider justifications also include self-respect, societal obligations and beliefs in human rights.	*small minority of secondary*

Evaluation
- Contrary to Kohlberg's view other-oriented reasoning emerges relatively early on, and children at the later stages may occasionally revert back to lower-level reasoning depending on the situation.
- Eckensberger notes that the emphasis on positive emotions reflects a more general shift away from Kohlberg's theory and a return to Piaget's in which empathy is seen as having a central role.
- In general, all three stage theories contain implicit moral judgements. For example, each implies that to have a predominantly hedonistic orientation is a more primitive or less sophisticated moral position than the alternatives.

Moral Development

- Children progress through *qualitatively different* stages of moral reasoning, linked to cognitive development.
- Morality of younger children is *heteronomous* (subject to another's rules) and older children *autonomous* (morality of social agreement). Change at 9/10 years, due to a reduction in egocentric thought (at 7).

Rules of marbles
Piaget studied children's beliefs about the rules of marbles to study morality.

Moral stories
Piaget told short stories in which children had to make moral judgements about another child.

5–9 yr-olds	**Unilateral respect**	**External responsibility**
	- Rules have always existed and been created by older children/adults/God. - Rules cannot be changed (external laws) but children broke them unashamedly.	- Could distinguish intentional/unintentional acts, but judged guilt on amount of damage done. - People should pay for their crimes (expiatory punishment). - Punishments accepted because of their source in authority. - Collective punishment seen as fair when someone doesn't 'own up'. - Naughty people who suffer misfortune are being punished (immanent justice).
10+ yr-olds	**Mutual respect**	**Internal responsibility**
	- Rules were invented by children and could be changed. - Rules function to ensure fair play. - Adhered rigidly to rules.	- Saw intention as most important in determining naughtiness. - Saw punishment as bringing home the nature of the offence and as a deterrent. - Punishing many for the misdeeds of one is immoral. - Principle of reciprocity – the punishment should fit the crime. - Moral relativism – justice is not solely tied to authority.

Conflicting research
- Nelson (1980): even 3-year-olds form moral judgements based on a person's intentions – but only if these are made explicit (they find it hard to discriminate intentions from consequences).
- Information-processing theorists argue that aspects of development which Piaget attributed to increasing complexity & quality of thought are actually due to increasing capacity for the storage & retrieval of information.
- Lee *et al.* (1997): compared Canadian & Chinese children's understanding of lying. When evaluating stories containing 'antisocial lying' both groups rated lie-telling negatively, but where lying was 'prosocial' ('white lies') the Chinese children rated lie-telling more positively than did the Canadian children.

- Like Piaget, argued that children pass through stages of moral development.
- Kohlberg (1963): presented 58 males aged 7 to 17 with moral dilemmas (e.g. 'should poor Heinz steal the expensive drug to save his dying wife?') and classified the responses in three levels and six stages:

Level 1: Pre-conventional morality

Stage 1: *punishment and obedience orientation*	Right and wrong are determined by what is punishable or not. Moral behaviour is the avoidance of punishment.
Stage 2: *instrumental relativist orientation*	Right and wrong are determined by what brings rewards and what people want. Others' needs are only important because they affect us.

Level 2: Conventional morality

Stage 3: *interpersonal concordance orientation*	Moral behaviour is whatever pleases/meets with approval from others. What the majority thinks is right by definition.
Stage 4: *maintaining the social order orientation*	Being good means maintaining the social order for its own sake and respecting authority. Laws are accepted without question.

Level 3: Post-conventional morality

Stage 5: *social contract-legalistic orientation*	Laws are mutually agreed and can be changed by mutual agreement. Individual rights can sometimes become more important than laws.
Stage 6: *universal ethical principles orientation*	The ultimate judge of morality is a person's own conscience guided by universal principles. Society's rules are less important than these.

Conflicting research
- Gilligan (1982): Kohlberg's stages are based on male morality and female morality is oriented more towards compassion.
- Gibbs & Schnell (1985): moral reasoning and actual behaviour do not always match – Kohlberg does not discover what people really do.
- Kohlberg (1978): later acknowledged that there may not be a separate sixth stage.

Are females & males morally different?
- Walker (1989): studied a large sample of females & males aged between 5 and 63.
Results: the only difference was between adults reporting on real-life dilemmas – females reported more 'relational/personal' dilemmas (e.g. telling a friend about her husband's affair), and males more 'non-relational/impersonal ones' (e.g. pointing out incorrect change in a store). Generally, Walker's findings do not support the claim that Kohlberg's stages contain an inherent gender bias.

PERSONALITY DEVELOPMENT

KEY QUESTIONS
- What are personality and temperament?
- How does Freud explain personality development?
- How does Eriksson explain personality development?
- How do social learning theorists explain personality development?

Section 1: Temperament and personality

1 Complete the sentence: 'According to Bee (2000) 'personality' describes those ____ ____ ____ in how children and adults go about relating to the people and objects in the world around them'.
2 What is the relationship between temperament and personality?
3 Name two of the best known classifications of temperament.

Section 2: Freud's psychoanalytic theory

4 Name the three interacting structures which Freud believed comprise the personality.
5 Which component of the personality is governed principally by the pleasure principle?
6 What is the role of the *ego* in Freud's model of the personality?
7 Which component of the personality is responsible for enforcing morality?
8 At what age do children acquire their sense of right and wrong?
9 What name does Freud attach to a preoccupation with orderliness, punctuality and routine?
10 What is the *Oedipus complex*?
11 What is the role of *castration anxiety* in the formation of morality?
12 Why did Freud believe that boys came to have a stronger sense of morality than girls?
13 What other influences might there be on childhood morality which are not taken into account by Freud's theory?
14 According to Freud, which *psychosexual stage* of development is experienced between the ages of three and five or six?

Section 3: Erikson's psychosocial theory

15 What view of the personality did Erikson (1963) challenge in proposing his *psychosocial stages*?
16 What does Erikson's (1963) *epigenetic principle* maintain about the pattern of social and psychological growth in an individual?

17 According to Erikson, what is the major conflict facing the individual during adolescence?
18 What are the possible positive and negative outcomes of this crisis?
19 What is meant by saying that Western societies see adolescence as a *moratorium*?
20 What is *ego identity*?
21 Name four ways in which *role confusion* may show itself during adolescence.
22 What did Simmons & Rosenberg (1975) discover when investigating self-esteem in girls?
23 Why has Erikson's research been criticised for being biased (Gilligan, 1982)?

Section 4: Social learning theory

24 In what important way does the social learning approach differ from 'stimulus–response' approaches in explaining human behaviour?
25 What name do social learning theorists give to that type of learning which occurs spontaneously, with no deliberate effort by the learner?
26 What important factor is likely to influence whether or not an individual imitates behaviour which they have seen?
27 In Bandura's (1965) 'bobo doll' study, what did the control group observe?
28 Complete the sentence: 'For Bandura, reinforcement provides the learner with ____ about the likely consequences of certain behaviour'.
29 To which cognitive variable do the terms *vicarious* and *self-reinforcement* apply?
30 What term is used to describe the way in which a child who has internalised societal standards uses them to regulate its own behaviour?
31 To what does the term *self-efficacy* refer?
32 What expression is used to describe Bandura's view that behaviour influences the environment and the environment, in turn, influences behaviour?

Section 1: Temperament and personality

1 'According to Bee (2000) 'personality' describes those *enduring individual differences* in how children and adults go about relating to the people and objects in the world around them.'

2 Temperament is genetically determined whilst personality is a product of the interaction between temperament and the environment.

3 'Easy', 'difficult', 'slow-to-warm-up', 'emotionality', 'activity', 'sociability' and 'behavioural inhibition' are amongst the best known classifications of temperament.

Section 2: Freud's psychoanalytic theory

4 The id, the ego, and the superego.

5 The id.

6 The role of the ego in Freud's model is to negotiate compromises between instincts (in the form of the id), morality (in the form of the superego) and reality (often taking the form of social constraints).

7 The superego is responsible for enforcing morality, and is the internalisation of parental standards.

8 Freud suggests that a child acquires a sense of right and wrong at the age of about five or six.

9 Freud termed such a trait *anal retentive*.

10 The Oedipus complex refers to the sexual attraction of the male child to its mother and the perception of the father as a rival.

11 According to Freud, castration anxiety, arising from the Oedipus complex, causes the male child to identify with the feared parent (identification with the aggressor) and subsequently internalise (introject) the parent's standards, which become the superego.

12 Since girls have no fear of castration, they identify with the mother only through fear of losing her love (anaclitic identification) and hence do not develop such strong superegos.

13 Freud's theory does not take into account the influence of the media (especially television – understandably so) and other extra-familial influences on morality.

14 The phallic stage.

Section 3: Erikson's psychosocial theory

15 Erikson (1963) challenged the view that personality development stops early in life (as was suggested by Freud, among others).

16 Erikson's (1963) epigenetic principle holds that the pattern of social and psychological growth in an individual is genetically determined.

17 Erikson believes that adolescents face the identity vs role confusion conflict, in which they must decide on an occupational role.

18 The positive (adaptive) outcome of this conflict is 'a sense of who one is', whereas the negative (maladaptive) outcome is a prolonged uncertainty about one's role in life.

19 Western societies see adolescence as a moratorium – an authorised delay of adulthood which frees adolescents from most responsibilities and helps them to make the transition into adulthood.

20 Ego identity is a firm sense of who one is and what one stands for.

21 Role confusion may show itself as an aimless drifting through occupations, as negative identity (drug-taking or suicide), as fear of intimacy, or an inability to plan, work or study well.

22 Simmons & Rosenberg (1975) discovered that low self-esteem is more common in girls during early adolescence than in late childhood or late adolescence.

23 Erikson's research was largely based on white males from the middle classes and has therefore been criticised for androcentrism (Gilligan, 1982).

Section 4: Social learning theory

24 The social learning approach differs from 'stimulus–response' approaches in explaining human behaviour in proposing cognitive/mediating variables which intervene between stimulus and response.

25 Observational learning (or 'modelling') learning occurs spontaneously, with no deliberate effort by the learner.

26 The consequences for the individual observed are likely to influence the likelihood that the observer will imitate behaviour which they have seen.

27 In Bandura's (1965) 'bobo doll' study the control group observed an adult who kicked, pummelled and punched an inflatable toy.

28 'For Bandura, reinforcement provides the learner with *information* about the likely consequences of certain behaviour.'

29 The terms vicarious and self-reinforcement both apply to motivation.

30 *Self-monitoring* describes the way in which a child who has internalised societal standards uses them to regulate its own behaviour.

31 The term self-efficacy refers to our belief that we can act effectively and exercise some control over our lives.

32 Bandura uses the expression *reciprocal determinism* to refer to the view that behaviour influences the environment and the environment, in turn, influences behaviour.

The psychic apparatus

The personality is composed of three interacting structures:

ID (operates on the pleasure principle): present at birth, impulsive and pleasure-seeking.

EGO (operates on the reality principle): negotiates compromises between id and superego and helps us cope with reality.

SUPEREGO (conscience + ego-ideal): governs moral judgements and feelings.

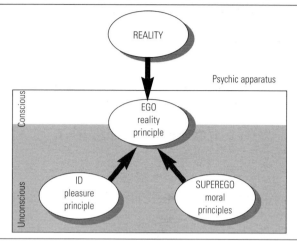

Psychic apparatus

Psychosexual stages

Oral stage (0–1 yr): pleasure achieved through the mouth.
Anal stage (1–3 yrs): pleasure achieved through anal membranes.
Phallic stage (3–5/6 yrs): pleasure through self-manipulation of genitals.
Latency stage (5/6–12 yrs): sexual motivations recede in importance.
Genital stage (after puberty): pleasure through heterosexual relationships.

The Oedipus complex, identification and the superego

- The child begins life with only sexual and aggressive instincts (ID).
- The EGO develops to negotiate compromises between the ID and REALITY (including social constraints).
- Young boys and girls become attracted to the opposite-sex parent (Oedipus/Electra complex, respectively).
- Boys become anxious that the father will punish them (castration anxiety).
- Boys identify with the father to resolve the conflict and the internalised voice of the parent becomes the SUPEREGO (roughly, the conscience).
- Girls do not fear castration, only loss of the mother's love and this anaclitic identification leads to weaker superegos & identities.

- SL theorists are interested in human learning (e.g. morality).
- SL theorists argue that cognitive variables (e.g. beliefs and memories) intervene between stimulus and response.
- SL theorists emphasise observational learning which takes place spontaneously, without reinforcement.
- Imitation of another's behaviour ('modelling') depends partly on the consequences of the behaviour for the model.

'Bobo doll' study (Bandura, 1965)

Children watched a video of an adult being aggressive towards an inflatable 'bobo doll':

- **Group A:** (*control*) saw an adult kicking, punching & pummelling the bobo doll.
- **Group B:** (*model-rewarded*) saw the same as group A but the adult was commended and offered sweets & lemonade by a second adult.
- **Group C:** (*model-punished*) saw the same as group A but the adult was scolded & warned against doing it again.

Results: Children who observed the adult being rewarded for behaviour were significantly more aggressive than those who had seen the adult punished (or not rewarded) when placed in the same situation.

Five major functions in observational learning (Bandura, 1974):

- **Attention:** learner must attend to important aspects of the stimulus situation.
- **Coding:** learner must form an image or semantic code in order to transfer the modelled behaviour to memory.
- **Memory permanence:** information must be retained.
- **Reproduction:** observed motor activities must be reproduced accurately and this may involve practice.
- **Motivation:** relates to the role of reinforcement (which provides us with information about what results we may achieve in the future).

Self-concept, self-monitoring, and self-efficacy

Bandura claims that children can also learn abstract skills and information through modelling – for example, extracting the rules for a model's behaviour and applying it to their own:

- This ability to internalise societal standards allows the child to engage in 'self-monitoring' and to regulate behaviour even in the absence of reinforcement. Our own self-appraisal may affect our self esteem.
- A particularly influential internalised standard is our self-efficacy – our belief that we can be effective and control events around us. This is critically important for motivation.

Personality Development

- Epigenetic principle: the entire pattern of psychological and social growth is governed by genetics.
- Psychosocial stages: are universal, each centring around a crisis with two possible outcomes.
- The adolescent struggles to establish a strong sense of identity (*ego identity*).

Role confusion

The failure to integrate perceptions of the self into a coherent whole, shown in:

- fear of intimacy
- inability to plan for the future
- inability to work/study industriously
- negative identity (e.g drug addict/yob).

Research

- Offer *et al.* (1988): no increase in the disturbance of self-image during adolescence.
- Gilligan (1982): Erikson's sample was biased (largely middle-class, white males) and is only applicable to that group.

Stage	Personal and social relationships	Crisis or conflict	Possible outcome
0–1 year	Mother	Trust vs mistrust	Trust and faith in others or a mistrust of people.
2 yrs	Parents	Autonomy vs shame and doubt	Self-control and mastery or self-doubt and fearfulness.
3–5 years	Family	Initiative vs guilt	Purpose and direction or a loss of self-esteem.
6–11 years	Neighbourhood and school	Industry vs inferiority	Social and intellectual competence or failure to thrive and develop.
Adolescence	Peer groups, outgroups, leaders	Identity vs role confusion	A sense of 'who one is' or prolonged role uncertainty.
Early adult	Friends, sexual partners	Intimacy vs isolation	Formation of deep relationships or failure to love others.
Middle age	Divided labour and shared household	Generativity vs stagnation	Expansion of interests and caring for others or turning in on one's own problems.
Old age	'Mankind', 'My kind'	Integrity vs despair	Satisfaction with the triumphs and disappointments of life or unfulfilment and a fear of death.

GENDER DEVELOPMENT

SYLLABUS

13.4 Social and personality development – gender development
- explanations of the development of gender identity and gender roles (e.g. social learning theories, cognitive–developmental theories and gender schema theory)

KEY QUESTIONS
- What biological variations may affect sexual identity?
- What psychological differences exist between the sexes?
- How do theories of gender development account for gender differences?

Section 1: Introducing gender

Q

1 What interpretation does the *feminist perspective* place on sex differences?
2 What is the view of *evolutionary psychologists* regarding sex differences?
3 What is the difference between *sex* and *gender*?
4 How do *gender roles* and *gender stereotypes* differ?
5 By what age do most children demonstrate some knowledge about their gender?
6 Name the five categories of biological sex.
7 What is the difference between a *hermaphrodite* and a *pseudohermaphrodite*?
8 Imperato-McGinley *et al.* (1979) found that of 18 DHT-deficient males who were raised as girls, all but two reverted to male gender roles at puberty. What does this suggest?
9 According to McGlone (1980), which of the two cerebral hemispheres is generally more dominant in men?
10 Which brain structure is larger in women?

Section 2: Gender stereotypes and differences

11 Identify the female characteristics and the male characteristics which Williams & Best (1994) found were associated with these gender groups.
12 How does verbal ability differ between the sexes, over the course of their development?
13 Which ability is consistently better in males during adolescence and adulthood (Maccoby & Jacklin, 1974)?
14 Complete the sentence: 'According to Eagly (1983), research has actually tended to ___ rather than ___ sex differences'.

Section 3: Theories of gender

15 What does *biosocial theory* see as central to the development of gender?
16 What did the 'baby X' experiments (Smith & Lloyd, 1978) discover?

17 What was Money & Ehrhardt's (1972) view as to whether or not it is possible to change the sex of rearing?
18 According to Money (1974), what view is supported by the case of the penectomised twin?
19 What is the central argument made by *sociobiological/evolutionary theorists*, regarding gender?
20 According to Buss (1994), what do females universally find attractive in men?
21 Outline any one criticism of the sociobiological approach.
22 According to Freud, how does the *Oedipus complex* relate to the development of gender identity?
23 To what extent do studies of children who grow up in 'atypical' families support Freud's theory?
24 According to *social learning theory*, which two processes account for the different behaviour of boys and girls?
25 What did Sears *et al.* (1957) find, when looking at parents' response to their children's aggressive behaviour?
26 According to Smith & Daglish (1977), whom do children prefer to model?
27 What feature is emphasised by the *cognitive–developmental approach* to understanding the development of gender?
28 According to this approach, what is the first stage in the development of gender identity?
29 What do children recognise during the second stage (*gender stability*)?
30 How does this stage differ from the third stage (*gender constancy* or *consistency*)?
31 What is a major problem for cognitive–developmental theory?
32 Complete the sentence: 'According to gender-schematic processing theory, then, children learn to judge themselves according to the ___ considered to be ___ to their genders'.

Section 1: Introducing gender

1 The feminist perspective believes that social, political, economic and cultural factors determine gender.

2 Evolutionary psychologists regard sex differences as 'natural', having evolved as part of the adaptation of the human species to its environment.

3 *Sex* refers to some biological fact about us (e.g. our reproductive anatomy or genetic make-up), whilst gender is what culture makes out of biological sex (the 'social interpretation' of sex).

4 Gender roles are the behaviours, attitudes, values and beliefs which a particular society considers appropriate to males and females, whilst gender stereotypes are widely held beliefs about psychological differences between males and females.

5 By the age of three or four, children demonstrate some knowledge about their gender.

6 The five categories of biological sex are: chromosomal sex, gonadal sex, hormonal sex, sex of the internal reproductive structures, and sex of the external genitals.

7 Both hermaphrodites and pseudohermaphrodites possess ambiguous external and internal reproductive structures; pseudohermaphrodites possess gonads which match their chromosomal sex (unlike true hermaphrodites).

8 Imperato-McGinley *et al.*'s (1979) finding suggests that testosterone had somehow pre-programmed masculinity into their brains.

9 McGlone (1980) claims that the right hemisphere is generally more dominant in men.

10 The corpus callosum is larger in women.

Section 2: Gender stereotypes and differences

11 Williams & Best (1994) found that terms such as 'aggressive', 'determined', and 'sharp-witted' were associated with males, whilst 'cautious', 'emotional', and 'warm' were associated with females.

12 The sexes are similar with respect to verbal ability until age 11, when females become superior, this difference increasing during adolescence and possibly beyond.

13 Spatial ability is consistently better in males during adolescence and adulthood (Maccoby & Jacklin, 1974).

14 'According to Eagly (1983), research has actually tended to *conceal* rather than *reveal* sex differences.'

Section 3: Theories of gender

15 Biosocial theory sees the interaction between biological and social factors as central to the development of gender.

16 The 'baby X' experiments (Smith & Lloyd, 1978) showed that adults treated babies according to the gender they believed them to be (and not their true gender).

17 Money & Ehrhardt (1972) believed that it is possible to change the sex of rearing with little psychological harm being done, provided this occurs within a 'critical' or 'sensitive' period of about two-and-a-half to three years.

18 According to Money (1974), the case of the penectomised twin supports the view that gender identity is learned.

19 The central argument made by sociobiological/evolutionary theorists, regarding gender, is that gender (and gender roles) has evolved gradually as part of our adaptation to the environment.

20 Buss (1994) claims that females universally find attractive in men the characteristics associated with the provision of resources.

21 The sociobiological approach assumes that dominance patterns are to be equated with greater aggression in males, when in fact these are more often related to status. Sociobiological approaches are difficult to test. Our hunches about which characteristics were adaptive in our evolutionary past are at best 'educated guesses'.

22 According to Freud, the Oedipus complex is resolved through identification with the same-sex parent, which results in the acquisition of a gender identity.

23 Studies of children who grow up in 'atypical' families do not show adverse affects in terms of their gender identity, and so do not support Freud's account.

24 According to social learning theory, observational learning and reinforcement play central roles in the development of gender.

25 Sears *et al.* (1957) found that parents allowed their sons to be more aggressive in their relations to other children, and intervened more frequently and quickly when girls behave aggressively.

26 According to Smith & Daglish (1977), children prefer to model the behaviour of those with whom they have most contact.

27 The cognitive–developmental approach emphasises the child's participation in the construction of his/her gender.

28 The first stage is gender labelling or basic gender identity.

29 During the second stage (gender stability), most children recognise that people retain their gender for a lifetime.

30 In the third stage (gender constancy or consistency) children realise that gender is immutable (i.e. remains constant despite transformations in appearance).

31 Cognitive–developmental theory cannot account for the appearance of gender-appropriate behaviour before gender constancy is achieved.

32 'According to gender-schematic processing theory, then, children learn to judge themselves according to the *traits* considered to be *relevant* to their genders.'

A

Aggression
Maccoby & Jacklin (1974): boys are more verbally and physically aggressive than girls, beginning as soon as play begins (2½ yrs).

Verbal ability
Maccoby & Jacklin (1974): sexes score similarly until age 11 when females are superior. Gap is small but increases during adolescence.

Spatial ability
Maccoby & Jacklin (1974): males' ability is consistently higher in adolescence and adulthood. However, difference is small.

Mathematical ability
Maccoby & Jacklin (1974): increases faster in boys, beginning around 12 or 13.

Gender differences

Pseudohermaphrodites
Pseudohermaphrodites possess ambiguous external and internal reproductive structures:
- Imperato-McGinley *et al.* (1979): studied 18 DHT-deficient males. Sexually, they appeared and were raised female but at puberty changed into males. All but two adopted male gender roles (suggesting masculinity is pre-programmed).
- Goldwyn (1979): cites the case of Daphne Went, who though genetically male has a female appearance and has lived happily as a woman.

Biological and sexual identity

Brain differences
- McGlone (1980): the right hemisphere is generally dominant in men, and the left in women.
- The *corpus callosum*, which connects the two hemispheres, is larger in women.
- Bryden & Saxby (1985): found greater activity in right hemisphere of males performing spatial tasks – both hemispheres activated in women.

However, it is unclear how and if these differences influence gender.

Sex: a biological fact about us, such as our genetic makeup or anatomy.
Sexual identity: our biological status.
Gender: what our culture makes out of the 'raw material' of biological sex.
Gender identity: our own classification of ourselves (can differ from sexual identity).

Gender Development

Gender/sex role: behaviours which a society considers appropriate to males or females.
Gender stereotypes: widely held beliefs about psychological differences between males and females.
Sex typing: the acquisition of a gender identity and learning the appropriate behaviours.

Biosocial theory
- Stresses the importance of the interaction between biological and social factors in producing gender and argues that they are inseparable.
- Money & Ehrhardt (1972): 'anatomy is destiny' – how an infant is labelled sexually determines how it is raised, which in turn determines gender identity and gender role.

Money & Ehrhardt (1972)
- Studied girls with *adrenogenital syndrome* who were raised as boys until age 3. At 3 they had surgery and were raised as girls.
- Children *can* change gender, provided this occurs before 3 years old.

Money (1974)
- Studied a twin who lost his penis during circumcision. He had surgery at 17 months and was raised as a girl.
- He adapted to a female role, supporting the idea that gender is learned.

Social learning theory
- Emphasises the different treatment of boys and girls by parents, who are treated in line with gender-role expectations.
- Observational learning and reinforcement of roles: children observe others and receive reinforcement for behaviours considered 'sex-appropriate' (Bandura, 1977).
- Parents tend to reinforce boys for independence and emotional control, girls for dependence and emotional expression.

Research
- Sears *et al.* (1957): parents allowed sons to be more aggressive than daughters.
- Bandura *et al.* (1961, 1963): boys were more likely to imitate aggressive male models than were girls.
- Maccoby & Jacklin (1974): no consistent differences in reinforcement for aggressiveness or autonomy between boys and girls.

Psychoanalytic theory
Gender identity is assumed to be flexible up until the resolution of the Oedipus complex, which is resolved via identification with the same-sex parent, leading to gender identity.

Conflicting research
- Krebs & Blackman (1988): children acquire gender-identity gradually, not in a single step.
- Golombok *et al.* (1983): parents who grow up in single-parent or lesbian families may well have 'normal' gender identity.
- Children are aware of gender roles long before the age of 5 or 6 which Freud proposed for identification.

Sociobiological theory
- Sociobiologists (evolutionary theorists) argue that gender has evolved as part of our adaptation to our environment.
- Males and females have evolved differently in line with their different contributions to domestic labour and reproduction (e.g. greater physical strength for hunting – males, milk-producing capacities – females).

Parental investment theory (Kenrick, 1994)
- Male–female partnerships arose from the needs for sexual exclusivity and protection, respectively.
- This led to different courtship displays and roles which are still evident.
- Women look for mates who can provide resources, whilst men look for mates who are capable of reproducing well.

Other theories

Cognitive–developmental theory (Kohlberg, 1969)

Three stages in the development of gender identity
- **Stage 1** (*gender labelling*): by 3 years the child recognises that it is male or female (but unaware that this is permanent).
- **Stage 2** (*gender stability*): by 4/5 child realises that gender is permanent – but judges gender superficially (e.g. by hair).
- **Stage 3** (*gender constancy*): by 6/7 child realises that gender is immutable – i.e. cannot be changed (e.g. by cutting hair).

Gender-schematic processing theory (Bem, 1985)
- Children learn to judge themselves according to the traits considered relevant to their genders, depending on the label 'boy' or 'girl'.
- The self-concept becomes mixed with the gender-schemas (gender roles) of a particular culture.
- The child's self-esteem then becomes linked with how well it performs against the gender-schema.

ADOLESCENCE

SYLLABUS

13.4 Social and personality development – adolescence
- research into social development in adolescence, including the formation of identity (e.g. Marcia).
- research into relationships with parents and peers during adolescence and cultural differences in adolescent behaviour

KEY QUESTIONS
- What is adolescence?
- What explanations of adolescence have been proposed by Hall, Coleman, Erikson, and Marcia?

Section 1: The concept of adolescence

1 What does *adolescence* mean?
2 What ages does adolescence tend to span in Western societies?
3 What is the important period which marks the beginning of adolescence?
4 Complete the sentence: 'Some researchers maintain that adolescence is difficult to define because it has been _____ _____ by Western culture and is a recent _____ of Western capitalist society'.
5 What can Plato tell us about adolescence?
6 What are the three main components of adolescence according to the classical view?

Section 2: Hall's and Erikson's theories

7 According to Hall (1904), what does each individual's psychological development 'recapitulate'?
8 What was the most revealing finding in Csikszentmihalyi & Larson's (1984) study in which students wrote a description of what they were doing and how they felt every two hours?
9 What did Rutter *et al.* (1976) discover when comparing the rates of mental disorders between ten-year-olds, 14-year-olds and adults?
10 In general, is Hall's theory well-supported by research into adolescence?
11 What view of the personality did Erikson (1963) challenge in proposing his *psychosocial stages*?
12 What does Erikson's (1963) *epigenetic principle* maintain about the pattern of social and psychological growth in an individual?
13 According to Erikson, what is the major conflict facing the individual during adolescence?
14 What are the possible positive and negative outcomes of this crisis?
15 What is meant by saying that Western societies see adolescence as a *moratorium*?
16 What is *ego identity*?

17 Name four ways in which *role confusion* may show itself during adolescence.
18 What did Simmons & Rosenberg (1975) discover when investigating self-esteem in girls?
19 Why has Erikson's research been criticised for being biased (Gilligan, 1982)?

Section 3: Marcia's and sociological theories

20 According to Marcia's four statuses of adolescent identity, what is the difference between *identity diffusion* and *identity foreclosure*?
21 Are Marcia's statuses necessarily sequential, in the way that Erikson's stages follow one after the other?
22 What did Meilman (1979) find which casts doubt on Marcia's theory?
23 What, according to sociologists, is one of the features which drives adolescent development by producing different expectations of the adolescent?
24 How does the *generation gap* relate to adolescent development?
25 Does the majority of research support the view that during adolescence there is a large amount of conflict between parents and children?
26 Name two areas in which research has shown significant disagreements between children and parents.

Section 4: Coleman's focal theory

27 What, according to Coleman & Hendry (1990), is the principal problem with other theories of adolescence?
28 What is it that *focal theory* tries to explain?
29 What did Coleman find when investigating the concerns of 800 six-, 11-, 13-, 15- and 17-year-olds?
30 What was Coleman's explanation for this important finding?
31 What prediction does focal theory make about which adolescents are most likely to experience difficulties during adolescence?
32 Overall, does the evidence support the notions of '*storm and stress*', *identity crisis* and the *generation gap* during adolescence?

Q

Section 1: The concept of adolescence

1 Adolescence comes from the Latin *adolescere* meaning 'to grow into maturity' and is regarded as a prelude to and preparation for adulthood.

2 Adolescence tends to span the ages of 12–20 in Western societies, though many other cultures view this as unusually long.

3 Puberty, the onset of sexual maturation, marks the beginning of adolescence.

4 'Some researchers maintain that adolescence is difficult to define because it has been *artificially created* by Western culture and is a recent *invention* of Western capitalist society.'

5 Plato, writing 2000 years ago, regarded the young as being most likely to challenge the existing social order, suggesting that adolescence has been around for a long time.

6 The three main components of adolescence according to the classical view are 'storm and stress', identity crisis, and the generation gap.

Section 2: Hall's and Erikson's theories

7 According to Hall (1904), each individual's psychological development 'recapitulates' the biological and cultural evolution of the human species.

8 Csikszentmihalyi & Larson's (1984) study of students showed that they were subject to extreme mood swings and could go from extreme happiness to deep sadness (and vice versa) in the space of an hour.

9 Rutter *et al.* (1976) discovered that there was very little difference in the rates of mental disorders between the three groups, suggesting that adolescence is not quite the period of 'storm and stress' which Hall suggests.

10 No, Hall's theory is not well-supported by research. For example, Siddique & D'Arcy (1984) found that 30 per cent of adolescents reported no symptoms of psychological distress and 40 per cent reported only mild levels.

11 Erikson (1963) challenged the view that personality development stops early in life (as was suggested by Freud, among others).

12 Erikson's (1963) epigenetic principle holds that the pattern of social and psychological growth in an individual is genetically determined.

13 Erikson believes that adolescents face the identity vs role confusion conflict, in which they must decide on an occupational role.

14 The positive (adaptive) outcome of this conflict is 'a sense of who one is', whereas the negative (maladaptive) outcome is a prolonged uncertainty about one's role in life.

15 Western societies see adolescence as a moratorium – an authorised delay of adulthood which frees adolescents from most responsibilities and helps them to make the transition into adulthood.

16 Ego identity is a firm sense of who one is and what one stands for.

17 Role confusion may show itself as an aimless drifting through occupations, as negative identity (drug taking or suicide), as fear of intimacy, or an inability to plan, work or study well.

18 Simmons & Rosenberg (1975) discovered that low self-esteem is more common in girls during early adolescence than in late childhood or late adolescence.

19 Erikson's research was largely based on white males from the middle classes and has therefore been criticised for androcentrism (Gilligan, 1982).

Section 3: Marcia's and sociological theories

20 Identity diffusion is a state in which the individual is in crisis and unable to formulate clear self-definition, goals or commitments, whereas identity foreclosure involves avoiding the crisis by rapidly committing oneself to a conventional goal without exploring other options.

21 No. Marcia's statuses are not necessarily sequential, and need not occur one after the other.

22 Meilman (1979) found that relatively few men achieve identity moratorium, an important status within Marcia's theory since he claims that it must precede identity achievement.

23 Sociologists see role change as an integral feature of adolescent development.

24 The generation gap represents the difference between the social norms of adults and adolescents and is significant, since sociologists claim that socialisation in adolescents is influenced more by their peer's generation than by their parent's.

25 No. In fact researchers such as Bandura & Walters (1959) and Fogelman (1976) found little disagreement between adolescents and parents.

26 Music, fashion, sexual behaviour (Noller & Callan, 1990), together with appearance and evening activities (Fogelman, 1976), are the areas likely to be most contentious.

Section 4: Coleman's focal theory

27 Coleman & Hendry (1990) point out that most other theories try to explain abnormal development through adolescence.

28 Focal theory tries to explain the relatively stable and stress-free transition which most adolescents manage to make into adulthood.

29 Coleman found that these concerns peaked at different ages, so that different concerns were paramount at different times.

30 Coleman believed that adolescents were able to cope with their concerns by dealing with them one at a time.

31 Focal theory predicts that adolescents forced to deal with more than one concern at a time will experience most stress.

32 No. Storm and stress, identity crisis and generation gap have not been found to occur in anything like the degree suggested by the classical view of adolescence.

Adolescence: begins at puberty and regarded as a prelude and preparation for adulthood. Spans ages 12–20 in Western societies.

Puberty: onset at 10 for girls and 12 for boys. Both males and females experience a growth spurt, peaking at 12 (girls) and 14 (boys) and experience sexual changes.

Hall's theory

- Hall believed that psychological development *recapitulates* the cultural and biological evolution of the human species.
- Adolescence was seen as a time of 'storm and stress', mirroring the conflicts of the last 2000 years.

Csikszentmihalyi & Larson (1984):
- Monitored the activities and feelings of high-school students every 2 hrs.
- Moods swung from extreme happiness to deep sadness within the course of 1 hour.

Most research rejects Hall
- Bandura & Walters (1959): adolescence is no more stressful than childhood or adulthood.
- Rutter *et al.* (1976) found only small differences in the rates of mental disorders between children, adults and adolescents.

Marcia's theory

Identified four 'statuses' of adolescent identity

Identity diffusion: Individual is in crisis, unable to define self, goals or commitments.

Identity foreclosure: Avoidance of uncertainties by rapid commitment to conventional goals.

Identity moratorium: Decisions about identity postponed whilst alternative identities are explored.

Identity achievement: Individual has experienced crisis but emerged with firm goals and ideology.

- Marcia does not see the stages as sequential; however, moratorium is necessary for identity achievement.
- Research suggests that relatively few men achieve moratorium, casting doubt on the four stages.

Coleman's focal theory

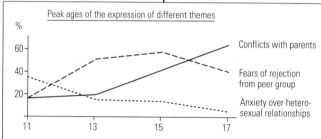

Peak ages of the expression of different themes

Conflicts with parents

Fears of rejection from peer group

Anxiety over hetero-sexual relationships

Coleman & Hendry (1990): *other* theories explain individuals (who are *abnormal*) with serious problems. They propose a theory of *normal* development, which accounts for the relatively *stable* transition made by most adolescents.
- Studied 800 boys and girls: concerns about issues reached peaks (*focused*) at different ages (see above).
- Adolescents cope with change by dealing with *one issue at a time*, spreading adaptation over years.
- Those who have to deal with more than one problem at a time are most likely to experience difficulties.

Sociological theory

Role change: starting college, starting work etc. produce new expectations which speed up the socialisation process.
Conflicting demands: made by family, mass media and peers may make this a difficult time.

Generation gap: may add to these problems as adolescents are more dependent on their own generation for socialisation.

Conflicting research
- Bandura & Walters (1959): the typical American adolescent tended to *accept* most parental values quite freely and associated with other adolescents who shared such values.
- The National Children's Bureau (Fogelman, 1976): in fact both children and adults agreed on most of the issues commonly thought to be areas of disagreement. Only major disagreements were *appearance* and *evening activities*.

Erikson's theory

- **Epigenetic principle:** the entire pattern of psychological and social growth is governed by genetics.
- **Psychosocial stages:** are universal, each centring around a crisis with two possible outcomes.
- The adolescent struggles to establish a strong sense of identity (*ego identity*).

Role confusion
The failure to integrate perceptions of the self into a coherent whole, shown in:
- fear of intimacy
- inability to plan for the future
- inability to work/study industriously
- negative identity (e.g drug addict/yob).

Research
- Offer *et al.* (1988): no increase in the disturbance of self-image during adolescence.
- Gilligan (1982): Erikson's sample was biased (largely middle-class, white males) and is only applicable to that group.

Stage	Personal and social relationships	Crisis or conflict	Possible outcome
0–1 year	*Mother*	Trust vs mistrust	Trust and faith in others or a mistrust of people.
2 yrs	*Parents*	Autonomy vs shame and doubt	Self-control and mastery or self-doubt and fearfulness.
3–5 years	*Family*	Initiative vs guilt	Purpose and direction or a loss of self-esteem.
6–11 years	*Neighbourhood and school*	Industry vs inferiority	Social and intellectual competence or failure to thrive and develop.
Adolescence	*Peer groups, outgroups, leaders*	Identity vs role confusion	A sense of 'who one is' or prolonged role uncertainty.
Early adult	*Friends, sexual partners*	Intimacy vs isolation	Formation of deep relationships or failure to love others.
Middle age	*Divided labour and shared household*	Generativity vs stagnation	Expansion of interests and caring for others or turning in on one's own problems.
Old age	*'Mankind', 'My kind'*	Integrity vs despair	Satisfaction with the triumphs and disappointments of life or unfulfilment and a fear of death.

EARLY AND MIDDLE ADULTHOOD

SYLLABUS

13.4 Adulthood – early and middle adulthood
- theories of development in early and middle adulthood (e.g. Levinson, Gould) including evidence for the existence of crises and transitions

KEY QUESTIONS
- How does Erikson view the changes which accompany adulthood?
- What does Levinson *et al.*'s *Seasons of a Man's Life* theory suggest?
- How does adult consciousness evolve, according to Gould?

Q Section 1: Erikson's theory

1 What name did Erikson give to the two crises which he believed everyone encounters in adulthood?
2 What is meant by the term *intimacy*?
3 Explain why *identity* is seen by Erikson as being a prerequisite for intimacy.
4 When would a person normally be expected to achieve intimacy?
5 What is the central task during the middle years of adulthood (40s and 50s)?
6 What is the negative consequence of failing at this task/crisis?
7 What important difference exists between the ways in which women and men achieve 'identity'?
8 According to Sanguiliano's (1978) research, what happens to a woman's identity, compared with a man's?
9 According to Sheehy (1996), to what age are many adults prolonging their 'adolescence'?
10 According to Orbach (cited in Beaumont, 1996), what is one problem with adults who refuse to grow up?

Section 2: Levinson *et al.*'s theory

11 How did Levinson *et al.* (1978) collect the data necessary to construct the *Seasons of a Man's Life* theory?
12 Complete the following sentence: 'According to Levinson *et al.*, adult development alternates between phases or periods which are _____ (or structure-_____) and _____ (or structure-_____)'.
13 What, according to Levinson *et al.*, is a person's *life structure*?
14 *Separation* is one of the key themes of the *early adult transition*. What is the difference between *internal* and *external* separation?
15 What are we trying to achieve when we work towards the *entry life structure for early adulthood*?

16 What is done during the *age-30 transition*?
17 Levinson *et al.* refer to the period between the ages of 33 and 40, as *settling down*. What is settling down?
18 What does BOOM stand for and what does it involve?
19 What are *marker events* and which of Levinson *et al.*'s phases are they most likely to accompany?
20 Complete the sentence: 'It is not possible to get through middle adulthood without having at least a moderate crisis in either _____-_____ _____ or _____-____ ____'.
21 Tredre (1996) believes that *downshifting* is often mistaken for a *mid-life crisis*. What is downshifting?

Section 3: Evaluating Levinson *et al.*

22 According to Durkin (1995), what percentage of people actually report experiencing a *crisis*?
23 Which marker events may accompany the *age-50 transition*?
24 Sheehy (1976) claims that men in their 40s begin exploring another aspect of themselves – what aspect?
25 According to Levinson's (1986) *gender-splitting* account, how do women and men differ in their dreams?
26 What is the key criticism of 'stage' theories of adult development (such as Levinson *et al.*'s and Erikson's), which suggest that we progress through inevitable and universal stages?
27 What consequences might *age deviancy* have for a person?

Section 4: Gould's theory

28 What, according to Gould's theory of the *evolution of adult consciousness*, is the thrust of adult development?
29 What name does Gould give to the illusion which he believes dominates our thinking during childhood?
30 With what do we replace a sense of parental dependency?
31 How is our *sense of time* affected during our mid-30s to mid-40s?

Section 1: Erikson's theory

1 Intimacy vs isolation and generativity vs stagnation are the names which Erikson gives to the two crises which everyone encounters in early and late adulthood respectively.

2 Intimacy is used by Erikson to refer to the ability to form close and meaningful relationships with others without fear of losing oneself.

3 Erikson views identity as the reconciliation of all our various roles into a stable personality, whilst intimacy requires us to give up some of our separateness. In order to do this we must first have established a stable sense of who we are.

4 Intimacy is usually achieved in a person's 20s or 30s.

5 The central task during the middle years of adulthood is to establish life's purpose and to focus on aims and achievements, including the aim of contributing to the well-being of others.

6 If we fail in the task of achieving generativity we 'stagnate', becoming preoccupied with our own needs and desires.

7 Men generally achieve identity before intimacy, but for many women these two tasks are fused. Women come to know themselves as they are known by others.

8 Sanguiliano (1978) claims that a woman's identity is submerged into that of her partner; she seeks separate identity only in mid-life.

9 Sheehy (1996) claims that many adults are prolonging adolescence into their 30s.

10 Adults who refuse to grow up may encounter problems with their own parenting, looking to their children for emotional support (Orbach: cited in Beaumont, 1996).

Section 2: Levinson *et al.*'s theory

11 Levinson *et al.*'s (1978) data were collected by interviewing 40 men aged 35–45 from a variety of backgrounds over a period of several months.

12 'According to Levinson *et al.*, adult development alternates between phases or periods which are *stable* (or structure-*building*) and *transitional* (or structure-*changing*).'

13 Life structure is the underlying pattern or design of a person's life at any given time.

14 Internal separation involves greater psychological separation from the family, whilst external separation involves greater physical separation (e.g moving out, financial independence).

15 The entry life structure for early adulthood is the first life-structure which we construct and its function is to provide a workable link between the valued self and adult society (i.e. to be the person you have become during adolescence, whilst at the same time taking on an adult role).

16 The age-30 transition is a time when the first life-structure can be reviewed and its flaws and limitations worked on.

17 Settling down is a consolidation of the second life-structure, a time when the individual makes strong commitments to a personal, familial and occupational future.

18 BOOM stands for becoming one's own man and involves striving to improve our skills, contribute to and be recognised by society whilst becoming self-sufficient.

19 Marker events are major life-events (such as divorce, illness, death of a loved one) and are most likely to accompany middle adulthood.

20 'It is not possible to get through middle adulthood without having at least a moderate crisis in either the *mid-life transition* or the *age-50 transition*.'

21 Downshifting is a term used by Tredre (1996) to describe voluntarily opting out of a pressurised career in pursuit of a more fulfilling way of life.

Section 3: Evaluating Levinson *et al.*

22 According to Durkin (1995), only ten per cent of people actually report experiencing a crisis.

23 Divorce, re-marriage, redundancy, serious illness, the death of a loved one and children leaving home, are all marker events which may accompany the age-50 transition.

24 Sheehy (1976) claims that men in their 40s begin to explore their feminine selves (by becoming more nurturant, affiliative and intimate).

25 Levinson's (1986) gender-splitting account maintains that men's dreams are usually unified, focusing on career goals, whereas women's dreams are often split between career and family.

26 'Stage' theories of adult development (such as Levinson *et al.*'s and Erikson's) are often criticised for overlooking the degree of individual variability in development from one person to the next.

27 Age deviancy (failure to comply with the norms for one's age-group) can result in social penalties such as ridicule, pity or rejection.

Section 4: Gould's theory

28 The thrust of adult development is the realisation and acceptance of ourselves as creators of our own lives, away from the dependencies of childhood.

29 The illusion of absolute safety is the name given by Gould to the illusion which dominates our thinking during childhood.

30 Parental dependency must be replaced with autonomy.

31 During our mid-30s to mid-40s, we feel that time is running out and develop a sense of urgency.

A

Erikson's theory

The individual faces two **crises**, each corresponding to a stage of development:

Intimacy vs isolation
Early adulthood (20s and 30s)
- The individual must be able to form close, meaningful relationships without fear of losing him-/herself (intimacy).
- To accomplish this, we need first to have established a firm sense of identity.
- If this does not happen, then isolation can result.

Generativity vs stagnation
Middle age (40s and 50s)
- The individual focuses on determining goals and achieving aims.
- **Generativity** means a concern for others beyond the family.
- Failure leads to **stagnation,** in which people become preoccupied with their own needs and desires.

- Men seem to achieve identity before intimacy, whereas for women the two tasks are often fused.
- Sangiuliano (1978): many women submerge their identities in partnerships and only search for separate identities in middle age.

Gould's theory

The evolution of adult consciousness
Adulthood is attained through freeing ourselves from childhood consciousness and illusions.

Gould's theory is an extension of the Freudian notion of *separation anxiety*.
- As we grow up, we have to free ourselves from **the illusion of absolute safety** which dominated childhood.
- This involves *transformations* which enable us to give up the past in order to form our own ideas.
- Parental dependency is replaced with a sense of **autonomy**.
- Our sense of *time* changes:
  – Up until 18 we are 'timeless' with infinite time before us.
  – In our 20s we are hurrying down a chosen path.
  – At the end of our 20s we must choose between options as we do not have time for them all.
  – During our mid-30s to mid-40s we feel that time is running out and become aware of our own mortality.

Levinson *et al.'s* theory

Seasons of a man's life
(Levinson *et al.*, 1978)
- Adult development comprises *eras* and *cross-era* transitions.
- Phases alternate between stable (*structure-building*) and transitional (*structure-changing*) periods.

Age	
65	**LATE ADULT TRANSITION**
60	Culmination of middle adulthood
55	Age-50 transition
50	Entering middle adulthood
45	**MID-LIFE TRANSITION**
40	Settling down
33	Age-30 transition
28	Entering the adult world
22	**EARLY ADULT TRANSITION**
17	Childhood & adolescence

Late adulthood / *Middle adulthood* / *Early adulthood*

Seasons of a man's life
Levinson *et al.* (1978)
- Interviewed 40 men aged 35–45, from a variety of occupations.
- Analysed tape-recordings made over several months.
- Advanced a *life-structure theory* (the underlying pattern of a person's life at a given time), according to which adult development passes through stable and transitional phases.
- Family and work roles are seen as central to the life structure at any time.

Seasons of a woman's life
Levinson's original work focused only on men. However, Levinson (1986) argues that a *gender-splitting* phenomenon occurs:
- Men tend to have *unified* 'dreams' which focus on career.
- Women's 'dreams' are more likely to be *split* between career and marriage.
- In addition, the transitory instability of early 30s lasts *longer* for women and the 'settling down' is much less clear cut for women, who may try to balance family and career.

Early adulthood (17–40)

Early adult transition (17–22)
Acts as a developmental 'bridge' between adolescence and adulthood.
- Incorporates the two themes of **separation**, both internal (e.g. less emotional dependence) and external (e.g. moving out) and **attachments** (forming links to the adult world).

Entering the adult world (22–28)
The first *structure-building* phase where we try to define ourselves as adults and live with our initial job, relationship and value choices.
- We try to strike a balance between '*keeping our options open*' and '*putting down roots*'.
- We try to keep the thread of our '**dreams**' alive in our choices and may look to *mentors* (more experienced others) for help.

Age-30 transition (28–33)
We work on the problems with the first life structure.
- Most people experience an **age-30 crisis** as they realise that life is becoming more serious and less provisional.

Settling down (33–40)
A consolidating period with more commitment to choices and planning for the future. Comprises two sub-stages:
- Early settling down (33–36).
- **BOOM** (36–40) '*becoming one's own man*': we want to contribute to society and be recognised as well as being self-sufficient.

Middle adulthood (40–60)

Mid-life transition (40–45)
A time of soul-searching when we terminate one life structure, initiate another, continuing the process of individuation started in BOOM.
- Sometimes referred to as a *mid-life crisis* where a re-assessment of life brings uncertainties and pain – though some find it fairly easy.

Entering middle adulthood (45–50)
We have resolved whether or not our commitments are worthwhile and make choices regarding a new life-structure.
- Changes may be influenced by *marker events* such as the death of a loved one, divorce, illness or change of job.

Age-50 transition (50–55)
Levinson *et al.* argue that middle adulthood cannot be reached without a crisis at either the mid-life transition or the age-50 transition.

Research
- Durkin (1995): only 10% of middle-aged people reported experiencing a crisis.
- Tredre (1996): the term 'crisis' is *misleading* in that often people are just *downshifting* (opting out of high-pressure lifestyles in favour of more fulfilling lives).
- Sheehy (1976): men begin to explore their more feminine sides and women their more masculine sides at this age.

Overall, although significant changes will occur at this age (such as death of parents, children leaving home), a crisis is not inevitable.

FAMILY AND RELATIONSHIPS IN ADULTHOOD

KEY QUESTIONS
- How are individuals affected by marriage and divorce?
- How are individuals affected by parenthood?
- How has the role of women in the workforce changed over the past 50 years?

Section 1: Introduction
1. What is a *normative age-graded influence?*
2. What is a *non-normative influence?*
3. What is the term used by Levinson (1986) to refer to events such as divorce, marriage and parenting?

Section 2: Marriage and divorce
4. What percentage of adults marries at least once?
5. When Davies (1956) looked at mental disorders occurring in those engaged to be married, what did he find regarding the sorts of events which triggered the disorders, and the sorts of events associated with their improvement?
6. Are cohabiting couples more or less likely to get divorced than couples who have not lived together before getting married? Why?
7. How are marriage and happiness, health and longevity related?
8. Bee (1994) argues that the greatest beneficiaries of marriage are men. Why is this?
9. According to Turnbull (1995), what pattern do divorce rates take?
10. When Woollett and Fuller (cited in Cooper, 1996b) investigated how mothers who had been divorced subsequently felt about their daily activities, what did they find?

Section 3: Parenthood
11. Describe the pattern of changes in marital satisfaction which takes place before and during parenthood?
12. What explanation do Levinson *et al.* (1978) offer for why unhappy couples might stay together?
13. What is the difference between *empty-nest distress* and *crowded-nest distress?*
14. What term is used to apply to the belief that women are born and reared to be, first and foremost, mothers?
15. Which implication of this belief may lead to women who do not bond immediately with their children feeling 'inadequate'?

16. What percentage of UK women, born between 1960 and 1990 are unlikely ever to become mothers?
17. According to the Pre-Family Lifestyles Report (1999), what percentage of people felt that having children early in adulthood outweighed the financial and career advantages?
18. Identify one further important implication of the belief that women are 'born mothers'.
19. How does the secondary employment sector differ from the primary employment sector?
20. Complete the sentence: 'Women comprise about half the workforce (although a far higher proportion are likely to be ____-____ than men)'.
21. What general conclusion was drawn by Kremer (1988) when reviewing several surveys into women's attitudes towards paid employment?
22. In what way does Hrdy (1999) use the term *compartmentalisation?*
23. Roughly what proportion of working women want to be homemakers, according to a recent UK survey conducted by *Top Sante* magazine and BUPA?
24. In a dual-earner family, which two main responsibilities is the woman nearly always responsible for?
25. Complete the sentence: 'Montgomery (1993) found that 82% of husbands had never ____, 73% had never ____ ____, and 24% had never ____'.
26. Which two aspects of fathers' behaviour did Pleck (1999) find had increased between the 1960s and the 1990s?
27. What does it mean to say that Pleck's findings suggest that American family life is changing in two contradictory directions?
28. According to Kitzinger *et al.* (1998), what was the main concern of initial research into gay/lesbian parenting?
29. How might one sum up the conclusions of this initial research into gay/lesbian parenting, according to Kitzinger?

Q

Section 1: Introduction

1 A normative age-graded influence is a biological or social change which occurs at a fairly predictable age (such as the menopause or retirement).

2 A non-normative influence is a change which is unpredictable and may occur at any time to different individuals (e.g. illness, unemployment).

3 Levinson (1986) uses the term *marker events* to refer to events such as divorce, marriage and parenting.

Section 2: Marriage and divorce

4 Ninety per cent of adults marry at least once.

5 Davies (1956) found that events which hinged on the marriage date (such as booking the reception) were most likely to trigger the disorders, whilst either breaking off the engagement or getting married tended to be associated with their improvement.

6 Cohabiting couples are more likely to get divorced than couples who have not lived together before getting married, possibly because of the type of individuals they tend to be, e.g. less conventional (Bee, 1994).

7 Married people are happier, healthier and live longer (on average) than their unmarried counterparts.

8 Bee (1994) believes that men are less likely to provide emotional support for their spouses than are women, leading to an inequitable exchange.

9 Turnbull (1995) claims that divorce rates are highest during the first five years of relationships, then subside, peaking again at between 15 to 20 years.

10 Woollett and Fuller (cited in Cooper, 1996b) found that mothers who had been divorced experienced a sense of achievement and of 'a job well done' in their everyday activities. Apparently, this is because their divorce 'galvanises' them into taking charge of their lives.

Section 3: Parenthood

11 Before parenthood, marital satisfaction is at its highest, dropping and remaining low with the arrival of children, then picking up when the children leave home.

12 Levinson *et al.* (1978) believed that unhappy couples might nevertheless stay together because of the satisfaction which they gain through their parenting roles.

13 Empty-nest distress is distress resulting from the departure of dependants, whilst crowded-nest distress results from the non-departure of dependants who have grown up but decide not to leave home.

14 The term *motherhood mystique/mandate* applies to the belief that women are born and reared to be, first and foremost, mothers.

15 The belief that motherhood comes 'naturally' may lead to women who do not bond immediately with their children feeling inadequate.

16 Twenty per cent of UK women, born between 1960 and 1990, are unlikely ever to become mothers (according to Jones, 1995).

17 Only three per cent of people felt that having children early in adulthood outweighed the financial and career advantages.

18 Further important implications are that many people would consider it 'unnatural/wicked' for a mother to leave her children, and that it is 'unnatural/wrong' for a mother of young children to go out to work.

19 The secondary employment sector is typically unstable, and offers poor working conditions and career prospects.

20 'Women comprise about half the workforce (although a far higher proportion are likely to be *part-time* than men).'

21 Kremer's (1988) review concluded that the overwhelming majority of working women preferred to be in paid employment, and most of those not in work would prefer to be.

22 Hrdy (1999) uses the term compartmentalisation to refer to the way in which modern women's lives separate out their productive and reproductive activities.

23 Roughly a third of working women want to be homemakers, according to a recent UK survey conducted by *Top Sante* magazine and BUPA.

24 In a dual-earner family the woman is still nearly always responsible for housework and childcare.

25 'Montgomery (1993) found that 82 per cent of husbands had never *ironed*, 73 per cent had never *washed clothes* and 24 per cent had never *cooked*.'

26 Pleck (1999) found that fathers' engagement and availability increased between the 1960s and the 1990s.

27 Pleck's findings suggest that whilst paternal involvement in childcare within two-parent families is increasing, the proportion of two-parent families is decreasing.

28 According to Kitzinger *et al.* (1998), the main concern of initial research into gay/lesbian parenting was whether or how far the children of gay/lesbian couples could be distinguished psychologically from those of heterosexuals.

29 Initial research into gay/lesbian parenting found that children of gay/lesbian parents were no more 'at risk' than children raised in heterosexual families.

Marriage and divorce

- Over 90% of adults marry at least once (so it is a normative age-graded influence).
- Involves personal commitment and financial responsibilities, and can be stressful.

Marriage
- Cramer (1994): married people tend to live longer, be **happier**, **healthier** and less likely to suffer mental disorders.
- Bee (1994): **men tend to benefit more** from marriage since women are more likely to provide emotional support than are men.
- Rutter & Rutter (1992): women are more likely to experience **career/family conflict**.

Divorce
- Turnbull (1995): divorce rates are highest during the first **5 years** of marriage, then peak again at **15–25 years**.
- Divorce is stressful on parents and children, with men experiencing more stress than women.
- Woollett & Fuller (cited in Cooper, 1996b): divorced mothers experience a greater **sense of achievement** in their everyday activities.

Cohabitation
Couples who live together before marriage are more likely to divorce later on and express less satisfaction with their marriage.
- Bee (1994): this is because cohabitees are likely to be less conventional and more likely to flout social traditions.

Parenthood

- 90% of people will become parents (Bee, 1994).
- Parenthood varies in meaning and impact more than any other transition and may occur within a wide range of ages.
- Turnbull (1995): the trend towards postponing childhood has led to increasing numbers of middle-aged parents with young children.

Adaptations
- Marital satisfaction tends to be highest before children and remains low whilst children are in the home, rising again in the post-parental phase.
- Bee (1994): new parents have less time for each other (e.g. conversation, sex, affection).
- Levinson *et al.* (1978): couples who are dissatisfied with the relationships may nevertheless stay together because of the satisfaction of the parental role.

Crowded and empty nests
- Durkin (1995): most parents do not find children's departure a distressing time (*empty-nest distress*).
- Durkin (1995): empty-nest distress in women may be related to the period in which they were brought up.
- Datan *et al.* (1987): 'crowded nests' (where grown-up children opt not to leave home) can be stressful.

Womanhood & motherhood

The **motherhood mystique/mandate** (the belief that women are born and reared to be, first and foremost, mothers) still exerted a powerful influence in the 1990s, with at least three important implications (identified by Berryman (in Lacey, 1998)):
- *Parenthood is seen as 'natural' and central to women* in a way that it isn't for men. Because families are smaller nowadays, many more women have only limited experience of children when they start their own families and they may experience the discovery that mothering doesn't come naturally with shock or even guilt. Jones (1995) found that 20% of women born between 1960 & 1990 are unlikely ever to become mothers, feeling that 'it's OK to go through life without ever having children'.
- *Women who leave their children are believed to be acting 'unnaturally'* or 'wickedly' in a way in which men would not. However, one in twenty absent parents is a woman suggesting that maternal absence is far more common than the 'motherhood mandate' would suggest.
- The third implication is that *it is 'unnatural' or 'wrong' for mothers of young children to go out to work*. This is discussed in more detail below.

Women in the work force
- Traditionally men have been seen as dominating the primary employment sector, typically with unbroken employment histories between leaving school & retirement, whilst women predominate in the secondary employment sector which is typically unstable and offers poor working conditions and prospects.
- At the end of the 1990s women comprise about *half* the workforce, although far more of these jobs are part-time and women are still more likely to interrupt their careers to look after children.

Attitudes to paid employment
- Kremer (1998): despite poorer working conditions, the vast majority of women prefer to be in employment and express higher job satisfaction than do men.
- Hrdy (1999): argues that from an evolutionary perspective women *should* be as ambitious as men, having to combine reproduction with work and compete for status among her female peers.
- However, a recent survey of 5000 UK women (conducted by *Top Sante* magazine & BUPA) found that 77% of employed women would give up their work tomorrow if they could, and almost a third wanted to be homemakers.

Atypical parenting

'New man'
- In families where both couples work, husbands report more marital dissatisfaction and conflicts over responsibilities than in 'traditional' couples (Nicholson, 1993).
- Although some domestic tasks are shared in 'dual-earner couples' the woman is still nearly always responsible for housework and childcare.
- A survey of UK husbands (Montgomery, 1993) found that 82% had never ironed, 73% had never washed clothes and 24% had never cooked.
- Pleck (1999) found that between the two periods 1960–1980 and 1980–1990 there had been increases in fathers' **engagement** with their children (the amount of interaction) and their **availability** (the amount of time spent near children). However, where couples were separated or divorced the *opposite* was true.

Step-parenthood
- In the early 1960s almost 90% of children grew up in homes with two biological, married parents. Now this is true for about 50% of children in the UK (Hetherington & Stanley-Hagan, 1999).
- This change is due to increases in divorce, cohabitation and out-of-wedlock childbearing.
- Nicholson *et al.* (1999) studied over 900 New Zealand children all of whom had lived in step-families between ages 6 & 16. They were found to be more likely to become juvenile offenders, nicotine-dependent, to abuse illegal substances, leave school without qualifications, engage in early sexual activity and have multiple sexual partners. However, many of these differences disappeared when factors such as socioeconomic status or histories of instability were taken into account.

Lesbian and gay parenting
- Early research into homosexual parenting focused on how the children of lesbian relationships differed from those of heterosexuals.
- Such studies showed that children of homosexual parents showed no increased likelihood of being disturbed or of suffering gender identity confusion than those of heterosexual parents. Barrett & Robinson (1994) showed that children of homosexual parents were in little danger of being sexually abused, and adjust well to their family situations.
- More recent research has attempted to consider homosexual relationships without simply comparing them to heterosexual ones – for example, by considering how homosexual individuals may develop a positive self-image in a predominantly heterosexual culture.

167

COGNITIVE CHANGES IN LATE ADULTHOOD

KEY QUESTIONS
- What is old age?
- What physical and psychological changes take place in old age?
- What theories have been advanced to explain social changes in old age?

Q

Section 1: Introducing old age

1 Kastenbaum (1979) identified four distinct 'ages of me' – to which of these does the expression 'You're only as old as you feel' refer?
2 What is a person's *biological age*?
3 What is one of the dangers, related to these 'ages of me', associated with *ageism*?
4 What are some of the difficulties shared by all of the sub-groups of 'the elderly'?
5 According to the *accumulated-damages theory*, why does ageing occur?

Section 2: Physical and psychological changes

6 Why do the elderly take longer to recover from stressful conditions than the young?
7 What general conclusions about the relationship between ageing and cognitive abilities can be drawn from *longitudinal studies*?
8 What is the difference between *crystallised intelligence* and *fluid intelligence*?
9 Which of these two types of intelligence is most likely to decrease with age?
10 Does recall decline or improve in older adults, as compared with younger adults?
11 What percentage of people over 65 show significant deterioration of the kind associated with dementia?
12 Complete the following sentence: 'When Levy & Langer (1994) compared hearing Americans, deaf Americans and Chinese on their performance on memory tasks, they found that, amongst older participants, _____ towards _____ and memory performance were positively correlated'.
13 What explanation did Levy and Langer offer for the decline of memory abilities?

Section 3: Theories of ageing

14 According to Cumming (1975), social disengagement involves two related withdrawals. What are they?
15 According to *social disengagement theory*, what is the appropriate and successful way to age?

16 Bromley (1988) offered three main criticisms of social disengagement theory. What was his *practical* criticism of it?
17 Some psychologists believe that disengagement is not the most successful way of entering old age. How did Havighurst *et al.*'s (1968) study support this view?
18 According to *activity theory*, from what does decreased social interaction in old age result?
19 What is meant by saying that it is important for older adults to maintain their role counts?
20 In what way do *lifespan theorists* differ from activity or disengagement theorists in their views of adjustment to old age?
21 *Social exchange theory* sees the process of adjusting to old age as a sort of *contract* between the individual and society. What is involved in this contract?
22 According to Erikson (1963), why is it inevitable that we face a conflict between *ego-integrity* and *despair* in old age?

Section 4: Retirement and bereavement

23 What is an important difference between unemployment and retirement?
24 What change are many couples likely to experience in their relationship, immediately following retirement?
25 What factors are most likely to contribute to *disenchantment* during this phase of retirement?
26 What happens during the *termination phase*?
27 Complete the following sentence: 'Bromley (1988) believes that it is the _____ between employment and retirement that causes adjustment problems'.
28 Define the terms *bereavement*, *grief* and *mourning*.
29 Engel (1962) believes there are three phases of *griefwork*, of which *developing awareness* is the second. What are the other two?
30 Ramsay & de Groot (1977) believe that grief comprises not phases but components. Name any five.
31 What is Lieberman's (1993) criticism of traditional bereavement research and its underlying assumption about bereavement?

Section 1: Introducing old age

1 The expression 'You're only as old as you feel' refers to a person's subjective age, according to Kastenbaum's (1979) 'ages of me'.

2 A person's biological age refers to the state of the face and body (how old a person appears to others).

3 Ageism encourages us to think that people's chronological age is an accurate indicator of their biological, subjective and functional ages – it may well not be.

4 All of the sub-groups of 'the elderly' share to some degree the problems of reduced income, failing health and the loss of loved ones.

5 Accumulated-damages theory claims that ageing is a consequence of the damage resulting from the wear-and-tear of living.

Section 2: Physical and psychological changes

6 The elderly take longer to recover from stressful conditions, because their immune systems function less effectively.

7 Longitudinal studies have suggested that some people retain their intellects well into middle age and beyond, contradicting the cross-sectional studies. However, these studies did find some changes in the nature of intelligence and memory.

8 Crystallised intelligence results from accumulated knowledge, whilst fluid intelligence refers to the ability to solve novel and unusual problems.

9 Fluid intelligence is most likely to decrease with age.

10 Generally, recall declines in older adults. However, some studies (e.g. Maylor's (1994) study of *Mastermind* contestants) have found improvements.

11 Ten per cent of people over 65 show significant deterioration of the kind associated with dementia.

12 'When Levy & Langer (1994) compared hearing Americans, deaf Americans and Chinese on their performance on memory tasks, they found that amongst older participants, *attitudes* towards *ageing* and memory performance were positively correlated.'

13 Levy and Langer argued that the self-fulfilling prophecy could account for the findings, whereby people with low expectations maintain their abilities less.

Section 3: Theories of ageing

14 Social disengagement involves withdrawal of society from the individual and withdrawal of the individual from society (Cumming, 1975).

15 According to social disengagement theory, the appropriate and successful way to age is to withdraw from society and to accept this withdrawal.

16 Bromley's (1988) practical criticism of social disengagement theory was that it encouraged segregation of and negative attitudes towards the elderly.

17 Havighurst *et al.*'s (1968) study found that the most active and 'engaged' of the elderly were the most content individuals.

18 Decreased social interaction in old age results from a withdrawal of society from the ageing individual which is not desired by the individual.

19 It is important for older adults to maintain their role counts (that is, the different roles which they have to play in society) if they are to maintain their levels of activity.

20 Lifespan theorists see adjustment to old age as an extension of personality styles, and as continuous with other periods in an individual's life rather than discontinuous.

21 The contract proposed by social exchange theory involves individuals giving up their roles as economically active members of society in exchange for increased leisure time and fewer responsibilities.

22 Erikson (1963) claims that the psychosocial stages are an inevitable result of biological, psychological and social forces.

Section 4: Retirement and bereavement

23 In most cases, retirement is anticipated whereas unemployment is usually sudden and unexpected.

24 Many couples will find themselves spending an increased amount of time together, following retirement.

25 Unrealistic pre-retirement fantasies and inadequate preparation for retirement are both likely to contribute to disenchantment.

26 The termination phase involves illness or disability which makes self-care difficult, possibly resulting in a sick or disabled role.

27 'Bromley (1988) believes that it is the *transition* between employment and retirement that causes adjustment problems.'

28 Bereavement refers to the loss, through death, of a loved one, grief to the psychological and physical reactions to bereavement, and mourning to the observable expression of grief.

29 The other two phases of griefwork are disbelief and shock, and resolution (Engel, 1962).

30 Ramsay & de Groot (1977) believed that shock, disorganisation, denial, depression, guilt, anxiety, aggression, resolution and reintegration, comprise the nine components of grief.

31 Lieberman (1993) criticises traditional bereavement research for its assumption that we need to 'recover' from bereavement and 'return to normal', rather than adapting to it.

Adjustment to Late Adulthood

The meaning of 'old'

Ages of me (Kastenbaum, 1979)
- **Chronological age:** my age in years starting from birth.
- **Biological age:** the state of my face and body.
- **Subjective age:** the age that I feel.
- **Functional age:** my status and lifestyle.

Ageism: beliefs about a group based solely on their chronological age. Dangerous since chronological age is not an accurate indicator of the other ages.

Theories of ageing
Genetic clock/programmed theory: ageing is built into every organism through a genetic code which tells cells when to stop working.
Accumulated damages theory: ageing is a consequence of damage resulting from the wear-and-tear of living.

Sub-groups of 'the elderly' (Burnside *et al.*, 1979)
- **The young old (60–69):** a major transition – adaptations to new roles and the loss of income.
- **The middle-aged old (70–79):** loss of friends and illness. Reduced participation and declining health.
- **The old old (80–89):** difficulty in adapting/interacting with surroundings. Need help maintaining social contacts.
- **The very old old (90–99):** altering activities to make the most of what they have – can be joyful and serene.

Decrement model: sees ageing as a process of decay or decline in physical and intellectual abilities and in social relationships.

Personal growth model: stresses the advantages of 'old age' (e.g increase in leisure time, reduced responsibilities).

Cognitive changes

Intelligence

Crystallised intelligence
Results from accumulated knowledge (e.g. reasoning skills). Linked to background and education and is measured by tests of general information.

Performance *increases* with age and improves until near the end of life (Horn, 1982).

Explanations
- A tendency to add to our knowledge as we grow older.
- Regular use of crystallised intelligence (Denney & Palmer, 1981).

Fluid intelligence
The ability to solve novel and unusual problems. Allows us to perceive and draw inferences about patterns of stimuli. Measured by tests using novel problems.

Performance *declines* with age, peaking between 20 and 30 (Schaie & Hertzog, 1983).

Explanations
- May be due to reduced neurological functioning.
- Low use – few challenges to use our fluid intelligence (Cavanaugh, 1995).

Memory

Research
- **Recall tests:** older adults generally perform more poorly. However, older Mastermind contestants tended to score more highly (Maylor, 1994).
- **Recognition tests:** differences between older and younger people are slight.
- **Everyday memory:** the elderly do have difficulty recalling events from their youth (Miller & Morris, 1993).
- **Dementia** (e.g Alzheimer's disease): 90% of people above 65 show little deterioration (Diamond, 1978).
- **Activity:** Rogers *et al.* (1990) found that those who kept mentally active were most likely to keep their cognitive abilities.

The influence of stereotypes
- Levy & Langer (1994): studied Americans, deaf-Americans and Chinese. Positive attitudes towards ageing and memory performance were positively correlated.

Conclusion: negative attitudes about ageing may become self-fulfilling prophecies, where low expectations cause a reduction in activities that help maintain memory abilities.

Social changes

Social disengagement theory
- Cumming (1975): social disengagement is the withdrawal of society from the individual and the withdrawal from society of the individual.
- Cumming: three aspects of disengagement:
  1. Shrinkage of life space: fewer interactions and roles.
  2. Increased individuality: governed by fewer rules/expectations.
  3. Acceptance of change: the individual accepts disengagement.

Evaluation: Bromley (1988) 1. the theory encourages negative attitudes towards and segregation of the elderly, 2. it is not a proper theory but a collection of loosely related assumptions, 3. that older people may in fact be more likely to seek engagement.

Psychosocial theory
Erikson (1963): the individual faces a conflict between *ego-integrity* (positive) and *despair* (negative).
Ego integrity involves:
- believing that life does have a purpose and makes sense
- believing that all of life offers something of value
- seeing our parents in a more sympathetic light
- seeing that we share with all others the cycle of birth, life and death.

Despair involves a fear of death and the feeling that it is too late to undo the past.

Activity (re-engagement) theory
- Older people are essentially the same as middle-aged people with similar psychological and social needs. Decreased social interaction is the result of society withdrawing and is often not wanted.
- Optimal ageing involves staying active and maintaining interactions, especially by maintaining a high number of roles.

However, each individual selects styles best suited to them.

Social exchange theory
- Dyson (1980): both disengagement and activity theories fail to take into account physical and economic factors and as a result are *prescriptive* (tell us what the elderly *should* be doing).
- It is more useful to see adjusting to ageing as a *contract* between the individual and society, in which we give up our economically active roles in return for more leisure time and fewer responsibilities.

Retirement

Unlike unemployment, retirement is expected and bearable. Couples may find themselves spending more time together and the transition to an economically unproductive role can be stressful. People who retire *voluntarily* have less difficulty adjusting, but it's important to bear in mind that retirement is a role and a process involving stages:

6 phases in retirement (Atchley, 1982)

Pre-retirement: anxiety about lifestyle changes, ➤ **Honeymoon:** euphoria, sense of freedom ➤ **Disenchantment:** 'let down', depression ➤ **Reorientation:** more realistic expectations, new avenues explored, ➤ **Stability:** mastery of the retirement role ➤ **Termination:** illness/disability role.

Research
- Bromley (1988): it is the *transition* from work to retirement which causes problems. People who are active in retirement experience fewer problems.
- Campbell (1981): retirement is an 'honourable' status, unlike unemployment and a proper reward, not a symbol of failure.

Bereavement

Three phases of 'griefwork'
Engel (1962)
Griefwork: the process of mourning through which the bereaved adjust to loss:
1. **Disbelief and shock:** refusal to accept truth.
2. **Developing awareness:** gradual realisation of what has happened. Often accompanied by guilt, apathy, exhaustion and anger.
3. **Resolution:** The individual fully accepts what has happened and establishes a new identity.

Components of grief Ramsay & de Groot (1977)
Shock: 'numbness' can include *depersonalisation* and *derealisation*.
Disorganisation: inability to do simple tasks.
Denial: behaving as if deceased were still alive.
Depression: 'despair' or 'desperate pining' are common following denial.
Guilt: over angry thoughts or imagined neglect.
Anxiety: fear of losing control, the future.
Aggression: irritability and outbursts towards God, doctors, deceased, family.
Resolution: emerging acceptance of the death.
Reintegration: reorganising one's life alone.

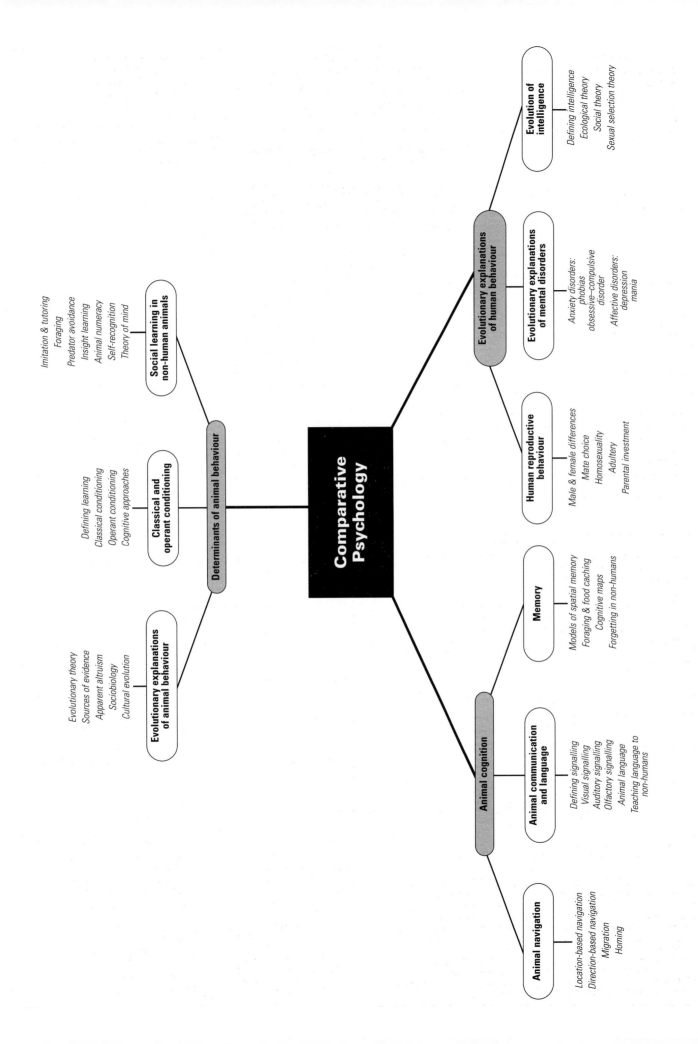

Comparative Psychology

Determinants of animal behaviour

Evolutionary explanations
of animal behaviour

Evolutionary theory
Sources of evidence
Apparent altruism
Sociobiology
Cultural evolution

Classical and
operant conditioning

Defining learning
Classical conditioning
Operant conditioning
Cognitive approaches

Social learning in
non-human animals

Imitation & tutoring
Foraging
Predator avoidance
Insight learning
Animal numeracy
Self-recognition
Theory of mind

**Evolutionary explanations
of human behaviour**

Human reproductive
behaviour

Male & female differences
Mate choice
Homosexuality
Adultery
Parental investment

Evolutionary explanations
of mental disorders

Anxiety disorders:
phobias
obsessive–compulsive
disorder
Affective disorders:
depression
mania

Evolution of
intelligence

Defining intelligence
Ecological theory
Social theory
Sexual selection theory

Animal cognition

Animal navigation

Location-based navigation
Direction-based navigation
Migration
Homing

Animal communication
and language

Defining signalling
Visual signalling
Auditory signalling
Olfactory signalling
Animal language
Teaching language to
non-humans

Memory

Models of spatial memory
Foraging & food caching
Cognitive maps
Forgetting in non-humans

44

EVOLUTIONARY EXPLANATIONS OF ANIMAL BEHAVIOUR

SYLLABUS
13.5 Determinants of animal behaviour – evolutionary explanations of animal behaviour
- evolutionary explanations of the behaviour of non-human animals including biological explanations of apparent altruism

KEY QUESTIONS
- How does evolution explain the origin of species?
- How can apparent altruism between individuals be explained?
- How does sociobiology explain the evolution of behaviour?

Q

Section 1: Evolution
1 How can *comparative psychology* be defined?
2 Complete the sentence: 'Comparative psychologists believe that most of the differences between animals are ____ rather than ____'.
3 Who is the author of the '*theory of evolution by natural selection*'?
4 Why are some members of a species more likely to survive than others?
5 What are the two factors which must occur for evolution to take place?
6 What is the *nature vs nurture debate* as it applies to the evolution of species?
7 What is *penetrance*, in this context?
8 What is the difference between *phylogeny* and *ontogeny*?
9 Name two sources of evidence for evolution.
10 What was Kettlewell's (1955) explanation for the increase in numbers of the dark form of the peppered moth in areas like Manchester?
11 Define *fitness*.
12 Define *inclusive fitness*.
13 In what way is the song of the white-crowned sparrow subject to both instinct and learning?
14 What is *convergent evolution*?
15 What is a common explanation for the emergence of analogous behaviours between species?
16 What does Skuse (1997) believe that girls are genetically pre-programmed to do?

Section 2: Apparent altruism
17 Define *altruism*.
18 In what way is the blackbird frequently altruistic?
19 How does *kin selection theory* (Hamilton, 1964) explain apparent altruism?

20 How much more altruistic would we expect an individual to be towards its own offspring than towards a nephew?
21 Which observation made by Bertram (1976) regarding the behaviour of lionesses is difficult for kin selection theory to explain?
22 What explanation for non-kin helping is proposed by reciprocal altruism theory?
23 Which impressive example of reciprocal altruism is used by Wilkinson (1984)?
24 Under what conditions would 'cheating' be an effective strategy in a population of reciprocal altruists?
25 What is the name of the game used by Axelrod & Hamilton (1981) to model co-operation or defection between two individuals?
26 What name is given to the winning strategy in this game?

Section 3: Additional approaches
27 How can *sociobiology* be defined?
28 How does sociobiology differ from classical studies of animal behaviour?
29 What name is given to the theory which proposes that what appears to be altruistic at the individual level is actually selfish at the gene level?
30 On a human level what process may be considered to have overtaken genetic evolution?
31 What name is given to a set of behaviour patterns which, if adopted by most of the population, cannot be bettered by any other strategy?
32 What is the main reason why cultural transmission of behaviour is more powerful than genetic transmission of behaviour?
33 What example of cultural transmission of behaviour was observed by Sherry & Galef (1984) amongst blue tits?

Section 1: Evolution

1 Comparative psychology may be defined as the study of the behaviour of animals with a view to drawing comparisons between them.

2 Comparative psychologists believe that most of the differences between animals are *quantitative* rather than *qualitative*.

3 Charles Darwin.

4 Because there is competition for resources, some members of a species will be better equipped to survive.

5 In order for evolution to take place the environment must select certain individuals (natural selection) and the differences between individuals must be inherited to some extent.

6 In relation to evolution, the nature vs nurture debate concerns how much variability within a species is due to genetic factors, and how much depends on the environment.

7 Penetrance refers to the degree to which learning and inheritance interact.

8 Phylogeny refers to inherited, species-specific behaviour patterns, whilst ontogeny refers to behaviour patterns acquired during the lifetime of the individual.

9 Sources of evidence for evolution include palaeontology, comparative anatomy, geographical distribution and artificial selection.

10 Kettlewell believed that the darker form of the moth was better camouflaged in industrial areas and less likely, therefore, to be spotted by predators.

11 Fitness can be defined as a measure of the ability of individuals to leave behind offspring.

12 Inclusive fitness may be defined as the total number of an animal's genes present in subsequent generations.

13 If isolated from other white-crowned sparrows during the first 50 days of life, a male sparrow will produce 'sub-song' but not the full adult song.

14 Convergent evolution occurs when similar behaviours evolve independently in a number of unrelated species.

15 Analogous behaviours may emerge between unrelated species when both are subject to similar environmental pressures.

16 Skuse believes that girls are genetically pre-programmed to learn to interpret social cues.

Section 2: Apparent altruism

17 Altruism can be defined as the performance of a behaviour which enhances the fitness of the recipient whilst lowering the fitness of the performer (the altruist).

18 A blackbird will give an alarm call on detecting a potential predator – this benefits individuals nearby whilst drawing attention to the bird giving the call.

19 Kin selection theory suggests that traits which directed an individual's altruism towards its relatives, but not its non-relatives, would evolve.

20 Since an individual shares 50 per cent of its genes with offspring and only 25 per cent with nephews we would expect it to be twice as altruistic.

21 Lionesses will allow cubs from another lioness in the pride to suckle from them.

22 Reciprocal altruism theory proposes that an altruist may help another individual, so long as they are later 'repaid' by this individual.

23 Wilkinson uses the example of vampire bats, which will regurgitate blood for starving roost-mates.

24 Cheating could only be effective if the altruists had poor memories, and could therefore not remember which individuals had not reciprocated.

25 Axelrod & Hamilton (1981) used the prisoner's dilemma to model co-operation or defection.

26 Tit for tat is the name of the winning strategy.

Section 3: Additional approaches

27 Sociobiology can be defined as the systematic study of the biological basis of all social behaviour.

28 Sociobiology differs from classical studies of animal behaviour in that it considers the set of genes, rather than the individual, as the basic unit of evolution.

29 This theory has been called the *selfish gene theory*.

30 Cultural evolution may be considered to have overtaken genetic evolution.

31 Such strategies are termed *evolutionarily stable strategies*.

32 Cultural transmission of behaviour is considerably faster than genetic transmission of behaviour.

33 Sherry & Galef (1984) observed that blue tits had learned from one another how to remove foil tops from milk bottles in order to drink the milk.

A

Nature vs nurture

This debate concerns the relative contributions to the individual made by nature (inherited characteristics) and nurture (acquired characteristics).

- Any behaviour has an element of both *phylogeny* (inherited, species-specific behaviour) and *ontogeny* (idiosyncratic behaviours acquired by an individual during their lifetime).

- Charles Darwin's **'theory of evolution by natural selection'** explained the way in which new species arise.
- Individuals within a species differ from one another. Much of this variation is inherited (*genetic variation*). These same individuals compete for scarce resources so competition means that certain members are more likely to survive and reproduce than others. Over time, this *'natural selection'* can lead to the considerable differences between species.

Evidence for evolution

- Paleontology: fossil records may show change.
- Comparative anatomy: resemblances between the anatomy of animals.
- Geographical distribution: similar animals in different areas of the world may suggest a common ancestor.
- Artificial selection: breeding of domesticated animals mimicks natural selection and leads to differences.

Evolution

Comparative psychology: the study of the behaviour of animals with a view to drawing comparisons (similarities and differences) between them.

Evolutionary Explanations of Animal Behaviour

Research – the peppered moth

Exists in two genetically determined forms – light and dark. The dark type was first reported in Manchester in 1849 but by 1900 had almost replaced the light type.

Explanation: Kettlewell (1955) found that in areas of industrial pollution the lighter moths were more likely to be eaten by birds, as they were less well camouflaged.

Behaviour

Darwin claims that all species are genetically related, whilst Grier & Burk (1992) suggest that nearly all behaviour is influenced by genetic factors. It seems likely, therefore that behaviours are shared within and across species. Since these behaviours may affect the reproductive success of an individual they will be subject to natural selection & evolution. The central question when examining animal behaviour is 'how does this behaviour affect the individual's ability to reproduce?'.

Instinctive and learned behaviour

- Instinctive behaviours are especially important for animals with short lifespans or little/no parental care, whilst learned behaviours can help animals to adapt their behaviours to their environment. An interaction between the two is the norm.
- Seligman (1970) suggested that animals are biologically *prepared* to learn some things more readily than others (e.g. humans fear spiders more commonly than would be predicted by learning alone).
- Ridley (1995) observes that young male white-crowned sparrows, if isolated from other sparrows during the 'sensitive period' do not produce the fully developed adult song, but only 'sub-song'. This suggests that the birdsong requires both instinct and learning.

Evidence for the evolution of behaviour

The best evidence comes from intraspecies comparisons. From the *phylogenetic tree* we can infer whether common behaviour patterns are *homologous* (species share a common ancestor) or *analogous* (unrelated organisms have developed similar behaviours in isolation).

- *Convergent evolution:* similar behaviours evolve in unrelated species (e.g. termites & bees). Often due to common environmental pressures. *Divergent evolution:* the emergence of different behaviours among related species (e.g. mating rituals among ducks).
- Skuse (1997) suggests that girls are genetically preprogrammed to learn to interpret social cues – since normal females may possess a cluster of 'social skills' genes present on the X chromosome but absent on the Y chromosome (which males possess).

Apparent altruism

- **Altruism** can be defined as the performance of a behaviour which enhances the fitness of the recipient, whilst lowering the fitness of the performer (the altruist).
- *Example:* a blackbird will give an alarm call when detecting a predator. This benefits individuals nearby whilst drawing the predator's attention to the blackbird sounding the alarm.
- **The paradox of altruism:** animals which performed selfless behaviours in a competitive world would lose out in the race for survival and should die out. They should not exist.
- **Inclusive fitness:** 'the total number of an animal's genes present in subsequent generations' (Dawkins, 1989) may help to solve the problem.

Kin selection theory (Hamilton, 1964)

- Suggests that traits which directed an individual's altruism towards its relatives but not to non-relatives would evolve. Genes promoting altruism therefore survive via inclusive fitness.
- Since kin selection relies on altruists helping relatives, the closer the relative the more altruistic behaviour we would expect (since close relatives share more genetic material).
- Bertram (1976): in a 'typical' pride of lions the males tended to be more closely related than the females. He found that males were, indeed, more likely to demonstrate altruism towards one another than the females. However, females allow the cubs of another female to suckle from them – which cannot be explained by kin selection.

Reciprocal altruism

- Animals that help one another are not always related. Packer & Pusey (1983) found that Tanzanian lions would form co-operative groups of non-relatives. Trivers (1971) proposed that one individual may help another in order to be later 'repaid' (i.e. altruism is an 'investment').
- Wilkinson (1984) found that vampire bats would demonstrate altruism towards relatives or unrelated roost-mates: bats will regurgitate blood for individuals who might otherwise starve. In the long run the benefit of avoiding starvation outweighs the cost of giving up a small amount of food. However, this system can only work if animals remember and recognise individuals who will reciprocate, thereby avoiding 'cheats'.
- Axelrod & Hamilton (1981) used the '*prisoner's dilemma*' to model co-operative/ cheating strategies. They found the best strategy to be a '*tit-for-tat*' approach in which individuals retaliate in response to cheating but are forgiving and resume co-operation.

Sociobiology

Sociobiology: the systematic study of the biological basis of all social behaviour, including altruism, aggression and sexual behaviour (Hamilton, 1964; Wilson, 1975).

- Considers the set of genes (rather than the individual) to be the basic unit of evolution.
- Dawkins' (1989) '*selfish gene*' theory suggests that it is not as important for the individual to survive as it is for their genes to survive. Behaviours may ultimately be in the 'interests' of genes rather than individuals (though these often coincide).
- From 'the gene's point of view' the body is a sort of survival machine/host created to enhance its chances of replication.
- In humans '*cultural evolution*' can be seen as analogous to genetic evolution. Ideas or behaviours compete with one another to bring about success. Unlike genes, however, cultural evolution can happen very rapidly and does not require genetic transmission.

Sociobiologists will sometimes talk about genes as though they were sentient (e.g. the 'interests' of genes). This is really only a shorthand way of describing the complex adaptive strategies which develop as a result of 'blind' natural selection.

Evolutionarily stable strategies

Kin selection theory

- An *evolutionarily stable strategy* (ESS) is a behaviour pattern which cannot be bettered by any other strategy if most of the population adopt it. This does not mean that, in isolation, it is the best strategy but simply that in a population an individual cannot behave differently and be more successful.
- For example: you might think that a male who, instead of parenting, abandoned his offspring in favour of mating with as many females as possible would have more offspring. However, if the female is less able to raise offspring when on her own, it is likely that this genetic type of male will die out.
- The *optimum strategy* can vary according to environmental conditions: the male dunnock (a type of bird) will desert his mate and fledgelings if the season has provided an abundance of food.

174

45

CLASSICAL AND OPERANT CONDITIONING

SYLLABUS

13.5 Determinants of animal behaviour – classical and operant conditioning
- the nature of classical and operant conditioning and their role in the behaviour of non-human animals

KEY QUESTIONS
- How can learning be defined?
- What processes are involved in classical conditioning?
- What processes are involved in operant conditioning?
- What other theories of learning exist?

Section 1: Introducing learning

1 Why is learning theory so important from the behavioural perspective?

2 What does it mean to say that learning is a *hypothetical construct*?

3 Complete the definition: 'Learning is the process by which relatively permanent changes occur in __ __ as a result of experience'.

4 What is the distinction between *learning* and *performance*?

5 What is the name of the theorist responsible for drawing a distinction between *operant* and *respondent* behaviour?

Section 2: Classical conditioning

6 What is the technical name for a stimulus which naturally produces a response?

7 What happens during the second stage of classical conditioning (during learning)?

8 What is a *neutral* stimulus?

9 What is the difference between *delayed conditioning* and *trace conditioning*?

10 How effective is *backward conditioning*?

11 How does *generalisation* differ from *discrimination*?

12 What technical term is used to describe the cessation of a conditioned response after the conditioned stimulus is repeatedly presented in the absence of the unconditioned stimulus?

Section 3: Operant conditioning

13 What, according to Skinner (1938), are the important differences between *classical* and *operant conditioning*?

14 What behaviours did Thorndike (1898) observe when he placed cats in 'puzzle-boxes', rewarding them when they escaped?

15 What is Thorndike's (1898) *law of effect*?

16 What are the key features of a Skinner box?

17 What terms did Skinner introduce to replace Thorndike's 'stamping in' and 'stamping out' of a response?

18 What, according to Skinner's analysis of behaviour, is the *ABC of operant conditioning*?

19 Complete the following Skinnerian quotation: 'Behaviour is ___ and maintained by its ___'.

20 What three classes of consequence can result from a behaviour?

21 Which of these three *strengthen* behaviours?

22 What is the difference between a *primary reinforcer* and a *secondary reinforcer*?

23 Which schedule of reinforcement leads to behaviours which are the most easily extinguished?

24 Which schedule of reinforcement leads to the most resistant behaviours?

25 What type of reinforcement schedule is involved in being paid on commission?

26 What is *shaping*?

27 What applications has *shaping* had in the area of human behaviour?

28 Why, according to Skinner, is positive reinforcement a much more potent influence on behaviour than punishment?

29 What is the *law of contiguity*?

30 What, according to Seligman (1970), is *preparedness*?

31 Why, according to Mackintosh (1978, 1995), can we not reduce conditioning to the strengthening of stimulus–response connections through an automatic process called reinforcement?

Section 4: Cognitive approaches

32 In Tolman & Honzik's (1930) experiment with rats running mazes, what behaviour was especially significant?

33 How did Tolman explain this significant behaviour?

34 What is a *cognitive map*?

35 What do *social learning theorists* believe intervenes between stimulus and response?

36 What is *observational learning*?

37 What is a key factor in determining whether or not a model's behaviour is imitated?

Section 1: Introducing learning

1 Behaviourists believe that psychology is the study of behaviour, and that learning plays a central role in determining behaviour.

2 It means that learning cannot be directly observed but only inferred from observable behaviour.

3 'Learning is the process by which relatively permanent changes occur in *behavioural potential* as a result of experience.'

4 Learning can be seen as an organism's behavioural potential, whilst performance is the actual behaviour exhibited by an organism.

5 B.F. Skinner was the first psychologist to draw a distinction between operant and respondent behaviour.

Section 2: Classical conditioning

6 An unconditioned stimulus is a stimulus which naturally produces a response.

7 During learning, the unconditioned stimulus is paired with a conditioned stimulus until the conditioned stimulus produces the response previously produced by the unconditioned stimulus.

8 A neutral stimulus is a stimulus which does not produce the conditioned response.

9 Delayed conditioning involves presenting the CS before and during the UCS, whilst in trace conditioning the CS is presented and removed before the UCS is presented.

10 Backward conditioning produces little, if any, learning in laboratory animals.

11 In generalisation the CR transfers spontaneously to stimuli similar to the original CS, whilst in discrimination the organism makes a different response to stimuli which differ from the CS.

12 Extinction describes the cessation of a conditioned response after the conditioned stimulus is repeatedly presented in the absence of the unconditioned stimulus.

Section 3: Operant conditioning

13 Skinner (1938) saw operant conditioning as an active process in which organisms operate on their environment, bringing about certain consequences, which in turn affect the likelihood of the behaviour being repeated.

14 Thorndike (1898) found that learning was initially trial-and-error; after the cats had escaped once, their escape times on successive trials decreased rapidly (from five minutes to five seconds after ten to twenty trials).

15 Thorndike's (1898) law of effect states that a stimulus–response connection is 'stamped in when pleasure results from the act and stamped out when it doesn't'.

16 A Skinner box is a box containing a food dispenser, a lever (or illuminated disc) and sometimes an electrified floor or light bulb.

17 Skinner replaced Thorndike's 'stamping in' and 'stamping out' of a response with the terms strengthening and weakening of a response respectively.

18 The ABC of operant conditioning is a representation of the relationships between antecedents (the stimulus conditions), behaviours (or operants), and consequences (results of operant behaviours).

19 'Behaviour is *shaped* and maintained by its *consequences*.'

20 Behaviour can result in positive reinforcers (rewards), negative reinforcers (threats) or punishers.

21 Both positive and negative reinforcers strengthen behaviours.

22 A primary reinforcer is a stimulus which is rewarding in itself (such as food, water), whereas a secondary reinforcer is a stimulus which acquires its reinforcing properties by being associated with a primary reinforcer.

23 Continuous reinforcement (reinforcing every single desired response) leads to behaviours which are very easily extinguished.

24 Variable ratio reinforcement schedules lead to behaviours which are highly resistant to extinction.

25 Being paid on commission involves a fixed ratio reinforcement schedule.

26 Shaping refers to the reinforcement of successive approximations to the desired response.

27 Shaping has been used to teach individuals with learning difficulties to use the toilet and other social skills, and in speech training with autistic children.

28 Positive reinforcement strengthens behaviours, whereas punishment can only make certain responses less likely. Nothing new can be taught by punishment.

29 The law of contiguity states that events which occur close together in time and space are likely to become associated with one another.

30 Preparedness is the idea that animals are biologically predisposed to learn actions that are closely related to the survival of their species (Seligman, 1970).

31 Mackintosh (1978, 1995) claims that conditioning is not an automatic response, but involves detecting and learning the relations between environmental events.

Section 4: Cognitive approaches

32 Tolman & Honzik (1930) found that if they reinforced a group of rats for finding their way to a goal box, having allowed these rats to wander around the maze for ten days, they reached the goal box very quickly.

33 Tolman concluded that the rats had been learning their way around the maze during the first ten days, but that this learning did not show itself until it was reinforced (i.e. learning was 'latent').

34 A cognitive map is a set of expectations about which part of an environment is followed by other parts.

35 Social learning theorists believe that cognitive or mediating variables intervene between stimulus and response.

36 Observational learning is learning through watching others (called models).

37 A model's behaviour is likely to be imitated if the consequences for the model are positive.

Classical and Operant Conditioning

Classical/respondent conditioning

Operant conditioning

Pavlov – conditioning in dogs
- A *neutral stimulus* (which does not normally produce a response) will produce a response if associated/paired with a stimulus which *does* produce that response.
- Learning is automatic, and the learner is passive. Responses and learning are not under conscious control.

Learning: '… the process by which relatively permanent changes occur in behavioural potential as a result of experience' (Anderson, 1995a).

Thorndike – conditioning in cats
- Cats would learn to escape from 'puzzle-boxes' if rewarded with fish.
- Initially behaviour was *trial-and-error*, escape times improving when behaviour was rewarded.
- Formulated '*law of effect* (1898)': behaviours are 'stamped in when pleasure results from the act and stamped out when it doesn't'.

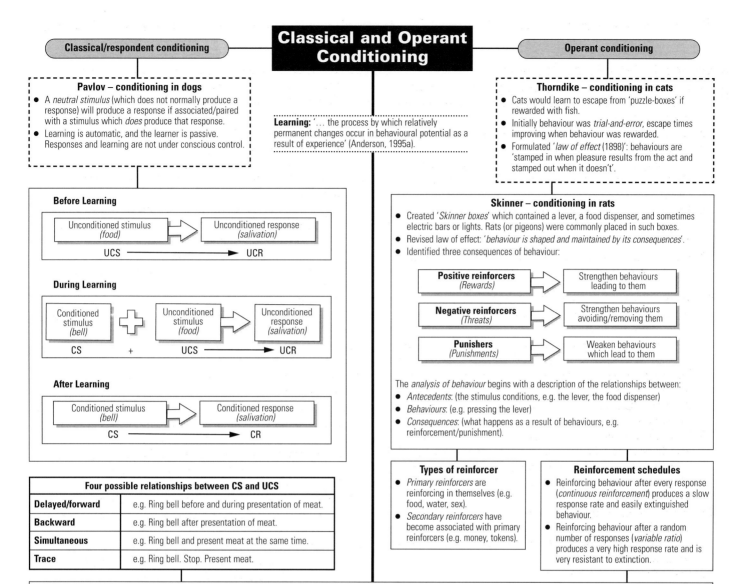

Skinner – conditioning in rats
- Created '*Skinner boxes*' which contained a lever, a food dispenser, and sometimes electric bars or lights. Rats (or pigeons) were commonly placed in such boxes.
- Revised law of effect: '*behaviour is shaped and maintained by its consequences*'.
- Identified three consequences of behaviour:

Positive reinforcers *(Rewards)*	Strengthen behaviours leading to them
Negative reinforcers *(Threats)*	Strengthen behaviours avoiding/removing them
Punishers *(Punishments)*	Weaken behaviours which lead to them

The *analysis of behaviour* begins with a description of the relationships between:
- *Antecedents*: (the stimulus conditions, e.g. the lever, the food dispenser)
- *Behaviours*: (e.g. pressing the lever)
- *Consequences*: (what happens as a result of behaviours, e.g. reinforcement/punishment).

Before Learning

Unconditioned stimulus *(food)* →	Unconditioned response *(salivation)*
UCS ——————→	UCR

During Learning

Conditioned stimulus *(bell)*	+	Unconditioned stimulus *(food)* →	Unconditioned response *(salivation)*
CS	+	UCS ——→	UCR

After Learning

Conditioned stimulus *(bell)* →	Conditioned response *(salivation)*
CS ——————→	CR

Types of reinforcer
- *Primary reinforcers* are reinforcing in themselves (e.g. food, water, sex).
- *Secondary reinforcers* have become associated with primary reinforcers (e.g. money, tokens).

Reinforcement schedules
- Reinforcing behaviour after every response (*continuous reinforcement*) produces a slow response rate and easily extinguished behaviour.
- Reinforcing behaviour after a random number of responses (*variable ratio*) produces a very high response rate and is very resistant to extinction.

Four possible relationships between CS and UCS

Delayed/forward	e.g. Ring bell before and during presentation of meat.
Backward	e.g. Ring bell after presentation of meat.
Simultaneous	e.g. Ring bell and present meat at the same time.
Trace	e.g. Ring bell. Stop. Present meat.

Generalisation, discrimination, extinction and spontaneous recovery
- **Generalisation:** making *similar* conditioned responses to stimuli which are similar to the conditioned stimulus, e.g. Pavlov found that his dogs would salivate at bells whose tones were similar to the original.
- **Discrimination:** making *dissimilar* responses to a stimulus which differs from the conditioned stimulus, e.g. by presenting his dogs with meat for some tones and not for others, Pavlov taught his dogs to make fine discriminations between tones.
- **Extinction:** the *weakening* of the conditioned response in the absence of the unconditioned stimulus, e.g. Pavlov found that his dogs would gradually stop salivating if he repeatedly rang bells without presenting meat.
- **Spontaneous recovery:** the *reappearance* of the conditioned response after it has stopped, e.g. Pavlov found that his dogs would salivate at the sound of a bell following extinction, after a period of rest.

Latent learning and cognitive maps

Cognitive approaches

Social learning theory

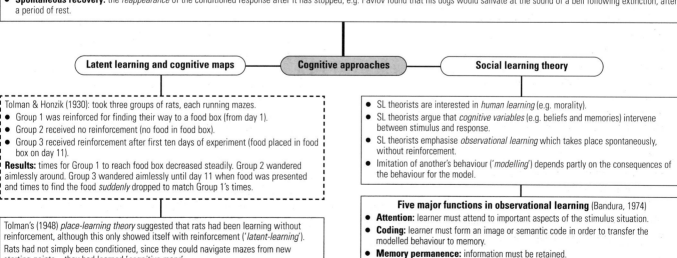

Tolman & Honzik (1930): took three groups of rats, each running mazes.
- Group 1 was reinforced for finding their way to a food box (from day 1).
- Group 2 received no reinforcement (no food in food box).
- Group 3 received reinforcement after first ten days of experiment (food placed in food box on day 11).

Results: times for Group 1 to reach food box decreased steadily. Group 2 wandered aimlessly around. Group 3 wandered aimlessly until day 11 when food was presented and times to find the food *suddenly* dropped to match Group 1's times.

- SL theorists are interested in *human learning* (e.g. morality).
- SL theorists argue that *cognitive variables* (e.g. beliefs and memories) intervene between stimulus and response.
- SL theorists emphasise *observational learning* which takes place spontaneously, without reinforcement.
- Imitation of another's behaviour ('*modelling*') depends partly on the consequences of the behaviour for the model.

Tolman's (1948) *place-learning theory* suggested that rats had been learning without reinforcement, although this only showed itself with reinforcement ('*latent-learning*'). Rats had not simply been conditioned, since they could navigate mazes from new starting-points – they had learned '*cognitive maps*'.

Five major functions in observational learning (Bandura, 1974)
- **Attention:** learner must attend to important aspects of the stimulus situation.
- **Coding:** learner must form an image or semantic code in order to transfer the modelled behaviour to memory.
- **Memory permanence:** information must be retained.
- **Reproduction:** observed motor activities must be reproduced accurately and this may involve practice.
- **Motivation:** relates to the role of reinforcement (which provides us with information about what results we may achieve in the future).

SOCIAL LEARNING IN NON-HUMAN ANIMALS

KEY QUESTIONS
- What are imitation and tutoring?
- In what ways do foraging and predator avoidance demonstrate social learning?
- What evidence is there of insight, self-recognition or a theory of mind in non-human animals?

Section 1: Imitation and tutoring

1　Define *social learning*.
2　Complete the sentence: 'We would expect to find social learning in ＿＿ species with good ＿＿'.
3　What occurs during the process of imitation?
4　What did Herbert & Harsh's (1944) experiments with cats and puzzle boxes discover?
5　What occurs during the process of *tutoring*?
6　How do mother chimpanzees facilitate infants' attempts to crack open nuts?
7　What makes *mimicry* a special case of imitation?
8　Why is imitation an efficient way of acquiring new behaviours (as compared with operant conditioning)?
9　What term is used to describe the increased attractiveness of an object which is the subject of another's attention?
10　What was the crucial factor determining the likelihood that a rat would try food in Galef's (1988) experiments?
11　Which of the following demonstrators were Nicol & Pope's (1999) 'observer chickens' most likely to copy: a dominant hen, a submissive hen or a cockerel?

Section 2: Foraging and predator avoidance

12　What aspect of potato washing by a troop of Japanese macaques led to the conclusion that the behaviour was acquired by social learning?
13　In what way was this conclusion challenged by Galef (1996)?
14　Provide another plausible explanation for the spread of potato washing amongst the Koshima macaques.
15　Why is it unlikely that inheritance can account for the spread of milk bottle opening behaviour among British blue tits?
16　Why is it also unlikely that imitation alone could account for the spread of this behaviour?
17　What general conclusion can be drawn from Sherry & Galef's (1984) experiments with black-capped chickadees?
18　'The mere presence of another bird may have motivated the bird to peck at and open the container.' What phenomenon is this an example of?

19　How did the presence of a model in Fritz & Kotrschal's (1999) experiments influence the observing ravens?
20　What interesting observation was made by Cheyney & Seyfarth (1986) regarding the 'inappropriateness' of juvenile vervet monkey alarm calls?
21　What did Seyfarth & Cheney (1986) observe when playing recordings of eagle alarm calls to infants?
22　What evidence for the involvement of both nature and nurture in vervet calls was reported by Bright (1984)?

Section 3: Learning and intelligence

23　To what does the expression *insight learning* refer?
24　What example of insight learning was demonstrated by Sultan, using bamboo rods?
25　Complete the sentence: 'Epstein *et al.* (1984) suggested that the behaviour of Kohler's chimpanzees could simply be built up from ＿＿ ＿＿'.
26　In what way did Hauser *et al.* (1996) investigate numeracy in wild rhesus monkeys?
27　How did Brannon & Terrace's (1998) experiments suggest that monkeys were able to abstract the concept of number?
28　In what way did Gallup (1970) provide convincing evidence for self-recognition in chimpanzees?
29　What did Swartz & Evans (1991) discover when attempting to replicate Gallup's findings?
30　How were Beninger *et al.* (1974) able to demonstrate self-recognition in rats?
31　In what sense do human children have *a theory of mind*?
32　What are the two ways in which we can approach the question regarding whether or not animals have a theory of mind?
33　Describe the apparatus used by Povinelli *et al.* (1992) to investigate the ability of chimpanzees to consider the perspective of others.

Section 1: Imitation and tutoring

1 Social learning can be defined as the acquisition of some new skill as the result of the direct effect of other individuals.

2 'We would expect to find social learning in *gregarious* species with good *memories*.'

3 In imitation a 'learner' observes a 'model' that demonstrates a behaviour which the learner may or may not imitate.

4 They discovered that cats escaped faster from a puzzle-box if they had previously watched another cat escaping.

5 In tutoring one animal takes the 'tutor' role, involving direct instruction, and the other the 'learner' role.

6 Mother chimpanzees facilitate this process by providing effective hammer stones and nuts.

7 In mimicry there is no obvious reward.

8 Imitation removes the need for a lengthy period of trial and error.

9 *Stimulus enhancement* is the term used to describe the increased attractiveness of an object which is the subject of another's attention.

10 The experience of another healthy conspecific animal seemed to be crucial.

11 Nicol and Pope's observer chickens were most likely to copy a dominant hen.

Section 2: Foraging and predator avoidance

12 This conclusion was based on the patterned way in which the behaviour spread from a single juvenile, to that individual's playmates and peer group, then finally to the adults.

13 Galef pointed out that the behaviour took a long time (five years) to spread and that this was inconsistent with the notion of social learning as a fast track process.

14 It may be that each macaque independently discovered the behaviour and was operantly conditioned to repeat it by humans.

15 The behaviour spread far too rapidly to be explained by inheritance.

16 Imitation alone would seem to be an unlikely explanation since the behaviour arose simultaneously in several different areas.

17 Sherry & Galef (1984) found that birds were just as likely to learn bottle opening if exposed to open bottles, as if exposed to another bird that modelled this behaviour.

18 The motivating effect of the mere presence of others is termed *social facilitation*.

19 Ravens which were exposed to the models learned to open boxes by pulling a blue tab.

20 Cheyney and Seyfarth noted that the juvenile calls, whilst inappropriate, had a certain 'logic' to them, suggesting a genetic predisposition to respond to categories of objects.

21 Seyfarth & Cheney (1986) noted that initially infants appeared startled and looked for their mothers, watching their mothers' responses and eventually responding in the same way.

22 Bright found that the calls given by vervets in Senegal and Kenya are very alike, despite the populations having been separated for thousands of generations.

Section 3: Learning and intelligence

23 Insight learning refers to the sudden solution of a problem in the absence of any trial-and-error process.

24 Sultan joined the rods together in order to make a single rod long enough to reach some fruit outside his cage.

25 'Epstein *et al.* (1984) suggested that the behaviour of Kohler's chimpanzees could simply be built up from *conditioned responses*.'

26 Hauser *et al.* (1996) placed two aubergines behind a screen as a monkey watched. When the screen was removed only one aubergine remained. The monkeys seemed surprised.

27 Brannon and Terrace trained monkeys to touch panels displaying items numbering 1, 2, 3, 4 in order. The monkeys were then able to touch panels numbered from 5 to 9 in order without any further training.

28 Gallup (1970) anaesthetised chimpanzees and applied spots of red dye to their faces. When they regained consciousness the chimps used the mirrors to touch these areas with their fingers.

29 Swartz and Evans found that not all chimps showed evidence of mirror self-recognition.

30 In Beninger *et al.*'s experiment rats were required to press a 'correct' lever in order to receive a food reward. The correct lever depended on which behaviour they were performing when a buzzer sounded.

31 Human children have a conception of the knowledge, intentions or beliefs held by another individual.

32 We can approach the question by asking whether or not animals can attribute knowledge to others, and by asking whether they can employ the tactic of deception.

33 Povinelli *et al.*'s apparatus consisted of a box with handles on two sides which allowed food trays visible inside the box to be moved back and forth.

Social Learning in Non-human Animals

Imitation and tutoring

This debate concerns the relative contributions to the individual made by nature (inherited characteristics) and nurture (acquired characteristics).

- **Imitation:** a passive process occurring in the absence of reinforcers, in which a learner observes a 'model' whose behaviour the recipient may or may not imitate (e.g. Herbert & Harsh, 1944) found that cats escaped faster from a puzzle box if they had previously observed other cats escaping).
- **Tutoring:** an active process involving direct instruction, in which animals take 'tutor' and 'learner' roles – the tutor encountering some cost as the learner benefits (see below).

Tutoring in chimpanzees (Boesch, 1991)

- Adult chimpanzees will facilitate infants' attempts to crack open nuts by leaving small 'hammer' stones on larger 'anvil' stones, together with unopened nuts. A mother will even facilitate the process by producing tools and unopened nuts for the infant to practise with. Finally, a mother will observe their infant's performance and demonstrate how to overcome difficulties.

Mimicry

- Mimicry is a special case of imitation, in which there is no obvious reward (e.g. copying of human behaviour by captive orang-utans).
- The key advantage of mimicry is that it removes the need for a lengthy period of trial & error (as with operant conditioning) and allows the learner to approximate desired behaviours quickly.

Stimulus enhancement

- McQuoid & Galef (1992): showed that jungle fowl seemed to be attracted to a food bowl, having seen another fowl feeding from it – this is an example of 'stimulus enhancement'.
- Galef (1988): found that rats would taste a food which they smelled on another individual – rather than simply on a pad. It seems the stimulus needed to be coupled with a healthy individual to be most effective.

What makes a good demonstrator?

- Nicol & Pope (1999): operantly conditioned chickens to find food in a chamber. 'Observer' chickens were then allowed to watch these demonstrators on successive days and then placed in the chamber themselves.
  Results: responses were more likely to be appropriate if they had observed a dominant hen rather than a submissive hen or a cockerel, suggesting that 'status' may affect salience as a demonstrator.

Application 1 – Foraging

Macaque monkeys – sweet potato washing

- Kawai (1965) describes a single 18-mth-old female macaque who was observed to wash sand-coated pieces of sweet potato in the sea before eating them. Within 5 yrs 14 of the troop's 15 juveniles and 2 of the 11 adults were washing potatoes, leading to the claim that the behaviour was acquired by social learning. However Galef (1996) questions why learning should have taken so long to occur and it may be that each monkey learned the behaviour for itself.

Blue tits – opening milk bottles

- Milk bottle opening behaviour spread rapidly across the British blue tit population between the years 1921 & 1947 (faster than can be explained by inheritance) leading Fisher & Hinde (1949) to suggest that it was spread by imitation. However Sherry & Galef (1990) found that social facilitation (the motivating effect of the mere presence of other birds) could be sufficient to explain the behaviour.

Further research: Fritz & Kotrschal (1999) found that after exposure to trained 'models' ravens could learn to open boxes by pecking at a blue tab rather than just pecking at the boxes themselves.

Application 2 – Predator avoidance

Blackbirds – alarm calls

Survival depends on the rapid acquisition of antipredator behaviour:

- Curio et al. (1978) exposed two blackbirds simultaneously to different stimuli (e.g one saw an owl whilst the other saw a honeyeater). The learner would begin to respond with inappropriate alarm calls as a consequence.

Vervet monkeys – alarm calls

Juveniles learn appropriate alarm calls from adults, who use different calls for different classes of predator:

- Cheney & Seyfarth (1986): found that infant vervets would make inappropriate calls (e.g. an eagle alarm in response to a falling leaf), but the 'logic' to their mistakes suggested a genetic predisposition to respond to different categories of objects. Feedback from adults could then reinforce appropriate calling. The infants' responses to adult calls were also observed: infants would appear startled and look to their mothers. Eventually infants would behave in the same way as their mothers, as if modelling their behaviour on the adults'.

Insight learning

Insight learning refers to the sudden solution of a problem, in the absence of any trial-and-error learning:

- Kohler (1925) observed the behaviour of his chimpanzees (particularly 'Sultan'). In one study Sultan, having played with some sticks, suddenly joined two short ones in order to make a stick long enough to reach bananas outside his cage. In addition, Sultan was observed to pile boxes on top of one another in order to reach bananas suspended from the ceiling.

Evaluation: Kohler's experiments are problematic – in fact Sultan made many errors before achieving the 'insightful' solution and at one point was assisted by an observer. In addition, Epstein et al. (1984) trained pigeons to push boxes around and to stand on them. He found that they would perform these conditioned responses in order to peck at food and argued that the same conditioning process might explain the chimps' behaviour.

Animal numeracy

- Human infants are surprised if objects which disappear subsequently reappear as a different number of objects (see Ch 35) – suggesting that they have a rudimentary concept of number. Hauser et al. (1996) hid a two aubergines behind a screen as a rhesus monkey watched. When the screen was removed only one aubergine could be seen. This seemed to surprise monkeys, suggesting that they expected a different number.
- Brannon & Terrace (1998) presented monkeys with groups of 1, 2, 3 & 4 items on a screen. In order to gain a reward they had to touch the groups of items in numerical order. After 5 days they were able to do this, and were then presented with groups of 5, 6, 7, 8, 9 items. The fact that they were able to perform this task immediately, with 75% accuracy, suggests that they had abstracted an understanding of number.

Learning and intelligence

Self-recognition

- Gallup (1970) gave chimpanzees the opportunity to learn to recognise themselves in a mirror (initially they reacted as if to another chimp). Once they had accepted the reflection, he anaesthetised the chimps and applied a coloured dye to one eyebrow and the opposite ear. On regaining consciousness, the chimps became interested in these coloured areas once given a mirror, implying self-recognition.

Evaluation: Some experimenters have been unable to reproduce Gallup's findings, and it may be that the age of chimps together with distractions may influence the result (Bard, 1994). It is also possible that some form of 'self-recognition' is a conditioned response: Beninger et al. (1974) reinforced rats for pushing one of four levers – the correct choice depending on the behaviour they had been performing when a buzzer sounded. Despite it being unlikely that the rats were 'self-aware' they were nevertheless able to push the correct lever.

Theory of mind

A 'theory of mind' is a conception of the beliefs, intentions or desires of another individual. Adult humans regularly anticipate what other individuals may be thinking as part of everyday interaction. But can animals do this – for example by attributing knowledge to others or employing deception?

- Povinelli et al. (1992) had chimps point to one of two trainers who in turn lifted cups under which food had been hidden. The chimps would consistently point to the trainer who had hidden the food, rather than the trainer who entered the room later on. However, such results can be accounted for by simple association.
- Povinelli et al. (1992) had 'informant' chimps indicate to 'operator' chimps which of a number of handles to pull in order to gain a food reward. The chimps quickly developed a signalling system and, when the roles were reversed immediately responded correctly using this system, suggesting that they had learned each other's roles.

ANIMAL NAVIGATION

SYLLABUS
13.5 Animal cognition – animal navigation
- explanations and research studies into animal navigation, including homing and migration

KEY QUESTIONS
- In what ways might animals navigate?
- What evidence is there that these means of navigation are used?
- How is navigation used in migration and homing?

Section 1: Navigation
1 Define *homing*.
2 What two aspects of knowledge does navigation require?
3 What is involved in *true navigation*?
4 Identify four sources of information which may be used in navigating.
5 What term is used to describe navigating using familiar landmarks?
6 In what important way do the navigational strategies employed by gerbils and bees differ, according to Cartwright & Collett (1983)?
7 What did Hasler & Larsen (1955) suggest regarding the navigational technique employed by salmon?
8 How did Hasler & Wisby (1954) confirm this suggestion, experimentally?
9 What is *dead reckoning*?
10 What did Wehner & Srinivansan (1981) discover by moving foraging desert ants 600 metres away from their nests?
11 How did Saint Paul's (1982) experiment using geese differ from Wehner and Srinivansan's experiment using ants?
12 How was Kramer (1951) able to demonstrate that some animals can use the sun as a source of navigational information?
13 What was the purpose of housing pigeons under artificial lighting schedules in Schmidt-Koenig's (1961) experiments?
14 What was the result of Ganzhorn et al.'s (1989) experiments with 'clock-shifted' pigeons?
15 What is *polarised light*?
16 Under what conditions are polarised rays most likely to reach the earth's surface?
17 Which animals did Von Frisch (1956, 1967) discover were able to utilise polarised light to navigate?
18 How were Larkin & Keeton (1976) able to cause pigeons to lose their navigational ability on overcast days?
19 Why were the initial directions of pigeons released by Walcott & Brown (1989) on Jersey Hill initially random?
20 What experimental set-up did Beason (1989) use in order to investigate the navigational abilities of the bobolink?
21 What is the name of the naturally occurring iron compound present in the heads of bobolinks?
22 What did Murphy (1989) discover when comparing magnetic sense in boys and girls aged 9–19 years?
23 Describe the apparatus used to study migratory restlessness in warblers.
24 What was the purpose of rearing indigo buntings in a planetarium where the nightly movements of the stars rotated around Betelgeuse (Emlen, 1972)?

Section 2: Migration and homing
25 To what does the term *migration* refer?
26 Complete the sentence: 'In general, animals migrate between a ____ place to spend winter and an area of ____ to mate during the summer'.
27 Where do the monarch butterflies of North America spend the winter?
28 What triggers migration in African wildebeest?
29 What is the key seasonal indicator, which triggers migration in many birds?
30 What did Biebach (1983) find when he allowed non-migrant/migrant and non-migrant/non-migrant pairs of robins to mate?
31 How are researchers able to study the migratory routes followed by turtles and whales?
32 Identify one of the two ways in which the term *homing* may be used.
33 How are whales able to navigate through the oceans?

Section 1: Navigation

1 Homing is navigating back to a known location.
2 Navigation requires knowing where to go and how to get there.
3 True navigation requires the use of a 'map' (which locates the goal) and some form of 'compass' (which indicates direction without reference to landmarks).
4 Navigation may make use of landmarks, smell, the sun, geomagnetism, poles, field lines or the stars.
5 Navigating using familiar landmarks is termed *piloting*.
6 Cartwright & Collett (1983) found that bees seemed to be using the size of a retinal image to navigate, whilst gerbils seemed to rely on dead reckoning.
7 Hasler & Larsen (1955) suggested that salmon may be using a sense of smell to navigate.
8 Hasler & Wisby (1954) blocked the nostrils of migrating salmon and found that they failed to return successfully.
9 Dead reckoning is a navigational technique involving 'knowing the location of the target with respect to yourself' (e.g. the pin is on the floor five paces in front of me). This is not an effective technique if either the goal or the individual are displaced.
10 Wehner & Srinivansan (1981) found that the ants behaved as if they had not been moved at all – presumably because they were unable to take into account their displacement.
11 Saint Paul (1982) allowed the geese to see part of their relocation journey, but covered their eyes for the rest. The geese were only able to correct for the part of the journey that they had seen.
12 Kramer (1951) trained caged starlings to search for food located at a particular compass direction, with only the sun and sky as cues. When released they were able to forage successfully, regardless of time of day.
13 The pigeons were housed under artificial lighting schedules to alter their internal clocks. When returned to natural daylight they misinterpreted the sun's position, based on the 'new' time of day.
14 Ganzhorn *et al.* (1989) found that pigeons could navigate correctly despite clock-shifting, suggesting that they use multiple navigation mechanisms.
15 Polarised light is light which consists of waves of the same orientation.
16 Polarised rays are most likely to reach the earth's surface when the sun is low in the sky (i.e. dawn and dusk).

17 Von Frisch (1956, 1967) discovered that bees were able to utilise polarised light.
18 Larkin & Keeton (1976) were able to cause pigeons to lose their navigational ability on overcast days by attaching magnets to their heads.
19 Jersey Hill is known to be an area of magnetic anomaly and may have interfered with the pigeons' magnetic sense.
20 Beason placed captive bobolinks under a planetarium sky, so that both star patterns and magnetic fields could be reversed around the birds.
21 Magnetite is the naturally occurring iron compound present in the heads of bobolinks.
22 Murphy (1989) discovered that girls performed significantly better than boys at all ages from 9–19 years.
23 The apparatus consists of a funnel with an inky pad at the base, on which the bird stands. The top of the funnel is closed – either by a wire mesh or an opaque screen.
24 The purpose of this experiment was to discover the extent to which stellar navigation is learned or innate. In fact the birds raised in this fashion headed off in the wrong direction under a normal night sky, suggesting an important role for learning.

Section 2: Migration and homing

25 Migration refers to cyclical, long-distance travel between two specific locations.
26 'In general, animals migrate between a *safe* place to spend winter and an area of *plenty* to mate during the summer.'
27 Monarch butterflies migrate to the mountains of Mexico for the winter.
28 Their migration is primarily controlled by scarcity of resources (food and water).
29 For many birds day length is the key seasonal indicator.
30 Biebach found that for both these pairings, roughly half of the offspring were migrants, suggesting a complex genetic component to migration.
31 Researchers attach radio transmitters to these animals in order to track their movements.
32 Homing may be used to refer to either the return of animals to their hatching/birth place after natural displacement or following artificial transportation by a captor.
33 Whales are able to use echolocation to map the ocean floor.

Navigation: requires two aspects of knowledge – knowing where to go and how to get there. True navigation differs from other forms of navigation in that the individual can locate the goal from any starting point.

Animal Navigation

Means of navigation
- The following are possible types of knowledge used to navigate: landmarks, smell, the sun, geomagnetism, geomagnetic poles, magnetic field lines, the stars.

Location-based navigation

Piloting by sight
Some animals navigate by remembering visual landmarks, enabling them to create a mental 'set of directions':
- Cartwright & Collett (1983) trained bees to find a sucrose solution and gerbils to find sunflower seeds at a fixed distance & bearing from a 40-cm tower.

Results: both animals learned to search in the correct position relative to the tower. However, varying the height of the tower affected the bees' ability to locate the food, but not the gerbils – suggesting that bees use visual comparisons to guide their position whilst gerbils may rely on 'dead reckoning'.

Dead reckoning
- This system works by 'knowing the goal location with respect to yourself':
- Wehner & Srinivansen (1981): took foraging desert ants 600 metres from their nest. They were unable to correct for their new location and foraged as if they had not been displaced at all.
- Saint Paul (1982) transported geese from their home, and they were able to see only part of the journey. On release they headed off in the wrong direction, only correcting for the part of the journey that they had seen.

Piloting by smell
After several years in the open sea salmon are able to return to the river where they hatched, to spawn:
- Hasler & Wisby (1954): blocked the nostrils of migrating salmon in order to determine whether or not the salmon were using smell to navigate.

Results: the migrating salmon were unable to return successfully. Similar results were obtained by severing the olfactory nerve of salmon. However, it is not clear what causes a river to have a particular 'smell'.

Direction-based navigation

Sun compass
Schmidt-Koenig (1961): tested the claim that birds can use the sun to guide them by housing pigeons under artificial lighting to alter their internal clocks. When released their foraging behaviour was altered as a result of misinterpreting the sun's position.

Multiple navigation mechanisms
Ganzhorn *et al.* (1989): found that clock-shifted (as above) pigeons would *ignore* incorrect information regarding the sun and fly in the right direction – suggesting that they use *additional* mechanisms to navigate.

Polarised light
The earth's atmosphere deflects polarised light when the sun is high in the sky, but allows polarised light through when the sun is lower in the sky (dawn or dusk). Pigeons can detect polarised light and might use this as a cue.

Research
Von Frisch (1956, 1967): showed that honey bees could accurately indicate direction even when it was cloudy, and that the bees' 'dance' could be altered by exposing them to light which had been altered.

Magnetic sense
Lines of magnetic force extend from one of the earth's poles to the other. Animals capable of detecting these could use them to navigate:
- Larkin & Keeton (1976): found that on overcast days pigeons lose their navigational ability when magnets are attached to their heads.

Research
- Walcott & Brown (1989): found that pigeons released on Jersey Hill (an area of magnetic anomaly) initially flew in random direction.
- Beason (1989): studied bobolink birds. By placing them in a planetarium so that he could alter the pattern of the stars, he found that birds would follow magnetic cues in preference to the (reversed) stellar map.

Stellar map
The stars seem to rotate around a single point (north or south depending on the hemisphere you are in) and this can be used to gain a compass bearing.

Research
- Birds placed on an inky pad in a funnel with a transparent lid will leave inky marks in their 'preferred' direction of travel. When placed in a planetarium Sauer & Sauer (1955) found that warblers would 'hop' in the direction indicated by the stars.
- Emlen (1972): reared indigo buntings in a planetarium where the stars rotated around Betelgeuse (i.e. abnormally). When released the young birds headed in the wrong direction, suggesting that stellar maps may be partially learned.

Migration

Researchers label animals with rings or tags in order to enable them to answer two key questions: '*Where do animals go?*' and '*How quickly do they get there?*'. Capturing incoming migrants can then provide useful information, providing their destination goal is known. In some cases (e.g. turtles and whales), radio transmitters are used to track the animals' migratory patterns.

Costs and benefits
Possible costs: energy expenditure, risk of predation, geographical barriers, unpredictable weather.
Benefits: improved temperature, food supply, more mates, fewer predators.

The monarch butterfly
Flies from Canada & N. America to over-wintering sites in the Mexican mountains (6700km round trip). It spends the winter in near-freezing temperatures (perhaps allowing it to survive by lowering its metabolic rate).

What triggers migration?
- Wildebeest migration is probably controlled by the availability of food and water – absence of these providing the impetus to move.
- Loggerhead turtles lay their eggs in Florida's beaches. The hatchlings use the light of the moon to guide them to the water, where they follow the gulf stream to the Sargasso sea.

Anticipating changes
Anticipating changes allows animals to prepare for migration, and to move before it is too late.
- The key predictor is probably day length, which shortens as autumn approaches. Birds respond to this change with increased pituitary gland hormones which stimulate eating.

Migratory routes
Long-lived species can learn migratory patterns from adult individuals; however for many species some innate mechanisms may also be involved.
- Perdeck (1958): took adult and hatchling starlings from Holland to a release site in Switzerland. Whilst the adults were able to find their normal wintering grounds, the hatchlings were not and flew as if they had not been displaced.

Breeding robins
- Biebach (1983): hand-reared robins from a population where some, but not all, tended to migrate. He bred migrant/migrant, migrant/non-migrant and non-migrant/non-migrant pairs.
Results: 90% of the offspring of the migrant/migrant pairings migrated, compared with only 53% of the other pairings – suggesting a complex genetic relationship.

Homing

Examples
- Kenyon & Rice (1958): report the Laysan albatross homing over distances in excess of 4100 miles.
- Homing pigeons can home over hundreds of miles using navigational skills including landmarks, piloting, dead reckoning, sun compass & internal clock and a magnetic compass. They may even be able to use two sources of information to establish their co-ordinates.

Homing: refers to either the return of animals to their hatching/birth place after displacement or following artificial transportation and release.

Other cues which may be used
- Tactile cues (e.g. the feeling of swimming upstream: Hasler, 1960)
- Flying into the prevailing wind (Bellrose, 1967)
- Auditory cues (e.g. whales using echolocation to map the ocean floor: Norris, 1967).

ANIMAL COMMUNICATION AND LANGUAGE

Section 1: Signalling systems

Q
1. Define *communication*.
2. What is a *signal*?
3. What signal causes herring gulls to regurgitate food for their chicks?
4. What term is used to describe legitimate signalling which is received illegitimately?
5. In what way does the hoverfly send a deceitful signal?
6. In what three ways can visual signals vary?
7. What is the role of the elaborate gestures performed by the great crested grebe?
8. Describe one signalling behaviour carried out by the common tern which has obvious functional significance.
9. What is the *wedding gift* of the male balloon fly?
10. Complete the sentence: 'Ritualisation makes signals ____ (improving detection by the receiver) and ____ (reducing the likelihood of misunderstanding)'.
11. Identify two disadvantages associated with the use of visual signals.
12. Why does the pitch of a male toad's croak matter?
13. What form of auditory signalling system was identified by Seyfarth *et al.* (1980) in vervet monkeys?
14. Identify two advantages of auditory signals.
15. What is the most likely explanation for the change of song in male great tits as they move from perch to perch?
16. What is a *pheromone*?
17. Identify a function of pheromones common to mice, badgers, cats and dogs.
18. What sexual function of pheromones was identified by Simmons (1990)?
19. Identify two disadvantages of olfactory signalling systems.

Section 2: Animal language

20. What is the difference between the discontinuity school and the continuity school in relation to non-human language?
21. What is meant by the *displacement* criterion for language?
22. To what extent do the calls of vervet monkeys exhibit phonological and lexical syntax?
23. Why is it fair to describe the alarm calls of vervets as *symbolic*?
24. What is the role of the *waggle dance* used by bees (von Frisch, 1956, 1967)?
25. How does the meaning of the 'round dance' differ from that of the 'waggle dance'?
26. Identify three criteria for language which are not met by honey-bee communication.
27. Identify three criteria for language which are satisfied by birdsong.
28. What species of animal was Akeakamai?
29. Complete the sentence: 'Herman *et al.*'s (1993) findings suggest that Akeakamai could use a ____-____ language as she would sometimes reject an anomalous sequence of gestures'.

Section 3: Teaching language to non-humans

30. What is the reason for the failure of early attempts at teaching chimpanzees to speak?
31. Name two of the four features which Aitchison (1983) proposes distinguish true language from non-human communication.
32. How did the language system used with Washoe (Gardner & Gardner, 1969, 1977) differ from that used with Lana (Savage-Rumbaugh *et al.*, 1977, 1980)?
33. What general conclusion regarding attempts to teach language to non-humans was reached by Terrace (1985)?
34. What were the findings of Savage-Rumbaugh *et al.*'s (1993) experiment in which Kanzi's comprehension of language was tested against that of a two-and-a-half-year-old human child's?

Section 1: Signalling systems

1 Communication is a two-way process in which a message is conveyed from a sender to one or more recipients.

2 A signal is a deliberate message sent to one or more recipients.

3 Herring gulls will regurgitate food when the chicks peck at a red spot on the adult's bill.

4 Illegitimate reception of legitimate signals is termed *eaves-dropping*.

5 By mimicking wasps hoverflies send the deceitful message that they are dangerous to predators.

6 Visual signals can vary according to position, movement and colour.

7 The gestures (such as the 'weed' or 'penguin' dance) form part of the courtship ritual of the grebe.

8 As part of courtship the male tern will provide the female with a fish to eat as evidence of its ability to provide.

9 The wedding gift is a hollow silken ball (not a balloon!).

10 'Ritualisation makes signals *conspicuous* (improving detection by the receiver) and *stereotyped* (reducing the likelihood of misunderstanding).

11 Visual signals rely on encountering conspecifics, may be transient and require energy (in the case of gestures) as well as requiring the recipient's attention. Visual signals are rarely useful by night and require a line of sight by day.

12 The pitch of the toad's croak indicates his size, with females preferring deeper croaks.

13 Vervet monkeys use alarm calls to warn of predators (such as eagles, leopards and snakes).

14 Auditory signals can carry long distances and travel through and around obstacles. They can be varied and complex and are difficult for a receiver to miss.

15 The most likely explanation is that the male's scope for song indicates to rivals his age or strength.

16 A pheromone is a volatile chemical released by animals which has an effect on the behaviour or physiology of other members of the species.

17 Mice, badgers, cats and dogs all use pheromones to mark out their territory.

18 Simmons (1990) demonstrated that female crickets used scent cues to avoid related males thereby reducing inbreeding.

19 Pheromonal signals can be interrupted by poor weather or blown in the wind.

Section 2: Animal language

20 The discontinuity school sees language as uniquely human and qualitatively different from communication in non-humans whilst the continuity school sees language as part of a cognitive continuum.

21 The displacement criterion is the criterion that a language system can be used to describe things which are absent in time or space.

22 The calls of vervet monkeys do not exhibit phonological or lexical syntax. They cannot be combined to form more meaningful 'sentences'.

23 The description is fair because the calls are arbitrary (the sounds are not related to the meaning).

24 The waggle dance is used by bees to communicate the distance and direction of food some distance from the hive.

25 The round dance indicates that food has been found near the hive (up to 50 metres away) while the waggle dance is used to communicate information relating to more distant food.

26 Honey-bee communication would not seem to meet the criteria for conversation, phonological/lexical syntax, spontaneous acquisition, critical period or cultural transmission.

27 Birdsong is symbolic and highly specialised, and is acquired spontaneously within a critical period. In addition, songs involve an element of cultural transmission.

28 Akeakamai was a bottlenosed dolphin.

29 'Herman *et al.*'s (1993) findings suggest that Akeakamai could use a *rule-based* language as she would sometimes reject an anomalous sequence of gestures.'

Section 3: Teaching language to non-humans

30 Chimpanzees lack the vocal apparatus and brain mechanisms which might allow them to speak.

31 Aitchison (1983) proposes semanticity, displacement, creativity and structure dependence as the distinguishing features.

32 Washoe was taught to use American sign language whilst Lana was taught using symbols on a computer keyboard.

33 Terrace concluded that no research had demonstrated spontaneous utterances, and that non-humans were merely imitating their trainers' actions.

34 Kanzi scored more highly than the child (she was correct 74 per cent of the time vs the 65 per cent for the child).

Communication: a two-way process in which a message is conveyed from a sender to one or more recipients, causing a change in behaviour of the recipient.
Signal: a deliberate message sent to one or more recipients.

Eavesdropping: occurs when a legitimate signal is received by an illegitimate receiver (e.g. female bark beetles use scent to attract a mate but other females may eavesdrop & locate her valuable egg-laying site).
Deceitful signalling: occurs when an illegitimate signal is received by a legitimate receiver (e.g. hoverflies send the deceitful signal that they are wasps to predators).

Herring gull chicks (Tinbergen & Perdeck, 1950)
The chicks peck at a red spot on the parent's bill to trigger the parent to regurgitate food for the chick. The chick's signalling is *active*, whilst the parent's is *passive*.

Visual signalling systems

Basic facts
A flexible system, with messages varied according to:
- **Position:** animals may adopt static postures sometimes exaggerated by physical structures (e.g. the threatening stance of a robin enhanced by fluffed up breast feathers).
- **Movement:** postures may form a sequence of movements (*gestures*) e.g. the courtship of the great crested grebe.
- **Colour:** e.g peacocks or robins (robins will ignore an invading stuffed robin painted brown, but attack a few red feathers).

The origin of signalling systems
Ritualisation describes the process by which evolution acts on signals to make them more effective – often by making them more conspicuous and stereotyped:
- The male balloon fly offers the female a hollow silken ball as a prerequisite to mating (Kessel, 1955). One possible explanation is that the balloon once housed a nutritious insect.

Advantages & disadvantages
Advantages: variation of colour, position & movement offers an enormous variety of messages which can be of great complexity. Colour signalling is an enduring, low-cost means of signalling.
Disadvantages: the receiver has to be able to see the signal, and such signals may also attract predators. Vigorous movements require energy.

Olfactory signalling systems

Basic facts
Pheromones are volatile chemicals released by animals which have an effect on the physiology or behaviour of conspecifics:
- **Releaser pheromones:** typically have short-term behavioural effects.
- **Primer pheromones:** typically have longer-term physiological effects.
- Pheromones are often used to mark out territories (e.g. dogs, cats, mice).

Incest avoidance
Simmons (1990) demonstrated that female crickets were sensitive to scent cues, preferring males who were not related to them.

Advantages & disadvantages
Advantages: smells can carry over long distances and around obstacles, reaching receivers who are not attending to them.
Disadvantages: smells can be interrupted by poor weather or blown away by the wind.

Auditory signalling systems

Basic facts
A flexible system with messages varied according to:
- **Pitch:** in toads, the pitch of the croak indicates the size of the male, females preferring deeper croaks.
- **Sequence:** the sequence of notes produced by crickets informs potential mates of their species.
- **Volume:** many species vary this in addition to pitch & sequence.

Vervet monkey alarm calls (Seyfarth *et al.*, 1980)
In vervet monkeys alarm calls fall into three types which indicate the type of predator & the appropriate response: leopard, snake and eagle.

Advantages & disadvantages
Advantages: sound is highly flexible and can carry across great distances or through obstacles. Sounds are also difficult to miss.
Disadvantages: errors are more likely and cheating is easier. Predators can use sounds to locate prey.

Animal language

Does language exist in non-humans?
Opinion is divided: the *discontinuity school* sees language as uniquely human, whilst the *continuity school* sees language as part of a quantitative continuum, connecting humans to primates.
Ten features of languages: symbolic, specialisation, displacement, generativity, syntax, spontaneous acquisition, critical period, cultural transmission, interchangeability, conversation.

Vervet monkeys
Symbolic/semantic: alarm calls *are* interpreted consistently by conspecifics.
Specialisation: unlikely that monkeys are merely vocalising in response to fear.
Generativity & displacement: communication limited, but response doesn't require predator.
Syntax: alarm calls cannot be combined to convey additional information.
Spontaneous acquisition, critical period, cultural transmission: Cheney & Seyfarth's (1990) studies suggest that there are both genetic and cultural elements to call acquisition.
Interchangeable roles & conversation: sender/receiver roles exchanged but not conversation.

Honey bees (von Frisch, 1956, 1967)
Symbolic/semantic: bees use a 'waggle dance' to communicate food distance & direction.
Specialisation: circular movements, waggles, vigour and sounds are all specialised.
Generativity & displacement: confined to food locations, though food itself is absent.
Syntax, spontaneous acquisition, critical period, cultural transmission: no evidence.
Interchangeable roles & conversation: sender/receiver roles exchanged but not conversation.

Birds
Birdsong is *symbolic* (e.g. communicating territoriality) but is really only comprised of elaborate signals. Though highly *specialised* it is not *generative* and lacks *syntax*. Birds do not alternate exchanges suggesting that it is not used for *conversation*. However, birds do *spontaneously acquire* language during a *critical period* and learn elements of songs (*cultural transmission*).

Chimpanzees
Chimpanzees use facial expressions, sounds and gestures to communicate although none seems varied or complex enough to be language. However, chimpanzees have demonstrated the ability to take another's perspective and to take on roles – suggesting a capacity to *acquire* language (see below).

Teaching language to non-human animals

Research
- **Washoe (chimp)** (Gardner & Gardner, 1969, 1977): could use 160 signs (American sign language) after 5 years and could ask for absent objects/people. Though word order was initially inconsistent Washoe combined signs spontaneously.
- **Sarah (chimp)** (Premack, 1971 & Premack & Premack, 1972): learned the meaning of over 100 plastic symbols including complex concepts (e.g. 'colour of'). No evidence of displacement or spontaneity.
- **Lana (chimp)** (Savage-Rumbaugh *et al.*, 1977, 1980): learned the meaning of over 100 computer keyboard symbols and could generalise these and combine them to refer to objects she had no word for. Able to distinguish meaning according to word order and refer to things not physically present.
- **Koko (gorilla)** (Patterson, 1980): after 7 years could use over 400 ASL signs and understood many English words for those signs. Was able to combine words to refer to objects she had no word for, though no evidence for word order dependence.
- **Akeakamai (dolphin)** (Herman *et al.*, 1993): learned a language based on visual signs, responding with complex behaviours. Responded accurately to new sentences whose meaning was dependent on word order, and rejected sentences which broke these rules.

Evaluation
- Early attempts into non-human language involved trying to get chimpanzees to speak. Since chimpanzees lack the appropriate vocal apparatus these were largely unsuccessful.
- Aitchison (1983) suggested four features which could be used to distinguish true language and non-human communication systems: **semanticity** (the use of symbols to refer to objects etc.), **displacement** (reference to events/objects in another time or place), **creativity** (combining symbols to produce new meanings), **and structure dependence** (an understanding of the patterns of language, such as word order).
- Terrace (1979) reviewed the results of research into non-human language, including those of his own chimpanzee studies (with 'Nim Chimpsky'). He concluded that none of the studies demonstrated language comprehension but merely reproductions of the teacher's utterances.
- Rumbaugh & Savage-Rumbaugh (1994) created environments in which chimpanzees could be immersed in language without any explicit training. Kanzi learned symbols from a lexigram keyboard and spontaneously made requests and named things. Kanzi was able to understand complex sentences and was tested on comprehension of novel instructions at age 9. Kanzi responded correctly 74% of the time, whilst a human child aged 2½ responded correctly 65% of the time.

MEMORY IN NON-HUMANS

KEY QUESTIONS

- To what extent do non-human animals possess spatial memory?
- How is memory used in foraging and food caching?
- How are animals able to make use of cognitive maps?

Section 1: Spatial memory

1 What is perhaps the sharpest contrast between memory in humans and in non-humans?
2 To what does the term *spatial memory* refer?
3 What did Regolin & Rose (1999) discover when testing spatial memory in two-day-old chicks?
4 Why does the female digger wasp leave the burrow in which she has laid her eggs?
5 What procedure did Tinbergen (1952) carry out in order to investigate spatial memory in the digger wasp?
6 How was Tinbergen able to test that it was the spatial arrangement of objects that the wasp was relying upon?
7 Identify one adaptive advantage to a non-human of possessing spatial memory.
8 Why is there a significant difference in the spatial memory ability of the male and female *meadow* vole, but little difference between the spatial memory of the male and female *prairie* vole?
9 Complete the sentence: 'The spatial-adaption model suggests a correlation between _____ and spatial ability'.
10 In what way does the *pliancy model* of spatial memory differ from the spatial-adaption model?
11 What task did Day *et al.* (1999) set their lizards in order to test their spatial memory?
12 Which of the two types of lizard – 'active' or 'sit-and-wait' – performed best at this task?

Section 2: Foraging and caching

13 Identify one advantage of a *food caching* strategy.
14 What procedure did Srinivasan *et al.* (1997) employ in order to investigate the way in which honey bees learn forage locations?
15 Under what conditions did the honey bees fail to stop at the correct location?
16 What experiment did Menzel (1971) carry out in order to investigate spatial memory in chimpanzees living in naturalistic conditions?

17 Jacobs & Liman (1991) released grey squirrels into an area where nuts had been hidden at the squirrels' own cache locations and at other random sites. What did they find?
18 What experimental procedure was used by Sherry (1984) to investigate spatial memory in black-capped chickadees?
19 Nutcrackers hide their seeds in holes that they dig. Over what period of time did Balda & Kamil (1992) find that they could recall the location of their caches?
20 In what way do the brains of 'food-hoarders' differ from those of non-hoarding species?

Section 3: Cognitive maps

21 What is a *cognitive map*?
22 How do rats typically behave when placed in a radial arm map?
23 What did Roberts (1979) discover when placing rats in a 24-arm radial maze?
24 How were Maier & Schneirla (1935) able to demonstrate the use of cognitive maps by rats navigating complex mazes?
25 What was the effect of hippocampal lesions on rats placed in a circular tank filled with powdered water and milk, in Morris *et al.*'s experiments?
26 What difference between racing pigeons and other breeds of pigeon did Rehkamper *et al.* (1988) discover?
27 What name is given to the type of cell, present in a rat's hippocampus, which responded only when the rat was in a particular location in the maze?
28 What is a *proprioceptive* cue?
29 What is the name of the neurotransmitter whose receptor sites are blocked by the action of the drug scopolamine?
30 How were Nilson *et al.* (1987) able to reduce memory deficits in rats which had undergone hippocampal lesions?
31 What type of forgetting did Dallenbach (1924) investigate, using groups of cockroaches?

Section 1: Spatial memory

1 Perhaps the sharpest contrast is that non-humans seem to be programmed to remember some pieces of information more readily than others (i.e. they are more selective and less flexible).

2 Spatial memory refers to the learning of an environmental layout in order to recall the objects or activities associated with particular places.

3 Regolin & Rose (1999) found that the chicks could retain spatial memories for at least 24 hours.

4 The wasp leaves the burrow in order to hunt for insects with which to feed the larvae.

5 Tinbergen (1952) surrounded a wasp's burrow with pinecones, then moved them 30 cm away while she was out hunting.

6 Tinbergen made the original circle of cones into a triangle and created a circle of stones. Wasps headed for the circle of stones rather than the re-arranged cones.

7 Spatial memory is adaptive in that it allows an individual to spend less time and energy travelling, so that they use their resources more efficiently and expose themselves to fewer dangers.

8 In the case of the meadow vole the male must cover far more territory than the female, whilst both male and female prairie voles cover similar territories.

9 'The spatial-adaption model suggests a correlation between *ecology* and spatial ability.'

10 The pliancy model suggests that it is a more general enhancement in memory which is favoured by natural selection, rather than a specific improvement in spatial memory.

11 The lizards were placed in an enclosure in which they had to find a hot rock from which to escape the cold water.

12 Both 'active' and 'sit-and-wait' types performed equally well.

Section 2: Foraging and caching

13 Caching food ensures that it keeps for longer, is protected from competitors, and is therefore available at times of scarcity.

14 Srinivasan *et al.* (1997) trained bees to find a sugar solution in the middle of a tunnel, whose walls were marked with stripes.

15 When the orientation of the stripes was changed (from vertical to horizontal) the honey bees were unable to home in on the food.

16 Menzel brought the chimpanzees indoors and took them on a long journey during which they saw food being hidden at 18 outside locations. They were then released and allowed to search for the food.

17 Jacobs & Liman (1991) found that the squirrels were more likely to recover nuts from their own cache locations than other sites.

18 Sherry (1984) allowed the chickadees to hide four or five sunflower seeds in trees with 72 specially drilled holes. The holes were later covered and the searching behaviour of the birds observed.

19 Balda & Kamil (1992) found that nutcrackers could find their caches up to 40 weeks later.

20 Food-hoarders' brains seem to have more neurones in the hippocampus.

Section 3: Cognitive maps

21 A cognitive map is an internal representation used by an animal to map its environment.

22 When placed in a radial arm map rats explore each arm (though not in a systematic way) and will avoid re-entering a previously encountered arm.

23 Roberts (1979) found that rats could only find food effectively by employing a fixed search pattern, suggesting that their memories had reached full capacity.

24 Maier & Schneirla (1935) removed walls within a complex maze with which rats were familiar. The rats took advantage of the short-cuts created.

25 The rats were unable to recall the location of a submerged platform and swam in random directions on every trial.

26 Rehkamper *et al.* (1988) discovered that racing pigeons had larger hippocampal regions than other breeds of pigeon.

27 Such cells are called *place cells*.

28 A proprioceptive cue is a body position.

29 Receptor sites for acetylcholine are blocked by the action of the drug scopolamine.

30 Nilson *et al.* transplanted healthy cells into the brains of rats with hippocampal lesions.

31 Dallenbach (1924) investigated interference using groups of cockroaches.

What can animals remember?

Human memory involves a variety of mechanisms (Ch 2). To what extent are these shared by animals? It seems likely that animals possess the following to some degree:

- *Procedural memory* – remembered actions
- *Declarative memory* – e.g. memory of locations
- *Episodic memory* – e.g. for painful events.

However, non-humans' memories seem to exhibit strong preferences for certain types of information.

Memory in Non-humans

Spatial memory

Facts

- **Spatial memory** refers to the learning of an environmental layout, in order to recall the objects or activities associated with particular places.
- Locations may be sources of resources, or sources of danger, so memory is important.
- Long-term spatial memory appears early in an animal's life. Regolin & Rose (1999) found that two-day-old chicks could learn a route and remember it after 24 hours.
- Having an effective spatial memory also allows animals to expend less energy in travelling and therefore to use their resources more efficiently.

Key study: Memory in digger wasps (Tinbergen, 1952)

A female digger wasp excavates a burrow in which to lay eggs. Having laid the eggs, she leaves the burrow, returning with paralysed insects for the larvae:

- Tinbergen surrounded a wasp's burrow with pinecones, then moved them 30 cm away while she was hunting for insects.

Results: the wasp was unable to find the burrow on her return.

- To test the hypothesis that the wasp relies entirely on spatial arrangements Tinbergen surrounded a burrow with a circle of cones. On departure, Tinbergen altered the cones to form a triangle and created a circle of stones. The wasp searched inside the circle of stones rather than the triangle of pinecones – *supporting* the hypothesis.

Models of spatial memory

Spatial adaption model

- Some animals have a greater need to remember particular places: if food or potential mates are clustered at regular venues then location memory will be of greater benefit.
- The model suggests that a spatially demanding ecological niche will naturally select improved navigational skills.

Key study: Spatial ability in voles

Gaulin & FitzGerald (1989): compared the maze learning ability of meadow voles and prairie voles. Male meadow voles have a much larger territory to navigate than do the females. However, in prairie voles male & female voles navigate a similar size of territory.

Results: as expected, male meadow voles made far fewer errors than female meadow voles, with male and female prairie voles making similar numbers of errors.

Pliancy model

The pliancy model contradicts the spatial-adaptation model, suggesting that natural selection merely favours a more general enhancement in memory.

Key study: Spatial ability in lizards

Day *et al.* (1999): compared the learning ability of two related species of lizard, one foraging for clumped sedentary prey ('active' approach), the other distributed mobile prey ('sit-and-wait' approach). The 'Barnes maze' required lizards to find a hot rock to escape cold water.

Results: both species performed similarly on the maze task. However, the active lizards were quicker to learn to associate a colour with palatable/unpalatable food, supporting the view that it is a more adaptable memory (not spatial ability) which is selected.

Foraging and food caching

Learning forage locations

When an animal forages successfully, it may need to find its way back to the same location at a later date.

- Srinivasan *et al.* (1997): trained bees to find food in a tunnel marked with vertical stripes. Changing the number of stripes did not affect this ability, but replacing the stripes with horizontal stripes caused them to fail, suggesting that they use visual indicators of motion to locate.

Key study

Menzel (1971): took chimpanzees on a circuitous indoor journey during which they saw food hidden in 18 outside locations. When released they took the shortest route between hiding places (rather than retracing the roundabout route). They were later shown fruit or vegetables being hidden and went immediately to find the fruit – showing that their spatial memory stores information about places *and* facts associated with them.

Locating food caches

A foraging animal may find more food than they can eat at one time, so may store (or 'cache') food for times when it is scarce.

- Jacobs & Liman (1991): allowed squirrels to bury 10 nuts in a 45 square metre area. The locations of each cache were recorded, and up to 12 days later the squirrels were released into an area where nuts had been buried at the same locations, together with random locations. They were more likely to discover nuts at their own sites.

Key study

Sherry (1984): placed chickadees in an aviary containing trees with 72 specially drilled holes. Each bird was allowed to hide 4 or 5 sunflower seeds and then taken into a holding cage for 24 hours. The seeds were removed and velcro covers placed over the holes (to eliminate visual & olfactory cues). When returned to the aviary the chickadees spent more time pecking at the covers where they had stored seeds.

Research studies   Cognitive maps   Neurobiological basis

Radial arm maze studies

A typical radial arm maze might have eight arms arranged in a star orientation.

- Though rats do not explore the arms in a systematic fashion, they do avoid re-entering arms that they have explored.
- Rats will quickly learn how to locate food in such a maze, based on visual cues in the surrounding environment.
- Roberts (1979): devised a 24-arm radial maze. Rats in this maze seemed able to find food only by employing a fixed search pattern (suggesting that their spatial memory capacity had been exceeded).

Detour studies

If animals build up cognitive maps (internal representations) of an area through exploration then they should be able to minimise journey time or take 'short cuts':

- Maier & Schneirla (1935): allowed rats to explore a complex maze. When they removed an obstacle creating a short-cut, rats noticed and used the shorter route.

Hippocampal lesions

- Morris *et al.* (1982): placed rats in circular tanks containing murky water which concealed a platform. Normal rats found the platform by chance, then remembered its location. Rats with hippocampal lesions swim randomly on every trial, suggesting that they are unable to learn the platform's location.

Hippocampal place cells

- O'Keefe & Dostrovsky (1971): recorded the activity of individual hippocampal cells. Some (called place cells) had specific spatial receptive fields, responding to environmental cues (such as furniture) in a specific geographical location.
- Hill & Best (1981): suggested that since these cells are still active in blind and deaf rats, they may be using proprioceptive (body position) cues.

Neurotransmitters in the hippocampus

- The drug scopolamine blocks receptor sites for the neurotransmitter acetylcholine and prevents rats from recalling which arm of a maze they have most recently entered.
- Damage to acetylcholine-producing cells causes rats to perform less well on spatial learning tasks. Transplants of healthy cells reverses this effect (Nilsson *et al.*, 1987).

50

HUMAN REPRODUCTIVE BEHAVIOUR

SYLLABUS

13.5 Evolutionary explanations of human behaviour – human reproductive behaviour
- the relationship between sexual selection and human reproductive behaviour including evolutionary explanations of sex differences in parental investment

KEY QUESTIONS
- How can evolutionary theory explain human mate selection?
- How may evolutionary theory help us to understand parental investment?
- What problems are associated with this approach?

Q ## Section 1: Evolutionary psychology

1 Define *evolutionary psychology*.
2 What do the letters EEA (Davies, 1995) stand for?
3 Complete the sentence: 'According to Miller (1998), the application of ____ ____ theory to human behaviour has been the greatest success story in evolutionary psychology'.
4 What is a *sexually dimorphic* species?
5 What term is used to describe the difference in gamete size between males and females?
6 What is the key difference in biological resources that underpins human reproductive behaviour?
7 Why was it necessary for Darwin to propose the theory of sexual selection?
8 What does it mean to say that 'humans are a *mutually sexually selected species*'?
9 According to Ridley (1993), what kind of people are we attracted to?

Section 2: Mate choice

10 Why are small noses and large eyes attractive female features, according to evolutionary psychology?
11 What did Concar (1995) discover, when presenting men and women with photographs of the opposite sex?
12 Why might a strong jawline in males relate to their fitness?
13 Complete the sentence: 'Concar's (1995) research indicates that women with ____ male partners have the most ____'.
14 Identify one explanation for the discovery that the human male penis is the longest, thickest and most flexible of any living primate.
15 Identify two female anatomical features which are likely to be a consequence of sexual selection.
16 What does Singh's (1993) ratio of 0.7 apply to?
17 Which two hormones (and their levels) are associated with a high level of fertility in human females?
18 Give two reasons why physical attractiveness is more important in females than males (according to the evolutionary account)?

19 Give one likely explanation for the finding that American men who marry in a given year earn about 50 per cent more money than married men of the same age.
20 Why might male expressions of love and kindness be important to a human female?
21 Identify two specific predictions which sexual selection theory is able to make regarding the nature of female deception.
22 Complete the sentence: 'Dunbar (1995) studied 'lonely hearts' columns and found that men predominantly offer ____ and seek ____, whilst the reverse is true for females'.

Section 3: Human sexuality

23 Why does homosexuality present a major puzzle for evolutionary psychology?
24 How do theories which suggest that homosexuality is influenced by recessive genetic factors explain homosexuality?
25 What does the dominance failure theory suggest regarding the origins of homosexuality?
26 Identify one of the differences between gay men and gay women discovered by Symons (1979).
27 According to Ridley's (1993) UK study, what percentage of children are the offspring of males other than their ostensible fathers?
28 In what two ways do women ensure fidelity by their partners, according to evolutionary explanations?
29 Which female trait does evolutionary theory predict that males will value highly as an indicator of fidelity?
30 Complete the sentence: 'To maximise her fitness a female should select a mate on the basis of 'good' genes *and* ____ ____'.
31 What are the two evolutionary consequences of the fact that females have more to lose than males from a poor choice of mate?
32 What is Alcock's (1993) explanation for the relatively large contribution to parenting made by human males (in relation to other higher primates)?

Section 1: Evolutionary psychology

1 Evolutionary psychology may be defined as the application of Darwinian principles to human behaviour.
2 EEA stands for Environment of Evolutionary Adaptedness.
3 'According to Miller (1998) the application of *sexual selection* theory to human behaviour has been the greatest success story in evolutionary psychology.'
4 A sexually dimorphic species is one in which the male and female of the species are physically or behaviourally distinct.
5 *Anisogamy* is the term used to refer to this difference.
6 The key difference is that females bearing fertile eggs are a scarce resource, whilst fertile males are common.
7 The theory was necessary because natural selection cannot explain the evolution of behaviours/structures which appear to reduce the chance of survival (e.g. the peacock's tail).
8 Mutually sexually selected means that both males and females have evolved preferences for certain behavioural and/or anatomical features in the opposite sex.
9 Ridley claims that we 'are attracted to people of high reproductive and genetic potential'.

Section 2: Mate choice

10 Large eyes and a small nose are more child-like features and suggest youth (and therefore reproductive potential).
11 Concar (1995) found that both males and females preferred photographs of symmetrical faces.
12 Jawlines lengthen and broaden during puberty as a result of increased testosterone – which also suppresses the immune system. It may be that only very fit individuals can develop strong jawlines.
13 'Concar's (1995) research indicates that women with *symmetrical* male partners have the most *orgasms*.'
14 It seems likely that the main influence on the evolution of the male penis was female choice.
15 The buttocks and breasts of human females are likely to have undergone sexual elaboration through mate choice by males.
16 Singh argues that 0.7 describes the ideal ratio of a woman's waist to her hips, based on studies of female attractiveness.
17 High levels of oestrogen and low levels of testosterone are associated with high levels of fertility.

18 Female reproductive success is not as limited by the problem of obtaining fertile mates; male fertility is less dependent on age, male fertility cannot be accurately assessed from physical appearance; male attractiveness is more likely to relate to other features (such as ability to provide).
19 It is likely that females seek males with resources connected with parenting.
20 Expressions of love and kindness may provide reliable clues to a man's willingness to devote resources to a female and her offspring.
21 Sexual selection theory would predict that females would lie about their age, alter their appearance and conceal prior sexual encounters.
22 'Dunbar (1995) studied 'lonely hearts' columns and found that men predominantly offer *resources* and seek *attractiveness*, whilst the reverse is true for females.'

Section 3: Human sexuality

23 Homosexuality would appear to be a maladaptive behaviour (since it produces no offspring) and should therefore be rapidly eliminated by natural selection.
24 Such theories propose that the gene is recessive in heterosexuals but could provide reproductive advantages when combined with other genes in these individuals.
25 The dominance failure theory suggests that subordinate males are unable to find female partners, and consequently develop a homosexual orientation.
26 Symons found that gay men were more likely to be promiscuous than gay women, and were more likely to be unfaithful to their partners.
27 The study found that 20 per cent of children are the offspring of males other than their ostensible fathers.
28 Women ensure fidelity by exhibiting long periods of sexual receptivity and by concealing ovulation.
29 Chastity is the female trait most likely to be indicative of future fidelity.
30 'To maximise her fitness a female should select a mate on the basis of 'good' genes *and parental investment*.'
31 The two consequences are that females are more reluctant to begin an investment (more selective in their choice of mate) and once committed, less likely to abandon their goal.
32 Alcock suggests that women concealed oestrus in order to encourage the males to guard them closely. Having thereby ensured their own paternity, males would be more likely to ensure the survival of offspring.

A

191

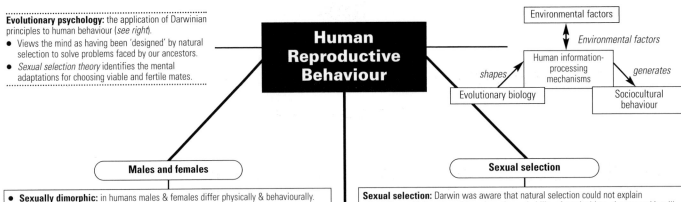

Evolutionary psychology: the application of Darwinian principles to human behaviour (*see right*).
- Views the mind as having been 'designed' by natural selection to solve problems faced by our ancestors.
- *Sexual selection theory* identifies the mental adaptations for choosing viable and fertile mates.

Human Reproductive Behaviour

Environmental factors

↕ *Environmental factors*

Human information-processing mechanisms

shapes ↗

Evolutionary biology

generates ↘

Sociocultural behaviour

Males and females

- **Sexually dimorphic:** in humans males & females differ physically & behaviourally.
- **Gametes:** males & females produce different size gametes (*anisogamy*); males producing sperm which are numerous, small & mobile and females producing a small number of large immobile eggs.

A human female is only fertile for a couple of days each month, and only able to produce eggs for a small proportion of her lifespan. Whilst females bearing fertile eggs are a scarce resource, fertile males are common.

Sexual selection

Sexual selection: Darwin was aware that natural selection could not explain adaptations which appeared to reduce the probability of survival (e.g. the peacock's tail). He proposed the theory of sexual selection, which depends on the advantage which individuals have solely in respect of reproduction.
- **Peacocks:** females appear to prefer males with the longest & most brightly coloured tails. The effects of sexual selection outweigh the disadvantages of having such a cumbersome appendage (Clamp & Russell, 1998).

Mate choice

Humans differ from other anthropoid apes in several respects, e.g. facial features, enlarged breasts & buttocks (female) and long penises (male). Findings suggest that average faces are attractive, and that females with more child-like features (large eyes, small noses & full lips) and males with testosterone-enlarged features (strong jaws, large noses) are preferred.

Symmetry
- Concar (1995) found that men prefer photographs of women with symmetrical faces and vice versa. Bodily symmetry is also preferred.
- Concar (1995) found that women with symmetrical breasts are most fertile, and women with symmetrical partners have the most orgasms.

It may be that symmetry is a good indicator of biological quality; such as good reproductive vigour and an effective immune system.

Vital statistics
- The penis of the human male is the longest & thickest of any living primate. This may be due to sexual selection.
- Female breasts & buttocks have undergone sexual elaboration through mate choice by males. Their reserves of fat may indicate nutritional status.
- Singh (1993) argues that the ideal female waist to hip ratio is 0.7. This seems to be stable across time & cultures.

Physical attractiveness
Male/female differences are more marked in humans than among apes & monkeys:
- Male size and strength may partly be due to rivalry in acquiring and protecting females from rivals.
- Physical attractiveness is a better way of assessing reproductive fitness of females than of males (whose fertility is less dependent on age).
- Female fertility indicators include white teeth, clear skin, energy & reputation.

Other factors
Females should seek males who are willing not simply to mate, but to invest resources connected with parenting. This may require females to predict their potential:
- Dunbar (1995) studied lonely hearts columns and found that men typically offer resources and seek attractiveness whilst the reverse is true for women.
- Willerman (1979) suggests that women may use cues such as ambition, industriousness and intelligence.

Homosexuality

Homosexuality presents a major puzzle for evolutionary psychology. Studies have discovered a genetic component to male homosexuality, which in turn probably influences sensitivity to testosterone. If the genes were not adaptive in some way, they would be eliminated:
- **Recessive vs dominant:** if the genetic factors are predominantly recessive (i.e. not expressed in the presence of other dominant genes) they may confer other reproductive advantages in heterosexual carriers.
- **Promiscuity:** before the advent of AIDS male homosexuals were typically more promiscuous than male heterosexuals, and more likely to be unfaithful. However the reverse is true for lesbians who usually form long-term partnerships with little risk of infidelity. This may be due to an evolved male tendency to seek variety.

Human sexuality

Adultery

Adultery can be advantageous to both sexes within a monogamous relationship: the male increasing the quantity of his offspring, the female increasing the quality of hers.
- Ridley (1993): found that in the UK more than 20% of children are the offspring of males other than their ostensible father.
- Since both sexes risk losing their partners, both have evolved strategies for ensuring fidelity: females exhibit long periods of sexual receptivity and conceal ovulation, so that men must copulate regularly and guard them against rivals. Males are more likely to place a high value on female chastity (as an indicator of future fidelity of a selected mate). Buss (1989) found that in 62% of cultures males valued chastity more highly than females did.

Parental investment

Parental investment: '... any investment by the parent in an individual offspring that increases the offspring's chance of surviving at the cost of the parent's ability to invest in other offspring' (Trivers, 1972). A female may choose a mate who is likely to invest in this way, in preference to one who merely possesses 'good genes'. Because of this the sexes are essentially in conflict, since males would benefit most from females who are prepared to raise their children alone ('stay vs stray'). However, other factors (such as social groups) are significant.

The burden of motherhood
- Females have far more to lose from making a poor mate choice: whilst ancestral men might have walked away from a poor mate, a woman may become pregnant and risk having to raise the child alone.
- Whilst males benefit from choosing a female who is fertile and a good mother, this may apply only to long-term relationships and not to casual sex partners.
- As a result of the 9-month investment in childbearing and the lengthy investment of breastfeeding, women are likely to be more selective in their choice of mates, and less likely to abandon her goal once committed.

The role of the father
Until recently fathers typically took on the 'breadwinner' role, providing food and resources which enabled his wife to care for children.
- From an evolutionary perspective, males who were able to offer material benefits may have been preferred as partners by females. This may also help to explain the practice of taking females out to restaurants: in the ancestral environment food would have been scarce, and mothers with children would have had limited opportunities to forage.
- Alcock (1993) suggests that the relatively long period during which males care for their young may have arisen from the female strategy of concealing ovulation. As a result, the male must guard the female over an extended period to ensure paternity. Having invested to this extent he may then wish to 'secure' his investment by looking after the offspring which he can be confident are his own.

51

EVOLUTIONARY EXPLANATIONS OF MENTAL DISORDERS

KEY QUESTIONS
- How can evolutionary theory explain anxiety disorders?
- How can evolutionary theory explain affective disorders?

Section 1: Introduction
1 What is Darwinian medicine?
2 What does Darwinian medicine suggest regarding symptoms such as fever, coughing and vomiting?
3 In what way may obsessive–compulsive disorder be linked to Sydenham's chorea?

Section 2: Anxiety disorders
4 Define *anxiety*.
5 Complete the sentence: 'In many ways, anxiety may be considered as synonymous with ____'.
6 What is *hypophobia*?
7 What was the outcome of Pinker's (1997) experiment in which timid, normal and bold guppies were placed in a tank with a predatory fish?
8 What, according to Marks (1987), is the evolutionary function of fear?
9 Roughly what percentage of the US population has experienced a clinical anxiety disorder?
10 Identify one disadvantage and one advantage of increased anxiety levels.
11 Identify two of the four pieces of information which we need to know in order to assess the appropriateness of a given anxiety reaction.
12 What is a *phobia*?
13 What are the three main types of phobia?
14 What were Watson & Rayner (1920) able to demonstrate regarding the origin of phobias?
15 What interesting observation regarding phobias led Seligman (1971) to propose the principle of *preparedness*?
16 What is *preparedness*?
17 In what way did Hunt's (1995) experiments with monkeys support the preparedness argument?

18 Which type of phobia is it difficult for preparedness to explain?
19 What are *obsessions*?
20 What are *compulsions*?
21 What evolutionary explanation of compulsive checking behaviours has been proposed?
22 Why might cleaning behaviours have evolved?

Section 3: Affective disorders
23 What are *affective disorders*?
24 Identify four characteristics of *depression*.
25 How does mania compare with depression?
26 In what way does Jamison's (1989) study suggest an adaptive advantage to genes causing bipolar disorder?
27 What does Kender *et al.*'s (1992) finding that the genetic co-variance between depression and anxiety is close to 100 per cent mean?
28 Complete the sentence: 'In general it seems that anxiety results from the ____ of loss, whereas depression comes from the ____ of loss'.
29 Which neurotransmitter seems to play a significant role in affective disorders?
30 How can depression in vervet monkeys be alleviated?
31 Give one plausible explanation for Nesse & Williams' (1996) finding that young people are more likely to have experienced depression than their elders.
32 Identify one of the two features of sadness which might increase fitness.
33 What do the letters SAHP stand for?
34 Which type of individual is particularly likely to develop depression, according to attachment theory?
35 What does rank theory propose, regarding the function of depression?

Q

Section 1: Introduction

1 Darwinian medicine is an evolutionary approach to understanding disease.

2 Darwinian medicine suggests that such 'symptoms' may actually be a vital part of the body's adaptive response towards infection.

3 The brain areas apparently involved in obsessive–compulsive disorder are very close to those damaged by Sydenham's chorea.

Section 2: Anxiety disorders

4 Anxiety is a general feeling of dread or apprehensiveness, which is typically accompanied by various physiological reactions.

5 'In many ways, anxiety may be considered as synonymous with *arousal*.'

6 Hypophobia is a deficient anxiety response to a situation or object.

7 After a few days many of the timid guppies had survived, a few of the normal guppies had survived and none of the bold guppies had survived.

8 Marks claims that 'Fear is a vital evolutionary legacy that leads an organism to avoid threat, and has obvious survival value'.

9 Roughly 15 per cent of the US population has experienced a clinical anxiety disorder.

10 Increased anxiety levels have the disadvantages of depleting energy reserves, impairing everyday activities and damaging bodily tissue but the advantage of preparing the individual for responding to danger (and thereby increasing chances of survival).

11 We need to know the likelihood of a stimulus signalling danger, the relative frequency of dangerous stimuli in a location, the cost of responding to a false alarm and the cost of not responding to a true emergency.

12 A phobia is a type of anxiety disorder, in which there is a persistent and unreasonable fear of an object or situation.

13 The three main types of phobia are: agoraphobia, social phobia and specific phobias.

14 Watson and Rayner were able to demonstrate that a phobia can be acquired through classical conditioning.

15 The interesting observation is the observation that people are more likely to become phobic towards some stimuli (such as spiders) than others (such as cars).

16 Preparedness is a psychological predisposition to be sensitive to and become phobic about some stimuli rather than others.

17 Hunt found that monkeys raised in the laboratory did not fear snakes, but would develop a phobia after only one exposure to a video of a monkey showing a fear reaction to a snake.

18 It is difficult for preparedness to explain social phobias.

19 Obsessions are involuntary thoughts or images that are recurrent and generally unpleasant.

20 Compulsions are irresistible urges to engage in repetitive behaviours.

21 Evolutionary theory suggests that checking behaviours may have arisen in relation to the defence of resources, such as food, territories, possessions and mates.

22 Cleaning behaviours might have evolved as a defence against micro-organisms.

Section 3: Affective disorders

23 Affective disorders are exaggerations of the human capacity to experience sadness and euphoria.

24 Depression is characterised by low mood, reduced energy, pessimistic thinking, disturbances of sleep and appetite, feelings of worthlessness, guilt and hopelessness.

25 Mania can be thought of as the mirror image of depression.

26 Jamison found a higher incidence of bipolar disorder among creative people.

27 Kendler *et al.*'s finding means that the genes that cause anxiety almost certainly cause depression as well.

28 'In general it seems that anxiety results from the *anticipation* of loss, whereas depression comes from the *experience* of loss.'

29 Serotonin seems to play a significant role in affective disorders.

30 Their depression can be alleviated by administering fluoxetine (*Prozac*).

31 This finding may partly be due to the effects of mass communication which encourages individuals to feel in competition with a wider group – leading to dissatisfaction.

32 Sadness may motivate us to stop activities that may be causing losses, and it may dampen our optimism and enable us to assess our lives more objectively.

33 SAHP stands for 'social attention-holding potential'.

34 According to attachment theory individuals who have failed to develop a mature capacity to deal with loss, as a result of ineffective attachment in childhood, are most likely to experience depression.

35 If depression is a consequence of conflict in which the losing individual submits, it may be that women are more likely to lose out in conflicts with men, causing depression.

Evolutionary Explanations of Mental Disorders

- Darwinian medicine suggests that many symptoms (e.g. fever, vomiting, fussiness over food) may form a vital part of the body's adaptive response towards infection (Davies, 1996).
- Natural selection may not have had time to change our bodies to cope with modern environments. This mismatch may be the root cause of some physical and mental illnesses.

Anxiety

- **Anxiety:** a general feeling of dread or apprehensiveness, which is typically accompanied by various physiological reactions (e.g. shallow breathing, sweating and muscle tension).
- **The function of anxiety:** anxiety prepares us to deal with and avoid threats and is synonymous with arousal. It is similar to the immune system, in that it has both general and specific forms. Generalised anxiety occurs in response to general threats (such as stress at work) whilst specific anxiety may occur in response to specific situations or objects (e.g. a phobic reaction to spiders). Whilst the general function of anxiety is to prepare for avoidance, attack or escape, both over-anxiety (*panic*) and under-anxiety (*hypophobia*) can be harmful.
- **The optimum level of anxiety:** we use *four* types of information to assess the appropriateness of anxiety: the likelihood that a stimulus is dangerous, the frequency of dangerous stimuli in this situation, the cost of responding to a false alarm, the cost of not responding to a true emergency. Whilst increased anxiety prepares us for danger and increases our chances of survival it also depletes our energy and damages bodily tissues. Decreased anxiety, on the other hand, saves energy but may leave us unprepared for a dangerous situation.

Phobias

- **Phobia:** a type of anxiety disorder in which there is a persistent and unreasonable fear of an object or situation.
- **3 main types:** agoraphobia (fear of open spaces), social phobia (fear of social situations), and specific phobias (fear of a specific object or situation).
- **The origin of phobias:** Watson & Rayner's (1920) experiments with 'little Albert' showed that phobias can be acquired by through classical conditioning. However people seem more likely to become phobic towards some stimuli (such as spiders) than others (such as cars – despite the fact that the latter cause more injuries!).

Preparedness
Seligman (1971) argues that we have a psychological predisposition to become phobic about certain stimuli (such as spiders) since these were real sources of danger hundreds of thousands of years ago.
- Hunt (1995): monkeys raised in a laboratory have no fear of snakes, but will develop a phobia after watching a single video showing a monkey reacting with alarm to a snake. However, they do not develop a fear of *flowers* in the same manner.
- It is difficult to see how this approach could explain certain simple phobias (such as a fear of straight lines) and most social phobias.

Obsessive–compulsive disorders

- **Obsession:** an involuntary thought or image that is recurrent and generally unpleasant.
- **Compulsion:** irresistible urges to engage in repetitive behaviours.
- **Incidence:** roughly 1.5 million people in Britain suffer from O–C disorders.
- **Role:** compulsive behaviours are usually aimed at reducing or preventing the discomfort associated with some future undesirable event. Compulsives realise that their behaviours are senseless but experience intense anxiety if prevented from performing them.

Checking & cleaning behaviours
- **Checking:** checking behaviours may have arisen in relation to the defence of resources, such as food supplies, territories and mates. Evolutionary theory would predict that genes responsible for excessive or inadequate checking would be lost from the gene pool over time.
- **Cleaning:** cleaning behaviours may have arisen as a defence against micro-organisms. The notion of 'contamination' is common among sufferers of OCD. OCD may represent an exaggerated form of behaviours which are normally adaptive.

Affective disorders

- **Affective disorders:** essentially exaggerations of sadness and euphoria, these are judged to be mental disorders when they are extreme (*depression* or *mania*), incapacitating, chronic or unresponsive to outside influences. They are the most common type of psychological problem and carry a 12% lifetime risk for men and 20% for women.
- **Depression:** characterised by low mood, reduced energy, pessimistic thinking and disturbances of sleep and appetite. Also involves feelings of worthlessness, hopelessness and guilt.
- **Mania:** a 'mirror image' of depression. Characterised by elation, inflated self-esteem, insomnia, high energy levels and extreme optimism. Appetite and libido are increased.
- **Genetic factors:** Jamison (1989) reported a higher incidence of bipolar disorder (depression and mania) in creative people, suggesting some adaptive advantage from the genes. Kendler *et al.*'s (1992) research suggests that the same genes cause both anxiety and depression (anxiety resulting from the anticipation of loss and depression from the experience of loss).
- **Neurotransmitter levels:** The neurotransmitter *serotonin* plays a significant role in affective disorders. Raleigh & McGuire (1991) found that the highest ranking male in groups of vervet monkeys had serotonin levels twice as high as those of other males. When they lose their position, their serotonin levels fall and they show signs of depression. This effect can be prevented by administering *Prozac*, and if *Prozac* is administered to a randomly chosen male this male always becomes the highest ranking male.

- **Key study:** Nesse & Williams (1996) examined data from 39,000 people in 5 different parts of the world and found that young people are far more likely than their elders to have experienced an episode of major depression. In addition, rates were higher in societies with higher levels of economic development. One explanation may be mass communication, which forces people to feel that they are competing with the rest of the world (rather than a small group), causing them to become dissatisfied with themselves.

The role of sadness
Sadness is universal, has relatively consistent characteristics and is reliably elicited by a loss of reproductive resources.
- It may be adaptive in motivating us to stop activities that may be causing losses. It may also cause us to assess ourselves more objectively.
- SAHP (*social attention-holding potential*) is used by Gilbert (1990) to refer to the quality and quantity of attention that others pay to a person and varies according to status. Extreme changes in SAHP may lead to mania or depression – the anticipation of such a change may explain social phobias.

Attachment theory
Stevens & Price (1996) argue that warm, intimate and lasting relationships form the basis of human happiness.
- Threats to a relationship may cause anxiety, whilst loss of a relationship may cause depression.
- Pathological depression is especially likely in individuals who have failed to develop effective attachments in childhood.
- One problem with attachment theory is that many causes of depression are not attributable to the loss of an attachment figure.

Rank theory
Proposes that depression is an adaptive response to a loss of status. The function of depression is to promote the acceptance of a subordinate role.
- Claims that depression originally arose as a submitting component of ritual conflict. An important part of conflict and ensuing changes in rank is *self-assessment*.
- Mental well-being involves forming an accurate assessment of our RHP (*resource holding power*) based on social cues. Mania and depression are relatively common amongst people who are insensitive to social cues. Depression may also elicit nurturance from others.

Sex differences
Theories relating depression to rank imply that depression should be more common in men. In fact, it is twice as common in women.
- Depression might reduce reproductive success more in males than in females, causing it to be 'bred out of' the male population to a greater extent.
- Conflict between males and females might result in females submitting more commonly than males.
- The burden of motherhood and post-natal depression may also contribute to the difference.

52

THE EVOLUTION OF INTELLIGENCE

SYLLABUS

13.5 Evolutionary explanations of human behaviour – evolution of intelligence
- evolutionary factors in the development of human intelligence including the relationship between brain size and intelligence

KEY QUESTIONS
- What is the role of intelligence?
- How can ecological theory explain intelligence?
- How can social theory explain intelligence?
- How can sexual selection theory explain intelligence?

Q

Section 1: Introduction

1 How do Binet & Simon (1915) define intelligence?
2 Identify two of the three aptitudes which are likely to be included in intelligence.
3 Complete the sentence: 'For most psychologists, intelligence can be attributed to an interaction between ____ and the ____'.
4 Roughly what percentage of our intelligence may be attributed to heredity?
5 What is the core concept for an understanding of why intelligence evolved, according to Plotkin (1995)?
6 How does the comparative approach establish the history of intelligence?
7 How long ago did *Homo sapiens* first appear?

Section 2: Ecological theory

8 Complete the sentence: 'According to ecological theory one of the main selection pressures that promoted the development of intelligence may have been efficiency in ____'.
9 What special adaptation may allow some species to find items over a large area?
10 How does Boesch & Boesch's (1984) study of chimpanzees in West Africa support the ecological theory?
11 Describe the tools which have found to have been used by *Homo erectus*.
12 Why is tool use an unlikely explanation for increases in intelligence in humans?
13 Identify two of the three skills required by hunting.
14 In what way do lions relate to the ecological theory of intelligence?
15 Which area of the brain is chiefly responsible for the increase of overall brain size in primates over other mammal groups?

Section 3: Social theory

16 What explanation of intelligence is offered by social theory?

17 Identify the two reasons why group living could have set the stage for the evolution of intelligence.
18 What is it that our ancestors should have evolved to detect, according to Cosmides & Tooby (1997)?
19 In what way did Watson (1983) demonstrate that our reasoning powers are affected by the content, not merely the logical structure, of arguments?
20 What name does Cosmides (1989) give for the procedure used by people in applying conditional rules to social contracts?
21 What is *tactical deception*?
22 What name is given by evolutionary psychologists to the type of reasoning which is principally concerned with *social manipulation*?
23 What physical characteristic is strongly positively correlated with this type of intelligence?
24 What name is given to the specialised cognitive system used to assign beliefs or desires to the actions of others?
25 What type of disorder is thought to result from damage to this system in humans?
26 What does neocortical enlargement correlate positively with?

Section 4: Sexual selection theory

27 What is Ridley's (1993) explanation for the evolution of human intelligence?
28 What are the specific evolutionary functions of the human brain, according to sexual selection theory?
29 What did Miller's (1992) review of survey data discover concerning intelligence?
30 How might food provision provide a link between ecological and sexual selection theories?
31 What is neotony?
32 What, according to Ridley (1993), is the mechanism by which apemen turned into humans?
33 Why might male sexual selection favour neotony?

Section 1: Introduction

1 Binet & Simon (1915) define intelligence as 'the faculty of adapting oneself to circumstances'.
2 Intelligence probably includes learning a wide range of information, applying learned information to new situations and thinking and original planning.
3 'For most psychologists, intelligence can be attributed to an interaction between *genes* and the *environment*.'
4 Roughly 50–60 per cent of our intelligence may be attributed to heredity.
5 Plotkin (1995) suggests that unpredictability is the core concept for an understanding of intelligence.
6 The comparative approach infers the history of intelligence from its pattern of occurrence in surviving species.
7 *Homo sapiens* first appeared about 45,000 years ago.

Section 2: Ecological theory

8 'According to ecological theory, one of the main selection pressures that promoted the development of intelligence may have been efficiency in *foraging*.'
9 Some species may use cognitive maps to find items over a large area.
10 Boesch & Boesch's (1984) study suggested that chimpanzees could use cognitive maps to remember the environment and objects within it.
11 *Homo erectus* used hand axes and teardrop-shaped stone devices.
12 Tool use increased dramatically about 200,000 years ago – too late to explain intelligence which had been increasing over three million years.
13 Hunting requires the skills of forethought, cunning and co-ordination.
14 Lions show that it is possible for skilled hunting to occur with brains only half the size of ours, suggesting that hunting is not a sufficient explanation of brain size.
15 The neocortex is chiefly responsible for the increase of brain size in primates over other mammal groups?

Section 3: Social theory

16 Social theory suggest that interactions with others present intellectual challenges to which intelligence is an evolved response.
17 Group living increases the value of having better information, and poses new cognitive challenges (such as communication and social exchanges).

18 Cosmides & Tooby (1997) argue that our ancestors should have evolved to detect violations of social conventions.
19 Watson gave participants two logical tasks involving identifying cards. The tasks shared the same logical structure, but one involved letters and numbers and the other a social problem. Participants found the latter easier to solve.
20 Cosmides (1989) calls the strategy which we employ a search-for-cheats procedure.
21 Tactical deception involves deliberately deceiving others in order to secure a goal.
22 Psychologists call this type of reasoning Machiavellian intelligence.
23 Neocortex size is strongly positively correlated with Machiavellian intelligence.
24 The specialised cognitive system used to assign beliefs or desires to the actions of others is called a *theory of mind module*.
25 Damage to this system may result in autism in children.
26 Neocortical enlargement correlates positively with group size.

Section 4: Sexual selection theory

27 According to Ridley (1993), the evolution of sexual intelligence was the result of sexual competition between individuals of the same sex.
28 Sexual selection theory suggests that the brain evolved to stimulate and entertain potential partners and to assess the stimulation attempts of others.
29 Miller found that surveys consistently place intelligence high in lists of desirable characteristics in both sexes (even above things such as beauty and wealth).
30 It may be that early humans exchanged food for sex, with the females mating with successful hunters.
31 Neotony is the retention of juvenile features into adult life.
32 Ridley (1993) suggests that the mechanism by which ape-men turned into humans was simply a genetic switch which slowed the developmental clock.
33 Males may favour females who have features suggesting youth, and neotonous females are more likely to appear youthful.

A

Intelligence: the ability to devise flexible solutions to problems.

Component aptitudes:
- learning a wide range of information
- applying learned information in new situations
- thinking, reasoning and original planning.

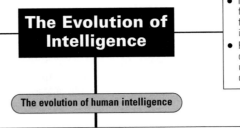

The Evolution of Intelligence

- Intelligence is a combination of special-purpose functions (e.g. face recognition) and general purpose functions (e.g. vision) which are subject to the interaction between genes and environment.
- Plotkin (1995) argues that the abnormally large (and costly) human brain is designed to cope with an unpredictable environment in a way that instincts cannot.

The evolution of human intelligence

The comparative approach

According to the comparative approach, the history of intelligence can be inferred from its pattern of occurrence in surviving species. There are three main components to the approach:
1. Find reliable differences in the intelligences of living animal species and ascertain how these affect the species' ability to survive under different circumstances.
2. Deduce from the above the likely intelligence of the species' extinct ancestors.
3. Look for plausible selection pressures which could have favoured the evolutionary changes uncovered (i.e. problems to which they seem to be solutions).

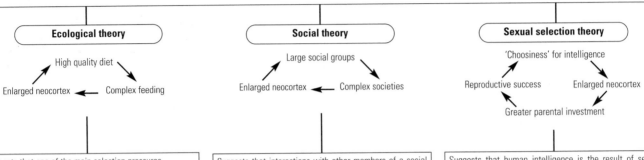

Ecological theory

High quality diet
Enlarged neocortex ← Complex feeding

Social theory

Large social groups
Enlarged neocortex ← Complex societies

Sexual selection theory

'Choosiness' for intelligence
Reproductive success — Enlarged neocortex
Greater parental investment

Suggests that one of the main selection pressures promoting the development of intelligence may have been efficiency in *foraging*:
- Many primates have to balance their diets via wide-ranging & selective eating, which favours individuals with adaptations such as *cognitive maps*.
- Boesch & Boesch (1984) showed that chimpanzees encountering nuts will often go straight to the nearest stone of the right type required to crack them, suggesting that they create cognitive maps containing features such as rock locations.

Tool use in humans
Obtaining food requires skills such as hunting, tool use and complex food processing:
- The first stone tools (chipped rocks) of *Homo habilis* appeared about 2.5 million years ago in Ethiopia.
- These were replaced by the hand axes of *Homo erectus* but there was little further development until about 200,000 years ago when there was a sudden explosion of tool variety and sophistication at about the time that *Homo sapiens* appeared.

Problem: Unfortunately this increase in tool use came too late to explain human intelligence which had been increasing steadily over the last 3 million years.

Evaluation
- Such 'hunting explanations' suggest that this ability requires forethought, cunning & coordination. However this applies equally to lions who manage with much smaller brains than ours.
- 'Gathering explanations' are similar but apply equally to baboons and chimpanzees (which do not have brains as large as ours.
- Our brains are larger because of a larger neocortical area. If this is a result of environment complexity as the theory suggests, then species inhabiting complex environments should tend to have larger neocortical areas. This is not the case (Byrne, 1995).

Suggests that interactions with other members of a social group present intellectual challenges to which primate intelligence is the evolved response:
- Generally, the most intelligent species are social (e.g. dolphins, wolves, elephants and monkeys). Social creatures benefit from information and communication.
- Cosmides & Tooby (1997) suggest that we evolved abilities which enable us to *search-for-cheats* and are therefore adept at solving puzzles to do with social exchanges (i.e. identifying people who take but don't give).
- Apes and humans are adept at *tactical deception* which involves deceiving others in order to secure a goal. Several psychologists argue that this type of 'Machiavellian intelligence' is the focus of a cognitive arms race which led to the evolution of intelligence. There is a strong positive correlation between neocortex size and tactical deception in primates.

Watson's selection task
Watson (1983) tested individuals' ability to determine if a rule had been violated by which cards they would need to turn over:
- 'If a card has the letter D on the one side it must have the number 3 on the other' (Cards: D, F, 3, 7)
- 'If a person is drinking beer then s/he must be over 18 years old' (Cards: drinking beer, drinking coke, 25 yrs old, 16 yrs old)

Results: individuals were far better at solving the social problem.

Theory of mind
Research suggests that humans and apes possess an evolved ability to assign beliefs or desires to the actions of others, resulting from a specific cognitive system.
- This ability is not present at birth but develops between the ages of 3 & 5 in a universal pattern.
- A theory of mind may have initially evolved to enable us to predict the behaviour of others and may later have been used for tactical deception.

Evaluation
- The Machiavellian theory applies to every social species so it is not clear why humans have broken away from the pack. Language may be part of the answer.
- Group size does correlate strongly with neocortex size providing strong support for the theory.
- Selection for Machiavellian intelligence would predict much larger brains in apes and monkeys than we actually observe.

Suggests that human intelligence is the result of sexual competition between individuals of the same sex. The brain is an elaborate courtship device designed to attract and retain sexual mates.
- The brain's evolutionary function is to stimulate and entertain potential partners. Intelligent people are more attractive than others and able to outwit their competitors.
- Miller (1992) found that surveys consistently place intelligence high in lists of desirable characteristics in both sexes.
- Mutual sexual selection for big brains may have influenced our mating systems: infants with large heads must be born relatively premature (if they are to pass through the birth canal) leaving them helpless & requiring long-term parental bonds to care for them.

The importance of neotony
Neotony refers to the retention of juvenile features into adult life. Humans are born more immature and remain more immature for a longer period than any other species (Montagu, 1961).
- Neotony may have come about as a result of sexual selection with men selecting mates with youthful features, who are more likely to possess genes which slow the rate of development.
- Such a 'neotony gene' would probably make males and females appear more youthful – females may also have selected younger-looking males.

Overall, the conclusion is that increased intelligence is favoured by neotony, and neotony is a consequence of sexual selection.

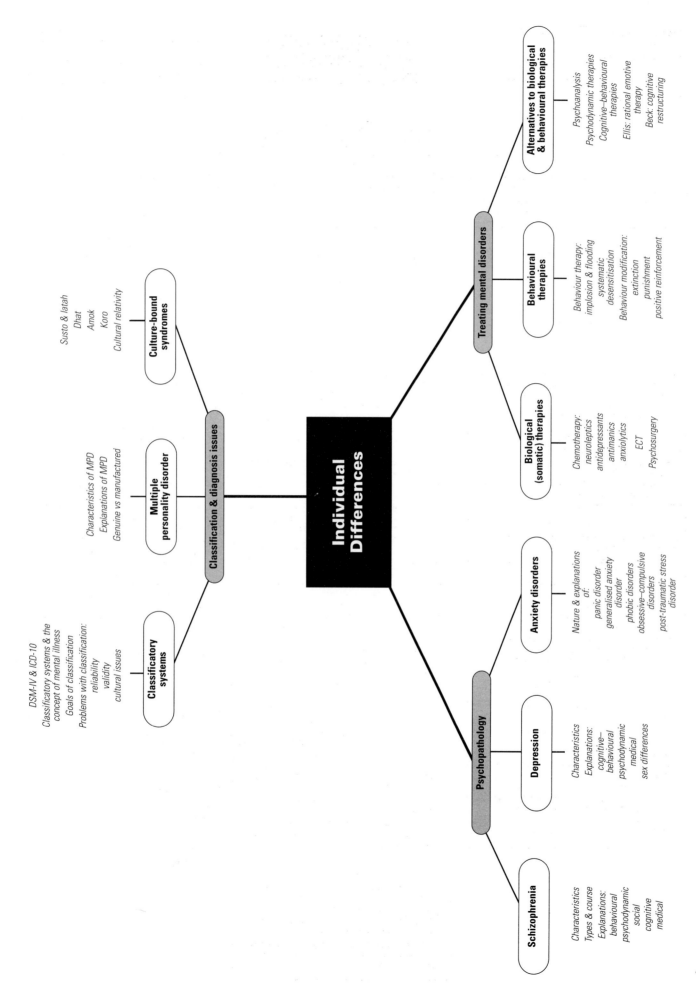

Individual Differences

Classification & diagnosis issues

Classificatory systems
DSM-IV & ICD-10
Classificatory systems & the concept of mental illness
Goals of classification
Problems with classification:
reliability
validity
cultural issues

Multiple personality disorder
Characteristics of MPD
Explanations of MPD
Genuine vs manufactured

Culture-bound syndromes
Susto & latah
Dhat
Amok
Koro
Cultural relativity

Treating mental disorders

Biological (somatic) therapies
Chemotherapy:
neuroleptics
antidepressants
antimanics
anxiolytics
ECT
Psychosurgery

Behavioural therapies
Behaviour therapy:
implosion & flooding
systematic desensitisation
Behaviour modification:
extinction
punishment
positive reinforcement

Alternatives to biological & behavioural therapies
Psychoanalysis
Psychodynamic therapies
Cognitive–behavioural therapies
Ellis: rational emotive therapy
Beck: cognitive restructuring

Psychopathology

Schizophrenia
Characteristics
Types & course
Explanations:
behavioural
psychodynamic
social
cognitive
medical

Depression
Characteristics
Explanations:
cognitive–behavioural
psychodynamic
medical
sex differences

Anxiety disorders
Nature & explanations of:
panic disorder
generalised anxiety disorder
phobic disorders
obsessive–compulsive disorders
post-traumatic stress disorder

53

CLASSIFICATORY SYSTEMS

SYLLABUS
14.1 Issues in the classification and diagnosis of psychological abnormality – classificatory systems
- current versions of ICD and DSM as alternative approaches to the classification of psychological abnormality, including research into the reliability and validity of classification and diagnosis (e.g. Rosenhan)

KEY QUESTIONS
- What are DSM-IV and ICD-10?
- How do psychosis and neurosis differ?
- What issues surround the use of the term 'mental illness'?
- What are the goals of classification and difficulties in achieving these goals?
- What other issues surround classificatory systems?

Q

Section 1: Introducing DSM-IV and ICD-10

1 Who was the first person to attempt a comprehensive classification of abnormal behaviours?

2 What is the full name of the classificatory system introduced by the World Health Organisation in 1948?

3 What are the three categories of mental disturbance or mental disorder identified in the 1983 Mental Health Act (England and Wales)?

4 Identify any one *organic mental disorder* identified in ICD-10.

5 Into which ICD-10 category would an individual suffering from *bipolar disorder* fall?

6 Into which DSM-IV category would *multiple personality disorder* fall?

7 Into which DSM-IV category would *anorexia nervosa* fall?

8 Which of ICD-10 and DSM-IV has the larger number of *discrete categories*?

Section 2: Neurosis, psychosis and mental illness

9 In what way do *neurotics* and *psychotics* differ with regard to 'contact with reality'?

10 What is the relationship between neurosis, psychosis and the *pre-morbid personality*?

11 Do ICD-10 and DSM-IV use the terms 'neurotic' and 'psychotic'?

12 Identify the four reasons given by Gelder *et al.* (1989) for abolishing the distinction between neurosis and psychosis.

13 How does Blaney (1975) defend the decision to think of abnormal behaviour as indicative of some kind of underlying *illness*?

14 According to Szasz (1974, 1994), what political purpose is served by labels such as *mentally ill*?

15 What, according to Szasz, is the difference between *diseases of the brain* and *problems in living*?

16 Which term, used to describe conditions resulting in abnormal behaviour, is used by both ICD-10 and DSM-IV?

17 Why has DSM-IV removed the category *organic mental disorder* from the classificatory system?

Section 3: Goals and problems with classification

18 Identify the three common goals shared by ICD-10 and DSM-IV.

19 Briefly describe Rosenhan's (1973) first experiment which questions the *reliability* and *validity* of classification of mental disorders.

20 What did Rosenhan's follow-up experiment involve?

21 What does the term *reliability* refer to when used to describe a diagnosis?

22 What did Cooper *et al.* (1972) discover about the diagnoses given by American and British psychiatrists?

23 In what way were Cooper *et al.* able to reduce these differences?

24 What is *multiaxial classification*, as introduced by DSM-III (1980)?

25 Name the five *axes* used by the DSM system.

26 Which of DSM-IV and ICD-10 gives more prominence to the *aetiology* of disorders?

27 What does the term *validity* refer to when used to describe a diagnosis?

28 What did Bannister *et al.* (1964) discover when investigating the relationship between diagnosis and treatment?

29 How do critics of Rosenhan's study argue that the *pseudopatients'* behaviour after admission was not normal?

30 What percentage of the general population and what percentage of the psychiatric population are black?

31 What is an *adaptive paranoid response*?

32 According to Littlewood & Lipsedge (1989), mental illness in minorities is an intelligible response to what?

33 Why does Littlewood (1992) criticise DSM-IV for being *ethnocentric*?

Section 1: Introducing DSM-IV and ICD-10

1 Kraepelin (1913) was the first to attempt a comprehensive classification of abnormal behaviours.
2 The full name is the International Standard Classification of Diseases, Injuries and Causes of Death.
3 The 1983 Mental Health Act identifies mental illness, personality disorder and mental impairment as the three categories of mental disturbance.
4 Dementia in Alzheimer's disease, personality and behavioural disorders due to brain disease, damage and dysfunction (e.g. BSE) are all examples of organic mental disorders (ICD-10).
5 Bipolar disorder falls into the category mood (affective) disorders.
6 Multiple personality disorder falls into the category dissociative disorders in DSM-IV.
7 Anorexia nervosa falls into the DSM-IV category, eating disorders.
8 DSM-IV has the larger number of discrete categories and ICD-10 a smaller number of more general categories.

Section 2: Neurosis, psychosis and mental illness

9 Neurotics maintain contact with reality, whereas psychotics lose contact (e.g. hallucinations and delusions).
10 Neurotic disturbances are related to the individual's personality prior to the disorder (the pre-morbid personality), whereas psychotic disorders are not.
11 ICD-10 uses the term *neurotic* and DSM-IV the term *psychotic*.
12 Gelder *et al.* (1989) believe that disorders included under these categories actually have little in common; these categories are less informative than more specific classifications (e.g. schizophrenia); the criteria used to distinguish neurosis and psychosis all have exceptions; the groupings are based on supposed common origins (related to the psychodynamic model) rather than observable commonalities.
13 Blaney (1975) argues that the term 'ill' is more humane than alternatives, since a person so described is seen as a 'victim' and not blameworthy.
14 Szasz (1974, 1994) believes that labels such as mentally ill may serve the political purpose of excluding those who have upset the social order.
15 Szasz argues that the term diseases of the brain should be applied to mental disorders resulting from a known organic cause, and problems in living to describe 'functional disorders' (i.e. those for which there is no known physical basis).
16 Mental disorder is the term used by both ICD-10 and DSM-IV.
17 The category organic mental disorder has been removed from DSM-IV because it implies that other disorders in the manual do not have an organic component.

Section 3: Goals and problems with classification

18 ICD-10 and DSM-IV share the goals of providing a common shorthand language (L), understanding the origins (O) of mental disorders, and identifying appropriate treatment (T) plans (LOT).
19 Rosenhan (1973) instructed eight psychiatrically normal people to present themselves to psychiatrists, complaining of hearing voices. Each was able to gain admission to psychiatric hospitals and most were diagnosed as schizophrenic.
20 In Rosenhan's follow-up experiment, he warned members of a teaching hospital that pseudopatients would be trying to gain admittance and to try to identify them. There were no pseudopatients; nevertheless, roughly one-quarter of (presumably) genuinely disturbed individuals were suspected of being pseudopatients by at least one member of staff.
21 Reliability refers to the consistency of a diagnosis across repeated measurements.
22 Cooper *et al.* (1972) found that American psychiatrists were far more likely to diagnose schizophrenia whereas manic depression was more likely to be diagnosed by British psychiatrists.
23 Cooper *et al.* were able to reduce these differences by establishing specific criteria and training clinicians in these.
24 Multiaxial classification involves assessing patients on five different axes which represent different areas of functioning. This gives a broader and more in-depth picture.
25 The five axes are clinical syndromes and other conditions that may be a focus of clinical attention, personality disorders, general medical conditions, psychosocial and environmental problems, and global assessment of functioning.
26 ICD-10 gives more prominence to the aetiology (cause) of disorders within its various categories.
27 Validity refers to the extent to which a diagnosis reflects an actual disorder (i.e. how accurate it is).
28 Bannister *et al.* (1964) discovered no clear-cut relationship between diagnosis and treatment.
29 Critics argue that a normal person would say 'I'm not crazy, I just pretended to be. Now I want to be released'.
30 Black people make up five per cent of the general population and 25 per cent of the psychiatric population.
31 Adaptive paranoid response describes a mental disorder brought about by a hostile environment.
32 Littlewood & Lipsedge (1989) see mental illness in minorities as an intelligible response to disadvantage and racism.
33 Littlewood (1992) believes that Axis V (global assessment of functioning) of DSM-IV's multiaxial classification makes ethnocentric assumptions regarding family life, occupation and education.

A

(International Standard Classification of Diseases, Injuries and Causes of Death)

Major categories

- **Organic, including symptomatic, mental disorders:** e.g. Alzheimer's disease.
- **Mental and behavioural disorders due to psychoactive substance use:** e.g. alcoholism.
- **Schizophrenia, schizotypal and delusional disorders:** e.g. paranoid schizophrenia.
- **Mood (affective) disorders:** e.g. bipolar affective disorder.
- **Neurotic, stress-related and somatoform disorders:** e.g. phobias.
- **Behavioural syndromes associated with physiological disturbances and physical factors:** e.g. anorexia nervosa.
- **Disorders of adult personality and behaviour:** e.g. dissocial personality disorder.
- **Mental retardation:** e.g. profound mental retardation.
- **Disorders of psychological development:** e.g autism.
- **Behavioural and emotional disorders with onset usually occurring in childhood and adolescence:** e.g. hyperkinetic disorder.

Comparing DSM-IV and ICD-10

- DSM and ICD overlap extensively and, for many categories, are virtually identical.
- DSM-IV uses a larger number of discrete categories, whereas ICD-10 uses a smaller number of more specific categories.
- The single category 'neurotic, stress-related and somatoform disorders' in ICD-10 accounts for 4 categories in DSM-IV (anxiety disorders, somatoform disorders, dissociative disorders and adjustment disorders).
- DSM-IV has a single category for 'disorders first diagnosed in infancy, childhood and adolescence' which corresponds to 3 categories in ICD-10.

ICD-10 & DSM-IV

DSM-IV *(Diagnostic and Statistical Manual of Mental Disorders)*

Major categories

- **Delirium, dementia, amnestic and other cognitive disorders:** e.g. Alzheimer's disease.
- **Substance-related disorders:** e.g alcoholism.
- **Schizophrenic and other psychotic disorders:** e.g. paranoid schizophrenia.
- **Mood disorders:** e.g bipolar disorder.
- **Anxiety disorders:** e.g. phobias.
- **Somatoform disorders:** e.g. hypochondriasis.
- **Dissociative disorders:** e.g. multiple personality disorder.
- **Adjustment disorders:** e.g. adjustment disorder with disturbance of conduct.
- **Disorders first diagnosed in infancy, childhood or adolescence:** e.g. retardation.
- **Personality disorders:** e.g. borderline personality disorder.
- **Sexual and gender identity disorders:** e.g. paraphilias.
- **Impulse control disorders not elsewhere classified:** e.g. kleptomania.
- **Factitious disorders:** e.g. factitious disorder.
- **Sleep disorders:** e.g. narcolepsy.
- **Eating disorders:** e.g. anorexia nervosa.
- **Mental disorders due to a general medical condition not elsewhere classified:** e.g. catatonic disorder due to medical condition.
- **Other conditions that may be a focus of clinical attention:** e.g. sexual abuse.

Classificatory Systems

Psychosis & neurosis

The concept of mental illness

Distinctions between neurosis and psychosis

Personality: only a part of the personality is affected in neurosis.
Reality: the neurotic maintains contact with reality, whereas the psychotic does not.
Insight: the neurotic recognises that a problem exists.
'Normal' behaviour: neurotic behaviours are exaggerations of normal behaviour.
Pre-morbid personality: neurotic disorders are related to the individual's personality prior to the disorder.

- Present classificatory systems have dropped the distinction, although ICD-10 still uses the term 'neurotic', and DSM-IV, 'psychotic'.
- The categories are too broad and unspecific to be of much use, and the distinction stems from the psychodynamic model, not current observations of disorders (Gelder *et al.*, 1989).

Neither DSM-IV nor ICD-10 uses the term 'mental illness', although much of the vocabulary is medical (e.g. symptoms, diagnosis, cure).
Blaney (1975): the label 'ill' is more humane than 'mad' since it removes any sense of blame.
Szasz (1974, 1994):

- There is no such thing as mental illness, only illnesses ('diseases of the brain') or 'problems in living' (where an organic cause is not known: *The Myth of Mental Illness*).
- There is no known organic basis for the majority of 'mental illnesses'.
- Such labels are used to stigmatise and exclude those who have upset the social order, and psychiatry is largely 'social policing'.

DSM-IV has removed the category 'organic mental disorders' because it implies that the other disorders do not have an organic component.

The goals of classification

3 goals common to ICD-10 and DSM-IV: language, origins, treatment (LOT)
Providing a common shorthand language: i.e. a common set of terms with agreed-on meanings, enabling effective communication.
Understanding the origins of disorders: grouping people with similar behavioural symptoms into categories can help to identify common causes.
Treatment plans: accurate diagnosis is necessary to match a disorder to a treatment to ensure maximum benefit for the individual.

Problems with reliability

- Reliability refers to the consistency of a diagnosis across repeated measurements.
- Cooper *et al.* (1972): the same video of a patient was more likely to lead to a diagnosis of schizophrenia in America and manic depression in Britain.
- Agreement can be increased using standardised interview schedules.
- DSM-III (1980) introduced a multi-axial system of classification according to which patients are assessed on 5 different axes: clinical syndrome, personality disorders, general medical conditions, psychosocial and environmental problems, global assessment of functioning.

Rosenhan (1973):

- Instructed 8 psychiatrically normal people to complain of hearing voices. All 8 *'pseudopatients'* were admitted to hospital, most with a diagnosis of schizophrenia. Once admitted, patients acted normally, although it took between 7 and 52 days for staff to be convinced they were well enough to be discharged (with a diagnosis of 'schizophrenia in remission').
- In a second study, Rosenhan warned institutions to be on the look out for 'pseudopatients'. Roughly 1/4 of genuine individuals admitted were thought to be 'faking' by at least one member of staff. However, there were **no** pseudopatients.

Problems with validity

- Validity refers to an estimation of a particular measure's accuracy (whether the diagnosis reflects the actual disorder).
- Since there is no objective test for most disorders, validity is difficult to assess.
- Bannister *et al.* (1964) found no clear-cut relationship between diagnosis and treatment. This suggests diagnoses may lack validity.
- Defenders of psychiatric diagnosis point out that medical diagnoses are often incorrect (e.g. 34% of 'causes of death' disagree with later post-mortems).

- 5% of the British population are black, but 25% of hospitalised psychiatric patients are black.
- Black patients are more likely to see a junior, rather than senior doctor (Littlewood & Lipsedge, 1989).
- Of those Afro-Caribbeans diagnosed as schizophrenic, only 15% show the classic diagnostic indicators.

Transcultural psychiatry

Until recently, Western diagnostic categories were seen as applicable to all cultures. Increasingly, this assumption is being questioned.

- Littlewood & Lipsedge (1989): the delusion of persecution displayed by ethnic minorities is actually an intelligible response to disadvantage and racism.
- Littlewood (1992): DSM-IV is **ethnocentric**, especially the assessment of the global level of functioning (Axis V).

54

MULTIPLE PERSONALITY DISORDER
(DISSOCIATIVE IDENTITY DISORDER)

KEY QUESTIONS
• What is multiple personality disorder (MPD)?
• What explanations of MPD exist?
• Is MPD a genuine or 'manufactured' disorder?

Section 1: Introducing MPD

1 How is multiple personality disorder (MPD) classified in DSM-IV?
2 How is MPD defined?
3 What does it mean to say that two personalities are *mutually amnesic*?
4 Complete the sentence: 'In complex forms of the disorder ____ personalities are fully aware of the thoughts of the ____ personality which is controlling behaviour'.
5 In MPD, which term is used to refer sub-personalities which differ completely from the core personality?
6 How did Maud and Sarah's IQs differ (Lipton, 1943)?
7 What is the *fugue* which frequently accompanies MPD?
8 What term is used to describe the transition from one personality to another?
9 How many additional personalities did Jonah (Ludwig *et al.*, 1972) possess, besides his own primary personality?
10 What is galvanic skin response a measure of, and what is it taken to be indicative of?
11 How did Ludwig *et al.* make use of galvanic skin response in assessing Jonah's personalities?

Section 2: Explaining MPD

12 How does the psychodynamic model explain MPD?
13 How does the *state-dependent learning model* explain MPD?
14 Complete the sentence: 'The number of reported cases of MPD peaked in the late nineteenth century when there was much fascination with ____ as a pathway to the unconscious mind'.
15 What was the effect of publishing *The Three Faces of Eve* (Thigpen & Cleckley, 1957) on cases of MPD?

16 What was the first indication that Thigpen & Cleckley (1954) had of Eve's multiple personalities?
17 At what point did 'Jane' (Eve's third personality) first appear?
18 What reason does Mersky (1992) give for suspecting that at least some cases of MPD are merely simulations?
19 Why, for Spanos *et al.* (1985) does a *role-playing* explanation of MPD not necessarily mean that cases of MPD are faked?
20 What was the name of the scale used by Thigpen & Cleckley (1954) to determine the validity of Eve's multiple personalities?
21 What term is used to describe the slight differences in eye positions shown by Eve's personalities and studied by London *et al.* (1969)?
22 What is a *doxogenic disorder*?
23 What motivation for simulating MPD is proposed by Wesley (1993)?
24 How was the 'Hillside Strangler's' simulation of MPD discovered?
25 What explanation for MPD is suggested by the fact that the majority of MPD patients are young women, and the majority of therapists older men?
26 What is an *iatrogenic disorder*?
27 How common is MPD outside of the USA?
28 What two criteria for determining whether or not MPD cases are genuine have been suggested by Berman (1975)?
29 What do Carson *et al.* (1988) believe regarding the genuineness of MPD?
30 When do the first signs of *dissociation* usually develop?
31 What was the proposed cause of MPD in Lucy (Coons *et al.*, 1982)?

Q

A

Section 1: Introducing MPD

1 DSM-IV classifies multiple personality disorder as a dissociative disorder.

2 MPD is defined as the existence within a person of two or more distinct personalities, at least two of which recurrently take full control of the person's behaviour.

3 This means that each personality is unaware of the thoughts and behaviours of the other.

4 'In complex forms of the disorder *subordinate* personalities are fully aware of the thoughts of the *dominant* personality which is controlling behaviour.'

5 In this case, the personalities are described as polar opposites.

6 Whilst Sara's IQ was well above average (128) Maud's was very low (43).

7 Fugue ('flight') is a kind of amnesia in which an individual flees from home and self by wandering off on a journey and being unable to remember their identity.

8 The transition from one personality to another is termed *switching*.

9 Besides his own primary personality, Jonah possessed three other distinct personalities.

10 Galvanic skin response is a measure of the electrical response (conductance) of the skin and is taken to be indicative of physiological arousal.

11 Ludwig *et al.* asked each of the personalities to supply words of emotional significance, and then tested the galvanic skin response of each personality in turn as the words (together with neutral words) were presented.

Section 2: Explaining MPD

12 The psychodynamic model views MPD as extreme repression, in which a child regularly exposed to trauma and abuse takes flight from the world by pretending to be another person.

13 The state-dependent learning model points to the fact that we remember best under the same conditions present during learning, and suggests that different arousal states may be tied exclusively to certain memories, thoughts and abilities.

14 'The number of reported cases of MPD peaked in the late nineteenth century when there was much fascination with *hypnosis* as a pathway to the unconscious mind.'

15 The number of reported cases of MPD rose dramatically, following the publication of *The Three Faces of Eve*.

16 Thigpen and Cleckley received a letter from Eve in which the handwriting and message in the last paragraph differed dramatically from the remainder of the letter.

17 Jane first appeared after eight months of treatment.

18 Mersky identifies that there is at least one patient who admitted that she was reporting her multiple personalities in order to please the doctors.

19 Spanos *et al.* claim that individuals predisposed to MPD may also be uniquely capable of adopting roles and inhabiting a fantasy world.

20 Thigpen and Cleckley used the semantic differential attitude scale.

21 These slight differences in the positioning of the eyes are termed *transient microstrabismus*.

22 A doxogenic disorder is a disorder produced as a result of a person's opinions (which are in turn susceptible to media influences).

23 Wesley points out that attributing antisocial acts to alternate personalities may be a way of avoiding blame – for example as a defence in criminal cases.

24 The Hillside Strangler was caught out when, having been told by a psychiatrist that most cases of MPD have a third personality, he promptly produced a third.

25 It may be that alternate personalities are generated in order to maintain the interest and attention of the therapist.

26 An iatrogenic disorder is a disorder produced by the therapist (through mechanisms such as reinforcement, selective attention, expectations).

27 MPD is virtually unheard of outside of the USA.

28 Berman suggested that genuine cases can be detected by discovering whether the split appeared before therapy, and by examining whether or not the separate personalities lead separate lives beyond the therapeutic setting.

29 Carson *et al.* believe that MPD cases may involve elements of performance which are not consciously contrived but more absorption in the 'role'.

30 The first signs of dissociation usually develop in early childhood, before the age of eight.

31 Sexual abuse. Lucy was sexually abused by an alcoholic father when she was five.

Characteristics

- In classic cases the personalities have unique memories, behaviour patterns and social relationships.
- In more complex forms, personalities 'eavesdrop' on their rivals when one personality is 'dominant' and controlling behaviour. 'Subordinate' personalities are fully aware of the dominant personality (but not the other way round).
- The transition from one personality to another is called 'switching' and is often triggered by traumatic or stressful events. MPD is often accompanied by *fugue* (a kind of extension of amnesia) in which the individual flees from home and self by wandering off on a journey.

Multiple Personality Disorder

MPD: the existence within a person of two or more distinct, integrated and well-developed personalities or personality states. At least two of these personalities recurrently take full control of the person's behaviour.

Explanations

Psychodynamic model

- Sees MPD as extreme repression in which memories of a traumatic event are repressed dysfunctionally.
- The reaction is believed to have its roots in abusive parenting, from which the child takes flight by pretending to be another person.

Biological (medical) model

- 'Double brain theory' suggests that MPD is the alternate functioning of the left & right hemispheres.
- *Commissurotomy* (in which the two halves of the brain are surgically separated) reveals that we have two 'selves' and extreme stress may cause MPD.

State-dependent learning

- When we learn something in one state or context, it is better remembered in the same state or context.
- Physiological arousal is an internal state, and it may be that in MPD a particular arousal state becomes tied exclusively to certain memories, thoughts and abilities.

Self-hypnosis

- In self-hypnosis people actively induce themselves to forget unpleasant events.
- Abused and traumatised children may escape their threatening world by self-hypnosis, mentally separating themselves from their bodies and surroundings, and fulfilling a wish to become some other person.

Genuine vs manufactured

- History: the first case of MPD recorded in detail is that of Mary Reynolds (Mitchell, 1816) who exhibited two personalities. The number of reported cases peaked in the late 19th century (coinciding with a fascination with hypnosis as a pathway to the unconscious mind). Taylor & Martin (1944) identified 76 cases that had occurred over the last 128 years.
- *The Three Faces of Eve*: Thigpen & Cleckley (1954) studied a 25-yr-old woman whose dominant personality 'Eve White' was serious, quiet and bland whilst 'Eve Black' was carefree, mischievous and uninhibited. Eve Black was aware of Eve White but the reverse was not true. A third personality, 'Jane' emerged after eight months of treatment. Following the publication of the book, and subsequent movie, the number of cases and personalities increased almost exponentially.

Simulation & MPD

Many psychiatrists and clinical psychologists believe that at least some cases of MPD are simulations:

- **Role-playing explanations:** the finding that MPD can be induced experimentally using hypnosis supports the view that MPD may be faked – however, Spanos *et al.* (1985) point out that individuals predisposed to MPD may also be suggestible & susceptible to cues from therapists. From this perspective the MPD individual may simply be adept at taking on roles and entering a fantasy world.
- **Eve – a skilful actress?:** Thigpen & Cleckley (1954) gave each of Eve's personalities the Semantic Differential attitude scale at two monthly intervals. The results suggested that since each personality was more similar to themselves than the others on re-testing, that the personalities were distinct and stable. This was confirmed by London *et al.* (1969) who found that each of the three personalities showed different 'transient microstrabismus' patterns in their eye movements.

MPD as a legal defence

In America, MPD has been used successfully as a defence in rape and other serious crimes.

- Case studies: Arthur D. Wyne Bicknall was acquitted of drink-driving in 1976 on the grounds that it was another personality that was the true criminal. By contrast Kenneth Bianchi (the 'Hillside Strangler') attempted to simulate MPD in order to escape the death penalty, but was caught out when he produced a third personality in response to a psychiatrist's remark that three personalities is the norm for MPD cases.

Diagnosing MPD

Doubts over the genuineness of MPD make diagnosis difficult – Rathus (1984) claims to have seen 'mini outbreaks' of MPD amongst psychiatric patients who use MPD as an explanation for unacceptable behaviour:

- **Therapist–patient relationship:** MPD is diagnosed in women at least 3 times as often as in men. Most of the females are young, and most of the therapists are older men. Multiple personalities may be a means of maintaining the therapist's interest.
- **Detecting simulation:** Body posture, voice & questionnaire results are easy to simulate and although it has been suggested that an EEG may be used to detect differences in evoked potentials between personalities, some researchers remain sceptical.

Iatrogenesis & MPD

An iatrogenic disorder is a disorder produced by the therapist through mechanisms such as selective attention, reinforcement & expectations:

- Thigpen & Cleckley (1984): discussed the epidemic of MPD cases in the USA following the publication of *The Three Faces of Eve*. They suggested that 'a competition [seems] to have developed among some doctors to see who could diagnose the most cases'. Therapists eager for publicity may have wittingly or unwittingly encouraged MPD.
- **Cross-cultural incidence:** since MPD is virtually unknown outside of the USA, it may be thought of as a culture-bound syndrome. This also suggests that MPD may be an artificial creation.

Consciously contrived or absorption in the 'role'?

Carson *et al.* (1988) argue that some elements of MPD are not consciously contrived performances but absorption in the 'role'.

- Berman (1975): believes that the use of hypnosis in getting MPD sufferers to switch from one personality to another indicates that the power of suggestion (and the patient's desire to please the therapist) may play a role in transforming simpler emotional responses into MPD. MPD may represent unconscious efforts by the person to play out the roles required by the therapist.

Childhood abuse & MPD

Whilst MPD is usually first diagnosed in late adolescence/early adulthood the initial signs of dissociation usually develop before the age of eight. The vast majority of cases are female and most have been physically, often sexually, abused as children.

- The link between childhood abuse and MPD is a dominant perspective, with some therapists believing that MPD is caused by abuse.
- Despite this, there is little factual evidence of a link: many MPD cases claim to have been abused but corroboration of potentially unreliable reports is difficult.

55

CULTURE-BOUND SYNDROMES

SYLLABUS
14.1 Issues in the classification and diagnosis of psychological abnormality – culture-bound syndromes
- case studies of syndromes apparently bound by culture (e.g. koro, dhat). Arguments for and against the existence of these culture-bound syndromes

KEY QUESTIONS
- What is a culture-bound syndrome?
- What are the characteristics of susto, latah, dhat, amok and koro?
- To what extent are these genuinely culture-bound syndromes?

Q

Section 1: Introducing CBS

1 How does DSM-IV define a *culture-bound syndrome*?
2 What are the characteristics of *pibloqtoq* (found in Greenland, Alaska and the Canadian arctic)?
3 Why might a sufferer of *windigo* plead for death?
4 What name is given to the disorder which appears widely in African students and is characterised by 'tiredness of the brain'?
5 What, according to Dein (1994) is *transcultural psychiatry* preoccupied with?
6 Why is kuru, a progressive psychosis found in cannibalistic groups in New Guinea, not a truly culture-bound syndrome?
7 Complete the sentence: 'Susto and latah are regarded as being examples of ____ rather than ____ culture-bound syndromes'.
8 Identify two of the characteristics of susto.
9 What is the principle characteristic of latah?
10 What important similarity do both disorders share?
11 Complete the sentence: 'In Yap's (1974) view this is sufficient for both to be regarded as local expressions of ____ ____ ____.'

Section 2: Dhat and amok

12 What is the central characteristic of *dhat*?
13 What name was given by Dangerfield (1843) to a disorder closely related to dhat?
14 What is Singh's (1992) view on the question as to whether or not dhat is a culture-bound syndrome?
15 What does *amok* mean, literally?
16 What is the origin of amok behaviour?
17 What name is given to an individual who suffers from amok?
18 What is it that Malays are taught from birth (according to Carr, 1978) which might help to explain amok?

19 What interesting discovery did Carr & Tan (1976) make when studying those individuals who had suffered from amok?
20 Westermeyer (1973) reported on 18 cases of amok with grenades, in Laos. Identify two of the events which preceded most of these incidents.
21 Which relatively recent British case fits the general description of amok?
22 What are the three ingredients necessary for amok to occur in any culture, according to Arboleda-Florez (1979)?
23 What did Kline (1963) find when investigating the incidence of amok in Chinese immigrants to Indonesia?

Section 3: Koro

24 What does *suk-yeong* (the alternative name for koro) mean, literally?
25 What are the three beliefs that characterise koro amongst men?
26 When was the disease first described?
27 What treatment measures were effective in treating the Singapore epidemic of koro reported on by the koro study team?
28 Identify two of the mental disorders in terms of which koro has been explained.
29 What was the general finding of Oyebode *et al.*'s (1986) research into whether or not beliefs in koro were delusional.
30 Why has the term *atypical koro* been applied to non-Chinese cases of koro?
31 How does *incomplete koro* differ from *complete koro*?
32 What are the two disorders which Fernando (1991) believes may be examples of culture-bound syndromes in Western societies?

Section 1: Introducing CBS

1 DSM-IV defines a culture-bound syndrome as a recurrent, locality-specific pattern of aberrant behaviour and troubling experience that may or may not be linked to a particular DSM-IV category.

2 Pibloqtoq is characterised by the uncontrollable urge to leave one's shelter, tear off one's clothes and expose oneself to the Arctic weather.

3 A person suffering from windigo may plead for death to avoid cannibalistic desires.

4 The disorder is called *brain fag*.

5 According to Dein (1994), transcultural psychiatry is preoccupied with the pursuit of culture-bound syndromes and the attempt to fit them into Western categories.

6 Kuru is not a truly culture-bound syndrome since it has been identified with a form of Creutzfeldt–Jakob disease and would be classified as an organic mental disorder.

7 'Susto and latah are regarded as being examples of *apparent* rather than *real* culture-bound syndromes.'

8 Susto is characterised by insomnia, apathy, depression and anxiety.

9 The principle characteristic of latah is uncontrollable imitative behaviour.

10 Both disorders are brought on by a frightening or startling stimulus.

11 'In Yap's (1974) view this is sufficient for both to be regarded as local expressions of *primary fear reaction*.'

Section 2: Dhat and amok

12 The central characteristic of dhat is severe anxiety (and hypochondriacal concerns) with the discharge of semen.

13 Dangerfield (1843) identified spermatorrhoea as a disorder whose primary symptoms were bodily complaints, anxiety, depression and sexual difficulties as a result of semen loss.

14 Singh (1992) believes that it is not a result of culture, but of medical ignorance.

15 Literally, amok means 'to engage furiously in battle'.

16 Amok probably originated in training for warfare, in which warriors were encouraged to charge forwards brandishing their daggers and shouting 'Amok!'.

17 An individual suffering from amok is called a *pengamok*.

18 According to Carr, Malays are taught from childhood that one never confronts another person, let alone expresses aggression.

19 Carr & Tan (1976) found that there was very little evidence of mental disturbances before or after the episode of amok.

20 Westermeyer found that most episodes were preceded by interpersonal discord, insults, or personal loss.

21 In 1987 Michael Ryan stalked the Berkshire town of Hungerford, killing 15 people before shooting himself.

22 Arboleda-Florez (1979) claims that the ingredients are: a society in transition, a feeling of alienation and a need for assertiveness.

23 Kline found that the incidence of amok in Chinese immigrants to Indonesia was as high as the local Indonesians (unlike the low incidence in China itself).

Section 3: Koro

24 Literally, suk-yeong means 'shrinking penis'.

25 Amongst men, koro is characterised by the belief that the penis is shrinking, it will disappear into the abdomen and that its disappearance will result in death.

26 The disease was first described in 3000BC in *The Yellow Emperor's Book of Medicine*.

27 The koro study team reported that simple treatment measures, such as reassurance and suggestion, were all that was required.

28 Koro has been explained in terms of obsessional disorder, castration fear, anxiety reaction, schizophrenia, depersonalisation syndrome and psychophysiological dysfunctions.

29 Oyebode *et al.* found that they were not delusional, since the convictions did correspond with a decrease in penile circumference.

30 The term atypical koro has been applied to non-Chinese cases of koro since most are secondary to a major mental disorder.

31 Incomplete cases of koro lack the belief that the penis will disappear into the abdomen and/or the fear of death as a consequence.

32 Fernando (1991) believes that anorexia nervosa and premenstrual syndrome may be examples of culture-bound syndromes in Western societies.

A

Culture-bound Syndromes

Culture-bound syndrome (CBS): recurrent, locality-specific patterns of aberrant behaviour and troubling experience that may or may not be linked to a particular DSM-IV category.

Examples: at least 36 apparent CBSs have been identified, including *pibloqtoq* (characterised by an uncontrollable urge to leave one's shelter, tear off one's clothes, and expose oneself to the Arctic weather), and *brain fag* (in which the individual complains of tiredness of the brain).

Cultural relativism and ethnocentrism.

- Culture-bound syndromes (CBSs) are those which fall outside of the classifications (DSM & ICD) defined by the West. This leads to a form of *ethnocentrism* in which Western mental disorders are seen as culturally neutral and on a different plane from those of non-Western societies.
- Disorders such as *anorexia nervosa* and premenstrual syndrome may represent Western CBSs (Fernando, 1991).

Dhat

Dhat: has been described as a 'culture-bound sex neurosis' to be found in India. Characterised by severe anxiety and hypochondriacal concerns with the discharge of semen. However, it seems unlikely that Dhat is a truly CBS.

- Many cultures share the Hindu belief that loss of semen produces mental & physical impairments, e.g. China and England in Victorian times (see below).
- Singh (1992) argues that it is not culture but ignorance which creates the belief: similar Western beliefs have vanished as medical knowledge & sexual awareness have increased; in India taboos and a lack of sex education help perpetuate such 'myth-oriented' beliefs.

Spermatorrhoea

In 1840 the *Lancet* medical journal carried an editorial on the mental and physical impairment caused by loss of semen.

- Dangerfield (1843) described spermatorrhoea as a disorder resulting from semen loss and characterised by symptoms such as bodily complaints and depression.
- Treatments included the insertion of egg-sized wooden blocks into the rectum and the attachment of an electric alarm to the penis.

Koro

Koro means 'head of the turtle' and is characterised amongst men by 3 beliefs: their penis is shrinking; it will disappear into the abdomen; this will result in death.

- Koro was first described in 3000BC and has its basis in traditional Chinese beliefs, for example that ghosts possess no genitals, and the activity of Yin & Yang humours.
- Characterised by intense anxiety and associated reactions (e.g. palpitations, sweating, breathlessness).

Incidence of koro

Koro is primarily a disorder of the young but may affect the elderly. Attacks tend to be short-lived and can be recurrent. It may affect single individuals or occur in epidemics:

- The Koro Study Team (1969) reported an epidemic in Singapore. 95% of the 450 cases were young Chinese males, some had tied chop-sticks to their sex organs in an attempt at self-treatment although the only treatment required was reassurance & suggestion. 17% had recurrent attacks.

Explanations

Koro has been explained in terms of disorders such as obsessional disorder, castration fear, anxiety reaction and schizophrenia.

- **Delusions:** Oyebode *et al.* (1986) investigated sufferers' beliefs and found that in fact their penises *were* shrinking. It might be that these changes are normal (and usually go unnoticed) or a result of dysfunctional autonomic control.

A genuine CBS or not?

- Examples of Koro in other cultures suggest that it may not be a truly CBS – although non-Chinese cases are usually secondary to a major disorder.
- Non-Chinese cases typically lack the belief that shrinkage will cause death and so are 'incomplete' forms of koro.
- Whilst 'true' cases of koro seem culture-bound, koro-like states are found in other cultures (e.g. a 44-yr-old English man who believed that his penis recurrently shrank into his abdomen, and who was successfully treated with psychotherapeutic drugs and behavioural therapy).

Amok

Amok means 'to engage furiously in battle' and probably originated in Javanese & Malay warfare: warriors were encouraged to charge forwards, brandishing their daggers and shouting 'Amok! Amok!'.

- Amok outside of battle was first described in the mid-sixteenth century. Sufferers would attack, without warning, anyone within reach, until overwhelmed or killed.

Basis in a belief system

- Epic poems praised legendary warriors who behaved in this way & during the fourteenth century it was occasionally an act of religious fanaticism.
- Kon (1994): Malays have a fatalistic view of courage in which one is willing to face up to overwhelming odds.
- Carr (1978): Malays are taught never to confront another person or show aggression.

The latter belief might easily lead an individual being treated as weak or inferior and amok would act as a 'loophole' which allowed the individual to restore his integrity.

Examples in other cultures

- Laos: Westermeyer (1973) reported 18 cases of amok with grenades, most of which were preceded by insults or personal loss.
- United Kingdom: In 1987 Michael Ryan stalked Hungerford killing 15 people, and finally himself. There was no history of mental disorder.
- Other cases have been reported in the USA, Trinidad, India, Liberia, Africa, Siberia and Polynesia.

A genuine CBS or not?

- Carr & Tan (1976): there is very little evidence of mental disorder in sufferers before or after the attack.
- Arboleda-Florez (1979): amok is not culture-bound and can occur in any culture when the following ingredients are present: a society in transition, a feeling of alienation, a need for assertiveness.
- Kline (1963): found Amok in Chinese immigrants living in close proximity to the Malays (but not in native Chinese), suggesting that Malay culture facilitates the behaviour.

Susto and latah

Susto and latah are regarded as examples of apparent, rather than real CBSs (i.e. they are merely local expressions of universal disorders already classified):

- **Susto:** occurs in the Andean highlands of Peru, Bolivia and Columbia. Characterised by insomnia, apathy, depression and anxiety and is believed to result from contact with supernatural beings which cause the soul to leave the body.
- **Latah:** (meaning 'ticklish'): occurs in Malaysia and Indonesia, usually amongst uneducated, middle-aged or elderly women. Characterised by uncontrollable imitative behaviour (of speech & movements) and the individual complies to the demands of others and behaves in ways they normally would not (e.g. uttering obscenities).

Explanation

Susto is typically brought on by fright and latah is often the result of a sudden or startling stimulus (e.g. being tickled).

- Yap (1974): regards both as local expressions of *primary fear reaction* which is recognised & classified in Western systems.

Matiruku

Matiruku describes a condition of 'periodic insanity' in which sufferers are 'cranky':

- Price & Karim (1978): argue that it is a form of hypomania – supported by the finding that it does not occur in children, and involves elevated mood, sleep disorders and talkativeness.

SCHIZOPHRENIA

KEY QUESTIONS
- What are the characteristics of schizophrenia?
- How many types of schizophrenia are there?
- What phases are there in schizophrenia's development?
- How do genetic/neurological and social/psychological factors contribute to schizophrenia?

Section 1: The nature of schizophrenia

1 Bleuler coined the term *schizophrenia* in 1911. To what does it refer?
2 In what way are *first rank symptoms* more significant than other symptoms?
3 What is *thought broadcasting*?
4 Define the term *hallucination*.
5 What form of hallucination is the most common in schizophrenics?
6 Define the term *delusion*.
7 What is a *delusion of reference*?
8 How can *thought process disorders* such as the loosening of associations, be explained?
9 What is '*word salad*'?
10 Name the three types of *disturbance of affect*.
11 What is the difference between *catatonia* and *stereotypy*?

Section 2: Types and phases of schizophrenia

12 Name the five types of schizophrenia.
13 Which type of schizophrenic shows the highest level of functioning and the least impairment in ability to carry out daily functions?
14 Which type of schizophrenia tends to appear during late adolescence, have a slow, gradual onset, and be characterised by aimlessness, a decline in academic/occupational performance and a withdrawal from reality?
15 Name the three *phases* which occur in the course of schizophrenia.
16 What percentage of schizophrenics regain the capacity to function normally?
17 Why do some psychologists argue that the concept of schizophrenia is 'almost hopelessly in tatters' (Carson, 1989; Sarbin, 1992)?

Section 3: Explaining schizophrenia

18 What is Ullman & Krasner's (1969) *behavioural* explanation for schizophrenia?

19 What is the principal problem with this explanation?
20 Complete the sentence: 'Freud believed that schizophrenia results from _____ to an infantile stage of development'.
21 Identify one criticism of the *psychodynamic* explanation of schizophrenia.
22 According to Bateson *et al.* (1956), what is a *double-bind communication*?
23 According to Fromm-Reichman (1948), what is a *schizophrenogenic mother*?
24 Donne *et al.* (1985) found that the recurrence of schizophrenic symptoms in sufferers could be reduced by changes in their parents' behaviours. Identify these changes.
25 According to the *cognitive model*, which 'mechanism' is impaired in schizophrenics?
26 What is the likelihood of an individual developing schizophrenia if they have one schizophrenic parent?
27 What does Gottesman & Shields' (1972) discovery of a *concordance rate* of 42 per cent for schizophrenia in MZ (monozygotic) twins suggest?
28 What did Gottesman (1991) find when comparing concordance rates for MZ twins raised together with rates for MZ twins separated at birth?
29 What explanation for schizophrenia is offered by the *inborn-error of metabolism hypothesis*?
30 Which type of receptor sites were found to be far more prevalent in the brains of schizophrenics than non-schizophrenics?
31 How does the *diathesis–stress model* explain the cause of schizophrenia?
32 When Chua & McKenna (1995) reviewed the literature concerning structural abnormalities in the brains of schizophrenics, what did they discover was the most well-established difference?
33 Why is the finding that more schizophrenics are born in late winter and early spring significant?

Section 1: The nature of schizophrenia

1 Schizophrenia originally referred to a splitting of the mind's various functions so that the personality loses its unity.

2 First rank symptoms are significant in that (in Britain) the presence of one or more of these is likely to lead to a diagnosis of schizophrenia.

3 Thought broadcasting is a thought disturbance in which people believe their thoughts are being broadcast or otherwise made known to others.

4 The term hallucination refers to perceptions of stimuli that are not actually present.

5 Auditory hallucinations (hearing voices) are the most common form of hallucination in schizophrenics.

6 A delusion is a false belief which persists even in the presence of disconfirming evidence.

7 A delusion of reference is the belief that objects, events and so on have a (typically negative) personal significance.

8 Thought process disorders can be explained in terms of a failure to maintain an attentional focus, as a consequence of an impairment of selective attention.

9 'Word salad' refers to the complete incoherence of some schizophrenic speech resulting from an extreme loosening of associations.

10 Disturbances of affect include blunting, flattened affect, and inappropriate affect.

11 Catatonia involves assuming a posture which is maintained for hours or days, whilst stereotypy refers to a pattern of purposeless, repetitive movements such as rocking back and forth.

Section 2: Types and phases of schizophrenia

12 The five types of schizophrenia are hebephrenic, simple, catatonic, paranoid, and undifferentiated.

13 Paranoid schizophrenics show the highest level of functioning and the least impairment in their ability to carry out daily functions.

14 Simple schizophrenia.

15 The course of schizophrenia usually occurs in the following phases: prodromal phase, active phase, and residual phase.

16 Approximately 25 per cent of schizophrenics regain the capacity to function normally.

17 With the exception of paranoid schizophrenia, other forms of schizophrenia are difficult to distinguish in practice, and may in fact be different disorders rather than types of one disorder. Hence, it is argued, diagnoses of schizophrenia lack validity.

Section 3: Explaining schizophrenia

18 Ullman & Krasner (1969) argue that people show schizophrenic behaviour when it is more likely than normal behaviour to be reinforced.

19 The explanation cannot account for the acquisition of schizophrenic behaviours when there has been no opportunity to learn them.

20 'Freud believed that schizophrenia results from *regression* to an infantile stage of development.'

21 Schizophrenic behaviour does not resemble infantile behaviour, and the psychodynamic model has poor predictive power.

22 A double-bind communication is one in which a child is placed in a 'no-win' situation by its parents, for example by their giving contradictory verbal and non-verbal messages.

23 A schizophrenogenic mother (Fromm-Reichman, 1948) is a mother who produces schizophrenic children because she is domineering, cold, rejecting and guilt-producing.

24 Donne *et al.* (1985) found that a reduction in parents' hostility, criticism and intrusiveness could reduce the recurrence of schizophrenic symptoms.

25 The selective attention mechanism is impaired in schizophrenics, according to the cognitive model.

26 An individual with one schizophrenic parent has a one in five chance of developing schizophrenia themselves.

27 Gottesman & Shields' (1972) discovery suggests that genetics play an important role in the likelihood of schizophrenia. However, other factors, such as environmental influences, also play an important role.

28 Gottesman (1991) found that the concordance rates for MZ twins raised together were the same as rates for MZ twins separated at birth.

29 The inborn-error of metabolism hypothesis suggests that some people inherit a metabolic error which causes the body to break down naturally occurring chemicals into toxic ones which cause schizophrenia.

30 Dopamine receptor sites are far more likely to be found in the brains of schizophrenics than in non-schizophrenics.

31 The diathesis–stress model argues that we inherit a genetic pre-disposition towards schizophrenia (a diathesis) which may be triggered by environmental stress (such as exams, leaving home, job loss).

32 Chua & McKenna (1995) argue that the only well-established structural abnormality in schizophrenia is lateral ventricular enlargement (and that even this is modest and overlaps with the non-schizophrenic population).

33 The finding that more schizophrenics are born in late winter and early spring (Torrey *et al.*, 1977) supports the theory that schizophrenia may result from a viral infection affecting children during the second trimester of pregnancy, when crucial brain interconnections are formed.

Characteristics

first rank symptoms

Passivity experiences & thought disturbances

Thought insertion: belief that thoughts are being inserted into the mind from outside.
Thought withdrawal: belief that thoughts are being removed from the mind.
Thought broadcasting: belief that thoughts are being 'broadcast' to others.

Hallucinations

Hallucination: the perception of stimuli not actually present.
Auditory hallucinations: (most common) typically involve voices offering a running commentary, commands, or insults.
Somatosensory hallucinations: changes in how the body feels.
Depersonalisation: the person feels separated from the body.

Primary delusions

Delusion: a false belief which persists even in the presence of disconfirming evidence.
Delusion of grandeur: belief that person is or was very important.
Delusion of persecution: belief that others are conspiring against the person.
Delusion of reference: belief that events (e.g. the news) have personal relevance.

other symptoms

Thought process disorder

Schizophrenics are unable to maintain an attentional focus, resulting in:
- **loose associations**
- **word salad**
- **clang associations**
- **neologisms**

Disturbances of affect

Emotional disturbances include:
- **Blunting:** lack of emotional sensitivity or response.
- **Flattened affect:** general absence of emotional expression.
- **Inappropriate affect:** displaying incongruous emotions.

Psychomotor disorders

May take the form of:
Catatonia: a (unusual) posture is maintained for hours/days.
Stereotypy: purposeless, repetitive movements

Lack of volition

The tendency to withdraw from interactions with others. More disturbed individuals may be oblivious to the presence of others.

Schizophrenia

Types of schizophrenia

- **Hebephrenic:** ('silly mind') predominantly active symptoms, e.g. disorganised behaviour and speech, delusions, hallucinations, flattened/inappropriate affect.
- **Simple:** slow onset, withdrawal from reality, deterioration of academic/occupational performance.
- **Catatonic:** impairment of motor activity often with catatonia.
- **Paranoid:** delusions and hallucinations (usually of persecution). Otherwise relatively unaffected.
- **Undifferentiated:** 'catch-all' category for people not clearly falling into one type.

The course of schizophrenia

Prodromal phase
Usually occurs in early adolescence or early adulthood. The individual becomes more withdrawn, eccentric, emotionally flat, unkempt, with reduced productivity.

Active phase
Major characteristics of schizophrenia appear. Varies in duration from months to a lifetime.

Residual phase
Lessening of the major characteristics and more-or-less return to the prodromal phase.

Explanations

Behavioural
- Ullman & Krasner (1969): schizophrenia results from reinforcement of bizarre behaviour or the absence of reinforcement for appropriate behaviours.
- However, without an opportunity to observe such behaviours, the model cannot explain how they are acquired.

Psychodynamic
- **Regression** to an earlier stage of functioning occurs when the ego is overwhelmed by the id or superego. The individual returns to the oral stage when self and world are no longer distinguished. Fantasies and reality are confused.
- However, schizophrenic behaviour is not similar to infantile behaviour.

Social/family relationships
- Bateson *et al.* (1956): parents predispose children to schizophrenia by communicating in ways which leave them in 'no-win' situations ('double binds').
- **Schizophrenogenic mothers** (Fromm-Reichman, 1948) may generate schizophrenic children by being cold, domineering, rejecting and guilt-producing.

Cognitive
- Sees schizophrenia as resulting from disturbances of thought and perception.
- Maher (1968): bizarre language use is a result of faulty information processing.
- Catatonia may result from a breakdown of selective attention, resulting in the senses being overloaded.

Medical

Genetic
Schizophrenia tends to run in families: the likelihood of developing it is 1 in 100, but this rises to 1 in 5 with one schizophrenic parent, and 1 in 2 with two schizophrenic parents.

- Gottesman & Shields (1972) looked at concordance rates for MZ (identical) and DZ twins. The concordance rate was 42% for MZ twins (but not 100%), suggesting that both genetics and environment play a role.
- Gottesman (1991): the concordance rate for MZ twins reared together and apart is the same.
- Attempts to identify the gene responsible have not yet been successful.

Biochemical
- **Inborn-error of metabolism hypothesis:** a tendency to break down naturally-occurring chemicals into toxic ones (resembling hallucinogens) is inherited.
- **Excess dopamine utilisation:** schizophrenics possess an abnormally large number of dopamine-receptor sites. Drugs which block the functioning of these sites reduce schizophrenic symptoms (Kimble, 1988).
- **Diathesis–stress model:** genes may cause a biological vulnerability (*diathesis*) which puts a person at risk from environmental *stressors* (like exams, leaving home, losing a job).

Neurodevelopmental
- **Brain damage:** resulting from disease, difficult birth, (resulting in lack of oxygen) may be related to schizophrenia.
- **Structural abnormalities:** Chua & McKenna (1995) identify lateral ventricular enlargement as the most well-established structural abnormality, although even this is slight and overlaps with the normal population.
- **Viral theories:** significantly more people who develop schizophrenia are born in late winter and early spring (Torrey *et al.*, 1977). This may relate to infection with the influenza virus during the stage when crucial inter-connections in the brain are being formed.

DEPRESSION

SYLLABUS
14.1 Psychopathology – depression
- clinical characteristics of depression (unipolar disorder). Biological (e.g. genetics, biochemistry) and psychological (e.g. learned helplessness) explanations of depression, including the evidence on which they are based

KEY QUESTIONS
- What are the characteristics of depression?
- What sex differences are there in depression?
- How do genetic/neurological and social/psychological factors contribute to depression?

Q Section 1: Characteristics of depression

1 What name is given to the disorder characterised by alternating phases of *mania* and *depression*?

2 Why does Seligman (1973) refer to depression as the 'common cold' of psychological problems?

3 Identify any three of the characteristics which need to accompany persistent low mood in order for a diagnosis of depression to be made.

4 What percentage of adults in Britain will experience serious depression at some time?

5 What is the difference between *endogenous* and *exogenous depression*?

6 Which of the mood disorders is equally prevalent in men and women?

Section 2: Explanations of depression

7 What was Ferster's (1965) *behavioural explanation* for depression?

8 According to Lewisohn's (1974) expansion of Ferster's theory, what important role do friends and relatives play in depression?

9 Why, according to Lewisohn's account, are people lacking in *social skills* most at risk from depression?

10 How did Seligman & Maier (1967) demonstrate *learned helplessness*?

11 According to Abramson *et al.* (1978), what types of *attribution* do depressed people make for failure and success?

12 According to Beck (1974), depression may result from a *cognitive triad*. What is a cognitive triad?

13 According to Freud's psychodynamic model, to what is depression a response?

14 What is the relationship between depression and childhood, according to Freud?

15 What is Freud's explanation for feelings of guilt, unworthiness or despair, which may accompany depression?

16 What explanation do psychodynamic theorists propose for *bipolar disorder*?

17 Complete the following sentence: 'There is little evidence for a direct connection between early ___ and the risk of ____ in adult life (Crook & Eliot, 1980)'.

18 How much more likely is an individual to suffer from a mood disorder if they have a first degree relative with a mood disorder, than if they do not?

19 What conclusion can be drawn from the fact that *concordance rates* for bipolar disorder and major depression differ significantly?

20 What difficulty in investigating the *genetic* contribution to depression is overcome by *adoption studies*?

21 What did Wender *et al.* (1986) discover when investigating adopted children who developed mood disorders as adults?

22 What might the link be between a gene called SERT and depression?

23 Name the two neurotransmitters which are thought to be involved in affective disorders.

24 How does the urine of depressives differ from that of manics?

25 According to Kety's *permissive-amine theory of mood disorder*, what is the relationship between the two key neurotransmitters?

26 What reason do we have for suspecting that drugs which alleviate depression (such as *Prozac*) do not do so simply by increasing levels of key neurotransmitters?

27 According to Wehr & Rosenthal (1989), what is the cause of *winter depression*?

28 What other naturally occurring phenomenon has been identified by some researchers as a possible contributor to depression?

Section 3: Sex differences in depression

29 Identify three potential sources of *hormonal changes* in women which may contribute to depression.

30 Complete the sentence: 'Girls are very much more likely to be victims of ____ as children than are boys'.

Section 1: Characteristics of depression

1 Bipolar disorder.
2 Because depression is the most common psychological problem people face.
3 The characteristics are: poor appetite and weight loss or increased appetite and weight gain, difficulty in sleeping or sleeping longer than usual, loss of energy or extreme tiredness, observable slowing down or agitation, loss of interest/pleasure in previously enjoyable activities, feelings of self-reproach or excessive guilt, diminished ability to concentrate, and recurrent thoughts of death and/or suicide.
4 Five per cent of British adults will experience serious depression at some time.
5 Endogenous depression describes depression which 'comes from within' (biological disturbances), whilst exogenous depression 'comes from outside' (stressful life experiences).
6 Bipolar disorder is equally prevalent in men and women.

Section 2: Explanations of depression

7 Ferster (1965) believed that depression results from a reduction in reinforcement.
8 Lewisohn (1974) argues that friends and relatives may reinforce the depressed behaviour by giving the individual their concern and attention.
9 People lacking in social skills are least likely to receive positive reinforcement from those around them (e.g. laughter at their witty comments), and are therefore most at risk from depression.
10 Seligman & Maier (1967) subjected dogs to unavoidable electric shocks, then later placed them in a situation in which they could avoid the shocks. They made no attempt to avoid them.
11 Abramson *et al.* (1978) believe that depressed people attribute failure to internal, stable and global factors, and success to luck.
12 A cognitive triad (Beck, 1974) consists of three interlocking negative beliefs concerning the self, the world and the future.
13 Freud's psychodynamic model claims that depression is a response to loss which may be either actual (e.g. the loss of a friend) or symbolic (e.g. the loss of a job).
14 According to Freud, the greater the experience of loss during childhood, the greater the susceptibility to, and depth of, depression.
15 Freud believed that such feelings represent the individual's hostility (towards parents) which is repressed and directed inwards, towards the self.

16 Psychodynamic theorists propose that bipolar disorder results from the alternating domination of the personality by the superego and the ego.
17 'There is little evidence for a direct connection between early *loss* and the risk of *depression* in adult life.' (Crook & Eliot, 1980)
18 An individual who has a first degree relative with a mood disorder is ten times more likely to suffer from a mood disorder than one who has not.
19 The difference in concordance rates suggests that the genetic factors involved in the disorders are different.
20 Adoption studies overcome the problem that children who share the same genes often share similar environments, so that is it difficult to determine their respective contributions.
21 Wender *et al.* (1986) discovered that such children were far more likely to have biological parents with a mood disorder, or who suffered from alcoholism or committed suicide, than children who did not suffer from a mood disorder.
22 Ogilvie *et al.* (1996) discovered that cells use SERT in the production of serotonin transporter proteins, and that the SERT gene is shortened in depressives. Serotonin is strongly linked to mood disorders.
23 Serotonin and noradrenaline.
24 The urine of depressives contains low levels of compounds produced when noradrenaline and serotonin are broken down, whereas the urine of manics contains high levels of these compounds.
25 Kety's permissive-amine theory of mood disorder suggests that one of the neurotransmitters (serotonin) acts to regulate the level of the other (noradrenaline).
26 Drugs which alleviate depression alter levels of neurotransmitters for only a short period (immediately after they are taken), and their anti-depressant effects do not occur during this period.
27 Wehr & Rosenthal (1989) claim that winter depression is caused by the desynchronisation of melatonin production as a result of decreasing light exposure.
28 Geomagnetic phenomena (e.g. the aurora borealis which is a source of geomagnetic changes) may be linked with depression.

Section 3: Sex differences in depression

29 The menstrual cycle, childbirth, the menopause, oral contraceptives, brain chemistry and diet are all sources of hormonal changes in women, and may contribute to depression.
30 'Girls are very much more likely to be victims of *abuse* as children than are boys.'

Depression

Characteristics — **Depression** — **Gender differences**

Clinical depression

Persistent low mood for at least 2 weeks plus at least 5 of the following:

- poor appetite or weight loss, or increased appetite or weight gain
- difficulty in sleeping (insomnia) or sleeping longer than usual (hypersomnia)
- loss of energy or tiredness to the point of being unable to make the simplest everyday decisions
- an observable slowing down or agitation (e.g. hand wringing)
- a markedly diminished loss of interest or pleasure in activities that were once enjoyed
- feelings of self-reproach or excessive or inappropriate guilt over real or imagined misdeeds
- complaints/evidence of diminished ability to think or concentrate
- recurrent thoughts of death, suicide, suicidal thoughts without a specific plan, or a suicide attempt or a specific plan for committing suicide.

- **Unipolar depression** (depression without mania): can occur at any age. In the USA, 15% of adults experience serious depression at some time, and is far more prevalent in women.
- Psychiatrists distinguish *endogenous* ('coming from within'/biochemical) depression from *exogenous* ('coming from the outside'/stressful experience) depression.
- **Bipolar disorder** (alternating depression and mania, or mania on its own): is equally prevalent in men and women and generally appears in the early 20s.

Women are 2–3 times more likely than men to be diagnosed as clinically depressed (Williams & Hargreaves, 1995).

Biological explanations

- Hormonal fluctuations may play a role in depression, and are associated with the menstrual cycle, childbirth, the menopause, oral contraceptives, brain chemistry and diet. However, a specific causal mechanism has not yet been identified.
- Diksic *et al.* (cited in Highfield, 1997d): men's brain stems manufacture serotonin at a rate 52% higher than do women's. One possibility is that dieting during teens may alter brain biochemistry.

Non-biological explanations

Cochrane (1995) has summarised non-biological explanations:

- Girls are far more likely than boys to be sexually abused, and victims of abuse are 2 times more likely than non-victims to suffer depression.
- The difference is greatest between the ages 20–50, when most women experience marriage, child-bearing, motherhood and the empty-nest syndrome.
- An acceptance of the traditional female role may contribute to learned helplessness, in which the woman sees herself as having little control over her life.
- Depression may be a coping strategy in response to the social and political circumstances in which women find themselves.

Explanations

The behavioural model — **The psychodynamic model** — **The cognitive–behavioural model**

Lewisohn (1974):

- Certain events (e.g. death of a loved one) reduce positive reinforcement. Less activity leads to concern and attention which reinforces the depression.
- Socially unskilled individuals are more at risk since they are less able to elicit positive reinforcement from others.

- Freud argued that actual losses (e.g. death of a loved one) and symbolic losses (e.g. loss of job) lead us to re-experience feelings of loss and dependence from our childhood.
- Repressed hostility towards one's parents is experienced as anger during loss. This anger is turned inwards and becomes guilt and despair and may lead to suicide.
- Bipolar disorder is seen as alternating dominance of the superego (depressive phase) and the ego (manic phase).

- However, there is little evidence that experience of loss in early life leads to an increased risk of depression, or that depressed people interpret the death of a loved one as desertion/rejection.

Learned helplessness

Seligman & Maier (1967): restrained dogs so that they could not avoid electric shock. Dogs became passively resigned to receiving shocks and made no attempt to escape when the opportunity arose.

- Argued that dogs' behaviours (including lethargy and loss of appetite) were similar to those of depressed humans.

Attributional style

Abramson *et al.* (1978): people who attribute failure to internal, stable and global causes ('It's my fault, it's always going to be like this, whatever I do'), and success to luck, are more likely to become depressed.

Beck's cognitive triad model

- Beck (1974): believes that certain childhood experiences lead to a cognitive triad of three interlocking negative beliefs concerning *self*, *world* and *future*.
- These lead people to magnify bad and minimise good experiences.

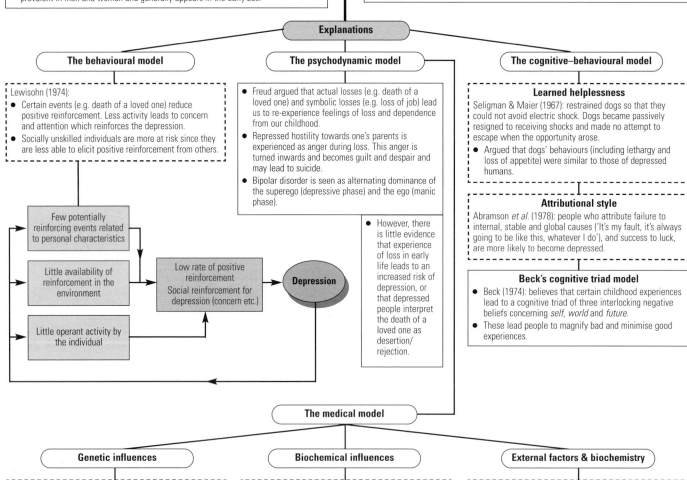

Few potentially reinforcing events related to personal characteristics

Little availability of reinforcement in the environment

Little operant activity by the individual

→ Low rate of positive reinforcement Social reinforcement for depression (concern etc.) → **Depression**

The medical model

Genetic influences — **Biochemical influences** — **External factors & biochemistry**

- Weissman (1987): people with first-degree relatives with a mood disorder are 10 times more likely to develop a mood disorder than people without affected relatives.
- Concordance rates are different for bipolar and unipolar depression, suggesting that different genetic factors are involved.

Serotonin transporter proteins

Ogilvie *et al.* (1996) found that cells use a gene called SERT to manufacture serotonin transporter proteins. Serotonin is strongly linked to depression. In a significant number of people with depression, this gene is shorter than normal.

- Schildkraut (1965): **noradrenaline** causes depression and mania in low and high amounts, respectively. Later research suggested that **serotonin** plays a similar role.
- Kety (1975): since serotonin can be low during mania, serotonin regulates noradrenaline levels and low levels permit noradrenaline to fluctuate.
- However, drugs that alleviate depression (e.g. Prozac) affect serotonin/noradrenaline levels immediately after taking them, but take weeks to work, suggesting that they affect the sensitivity of neurons utilising serotonin/noradrenaline.

Lower levels of noradrenaline and serotonin may be the *result* of, rather than the *cause* of, depression, e.g.:

- **Seasonal affective disorder** (SAD) such as summer depression and winter depression. Summer depression is associated with deficient serotonin levels, whilst winter depression is caused by the desynchronisation of melatonin production as a result of decreasing natural light exposure (Wehr & Rosenthal, 1989).
- Kay (1994): **geomagnetic storms** affect melatonin production and may partly account for both summer and winter depression.

ANXIETY DISORDERS

KEY QUESTIONS
- What are the characteristics of panic disorder, generalised anxiety disorder, phobic disorders, obsessive–compulsive disorder, and post-traumatic disorder?
- How do genetic/neurological and social/psychological factors contribute to these anxiety disorders?

Section 1: Panic disorder (PD) and generalised anxiety disorder (GAD)

1 Define *anxiety*.
2 What are the physiological reactions accompanying *panic attacks* similar to?
3 At what time of day do anxiety attacks occur?
4 What is *anticipatory anxiety*?
5 In what ways is *generalised anxiety disorder* different from *panic disorder*?
6 Clark (1993) proposes that abnormalities in thinking are the core disturbance in panic. What form do these abnormal cognitions take?
7 Outline two explanations proposed by the *psychodynamic model* for the origins of anxiety disorder.
8 What percentage of first degree relatives of sufferers of panic disorder have the disorder themselves?
9 According to Eysenck (1967), what exactly is inherited in panic disorder and generalised anxiety disorder?
10 What is *autonomic lability*?
11 Papp *et al.* (1993) argue that panic disorder is caused by a dysfunction of receptors in the brain. In what way do these receptors cause panic attacks?

Section 2: Phobic disorders

12 What is a *phobia*?
13 What is a *social phobia*?
14 In what ways does a *specific phobia* differ from a social phobia?
15 What is the third category of phobia identified by DSM-IV?
16 What was Freud's (1909) explanation for Little Hans' phobia of horses?
17 What alternative explanation for Hans's phobia is offered by the *behavioural model*?
18 How does Mowrer's (1947) *two-process* (or *two-factor*) *theory* explain the way in which phobias are maintained and are resistant to extinction?

19 What aspect of phobias is difficult for the behavioural model to explain?
20 What explanation did Rosenhan & Seligman (1984) propose to explain the finding that certain classes of stimuli (such as snakes) can more easily be made a conditioned stimulus than others (such as flowers)?

Section 3: Obsessive–compulsive disorder (OCD)

21 How do an *obsession* and a *compulsion* differ?
22 Identify the four most common characteristics of obsessive thought.
23 According to Tallis (1994), why might the finding that first degree relatives of sufferers of OCD often have some sort of anxiety disorder themselves not necessarily suggest a strong genetic component to the disorder?
24 What difference in brain activity do OCD sufferers show compared with non-OCD sufferers?
25 How does the *psychodynamic model* explain obsessive thoughts?
26 How does the *anxiety-reduction hypothesis* account for OCD's maintenance?
27 How can Skinner's (1948a) *superstition hypothesis* account for the behaviour of soccer players who insist on putting on the left sock before the right sock?

Section 4: Post-traumatic stress disorder (PTSD)

28 What is *post-traumatic stress disorder*?
29 Identify three of the symptoms of PTSD shown by Vietnam war veterans.
30 What did Hunt (1997) find when studying PTSD in people in their sixties and seventies who had been disturbed by their experiences during World War II?
31 How do explanations of PTSD differ from explanations of other disorders?
32 Why isn't classical conditioning the only mechanism involved in PTSD?
33 Identify three factors which may influence the likelihood that individuals experiencing trauma will develop PTSD.

Q

Anxiety Disorders

Panic disorder
- Panic attacks come 'out of the blue', and can occur during sleep.
- Sufferers often believe they are having a heart attack.
- Attacks can last from minutes to hours.
- Attacks may be followed by anticipatory anxiety (fear of having an attack) which may develop into agoraphobia.

Generalised anxiety disorder
- Characterised by persistent high levels of anxiety and worry.
- The sensations associated with PD are also present, though more persistent and less intense.
- May cause people to become tired, irritable and socially inept.

explanations

Psychodynamic
- GAD is the result of unconscious conflicts blocked by the ego. We repress these impulses but defences sometimes weaken, leading to a panic attack.
- PD may represent unresolved separation anxiety.

Cognitive
- Clark (1993): increased physiological activity is interpreted in catastrophic ways (e.g as a heart attack).
- This abnormal cognition leads to even more physio-logical activity which confirms the catastrophic belief.

Genetics and biochemistry
- 40% of 1st degree relatives of PD suffer from the disorder (Balon *et al.*, 1989). Eysenck (1967) claims that a predisposition is inherited in the form of a highly reactive ANS.
- Papp *et al.* (1993): PD is caused by a dysfunction in receptors that monitor oxygen levels in the blood.

Phobic disorders

- **Agoraphobia:** a fear of open spaces typically involving a fear of being unable to escape/be helped. Accounts for 10–50% of all phobias and mostly affects women.
- **Social phobia:** intense and excessive fear of being scrutinised by others and embarrassing or humiliating oneself.
- **Specific phobia:** an extreme fear of a specific object (e.g. spiders) or situation (e.g. enclosed spaces).

Phobias are the most common type of anxiety disorder and usually develop in childhood.

explanations

Psychodynamic
- Phobias are the surface expression of deeper conflicts.
- Freud (1909) described **'Little Hans'** – a 5-yr-old with a phobia of horses. Horses symbolised Hans's father, whom Hans saw as a rival for his mother's affection (Oedipus complex).

Behavioural
- Phobias may be acquired by classical conditioning (see Ch 45).
- The **two-process theory** (Mowrer, 1947) claims that phobias are acquired by classical conditioning then maintained by operant conditioning (avoiding the stimulus is reinforced by reduced anxiety).

Biological and genetic
- Rosenhan & Seligman (1984): we are genetically prepared to fear certain stimuli (e.g. spiders).
- Slater & Shields (1969): found a 41% concordance rate among MZ twins, but only a 4% rate between DZ twins.

Anxiety: a general feeling of dread typically accompanied by physiological reactions including increased heart rate, rapid and shallow breathing, sweating, muscle tension and dryness of the mouth.

Obsessive–compulsive disorder

- **Obsessions:** recurrent thoughts or images (often senseless or repugnant) which cannot be controlled.
- **Compulsions:** irresistible urges to engage in repetitive behaviours aimed at preventing some undesirable event.

Often compulsions arise from obsessions (e.g. a hand-washing compulsion from a fear of contamination).

In Britain, roughly 1½ million people suffer from the disorder. It is slightly more common in women than in men.

explanations

Psychodynamic
- Obsessions are **defence mechanisms** which occupy the mind so as to displace more disturbing thoughts.
- However, it is hard to see what thoughts of killing a loved one (which are common to sufferers of OCD) could displace.

Behavioural
- OCD is a way of reducing anxiety. If a behaviour or thought reduces anxiety, then it becomes reinforced and therefore more likely to occur.
- **Superstition hypothesis** (Skinner, 1948a): chance associations between behaviours and reinforcers leads the individual to repeat those behaviours.

Biological and genetic
- People with OCD show increased activity in the left frontal lobe. Drugs which reduce this activity reduce symptoms of OCD.
- Comings & Comings (1987): first degree relatives of OCD sufferers often have the disorder.

Post-traumatic stress disorder

- Occurs in response to an extreme psychological or physical trauma outside the range of normal human experience (Thompson, 1997).
- May result from involvement in a disaster, physical threats to self/family, and witnessing another's death.
- May occur immediately after the event or months later.
- Symptoms include tiredness, apathy, depression, social withdrawal, nightmares, flashbacks, hyperalertness.

Children and PTSD
- Yule (1993): child survivors of recent disasters show symptoms of PTSD, including distressing memories of the event, avoidance of reminders, disturbed sleep and poor concentration.

explanations

- Unlike other disorders, PTSD can be explained in environmental terms.
- Classical conditioning is involved (Kolb, 1987): sufferers often show reactions to stimuli present at the time of the trauma.

However, not everyone who suffers a traumatic event experiences PTSD.

- Green (1994): PTSD develops in about 25% of those who experience potentially traumatic events (12% for accidents, 80% for rape).
- Paton (1992): differences between what workers *expected* to find and what they *actually* found were a source of stress for relief workers at the Lockerbie disaster.

- **Individual differences** in how people perceive events, as well as the **predictability** of events, seem to influence the degree of stress experienced.
- The **recovery environment** (such as support groups) may also play an influential role.
- The effects of drugs on victims of PTSD suggest that disturbed opioid function may play a role (van der Kolk *et al.*, 1989), and the *locus coeruleus* (the brain's 'alarm centre') may also be involved.

BIOLOGICAL (SOMATIC) THERAPIES

KEY QUESTIONS
- How is chemotherapy used to treat mental disorders?
- How is ECT used to treat mental disorders?
- How is psychosurgery used to treat mental disorders?
- What ethical and other issues are involved in the use of these therapies?

Section 1: Chemotherapies

1 Identify one reason why the *neuroleptics* were seen as a great advance in the treatment of seriously disturbed individuals.
2 What are other names for the neuroleptics?
3 Identify three disorders which neuroleptics are commonly used to treat.
4 Identify the three inter-related but discriminable ways in which neuroleptics function.
5 What are *akathisia* and *tardive dyskinesia*, commonly reported by users of neuroleptics?
6 Are the *positive* or *negative* symptoms of schizophrenia least likely to be affected by typical neuroleptics?
7 Identify two criticisms relating to the use of neuroleptic drugs.
8 To what class of drug do the *antidepressants* belong?
9 Name any two disorders, not including depression, for which antidepressants are commonly prescribed.
10 Name any one member of the *tetracyclic* group of antidepressants.
11 Why are *monoamine oxidase inhibitors* (*MAOIs*) so called?
12 The tetracyclics are also known as *SSRIs*. What do the letters SSRI stand for?
13 Identify two side-effects common to both MOAIs and tricyclics.
14 Identify one drawback in using antidepressants with patients considering *suicide*.
15 What effect do *lithium salts* have on *bipolar disorder*?
16 What is the mode of action of *lithium carbonate*?
17 Identify two side-effects associated with lithium salts.
18 To what class of drug do the *anxiolytics* belong?
19 What disorders are the anxiolytics used for?
20 For which type of anxiety disorder are the anxiolytics of little use?
21 Complete the sentence: 'The general effect of anxiolytics is to depress ____ activity, which causes a decrease in activity of the ___ branch of the ___'.
22 Identify two side-effects associated with the use of anxiolytics.

23 What is *rebound anxiety*?
24 Identify two dangers associated with the use of anxiolytics.

Section 2: Electroconvulsive therapy (ECT)

25 What did von Meduna advocate, based on his observation that schizophrenia and epilepsy were *biologically incompatible*?
26 Which therapeutic technique was pioneered by Cerletti and Bini?
27 What is the purpose of giving ECT patients an *atropine sulphate* injection, 45–60 minutes before the treatment?
28 Which two other types of drug are administered to patients before treatment?
29 What current flowing at what voltage is passed across the electrodes, and for what period of time?
30 Name three disorders for which ECT is primarily used today.
31 Why is it unlikely that the effects of ECT are due to the memory disruption caused by the treatment?
32 Why is it unlikely that the effects of ECT can be attributed to patients denying their symptoms to avoid the 'punishment' of therapy?
33 What is the most plausible account of ECT's effectiveness?
34 What did Breggin (1979) discover when investigating the effects of ECT in non-humans?

Section 3: Psychosurgery

35 To what does the term *psychosurgery* refer?
36 What was the rationale behind Moniz and Lima's procedure in which the neural connections between the pre-frontal areas and the hypothalamus and thalamus were severed?
37 What was involved in the original *'apple corer' technique*?
38 What is the principal criticism of the theoretical rationale behind Moniz's operation?
39 What is involved in a *capsulotomy*?

Section 1: Chemotherapies

1 Neuroleptics were seen as a great advance since they lessened the need for the physical restraint of seriously disturbed individuals.

2 Neuroleptics are also called *antipsychotics* and *major tranquillisers*.

3 Neuroleptics are commonly used to treat schizophrenia, mania and amphetamine abuse.

4 Neuroleptics function by blocking dopamine receptors in the brain, by inhibiting the functioning of the hypothalamus, and by preventing arousal signals from reaching higher brain regions.

5 Akathisia is restlessness, whilst tardive dyskinesia is an irreversible movement disorder resembling Parkinson's disease.

6 Negative symptoms (such as apathy and withdrawal) are least likely to respond to typical neuroleptics.

7 Neuroleptic drugs are not cures but only treat the symptoms of pychosis. In addition, they do not treat social incapacity or assist the patient in adjusting to life outside a therapeutic setting.

8 Antidepressants are classed as stimulants.

9 Antidepressants are commonly prescribed for anxiety, agoraphobia, obsessive–compulsive disorder and eating disorders.

10 Prozac (fluoxetine) is a tetracyclic antidepressant.

11 Monoamine oxidase inhibitors (MAOIs) are so called because they inhibit the uptake of the enzyme which deactivates the monoamine neurotransmitters noradrenaline and serotonin.

12 SSRI stands for selective serotonin re-uptake inhibitors.

13 MOAIs and tricyclics are both associated with cardiac arrhythmias and heart block, dry mouth, blurred vision and urinary retention.

14 Antidepressants do not work immediately and may take weeks to begin working. For patients considering suicide this may be too long.

15 Lithium salts flatten out cycles of manic behaviour.

16 Lithium carbonate functions by increasing the re-uptake of noradrenaline and serotonin.

17 Lithium salts are associated with depressed reactions, hand tremors, dry mouth, weight gain, impaired memory and kidney poisoning. In high concentrations they may cause nausea, diarrhoea and death.

18 Anxiolytics are classed as depressants.

19 Anxiolytics are used to treat anxiety and tension in people whose disturbances are not severe enough to warrant hospitalisation.

20 Anxiolytics are of little use in treating panic disorder.

21 'The general effect of anxiolytics is to depress *CNS* activity, which causes a decrease in activity of the *sympathetic* branch of the *ANS*.'

22 Anxiolytics are associated with drowsiness, lethargy, tolerance, dependence, withdrawal and toxicity.

23 Rebound anxiety refers to anxiety which is even more intense than the original anxiety, and occurs when the drug is stopped.

24 Overdose of anxiolytics can lead to death, especially when taken with alcohol. They may also lead to addiction.

Section 2: Electroconvulsive therapy (ECT)

25 Von Meduna advocated inducing major epileptic fits in psychotics in order to 'cure' their schizophrenia.

26 Cerletti and Bini (Bini, 1938) were the first to advocate passing an electric current across the temples to induce an epileptic fit.

27 An atropine sulphate injection is given in order to prevent the heart's normal rhythm from being disturbed, and to inhibit the secretion of mucus and saliva.

28 A muscle relaxant and an anaesthetic are administered before treatment.

29 A current of 200 milliamps, flowing at 110 volts, for a period of 0.5–4 seconds.

30 ECT is primarily used to treat severe depression, bipolar disorder and certain obsessive–compulsive disorders.

31 Unilateral ECT minimises memory disruption, but is nevertheless effective at reducing depression.

32 Sub-convulsive shocks have been applied to patients, and although these are likely to be just as unpleasant and threatening as convulsive shocks, they do not seem to be as beneficial.

33 The most plausible account of ECT's effectiveness suggests that it produces biochemical changes in the brain, particularly in levels of serotonin and noradrenaline, which are greater than those produced by drugs.

34 Breggin (1979) discovered that ECT caused brain damage to non-humans, immediately following its administration.

Section 3: Psychosurgery

35 The term psychosurgery refers to surgical procedures that are performed on the brain to treat mental disorders, where the intention is to alter purposely psychological functioning.

36 Moniz and Lima's procedure aimed to disconnect thought (mediated by the cortex) from emotion (mediated by the lower brain centres).

37 The original 'apple corer' technique involved drilling a hole in the skull on either side of the head, then inserting a blunt instrument which was rotated in a vertical arc.

38 The theoretical rationale behind Moniz's operation was vague and misguided, with researchers not entirely clear why beneficial effects should occur.

39 A capsulotomy involves cutting two tiny holes in the forehead, which allow radioactive electrodes to be inserted into the frontal lobe, to destroy tissue by means of beta rays.

Psychosurgery

Facts

- Refers to surgical procedures which are performed on the brain with the intention of altering psychological function.
- Moniz and Lima pioneered the *leucotomy* or *prefrontal lobotomy*. The procedure involved severing the connections between the prefrontal areas ('rational area') and the hypothalamus and thalamus ('emotional areas').
- Original 'apple corer' technique involved inserting a blunt instrument into either side of the head and rotating it. A 70% 'cure' rate was claimed by Moniz and Lima after one year.
- Freeman & Watts (1942) popularised the prefrontal lobotomy, and Freeman developed the *transorbital lobotomy* involving the insertion of a probe into frontal area via the eye socket.

Reasons for abandoning psychosurgery

- **Psychotherapeutic drugs:** introduced in the late 1950s.
- **Lack of scientific basis:** David (1994) has suggested that, even today, knowledge of the frontal lobes is psychiatry's 'pseudoscience'.
- **Consistency and irreversibility:** psychosurgery is irreversible and its effectiveness varies between individuals.
- **Side-effects:** apathy, seizures, intellectual impairments, memory loss, hyperactivity, impaired learning ability, and death are possible.
- **Lack of evaluation:** the consequences of many forms of psychosurgery are poorly researched.
- **Consent:** psychosurgery was routinely used with people who could not give their consent to the operation.

Modern techniques

- Over 20 operations a year are still conducted in Britain (Snaith, 1994).
- Modern labotomies involve the insertion of radioactive rods into the frontal lobes, or the use of a heated electrode.
- Techniques are used with depressives and obsessive–compulsives, and reduce the risk of suicide in depressives from 15% to 1% (Verkaik, 1995).

Electroconvulsive therapy

Facts

- Involves passing an electric current across the brain in order to induce an epileptic fit.
- von Meduna claimed that schizophrenia and epilepsy were *'biologically incompatible'*, and used Cardiazol to induce epileptic fits.
- Cerletti and Bini (Bini, 1938) advocated the use of electric currents to induce epileptic fits.
- Typically, a number of treatments are administered over several weeks. Around 20,000 people per year undergo ECT in Britain.
- Originally used to treat schizophrenia, now mostly used to treat depression, bipolar disorder and obsessive–compulsive disorder.
- ECT has a negative public image and has been criticised on ethical grounds and even outlawed in Berkeley, California.
- Heather (1976): the treatment is unscientific, and Breggin (1979) cites studies of non-humans which suggest that ECT may cause brain damage.

Procedure

- An atropine sulphate injection is given to prevent disturbance of the heart's rhythm, followed by a short-acting anaesthetic and a muscle relaxant.
- In unilateral ECT, a current of around 200 milliamps at 110 volts is passed across the temples for between 0.5 and 4 seconds. In unilateral ECT, only one hemisphere (the non-dominant hemisphere) is affected.

Explaining ECT's effectiveness

- Benton (1981): whilst ECT is clearly effective in some cases, little is known about how it works.
- It is possible that a person denies their symptoms to avoid the 'punishment' that ECT is perceived as being. However, 'sub-convulsive shocks' are equally unpleasant but do not reduce depression equally.
- ECT may produce biochemical changes greater than those produced by drugs. It is difficult to establish which of the physical changes occurring during ECT is responsible. Lilienfeld (1995) suggests that *serotonin* and *noradrenaline* are most likely to be affected.

Biological Therapies

Chemotherapy

	Neuroleptics	Antidepressants and antimanics	Anxiolytics
Facts	• Also known as **antipsychotics/major tranquillisers.** • Introduced in the 1950s following the discovery that they calmed psychotics without impairing consciousness. • Seen as a great advance since they lessened the need for physical restraints. • Antipsychotics do not cure schizophrenia but reduce its prominent symptoms.	• Antidepressants are classified as **stimulants** and were introduced in the late 1950s. *Prozac* is popular today. • Used to treat depression, anxiety, agoraphobia, obsessive–compulsive disorders. • None of the antidepressants exerts immediate effects (most take two weeks). • Lithium salts flatten out cycles of manic behaviour.	• Classified as **depressants** and known as **anti-anxiety drugs** or **minor tranquillisers.** • Used to reduce anxiety and tension. • Anxiolytics are effective in reducing the symptoms of GAD, but less effective for panic attacks. • Overdose can lead to death, especially if mixed with alcohol, and they are addictive.
Examples	• Largely derive from phenothiazines and include Thorazine, *Largactil*. • Recently a dibezazepine *(Clozaril)* has been used and has fewer side-effects.	• MAOI (monoamine oxidase inhibitors) include *Nardil*. The tetracyclic group (selective serotonin reuptake inhibitors – SSRIs) include *Prozac*. • Lithium salts include *Camoclit* and *Litarex*.	• The propanediol group includes *Miltown*. • The benzodiazepine group includes Librium and *Valium*.
Mode of action	• Most neuroleptics block D2 dopamine receptors in the brain. • Also inhibit the hypothalamus, which secretes dopamine. • Prevent arousal signals from reaching higher brain regions.	• MAOIs block the uptake of an enzyme which deactivates noradrenaline and serotonin. Tetracyclics deactivate the enzyme which removes serotonin. • Antimanics increase the re-uptake of noradrenaline and serotonin.	• CNS activity is depressed, causing a decrease in the activity of the sympathetic branch of the ANS. • This produces decreased heart and respiration rate, reducing feelings of nervousness and tension.
Side-effects	• **Neuroleptic malignant syndrome:** delirium, coma and death. • **Extrapyramidal symptoms:** restlessness, abnormal body movements and tardive dyskinesia (irreversible shaking resembling Parkinson's disease).	• MAOIs can cause death if combined with certain foods (e.g. cheese and yeast extracts), whilst tetracyclics may impair sexual functioning and heighten aggression. • Antimanics may cause tremors, dry mouth, weight gain, impaired memory.	• Include drowsiness, lethargy, tolerance, dependence, withdrawal and toxicity. • *Rebound anxiety*, which is even more intense than the original anxiety, can occur when use is stopped.

BEHAVIOURAL THERAPIES

KEY QUESTIONS
- What do therapies based on classical conditioning involve?
- What do therapies based on operant conditioning involve?
- What ethical and other issues concern these therapies?

Section 1: Behaviour therapy

1 What did Watson & Rayner (1920) demonstrate in their experiments with 'Little Albert'?
2 What is the principle common to both *implosion therapy* and *flooding*?
3 Outline the procedures in implosion therapy.
4 What is *stimulus augmentation*?
5 How does flooding differ from implosion therapy?
6 Wolpe (1973) describes the case of an adolescent girl with a fear of cars. How was this fear overcome?
7 Identify one difficulty with the use of flooding as a form of therapy.
8 What is learned during *systematic desensitisation* (SD) that is not learned during either implosion therapy or flooding?
9 How was Jones (1924) able to eliminate fear responses in children?
10 What is an *anxiety hierarchy*?
11 What are the next two steps during SD which follow the construction of an anxiety hierarchy?
12 What does the *principle of reciprocal inhibition* maintain, as applied to phobias?
13 What source of variation between individuals poses a problem for SD?
14 What is meant by saying that *in vivo* desensitisation is always the most effective form of desensitisation?
15 Which of flooding, implosion therapy, and SD is the most effective?
16 What is the objective of *aversion therapy*?
17 In what way is aversion therapy applied in the treatment of *alcohol abuse*?
18 Identify one other behaviour which aversion therapy has been used to treat.
19 Identify one highly controversial (and non-fictitious) use of aversion therapy.
20 Complete the sentence: 'In some cases, ___ factors will "swamp" the conditioning process, and this is one reason why aversion therapy is not always effective'.

21 In what way does aversion therapy also involve *operant conditioning*?
22 How does *covert sensitisation* differ from aversion therapy?

Section 2: Behaviour modification

23 During any form of therapy based on *operant conditioning*, the first step is to identify the maladaptive behaviour. What is the next step?
24 What is the rationale behind therapies based on *extinction*?
25 Identify one problem which a therapist faces in attempting to implement therapies based on extinction.
26 How were Cowart & Whaley (1971) able to eliminate self-mutilating behaviour in an emotionally disturbed infant?
27 Identify two reasons why therapies based on *punishment* are not as effective as those based on positive reinforcement.
28 What name is given to therapies in which successive approximations to desired behaviours are rewarded?
29 How does Ayllon & Azrin's (1968) *token-economy system* work?
30 Ayllon & Azrin's (1968) therapies were effective in eliciting and maintaining desired behaviours. What further effect did they have on staff and patients?
31 Identify two problems associated with the use of token economies.

Section 3: Behavioural therapies – issues

32 Complete the sentence: 'Although critics accept that therapies based on the behavioural model can alter behaviour, they argue that such therapies fail to identify a disorder's ___ ___'.
33 What is *symptom substitution*?
34 Identify one further practical problem associated with the use of behaviour therapies.
35 Outline one ethical issue of behavioural approaches to therapy.

Section 1: Behaviour therapy

1 Watson & Rayner (1920) showed that a fear response to a neutral stimulus could be conditioned, by pairing the neutral stimulus with an unpleasant one.

2 Both implosion therapy and flooding work on the principle that a stimulus which evokes a fear response will lose this power if it is repeatedly presented without the unpleasant experience.

3 Implosion therapy involves the therapist repeatedly exposing the person to vivid mental images of the feared situation whilst in the safe therapeutic setting.

4 Stimulus augmentation is when verbal descriptions of the feared stimulus are used by the therapist to supplement the person's imagery.

5 Flooding differs in that the individual is forced to confront the feared object or event, rather than simply imagining it.

6 The girl's fear of cars was overcome by forcing her into the back of one and driving her around for four hours.

7 For some people, such therapies lead to increased anxiety or are too traumatic.

8 Systematic desensitisation teaches the adaptive and desirable response, whereas implosion therapy and flooding only extinguish the undesirable behaviour.

9 Jones (1924) was able to eliminate fear responses in children by gradually introducing the feared object, whilst at the same time giving them candy.

10 An anxiety hierarchy is a series of scenes or events rated from lowest to highest in terms of the anxiety they elicit.

11 Following the construction of an anxiety hierarchy, SD involves relaxation training, then relaxing whilst imagining scenes from the hierarchy.

12 The principle maintains that it is impossible to experience anxiety and relaxation at the same time.

13 Individuals differ in their abilities to conjure up vivid mental images.

14 *In vivo* desensitisation involves live encounters with the feared object or situation, and is more effective than other desensitisation techniques.

15 Flooding.

16 Aversion therapy aims to extinguish the pleasant feelings associated with socially undesirable behaviours.

17 Alcohol is paired with vomiting by giving people a drug which induces vomiting when combined with it, or inducing vomiting immediately after alcohol is taken.

18 Aversion therapy has also been used to treat cigarette smoking, overeating and children's self-injurious behaviour.

19 Aversion therapy has also been used to 'treat' homosexuality.

20 'In some cases, *cognitive* factors will "swamp" the conditioning process, and this is one reason why aversion therapy is not always effective.'

21 Aversion therapy also involves operant conditioning in that once the classically conditioned fear has been learned, the person is inclined to avoid contact with the stimulus in the future (operant response).

22 Covert sensitisation differs from aversion therapy in that people are trained to punish themselves using their imaginations (rather than aversive stimuli).

Section 2: Behaviour modification

23 Once the maladaptive behaviour has been identified, the next step is to identify the reinforcers that maintain such behaviour.

24 Therapies based on extinction maintain that operant conditioning can be used to eliminate abnormal behaviour by removing reinforcers which maintain such behaviour.

25 In order to be effective, the therapist must be able to identify and eliminate the reinforcer(s) which maintain the behaviour, and this is not always easy.

26 Cowart & Whaley (1971) were able to eliminate self-mutilating behaviour by delivering electric shocks to the infant via his leg, every time he showed the maladaptive behaviour.

27 Behaviours learned through punishment may overgeneralise to behaviours related to the punished behaviour, and punishment tends only to produce a temporary suppression of undesirable behaviours.

28 Behaviour shaping.

29 Ayllon & Azrin's (1968) token-economy system works by rewarding disturbed individuals with tokens for desirable behaviours. These tokens can then be exchanged for 'privileges'.

30 Token economies improved staff and patient morale, with patients less apathetic and irresponsible, and staff more enthusiastic about their patients and therapy.

31 Patients who are re-introduced to the community may not be successfully 'weaned off' the token, and token economies may lead to 'token learning' where patients only perform a behaviour if rewarded for it.

Section 3: Behavioural therapies – issues

32 'Although critics accept that therapies based on the behavioural model can alter behaviour, they argue that such therapies fail to identify a disorder's *underlying causes*.'

33 Symptom substitution occurs when removing one symptom simply results in another occurring in some other form.

34 Behaviour therapies may condition behaviours which, since they are learnt in a therapeutic setting, do not generalise well to other conditions.

35 Behavioural approaches to therapy have been criticised on a number of ethical grounds, in particular, techniques involving punishment have been seen as authoritarian, dehumanising and akin to 'brainwashing'. Others argue that behaviour therapies manipulate people and deprive them of their freedom.

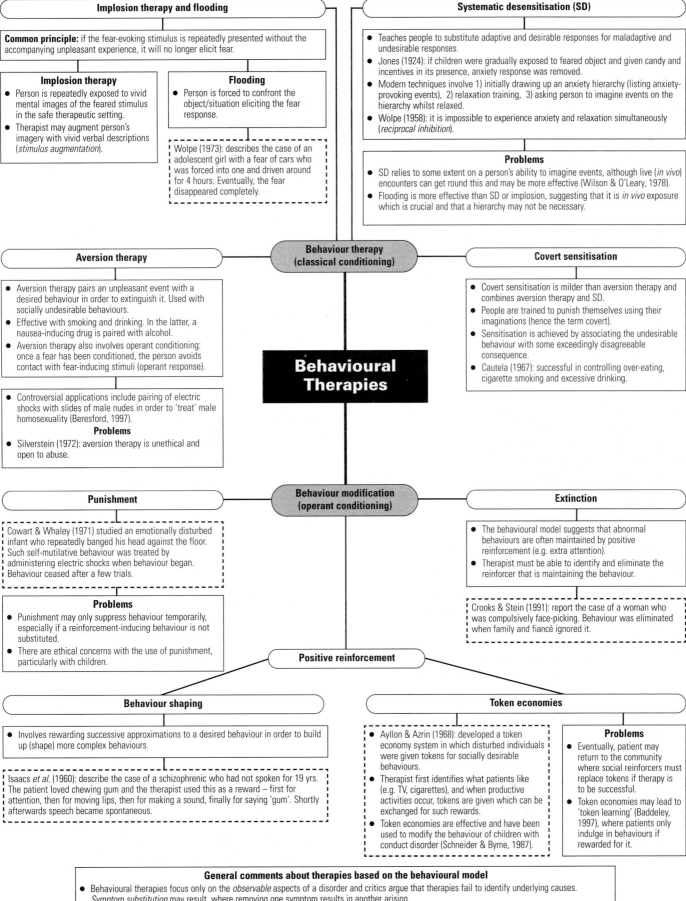

Implosion therapy and flooding

Common principle: if the fear-evoking stimulus is repeatedly presented without the accompanying unpleasant experience, it will no longer elicit fear.

Implosion therapy
- Person is repeatedly exposed to vivid mental images of the feared stimulus in the safe therapeutic setting.
- Therapist may augment person's imagery with vivid verbal descriptions (*stimulus augmentation*).

Flooding
- Person is forced to confront the object/situation eliciting the fear response.

Wolpe (1973): describes the case of an adolescent girl with a fear of cars who was forced into one and driven around for 4 hours. Eventually, the fear disappeared completely.

Systematic desensitisation (SD)
- Teaches people to substitute adaptive and desirable responses for maladaptive and undesirable responses.
- Jones (1924): if children were gradually exposed to feared object and given candy and incentives in its presence, anxiety response was removed.
- Modern techniques involve 1) initially drawing up an anxiety hierarchy (listing anxiety-provoking events), 2) relaxation training, 3) asking person to imagine events on the hierarchy whilst relaxed.
- Wolpe (1958): it is impossible to experience anxiety and relaxation simultaneously (*reciprocal inhibition*).

Problems
- SD relies to some extent on a person's ability to imagine events, although live (*in vivo*) encounters can get round this and may be more effective (Wilson & O'Leary, 1978).
- Flooding is more effective than SD or implosion, suggesting that it is *in vivo* exposure which is crucial and that a hierarchy may not be necessary.

Behaviour therapy (classical conditioning)

Aversion therapy
- Aversion therapy pairs an unpleasant event with a desired behaviour in order to extinguish it. Used with socially undesirable behaviours.
- Effective with smoking and drinking. In the latter, a nausea-inducing drug is paired with alcohol.
- Aversion therapy also involves operant conditioning: once a fear has been conditioned, the person avoids contact with fear-inducing stimuli (operant response).

- Controversial applications include pairing of electric shocks with slides of male nudes in order to 'treat' male homosexuality (Beresford, 1997).
Problems
- Silverstein (1972): aversion therapy is unethical and open to abuse.

Covert sensitisation
- Covert sensitisation is milder than aversion therapy and combines aversion therapy and SD.
- People are trained to punish themselves using their imaginations (hence the term covert).
- Sensitisation is achieved by associating the undesirable behaviour with some exceedingly disagreeable consequence.
- Cautela (1967): successful in controlling over-eating, cigarette smoking and excessive drinking.

Behavioural Therapies

Behaviour modification (operant conditioning)

Punishment

Cowart & Whaley (1971) studied an emotionally disturbed infant who repeatedly banged his head against the floor. Such self-mutilative behaviour was treated by administering electric shocks when behaviour began. Behaviour ceased after a few trials.

Problems
- Punishment may only suppress behaviour temporarily, especially if a reinforcement-inducing behaviour is not substituted.
- There are ethical concerns with the use of punishment, particularly with children.

Extinction
- The behavioural model suggests that abnormal behaviours are often maintained by positive reinforcement (e.g. extra attention).
- Therapist must be able to identify and eliminate the reinforcer that is maintaining the behaviour.

Crooks & Stein (1991): report the case of a woman who was compulsively face-picking. Behaviour was eliminated when family and fiancé ignored it.

Positive reinforcement

Behaviour shaping
- Involves rewarding successive approximations to a desired behaviour in order to build up (shape) more complex behaviours.

Isaacs *et al.* (1960): describe the case of a schizophrenic who had not spoken for 19 yrs. The patient loved chewing gum and the therapist used this as a reward – first for attention, then for moving lips, then for making a sound, finally for saying 'gum'. Shortly afterwards speech became spontaneous.

Token economies
- Ayllon & Azrin (1968): developed a token economy system in which disturbed individuals were given tokens for socially desirable behaviours.
- Therapist first identifies what patients like (e.g. TV, cigarettes), and when productive activities occur, tokens are given which can be exchanged for such rewards.
- Token economies are effective and have been used to modify the behaviour of children with conduct disorder (Schneider & Byrne, 1987).

Problems
- Eventually, patient may return to the community where social reinforcers must replace tokens if therapy is to be successful.
- Token economies may lead to 'token learning' (Baddeley, 1997), where patients only indulge in behaviours if rewarded for it.

General comments about therapies based on the behavioural model
- Behavioural therapies focus only on the *observable* aspects of a disorder and critics argue that therapies fail to identify underlying causes. *Symptom substitution* may result, where removing one symptom results in another arising.
- Behaviours which are learned under one set of conditions (e.g. therapeutic setting) may not *generalise* to another (e.g. real life). Therapists try to counter this by working in environments which are representative of real life.
- Behaviour therapies have been criticised for being unethical. Punishment techniques are authoritarian, and other therapies may manipulate people and deprive them of their freedom. Therapists respond that patients give consent, and are encouraged to control their own behaviours.

ALTERNATIVES TO BIOLOGICAL AND BEHAVIOURAL THERAPIES

KEY QUESTIONS
- What do alternative therapies based on the psychodynamic model offer?
- What do alternative therapies based on the cognitive–behavioural model offer?
- What did early attempts at assessing the effectiveness of therapies suggest?

Section 1: Psychoanalytic techniques

1 According to Freud's *psychodynamic model*, how does the ego defend itself from demands of the id or superego with which it is too weak to cope?
2 According to Freud, why is a change in behaviour not enough to bring about a permanent cure?
3 Why did Freud view a person's present problems as not belonging to the *psychoanalyst's* domain?
4 What is the purpose of *psychoanalysis*?
5 What is *insight*?
6 What is the rationale behind providing an analysand with insight?
7 What name is given to the technique in which an analysand is encouraged to say whatever comes to mind?
8 Why is it important that analysts should not reveal personal information about themselves, nor express emotion or evaluation of an analysand?
9 What does *resistance* demonstrate to a psychoanalyst?
10 What is the role of *transference* in the psychoanalytic process?
11 What is meant by Freud's claim that *working through* is necessary as troubles are usually *over-determined*?
12 Identify two ways in which *focal psychotherapies* differ from *classical psychoanalysis*.
13 What is the principal way in which *ego analysts* disagree with Freud's psychodynamic model?

Section 2: Evaluating effectiveness

14 According to Eysenck, what percentage of cases treated with psychoanalysis could be considered 'cured' or 'improved'?
15 What percentage of the control group in Eysenck's study underwent spontaneous remission?
16 Complete the sentence: 'Eysenck claimed that there appeared to be an ___ correlation between recovery and psychotherapy'.
17 What additional *ethical issue* did Eysenck raise?

18 What is a *meta-analytic study*?
19 Complete the sentence: 'On the basis of their meta-analytic study, Smith *et al.* (1980) concluded that the average person who receives therapy is better off at the end of it than __ per cent of persons who do not.'
20 What criticism did Smith *et al.*'s study attract, concerning the nature of its sample?

Section 3: Cognitive–behavioural approaches

21 What name do *social learning theorists* give to learning in which humans learn from others without direct experience?
22 Under what conditions is our restraint against performing an action likely to be lowered (*response disinhibition*)?
23 What is involved in *participant modelling*?
24 How is participant modelling applied in the area of *assertiveness training*?
25 Complete the sentence: 'Bandura (1977) believes that one reason for modelling's effectiveness is the development of ___-___.'
26 What is the aim of *rational–emotive therapy (RET)*?
27 In Ellis's *A-B-C model* what do the letters A, B and C stand for?
28 Identify two of the common maladaptive cognitions suggested by Ellis.
29 What does it mean to say that the therapist is an 'exposing and nonsense-annihilating scientist'?
30 Why do rational–emotive therapists not offer people warmth, love and support?
31 Name one characteristic of individuals for whom RET is effective.
32 For which types of disorders is RET ineffective?
33 What does Beck's *cognitive restructuring therapy* have in common with Ellis's RET?
34 What type of disorder is Beck's therapy specifically designed to treat?
35 What is the *cognitive triad* suffered by depressed people?

Section 1: Psychoanalytic techniques

1 The ego defends itself by repressing the demands into the unconscious.

2 In order to bring about a permanent cure, the problems giving rise to the behaviours must also be changed.

3 Present problems will already have received attention in the form of sympathy and advice from family and friends.

4 The purpose of psychoanalysis is to uncover the unconscious conflicts responsible for a person's mental disorder.

5 Insight is a conscious awareness of repressed conflicts.

6 The rationale is that once a person understands the reason for a behaviour, the ego can deal more effectively with it and resolve the conflict.

7 Free association.

8 It is important that the analyst remain anonymous since such an interaction ensures that the analysand does not form a close, personal relationship with the analyst, but views him/her as an ambiguous stimulus.

9 Resistance demonstrates that the analyst is getting close to the source of the problem, and that the unconscious is struggling to avoid 'giving up its secrets'.

10 Transference occurs when the unconscious conflict has been unearthed and displaced onto the analyst, who now becomes the object of the analysand's emotional responses. The conflict can then be 'lived out'.

11 Freud maintains that troubles seldom stem from a single source (i.e. are over-determined), and all aspects of the conflict and their implications must be dealt with before the conflict can be resolved (working through).

12 Focal psychotherapies are usually briefer, involve face-to-face interaction, and pay more attention to the analysand's current life and relationships than does classical psychoanalysis.

13 Ego analysts believe that Freud over-emphasised the influence of sexual and aggressive impulses, and underestimated the ego's importance.

Section 2: Evaluating effectiveness

14 Eysenck claimed that 44 per cent of such cases could be considered 'cured' or 'improved'.

15 Sixty-six per cent of the control group underwent spontaneous remission.

16 'Eysenck claimed that there appeared to be an *inverse (or negative)* correlation between recovery and psychotherapy.'

17 Eysenck claimed that it was unethical for therapists to charge people for their services, when research suggested that they were paying for nothing.

18 A meta-analytic study is one in which researchers combine the results of all the studies conducted in a given area to produce an 'averaged' result.

19 'On the basis of his meta-analytic study, Smith *et al.* (1980) concluded that the average person who receives therapy is better off at the end of it than *80* per cent of persons who do not.'

20 Most of the participants in Smith *et al.*'s study were students, who do not form a representative sample of the population as a whole.

Section 3: Cognitive–behavioural approaches

21 Observational learning.

22 Response disinhibition is likely to occur when we observe a positive outcome for a behaviour.

23 Participant modelling involves an individual observing the therapist's behaviour and then imitating it.

24 In assertiveness training, people with difficulty asserting themselves in interpersonal situations are required to perform in the presence of a group which provides feedback on the adequacy of the performance. The therapist may then model the appropriate behaviour, and the individual is required to imitate the therapist.

25 'Bandura (1977) believes that one reason for modelling's effectiveness is the development of *self-efficacy*.'

26 Rational–emotive therapy aims to help people find flaws in their thinking, and to replace these maladaptive cognitions with more rational ones.

27 The letters A, B and C stand for a significant activating event (A), a person's belief system (B), and the highly charged emotional consequence (C).

28 Ellis identifies people's beliefs that they are worthless unless they are perfectly competent at everything they try, and that they must be approved of and loved by everyone they meet.

29 The therapist is responsible for exposing irrational beliefs and substituting more rational alternatives in a scientific fashion, by reference to observations.

30 Rational–emotive therapists believe that offering people warmth, love and support may reinforce their need for love (which is often at the core of their circumstances), and create a dependence on therapy or the therapist.

31 RET tends to be effective with people who are self-demanding and feel guilty, or feel that they are not living up to their own standards of perfection.

32 RET is ineffective for people with severe thought disorders (such as schizophrenia).

33 Beck's cognitive restructuring therapy and Ellis' RET both assume that disorders stem primarily from irrational beliefs.

34 Beck's therapy is specifically designed to treat people suffering from depression.

35 Depressed people suffer from the cognitive triad of negative beliefs about themselves, their futures, and their experiences.

Free association

- The *analysand* is encouraged to say whatever comes to mind, no matter how trivial or frivolous.
- In so doing, the *ego* (which usually censors threatening impulses) may be bypassed.
- The analyst remains anonymous and makes no personal revelations.

Resistance

- During free association, the analyst may draw attention to the analysand's *resistances*.
- Jokes, changing the subject, disrupting the session, may all indicate an unwillingness to talk about some significant aspect of the analysand's life.
- In *confrontation*, the analyst tells the analysand exactly what is being revealed.

Achieving insight and working through

- Insight is achieved once the analysand understands the roots of the conflict.
- Since conflicts seldom stem from a single source, but rather are over-determined, analysands must consider *all* aspects of the conflict (*working through*) to prevent them from repressing it again.
- The goal is to allow the analysand to deal with the conflict without using defence mechanisms.

Psychoanalysis: aims to uncover the unconscious conflicts responsible for an individual's mental disorder, thereby 'making the unconscious conscious', and providing the analysand with insight into repressed conflicts.

Transference

- When conflicts are brought into consciousness, they are then 'lived out'.
- The original source of the conflict is displaced onto the analyst and the corresponding feelings *transferred*.
- Such feelings may include attachment to the analyst, jealousy, or overestimation of the analyst's qualities.

Countertransference

- Freud discovered that analysts may also transfer their own feelings onto the analysand (countertransference). He considered this a failing on the part of the analyst.
- Thomas (1990): countertransference is now considered an unavoidable outcome of the analytic process.

Issues

Freud's approach has been subject to much criticism:
- **Hard to study scientifically** – many of the concepts are vague or difficult to measure.
- **Evaluating the effectiveness of therapy is difficult**, especially where the evidence is related to case studies.
- **Analysts may blame analysands when therapy fails to produce changes**, or insights may not be accompanied by behavioural change.
- **Psychoanalysis is a closed system**: if it is effective, then this is attributed to insight; if it is not, then 'real' insight cannot have occurred.

Psychoanalysis

Psychoanalytically oriented therapies

Psychoanalytically oriented therapists differ from classical psychoanalysts:
- Therapies involve briefer treatment and use face-to-face interaction (focal psychotherapies).
- More attention is paid to current life and relationships than early childhood.
- Personality may also be shaped by the external environment.
- *Ego analysts* focus on the role of the ego, rather than that of the id.

Studies of effectiveness

Eysenck (1952)

Looked at studies conducted between 1920 and 1951, comparing psychoanalysis, eclectic therapies (a variety of approaches is used) and a control group (who received no therapy).
Results: Psychoanalysis – 44% improved, Eclectic – 64% improved, No therapy – 66% improved. Concluded that **no treatment is at least as effective or more effective than treatment**, and suggested that it was unethical for therapists to charge for treatment (Eysenck, 1992).

Alternative Therapies

Smith *et al.* (1980)

Attempted to overcome the possibility that certain types of measurement may favour certain therapies by looking at **all** types of measurement. Looked at 475 studies using a total of 1776 outcome measures.
Results: Concluded that the average person who receives therapy is better off than 80% of persons who do not.

Bandura

Cognitive–behavioural therapies

Ellis

Modelling (Bandura,1969)

Observational learning: Humans can learn simply by observing the behaviour of another. If we see a positive outcome for a behaviour, we are more likely to perform it (**response disinhibition**); if we see a negative outcome, we are less likely to perform it (**response inhibition**).
Modelling: Maladaptive behaviours can be eliminated by exposing sufferers to models who demonstrate the appropriate actions. Participant modelling involves the individual observing, then imitating, the therapist. Used effectively with a variety of phobias.

Assertiveness training

- Individuals demonstrate problem behaviours in front of a group who provide feedback. Therapist then models appropriate behaviour.
- Individual then tries again, alternating between modelling and behavioural rehearsal. Used in social skills training.

Self-efficacy

Bandura (1977): one reason for modelling's effectiveness is it increases a person's evaluation of the degree to which he/she can cope with difficult situations (*self-efficacy*), by encouraging them to perform behaviours which were previously impossible.

Beck

Cognitive restructuring therapy (Beck, 1967)

- Assumes that disorders stem primarily from *irrational beliefs*.
- Specifically designed to treat depressed people.
- Depressed people suffer from a *'cognitive triad'* of negative beliefs about themselves, their future and their experiences (Beck *et al.*, 1979 – see Ch 57).
- Therapy aims to identify *implicit* and *self-defeating assumptions*, substituting more adaptive ones.
- The approach is gentler and less confrontational than RET, disproving the person's negative self-image (Williams, 1992).
- Most effective in the treatment of depression (Andrews, 1991), but has also been used in treating eating disorders.

Rational–emotive therapy (RET)

- The aim of RET is to help people find flaws in their thinking and alter these *maladaptive cognitions* by creating a *dispute belief system* (D), which does not lead to severe emotional consequences (see below).
- Ellis proposes that two common cognitions are:
  1. *I am worthless if I am not perfectly competent.*
  2. *Everyone must approve of me and love me.*
- Therapy involves substituting more realistic thoughts in place of the self-defeating ones (the therapist is 'an exposing and nonsense annihilating scientist').
- People are seen as having the capacity for rational understanding and the resources for personal growth.

The A-B-C model

- Ellis (1991): significant activating events (A) are often followed by highly charged emotional consequences (C) because of a person's belief system (B).

Effectiveness

- Effective in producing change amongst the self-demanding or perfectionists (Brandsma *et al.*, 1978).
- Ineffective with severe thought disorders (Ellis, 1993).

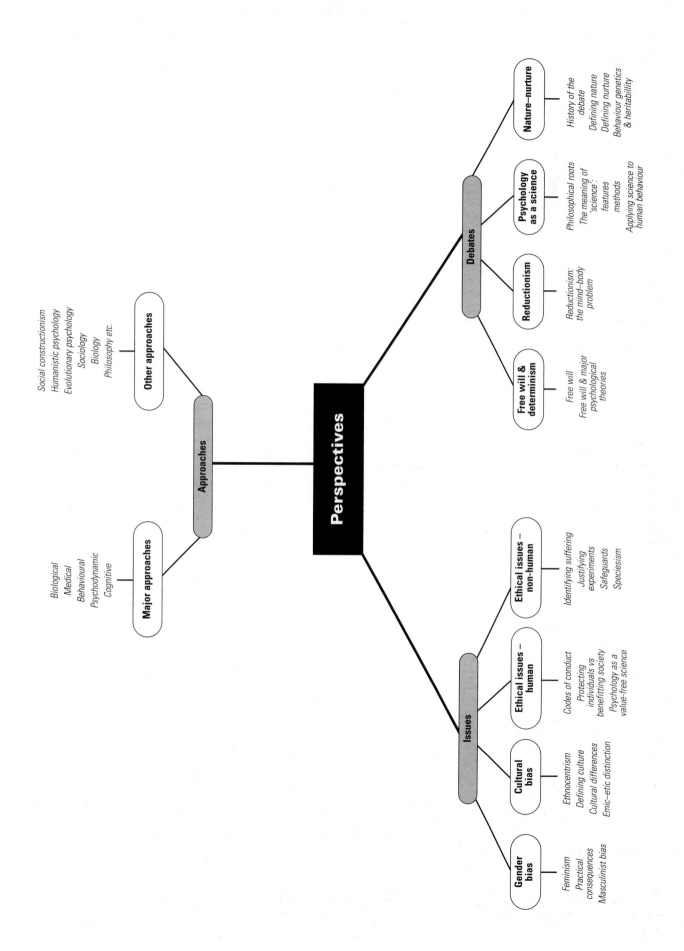

Perspectives

Approaches

Major approaches
- Biological
- Medical
- Behavioural
- Psychodynamic
- Cognitive

Other approaches
- Social constructionism
- Humanistic psychology
- Evolutionary psychology
- Sociology
- Biology
- Philosophy etc.

Issues

Gender bias
- Feminism
- Practical consequences
- Masculinist bias

Cultural bias
- Ethnocentrism
- Defining culture
- Cultural differences
- Emic–etic distinction

Ethical issues – human
- Codes of conduct
- Protecting individuals vs benefitting society
- Psychology as a value-free science

Ethical issues – non-human
- Identifying suffering
- Justifying experiments
- Safeguards
- Speciesism

Debates

Free will & determinism
- Free will
- Free will & major psychological theories

Reductionism
- Reductionism: the mind–body problem

Psychology as a science
- Philosophical roots
- The meaning of 'science': features methods
- Applying science to human behaviour

Nature–nurture
- History of the debate
- Defining nature
- Defining nurture
- Behaviour genetics & heritability

BIAS IN PSYCHOLOGICAL THEORY AND RESEARCH

SYLLABUS

14.2 Section B – issues and debates in psychology –
a issues
- **gender bias** in psychological theory and research
  (e.g. alpha/beta bias, androcentrism). **Cultural bias** in
  psychological theory and research (e.g.
  ethnocentrism, historical bias, the imposed etic)

KEY QUESTIONS
- In what ways do psychological theory and research
  demonstrate gender bias?
- In what ways do psychological theory and research
  demonstrate culture bias?

Q **Section 1: Gender bias**

1 Identify two common themes within *feminism*.
2 What is the role of *individualism* within psychology in
   relation to gender bias?
3 Complete the sentence: 'Most psychological research is
   conducted on ___ samples'.
4 Identify one way in which women's behaviour is often
   viewed when it differs from men's.
5 What do psychological explanations of women's behaviour tend to emphasise?
6 What is *heterosexism*?
7 Complete the sentence: 'Psychology's claims to be a science are based on its methods and the belief that it is a
   ___-___ discipline'.
8 Identify the two major problems identified by Nicholson
   (1995) which are associated with adherence to the 'objective' investigation of behaviour.
9 What is meant by the claim that 'scientific psychology
   has reified concepts such as personality and intelligence'?
10 What was the practical consequence of gender bias for
   many women living in the state of Virginia between 1924
   and 1972?
11 In what way did psychology influence the 1924 Immigration Restriction Act in the USA?
12 What is *androcentrism*?
13 According to Caplan (1991), what does *masochistic disorder*
   (proposed as an addition to DSM-III-R) represent in relation to women?
14 According to Tavris (1993), what type of causal attributions are often made for men's and women's socially
   unacceptable behaviours, respectively?
15 According to Tavris, what view is central to the 'mismeasure of woman'?
16 In what way may gender bias show itself in the formulation of research questions?

17 What problem is raised by the failure of many studies to
   report the sex and race of participants, researchers and
   any confederates?
18 In what way may gender bias enter into the conclusion
   formulation of studies?
19 Name one developmental theory which has been identified as sexist.

Section 2: Culture bias

20 According to Smith & Bond (1993), what does *cross-cultural
   psychology* study?
21 What is *ethnocentrism*?
22 According to Moghaddam (1987), which individuals comprise the core of psychology's 'First World'?
23 Complete the sentence: 'An implicit equation is made
   between "human being" and "human being from ___
   ___" (the Anglocentric bias)'.
24 What is the independent variable for cross-cultural psychologists?
25 How does Herskovits (1955) define *culture*?
26 Which terms are used to describe the two aspects of culture?
27 What does *cultural complexity* refer to?
28 What label is used to describe cultures in which identity
   is largely defined by personal choices and achievements?
29 What do *tight cultures* expect?
30 What is meant by an *etic approach* to the study of a culture?
31 What is an *imposed etic*?
32 According to Brislin (1993), why may etics cause difficulties with regard to the concept of intelligence?
33 What is the problem of *equivalence*, as identified by Brislin?
34 Complete the sentence: 'Cross-cultural research allows
   investigators to highlight ___ ___'.
35 Identify some other advantages of cross-cultural research.

Section 1: Gender bias

1 Two common themes within feminism are the valuation of women as worthy of study in their own right, and recognition of the need for social change on behalf of women.

2 Individualism obscures the social and structural operation of male power by concentrating its analysis on people as individuals.

3 'Most psychological research is conducted on *male* samples.'

4 Women's behaviour is often viewed as pathological, abnormal or deficient in some way when it differs from men's.

5 Explanations of women's behaviours tend to emphasise biological causes.

6 Heterosexism is taking heterosexuality to be the norm, so that homosexuality is seen as abnormal.

7 'Psychology's claims to be a science are based on its methods and the belief that it is a *value-free* discipline.'

8 Nicholson (1995) points out that the experimental environment takes the 'subject's behaviour,' as distinct from the 'subject' herself, as the unit of study (becoming deliberately blind to the behaviour's meaning), and occurs in a very specific context which typically disadvantages women.

9 Scientific psychology has treated abstract concepts (such as personality and intelligence) as if they were 'things' or entities.

10 More than 7500 women were forcibly sterilised, using mental age (as measured by the Stanford–Binet intelligence test) as a criterion.

11 The army alpha and beta tests of intelligence, which suggested that certain cultures were of 'inferior intelligence', influenced the 1924 Immigration Restriction Act.

12 Androcentrism refers to male-centredness, the tendency to take maleness as a standard or norm against which to compare women.

13 Caplan (1991) claims that masochistic disorder represents a way of calling psychopathological the behaviour of women who conform to social norms for a 'feminine woman'.

14 Tavris (1993) claims that such behaviours are likely to be attributed to men's upbringings and to women's psyches or hormones.

15 According to Tavris, the view that men are the norm and women the opposite, lesser or deficient beings, is central to the 'mismeasure of woman'.

16 It is often assumed that topics relating to white males are more important and 'basic' than those relating to females and/or ethnic minorities.

17 This failure may lead researchers to overlook the significance of interactions between variables, such as sex and race.

18 In the formulation of conclusions, results based on one sex only are often applied to both.

19 Both Erikson's (1950) theory of lifespan development and Kohlberg's (1969) theory of moral development have been criticised for sexism.

Section 2: Culture bias

20 Cross-cultural psychology studies variability in behaviour among the various societies and cultural groups around the world (Smith & Bond, 1993).

21 Ethnocentrism is the tendency to use our own ethnic or cultural group's norms and values to define what is 'natural' and 'correct' for everyone else.

22 Moghaddam (1987) points out that historically white, middle-class males living in the USA have comprised the core of psychology's 'First World'.

23 'An implicit equation is made between "human being" and "human being from *Western culture*" (the Anglocentric bias).'

24 For cross-cultural psychologists, the independent variable is culture.

25 Herskovits (1955) defines culture as the 'human-made part of the environment'.

26 Culture can be broken down into objective aspects and subjective aspects.

27 Cultural complexity refers to how much attention people within a culture pay to time.

28 Individualistic cultures.

29 Tight cultures expect their members to behave according to clearly defined norms.

30 An etic approach to the study of a culture looks at a behaviour from outside that cultural system.

31 An imposed etic refers to the imposition of concepts or research tools by a 'visiting' psychologist on an 'alien' culture, for which these are assumed to be valid.

32 Brislin (1993) points out that definitions of what constitutes a 'problem' (a common element of intelligence tests) vary between cultures.

33 The problem of equivalence refers to the difficulty in knowing that we are studying the same process across different cultures.

34 'Cross-cultural research allows investigators to highlight *implicit assumptions*.'

35 Cross-cultural research also allows investigators to separate a behaviour from its context, extend the range of variables available to study, separate the influence of variables which are frequently confounded within a particular culture, and test theories to discover whether they are relevant outside a particular cultural context.

A

The feminist critique of science

- Some feminists argue that scientific enquiry itself is biased.
- Nicholson (1995) identifies 2 major problems with the 'objective' investigation of behaviour:
  1. The experimental situation takes the 'subject's behaviour' as distinct from the 'subject' herself as the unit of study. Because of this it blinds itself to the behaviour's *meaning* and the personal, social and political contexts in which it occurs.
  2. Experimental psychology takes place in a context which disadvantages women. Women are stripped of their social roles and expected to respond to the needs of a (usually) male experimenter.

Gender bias

- *Feminist psychology* argues that women are worthy of study in their own right and that there is a need for social change on behalf of women.
- Feminist psychology challenges the way in which psychology excludes women or assimilates them to male norms.
- By focusing on the individual, psychology neglects the social context and the mechanisms of oppression.

Major feminist criticisms

- Much research is conducted on all-male samples, then generalised to women.
- Where women's behaviour differs from men's, it is often judged to be abnormal or deficient.
- Explanations tend to emphasise biological causes, ignoring social causes and giving the impression that psychological differences are inevitable.

Practical consequences of gender bias

Intelligence testing and sterilisation

- Prince & Hartnett (1993): psychologists have *reified* concepts such as personality and intelligence (treating them as if they really exist), and this has led to assaults on women. Between 1924 and 1972, more than 7500 women in the State of Virginia were forcibly sterilised, based on a measure of intelligence (using the Stanford–Binet intelligence test).

Complicity

- Gilligan (1982): psychologists have a responsibility to make their values explicit regarding social and political issues, and failure to do so may result in them (unwittingly) contributing to prejudice, discrimination or oppression.

The masculinist bias (androcentrism) – a closer look

The male norm as standard

2 examples (Tavris, 1993):

- In 1985: the mental disorder *'masochistic personality'* was proposed as an addition to DSM-III-R. It was to include symptoms such as putting others first and seeking failure at home and at work. Caplan (1991) argues that this would have labelled as pathological the behaviour of many women who conform to social norms (the 'good wife syndrome').
- When men behave in socially unacceptable ways, causes are looked for in their upbringing (*external attribution*), whereas women's problems are seen as a result of their psyches or hormones (*internal attribution*).

The 'mismeasure of woman'

Tavris (1993): man is viewed as the norm and woman as opposite and deficient by comparison (e.g. research which aims to discover why women aren't 'as something' as men).

Example:

- Wilson (1994): the reason why 95% of bank managers, company directors and professors in Britain are men is that men are more competitive and dominant (because of their hormones).
- Wilson also claims that men are more productive than women and that those women who do reach top positions probably have 'masculinised' brains.

Sexism in research

The APA's *Guidelines for Avoiding Sexism in Psychological Research* (Denmark *et al.* 1988) identify gender bias at all stages of research:

1. **Question formulation:** it is assumed that topics relating to white males are more important than others.
2. **Research methods and design:** often the sex and race of the researchers, participants and any confederates are not specified.
3. **Data analysis and interpretation:** where sex differences are found, these are often reported in misleading ways.
4. **Conclusion formulation:** results based on one sex are then applied to both.

Sexism in theory

Gilligan (1982): psychology describes the world from a male perspective and confuses this with truth:

- Erikson (1950): describes a series of 8 universal stages of lifespan development (based on a study of males only). Despite recognising that there are sex differences, his epigenetic chart remains the same.
- Kohlberg (1969): claimed that his six stages of moral development are universal, despite the fact that his sample comprised 84 boys. His theory also suggests that females rarely develop beyond stage 3 (so are relatively morally deficient).

Bias in Psychology

What is culture?

Culture: the human-made part of the environment (Herskovits, 1955).

Includes:

objective aspects (e.g. tools, roads)

subjective aspects (e.g. norms, roles)

- Humans make and are made by culture in an interactive way (Moghaddam *et al.*, 1993).
- Research often fails to identify the sub-cultural groups (e.g. Welsh) represented within a sample of a national culture (e.g. British). This can lead researchers to overlook important sub-cultural differences and also implies that national cultures are unitary, harmonious systems.

Culture

How do cultures differ?

Triandis (1990) identifies 3 cultural syndromes (patterns of beliefs and behaviour which can be used to contrast different cultures):

1. **Cultural complexity:** how much attention people pay to time (related to the number and diversity of roles which members of a culture play).
2. **Individualism–collectivism:** whether the person's identity is defined by personal choices and achievements (individualism) or by characteristics of the group to which the person is attached (collectivism).
3. **Tightness:** tight cultures define norms clearly and do not tolerate much deviation from these.

Ethnocentrism

Ethnocentrism: the human tendency to use our own ethnic or cultural group's norms and values to define what is 'natural' and 'correct' for everyone.

- Moghaddam (1987): historically, psychology has been dominated by white, middle-class male Americans (psychology's 'First World') who applied Anglocentric theory and research to people in general.
- *Cross-cultural psychology* helps to correct ethnocentrism by treating culture as the independent variable and identifying differences and similarities between cultures.

The emic–etic distinction

Pike (1954) used the distinction to refer to different approaches to the study of behaviour:

- **Etic:** looking at a behaviour from outside a particular cultural system. 'Etics' refers to culturally general concepts.
- **Emic:** looking at a behaviour from the inside. 'Emics' are culturally specific concepts.
- **Imposed etics:** occur when 'visiting' psychologists bring an emic valid for the 'home' culture, which they then assume to be valid in the 'alien' culture. This often leads to the imposition of cultural biases onto the phenomena being studied (e.g. 'intelligence').

Advantages of cross-cultural research

- **Highlighting implicit assumptions:** allowing researchers to examine the influence of their own beliefs and assumptions.
- **Separating behaviour from context:** allowing researchers to appreciate the impact of situational factors on behaviour.
- **Extending the range of variables:** expanding the range of variables which can be explored.
- **Separating variables:** allowing researchers to identify variables which are often confounded within a particular culture.
- **Testing theories:** discovering whether Western theories are relevant outside their own cultural contexts.

ETHICAL ISSUES IN PSYCHOLOGY

SYLLABUS
14.2 Section B – issues and debates in psychology – a issues
- ethical issues involved in psychological investigations using human participants, including the ethics of socially sensitive research. The use of non-human animals in psychological investigations, including constraints on their use and arguments (both ethical and scientific) for and against their use

KEY QUESTIONS
- What are the ethical issues surrounding human participants?
- What are the wider ethical concerns?
- What are the ethical issues surrounding non-human participants
- Which ethical concerns relate to psychologists as practitioners?

Section 1: Introducing ethics

1 Complete the sentence: 'Just as Orne (1962) regards the psychological experiment as a ___ situation, so every psychological investigation is an ___ situation'.
2 What are the two major *professional bodies* responsible for publishing ethical guidelines?
3 Identify one reason why ethical guidelines must be continually updated.

Section 2: Human participants

4 Complete the sentence: 'The essential principle is that the investigation should be considered from the ___ of all ___'.
5 Explain what is required for *informed consent* to be given.
6 What accusation did Baumrind (1964) level against Milgram?
7 In what ways did Zimbardo *et al.* (1973) follow the current *Ethical Principles* (BPS, 1993)?
8 In what way did Milgram contravene the principle of the *right to withdraw* (Coolican, 1990)?
9 Where participants are deceived, what procedure should be carried out at the earliest opportunity?
10 Which types of deception are the most serious?
11 What did Milgram (1974) point to as the central moral justification for his use of deception?
12 How great a risk of harm to participants is acceptable in psychological investigations?
13 Identify one purely pragmatic argument for guaranteeing confidentiality to participants.

Section 3: Wider ethical issues

14 Complete the sentence: 'Whilst individual participants may be protected from overt harm, the ___ ___ to which they belong may be harmed as a consequence of the research findings'.
15 Identify one area of research in which the above concern has not been considered sufficiently.

16 What is the nature of the *double obligation dilemma* which psychologists face?
17 What type of 'socially beneficial' studies were carried out by Latané & Darley (1968)?

Section 4: Non-human subjects

18 What are the two fundamental questions regarding the use of non-humans in psychological research?
19 According to Dawkins (1980), how can we discover if apparently healthy animals are actually suffering?
20 According to Gray (1987), what are the two main justifications for non-human experimentation?
21 According to Gray (1987), why is food deprivation not a source of suffering?
22 What is a *cost–benefit analysis* in relation to non-human experimentation?
23 Identify areas of medical advance in which non-human experimentation has played a vital role.
24 What do opponents of non-human experimentation argue, regarding medical advances?
25 Complete the sentence: 'Gray (1991) argues that not only is it ___ wrong to give preference to the interests of one's own species, one has a ___ to do so'.
26 Identify one major problem with this argument.

Section 5: Psychologists as practitioners

27 Identify the two beliefs which Fairburn & Fairburn (1987) believe may cause psychologists to overlook professional ethics.
28 In what important way do psychotherapists regard their work as different from behaviour modification?
29 In what way does Wachtel (1977) criticise the institutional use of the *token economy*.
30 What does Masson (1988) believe regarding the needs of individuals seeking therapy?

Section 1: Introducing ethics

1 'Just as Orne (1962) regards the psychological experiment as a *social* situation, so every psychological investigation is an *ethical* situation.'

2 The British Psychological Society (BPS) and the American Psychological Association (APA).

3 They must be updated to take into account changing political and social contexts.

Section 2: Human participants

4 'The essential principle is that the investigation should be considered from the *standpoint* of all *participants*.'

5 Participants need to be informed of the objective of the study and any other aspects which might reasonably be expected to influence their willingness to participate.

6 Baumrind (1964) accused Milgram of failing to protect his participants from stress and emotional conflict.

7 Zimbardo *et al.* (1973) terminated their study because of the prisoners' distress, obtained informed consent and consulted the legal council of Stanford University.

8 Milgram urged participants to continue when they wished to stop, using harsh verbal prods and prompts.

9 Where participants are deceived, a full debriefing should be carried out at the earliest opportunity.

10 Deceptions which affect the participants' self-image (especially self-esteem) are the most serious.

11 The central moral justification was that the participants had judged the experiment to be acceptable.

12 The risk of harm should be no greater than in ordinary life.

13 If participants' confidentiality is not guaranteed, it is unlikely that members of the public would volunteer for psychological experiments.

Section 3: Wider ethical issues

14 'Whilst individual participants may be protected from overt harm, the *social groups* to which they belong may be harmed as a consequence of the research findings.'

15 Research into the intellectual inferiority of races (or genders) fails to acknowledge the harm that may be caused by such research.

16 The double obligation dilemma refers to the ethical obligation which psychologists have towards individual participants and society at large.

17 Latané & Darley (1968) investigated the nature of bystander intervention.

Section 4: Non-human subjects

18 The two fundamental questions are 'How do we know non-humans suffer?' and 'What goals can ever justify subjecting them to pain and suffering?'.

19 According to Dawkins (1980), careful observation and experimentation with a species enables us to discover the signs of suffering.

20 The main justifications are the pursuit of scientific knowledge and the advancement of medicine (Gray, 1987).

21 Rats are maintained at 85 per cent of their 'free-feeding' body weight, and are actually healthier than if allowed to eat freely (Gray, 1987).

22 A cost–benefit analysis involves considering non-human pain, distress and death versus acquisition of new knowledge and the development of new medical therapies for humans.

23 The causes and vaccines for infectious diseases, the development of antibacterial and antibiotic drugs, open-heart surgery, organ transplantation, kidney failure, diabetes, malignant hypertension and gastric ulcers.

24 Opponents argue that medical advances have been delayed because of misleading results from non-human experiments.

25 'Gray (1991) argues that not only is it *not* wrong to give preference to the interests of one's own species, one has a *duty* to do so.'

26 Many medical advances are possible only after scientific understanding has been developed. In the early stages of this process, suffering is imposed on non-humans with little immediate benefit to humans.

Section 5: Psychologists as practitioners

27 The two beliefs that psychology is a value-free science and that therapists should be value-neutral (or 'non-directive') may detract from an explicit consideration of professional ethics.

28 Psychotherapists regard their work as fostering the autonomous development of the patient, whereas behaviour modification removes control from the patient.

29 Wachtel (1977) believes that the token economy is open to abuse in institutional settings and renders the patient powerless.

30 Masson (1988) believes that individuals seeking therapy need protection from the therapist's constant temptation to abuse, misuse, profit from and bully the client.

Ethical Issues

The Code of Conduct for Psychologists (British Psychological Society, 1985) identifies the responsibilities and obligations common to both the scientist and practitioner roles.

The psychological investigation is also a *social situation* (Orne, 1962) and therefore an *ethical situation*. Ethical guidelines are difficult to apply in a hard and fast way and must take into account the social and political context.

Human participants

The introduction to *The Ethical Principles for Conducting Research with Human Participants* (BPS, 1990, 1993) states 'The essential principle is that the investigation should be considered from the standpoint of all participants ...'.

Consent, informed consent and the right to withdraw
- The *Ethical Principles* state that participants should be informed of the objectives of the research and any aspects which might be expected to influence their willingness to participate.
- In addition, researchers should not pressurise participants to take part in or remain in the investigation.

Coolican (1990): Milgram (1963, 1965 – see Ch 6) violated this latter principle (by the use of harsh verbal 'prods').

Deception
- The *Ethical Principles* state that intentional deception of participants should be avoided where possible.
- Where there are no alternatives to deception, participants should be debriefed at the earliest possible opportunity.
- Social psychological research often makes use of 'stooges' and care must be taken with regard to participants' self-esteem.

- Milgram's study has been criticised for its use of deception. However, Aronson (1988) defended its use, pointing out that realistic results could not have been obtained otherwise.
- Psychologists must consider whether or not a means can be sufficiently justified by an end.
- In defence of his experiments, Milgram pointed out (1974) that all participants were debriefed and most were glad to have participated.

Protection of participants
- The *Ethical Principles* state that investigators have a responsibility to protect participants from physical and mental harm.
- Debriefing, confidentiality and the right to withdraw are all means of ensuring that this happens.

- Baumrind (1964): criticised Milgram for exposing participants to stress and emotional conflict.
- Milgram (1974): stress was neither an anticipated nor intended outcome and 'momentary excitement' is not harm.

Debriefing
The *Ethical Principles* state that investigators should provide the participants with any information necessary to complete their understanding of the research.

Milgram carried out thorough debriefings and one year later participants were assessed by an independent psychiatrist for signs of psychological harm.

Confidentiality
- The *Ethical Principles* state that information obtained about a participant is confidential unless otherwise agreed in advance.
- Only in situations where there are direct dangers to a human life might an investigator contravene this rule.

Non-human subjects

The *Guidelines for the Use of Animals in Research* (BPS Scientific Affairs Board, 1985) identifies four general obligations:
1. avoid or minimise discomfort to living animals
2. discuss any future research with colleagues and the HO inspector
3. seek advice as to whether the end justifies the use of animals
4. consider alternatives to the use of animals.
These raise two fundamental questions:

(a) How do we know that non-humans suffer?
1. Disease and injury are major causes of suffering. Brady's (1958) 'executive monkey' experiments are unacceptable today.
2. Mental suffering due to confinement may show in bizarre behaviours.
3. Careful study of a species can increase our knowledge of their requirements (Dawkins, 1980).
However, Bateson (1992) points out that the boundaries between organisms which can and cannot experience pain are 'fuzzy'.

(b) How can we justify experiments with non-humans?
Gray (1987): the main justifications are the *pursuit of scientific knowledge* and the *advancement of medicine*.
However, in some cases the scientific justification is clear but the immediate medical justification much less so.

Olds & Milner (1954) implanted electrodes in the brains of non-humans to study self-stimulation. Although such experiments had practical applications (e.g. pain relief), they were not conducted with this objective in mind.

Safeguards for non-human subjects
- Gray (1987): food deprivation in rats is not a source of suffering, as rats are maintained at 85% of their free-feeding weight. The level of electric shock is controlled by Home Office (HO) inspectors and does not cause extreme pain.
- Procedures causing pain and distress/surgical procedures are illegal unless the experimenter holds a HO licence.
- Experimenters are required to undertake a *cost–benefit analysis* before any non-human experiment can proceed.

The medical justification argument
- **Supporters** of such experiments argue that there are no basic physiological differences between laboratory animals and humans, and that vaccines and surgical techniques could not be developed without them.
- **Opponents** argue that tests on different species produce different results and that the stress of confinement may affect the outcome unpredictably. Some important medical advances have been delayed because of misleading results from such experiments.

Speciesism: Gray (1991) argues that discriminating against another species is justified since one has a duty to give preference to one's own species, where we have to choose between human and non-human suffering.
- However, many medical advances are only possible with the advancement of scientific knowledge, during which stage non-humans may be sacrificed with no saving of human life.

Psychologists as practitioners

Psychology as value-free science
The scientist–practitioner model of helping sees clinical psychology as being guided by the general scientific method. However, at the point where psychological knowledge is applied, the psychologist is responsible for the choice of technique and its application.

Therapists as value-neutral
- **Therapist influence:** therapist neutrality is a myth. Therapists influence their clients in subtle but powerful ways. Whether these influences are in the client's interests and whether they are aware of them are important questions.
- **Freedom and behavioural control:** therapies based on operant conditioning (e.g. token economies) may place the patient in a powerless position relative to the institution enforcing the therapy.
- **The abuse of patients:** Masson (1988) believes patients need protection from therapists who have emotional power over the patient and can cause emotional, sexual and financial abuse.

Wider ethical issues

Protecting the individual vs harming the group: whilst individual participants may be protected from harm, groups may not be protected from the wider implications of damaging research (e.g. Herrnstein's, 1971, research into the 'intellectual inferiority' of African Americans). Such research may be used to justify unacceptable attitudes or prejudices.

Protecting the individual vs benefiting society: focusing on the protection of individual participants may occasionally discourage psychologists from carrying out socially meaningful and beneficial research, e.g. Milgram's experiments may have been unethical but furthered our understanding of obedience (and in 1965 was awarded the prize for outstanding psychological research by the APA).

233

FREE WILL AND DETERMINISM,
AND REDUCTIONISM

KEY QUESTIONS

- What is free will?
- How do the major psychological theories view the issue of free will?
- What is reductionism?
- What is the mind–body problem?

Q

Section 1: What is free will?

1 What name is given to the condition characterised by uncontrollable verbal and behavioural tics?
2 What human 'ability' is described by the term *free will*?
3 Complete the sentence: 'Determinism implies that behaviour occurs in a regular manner which is (in principle), totally ___'.
4 What was demonstrated by Penfield's (1947) experiments, in which he stimulated the cortex of patients in order to produce movements of their limbs?
5 What is *psychological reactance*?
6 What are the two levels of functioning, besides deliberate control, which Norman & Shallice (1986) suggest we are capable of?
7 Identify two further ways in which free will can be defined (besides 'deliberate control' and 'behaving voluntarily').
8 According to Koestler (1967), what are the two enemies of free will?
9 In general terms, what is the relation between mental disorders and free will?
10 Identify three important roles which a psychiatrist may play in advising a court of law.
11 What are the implications of determinism for morality (is it possible to derive an 'ought' from an 'is')?

Section 2: Free will and psychological theories

12 According to James's *soft determinism*, what type of cause is required for our behaviours to be free?
13 What further distinction did James draw?
14 According to Freud, what is *psychic determinism*?
15 Which psychoanalytic technique most clearly demonstrates this principle?
16 What is *overdetermination*?
17 What does Skinner eliminate all reference to in his *radical behaviourism*?

18 According to Skinner, what determines what we do?
19 What is the principal argument in Skinner's (1971) book *Beyond Freedom and Dignity*?
20 With what does Skinner equate the terms 'good' and 'bad' in order to remove morality from human behaviour?
21 What is the *behaviour therapist's dilemma*?
22 Complete the sentence: 'For Rogers, therapy and life are about ___ human beings struggling to become more ___'.
23 According to Rogers, what are the two elements which determine whether or not impulses are translated into behaviour?

Section 3: Reductionism

24 According to *reductionism*, what can psychological explanations be replaced by?
25 Outline one way in which the *mind–body relationship* poses a problem.
26 What is the difference between *dualism* and *monism*?
27 What did Descartes believe regarding the relationship between mind and body?
28 What is the difference between an *epiphenomenologist* and a *psychophysical parallelist*?
29 What name is given to those reductionists who attempt to replace psychological accounts with neuro-physiological ones?
30 What argument does Penrose (1990) put forward, regarding the way in which individual neurons and their synaptic connections work?
31 Complete the sentence: 'Consciousness, intelligence, and memory are properties of the brain as a ___ which ___ from interactions between the units that compose it'.
32 According to Rose (1992), how is it possible to be a materialist without being a reductionist?

Section 1: What is free will?

1 Tourette's disorder is characterised by uncontrollable verbal and behavioural tics.

2 Free will describes the ability of people to choose their own courses of action.

3 'Determinism implies that behaviour occurs in a regular manner which is (in principle) totally *predictable*.'

4 Penfield's (1947) experiments demonstrated that the subjective experience which we have of voluntarily moving our limbs is not the same as that when the appropriate brain region is stimulated (implying that the former cannot be simply reduced to the latter).

5 Psychological reactance describes the attempt to regain or reassert our freedom when we feel that it is threatened.

6 Norman & Shallice (1986) identify fully automatic processing and partially automatic processing in addition to deliberate control.

7 Free will can also be defined as 'having a choice' and 'not being coerced or constrained'.

8 Koestler (1967) identifies habit and strong emotions as the two enemies of free will.

9 In general terms, mental disorders can be seen as the partial or complete breakdown of the control people normally have over their thoughts, emotions and behaviours.

10 Psychiatrists may advise the court about fitness to plead, mental state at the time of the offence, and diminished responsibility.

11 If determinism were true, then we could not be held responsible for our actions, and it would be impossible to say that behaviours were 'right' or 'wrong'.

Section 2: Free will and psychological theories

12 According to James's soft determinism, a behaviour is free if it has as its immediate cause processing by a system such as conscious mental life.

13 James also distinguished between the scientific and non-scientific worlds.

14 Psychic determinism refers to the idea that all behaviours (even apparently 'accidental' ones) have their causes in the unconscious mind.

15 Free association clearly demonstrates this principle.

16 Overdetermination refers to the idea that much of our behaviour has multiple causes, both conscious and unconscious.

17 Skinner eliminates all reference to mental or private states in his radical behaviourism.

18 Skinner claims that the environment, in the form of punishments, rewards and threats, determines what we do.

19 In *Beyond Freedom and Dignity*, Skinner (1971) argues that the notion of 'autonomous man' is both false and has many harmful consequences.

20 Skinner equates the terms 'good' and 'bad' with 'beneficial to others' and 'harmful to others' respectively.

21 The behaviour therapist's dilemma refers to the conflict between ethical and legal constraints on therapeutic practice, which obliges therapists to recognise the autonomy of the individual, and behaviour therapy, which does not.

22 'For Rogers, therapy and life are about *free* human beings struggling to become more *free*.'

23 According to Rogers, social conditioning and voluntary choice determine whether or not impulses are translated into behaviour.

Section 3: Reductionism

24 According to reductionism, psychological explanations will be replaced by explanations in terms of brain functioning, or even in terms of physics and chemistry.

25 It is difficult to see how the physical (body) and the non-physical (mind) could be related, since they do not share any properties. In addition, it is unclear how something non-physical could influence something physical.

26 Dualism proposes that there are two types of substance, mind and body, whilst monism proposes that there is only one (mind or body).

27 Descartes believed that the mind can influence the brain (or body), but not vice versa.

28 An epiphenomenologist sees the mind as a kind of by-product of the brain, whilst a psychophysical parallelist sees that there is no interaction between mind and brain at all (the two are synchronised).

29 Eliminative materialists.

30 Penrose (1990) argues that there is a built-in indeterminacy in the way that individual neurons and their synaptic connections work.

31 'Consciousness, intelligence, and memory are properties of the brain as a *system* which *emerge* from interactions between the units that compose it.'

32 According to Rose (1992), it is possible to have distinct and legitimate languages (levels of description) which are not reducible to one another.

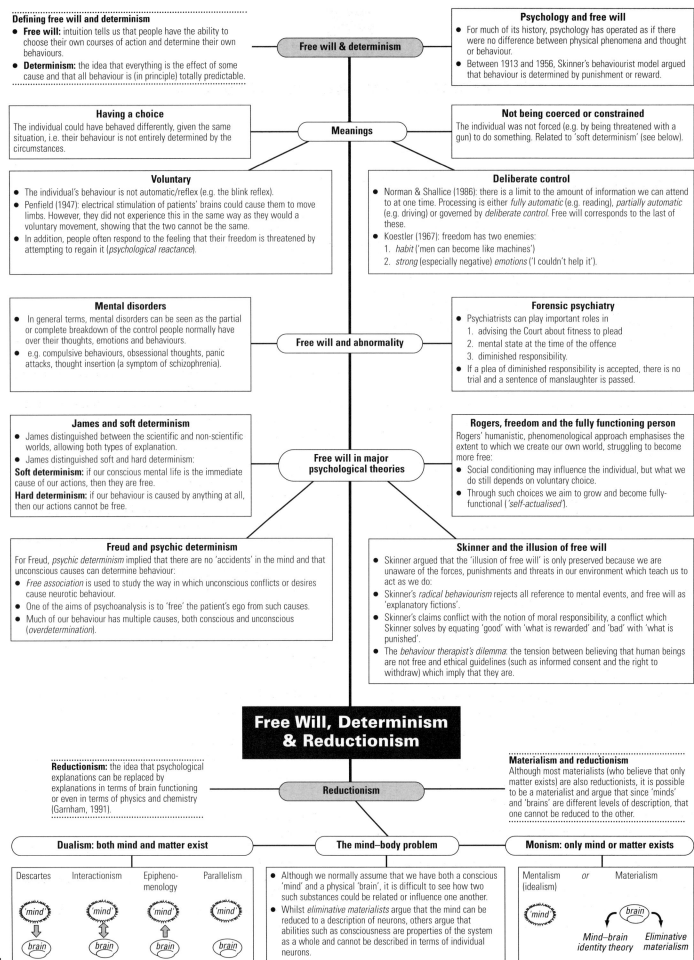

Defining free will and determinism
- **Free will:** intuition tells us that people have the ability to choose their own courses of action and determine their own behaviours.
- **Determinism:** the idea that everything is the effect of some cause and that all behaviour is (in principle) totally predictable.

Free will & determinism

Psychology and free will
- For much of its history, psychology has operated as if there were no difference between physical phenomena and thought or behaviour.
- Between 1913 and 1956, Skinner's behaviourist model argued that behaviour is determined by punishment or reward.

Having a choice
The individual could have behaved differently, given the same situation, i.e. their behaviour is not entirely determined by the circumstances.

Meanings

Not being coerced or constrained
The individual was not forced (e.g. by being threatened with a gun) to do something. Related to 'soft determinism' (see below).

Voluntary
- The individual's behaviour is not automatic/reflex (e.g. the blink reflex).
- Penfield (1947): electrical stimulation of patients' brains could cause them to move limbs. However, they did not experience this in the same way as they would a voluntary movement, showing that the two cannot be the same.
- In addition, people often respond to the feeling that their freedom is threatened by attempting to regain it (*psychological reactance*).

Deliberate control
- Norman & Shallice (1986): there is a limit to the amount of information we can attend to at one time. Processing is either *fully automatic* (e.g. reading), *partially automatic* (e.g. driving) or governed by *deliberate control*. Free will corresponds to the last of these.
- Koestler (1967): freedom has two enemies:
  1. *habit* ('men can become like machines')
  2. *strong* (especially negative) *emotions* ('I couldn't help it').

Mental disorders
- In general terms, mental disorders can be seen as the partial or complete breakdown of the control people normally have over their thoughts, emotions and behaviours.
- e.g. compulsive behaviours, obsessional thoughts, panic attacks, thought insertion (a symptom of schizophrenia).

Free will and abnormality

Forensic psychiatry
- Psychiatrists can play important roles in
  1. advising the Court about fitness to plead
  2. mental state at the time of the offence
  3. diminished responsibility.
- If a plea of diminished responsibility is accepted, there is no trial and a sentence of manslaughter is passed.

James and soft determinism
- James distinguished between the scientific and non-scientific worlds, allowing both types of explanation.
- James distinguished soft and hard determinism:
Soft determinism: if our conscious mental life is the immediate cause of our actions, then they are free.
Hard determinism: if our behaviour is caused by anything at all, then our actions cannot be free.

Free will in major psychological theories

Rogers, freedom and the fully functioning person
Rogers' humanistic, phenomenological approach emphasises the extent to which we create our own world, struggling to become more free:
- Social conditioning may influence the individual, but what we do still depends on voluntary choice.
- Through such choices we aim to grow and become fully-functional ('*self-actualised*').

Freud and psychic determinism
For Freud, *psychic determinism* implied that there are no 'accidents' in the mind and that unconscious causes can determine behaviour:
- *Free association* is used to study the way in which unconscious conflicts or desires cause neurotic behaviour.
- One of the aims of psychoanalysis is to 'free' the patient's ego from such causes.
- Much of our behaviour has multiple causes, both conscious and unconscious (*overdetermination*).

Skinner and the illusion of free will
- Skinner argued that the 'illusion of free will' is only preserved because we are unaware of the forces, punishments and threats in our environment which teach us to act as we do:
- Skinner's *radical behaviourism* rejects all reference to mental events, and free will as 'explanatory fictions'.
- Skinner's claims conflict with the notion of moral responsibility, a conflict which Skinner solves by equating 'good' with 'what is rewarded' and 'bad' with 'what is punished'.
- The *behaviour therapist's dilemma*: the tension between believing that human beings are not free and ethical guidelines (such as informed consent and the right to withdraw) which imply that they are.

Free Will, Determinism & Reductionism

Reductionism: the idea that psychological explanations can be replaced by explanations in terms of brain functioning or even in terms of physics and chemistry (Garnham, 1991).

Reductionism

Materialism and reductionism
Although most materialists (who believe that only matter exists) are also reductionists, it is possible to be a materialist and argue that since 'minds' and 'brains' are different levels of description, that one cannot be reduced to the other.

Dualism: both mind and matter exist

The mind–body problem

Monism: only mind or matter exists

Descartes | Interactionism | Epipheno-menology | Parallelism

- Although we normally assume that we have both a conscious 'mind' and a physical 'brain', it is difficult to see how two such substances could be related or influence one another.
- Whilst *eliminative materialists* argue that the mind can be reduced to a description of neurons, others argue that abilities such as consciousness are properties of the system as a whole and cannot be described in terms of individual neurons.

Mentalism (idealism) *or* Materialism

Mind–brain identity theory | Eliminative materialism

65

PSYCHOLOGY AS A SCIENCE

SYLLABUS

14.2 Section B – Issues and debates in psychology – a issues

- **psychology as a science**, including definitions/varieties of science, the development of psychology as a separate discipline, and arguments for and against the claim that psychology is a science (e.g. Kuhn's concept of a paradigm, objectivity, and the use of the experimental method)

KEY QUESTIONS

- What are the philosophical roots of science and psychology?
- What does 'science' mean?
- Are scientific methods appropriate for the study of human behaviour?

Section 1: Philosophical roots

1 What does the expression *philosophical dualism* mean?
2 Complete the sentence '___ became the ideal of science, and was extended to the study of human behaviour by Comte in the mid-1800s, calling it ___'.
3 What do *empiricists* believe about knowledge?
4 Why is 1879 widely accepted as the 'birthdate' of psychology?
5 According to Wundt, what were the two components of conscious experience?
6 What name is given to Wundt's attempts to analyse conscious experience?
7 What is the famous definition of psychology provided in James's *The Principles of Psychology*?
8 Which approach, which emphasises behaviour's purpose and utility, did James inspire?
9 For what reason did Watson (1913) reject introspective reports?
10 According to Watson, what should the subject matter of psychology be?
11 What did Watson see as the two *goals* of psychology?
12 Which approach emerged during the *cognitive revolution*?
13 What analogy is central to this approach?
14 What does *scientism* maintain, regarding the study of human behaviour?

Section 2: The meaning of 'science'

15 Identify the four major characteristics which must be possessed for a discipline to be a science.
16 What is a *theory*?
17 According to common belief, what is the starting point for scientific discovery?
18 What alternative view of this 'starting point' has been proposed?
19 Name the two phases which Kuhn (1962) identifies in the history of a science.
20 Complete Deese's (1972) equation: ___ = data + ___.

21 According to Popper's (1972) version, what is the starting point for the *scientific method*?
22 According to Kuhn (1962), under what condition can a field of study be legitimately called a science?
23 According to Kuhn, what name is given to the stage of development in which psychology remains?
24 What argument does Valentine (1982) give in support of the view that psychology is 'normal science'?
25 One view argues that psychology is not yet a normal science, since it does not have a paradigm. What are the two other views relating to this issue?
26 Complete the sentence: 'According to Richardson (1991), science is a very ___ business'.
27 What suggestion does Richardson (1991) make to increase the 'objectivity' of science?
28 Why, according to Kuhn, does 'scientific truth' have little to do with objectivity?

Section 3: Human behaviour and scientific method

29 What is the problem of *experimenter bias*?
30 In what way did Rosenthal & Fode (1963) and Rosenthal & Lawson (1961) illustrate the problem of *experimenter bias*?
31 What are *demand characteristics*?
32 In what way does experimental psychology adopt a *nomothetic approach*?
33 Why does psychology suffer from '*the problem of representativeness*'?
34 Why is *artificiality* in laboratory settings a source of problems?
35 What social factor makes the laboratory such an unnatural setting?
36 For what reason may psychological experiments lack *internal validity*?
37 Which types of variable pose a special problem for psychologists?

Q

Section 1: Philosophical roots

1 Philosophical dualism is the distinction between mind and matter (as two 'types' of substance).

2 '*Objectivity* became the ideal of science, and was extended to the study of human behaviour by Comte in the mid-1800s, calling it *positivism*.'

3 Empiricists believe that the only source of true knowledge is sensory experience.

4 In 1879 Wundt established the first 'laboratory' of experimental psychology at Leipzig.

5 According to Wundt, conscious experience is composed of sensations and feelings.

6 Wundt's attempts at analysis were called *structuralism*.

7 James defines psychology as 'the science of mental life'.

8 James inspired functionalism.

9 Watson (1913) rejected introspective reports, since they are impossible to verify accurately (as they are subjective experiences).

10 According to Watson, the only valid subject matter of psychology is behaviour (both human and non-human).

11 Watson saw the two goals of psychology as the prediction and control of behaviour.

12 The information-processing approach emerged during the cognitive revolution.

13 Central to this approach is the computer analogy.

14 Scientism maintains that human behaviour can and should be studied using the methods of natural science (such as the laboratory experiment).

Section 2: The meaning of 'science'

15 In order for a discipline to be a science, it must possess a definable subject matter, demonstrate theory construction, generate testable hypotheses, and use empirical methods of investigation.

16 A theory is a complex set of inter-related statements which attempts to explain observed phenomena.

17 According to common belief, the starting point for scientific discovery is simple, unbiased observation.

18 An alternative view of this 'starting point' argues that there is no such thing as 'unbiased' observation, and that our observation is always selective, interpretative, pre-structured and directed.

19 Kuhn (1962) claims that the history of a science demonstrates long peaceful periods called 'normal science', and 'scientific revolutions'.

20 *Fact* = data + *theory* (Deese, 1972)

21 Popper (1972) claims that the starting point for the scientific method is a problem (usually a refutation of an existing theory or prediction).

22 According to Kuhn (1962), a field of study can only be called a science if the majority of its workers subscribe to a common, global perspective or paradigm.

23 Psychology remains in a state/stage of pre-science, according to Kuhn.

24 Valentine (1982) argues that behaviourism comes as close as anything could to a paradigm.

25 The two other views maintain that psychology has had a number of paradigms and corresponding revolutions, and that psychology has, simultaneously, a number of paradigms.

26 'According to Richardson (1991), science is a very *social* business.'

27 Richardson (1991) suggests that researchers must universally agree conventions for reporting observations and findings, so that others can replicate them.

28 According to Kuhn, 'scientific truth' has more to do with the popularity and acceptance of a particular framework within the scientific community.

Section 3: Human behaviour and scientific method

29 The problem of experimenter bias refers to the way in which the particular characteristics of the researcher may, inadvertently, influence the participant(s).

30 Rosenthal & Fode (1963) and Rosenthal & Lawson (1961) found that researchers who were deceived into thinking they were using 'maze-bright' rats in their experiments found faster rates of learning in these rats than did those deceived into thinking their rats were 'maze-dull'.

31 Demand characteristics are those cues in an experimental situation which convey the experimental hypothesis to participants ('giving the game away').

32 Experimental psychology adopts a nomothetic approach in that it attempts to establish general laws of behaviour, by generalising from limited samples of participants to 'people in general'.

33 Psychology suffers from the problem of representativeness in that the participants in traditional experiments have not been representative of 'people in general' (e.g. they have largely been psychology undergraduates).

34 Artificiality is a source of problems since we cannot be sure whether the behaviour of people in a laboratory is an accurate indicator of how they are likely to behave outside it.

35 The fact that the experimenter has all the 'power' and is responsible for structuring the situation makes the laboratory an especially unnatural setting.

36 Psychological experiments may lack internal validity, since it is difficult to know when all extraneous variables have been controlled.

37 Participant variables pose a special problem for psychologists.

James's contribution

- James published *The Principles of Psychology* in 1890, in which he discusses instinct, brain function, consciousness, the self, attention, memory, perception, free will and emotion.
- James inspired *functionalism* – an approach which emphasises the utility and purpose of behaviour.

Watson's contribution

- Watson rejected introspectionism, arguing that psychology must be the *science of behaviour* and confine itself to *measurable* and *observable* events.
- The *goals* of psychology should be the *prediction* and *control* of behaviour.
- Watson believed that the *conditioned reflex* could become the foundation of psychology.
- Behaviour was seen as shaped by the environment and analysable into *stimulus–response* units.

The cognitive revolution

- The *information-processing approach* compared human cognition to the functioning of a digital computer (the *computer analogy*).
- It became acceptable again to study 'the mind' and psychologists began to explore the possibility of modelling human intelligence on computers.

Philosophical roots

Wundt's contribution

- Wundt founded the first psychological laboratory, at Leipzig in 1879.
- He attempted to analyse conscious mental states into their component *sensations* and *feelings* by the use of *introspection*.
- This approach is known as *structuralism*.

- Descartes was the first to distinguish between mind and matter (*philosophical dualism*).
- *Objectivity* became the ideal of science and Comte's *positivism* extended this approach to the study of human behaviour.
- Descartes also advocated *mechanism* and *reductionism* (the world can be reduced to physical interactions).
- *Empiricism* is the idea that the only source of knowledge about the world is sensory experience.

Mainstream psychology

- Central assumptions and practices have remained the same (referred to as mainstream psychology).
- *Scientism*: the borrowing of methods and vocabulary from the natural sciences (e.g. studying phenomena in the laboratory) in a value-free way (with no investigator bias).

Psychology as a Science

What is a 'science'?

The major features of science

- **A definable subject matter:** in psychology, this changed from human thought to behaviour to cognitive processes.
- **Theory construction:** e.g. Watson's attempt to account for human behaviour in terms of classical conditioning.
- **Hypothesis testing:** making and testing specific predictions deduced from the theory.
- **The use of empirical methods:** used to collect data relevant to the theory.

The scientific method

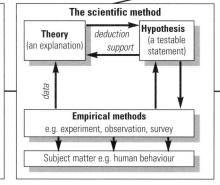

Common beliefs	Alternative views
Scientific discovery begins with unbiased observations.	Observations are always biased and influenced by our preconceptions.
From the resulting data/sense data genera-lised statements of fact will emerge.	Fact = Data + Theory. Facts do not exist objectively, all data is partly interpreted.
The essential feature of scientific activity is the use of empirical methods.	Data alone cannot make a science, since without theory data are meaningless.
Science discovers the objective truth about the world.	Scientific theories reflect the prevailing values and assumptions.
Science involves the steady accumulation of knowledge.	Sciences involves a series of peaceful periods and 'scientific revolutions' (Kuhn, 1962).

Can psychology be a science if psychologists cannot agree what psychology is?

- Kuhn (1962): a field of study is only a science if the majority of its workers subscribe to a common perspective or *paradigm*.
- Kuhn argues that there are three stages in the development of a science (and that psychology is still a pre-science):
  1. **Pre-science:** no paradigm has evolved and there are several schools of thought (Kline, 1988, sees psychology as having several paradigms).
  2. **Normal science:** a paradigm has emerged providing a framework for interpreting results. Workers explore the limits of the theory.
     Valentine (1982): behaviourism 'with its clearly defined subject matter, methodology and assumptions' is as close to a paradigm as you can get.
  3. **Revolution:** the old paradigm has to be abandoned and replaced by a new one because of the weight of conflicting evidence.
     Palermo (1971) and LeFrancois (1983): psychology has already undergone several paradigm shifts (see above).

The problem of objectivity

- Kuhn stresses the role of agreement and consensus among scientists, so the 'truth' of a theory may have more to do with its acceptability.
- Richardson (1991): argues for the importance of universally agreed conventions on reporting and measurement in order to ensure a theory's 'truth value'.

Human behaviour & scientific methods

The problem of representativeness

- The *nomothetic* ('law-like') approach to psychology involves generalising from experimental samples to 'people in general'.
- However, the participants in American psychology experiments are typically undergraduates who may not be representative of 'people in general', thus introducing *ethnocentrism*.

The problem of artificiality

- Heather (1976): we cannot be sure that the way people behave in the laboratory is an accurate indicator of how they will behave outside it.
- Particularly unnatural is the way in which one 'participant' (the experimenter) has all the power and structures the situation.

The psychology experiment as a social situation

Experimenters and participants influence each other:

1. **Experimenter bias:** the experimenter's expectations may cause participants to behave differently.
   - Rosenthal & Fode (1963) found that experimenters who had been informed that their rats were 'maze-bright' obtained better learning than did those with the 'maze-dull' group, despite the fact that the rats were actually randomly allocated!
2. **Demand characteristics:** any cues in the experimental situation which convey the expected outcome may be detected by the participant, who may then decide to play the role of 'good' or 'bad' participant.

Internal vs external validity

- Whilst an experiment may be *ecologically valid* (*external validity*), it will lack *internal validity* if all relevant extraneous variables have not been controlled.
- Participants vary and we cannot assume that they all perceive the IV in the same way.
- In attempting to increase the control, we also increase the situation's artificiality.

66

NATURE AND NURTURE

SYLLABUS

14.2 Section B – issues and debates in psychology
- nature–nurture, including definitions of the terms, the history of the debate, assumptions made about nature and nurture in psychological theory and research (e.g. Piaget's theory and sociobiology) and different views regarding their relationship (e.g. gene–environment interaction)

KEY QUESTIONS
- What is the nature–nurture debate?
- What is meant by 'nurture'?
- What is meant by 'nature'?
- In what ways do these two influence our development?

Section 1: The nature–nurture debate

Q

1 What is *nativism*?
2 What is *empirism*?
3 What does *tabula rasa* mean, literally?
4 To what does the term *maturation* refer?
5 Complete the sentence: 'For Watson (1925) ____ influence is all important and human beings are completely malleable'.
6 What does Bee (2000) point out regarding maturationally determined developmental sequences?
7 In what way is the environment involved in the maturation of the visual system?
8 What two responses to the sexual instinct are likely to produce long-term effects on the child's personality, according to Freud?
9 What are the twin processes which allow the child to adapt to the environment, according to Piaget?
10 Why, according to Bee (2000), would no developmental psychologist today take seriously the 'Is it nature or nurture?' form of the debate?
11 Which two theoretical approaches have contributed to a swing towards the nature side of the debate in recent years?

Section 2: The meaning of 'nature'

12 In which of two key areas concerning human nature does the nature–nurture debate 'properly' take place, according to Plomin (1994)?
13 What does *nature* refer to, from the perspective of genetics?
14 What is a *gene*?
15 How many pairs of genes does a normal human being inherit?
16 What number of X and Y chromosomes do males and females inherit?
17 Name the two major functions of genes.
18 What is the difference between *mitosis* and *meiosis*?

19 What interesting discovery did Carr & Tan (1976) make, when studying those individuals who had suffered from amok?
20 What is the role of *regulator genes*?
21 What is *neurogenetic determinism* in Rose's (1997) view?
22 What name is given to the material which acts as a set of instructions, telling the genes when to become active, and to what extent?

Section 3: The meaning of 'nurture'

23 Complete the sentence: 'In a psychological context the term "environment" usually refers to all those ____-____ influences lying ____ the individual's body'.
24 In what sense is it invalid to regard the environment as existing independently of the individual?
25 What does it mean to talk of the *relative differences* in the way in which parents raise their children?
26 What name is given to the gene–environment correlation in which children inherit from their parents an environment which is correlated with their genetic tendencies?
27 What has more influence on the development of children within the same family than their shared environment?
28 Complete the sentence: 'According to Horowitz (1987, 1990), a vulnerable child may do well in a highly ____ environment, whilst a ____ child may do quite well in a poor environment'.
29 What was the general conclusion of Werner's (1955) longitudinal study of 700 children born on Kanuai?
30 What are the three factors to which behaviour geneticists attempt to attribute variability for a given trait?
31 What are the two major methods used by behaviour geneticists in studying individual differences?
32 Why might some identical twins be more alike than others?
33 If a population of individuals shared exactly the same environment, what figure would the degree of heritability approximate to?

Section 1: The nature–nurture debate

1 Nativism is the philosophical theory according to which knowledge of the world is largely inborn (or innate).

2 Empiricism is the opposite view, namely that knowledge of the world is largely acquired through experience.

3 Tabula rasa means 'blank slate'.

4 Maturation refers to genetically programmed patterns of change.

5 'For Watson (1925) *environmental* influence is all important and human beings are completely malleable.'

6 Bee (2000) points out that even such maturational processes require some degree of environmental support (at least the environment must be benign).

7 At least some visual experience is required in order to trigger the gene which controls the development of the visual system.

8 Both excessive satisfaction and excessive frustration are likely to produce long-term effects on the personality, according to Freud.

9 According to Piaget, the twin processes of adaptation and assimilation enable us to adapt to our environment.

10 Bee argues that the modern developmental psychologist sees every facet of a child's development as the product of the interaction between nature and nurture.

11 In recent years both sociobiology and evolutionary psychology have contributed to a swing towards the nature side of the debate.

Section 2: The meaning of 'nature'

12 According to Plomin (1994), the nature–nurture debate 'properly' takes place in the area of individual differences (such as intelligence and schizophrenia).

13 From the perspective of genetics, nature refers to differences in genetic material that are transmitted from parent to offspring (heredity).

14 A gene is the basic unit of hereditary transmission and consists of a large molecule of DNA (deoxyribonucleic acid).

15 A normal human being inherits 23 pairs of chromosomes.

16 Females inherit two X chromosomes whilst males inherit an X and a Y chromosome.

17 The two major functions of genes are self-duplication and protein synthesis.

18 Mitosis is the process by which cells duplicate themselves, producing identical copies, whilst meiosis refers to the process by which reproductive cells (which contain only half the chromosomes of normal cells) are created.

19 Carr & Tan (1976) found that was very little evidence of mental disturbances before or after the episode of amok.

20 Regulator genes regulate the function and effect of other genes.

21 According to Rose, neurogenetic determinism is the claim that there is a direct causal link between genes and behaviour.

22 This material is known as the *epigenetic material*.

Section 3: The meaning of 'nurture'

23 'In a psychological context, the term *environment* usually refers to all those *post-natal* influences lying *outside* the individual's body.'

24 Not only do people's environments influence them, but people influence their environments.

25 Relative differences in child-rearing refer to the ways in which the same parents respond differently to their different children.

26 This type of correlation is termed a *passive gene–environment correlation*.

27 Differences in children growing up together are likely to be due to their non-shared environment.

28 'According to Horowitz (1987, 1990), a vulnerable child may do well in a highly *facilitative* environment, whilst a *resilient* child may do quite well in a poor environment.'

29 Werner concluded that as long as the balance between stressful events and protective factors (such as natural resilience) was favourable, children can adapt successfully.

30 Behaviour geneticists attempt to attribute variability for a given trait to genetic differences (heritability), shared environments, and non-shared environments.

31 The two major methods used by behaviour geneticists are twin studies and adoption studies.

32 Some identical twins share the same placenta during their time in the womb, whilst other have separate placentas.

33 Under these conditions the degree of heritability would approximate to 100 per cent.

Nature and Nurture

Nativism: the theory according to which knowledge of the world is largely innate or inborn: nature (heredity) is seen as determining certain abilities and capacities.

Empirism: the theory according to which knowledge of the world is largely acquired through experience and learning. Locke believed that at birth the human mind is a *tabula rasa* ('blank slate').

Are nativism and empirism mutually exclusive?
Many characteristics which are part of the maturational process nevertheless require some environmental input:
- Chomsky's language acquisition device (LAD) is innate but needs to be applied to a linguistic context. Similarly some visual experience is necessary to trigger the development of the visual system.
- Freud suggested that our personality is shaped by the frustrations and satisfactions which our inborn drives meet with, whilst Piaget suggested that the inborn mechanisms of assimilation and adaptation enable us to adapt to our environments.

Gesell (1925)
Maturation refers to genetically programmed patterns of change which cause all individuals to pass through the same series of changes in a way which is largely unaffected by the environment (e.g. crawling & walking in babies).

Watson (1925)
Environmental influence is all important: 'Give me a dozen healthy infants ... and my own specialised world to bring them up in and I'll guarantee to take any one at random and train him to become any type of specialist I might select ...'.

What do we mean by 'nature'?

Genetics
- **Genetics:** the science of heredity. Views 'nature' as inherited differences in genetic material which are transmitted from parents to offspring.
- **Genes:** the basic units of hereditary transmission, consisting of large molecules of DNA in a double helix structure.
- **Chromosomes:** structures containing the genes which are found within the nuclei of living cells. Normal human beings inherit 23 pairs of chromosomes, each pair being made up of one chromosome inherited from the male parent and one from the female parent.

The two major functions of genes
- **Self-duplication:** reproductive cells (sperm in males and ova in females) contain only one chromosome from each chromosome pair, determined at random. When these cells join to form a gamete, the offspring may be XX (female) or XY (male).
- **Protein synthesis:** DNA controls the production of RNA. RNA is then converted into amino acids – the building blocks of proteins and enzymes. Such genes are called *structural* genes. Genes can also produce products which regulate other genes. These genes are known as *regulator* genes.

Neurogenetic determinism
Refers to the claim that there is a direct causal link between genes and behaviour (e.g. criminality). Based on the false assumption that causes can be classified simply as genetic or environmental.
- **Phenotype:** refers to the observable characteristics of an organism. While these may seem to be determined by heredity (e.g. eye colour) they may depend on the complex interactions of many genes or even determined by biological factors other than genes (e.g. high blood pressure).
- **Epigenetic material:** all cells inherit the same genes but develop differently depending on the instructions contained in epigenetic material. Studies of women who were poorly nourished during the war showed that whilst their children were normal, the next generation grew into small adults suggesting that the epigenetic material somehow carried a 'marker'.

What do we mean by 'nurture'?

Environment
- **Environment:** usually refers to those post-natal influences lying outside of the individual's body.

Problems
- **Level of analysis:** it is not just the individual who is influenced by the environment – early on in development individual cells are subject to environmental changes.
- **Pre-natal influences:** some 'environmental influences' are pre-natal – such as a mother's alcohol consumption during pregnancy.
- **Reciprocal influence:** the inside/outside distinction is not a clear one – people influence their environments even as they are influenced by them.

Shared & non-shared environments
- **Shared environment:** when comparing influences such as socioeconomic status, family discord etc. it is often assumed that children within the same family share the same environment.
- **Non-shared environment:** in fact children within a family often differ greatly. This suggests that the non-shared environment has the greatest influence and that influences vary even within a single family.

Gene–environment correlations
Genetic differences between individuals may lead them to be treated differently or have different experiences. Plomin *et al.* identified 3 types of gene–environment correlations:
- **Passive gene–environment correlations:** parents provide environments correlated with their genetic tendencies (e.g. high IQ > rich environment).
- **Reactive gene–environment correlations:** children's genetic tendencies elicit certain behaviours from others (e.g. aggressive children elicit aggressive responses).
- **Active gene–environment correlations:** children construct/reconstruct experiences in a way consistent with their genetic tendencies.

Gene–environment interactions
Genetics and environment may interact. A child may be vulnerable or resistant and this trait may interact with facilitative or non-facilitative environments:
- Werner (1955): conducted a long-term study of 700 children born on Kanuai and found that even where environmental risk factors were high (e.g. impoverished home lives), the children who were resilient went on to cope well with adult life.

Behaviour genetics and heritability

Behaviour genetics
Behaviour geneticists attempt to determine how much of the variability in a trait can be attributed to heritability, shared-environments and non-shared environments.
- **Twin studies and adoption studies:** are used to determine the contributions made by each. With identical twins whom we know to be genetically identical, differences are likely to be due to environmental differences, whilst similarities between adopted children may suggest an environmental influence.

Identical twins
Some identical twins share a single placenta whilst in the womb, whilst others have separate placentas (meaning that they are exposed to different environmental toxins and diseases). If identical twins who have not shared a placenta are no more likely to be concordant for certain traits (such as schizophrenia) than are non-identical twins, then this suggests that it is uterine environment, *not* genetics, which makes MZs so similar.

Heritability
Heritability: A statistical measure of the genetic contribution to differences between individuals. It helps to explain what makes people different, not the relative contribution of genes & environment to an individual's makeup.
- **Heritability can change:** depending on the amount of variation in the environment (e.g. if environment was the same for all individuals then *all* differences would be due to heritability).
- **Heritability differs for different traits:** e.g. the heritability of IQ is higher than for many other traits.
- **Heritability of the same trait differs for different populations.**

EXAM PREPARATION

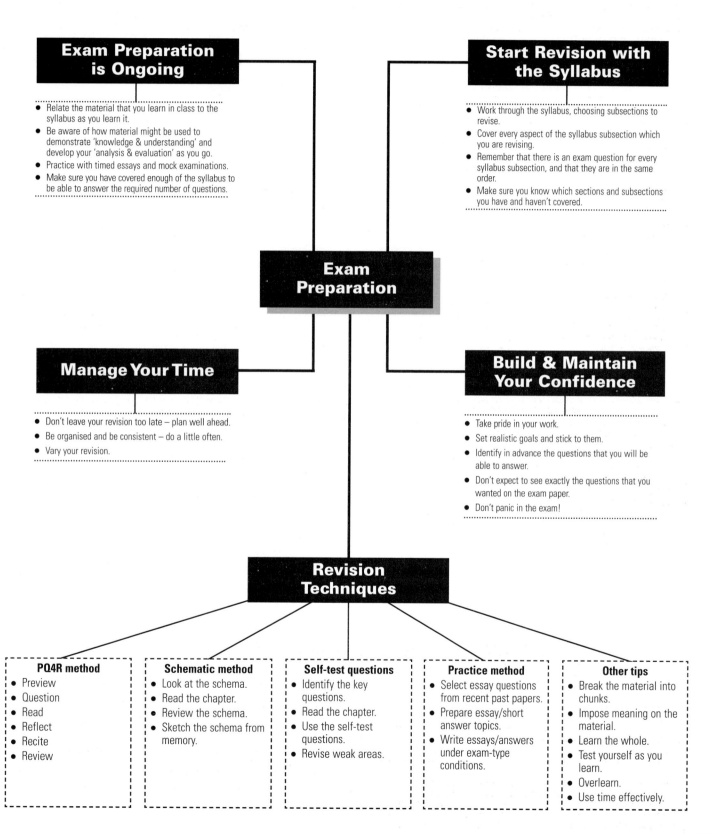

Exam Preparation is Ongoing

- Relate the material that you learn in class to the syllabus as you learn it.
- Be aware of how material might be used to demonstrate 'knowledge & understanding' and develop your 'analysis & evaluation' as you go.
- Practice with timed essays and mock examinations.
- Make sure you have covered enough of the syllabus to be able to answer the required number of questions.

Start Revision with the Syllabus

- Work through the syllabus, choosing subsections to revise.
- Cover every aspect of the syllabus subsection which you are revising.
- Remember that there is an exam question for every syllabus subsection, and that they are in the same order.
- Make sure you know which sections and subsections you have and haven't covered.

Exam Preparation

Manage Your Time

- Don't leave your revision too late – plan well ahead.
- Be organised and be consistent – do a little often.
- Vary your revision.

Build & Maintain Your Confidence

- Take pride in your work.
- Set realistic goals and stick to them.
- Identify in advance the questions that you will be able to answer.
- Don't expect to see exactly the questions that you wanted on the exam paper.
- Don't panic in the exam!

Revision Techniques

PQ4R method
- Preview
- Question
- Read
- Reflect
- Recite
- Review

Schematic method
- Look at the schema.
- Read the chapter.
- Review the schema.
- Sketch the schema from memory.

Self-test questions
- Identify the key questions.
- Read the chapter.
- Use the self-test questions.
- Revise weak areas.

Practice method
- Select essay questions from recent past papers.
- Prepare essay/short answer topics.
- Write essays/answers under exam-type conditions.

Other tips
- Break the material into chunks.
- Impose meaning on the material.
- Learn the whole.
- Test yourself as you learn.
- Overlearn.
- Use time effectively.

EXAM PREPARATION

One of the fundamental errors made by many A level students is to assume that revision and exam success can be achieved by 'knowing the facts'. Many students who think they 'know the facts' do badly, because they do not know *how* to use the information they know, *where* to use it, how to manage their *time*, and how to *comment* on what they know. Consequently, many students find themselves unable to relate what they know to the question, or comment on or evaluate information. Knowing information is, therefore, only a part of successful exam preparation. In this chapter, we will look at how best to prepare for a psychology exam and address some of the issues above.

A1 Exam preparation is ongoing

You must **relate material to the syllabus as you learn**, so that at any time you are able to answer questions such as 'Which areas of the syllabus have I covered'? It is an excellent idea to bring a copy of the syllabus to every lesson. By doing this, you ensure that you know how the material relates to specific sections and subsections, and are familiar with the precise wording of the syllabus, which is often used by examiners in setting A level questions.

In every examined essay, half of the available marks are awarded for 'AO1 skills' (knowledge and understanding) and half for 'AO2 skills' (analysis and evaluation). As you learn, you should **be aware of how the material can be used to demonstrate both AO1 and AO2 skills**.

Time management should develop as you learn – **timed essays and practice examinations** can be very useful in developing these skills.

Make sure you have covered enough of the syllabus to be able to answer the required number of questions in the exam. Most schools and colleges teach a couple of subsections from each of the syllabus sections (e.g. perceptual processes and development, and attention and pattern recognition from the Cognitive psychology section). It is unwise for you to study only one subsection from each syllabus section, since if the question is worded in such a way as to make it difficult for you to answer, you may be unable to answer the required number of questions.

A2 Revision must start with the syllabus

The best way to approach revision is to **work through the syllabus**, choosing syllabus areas to revise and 'ticking off' those areas as you cover them.

Make sure you **cover every aspect of the syllabus subsection** which you are revising. If you do not study *every* aspect of the subsections which you have chosen to cover, it is possible that you will be unable to answer *any* of the questions on the paper.

View the syllabus as a list of possible questions which may be asked. Increasingly, AQA examiners will set examination questions using wording drawn from the syllabus. This is helpful, in that it allows you to know precisely what material they are looking for in your answer, but *only* if you are familiar with the syllabus.

Remember that **there is an examination question for every subsection of the syllabus** (e.g. there will always be one question on 'attention and pattern recognition', one question on 'perceptual processes and development' and one question on 'language and thought' in the Cognitive psychology section of the examination paper).

The exam questions are in the same order on the paper as the topic material in the syllabus subsections (so it is possible to work out in advance of the examination the numbers of the questions you should be able to answer).

Exam questions rarely 'span' the a, b and c areas of syllabus subsections so that, for example, there are three areas under the heading 'Perceptual processes and development', and there are three basic 'types' of question corresponding to three areas of material relating to perceptual processes (the visual system, perceptual organisation and perceptual development).

It is important to know which questions you cannot answer. Exam questions relate to fairly specific areas of material on the syllabus, and if you have not covered this material your chances of answering an exam question successfully are greatly reduced.

A3 Manage your time

Many students underestimate how long it will take them to revise, and overestimate the amount of time which will be available for revision. **If you leave your revision too late it can be very demoralising**, as you realise that you do not have time to revise adequately.

Plan well ahead. Most A2 students will cover between 17 and 25 of the bullet points on the syllabus. If you were to cover two of these per week (e.g. 'perceptual organisation' and 'divided attention'), you might expect to revise for between 9 and 13 weeks. If you can only cover one bullet point per week, revision will take considerably longer.

Managing time involves organisation and consistency. It is important to set a realistic timetable in which you know *what* you are going to revise and *when* you are going to revise it. Like physical exercise, it is far more beneficial to do a little, regularly, than attempt a lot in one go. Work steadily through the syllabus.

Remember that **it is difficult to organise your time in a space which is cluttered with stuff and continual interruptions**. In the exam you will have a pen, a desk, some paper and three hours of silence. Your revision environment should not be too dissimilar.

Vary your revision, incorporating techniques such as studying with friends, timed essays, self-tests, 'sketches' from memory of syllabus areas, together with time in which you revise both your own notes and the contents of the textbook (see specific revision strategies below).

A4 Build and maintain your confidence

See your revision as developing strengths and competencies, not as a chore. If you take pride in your work, studying can become an important source of self-esteem, and others may respect you for it and look to you for advice and assistance.

Don't set unachievable goals ('I'm going to revise solidly all weekend'), but do stick to the goals which you set yourself (e.g. revising for 45 minutes, then taking a break for 15 minutes).

Reward yourself and remind yourself of the areas which you have covered, and how much you have achieved.

It may help to **identify in advance the questions which you will be able to answer** on the exam paper, once you have covered a bullet point thoroughly.

Don't expect to see precisely the question which you wanted to see on the paper. If a question looks unfamiliar or confusing, remember to slow down and remind yourself that although the question may be different, the material needed to answer it stays the same, and that you know this material. Do not simply revise from essays that have earned a high mark; 'prepared answers' will rarely be appropriate to the exam question. If someone asks you a question, you often have to think before you reply, and this is equally true of questions on a psychology examination paper. You are being asked to use material to answer a question, not just show that you know it. You can tackle *any* question by applying what you know thoughtfully.

Don't panic! It's easier said than done, but it is worth remembering that memory can be affected by your physical and mental state, and that flooding your system with adrenaline may temporarily leave you feeling that you can't remember anything at all! Plenty of practice examinations, timed essays, a good familiarity with the exam setting and procedures, and confidence in your own abilities will all prevent you from panicking. If you find yourself panicking, think about something pleasant, or think back to a psychology lesson that you enjoyed.

If you are opting for a modular route, avoid relying on the thought that you can always re-take modules. This can be dangerously de-motivating and lead you to settle for less than your best.

A5 Revision techniques

'THE PQ4R' METHOD
(Thomas & Robinson, 1972)

According to this approach, revising is best accomplished by carrying out the following steps:

Preview – the reader previews the material to familiarise him/herself with the topics and issues covered in a particular chapter.

Question – the reader prepares questions which focus on key concepts and issues.

Read – bearing the key questions in mind, the reader reads the material.

Reflect – the reader takes time to reflect on the meaning of the information, and its relation to what is already known.

Recitation – the reader then recites what has been read, using the questions as reminders.

Review – finally, the material is reviewed in the reader's mind, using questions to structure the task.

THE SCHEMATIC METHOD

The *schemas* contained in this Guide can be used to provide a 'road map' of a specific chapter before the chapter is covered, and can then be used to revise that chapter, for example, by using highlighter pens to highlight specific points, and then attempting to reproduce the information in structural form on a sheet of A3 paper.

An excellent way to prepare is to produce an essay plan/schema for example essays, drawn from each of the bullet points covered under a subsection. This is not as time-consuming as writing the essays themselves, but allows you to revise the factual content and practice structuring this content at the same time.

SELF-TEST QUESTIONS

Tests of recall (such as *self-test questions*) are a good way of determining how much information has been remembered and can be retrieved in an exam situation.

Teachers may use self-test questions, and then require students to mark each others' papers, or students may test themselves. When the answers are checked, new information can be learned and students can develop the ability to view their answers from an examiner's perspective, and judge the quality of what they have written more objectively.

THE PRACTICE METHOD

Skills in performing specific tasks, such as essay-writing under time constraints, are most likely to be best developed by practising the same skills. Students who prepare material by writing 'key notes' onto small cards may not develop skills which generalise perfectly to essay-writing.

Practice at timed essays under conditions similar to those in the examination setting can help students to develop skills such as time management, essay planning, and essay writing, as well as providing familiarity with the exam situation.

THE 'BLUE PETER' MODEL

One approach sometimes adopted by students is to write and memorise 'prepared answers' which they then reproduce in the exam ('Here's one I did earlier'). Typically, if a student covers twenty syllabus 'bullet points', then they might write twenty essays, one for each topic.

Although this technique is good at developing essay skills, and encourages students to learn and structure the material, it can lead to failing to answer the question asked, instead simply giving a set response. Since only material which is relevant to the question can be credited, this may in turn lead to them failing the exam, so **it is not a recommended approach**. However, if a student can adapt a prepared essay intelligently, in a way which makes it relevant to the examination question, then prepared essays can occasionally be useful.

OTHER APPROACHES
(adapted from Crooks & Stein, 1991, cited in Gross & McIlveen 1998)

- **Reduce the material to a manageable amount:** even if you could remember every single point in a textbook, not every one will be important. Revise efficiently, by focusing on the key points that you would need to make (and have time to make) in a forty-minute essay on the topic.
- **Impose meaning on the material:** material which is related in some way to other material, or to your own experiences, is more easily remembered, so try to relate the material to real life and understand the way in which material is structured (the schemas below are designed to help with this).
- **Learn the whole:** memory tends to be better if related material is revised as a whole, rather than in small parts.
- **Test yourself during learning:** it is quite possible to read material, then be unable to remember what you have just read! Test yourself as you go – if the material has not been learned, revise the material again. If this doesn't work, it may be time for a break!
- **Engage in overlearning:** continuing to learn material, after you have reached 100 per cent accuracy on recalling it, can improve the retention of that material in the longer term.
- **Use study breaks and rewards:** you can function at maximum efficiency only for a certain period of time before your concentration starts to wane. Taking a break every so often allows you to return refreshed.
- **Space study sessions:** two three-hour or three two-hour study sessions usually result in better retention than a single six-hour session.
- **Avoid interference:** revising similar topics (such as sociology and psychology) within a relatively short time period, can cause the memories to interfere. Plan your study sessions so that similar subjects are revised on different days.
- **Use time effectively:** try to develop a study schedule which incorporates revision time and leisure time. Once you have planned your schedule, stick to it!

ESSAY WRITING GUIDE

Skills	Process	Notes
	Read the Question	• Identify how many studies/theories you are required to discuss. • Check if question asks specifically for 'research studies'. • Does the question say 'including' or 'for example'?
Making the material relevant to the question	**Decide which Syllabus Area it Refers to**	• There is one question per syllabus subsection. • Questions are in the same order as the syllabus subsections. • Questions often use the syllabus wording.
Balancing the AO1 & AO2 skills (knowledge & evaluation) equally	**Identify AO1 & AO2 Skill Areas using Injunctions**	• Equal marks are awarded for AO1 & AO2 skills. • Injunctions inform you where AO1 and AO2 skills are required. • AO2 skills are analysis & evaluation, not just criticism, and demonstrate that you have thought about the material.
	Sketch a Quick Essay Plan	• Don't waste too much time drawing complex plans. • Don't cross essay plans out – they earn marks if the essay is incomplete.
Managing your time carefully	**Write an Introduction Defining Key Terms or Key Studies**	• Define key terms in the question. • Outline central issues/debates. • Describe an introductory study. • Do not waste time saying what you are going to do.
Leaving out personal opinion and waffle	**Set out Research/Theory Relevant to the Question**	• *Any* research/theory which informs the answer is credited. • Summarise clearly – don't spend too much time on one memorable study. • Names are more helpful than dates.
	Comment on the Research/Theory as Required	• Learn to distinguish between commentary and waffle. • Use the injunctions to tell you precisely where to comment on material – don't include commentary if not required.
Using link sentences to make sense of the material	**Relate each Paragraph back to the Question**	• Use link sentences to make material relate to the question. • Write a sentence at the end of each paragraph relating it back to the question. • Make comments informative.

ESSAY WRITING GUIDE

It is not difficult to describe a good A level Psychology essay. The examiner is simply looking for a considered and informed answer to the question which has been set. However, for most students, learning to write such an essay takes both hard work and practice, which involve the acquisition of new skills and a good awareness of the way in which essays are graded. This final point is very important: without knowing how your essays will be assessed by an examiner, you cannot know what is required of you in them. Many students assume that essay writing is simply a matter of putting what they *know* on paper, and fail to appreciate that this will only earn them, at best, half marks. In this chapter, we will be taking a close look at what an examiner is looking for in a psychology essay.

B1 Read the question

Students are often criticised for not answering the question. This is often due to a failure to read and understand it.

Every question requires you to do two things: demonstrate **knowledge & understanding** of a given area and demonstrate an ability to **analyse & evaluate** this area. These two skills (AO1 and AO2 skills – discussed below) are allocated the same proportion of marks in every essay question, with half of the marks available for each skill. One way to approach an essay question, therefore, is to ask yourself 'How do I demonstrate both AO1 and AO2 skills here?'.

The precise wording of essay questions is very important: if, for example, you are asked to *describe two theories* and you only describe one, you will incur a 'partial performance' penalty, which means that full AO1 skill marks cannot be obtained. Describing more than two theories will result in the examiner only crediting the best two.

The terms 'including' and 'for example' have very different meanings. If a question uses the term 'including', you *must* discuss whatever is included, whereas if the question says 'for example' you are *not required* to discuss the example(s) unless you wish to.

Where the question uses the term 'research studies' you *must* discuss empirical studies alone. Any other usage of the term 'research' (e.g. 'research into') permits you to discuss both empirical studies *and* theory.

Read the question more than once. Under pressure, students do misread questions!

Read *all* the questions on the paper: this will help you to separate those questions which you can answer from those which you can't, *before* you begin answering them.

B2 Decide which syllabus area the question refers to

It is very important that you get this right. In theory, it is easy: since **questions on each subsection on the AS & A2 papers follow the same order as they do on the syllabus**, you can work out in advance which questions correspond to which bullet point (e.g. 'Attention and pattern recognition' will always be the first question on the Cognitive section).

Just to make things easier, **the examiner tries to use the same wording in the exam questions as are in the syllabus**.

Finally, **there is always one question per syllabus subsection**, so there will always be a question corresponding to the subsections (e.g. memory) that you have learned.

Despite this, many students fail to produce material relevant to the question. Most commonly, this is because they do not know their syllabus and instead rely on words which they recognise (such as 'cognitive' or 'language'). This often fails, since these words may be used in questions which apply to entirely different areas of the syllabus (e.g. 'Discuss theories and research findings into the process of language acquisition' (Cognitive psychology) as opposed to 'Critically consider attempts to teach human language to non-human animals' (Comparative psychology)). Once again, you cannot succeed if you do not know your syllabus.

B3 Identify where AO1 and AO2 skills are to be demonstrated, using the injunctions

The AQA chooses from a limited list of terms (*injunctions*), each of which determines where the AO1 and AO2 skills are to be assessed within an essay question. **You must be familiar with the injunctions** to the extent that you are able to identify whether they call for AO1 skills, AO2 skills, or a combination of both.

In any essay, half of the marks are allocated for demonstrating skill AO1 and the other half for skill AO2. In practice, more than one injunction is often used to achieve this distribution of marks. Consider the following question:

(a) Describe *one constructivist* theory of perception.
(6 marks)

(b) Critically consider one other theory of perception.
(18 marks)

Where are the AO1 skill and AO2 skill marks to be found? 'Describe' is a skill AO1 term, so this accounts for six of the marks. Since 'critically consider' is a Skill AO1 and AO2 term, the other six of the AO1 skill marks must be found here, together with the twelve AO2 skill marks.

In this example, therefore, part **b** of the question would obviously require twice as much skill AO2 material as skill AO1 material.

The situation can be represented as a table:

Part **a**

AO1 skills (6 marks)
Description of one constructivist theory of perception

Part **b**

AO1 skills (6 marks) Demonstration of knowledge and understanding of one other theory	AO2 skills (12 marks) Awareness of strengths and weaknesses of this theory

Many students make the mistake of assuming that AO2 skills are equivalent to *criticism*, and that in order to demonstrate these skills they must come up with criticisms of the theories or research which they mention. In fact

AO2 skills are analysis and evaluation, which includes both positive and negative evaluative points (e.g. the strengths and weaknesses of a theory), as well as comparisons and informative comment. AO2 skills are demonstrated most clearly by commentary which goes beyond that given in the textbook. For this reason it is important that you consider the material carefully as you learn, discussing it wherever possible.

Exercise 1

Look at the following terms and try to sort them into skill AO1 terms, skill AO2 terms, and skill AO1 and AO2 terms:

analyse/critically analyse critically consider consider
explain distinguish between assess/critically assess
criticise justify examine
evaluate/critically evaluate describe discuss
define compare/contrast state

Now check your answers against the table at the bottom of the page. How did you do?

Exercise 2

Draw up tables to represent the balance of AO1 and AO2 skills for the following essays:

1 Discuss one theory of cognitive development.
2 Discuss any two methods used to study perceptual development.
3 Describe and evaluate two theories of interpersonal relationships.

Often, commentary will take the form of an explanation of a theory or piece of research which you have just introduced. For example, having just explained Piaget & Inhelder's (1956) 'three mountains scene', in a developmental psychology essay you might continue: 'This research demonstrates what Piaget called "egocentrism", which is the inability of the child to take another's point of view. However, other researchers dispute Piaget's conclusion, arguing that the task is particularly difficult and that on simpler tasks children *can* demonstrate an ability to take another's perspective'. All of the above constitutes commentary on the research.

Exercise 1 – answers

Skill AO1	Skill AO2	Skill AO1 & Skill AO2
consider	analyse/critically analyse	compare/contrast
define	assess/critically assess	critically consider
describe	criticise	distinguish between
examine	evaluate/critically evaluate	discuss
explain	justify	
outline/state		

249

Sometimes, **AO2 skills can be improved by the use of link sentences, or link structures**. These are pre-set ways of presenting or linking material, which enhance the style and quality of the essay. In the example above, the linking structure is 'This demonstrates that … . However, …'.

Below is a list of link sentences and structures which you could try to introduce into your work.

Link sentences and link structures

This suggests that …
This demonstrates that …
According to …
However, …
Clearly, …
Psychologists have investigated …
Research conducted into … has shown that …
Psychologists investigating … have found that …
Whilst some studies have supported … other researchers have found that …
… believes that …, whilst … believes that …
In an attempt to resolve the issue …
Despite this, other researchers …
There are, however, a number of weaknesses with …
Unfortunately, … cannot account for …
By contrast … believes that …

Many industrious and intelligent students make the error of writing essays which are condensed accounts of the facts relating to a given topic. Although it is important to be able to do this, such essays frequently score highly for their AO1 skills content but achieve low marks for their demonstration of AO2 skills. Often, this is largely because they have *failed to explain* what research means or demonstrates.

As a rule of thumb, you should **explain any technical term, and state the conclusion which can be drawn from any piece of research which you cite**. Link sentences can be used to encourage the 'framing' of research, and to enable students to produce essays which flow better, sound more professional, and score more highly on AO2 skills.

Exercise 3

Example essay: Stage 1

In the following exercise you can see how an essay which has high factual content can be improved to score more highly on AO2 skills. Read the essay below and try to identify material which can be cut without affecting the marks which the essay will gain. Focus on whether or not material is informative or adds to the reader's understanding of the topic, and on whether or not material is relevant to the essay question.

Discuss the view that perceptual abilities are largely innate. *(24 marks)*

This question forms a part of the wider 'nature–nurture' debate in psychology. In answering this question I will first say what the terms 'nature' and 'nurture' refer to, then I will discuss research findings relevant to the question. Psychologists on the 'nurture' side of the debate are called 'empirists' and argue that abilities develop largely as a consequence of learning and may be influenced by our experiences, whilst 'nativists' believe that abilities are largely innate and develop as a result of inherited genetic factors which pre-determine their development in a process called 'maturation'. I will now answer the question using psychological research which is relevant to the question, making reference to the question as I go.

The 'nature–nurture' debate as it applies to perception is a difficult one to answer. Psychologists have investigated perceptual abilities in a number of different ways in an attempt to resolve the issue including studies of human infants, human cataract patients, studies of sensory restriction in non-humans, perceptual readjustment studies and cross-cultural studies. In this essay I will discuss some of this research which is relevant to the question (and which I have time for!).

First of all I am going to discuss infants, who are extremely relevant to the study of perception. Bornstein (1976) used a technique called 'habituation' to investigate colour perception in infants. Using this technique Bornstein discovered that most babies possess largely normal colour vision at the age of two months. Infants also show the pupillary reflex and blink response at birth. This relates to the question of whether or not perception is inborn.

Fantz (1961) looked at pattern recognition and the perception of facedness in infants. In order to discover whether infants could discriminate pattern and form Fantz used the preferential looking technique. This is a technique which is used by psychologists to investigate perception. By presenting one- to 15-week-old infants with discs on which were painted colours, a bull's-eye, a patch of printed matter and a face, Fantz discovered a preference for more complex figures over simple ones, with infants spending most time looking at the human face. This was a very interesting finding as it showed us that children do have perceptual abilities fairly early on. Fantz presented infants with a normal face and a 'scrambled' face in which all the normal features were present but not placed in a normal arrangement on the disc. Fantz found that infants spent significantly longer looking at the normal face. Overall, I think that these studies tell us a great deal about perception and the way in which perception is either inborn or innate.

Gibson & Walk (1960) constructed an apparatus in which infants were placed on a sheet of plexiglass below which was a checkerboard pattern. Personally I think this was cruel and I don't know how the mothers of these children agreed to let them do it. On the 'shallow' side the pattern was immediately below the glass, whilst on the 'deep' side the pattern was placed at a distance of about four feet, giving the impression of a drop. I have drawn a detailed diagram of the apparatus used (see attached sheet). The researchers placed the infant on the shallow side of the visual cliff apparatus, and observed their behaviour when called by their mother from across the deep side. Gibson and Walk found that most babies aged between 6 and fourteen months would not crawl onto the deep side. I don't think this is very surprising, myself – I don't expect that adults would want to crawl onto the deep side! Some people said that the babies used by the researchers were too old. Campos *et al.* (1970) devised a method of assessing babies younger than six months. In their experiment babies were placed on either the shallow or deep sides of the cliff whilst their heart rates were monitored. Campos *et al.* found that heart rates would increase or decrease significantly. This showed that the babies were probably really scared by the experience.

'Sensory restriction' studies can be carried out on non-humans. Riesen (1947) raised chimpanzees in total darkness for the first sixteen months of life. As a result they failed to show a blink response and only noticed objects when they were accidentally bumped into. I think that these studies are unethical and should be banned since they cause harm to their participants. Weiskrantz (1956) argued that the visual deficiencies shown by Riesen's chimps were a consequence of degeneration of the retina in the absence of stimulation by light. Which demonstrated that Riesen's experiments were cruel and that they didn't prove anything.

Riesen (1965) conducted a second experiment in which he raised three chimps, Debi, Kova, and Lad. Lad was reared under normal conditions, Debi in total darkness and Kova was exposed to one-and-a-half hours of light per day whilst wearing opaque goggles. These goggles were worn by Kova for one and a half hours every day. Riesen found that though Kova's retina had developed normally, her receptive fields had failed to develop normally. This shows that wearing goggles can cause some blindness.

Some other psychologists have also investigated non-human perception. Blakemore and Cooper raised kittens in cylindrical chambers which had either vertical or horizontal stripes painted on the inside. The kittens were kept in the drums whether or not they wanted to be in the drums. The kittens wore collars to prevent them from seeing their own bodies and so were only exposed to lines of a particular orientation. When tested the kitten who had only been exposed to horizontal lines made no response to a rod which moved vertically, and kittens in vertical-only environments were equally 'behaviourally blind' to a rod moving in a horizontal direction. This means that kittens could not see things that they had not experienced in their lives. Studies of their visual cortex revealed that the kittens did not possess cells which were sensitive to lines of orientations which they had not experienced.

In conclusion, I think that such studies are really unnecessary. 'Is the value of this research worth the cost of life?' is the question we should ask. As for studies of infants they show that infants can perceive things from birth, although I feel that should have been obvious, really.

Example essay: Stage 2

In the essay below, irrelevant or unhelpful comments have been removed, leaving the factual material. It is interesting to note just how little factual material is required for a full answer to an essay question which you could reasonably be expected to produce in an exam. Read through the essay and try to decide where and how commentary can be introduced in order to increase the AO2 skills content of the essay.

Discuss the view that perceptual abilities are largely innate.   *(24 marks)*

This question forms a part of the wider 'nature–nurture' debate in psychology. Psychologists on the 'nurture' side of the debate are called 'empirists' and argue that abilities develop largely as a consequence of learning and may be influenced by our experiences, whilst 'nativists' believe that abilities are largely innate and develop as a result of inherited genetic factors which pre-determine their development in a process called 'maturation'.

Psychologists have investigated perceptual abilities in a number of different ways in an attempt to resolve the issue including studies of human infants, human cataract patients, studies of sensory restriction in non-humans, perceptual readjustment studies and cross-cultural studies.

Bornstein (1976) used a technique called 'habituation' to investigate colour perception in infants. Using this technique Bornstein discovered that most babies possess largely normal colour vision at the age of two months. Infants also show the pupillary reflex and blink response at birth.

Fantz (1961) looked at pattern recognition and the perception of facedness in infants. In order to discover whether infants could discriminate pattern and form Fantz used the preferential looking technique. By presenting one- to 15-week-old infants with discs on which were painted colours, a bull's-eye, a patch of printed matter and a face, Fantz discovered a preference for more complex figures over simple ones, with infants spending most time looking at the human face. Fantz presented infants with a normal face and a 'scrambled' face in which all the normal features were present but not placed in a normal arrangement on the disc. Fantz found that infants spent significantly longer looking at the normal face.

Gibson & Walk (1960) constructed an apparatus in which infants were placed on a sheet of plexiglass below which was a checkerboard pattern. On the 'shallow' side the pattern was immediately below the glass, whilst on the 'deep' side the pattern was placed at a distance of about four feet, giving the impression of a drop. The researchers placed the infant on the shallow side of the visual cliff apparatus, and observed their behaviour when called by their mothers from across the deep side. Gibson and Walk found that most babies aged between 6 and fourteen months would not crawl onto the deep side. Campos *et al.* (1970) devised a method of assessing babies younger than six months. In their experiment babies were placed on either the shallow or deep sides of the cliff whilst their heart rates were monitored. Campos *et al.* found that heart rates would increase or decrease significantly.

'Sensory restriction' studies can be carried out on non-humans. Riesen (1947) raised chimpanzees in total darkness for the first sixteen months of life. As a result they failed to show a blink response and noticed objects only when they were accidentally bumped into. Weiskrantz (1956) argued that the visual deficiencies shown by Riesen's chimps were a consequence of degeneration of the retina in the absence of stimulation by light.

Riesen (1965) conducted a second experiment in which he raised three chimps, Debi, Kova, and Lad. Lad was reared under normal conditions, Debi in total darkness and Kova was exposed to one-and-a-half hours of light per day whilst wearing opaque goggles. Riesen found that though Kova's retina had developed normally, her receptive fields had failed to develop normally.

Blakemore and Cooper raised kittens in cylindrical chambers which had either vertical or horizontal stripes painted on the inside. The kittens wore collars to prevent them from seeing their own bodies and so were only exposed to lines of a particular orientation. When tested the kitten who had only been exposed to horizontal lines made no response to a rod which moved vertically, and kittens in vertical-only environments were equally 'behaviourally blind' to a rod moving in a horizontal direction. Studies of their visual cortex revealed that the kittens did not possess cells which were sensitive to lines of orientations which they had not experienced.

Example essay: Stage 3

Here, commentary and link sentences have been added to the essay above in order to improve the A02 skills score, as well as assisting with the flow and style. The additional commentary is indicated by the use of italics.

Discuss the view that perceptual abilities are largely innate. (24 marks)

Psychologists have long been interested in the question whether perceptual abilities are predominantly inborn or whether they are a product of learning. This question forms a part of the wider 'nature–nurture' debate in psychology. Psychologists on the 'nurture' side of the debate are called 'empirists' and argue that abilities develop largely as a consequence of learning and may be influenced by our experiences, whilst 'nativists' believe that abilities are largely innate and develop as a result of inherited genetic factors which pre-determine their development in a process called 'maturation'.

Psychologists have investigated perceptual abilities in a number of different ways in an attempt to resolve the issue, including studies of human infants, human cataract patients, studies of sensory restriction in non-humans, perceptual readjustment studies and cross-cultural studies. *In this essay I will consider research from studies of human infants, and studies of sensory restriction in non-humans.*

Studying the perceptual abilities of newborn infants would seem to be the most direct way of assessing which perceptual abilities are inborn, since it is unlikely that abilities present at birth can have been learned. However, the study of infant perception poses some problems for researchers; in particular infants cannot tell us what they perceive. To get round this problem, researchers have developed a range of techniques which allow us to infer what infants can and cannot perceive. Bornstein (1976) used a technique called 'habituation' to investigate colour perception in infants. *The technique is based on the finding that infants attend less to stimuli that they recognise (to which they have become habituated). Novel stimuli presented after familiar stimuli will tend to re-excite attention.* Using this technique Bornstein discovered that most babies possess largely normal colour vision at the age of two months. Infants also show the pupillary reflex and blink response at birth. *This suggests that infants can perceive brightness and movement to some extent, and that such abilities are likely to be inborn.*

More complex perceptual abilities have also been investigated. Fantz (1961) looked at pattern recognition and the perception of facedness in infants. In order to discover whether infants could discriminate pattern and form Fantz used the preferential looking technique. *This involves presenting infants with two or more different stimuli. If the infant spends significantly longer looking at one stimulus rather than another we can conclude both that they can tell the stimuli apart, and that they prefer one over the other.* By presenting one- to 15-week-old infants with discs on which were painted colours, a bull's-eye, a patch of printed matter and a face, Fantz discovered a preference for more complex figures over simple ones, with infants spending most time looking at the human face, *suggesting that a preference for complexity is inborn.*

Whether a preference for faces is innate, or whether infants prefer looking at faces because they are complex, is unclear. In an attempt to resolve the issue, Fantz presented infants with a normal face and a 'scrambled' face in which all the normal features were present but not placed in a normal arrangement on the disc. Fantz found that infants spent significantly longer looking at the normal face. *This suggests that a preference for faces is inborn. However, the difference in looking times was small and other researchers have failed to replicate Fantz's findings.*

Another area of neonate studies has focused on the question 'Can infants perceive depth?'. In an ingenious experiment, Gibson & Walk (1960) constructed an apparatus in which infants were placed on a sheet of plexiglass below which was a checkerboard pattern. On the 'shallow' side the pattern was immediately below the glass, whilst on the 'deep' side the pattern was placed at a distance of about four feet, giving the impression of a drop. The researchers placed the infant on the shallow side of the visual cliff apparatus, and observed their behaviour when called by their mothers from across the deep side. *The researchers reasoned that if the infant was reluctant to crawl onto the deep side, then it can be inferred that they were able to perceive the drop.* Gibson and Walk found that most babies aged between 6 and fourteen months would not crawl onto the deep side. *This suggests that depth perception is innate. However, since infants needed to be at an age where they could crawl, it is possible that they may have learned to perceive depth by this age.* Campos *et al.* (1970) devised a method of assessing babies younger than six months. In their experiment babies were placed on either the shallow or deep sides of the cliff whilst their heart rates were monitored. Campos *et al.* found that heart rates would increase or decrease significantly *suggesting that babies were able to detect the change, and could therefore perceive depth from birth.*

Overall studies of neonates suggest that many perceptual abilities, such as the detection of brightness, pattern, depth and colour, are innate, although they may not mature fully until some time after birth.

One difficulty with studies of neonates is that it is not possible for ethical reasons to discover the extent to which the environment may influence the development of perceptual abilities by restricting their opportunities for perceptual learning to take place. 'Sensory restriction' studies can be carried out on non-humans. *Researchers typically deprive newborn animals of normal sensory stimulation and record the effect which this has on perception.*

Riesen (1947) raised chimpanzees in total darkness for the first sixteen months of life. As a result they failed to show a blink response and only noticed objects when they were accidentally bumped into. *This would seem to contradict the findings of infant studies which suggest that such abilities are innate. By way of explanation,* Weiskrantz (1956) argued that the visual deficiencies shown by Riesen's chimps were a consequence of degeneration of the retina in the absence of stimulation by light. *Because of this, abilities which may have been present at birth might have been lost due to retinal damage.*

In response to this observation, Riesen (1965) conducted a second experiment in which he raised three chimps, Debi, Kova, and Lad. Lad was reared under normal conditions, Debi in total darkness and Kova was exposed to one-and-a-half-hours of light per day whilst wearing opaque goggles. *The purpose of the opaque goggles was to allow light stimulation to maintain the retina, whilst preventing Kova from being exposed to patterned light.* Reisen found that though Kova's retina had developed normally, her receptive fields had failed to develop normally.

Riesen's studies show that some light is necessary for the development of the visual system and that patterned light is necessary for more complex visual abilities to develop.

Other researchers have attempted to investigate the impact of more specific aspects of the environment on perceptual development. Blakemore and Cooper raised kittens in cylindrical chambers which had either vertical or horizontal stripes painted on the inside. The kittens wore collars to prevent them from seeing their own bodies and so were only exposed to lines of a particular orientation. When tested, the kitten who had been exposed to only horizontal lines made no response to a rod which moved vertically, and kittens in vertical-only environments were equally 'behaviourally blind' to a rod moving in a horizontal direction. Studies of their visual cortices revealed that the kittens did not possess cells which were sensitive to lines of orientations which they had not experienced.

Although this research suggests that the environment can play an important role in the development of more complex perceptual abilities, it may be that these abilities were present at birth but deteriorated in the absence of appropriate stimulation. It is also important to note that we cannot necessarily assume that the findings of studies of non-humans can be generalised to human abilities, even when the systems are biologically similar.

In conclusion it is clear that many simple perceptual abilities mature in accordance with an innate programme. During maturation specific environmental factors may be required for perceptual development to proceed normally. The evidence regarding more complex perceptual abilities, such as recognising human faces, is less clear and such abilities may be more heavily dependent on learning.

B4 Sketch a quick essay plan

Essay plans are very useful: they encourage you to stop and **think about the structure of the essay before you begin writing** (rather than making it up as you go along), and to **put the key facts which you can remember down on paper for easy reference** (rather than hoping that you will remember them as you go along). They also allow you to concentrate on writing the essay, having taken care of the structure and the information.

In the event that the essay is unfinished or incomplete, essay plans will be marked by the examiner, so **don't cross them out!**

However, it is also true that detailed essay plans can waste time which would be better spent in writing the essay: *essay plans should be an overview of the main points and take no more than five minutes to sketch.*

Essay plans can be sequential or schematic depending on which you prefer. Sequential plans list the points that you aim to cover in the order in which you aim to cover them. Schematic plans present the points in diagrammatic form, showing how they relate to one another. Examples of both types of plans for a sample essay title are given overleaf:

Discuss constructivist and direct approaches to understanding perceptual processing. *(24 marks)*

Sequential plan

Intro

Define sensation and perception.
Explain constructivist and direct.

Body

Introduce Gregory's theory 'perception as interpretation'.
Support from illusions and constancies.
Give example – Müller–Lyer.
Identify problems (what is a hypothesis?, how is it formed?, how does theory relate to real life?).
Introduce Gibson's theory 'perception is direct'.
Explain optic array and three components: texture gradient, optic flow patterns, affordances.
Supporting research – swaying room.
Identify problems (difficulty (Marr), can't explain illusions, affordances).

Conclusion

Alternatives – transactionalists, Neisser (perceptual cycle).

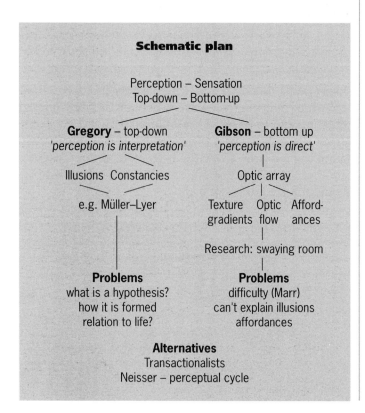

Schematic plan

Exercise 4

- Select six essay titles from different areas of the syllabus from *recent* past papers.
- Draw up essay plans for each from memory.
- Identify information that is missing from these plans.
- Go back to your notes and revise this information.
- Re-write the essay plans.

As pointed out earlier, drawing up essay plans is a very good way to assist revision. The plans can help you to think about how the material can be used in an essay, how it is structured and how much you need to know.

B5 Write an introduction

An introduction need not be very long but is usually necessary. **The primary role of an introduction is to link the question to your response** (your essay). Typically, an introduction will 'set the scene', such as with a single sentence like ' … is one of the most enduring questions which psychologists have faced'.

An introduction can often be used to **define or introduce the key terms of the question**, such as 'constructivist', 'obedience', 'memory', and to provide a brief overview of the subject area, e.g. 'Explanations of schizophrenia have focused on the genetic, biological and environmental factors which may contribute to the disorder'.

An introduction may also include a brief account of a key study relating to the area (perhaps the first research to be done in the area), or which illustrates the general importance of the question.

An introduction will often conclude with **a single sentence summary of what you intend to say in your essay** (**'In the following essay** I will …'). It is not necessary to say in advance precisely what you are going to do, since this will be clear from what you write.

B6 Set out research studies and/or theories relevant to the question

Examiners will credit any theory or research study which informs the question. However, they will be interested in *psychological* research, and are less likely to credit news reports (with a few notable exceptions, such as the case of Kitty Genovese). They are also highly unlikely to give you many marks for anecdotes (personal accounts of events).

It is a grave mistake not to answer the question. If material is not relevant to the question, it will gain no marks.

For this reason, it is very important not simply to read the question but to answer it as well.

Be aware of the syllabus. In most cases, the only material which will be relevant to an exam question will come from the corresponding syllabus subsection. Only sometimes can material from one syllabus subsection be used effectively in answer to a question on another section (exceptions include questions on major theoretical orientations in psychology). **You must be able to identify the syllabus subsection to which a question 'points', and know which material is covered in that subsection.**

Stay 'on task'. Make sure that you do not drift off into related areas, such as a discussion of ethical considerations and research in similar sounding areas (for example, an essay on animal language should not end up including Skinner's theory of language development in humans).

It is very important to develop the ability to **summarise research studies and theories clearly and concisely**. A good summary of a study should include key points such as who the participants were, what the experimental conditions were, what was manipulated and what the results were. Lengthy and lurid descriptions which include a lot of extraneous detail earn very few marks and are time-consuming. Summaries which simply include the conclusions of research, without saying how the researchers arrived at these conclusions are also inadequate. A good study to practice on is Milgram's study of obedience. Try summarising the key points in a single paragraph.

Students often worry about whether or not they have to memorise *names of researchers* and *publication dates of research*. The AQA examiner requires that research studies be *recognisable*, so often a clear description of research is adequate, although the name of the researcher lends clarity to the essay. A date is rarely very important, although a general idea of when research studies were carried out can be useful (e.g. Milgram's studies of obedience were carried out *after* the second world war).

B7 Comment on the research studies and/or theories as required

Remember that half of your marks come from commentary (A02 skills), and that commentary takes many forms.

The precise extent to which you are required to comment on theories will be determined by the injunctions used in the question. Students often make the mistake of wasting time *evaluating* studies or theories, despite the fact that the question only requires them to *describe* the research or theories. **Avoid the temptation to put down what you know, just because you know it!**

Whilst commentary is credited, waffle is not! Although the difference is not always obvious, waffle is generally uninformative, whilst commentary informs the answer. Commentary could therefore be an explanation or clarification of a previous point, but should not be a repetition of that point.

B8 Relate each paragraph back to the question

Although not strictly required, relating what you have said back to the question at the end of each paragraph can be a useful strategy, both because it draws the examiner's attention to the point that you have made and its relation to the question, and because it forces you to systematically relate what you say back to the question.

Even if you are only stopping to *check* at the end of each paragraph that what you have said relates to the question, this is a useful exercise: it will help you to address the question, rather than simply slipping into a recitation of whatever material you know.

B9 Make the most of your time

Learning how to manage your time, and concentrating for extended periods of time, are skills which you will master with practice. Timed essays are an important part of your preparation.

If you finish writing your essays before time, take a short break, relax, then review your work. Students invariably make errors when writing essays under pressure, and it may be possible to spot some of these and make corrections.

Writing an essay for the first time

All these comments make essay-writing seem more daunting than it really is. Many of these points are obvious, and the remainder you will probably learn to do automatically.

However, if you are writing an essay for the first time just remember that an essay should **summarise the psychological research and theory which relates to the question and say what it means.** If you do this, you cannot go far wrong.

If it helps, look at the way in which textbooks are written. They will be far more comprehensive than your essay, but they can give you a good idea of the 'style' to use (for example 'I think …' is never used).

COURSEWORK GUIDE

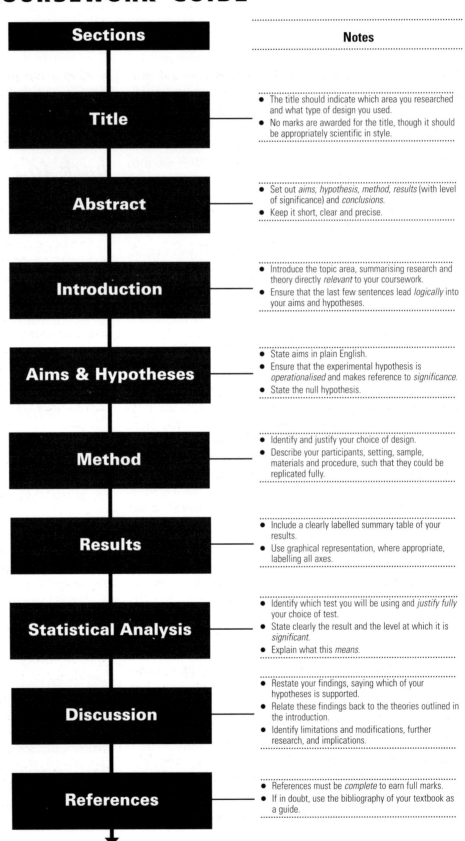

Guidelines (AQA)

Pieces of coursework must be drawn from different syllabus sections.

Coursework must comprise 1 experimental and 1 non-experimental design.

Marks are awarded for style and grammar.

Students may not work in groups larger than 3.

Pooled class data cannot be used.

Work within the 2000 word limit.

Title each subsection of your work clearly.

Have a copy of the marking scheme beside you as you write.

Sections

Title

Abstract

Introduction

Aims & Hypotheses

Method

Results

Statistical Analysis

Discussion

References

Notes

- The title should indicate which area you researched and what type of design you used.
- No marks are awarded for the title, though it should be appropriately scientific in style.

- Set out *aims, hypothesis, method, results* (with level of significance) and *conclusions*.
- Keep it short, clear and precise.

- Introduce the topic area, summarising research and theory directly *relevant* to your coursework.
- Ensure that the last few sentences lead *logically* into your aims and hypotheses.

- State aims in plain English.
- Ensure that the experimental hypothesis is *operationalised* and makes reference to *significance*.
- State the null hypothesis.

- Identify and justify your choice of design.
- Describe your participants, setting, sample, materials and procedure, such that they could be replicated fully.

- Include a clearly labelled summary table of your results.
- Use graphical representation, where appropriate, labelling all axes.

- Identify which test you will be using and *justify fully* your choice of test.
- State clearly the result and the level at which it is *significant*.
- Explain what this *means*.

- Restate your findings, saying which of your hypotheses is supported.
- Relate these findings back to the theories outlined in the introduction.
- Identify limitations and modifications, further research, and implications.

- References must be *complete* to earn full marks.
- If in doubt, use the bibliography of your textbook as a guide.

COURSEWORK GUIDE

Many students find coursework a bewildering and difficult part of their course. In fact, it is not difficult to write a good piece of coursework given that you **know the criteria against which your coursework will be assessed**. The most common mistake which students make is to fail to familiarise themselves with the precise *format* required by their examination board, with the consequence that they produce elaborate and original pieces of coursework which *cannot* be awarded many marks, because they fail to meet many of the marking criteria. A good piece of coursework can *only* be written by a student fully acquainted with the marking scheme. Below is a guide to writing your coursework, together with some suggestions for coursework designs and a sample piece in outline.

C1 *Choosing your design*

There are two important questions to raise when choosing a coursework design. Firstly, **'Will the results be easy to collect, quantify and analyse?'**: it may seem 'back-to-front' to consider your statistical test before you have obtained your results, but if you collect results which are difficult to analyse or quantify you may lose marks both for your analysis and your design decisions. Results should be in an *operationalised* form (for example 'scores', or 'number of participants', or 'seconds', rather than 'attitude' or 'feelings').

Secondly, **'Does the investigation relate closely to an area on the syllabus?'**. Students are required (by the AQA) to choose investigations which relate to the syllabus, but it is also wise to choose an area with full and straightforward literature support, so that you do not have to struggle to complete the introduction and discussion.

Try to keep things simple. It is usually a good idea to concentrate on a single variable, or measure. With more than one variable, you are likely to require more than one experimental hypothesis and corresponding increases in the complexity of the statistics and discussion.

Consider the BPS's *Ethical Guidelines* (1993). The BPS guidelines are summarised in your textbook, but the following are likely to be particularly relevant:

- **Avoid deceiving your participants** where possible.
- Always obtain **informed consent** (designs involving children should be avoided for this reason).
- Inform participants in advance of their **right to withdraw**.
- Inform participants in advance that their results will be **confidential**, and maintain this confidentiality.
- **Debrief** participants fully, and thank them for their participation.
- Undisclosed observations are unacceptable, except in situations where participants might reasonably expect to be observed.
- **Under no condition expose participants to conditions which might cause distress or pain** (for this reason avoid designs involving non-human animals).

Bear in mind that these considerations apply whatever the experimental design (for example, a 'survey' still requires informed consent).

Remember that the AQA requires that one design is **experimental**, and the other **non-experimental**. **Surveys**, **correlations** and **observations** are all non-experimental designs.

Be aware of the limitations on group size, and on the use of pooled class data (the AQA allows for a group of up to four students to count as a 'small group', but you will lose marks for larger group sizes).

Follow the advice of your teacher regarding your choice of design. Although you will lose some marks if your teacher has supported you, coursework produced with teacher support tends to score more highly on many of the other areas (bear in mind that your teacher will also probably be responsible for assessing your work!).

Ensure that procedures are standardised, and that methodological problems (such as participant variables, practice effects, and other extraneous variables) are anticipated, and the design adjusted to minimise their effects.

Don't worry if your results do not support your experimental hypothesis. Students are often disappointed if the experimental hypothesis is not supported. However, this makes no difference whatsoever to the marks awarded.

If you are working as part of a group, bear in mind that although both the design and results may be a 'joint effort', the 'write-ups' should not be (plagiarism can result in disqualification).

Below are some suggestions for coursework designs:

Suggested coursework outlines

SYLLABUS AREA 13.1 – SOCIAL COGNITION
Attribution of causality
Design: survey

Literature: attribution theory and biases

Procedure: students investigate the different attributions given by fellow students for failures/successes of their own/rival football teams

Results: nominal, in the form of external/internal attributions for failures/successes

Prejudice and discrimination
Design 1: experimental (independent subjects)

Literature: origins, maintenance and reduction of prejudice

Procedure: students present two groups of fellow students with the same description of an individual, in which only the name has been changed (male/female, Western/non-Western), asking participants to assess their suitability for interview

Results: nominal, in the form of 'suitable/unsuitable' judgements

Design 2: experimental (independent)

Literature: origins, maintenance and reduction of prejudice

Procedure: students leave copies of 'bogus' UCAS forms, together with instructions to return to reception if lost. Application materials are identical except for the name (male/female, Western/non-Western)

Results: nominal, in the form of how many of each type have been returned

SYLLABUS AREA 13.1 – RELATIONSHIPS
Attraction and the formation of relationships
Design: correlational

Literature: theories of relationships; the matching hypothesis

Procedure: students ask fellow students if they wish to join a pilot 'dating service'. Assured that information will be kept confidential, asked to complete a questionnaire concerning their traits and their desired partner's traits (all scored on a ten-point scale). Scores can be correlated

Results: ordinal in the form of ratings for own/partner's attractiveness

SYLLABUS AREA 13.2 –
PHYSIOLOGICAL PSYCHOLOGY
Theories of motivation
Design: natural experiment

Literature: theories of emotion and motivation

Procedure: fellow students either waiting for an important exam (anxiety condition) or a bus (low anxiety conditions) are asked to rate a photograph of a member of the opposite sex of 'near average' attractiveness for attractiveness. Aroused participants should rate the photograph more highly

Results: interval/ordinal in the form of attractiveness scores

SYLLABUS AREA 13.3 –
PERCEPTUAL PROCESSES AND DEVELOPMENT
Perceptual organisation
Design: experiment (independent)

Literature: theories of perception, perceptual set

Procedure: participants are asked to identify an ambiguous figure, having first been exposed to stimuli which create an expectation. (e.g. showing a rabbit/duck figure after either a series of rabbits or ducks)

Results: nominal, in the form of what was identified

SYLLABUS AREA 10.1 – HUMAN MEMORY

Forgetting

Design: experimental (related)

Literature: theories of memory and forgetting

Procedure: participants are instructed to use either imagery or rehearsal to remember a list of concrete word pairs. The first word of each word pair is presented, participants recall scores for the second word of each pair recorded in each condition

Results: interval, in the form of recall scores

SYLLABUS AREA 13.4 – COGNITIVE DEVELOPMENT

Development of thinking

Design: survey

Literature: Piagetian theory and theories of cognitive development

Procedure: tests of formal operational thinking are administered to participants aged 16+. Results are compared with Piaget's predictions

Results: nominal, in the form of correct/incorrect, or interval in the form of number of correct responses

C2 Project Brief

Students are required to submit a project brief in support of their report. The project brief accounts for twelve of the marks available, and outlines the rationale or 'thinking' behind the report. Like the report, the project brief needs to follow a set format:

Begin by restating your hypothesis (although marks for your hypothesis are awarded in the report).

Explain why you have chosen a 'directional' or 'non-directional' hypothesis. A directional hypothesis states that there will be a difference and the direction of this difference (e.g. girls will score more highly than boys) whilst a non-directional hypothesis only states that there will be a difference.

Identify the research method/design which you are going to use and evaluate the advantages and disadvantages of this particular method (e.g. laboratory experiments involve artificial conditions, whilst natural experiments permit less control over extraneous variables).

Identify sources of bias/confounding variables. Tell the examiner about factors which might reasonably be expected to influence the outcome (e.g. the experimenter–participant relationship) but don't just throw in variables for the sake of it (e.g. wind conditions). Explain how you are able to control these problems – if you are unable to control them, explain why.

Identify the level of statistical significance that you will be using (0.05 is normal).

Identify ethical considerations and explain the steps which you have taken to deal with these.

C3 Report Title

The title does not actually merit any marks by itself, but marks are allocated for the overall style of the coursework, so the title should be appropriately scientific.

A title should be suggestive of **the area you have investigated and the method which you have used**, such as '*An experiment into the effectiveness of different memory techniques*', or '*A survey into gender stereotypes*'.

C4 Abstract

An abstract is a **clear and concise summary of your investigation**, which allows the reader to understand what you did and what you discovered. The moderator will be checking for clarity and conciseness and ensuring that you have clearly stated your **aims, hypothesis, method, results and conclusions**. Below is a possible template for an abstract:

Abstract

The aim of this [experiment/survey/observation] was to investigate the relationship between [two variables]. The experimental hypothesis was that [experimental hypothesis – see below].

A [repeated measures/independent measures/matched pairs, experimental design]/ [survey/observational/correlation method] was used. Participants were selected using a [quota/opportunity] sample. Results obtained were in the form of ... [scores /ratings .../ seconds ...] and [were/were not] significant at the p < [0.05/0.01/0.001] level of significance. It was concluded that [conclusion].

C5 Introduction

An introduction is not dissimilar to an essay. It should **introduce the key terms relevant to the topic, outline** the general theoretical background, then describe any research studies directly relevant to the study. It is assessed according to AO1 skills, according to the *relevance* of the material to the investigation. Beware of being 'unselective' in your choice of material – you may lose a mark. **And remember the word limit!**

In order to gain the remaining marks which are awarded for the introduction, **you must write a logical lead in to your aims and hypothesis**. If you have outlined the relevant theories correctly, this should simply mean adding a couple of link sentences onto the end of the introduction, along the lines of 'If X's theory is correct it would be anticipated that ..., whilst if Y is correct ... . In this investigation it is intended to discover which of these outcomes is more likely, by ...'.

C6 Aims and hypotheses

The aims and hypotheses need to be **clear and testable** in order to earn full marks.

The aim is a **plain statement of what you intend to demonstrate**, for example 'This study aims to discover which of the memory techniques, rehearsal or imagery, is more effective in remembering word pairs', or 'The aim of this experiment is to find out whether or not participants' perceptions of an ambiguous figure will be influenced by the context of presentation'.

The experimental hypothesis is a **precise and testable statement**, and must be more exact than the aims. As a rule of thumb, the hypothesis usually makes reference to **significance**, and to **operationalised** terms (terms stated in a manner which is measurable, e.g. participants' 'recall scores' rather than participants' 'memories'). There is no set way to write a hypothesis, but below is a template which works for most designs.

Hypothesis Template

There will be a significant [difference/correlation] between the [scores, ratings, responses] of participants [condition1] and the [scores, ratings, responses] of participants [condition2].

e.g. There will be a significant difference between participants' scores in the divided attention condition and participants' scores in the control condition.

Where appropriate, you should state the direction of the difference/correlation and justify the direction.

e.g. There will be a significant positive correlation between [X] and [Y]. The hypothesis is [uni-/bi-directional] because ...

When you have written your hypothesis, judge for yourself whether or not it is unambiguous and testable.

The **null hypothesis should also be stated**. This is the same in any design and states simply that 'There will be no significant [difference/correlation] between ..., and any [difference/correlation] there is reflects the operation of chance factors'.

C7 Method

The central task in your reporting of the method is to **ensure that all aspects of the investigation are reported clearly and in sufficient detail for full replication to be possible**.

You should **state the design which you used and defend it** (e.g. a repeated measures experimental design was used because it reduces the effects of participant variables).

You should **describe the participants used** (without identifying them individually), **and the sampling method used to obtain them**, e.g. 'A total of twenty male students between the ages of 17 and 18 were used, selected on an opportunity basis, since this was the best sampling method given the available time and money'.

You should identify the experimenter(s), location, time, and any other relevant conditions under which the investigation was conducted.

In the case of an experimental investigation, you should **say which were the independent and dependent variables** and any confounding or extraneous variables, together with the level of measurement (i.e. whether the data is nominal, ordinal or interval). You should also **identify any experimental or control conditions**, and any measures which you have taken to reduce practice or order effects.

Your materials should be listed, and it would be a good idea to **include (in your appendix) one copy of any stimulus materials used**.

You should **state the procedure which was followed and include copies of any standardised instructions**, e.g. 'Students who appeared to be on their own were approached on an opportunity basis by the experimenter and asked if they wished to participate in an experiment into memory. If the participant replied that s/he would, s/he was read the standardised instructions (see Appendix)'.

C8 *Presentation of results*

Results should be presented clearly. This almost always means that you must **draw up a clearly labelled table**, using appropriate descriptive statistics.

Graphical representations (such as bar charts or line graphs) may then follow, if appropriate. Many students are now adept at producing such representations using spreadsheet software. Unfortunately, this has led to a tendency to prize aesthetic merits over genuine informativeness (e.g. students occasionally produce pie-charts which show that half of the participants are male, and half female). **Do not produce graphical representations simply because they can be produced.** A graphical representation of data should make the pattern of results clearer than does the summary table; **one well-chosen graphical representation is usually sufficient** to do this.

C9 *Statistical analysis*

In order to earn full marks for your use of inferential statistics, you must **state the statistical test which you intend to use, then justify it fully, making reference to your data**. The criteria for use of a statistical test can usually be found in textbooks which detail the methods used in psychological research.

The mathematical calculations can be presented in an appendix. Statistical tests can be performed by computer: no marks are lost so long as calculations are correct.

In the results section of your coursework, you must **state the observed value for your test of statistical significance** (i.e. the value produced by the statistical test) **and the critical value which it must exceed (or, in the case of some statistical tests, be smaller than) in order for the outcome to be significant. State which level of significance you are using, and how many degrees of freedom (or, in the case of some statistical tests, the 'N' value) are involved.** For example, if using the t-test of significance you might state 'the value of t for our results is 7.844, which exceeds the critical value of 3.84 ($p < 0.05$ with 20 degrees of freedom)'.

Say whether or not the outcome is significant, whether this allows you to reject or accept the null hypothesis and accept or reject the experimental hypothesis.

Finally, **say what your result means**, e.g. 'This means that participants recalled significantly more word pairs using the imagery rather than the rehearsal technique'.

C10 *Discussion*

A discussion must **begin with a restatement of the outcome**, e.g. 'The results showed that participants recalled significantly more word pairs using the imagery rather than rehearsal technique ($p < 0.05$)'.

Relate the outcome to the hypotheses (again), explaining which of the hypotheses has been accepted and rejected.

Relate the findings back to the research and/or theory which was outlined in the introduction. Explain which research and/or theory is supported and which not supported.

You can **broaden your discussion** to include criticisms of the research and/or theory outlined in the introduction or other areas of research or theory which relate to your findings.

Following this, **you must examine actual or potential limitations of your research design and suggest modifications which might remedy these**. Many students make only token attempts to do this, resulting in a loss of valuable marks. Try to identify *at least three actual or plausibly potential* problems with your design and *three plausible modifications* which might be made.

Identify implications of your findings and ideas for further research. Again, many students rush this part, unaware that as many marks are earned here as for other parts of the discussion. Do not confuse implications with suggestions for further research. **Try to include at least three of each.**

C11 *References*

Marks are awarded for full, appropriate references. You will not gain full marks if you have referred to any research or theory in the text which cannot be found in the references, or if your references are not appropriate.

If you are in doubt as to how to produce references in the appropriate format, you may look in the back of any textbook. These contain references to all publications cited in the main text.

C12 *Appendices*

Appendices should be included in your list of contents, and contain any **further information required for a full understanding of your study**. They are not intended to be a repository for any odd bits of paper, or illegible scribblings produced *en route* to the finished product. Neither should appendices contain, for example, every single questionnaire returned by participants (although they should contain one sample copy).

C13 Style and quality of language

The AQA awards marks for your report style and the quality of the language used.

Full marks for style are awarded for reports which are **concise, logically organised into sections and written in an 'appropriately scientific style'**. Guidelines on style can be found in the chapter on essay writing in this book; otherwise any textbook will give you a good idea as to what a scientific style is.

Full marks for quality of language are awarded for reports in which **ideas are expressed accurately, a broad range of specialist terms are used precisely, with only minor errors in spelling, punctuation or grammar**. The use of a spell-check facility (available on most word-processors) can help here.

C14 Submitting your coursework

Before you submit your coursework, use a copy of the examination board's marking criteria to check that, as far as possible, you have fulfilled the requirements.

Some examination boards permit students to revise a marked piece of coursework, then resubmit it before it receives a final grade. You will need to check with your teacher whether or not this is the case. If it is the case, then it is a good idea to submit your coursework well in advance of the examination board's deadline.

The AQA will award a grade X (no grade) for students who do not submit *any* coursework. However, it is clearly to your advantage to submit the required amount of coursework.

If you are re-sitting your A level examination, it might be possible to resubmit previously submitted pieces of coursework. Check with your teacher.

C15 Sample coursework outline

Below is a sample coursework outline that was submitted by a student. It has been written in 'note form' and is therefore not intended as a guide to appropriate report style. It identifies the report headings which you would be advised to use, together with the type of material and structure which *might* typically comprise a piece of coursework (although it is by no means perfect!).

Under no conditions should this sample be copied and submitted as a report (since this is likely to result in disqualification). However, bear in mind when deciding on a design that *it is permissible* for a design to be based on that of a previously published work. Have a copy of the marking scheme beside you as you write.

REHEARSAL AND IMAGERY

SAMPLE COURSEWORK OUTLINE

Title

An experimental investigation into the effectiveness of imagery and rehearsal as techniques of remembering word pairs.

Abstract

The aim of this investigation was to discover whether imagery or rehearsal is the more effective technique of remembering, as tested by recall of word pairs. Atkinson & Shiffrin (1971) suggest that repeating words to oneself (*rehearsal*) is the most effective technique, whilst Paivio (1984) proposes that forming a mental image of the words to be recalled (*imagery*) is better.

A repeated measures experimental design was used to gain the responses, in the form of rehearsal and imagery scores for each participant. There were two experimental conditions, participants remembering word pairs using either imagery or rehearsal. A total of 7 participants were used, all of whom were psychology students. Participants were selected on an opportunity basis.

The results were analysed using the repeated measure *t*-test, and there was a significant difference ($p < 0.05$) between the number of word pairs recalled in each condition. This suggests that imagery is indeed the superior technique of remembering.

Introduction

Definition of memory: 'the retention of learning and experience' (keep this brief).

Components: *registration, storage and retrieval*. In order to remember something we have to be able to store and retrieve it (keep this brief).

Theories of memory

- Theory 1: Multi-store model/dual-memory theory (Atkinson & Shiffrin, 1971) attempts to explain memory in terms of the transfer of information from short-term memory (STM) to long-term memory (LTM). The key process in doing so is *rehearsal*. Dual-memory theory suggests that rehearsal is the principal technique of remembering. But this model cannot explain memory for faces, or for things which we have not rehearsed.

- Theory 2: Paivio's dual-code hypothesis – Paivio (1986) says that we can store concrete nouns (but not abstract nouns) in both a verbal form and an imaginal form (images). Forming an image to go along with a word causes it to be stored in both forms, so we remember it better. Paivio (1984) would predict imagery to be the superior technique.

Logical lead into experiment: according to Atkinson & Shiffrin (1971), we might expect rehearsal scores to be higher, but Paivio (1986) believes the opposite … in this experiment we hope to discover which of these two theories is best supported.

Aims

The aim of this experiment is to discover which technique (imagery or rehearsal) is the more effective method of remembering word pairs.

Experimental hypothesis

There will be a significant difference between the recall scores of participants in the imagery and rehearsal conditions. Imagery scores will be higher. This is a uni-directional hypothesis because the direction the outcome will take has been stated.

Null hypothesis

There will be no difference between recall scores of participants in the imagery and rehearsal conditions. Any difference reflects the operation of chance factors.

Method

Design: repeated measures experimental design.

Justification: an experiment offers good control of extraneous variables, allowing us to manipulate an independent variable and draw inferences about cause and effect. Repeated measures are used, since by using the same participants twice we can reduce the number of participant variables and consequently need fewer participants.

Sample: selected on an opportunity basis, obviously biased but the best possible with the available time and money.

Participants: psychology students at school on a Monday morning. Aged 16–19.

Controlled variables: location, distractions kept to a minimum, quiet conditions, good lighting, time for each technique to be used. Procedure standardised (copy in appendix). The 'recency effect' eliminated by getting participants to count backwards for 30 seconds at the end.

Extraneous variables: the presence of other students may have affected performance. Difficult to control absolutely which technique was used. Word pairs were read out, not presented on a tachistoscope/computer, meaning that at least some

acoustic processing was necessary, even when forming an image. Age was not representative. Sex was not representative.

Independent and dependent variables: memory technique used, versus recall score for each technique.

Materials

Stop-watch
Copy of standardised procedure
Pencils
Paper
List of word pairs (copy in appendix)

Procedure

The experimenter asked a group of students, selected on an opportunity basis, whether they wished to participate in an experiment into memory.

Once consent had been obtained and participants had been informed of their right to withdraw, the experimenter explained that the experiment was into the effectiveness of recall techniques on word pairs and that participants would be required either to form a mental image of the word interacting in some way or rehearse the pair silently to oneself.

The experimenter explained that s/he would read the word pair to be remembered, followed by the technique to be used, after which participants would be allowed ten seconds to remember the words.

Finally, the experimenter explained that at the end of the experiment, on the instruction 'count', participants would be required to count backwards from 100 until the experimenter said 'stop'. At the end of this procedure, the experimenter read out the first of each word pair, and participants were required to write down the correct second word.

The experimenter asked if the participants had any questions, then began the experiment.

(copy of standardised procedure in appendix)

Results

1 Summary table showing participants' scores for each condition, with average score for each condition.
2 Bar chart showing difference in average performance.

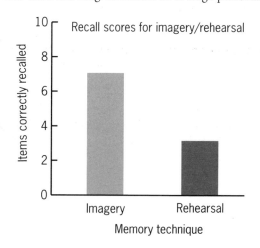

Statistical analysis: repeated measures t-test (workings in appendix). Justified because participants' scores were in the form of interval data, because participants were identical in each condition (so the design and test are *related*).

The value of t is calculated as 7.84, which exceeds the critical value of t ($t = 3.84$) at the $p < 0.05$ level, with 20 degrees of freedom. This means that participants recalled significantly more word pairs using the imagery technique (average = 7.1) as compared with the rehearsal (average = 3.2) technique.

Discussion

Restate the results.

Relate this back to the experimental and null hypotheses, which are supported or rejected.

Supports Paivio's dual-coding approach (1986) and rejects Atkinson & Shiffrin's (1971) dual-memory theory.

Clearly there are flaws in dual-memory theory. We remember faces, smells, sensations – and often our memory for distinctive events doesn't seem to require rehearsal.

In addition, rehearsal is sometimes ineffective, so Craik & Watkins (1973) distinguish *rote rehearsal* (which just keeps information in STM) and *elaborative rehearsal*, where the information is linked with other things, given more associations (which transfers information into long-term memory).

Craik & Lockhart's (1972) *levels-of-processing model* suggests that images are remembered better, not because of better memory for images, but because in forming an image we increase the number of associations the words have (a form of semantic processing). Could this have happened in this investigation?

Although the findings from this experiment support Paivio's theory, the dual-coding approach is not without its critics, who point out that storing images would require an impossible amount of memory space and that we would still need a system to 'decode' these images even if we could store them.

Summary

Perhaps it is not that images are stored better but just that the *way* in which images are stored is better.

Limitations of the design and modifications

The presence of other students may have affected performance; ideally, students should be tested individually under controlled conditions. However, this would be more time-consuming and expensive.

It was difficult to control absolutely which technique was used. This variable cannot be controlled, although PET scans *might* be able to ascertain which areas of the brain are active during a task.

Word pairs were read out, meaning that at least some acoustic processing was necessary, even when forming an image. Presentation of stimulus words on a tachistoscope/computer might be better.

The age and sex of participants was not representative of the population at large. A quota sample drawing people from each gender and age range might be preferable.

Further study

A comparison of males' and females' imagery and rehearsal scores could be carried out, based on suggestions by some researchers that males possess better visuo-spatial skills and females better verbal ability.

The experiment could be repeated using a recognition rather than recall test, in an attempt to discover whether the different techniques affected the *availability* of information or simply its *accessibility*.

Lists could be learned until they could be correctly recalled twice, using either imagery or rehearsal. Recall scores could then be tested one month later, to see if there was any difference in the 'durability' of the memory traces created by the two techniques.

Implications

We can remember information (like shopping lists or stories) better if we convert it to images (e.g. the 'method of loci' where items to be remembered are mentally 'placed' at locations along a familiar route).

This suggests that diagrams are valuable aides to memory, and should be used in teaching.

In advertising, 'an image is worth a thousand words'. The conclusion suggests that images will be better remembered than 'voice-overs', or text.

References

ATKINSON, R.C. & SHIFFRIN, R.M. (1971) The control of short-term memory. *Scientific American*, 224, 82–90.

PAVIO, A. (1986) *Mental Representations: A dual-coding approach*. Oxford: Oxford University Press.

CRAIK, F. & LOCKHART, R. (1972) Levels of processing. *Journal of Verbal Learning & Verbal Behaviour*, 12, 599–607.

CRAIK, F.I.M. & WATKINS M.J. (1973) The role of rehearsal in short-term memory. *Journal of Verbal Learning & Verbal Behaviour*, 12, 599–607.

Appendix

Copy of stimulus materials (word pairs)

Copy of standardised procedure

t-test workings